THE WORLD OF MUSIC

AN *Illustrated* Encyclopedia

THE

Volume II

WORLD OF MUSIC

MUSIC

AN *Illustrated* Encyclopedia

ABRADALE PRESS / *Publishers* / *New York*

Library of Congress Catalog Card Number: 63–14095

Special contents of this edition copyright © Abradale Press, Inc., New York, 1963. All rights reserved. No part of the contents of this book may be reproduced without the written permission of the publishers. In Norway, the copyright is held by Kjell B. Sandved and Sverre Hagerup Bull

DESIGNED BY HOWARD MORRIS

Printed in the United States of America

The paintings reproduced on this binding:

FRONT COVER: Degas' Father Listening to Pagans *(portion), by Edgar Degas (French, 1834–1917). Museum of Fine Arts, Boston (John T. Spaulding Collection)*

BACK COVER: M. Gaston Dufy at the Piano *(portion), by Raoul Dufy (French, 1877–1953) Private collection*

EAMES, Emma. American soprano (1865–1932). Born in Shanghai of American parents, she came to the United States at five years, and studied with her mother in Maine, then with Miss Munger in Boston, and finally with Mathilde Marchesi in Paris. After her Paris debut as Juliette in Gounod's *Roméo et Juliette* (1889), she sang at the Opéra for two years. Both her Covent Garden and her Metropolitan Opera debuts occurred in 1891, and she continued to sing at these two houses almost every year until her stage retirement in 1911, when she married the Spanish baritone, Emilio de Gogorza.

EASTMAN, George. American music patron (1854–1932). Inventor, industrialist, and founder of the Eastman Kodak Company, George Eastman was directly responsible for the founding of the Eastman School of Music, affiliated with the University of Rochester. In 1919 he contributed $3,500,000 in order to establish the school, and in the following year he gave $1,000,000 more to its permanent endowment fund.

EASTON, Florence. English soprano (1884–1955). Her operatic debut was made at Covent Garden in 1903. She sang for many years in Germany (Berlin and Hamburg) and from 1917–29 was a member of the Metropolitan Opera. Her repertory was enormous, covering over a hundred operas in four languages.

EATON, Quaintance. American writer. After newspaper experience in the Middle West, she became associate editor of *Musical America* and remained there until 1952. She has written several books on music, the latest being *Opera Caravan* (the history of the Metropolitan Opera Company's tours), and *Opera Production, A Handbook*.

ECCLES, John. English composer and violinist (1668–1735). The most famous of a large family of musicians, he wrote theater music and was a member of and later master of the King's Band. His father **Solomon**, also a violinist and composer, was a personal musician to William and Mary. One of his brothers, **Henry** (*c.*1672–*c.*1745), also a personal musician to William and Mary, later moved to Paris where he published as his own a book of violin solos written by others.

Emma Eames as the Countess in The Marriage of Figaro

ECKSTINE, William (Billy). American jazz and popular singer (1914–). After graduation from Howard University, Eckstine performed at various night clubs until he became vocalist with the Earl Hines band. In 1944, he organized his own band with which he sang and played trombone. He has been a leading exponent of the "bop" jazz style and his band has been the training ground of many luminaries in the field of jazz, including Dizzy Gillespie, Charlie Parker, and Miles Davis.

EDDY, Nelson. American baritone and film actor (1901–). His singing career began in opera, but he is most widely known for his concert, radio, and film work.

EDISON, Harry ("Sweets"). American jazz trumpeter (1915–). Edison was a member of the Count Basie band between 1937 and 1950, toured with Josephine Baker, and has led his own groups. He has appeared in films and made many records.

Editing and Publishing of Music

The Editor

We usually think of music as having three principal phases: the composer, who formulates music on paper; the performer, who translates it into sound; and the listener who perceives the work aurally. But between the composer and the performer, there is a fourth person, who can be almost as important as the other three. His is the task of editing the composer's manuscript, to make it accurate and practical.

One need only consult some of the hasty, crossed-up scores of composers to appreciate the importance of the editor and the difficulties he encounters. Even when the composer's handwriting is clearly legible, there will inevitably be some errors; the most careful composer will occasionally forget an accidental, a dynamic or staccato mark, or some other indication. It is the job of the editor to fill these in and to alter any inconsistencies in notation. Sometimes, for example, the editor will recommend some other method of barring that he thinks would be easier to read. Most publishing houses also have policies regarding the notation of transposed instruments, abbreviations, and various visual aspects of the music, so that all their publications will have some resemblance; thus, the editor may make minor changes in keeping with the "house style."

The editor's largest responsibility, however, is toward old music. Figured basses must be realized; ornamentation must be filled in; notation must be modernized; and performance practices of the period must be observed. Current-day editors are usually fairly conscientious in attempting to render everything as the composer meant it to be, but this has not always been true. There are notorious examples of unscrupulous editors who correct the "wrong notes" in original manuscripts, and many erroneous publications have resulted from these "corrections." Competent editing requires that the earliest sources be consulted, and that whatever discrepancies have arisen be meticulously reasoned out. Sometimes the editor must be a detective as well as a musician. In many cases several manuscripts and several editions were printed during the composer's life. It is then necessary to determine the chronology of the sources (older publications are frequently undated), and the role of the composer in each of them. Watermarks, handwriting, plate numbers, and spacing, may provide clues for determining the most authentic reading.

Editions based on original sources are often called "Urtext" editions, but the reliability of a publication can be better judged not by whether it is called an Urtext, but by other signs: are the exact sources given? Are the editor's own additions or corrections placed in brackets or set off in some other way? Are explanations of these changes given in footnotes or in a preface?

Scholars are often engaged by a publisher to edit Urtext editions which require considerable research; and small publishing houses usually employ free-lance musicians for all their editorial work. But the editing in large houses is mostly done by members of the publisher's editorial staff. Another extremely important function of the editorial staff is the reviewing of

Frontispiece of Encomium Musices, *a collection of songs published by Philippe Galle, after J. Stradanus,* circa *1590*

manuscripts submitted for publication. Here the editor is obligated to the music world as well as the business world, and may find himself at odds with the publisher. A conscientious editor judges manuscripts primarily for their lasting musical value, and gives only secondary consideration to their immediate commercial value.

Usually the editorial staff is also responsible for proofreading and other tasks involved in the production of publications. For example, if the publisher decides he would like to issue a concert-band version of a well-known symphony, or a book of art songs arranged for cello and piano, a staff member may be called upon to do the arrangement. Editors are often composers as well, and their own works may be published by their employer.

But editors are only a small part of a music-publishing house. As in most businesses, the majority of its employees are bookkeepers, billing and shipping clerks, salesmen, and so forth.

The Publisher

Before the eighteenth century, there were no music publishers as we know them today. The issuing of printed music was a comparatively simple procedure, the composers themselves taking care of many business details. The composers dealt directly with engraver-printers or, in a few cases, learned to engrave and print their own music. As the demands for printed music increased, however, and the protecting, distributing, and promoting of music became more involved, this procedure became inadequate. The music publisher stepped into the picture as a sort of business manager for composers and as an important part of the music world in his own right.

Today, the activities of a typical music publisher are numerous and varied. Besides making all arrangements for the editing, engraving, printing, and copyrighting of works, he must devote much time to promoting them. He distributes catalogues, sends complimentary copies to critics and conductors, and attempts to interest recording companies in the works he handles. He places advertisements in music publications and often sends representatives to concerts and to conventions of music organizations. The publisher usually maintains a rental library, where sets of parts for large orchestral works are available. It is also important for the publisher to build up his catalogue. Most publishers give careful consideration to the manuscripts that are submitted by composers, and try to obtain other works that interest them. In all, the publisher's work combines that of legal advisor, business manager, promotion director, talent scout, personal representative, and sales agent.

The contracts between composer and publisher vary from case to case, but it is common in the United States for the composer to receive royalties of about 10 per cent on the gross profits derived from his works. The publisher maintains the copyrights and assumes all the costs. Although a well-established composer may have an exclusive contract with one publisher, it is not uncommon for a composer to distribute his works among different houses. However, a composer may belong to only one protective rights society.

The above discussion pertains primarily to publishers of serious music and only partly applies to Tin Pan Alley. The main goal of popular-music publishers is to expose their publications by recordings, radio, television, juke boxes, and live performances. They attempt to interest recording stars in their publications, and to hire song "pluggers" to try to find outlets for them.

Copyrights

Since the earliest days of publishing, authors and composers have had difficulty in keeping their works from being stolen or "pirated." The first country to provide formal copyright protec-

tion was England, which adopted the Statute of Anne in 1709–10. Other countries were slow to follow: Denmark's first copyright law was enacted in 1741, France's in 1793, Spain's in 1847, and Germany's first national copyright law was set down in 1870. Although the first federal copyright act in the United States was passed in 1790, there was no specific protection for musical compositions until 1831.

The most important step in establishing an international copyright law was the formation in 1887 of the International Copyright Union at the Berne Convention. Under this agreement, the member countries grant to foreigners the same copyright protection of their own citizens. All the major European countries except Russia signed this agreement. The United States also maintains independent copyright procedures.

Today, in the United States, one may apply for a copyright of a piece of music by filling out an application and sending it, along with a small fee and one or two copies of the work, to the Library of Congress. If the copyright is secured, it will be valid for 28 years and may be renewed for an additional 28 years before the work falls into public domain. The owner of a copyright has the exclusive rights to print, reprint, copy, sell, dramatize, arrange, and adapt a work; to perform it publicly for profit; and to license its use on records.

Since a musical work may be original only in part, many intricacies arise in determining what part may be copyrighted and what may not. For example, if a piece of music in the public domain is sufficiently *adapted,* by changing the rhythm, harmony, accentuation, or tempo, then the adaptation (but not the original piece) may be copyrighted. However, merely to *set* a piece for contralto and piano does not justify a copyright. There are other fine points: the text of a song is usually copyrighted along with the music, unless the text is already copyrighted or in the public domain. A collection of lyrics may be copyrighted without their music as a book, but not as music. Permission should always be obtained for reprinting any copyrighted music—even when only a few measures are quoted as illustration.

By tradition, any unpublished manuscript is automatically protected by "common law." This means that a composer can collect damages against any pirating—even though his work has not been officially copyrighted—if he can prove he wrote the work, and has not sold the manuscript outright, or abandoned it, or authorized its publication, or otherwise given up his common-law rights. It is considerably safer and, in the long run, easier to take the formal legal precautions. A copyright lawyer should be consulted if there are unusual circumstances.

The protective law states that anyone who performs a copyrighted work publicly and for profit, without obtaining permission from the copyright holder, is liable to pay damages as well as profits. When these profits cannot be ascertained, the infringer must pay $100 for the first performance and $50 for every subsequent performance of a dramatico-musical, choral, or orchestral composition, and $10 for infringing performances of works in other mediums. In no case can the damages be less than $250.

However, the rights which a copyright gives to its holder are of little value if they are not enforced; with professional choruses, orchestras, concert artists, radio and television stations, and other musical outlets being so numerous it is impossible for individual copyright holders to police these mediums adequately. Thus, composers and publishers have banded together to form protective rights societies to enforce the laws, and to guard their rights more efficiently.

There are two main protective agencies in the United States: ASCAP (American Society of Composers, Authors and Publishers), formed in 1914, and BMI (Broadcast Music, Inc.), formed in 1940. Composers of all kinds of music, as well as lyricists and publishers, belong to these organizations. They maintain large staffs that police all the professional music mediums as

thoroughly as possible. Radio broadcasts are spot-checked; files of concert and recital programs are maintained; and representatives travel throughout the country visiting bars, night clubs, hotels, and other places where music is played publicly and for profit. The societies also issue "blanket licenses" which, for an annual fee, give organizations the right to present any works protected by the society. Members receive payments from the societies in accordance with the estimated number of performances of their works. Other countries have similar organizations that are, however, often affiliated with the composers' guild or union in that country, or are agencies of the government, rather than having the autonomy of the American societies.

The Printing of Music

People have been printing music almost as long as they have been printing books. The first attempts to print music came about 20 years after Gutenberg had introduced ordinary letterpress typography (*c.* 1455), and a number of publications containing music notation appeared before 1500. Probably the earliest of these was Johannes Gerson's *Collectorium super Magnificat,* printed by Conrad Fyner at Esslingen in 1473. Much of the earliest publication of music was German, but several Italian music printers were also active during the 1470s and 1480s. The first music to be published in England was Higden's *Policronicon* (1495). American publication of music seems to have begun with the ninth edition of the *Bay Psalm Book* (1698), which included thirteen tunes in two-part harmony.

A number of processes have been used in printing music, but the basic methods are only two. One is *block printing,* in which the impression of an entire page is engraved on a sheet of metal or carved in wood. The other is *type printing,* in which small pieces of movable type are fitted into the desired position. The latter process is always used for printing the words, but music, which requires so many basic shapes and symbols, makes type printing not so practicable. Despite this comparative awkwardness, however, much music has been set in type, and the method is still used in setting musical examples for books.

In the Gerson book of 1473, only the notes

One page from a double-printed anthology of secular songs, published by Ottaviano dei Petrucci in Venice, 1501

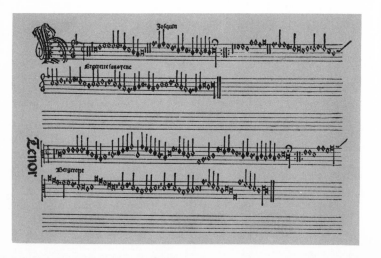

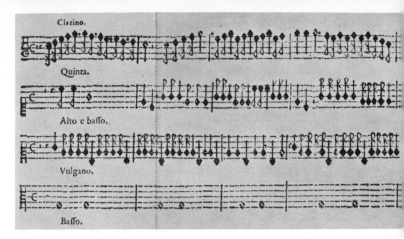

One page of Monteverdi's Orfeo, *printed from movable type. Each piece of type consists of one note and one segment of the five-line staff, producing the small spaces between notes and the uneven appearance of the staffs*

were printed; the staffs were drawn in by hand. In most early publications the staffs were printed, but in a separate impression, often with ink of a different color than that used for the notes. This *double printing* was a troublesome method, for it was difficult to line up the staffs with the notes. Exceptions to the usually poor quality of double-printed editions were issued by the Venetian publisher Ottaviano dei Petrucci (1501 and later), who achieved excellent results. Many attempts were made in the late fifteenth century to print from a woodcut in a single impression; but it was not always possible to carve the delicate musical symbols in wood with sufficiently fine precision. Printers soon discovered that it was easier to make the impression from metal plates, but these efforts were also rather crude at first. The first completely successful block printing using hand-engraved metal plates was done in Rome, late in the sixteenth century: Simone Verovio (*Diletto spirituale,* 1586) and Nicola Borbone (*Toccate di Frescobaldi*). This soon became the most common means of printing music, and is still used today. The engraving was first done entirely by hand until, early in the eighteenth century, engravers refined the method by employing different types of punches to impress the symbols on the metal. Thomas Johnston, who built the organ in Boston's Old North Church, and Paul Revere were two of the earliest American engravers of music; both worked in Boston during the third quarter of the eighteenth century.

Until the invention of the offset press in the twentieth century, music was printed on flatbed presses. An impression of a page was transferred from the engraved plate to a piece of transfer paper, and the transfer was pressed onto lithographic stone. The impression on the stone was rolled with ink, and spread with powdered rosin. Then it was etched with an acid, and the printing was done directly from the stone. The impressions could be polished off and the stones used again for another work after the edition was printed.

In the offset process (the most common method today), the transfer is merely photographed, and the picture is printed on a plate. The plate is etched and the music is printed from that. Since, in the offset process, all one needs in order to print music is a single master copy that may be photographed, it is no longer necessary to have music engraved. This fact has enabled

Engraved frontispiece of Agazzari's Del Sonare Sopra 'l Basso. . . , *1607*

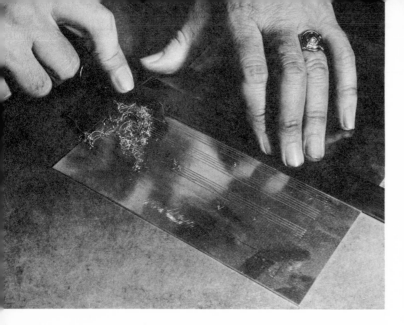

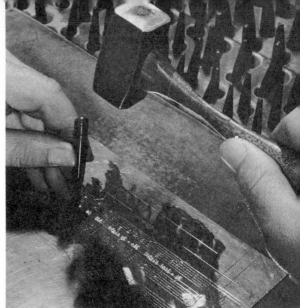

Engraving the musical staffs on a metal plate

Stamping letters of text between musical staffs, the notes being already in position

publishers to print facsimile editions of a composer's sketches, or even entire scores in the composer's handwriting. Offset printing has also had some less good effects, however, for cheap editions of new works can be printed from the composer's manuscript; if a publisher wishes the edition to have a better appearance than the original manuscript, he will still save by sending it to an autographer, who will copy it by hand with extreme precision. The recent invention of the music typewriter provides another source for neat master copies. The use of this machine is rather limited, since it requires a skilled operator; accurate horizontal spacing is difficult to achieve; and words and slurs must be filled in by hand. However, it does have advantages over autography, in that the notes and symbols are always exactly the same size and shape.

In the United States, the per-page rates for autography or typing are much less than for engraving, and many publishers employ these economical methods. Engraving, which is slower than either, requires more experience and more expensive equipment. It continues to be the best and the most common method; but not many of the younger generation are taking up the craft and, with the added threat of competing methods, music engraving may one day be a lost art.

Below is a list of some of the most distinguished music-publishing houses:

Bärenreiter-Verlag

Although a rather young company, the Bärenreiter firm has contributed numerous valuable editions. The company was founded in 1924 in Augsburg, but moved to its present location in Kassel, Germany, in 1928. Among its publications are the collected works of Schütz, a complete edition of Corelli's trio sonatas, many important works of Isaac and Buxtehude, and numerous publications of little-known Baroque chamber music. The firm has also revived many old German folk songs, and works by forgotten composers such as Othmayr, Hassler, and Senfl. In addition, Bärenreiter issues five periodicals: *Der Kirchenchor, Musica, Die Musikforschung, Musik und Kirche,* and *Hausmusik.*

The tools of music engraving

Boosey and Hawkes

This firm was founded by Thomas Boosey in 1816 in London. Highlights of the company's early years were publications of Bellini, Donizetti, and Verdi, and some of the earliest English editions of standard European works. Today the Boosey and Hawkes catalogue is particularly strong in twentieth-century music; the firm handles works by such composers as Rachmaninoff, Stravinsky, Copland, Prokofiev, Richard Strauss, and Britten.

Breitkopf und Härtel

The Breitkopf und Härtel firm was established in Leipzig by Bernhardt Christoph Breitkopf in 1719, but made its most important contributions when it came into the Härtel family several generations later. It was among the first firms to publish vast quantities of the standard works; between 1798 and 1818 it issued 17 volumes of Mozart, 13 of Clementi, and 12 of Haydn. The company was also publishing about that time the first editions of Beethoven's works. Later, it became the original publisher of early works by Wagner, Brahms, Sibelius, Elgar, and Fauré. Their Leipzig headquarters were heavily damaged in air raids during the second World War but were later rebuilt, and Breitkopf resumed activity under the East German government.

Durand et Cie.

In 1870, Marie-Auguste Durand formed, in partnership, a company that was first called Durand et Schönewerk. This firm, now known as Durand et Cie., has concentrated on publishing works by French composers. It has issued the complete works of Rameau, and numerous original publications of works by Lalo, Franck, Massenet, Debussy, and Ravel. The company, located in Paris, is the largest of the French music-publishing houses.

Novello and Co.

Novello and Co., one of the chief English music-publishing houses, was established in 1811 in London. The firm is particularly noteworthy for its innovations in publishing cheap, practical editions of large works. Their early editions of the vocal scores of oratorios were a boon to choral societies in England and else-

Printing from an engraved plate of music

Photographic negatives made from engraved music; inspection precedes the making of final photolithographs

where. The firm also publishes a periodical, *The Musical Times.*

C. F. Peters

This firm, originally located in Leipzig, was purchased by Carl Friedrich Peters in 1814, although it had been active under other names since before 1800. Important Peters editions include early complete collections of Bach, Mozart, and Haydn, and first editions of all but three of Grieg's works. The house, which has been in the Hinrichsen family since 1867, was greatly damaged during the second World War, and the family was forced to abandon the Leipzig location. The heirs jointly established a Peters firm in Frankfurt, and Max Hinrichsen founded Hinrichsen Publications, Ltd., in London. In 1948, his brother, Walter, established C. F. Peters for the Western Hemisphere in New York, where he publishes a great deal of serious American music and represents numerous European publishers in addition to continuing the old Peters catalogue of standard works.

G. Ricordi

Founded by Giovanni Ricordi in 1808, this house has long been the leading Italian music

The first office building of G. Schirmer, Broadway and 4th Street, New York

The first office building of G. Ricordi, in the Teatro alla Scala, Milan

publisher. The firm is centered in Milan, and is renowned for its publication of Italian music. Besides being the original publisher of most of the operas of Bellini, Verdi, Puccini, and others, the firm is in the process of compiling a complete Vivaldi series, and has revived many forgotten works by early Italian composers.

G. Schirmer

G. Schirmer, oldest of the major American music publishers, was established in New York in 1861 by Gustav Schirmer. The firm maintains an extensive catalogue of standard works, and publishes a certain amount of serious contemporary compositions. It is one of the few American houses that maintains its own engraving and printing plant, and is the only American house to publish an important music periodical: *Musical Quarterly,* a musicological journal begun in 1915.

B. Schott und Söhne

This house was founded in 1773 in **Mainz** by Bernhard Schott, and is responsible for a number of first editions of important works. B. Schott und Söhne was the original publisher of Beethoven's *Missa Solemnis,* his Ninth Symphony, and several of his late quartets. It issued first editions of nearly all the operas of Donizetti and Rossini, and several of Wagner's: *Die Meistersinger, Der Ring des Nibelungen,* and *Parsifal.* The firm also publishes the works of Hindemith and issues a journal called *Melos.*

Universal Edition

Universal Edition, established as a corporation in 1901, has been one of the leaders in twentieth-century music publishing. The firm has issued the complete works of Webern, and a number of volumes by such composers as Bruckner, Mahler, Delius, Schoenberg, Berg, and Bartók. Universal has published many works by more recent European composers such as Stockhausen and Boulez, and has also issued a number of works by Americans. The firm has offices in Vienna, Zurich, and London.

Others

A number of other houses have also made valuable contributions: **Editions Salabert,** a French firm founded by Edouard Salabert in 1896, handles many of the important works by modern French composers. The **Oxford University Press,** though primarily a book publisher, has issued many volumes of music by leading English composers.

Music publishing in Iron Curtain countries, because it is government controlled, cannot be compared to the private firms of other countries. However, particular mention should be made of Poland, which is currently issuing the definitive edition of Chopin's complete works. The music publishing agencies of Czechoslovakia, Hungary, and the Soviet Union have also published significant volumes of works by their native composers. Most of these editions are available in the West.

Several other American houses also deserve mention: **Theodore Presser,** founded in 1886, handles the New Music Editions series and publishes a number of serious contemporary works, besides maintaining a large catalogue of standard works. The **Carl Fischer** company, established in 1872, is one of the largest American houses, maintaining offices in New York, Boston, Dallas, and Los Angeles. Foss, Mennin, and Dello Joio are some of the composers represented in Carl Fischer study scores. The firm of **E. B. Marks** has recently become one of the leading American publishers of serious contemporary music.

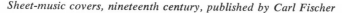

Sheet-music covers, nineteenth century, published by Carl Fischer

A scene from Goethe's Egmont

EDVINA, Louise (real name, **Martin**; stage name taken from her husband, the Hon. Cecil Edwardes). French-Canadian soprano (1885–1948). A pupil of Jean De Reszke, she made her opera debut at Covent Garden in 1908. She sang in Boston from 1912–14, and in Chicago in 1915. She was the first member of the British ruling class to become successful in opera.

EFFINGER, Cecil. American composer (1914–). Effinger's numerous compositions include three symphonies, military marches, concertos and concertinos (for piano, oboe, and other instruments), chamber music, piano compositions, choral works, and songs.

EGER, Joseph. American French-horn player and conductor. Eger was a scholarship graduate of the Curtis Institute of Music, a scholarship student at Tanglewood, and conductor of the Monteux Master Class. He spent more than three years in the United States Army Air Forces Band and was principal horn in major orchestras in Washington, New York, and Los Angeles. He is active as recitalist, soloist with orchestra, director of the Eger Players, soloist-conductor of the chamber orchestra Camera Concerti, and director of the Westside Symphony Orchestra, New York.

EGGE, Klaus. Norwegian composer (1906–). Studied with W. Gmeindl in Berlin. His works often have classical form and make use of folk materials. He has composed symphonies, concertos, chamber music, and piano pieces. Prominent among his works are Symphony No. 1, Op. 17; Symphony No. 3; the Violin Concerto, and Piano Concerto No. 2. He has worked as a music critic *(Arbeiderbladet)* and editor *(Tonekunst)* and since 1945 has been president of the Norwegian Composers Society.

EGK, Werner. German composer and conductor (1901–). Egk's sprightly opera *Die Zaubergeige (The Magic Violin)* brought him to public notice in 1935, and he was conductor at the Berlin State Opera 1938–41 and again 1949–50. He was then appointed director of the Berlin Hochschule für Musik.

His music developed from the simple, popular, and tuneful *Die Zaubergeige* to the sharp and ironic expression that characterizes his later works, e.g. *The Temptations of St. Anthony* (1947) and the singular ballet *Abraxas* (1948). He has written ballets, film music, orchestral works, cantatas, choral works, songs with orchestral accompaniment, and a piano sonata.

Best-known works:

> *Die Zaubergeige,* opera (1934–35), first performance 1935
> *French Suite After Rameau* (1949)
> *The Inspector-General,* opera (1957)

EGMONT OVERTURE. Composition for orchestra, Op. 84, by Beethoven: the prelude to Beethoven's incidental music to Goethe's tragedy *Egmont*. Beethoven wrote in a letter to Goethe: "I read the play with absorbing interest, thought it over, lived it through, and then gave it musical expression."

In addition to the overture, the incidental music consists of nine pieces: four entr'actes, two songs for Clärchen (the beloved of Count Egmont), the *Death of Clärchen,* a melodrama, and the *Victory Symphony,* which is related to the end of the overture. The first performance took place on May 24, 1810, in Vienna.

Goethe's play is laid in sixteenth-century Netherlands. The hero is the Flemish count Lamoral of Egmont (1522–68), who as governor of Flanders became the hope of the country against the reign of terror instituted by the Duke of Alba and the Inquisition. For his defense of his people against the Spaniards' cruelties he was imprisoned, sentenced as a traitor, and executed.

The main theme is:

EICHHEIM, Henry. American composer and violinist (1870–1942). He studied at the Chicago Musical College, played in the Thomas Orchestra, and then in the Boston Symphony. After 1913, he devoted himself to composition, drawing on Oriental sources for his numerous orchestral works. For example, his *Java* makes use of a "gamelan" section of 45 instruments.

EINE KLEINE NACHTMUSIK. Serenade for string orchestra (K. 525), composed in 1787 by Mozart. By *Nachtmusik* ("night music," the German for "serenade") Mozart and his contemporaries meant a musical work in several movements for performance, probably in the open air, on a festive occasion.

Eine kleine Nachtmusik was composed while Mozart was working on *Don Giovanni,* but was apparently never performed during his lifetime.

Eric Blom has called it, "a singularly perfect worklet, thoroughly polished in a classical way—the first movement is a faultless sonatina."

In Alfred Einstein's opinion, the orchestra should be composed of a double string quartet and one double bass. The movements are as follows: I. Allegro, II. Romance, III. Minuet, IV. Rondo.

EINEM, Gottfried von. Austrian composer (1918–), born in Switzerland. Von Einem was a coach at the Berlin State Opera, then studied with Boris Blacher, and finally settled in Salzburg. As a composer he was especially concerned with contemporary music—works of Hindemith, Stravinsky, Milhaud, and others—and also became interested in jazz and semiclassical music. He has written two operas, *Dantons Tod* (Büchner) and *Der Prozess* (*The Trial*) (Kafka); ballet music; piano pieces; songs; and orchestral works, the best known of which are Capriccio for Orchestra, Op. 2, and Meditations, Op. 18.

EINSTEIN, Alfred. German-American musicologist (1880–1952). Also an editor, critic, and teacher, Einstein is best known as a scholar of Mozart and of the Italian madrigal. He settled in the United States in 1939. Important books he wrote include *The Italian Madrigal; Gluck;*

A pre-war performance of Mozart's Eine kleine Nacht-musik *at the Zwinger Palace in Dresden*

A Short History of Music; Greatness in Music; Mozart: His Character, His Work; Schubert: A Musical Portrait; and *Music in the Romantic Era.*

EL-DABH, Halim. Egyptian composer (1921–). El-Dabh's formal musical education was taken at the Sulcz Conservatory in Cairo in 1941 where he first learned to read Western music notation. He came to the United States in 1950 and attended New Mexico University, the New England Conservatory, and Brandeis University. He studied composition with Irving Fine, Francis Cooke, and Aaron Copland. He has composed more than one hundred works, many of which have been performed in the United States, Europe, and the Middle East. His dance epic *Clytemnestra* was commissioned and performed by Martha Graham and her company in 1958 in New York and on tour. El-Dabh received a Guggenheim Fellowship in 1959.

ELECTRIC MUSICAL INSTRUMENTS. These can be divided into two groups; *electro-mechanical instruments,* in which the sounds are produced by means of vibrating strings (as in ordinary musical instruments) or rotating disks, electrically operated; and *electronic instruments,* in which the sounds are produced solely by electrical means with the help of radio tubes and oscillating circuits.

The Ondes Martenot

ELECTRIC STRING INSTRUMENTS

In these the vibrations are picked up by small microphones placed in the neighborhood of the strings; the vibrations do not pass through the air, but directly—either from the strings to the microphones electrically, or from the body of the instrument itself to the microphones.

The Neo-Bechstein Grand

This instrument was invented in 1931. As only quite weak vibrations are required, it is possible to use short strings which are struck by means of very small hammers ("microhammers"). By reducing the damping of the strings, notes are produced with a duration of up to three times that of ordinary piano notes, and by increased damping, tones similar to those of the spinet or harpsichord can be produced.

PHOTOELECTRIC SYSTEMS

A rotating black celluloid disk with holes or slits in it, is made to interrupt the light from an incandescent lamp in a rhythm dependent upon the shape and position of the holes or slits. The interrupted beam of light falls on a photoelectric cell, which transforms the varying light beam into electric current with corresponding variations.

Spielmann's Superpiano

Invented in 1927, this instrument resembles an ordinary piano in outward appearance. It contains photoelectric "sirens" totaling twenty-four disks, twelve of a type which produces vibrations rich in harmonics, and twelve of a type producing vibrations with few harmonics. The disks have an incandescent lamp for each row of light holes. The timbre can be varied by connecting different disks, and by the use of differently shaped apertures which control the beam of light falling on the holes in the disks. The superpiano has a compass of seven octaves.

ELECTROMAGNETIC SYSTEMS

These have an iron-toothed wheel rotating near an electromagnet. Changes occur in the magnetic field when a tooth moves into it, and differences in potential arise in the windings of the coil. By varying the number of teeth and the shape of the disk the character and the frequency of the current may be changed as desired.

The Hammond Organ

In this organ, invented by Laurens Hammond in 1935, the vibrations are produced by electromagnetic "sirens." It has ninety-six sets of disks producing the various semitones. Timbre is altered by adding tones from different disks, or by means of electric filters. The modern Hammond organ can also produce an artificial echo effect, so that the listener in a small room has the impression of hearing the music in a large concert hall or church.

ELECTRONIC SYSTEMS

An electric oscillation circuit consists, in its simplest form, of a capacitor and coil. If the circuit receives an impulse, electric oscillations of a fixed frequency arise. The frequency may be adjusted by varying the capacitance of the ca-

Rotating disks with light holes used in photoelectric systems

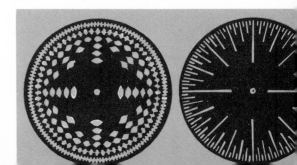

pacitor or the inductance of the coil. In a circuit as simple as this the oscillations would soon die out, but by connecting it to a radio tube it is possible to keep the circuit oscillating until it is purposely broken. Apparatus of this type is called an oscillator.

Leon Theremin's Spherical Musical Instrument

This early electric instrument was invented in 1924. The first radio sets with tubes had a tendency to "howl" when the hand was placed near them. Theremin's instrument was a specially built radio set in which the pitch of the "howl" was varied over a wide compass by moving the hand toward and away from a metal rod at the top of the cabinet (i.e. the capacitance of an electric circuit was varied). A switch was added to make it possible to play staccato.

Martenot's Musical Waves

An improvement on Theremin's invention was made by the French pianist and radio technician, Maurice Martenot, who produced what he called musical waves. His instrument, the Ondes Martenot, consisted of a wire stretched over a keyboard, which served as a guide. By moving the wire the capacitance of a capacitor, the pitch of the notes (frequency of the electric circuit) produced was varied. The timbre can be changed by electric filters. Music has been specially composed (by Honegger, André Jolivet, Florent Schmitt, and others) for Martenot's instrument.

The Hellertion and the Trautonium

A characteristic feature of Hellberger's Hellertion (1928) and Trautwein's Trautonium (1930) is the use of a resistance wire. Pitch is dependent upon the potential in one of the electrodes of the oscillator tube, and this potential is controlled by a resistance placed under a metal wire, the potential varying with the resistance. By depressing the wire, any desired length of the resistance is connected into the circuit, resulting in notes of the desired pitch. By means of finger pressure it is also possible to control the volume and the rate of transience and decay. The principle is similar to that of playing a conventional string instrument.

RCA Victor Electronic Music Synthesizer

A composite electronic instrument which can both transcribe and reproduce musical sounds.

The RCA Synthesizer produces sound from a punched tape, whose holes indicate pitch, loudness, timbre, growth, duration, and decay of sound. This tape, which can be made on the Synthesizer, can be created from a conventional score, in which case the Synthesizer will produce an electronic version of the sounds of actual instruments, or can be especially composed in terms of electronically produced sound. The sounds thus produced can then be transferred to magnetic recording tape, suitable for use at a performance. Conversely, sounds produced originally through electronic impulses and recorded immediately on tape, can be translated into the Synthesizer's punched paper roll, combined, altered, etc., at the will of the composer, and the resulting combinations re-recorded as they come out of the Synthesizer.

AMPLIFICATION AND FILTERS

Amplification of the very weak vibrations produced by an oscillator or mechanical generator is accomplished by means of an amplifier, to which one or more loudspeakers may be connected. It is possible to devise electric filters and circuits which pass only vibrations of certain frequencies, other frequencies being filtered out.

Electric musical instruments have some advantages over ordinary instruments with regard to the adjustment of volume, pitch, timbre, and duration of notes. While the volume of ordinary

The RCA Victor Electronic Music Synthesizer

instruments is limited, that of electric instruments may be varied by regulating the amplification from the most delicate pianissimo to a volume comparable to that of a large church organ.

The "artificial" generation of notes makes it possible to produce any pitch throughout the entire musical register; ordinary musical instruments, with the exception of the organ and piano, do not exceed a compass of four octaves.

Timbre is varied by adding or filtering out harmonics as desired, by means of electric filters. Electric string instruments are admittedly somewhat limited by the timbre of the vibrating string, but in other instruments it is possible, by means of a simple manual control, to change from the light tone of a flute to the dark timbre of the violin. It is also possible to regulate the transience and decay rate of the notes—that is to say, when and how rapidly individual harmonics are added or removed from the note.

ELECTRONIC MUSIC. Electronic music had its origin in the studios of various European radio stations. Its conception and execution are

based on the use of magnetic tape which provides the raw material, and, in a sense, may be compared to the instruments used in the performance of conventional music.

In electronic music musical instruments are rarely used. Sounds are produced electronically by means of generators and filters. Occasionally musical instruments are used in the laboratory to produce the initial sounds, which are later altered and deformed electronically and incorporated into the over-all electronic fabric. The extensive use of noises in combination with tones which produce no overtone vibrations is one of the aspects of electronic music. The entire movement is still in the experimental and developmental stages, and its possibilities seem virtually unlimited.

Several attempts have been made to combine electronic music with instrumental ensembles (Stockhausen, Boulez, Pusseur), but it has been most convincing in its pure form, and the new vistas of sound it has produced have already exerted an influence on conventional instrumental music.

The technical explanation which follows was

A magnetophone, an oscilloscope, a tone generator, and a cutting table

A magnetophone, an electronic musical score, and a model of a band cut

provided by Gottfried Michael Koenig, a composer and one of the experts in the field.

COMPOSITION AND NOTATION

Electronic music came into existence in the 1950s. The composer's intention (although theoretically formulated much later) was to graduate all musical elements unbrokenly, to relate them to one another, and, where possible, to replace one by another: intensity by timbre, timbre by time structure, etc. The technique of electromagnetic recording (by tape) made accessible an area which remains closed to instrumental music. Any "spectrum" (i.e. any timbre) can be produced from tones that are partials of instrumental timbre, or by noise-bands. Any rhythmic configuration can be prescribed by cutting and splicing the tape; any pitch and volume can be regulated by the employment of generators and volume indicators; and the sound can be made to appear to emanate from any position in the concert hall by using several loudspeakers.

As with instrumental music, the performance of an electronic composition depends on a score. The electronic music score is notated in units of measurement: in Hertz (frequency cycles per second) for the pitch, in centimeters (corresponding to a certain tape speed) for the time values, and in decibels for volume values. These data can be expressed either in a diagram or in a table of figures.

The technique of composition is basically similar to that of serial instrumental music. (See *Twelve-Tone Music.*)

TECHNIQUE

The main sound sources are three types of generators: the sinus tone generator (for continual-periodic processes); the noise generator (for continual-aperiodic processes); and the impulse generator (for discontinuous processes, periodic or aperiodic). Sinus tones are combined to spectra (timbres), and white noise and impulses (clicks) are filtered to colored noise and impulses with defined pitch. "White" and "colored" are terms derived from the analysis of light: white noise contains all frequencies and can be most easily compared to the sound of the sea.

The recorded sounds are determined in their length by cutting the tape, and in their volume (or alteration of volume) by dynamic regulation ("envelopes"). Possibilities of further transformation are: transposition (the simultaneous alteration of frequency and duration) by altering the tape speed; filtering (the sifting out of various frequency ranges); reverberation (spatial depth, aleatoric modulation); frequency and amplitude modulation; and ring-modulation (multiplicative mixing).

The results are combined—always according to the score—into the whole piece (synchronization). Should the spatial position of the sounds be determined, these must be distributed either among several synchronized tapes, or onto a tape with several tracks.

DEVELOPMENT

After the initial experiments with the Monochord (Trautwein) and Melochord (Bode), the first studio for electronic music began to operate regularly in May 1953 at the Westdeutscher Rundfunk (West German Radio) in Cologne, under the direction of Herbert Eimert. A studio for tape music in New York and a studio for *musique concrète* in Paris were already in existence. Each has exercised an important influence on the present-day work. After the foundation of the Cologne studio, studios were also set up in Milan, Tokyo, Brussels, Eindhoven, Hilversum, and Warsaw.

Electronic music has been presented in public concerts by the Cologne Radio Station: in 1953 on the occasion of the International Music Festival (ISCM), in 1954 in the second half of a concert in the series *Musik der Zeit,* in 1956 and 1958 in concerts consisting exclusively of electronic music. Electronically produced sounds have been used in the theater, motion pictures, and radio. Electronic music composers include Bülent Arel, Milton Babbitt, Luciano Berio, Robert Beyer, Herbert Brun, John Cage, Mario Davidovsky, Herbert Eimert, Halim El-Dabh, Franco Evangelisti, Karel Goeyvaerts, Paul Gredinger, Bengt Hambraeus, Hermann Heiss, Mauricio Kagel, Giselher Glebe, Gottfried Michael Koenig, Ernst Křenek, György Ligeti, Otto Luening, Bruno Maderna, Bo Nilsson, Henri Pousseur, Karlheinz Stockhausen, Vladimir Ussachevsky, and Edgar Varèse. Public concerts have been organized in Brussels, Darmstadt, Helsinki, Milan, Munich, New York, Paris, Salzburg, Stockholm, Tokyo, Vienna, Warsaw, and in several other cities in the United States and Canada.

OUTLOOK

Although none of the composers of electronic music has issued any program concerning the meaning and future of his métier, the future prospects of this art form can be seen from its development to date.

The student of the development of instrumental music will find in electronic music an impetus to ever-increasing expansion of technique and language (new instruments, new sounds, new rhythms, and new forms).

In seeking and finding new technical media in electric generators, magnetic tape, and the loudspeaker, composers have discovered new

Gerda Lammers as Elektra and Frances Yeend as Chrysothemis in the Metropolitan Opera production of Strauss' Elektra *in 1962*

timbres through new filter combinations, and technical processes have been simplified by new copying methods. The new technical possibilities have also been used to distribute several sound sources in the concert hall in order to make the structure of the music more clear. Technical development aims at the construction of an electronic brain, such as the RCA Music Synthesizer, which would combine the possibilities of the various generators and filters hitherto used and control the total acoustical range. Attempts are also being made to manipulate real stereophony without employing microphones or mobile loudspeakers.

ÉLÉGIE. Composition by Massenet. In 1873 the composer was asked to provide the incidental music for Leconte de Lisle's drama *Les Erinnyes*. The music as a whole failed to please, but it contained one beautiful melody—the tune now known as *Élégie*. This was published separately as a song with cello and piano accompaniment, and became perhaps the most popular of Massenet's two hundred songs.

ELEGY. Greek, "song of lamentation."

ELEKTRA. Opera in one act (1909) by Richard Strauss, with libretto by Hugo von Hofmannsthal. *Elektra* began the partnership of Strauss and Von Hofmannsthal which lasted twenty years, until the latter's death in 1929. Von Hofmannsthal's *Elektra* was originally a play, not intended for music, but when Strauss attended a performance he at once realized what a good opera libretto it would make. The subject is taken from Sophocles' tragedy of the same name.

Elektra has been termed "a dramatized symphonic poem." An orchestra of 111 players is required, and almost superhuman demands are made of the singers. The work was a *succès de scandale* at its first performance in 1909 in Dresden, and created a furor when it was conducted by Sir Thomas Beecham at Covent Garden the next year.

Time: *After the Trojan War*

Place: *Courtyard of the Royal Palace at Mycenae*

Elektra (soprano) is the daughter of Agamemnon, who, on returning from the Trojan War, was murdered by his wife Klytemnestra (contralto) and her lover Aegisthus. Day and night Elektra ponders how to

Inge Borkh as Elektra in the Salzburg Festival production of 1957

avenge her father. Some rebuke and others support her, but all fear her. Her sister, Chrysothemis (soprano), also suffers but cannot bear to think of revenge.

In a violent scene Elektra invokes the spirit of her father. She relives the dreadful murder, and in her imagination sees how, with the help of her sister and her brother, Orestes, who is abroad, she can wreak vengeance on the assassins.

Chrysothemis warns her sister against Klytemnestra, who is troubled by horrible dreams. A gruesome procession of sacrificial victims precedes Klytemnestra who asks Elektra if she knows a cure for her ghastly dreams. Elektra first replies that Klytemnestra will dream no more once the appointed victim has fallen to the ax. When she sees that Klytemnestra does not understand her, she tells her mother that it is *she* who will die.

Word of the death of Orestes is brought, and Elektra goes mad with grief and despair. A messenger is dispatched to Aegisthus, and Elektra resolves herself to wield the ax that she has kept hidden pending the coming of Orestes, and slay her mother and her mother's lover.

She is unable to persuade her sister to join her, and this infuriates her. Then the messenger who had brought the news of Orestes' death enters. At first Elektra does not recognize him, but she soon discovers that he is her brother Orestes (baritone), and hands him the ax.

Orestes goes to Klytemnestra's room and kills her. Aegisthus arrives, and is received with deceptive friendliness by Elektra. He goes into the palace, where Orestes is waiting, and is slain. Elated at her revenge,

Elektra flings herself into a convulsive dance of insane joy, but when it is at its height she falls to the ground dead.

ELGAR, Sir Edward. English composer (1857–1934). Although he received almost no formal musical training, Elgar grew up in a musical household and was immersed in practical music from an early age. His father was organist at St. George's Roman Catholic Church in Worcester, and Elgar substituted for his father while still a schoolboy. He also learned to play the violin and bassoon and sang in the Worcester Glee Club. When he left school, he went into a solicitor's office, but he continued his playing and he also composed. Some of his works were performed by local groups, but it was not until after his marriage in 1889 that he began to be known outside the vicinity of Worcester. His first major success came when his concert overture *Froissart* was played at the Worcester Festival in 1890. The *Enigma Variations,* probably his best-known piece outside England, dates from 1899, and his masterpiece, the oratorio *The Dream of Gerontius* (text by Cardinal Newman), from 1900. One of his five *Pomp and Circumstance* marches (1901–30), the one later known as *Land of Hope and Glory,* has had an extraordinary success.

During his lifetime he received many honors, among them the Order of Merit (1911) and several honorary degrees; he was made K.C.V.O. (1928) and a baronet (1931), and was appointed Master of the King's Musick (1924). He is appreciated far more in England than in other countries, although both Richard Strauss and Hans Richter were warm admirers. His output sharply declined after his wife's death in 1920, and he left behind several unfinished large-scale pieces.

ELGAR'S BEST-KNOWN WORKS

ORCHESTRAL

Symphonies:
  No. 1, A flat major, Op. 55 (1908)
  No. 2, E flat major, Op. 63 (1911)
Violin Concerto, B minor, Op. 61 (1910)
Cello Concerto, E minor, Op. 85 (1919)
Enigma Variations, Op. 36 (1899)
Falstaff: Symphonic Study, Op. 68 (1913)
Pomp and Circumstance, Op. 39, Marches
  1. D major, *Land of Hope and Glory* (1901)
  2. A minor (1901)

EDWARD ELGAR

ROSALIND ELIAS

  3. C minor (1905)
  4. G major, *Song of Liberty* (1907)
  5. C major (1930)

CHORAL

Coronation Ode, Op. 44, soloists and chorus (A. C. Benson)
  No. 6, *Land of Hope and Glory* (1901)
The Dream of Gerontius, Op. 38, oratorio (Newman) (1900)

ELIAS, Rosalind. American mezzo-soprano. Following studies at the New England Conservatory of Music, Rosalind Elias appeared with the New England Opera and the Boston Symphony Orchestra. After three summer scholarships at Tanglewood she went to La Scala, Milan, and the San Carlo Opera in Naples. Upon her return to the United States she won an American Theatre Wing scholarship and was signed to a Metropolitan Opera contract. She made her Metropolitan Opera debut in 1954. She created the role of Erika in Barber's *Vanessa* in its world première at the Metropolitan Opera, in addition to appearing in other leading roles. She has toured extensively in the United States and Canada and has appeared in Europe.

ELIJAH. Oratorio for soloists, chorus, and orchestra, Op. 70, by Mendelssohn. The composer's last great work, it was completed in 1846, the year before his death. In 1845 the Birmingham Musical Festival committee invited Mendelssohn to conduct at their next festival and to provide a work for performance on that occasion. The composer replied that he had begun an oratorio some time before and hoped to complete it in time for the festival. In May, 1846, when he had finished the first part and some numbers of the second, he wrote to Jenny Lind, for whose beautiful voice the soprano part was written: "I am jumping about my room for joy. If it only turns out to be half as good as I believe it is, how pleased I shall be!"

He completed the work by the end of July, and brought the instrumental parts and translation of the text with him to England in mid-August.

The work received its first performance at Birmingham, August 26, 1846. It was a fantastic success; the applause was deafening, and encores had to be given of four choruses and four solos.

"No other work of mine ever went so admirably at the first performance," Mendelssohn wrote that evening, "or was received with such enthusiasm by both musicians and public. . . . Never in my life did I hear a better performance."

Nevertheless, he at once set about making alterations to the score and was not satisfied with it until December. In April, 1847, on his last visit to England, he conducted four performances of the work in London, Queen Victoria and Prince Albert attending the second of them. He conducted it again in Manchester and Birmingham, and engaged to do the same in Berlin, and in Vienna where Jenny Lind was due to take part. But his last illness caused the cancellation of the Berlin performance and he died ten days before the date of the Vienna performance.

ELISIR D'AMORE, L' *(The Elixir of Love).* Comic opera in two acts by Donizetti, with libretto by F. Romani. With its gay and melodious music, amusing "whispering choir," attractive arias, and artless but charming story, this is a genuine Italian comic opera and a delightful work. First presented in Milan in 1832, it was for many years seldom performed, but it

Dieric Bouts, Elijah in the Desert. *Part of a triptych in the Church of St. Peter, Louvain*

has gained in popularity and is now often played at the larger opera houses.

Time: *End of the 18th Century*
Place: *A village in the north of Italy*

ACT I

Scene: *The village square*

Nemorino (tenor), a handsome but poor peasant, is in love with Adina (soprano), a wealthy and beautiful young woman, but she does not return his love:

Quanto è bel-la, quan-to è ca-ra! Più la ve-do,

Nemorino's unhappy state is made worse by the entrance of Sergeant Belcore, a vain and dashing soldier, who is trying to take Adina by storm.

A quack doctor, Dulcamara (bass), arrives and sells a "miraculous love potion," which he promises Nemorino will enable him to win Adina within twenty-four hours. Nemorino buys a bottle of the stuff (which is actually only red wine) and empties it at one gulp with the instantaneous effect that he begins to dance and sing but pays not the slightest attention to Adina.

Adina, annoyed at this treatment, promises herself to the sergeant. The latter receives orders to march with his section and must therefore marry immediately.

Adina agrees, thus throwing Nemorino once again into despair.

ACT II

Scene: *A farm*

The villagers are ready to celebrate Adina's marriage to Belcore, although she is alarmed by Nemorino's absence. Nemorino is not quite satisfied with the effects of the first bottle and wishes to buy another; as he has no money, he allows himself to be enlisted by Belcore, in order to pay the quack with his soldier's pay.

The village girls, having learned that Nemorino's uncle has just died and made his nephew rich, treat him with new respect. He of course thinks this is due to the second bottle of elixir which he has in the meantime purchased from Dr. Dulcamara. Adina learns from the doctor that Nemorino has signed up with the regiment in order to have money to buy the second bottle of elixir, and is so touched at the strength of Nemorino's affection that she realizes she loves him. Nemorino, having seen a tear in Adina's eye and realizing there is hope for his love, sings the famous aria, *Una furtiva lacrima:*

U - na fur - ti - va La - gri - ma ___   negl' oc - chi

Adina has bought out Nemorino's contract with the army. She presents the contract to him, but at first she behaves so shyly that he threatens to seek death in the war, whereupon she throws herself into his arms. Belcore takes his disappointment like a man, and Dulcamara is able to sell the remainder of his love potion on the strength of the happiness the two bottles have brought.

ELÍZAGA, José Mariana. Mexican theorist and composer (1786–1842). A child prodigy, Elízaga received all his training in Mexico. In 1825 he founded the first Mexican conservatory. He wrote two didactic works, *Elementos de música* (1823) and *Principios de la harmonía y melodía* (1835) and composed music for chorus and orchestra. He was one of the first in Mexico to promote the music of Mozart and Beethoven.

ELIZALDE, Federico. Philippine conductor and composer (1907–). Born in Manila, he studied at the Madrid Conservatory, and in England, then with Ernest Bloch in California. He became conductor of the Manila Symphony Orchestra in 1930, spent the second World War in France, and was appointed president of the Manila Broadcasting Company in 1948. A friend of Ravel, Debussy, Milhaud, Lorca, and above all De Falla, he has written an opera *Paul Gauguin* (1948), a violin concerto (1943),

The arrival of Dr. Dulcamara in Act I of L'Elisir d'Amore *at the Metropolitan Opera*

a piano concerto (1947), and much chamber music.

ELLINGTON, Edward Kennedy ("Duke"). American pianist, composer, and band leader (1899–). It was intended at first that Ellington should become a painter, and he studied for a time at the Pratt Institute in New York. But owing to lack of money he had to abandon his art studies, and he took a job as a pianist at a small café in his home town, Washington, D. C., where he wrote his first composition, *Soda Fountain Rag.*

About 1919 he formed a band with some school friends, and three years later he was taken into Wilbur Sweatman's band in New York. In 1923, however, Ellington again became the leader of his own band, and, after playing at various Harlem night clubs, he won an engagement at the Cotton Club in 1927. In the course of four years there the band became world-famous, thanks largely to Ellington's ability for getting the best out of such musicians as Bubber Miley, "Tricky Sam" Nanton, and Harry Carney.

Ellington's records of 1927–38 best reveal his quality as an arranger, both of the powerful mass orchestra in which he smoothly sets one section against another (as in *New Black and Tan Fantasy*) and of the soft, intimate moods with muted sound effects (as in *Mood Indigo* and *Solitude*). Among his arrangements with a more pronounced swing character are *Me and You, Harlem Air-Shaft,* and *Harlem Speaks.* He has also distinguished himself in a number of piano recordings, including the celebrated *Black Beauty* (with bass players Jimmy Blanton and Oscar Pettiford).

Swing style avowedly influenced him in several brilliant numbers, including *So Far So Good.* He has also created orchestral works which seem at first sight to be related to symphonic jazz, but display on closer inspection a truly intimate contact with genuine jazz. Examples of this style are the small concerto pieces for his soloists, who included such men as Cootie Williams, Johnny Hodges, Juan Tizol, Ben Webster, Louis Bellson, and Al Hibbler (*Concerto for Cootie, Trumpet in Spades,* and *Echoes of Harlem*), or the large suites, *Black, Brown and Beige,* with its moving blues-inspired section, and the *Liberian Suite* dedicated to the African Negro republic.

DUKE ELLINGTON

"The music of my race," Ellington has said, "is more than an American form of expression. . . . What we Negroes did not dare to say openly, we said in music, and what we call jazz is something more than mere dance music."

ELLIOTT, Don. American jazz instrumentalist (1926–). Elliott's instruments are the mellophone, vibraphone, and trumpet. He studied harmony at the Juilliard School of Music and arranging at the University of Miami. He has been a member of the George Shearing, Teddy Wilson, Benny Goodman, and Buddy Rich groups, and he has headed his own group.

ELLSTEIN, Abraham. American composer (1907–1963). He studied music first at the Third Street Settlement and then at the Juilliard Graduate School in New York, where he studied composition with Rubin Goldmark. He has written over thirty scores for the Yiddish operetta theater, three scores for Broadway musicals, and several scores for Warsaw-made films. He is well known as a composer of Jewish liturgical music. He wrote a one-act opera, *The Thief and the Hangman,* which won Ohio State University's competition for American chamber opera, and a full-length opera, *The Golem,* which opened the 1962 season of the New York City Opera Company. His last work, *The Redemption,* is an oratorio based on the Chanukah story.

ELMAN, MISCHA. Russian-American violinist (1891–). Elman's father, a rabbi and a keen amateur violinist, sent his son to the Royal School of Music in Odessa. When he was twelve years old, Elman gave a concert at which Leopold Auer heard him play and wanted to take him to St. Petersburg, where he could take charge of the boy's further training. At this time, Jews were not allowed to reside in St. Petersburg, but Auer used his influence, and an exception was made for Mischa Elman and his father.

Elman soon became Auer's favorite pupil, and before long was able to substitute for his teacher at a concert, playing Mendelssohn's Violin Concerto and Paganini's *Moto Perpetuo* almost as well as Auer would have played them himself.

ABRAHAM ELLSTEIN

MISCHA ELMAN

He appeared as a soloist in Paris with the Colonne Orchestra, and gave concerts in Vienna, Berlin, London, and other European cities. The Duke of Mecklenburg presented him with an Amati violin as a token of his admiration.

In 1908, the seventeen-year-old virtuoso arrived in New York, the first of many representatives of the great school of violinists from the St. Petersburg Conservatory; others were Heifetz, Zimbalist, and Milstein. His success was immediate. He became an American citizen in 1923, and in 1925 he married an American. For a wedding present he received a Stradivarius which had belonged to Mme. Récamier.

Elman, who founded his own string quartet in 1924, is beyond question one of the finest violinists of his time. From the musical point of view modesty is a notable trait in his character; he always puts the composition and its purely musical features first, and he subordinates himself entirely when playing in an ensemble. His tone is sensitive, warm, and vibrant. He has given more than three thousand concerts all over the world, and millions of his records have been sold. His repertoire includes more than six hundred concertos and sonatas.

ELSON, Louis Charles. American music scholar (1848–1920). He was for many years music editor of the Boston *Advertiser,* and edited musical publications and acted as correspondent for various newspapers. He wrote more than a dozen books on music, including dictionaries and analyses, and composed many works, as well as arranging innumerable songs.

ELWELL, Herbert. American composer and critic (1898–). He studied with Ernest Bloch in New York and Nadia Boulanger in Paris, and won a fellowship at the American Academy in Rome in 1926. Two years later he became head of the theory and composition department at the Cleveland Institute of Music, and for six years edited the program notes of the Cleveland Orchestra. He has been for many years music critic of the Cleveland *Plain Dealer*. Elwell's compositions include a ballet, *The Happy Hypocrite; Introduction and Allegro,* for orchestra; *I Was With Him,* cantata; *Blue Symphony,* for voice and string quartet; *Lincoln: Requiem Aeternam,* for chorus and orchestra; *Pastorale,* for voice and orchestra; *Ode,* for orchestra; and many others.

EMBOUCHURE. A term denoting the position of lips and mouth adopted in playing woodwind and brass instruments. The position of lips and mouth is the player's greatest single influence on the tone and intonation of his instrument, since this controls the shaping of the column of air supplied by the lungs as it is forced into the instrument. Unless a player develops a good embouchure, he will not become a good wind player, no matter how he develops his finger technique. The teeth and jaw are also important to the embouchure, since they form the scaffolding which supports the mouth, tongue, and lips. The term is also used for the mouthpiece of certain wind instruments, particularly the flute.

EMPEROR CONCERTO. Popular name for Beethoven's Piano Concerto in E flat major. See *Beethoven (Concertos).*

EMPEROR QUARTET. See *Haydn (Chamber Music).*

EMPEROR WALTZ *(Kaiserwalzer).* Composition for orchestra, Op. 437, by Johann Strauss the Younger, who wrote it to celebrate the fortieth anniversary (December 2, 1888) of the accession of the Emperor Francis Joseph. As the Emperor's life had been clouded with much

GEORGES ENESCO

sorrow, Strauss' homage was infused with majestic calm rather than gaiety.

ENCINA, Juan del. Spanish poet, dramatist, and composer (1468–1529). He served as master of ceremonies for the second Duke of Alba from about 1492 to 1500. He then entered on an ecclesiastical career, being ordained a priest in 1519. He did most of his composing before 1500, setting many of his own poems to music, and writing for the Duke a series of eclogues (pastoral plays) containing *villancicos* (rustic songs), the music for which also he wrote himself. He is considered one of the founders of Spanish secular drama and was the most important Spanish composer of his day.

ENDICH, Sara. American soprano (1930–). She attended Ohio State University and the Berkshire Music School in Lenox, Massachusetts. She first appeared in the Young Artists Series at the Brooklyn Academy of Music in 1951. Since 1952, she has been a regular soloist with the Boston Symphony Orchestra, has appeared with leading orchestras throughout the United States, and has made recital tours.

ENESCO, Georges. Romanian violinist, conductor, and composer (1881–1955). In his last years Enesco was regarded as his country's leading musician, and aroused the admiration of the whole world by his achievements in all branches of musical activity.

He entered the Musical Academy at Vienna when he was nine years old, and later studied at the Paris Conservatory, where he won the highest distinction as a violinist. His teachers, Massenet, Fauré, Gédalge, and Marsick, brought him to a certain extent under French influence, but he retained his national characteristics. Extensive tours in Europe and America established his fame as a violinist, particularly for his very individual interpretations of Mozart.

As a composer Enesco won fame with works like *Poème roumain, Symphonie Concertante,* the opera *Oedipus,* and his lively *Romanian Rhapsodies.*

Until the second World War Enesco lived alternately in Romania and France; afterward he settled in the United States. He taught at the Mannes Music School, New York, 1948–50, and then joined the faculty of the University of Illinois.

ENFANT ET LES SORTILÈGES, L' *(The Child and the Sorceries).* One-act opera ("lyrical fantasy") by Maurice Ravel with libretto by the novelist Colette; première in Monte Carlo, March 21, 1925. The plot concerns a naughty boy who will not do his lessons, abuses his playthings, and is rude to his mother. The toys and furnishings in his room and the animals in the garden, having become much larger than the boy, begin to torment him in revenge. The boy realizes how cruel he has been; when, in the ensuing fight, he tends the wounded paw of a squirrel and then faints, the animals and objects fetch his mother. Among the numbers are a duet in cat language between two cats *(Miinhou, Môrnâou, nâou),* and a duet in fake English between the Wedgewood tea pot and the Chinese tea cup. *(How's your mug?)*

ENGEL, Carl. American musicologist (1883–1944). He was chief of the Music Division of the Library of Congress from 1922–34 and was then appointed Honorary Consultant in Musicology. Editor of the *Musical Quarterly* from 1929 until his death, most of his writings were published in that magazine. He was one of the founders of the American Musicological Society.

A scene from L'Enfant et les Sortilèges *performed by the Opera Society of Washington (D. C.)*

ENGEL, Lehman. American composer and conductor (1910–). He studied at the Conservatory of Cincinnati and the Cincinnati College of Music, then with Rubin Goldmark at the Juilliard Graduate School in New York, and later with Roger Sessions. He began his career as a theater conductor, has also written much incidental music for theatrical productions, and two operas, *Malady of Love* and *The Soldier*. He founded and was head of the Madrigal Singers (1936–39) under the W.P.A. He has composed orchestral music, chamber music, and ballet (for Martha Graham and other dancers).

ENGLISH HORN (cor anglais). See *Wind Instruments*.

ENIGMA VARIATIONS. Composition for orchestra by Edward Elgar, consisting of fourteen variations on an original theme (Op. 36). Elgar began the work on February 5, 1899, and finished it fourteen days later. It was first performed on June 19, 1899, with Hans Richter conducting.

Each variation represents some aspect of the character of one of Elgar's friends, the friend's initials, or a pseudonym being attached to the appropriate section. All the personalities have been identified. The "enigma" of the title did not lie only in the mystery of the friends' identities, however. Elgar said that his theme is in counterpoint with another, unheard theme which is a well-known tune: "Through and over the whole set, another and larger theme 'goes,' but is not played." This "unheard" tune has never been discovered.

ENTFÜHRUNG AUS DEM SERAIL, DIE. See *Abduction from the Seraglio, The*.

ENTREMONT, Philippe. French pianist (1934–). Philippe Entremont studied with his mother, with Marguerite Long, and at the Paris Conservatory with Jean Doyen. In 1953 he was awarded the Harriet Cohen Piano Medal and won first prize in the Marguerite Long–Jacques Thibaud International Competition. He made his United States debut the same year, playing the American première of Jolivet's Piano Concerto in Carnegie Hall with the National Orchestral Association conducted by Leon Barzin. He has since been heard as soloist with the major orchestras in the United States, and has toured throughout the world.

Detail of an Erard piano made in London, c. 1880. The Metropolitan Museum of Art. Gift of Mrs. Henry McSweeney, 1959

ERARD, Sébastien. Alsatian piano and harp maker (1752–1831). After learning his father's trade of cabinetmaking, he learned harpsichord-making in Paris. His was the first pianoforte made in France (1777) and with his brother he set up a workshop which enjoyed the protection of Louis XVI. A London branch was established in 1786. His nephew, **Pierre Erard** (1796–1855), succeeded him. The firm was known for its many improvements in the harp (double action, 1811) and pianoforte (repetition action, 1809). After 1890 the firm ceased manufacturing in London, but it is still the leading French manufacturer of pianos and harps.

ERB, John Lawrence. American organist and teacher (1877–1950). He was music director of several prominent educational institutions, the last being Connecticut College for Women.

His books include a biography of Brahms, and studies on theory and appreciation. He composed songs, piano and organ pieces, and music for pageants.

ERB, John Warren. American educator and composer (1887–1948). He studied in Berlin with Scharwenka, Ochs, and Weingartner, and in the United States with Edgar Stillman Kelley. He held many distinguished posts, among them director of music at Lafayette College. His compositions include *An Early Greek Christmas, The Unfoldment* (strings), and others.

EREDE, Alberto. Italian conductor (1909–). After studying at the Genoa Conservatory and under Weingartner at the Basel Conservatory, he gained his first important post in 1934 when he became associate conductor, with Fritz Busch, of the Glyndebourne Opera. He continued to conduct at Glyndebourne until 1939. From 1935–38 he also held the post of musical director of the Salzburg Opera Guild. From 1945 to 1946 he conducted the Italian Radio Orchestra (Turin). He joined the staff of the Metropolitan Opera, New York, in 1954. In 1958, Erede was appointed general music director of the Deutsche Oper am Rhein in Düsseldorf, Germany.

ERKEL, Ferenc. Hungarian composer and conductor (1810–1893). Most of his musical education came from his father. He started his career as music master for various noblemen, until in 1836 he went to Pest as second conductor of the Municipal (German) Theatre. In 1838 he was appointed musical director with full powers of administration of the newly formed National Theatre at Pest.

He was absorbed by the problem of creating a true national Hungarian opera. Although he had previously composed very little music, his first opera, *Bátori Mária* (1840), was a great success. *Hunyadi László* (1844) had almost 300 performances in its first fifty years.

Erkel was important in the formation of the Philharmonic Society (1853) and was appointed President Conductor, directing its concerts until 1870. His sons also became musicians; one took over as director of the opera and another, a pianist, gave lessons to Bartók.

Erkel's earlier operas are based on traditional French and Italian models with set pieces, recitatives, etc., but he later developed a Mussorgskian kind of declamation, without set pieces. All of his operas used incidents from national history, which contributed to their popularity.

ERLANGER, Camille. French composer (1863–1919). A student of Delibes, Durand, and Matthias at the Paris Conservatory, he won the Grand Prix de Rome in 1888 for his cantata *Velléda*. His opera. *Le Juif Polonais* (1900), made him famous and has continued to be revived from time to time. His *Aphrodite* provided a famous role for Mary Garden.

ERLANGER, Baron Frédéric d'. French-born composer (1868–1943). He lived in London as a banker and was a director of Covent Garden Opera for many years. He wrote in many forms, including opera, publishing some of his post-1897 compositions under the pseudonym, Regnal.

ERLKING, THE (*Der Erlkönig*). Song by Schubert, a setting of a poem by Goethe. The poem had its origin in the Danish ballad of *Herr Olaf,* but a personal experience brought it to life for Goethe: one evening he saw a rider passing the garden gate at a furious pace, and next day he learned that it had been a farmer taking his sick child to a doctor.

The poem was also set by Loewe and Rei-

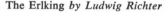

The Erlking *by Ludwig Richter*

Top: *Act II of* Ernani *at La Scala*. Bottom: *Act IV at the Metropolitan Opera*

chardt, but only Schubert's setting is still well known. It is his Op. 1 and was composed in 1815, when he was eighteen. Schubert's friend Spaun relates in his memoirs: "One afternoon I went with Mayrhofer to visit Schubert, who was then living with his father in Himmelpfortsgrund. We found Schubert in a state of great excitement over *Erlkönig,* which he was reading aloud from a book, pacing up and down as he read. He suddenly sat down, and in an incredibly short time the magnificent ballad was on paper. Schubert had no piano, so we ran down to the Konvikt with it, and there *Erlkönig* was sung the same evening with great enthusiasm."

Schubert's friends made every effort to get the composition printed, even sending it to Goethe, who did not reply. In 1817 Spaun sent it to the Leipzig publishers Breitkopf & Härtel. Unfortunately, there was another and better known Franz Schubert, the Saxon royal family's orchestra director in Dresden, and the publishers, suspecting forgery, sent the composition to him. He replied indignantly: "I will try to discover who has sent you such a bungling work in this impolite manner, and to expose the fellow who has misused my name."

Finally, Schubert's friends had *Erlkönig* published at their expense in February, 1821, and it was thus the first of Schubert's works to be printed. It soon became popular, and the singer Vogl had great success with it. An *Erlkönig* March and an *Erlkönig* Galop were also printed, and Schubert's friend Anselm Hüttenbrenner even rearranged the song as a waltz.

Wer rei - tet so spät durch Nacht und Wind?

"Who rideth so late through night and storm?" The ballad describes a father holding his little son safe and warm in his strong arms as his horse carries them swiftly through the stormy darkness. The boy hides his face in fright, for he has seen the Erlking, the chief of the evil spirits; but his father sees nothing and seeks to calm his son's fears by saying it is only a wisp of mist. Then the Erlking's voice, heard only by the child, tells of the merry games they will play, the pretty flowers he will see, and the golden robes he will wear if he will come away with him.

"My father, my father, cannot you hear what the Erlking is whispering to me?" cries the child, but his father tells him it is only the rustling of the leaves in the wind. The voice again tempts the boy, who now sees the Erlking's daughters singing and dancing. The child is terrified, but his father says it is only the old gray willow trees bending in the wind.

Then the Erlking's cajoling tones give way to angry commands. He declares that he loves the child and means to have him for his own. At the boy's last despairing cry, the father grows pale and spurs on his horse, but when he arrives in the town the child is dead in his arms.

ERNANI. Four-act opera by Giuseppe Verdi, with libretto by Francesco Maria Piave based on Victor Hugo's *Hernani*. First performed in Venice in 1844 and in the United States in 1847, the work was revived at the Metropolitan Opera in 1956, with Leonard Warren, Zinka Milanov, Cesare Siepi, and Mario Del Monaco in the leading roles, and Dimitri Mitropoulos conducting. Leontyne Price and Franco Corelli appeared in the 1962–63 revival.

Don Ruy Gomez de Silva (bass) is about to marry his ward Elvira (soprano) when two other suitors appear: her favorite, Ernani (tenor), the outlaw (really Don Juan of Aragon), and Don Carlo, King of Spain (baritone), who has ruined Ernani, but at this moment saves him. Silva is later to spare him under the rule of hospitality, but exacts a promise that Ernani will give his life when summoned by a horn blast. The King meanwhile has been elected Emperor. Silva and Ernani plot against him, but are captured. The new Emperor shows mercy and pardons all the conspirators, further-

Napoleon on the Pont d'Arcole *by Antoine-Jean Gros. The Louvre, Paris*

more giving Elvira's hand to Ernani. But before they can marry, Silva exacts his revenge, blowing the horn. Ernani kills himself.

EROICA SYMPHONY. Beethoven's Symphony No. 3, in E flat major. The composer's preliminary sketches show that work on the symphony was started in 1802, but it was in Baden and Ober-Döbling in 1803 that it seriously engaged Beethoven, and it was completed in 1804.

He had written in 1802: "I am not satisfied with my work up to the present. From now on I intend to turn to a completely new path." This new path, touched on in the scherzo of his First Symphony and in the coda of the Second, was followed throughout the Third Symphony. The *Eroica* thus marked the great change in Beethoven's career as a composer.

Beethoven once said (1823) that it was General Bernadotte, later King of Norway and Sweden, who suggested to him the idea of composing a herioc symphony with the Chief Consul, Napoleon Bonaparte, as the central figure. Bernadotte was the French Government's special ambassador in Vienna when Beethoven first met him in 1798. A revolutionary idealist himself, Beethoven ardently admired Bonaparte and saw in him not only a great leader of armies, but also Europe's future deliverer who would realize the ideals of the French Revolution.

Ries recounts how and why the dedication of the symphony was altered: "Several of his closest friends, including myself, had seen the score of the symphony lying on his desk and noticed that at the top of the title page was written 'Bonaparte.' When I brought him the news that Napoleon had had himself proclaimed Emperor, he was very upset and cried: 'So even he is no more than an ordinary human being! Now he will stamp on all the people's rights, and only be ruled by ambition. He will place himself above all others and become a tyrant!' Thereupon he rushed to his desk, tore out the title page from the score of the symphony and threw it on the floor."

The work was then given the title *The Heroic Symphony, composed in remembrance of a great man,* and was dedicated to Prince Lobkowitz.

The first performance was at a private concert at the house in Vienna of Prince Lobkowitz in 1804, and the first public hearing took place on April 7, 1805, at the Theater an der Wien, under Beethoven's direction. The work was one of Beethoven's own favorites, but both public and critics were puzzled by it. One Leipzig critic wrote in 1807 that it was a long and extraordinarily difficult composition: "in reality a broadly conceived and daring fantasy—that would gain much if the composer could decide to cut it down and bring more light, clarity, and unity into it."

The Director of the Prague Conservatory, Dionys Weber, regarded the symphony as the "most frivolous one" he had ever heard. Even Beethoven's most faithful followers were amazed at the defiant novelty of the work. When young Ries, for instance, first heard the passage in the first movement where the horns come in with their tonic chord theme while the dominant chord still sounds, he thought that they had come in at the wrong moment. When he said so, Beethoven "threw him a furious look and very nearly boxed his ears."

I. *Allegro con brio.* Two strong introductory chords are immediately followed by the main theme—

—first on the cellos, thereafter alternately on wind and strings, and then fortissimo by the whole orchestra. The theme is similar to one in Mozart's youthful *Bastien and Bastienne,* but Beethoven gave it a completely new character. Many small motifs follow the main theme before the second theme arrives. Finally, the movement gathers itself into a magnificent and powerful tension which is unique in the history of symphonies, and the main theme is again affirmed in a tremendous coda.

II. *Marcia funebre: Adagio assai.* This famous funeral march stands out in sharp contrast to the vivacious first movement.

III. *Scherzo: Allegro vivace.* This was Beethoven's first symphonic scherzo on a large scale. Those who interpret the symphony as describing a hero's life have called it *Fun in Camp.* To others the lively horns and haunting melodies give it a romantic air. In spite of the great contrast among all the first three movements, Beethoven retained a uniformly heroic spirit throughout the work.

IV. *Finale: Allegro molto.* The first half of the movement is a variation constructed on the following theme:

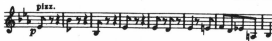

This theme forms the bass line for the following melody which Beethoven had already used in a very similar context in his Variations for piano, Op. 35 (commonly called *Eroica Variations*) and again in the incidental music to *The Creatures of Prometheus,* Op. 43.

After the third variation a melodious fugal interlude is inserted, following which the variation form returns. The movement then widens out into a joyous finale.

ERSKINE, John. American educator and writer on music (1879–1951). He was professor of English at Columbia University from 1909–37, president of Juilliard School of Music from 1928–37, a concert pianist and a writer of novels, essays, opera libretti, and books on music.

ESPAÑA. Orchestral rhapsody by Chabrier, composed in 1883, his best-known work. Shortly after Chabrier had decided to adopt music as his life work he traveled to Spain, where he collected many folk tunes, including several Andalusian gypsy melodies used in the rhapsody. A friend gave this account of the composer's visit to some Spanish gypsies: "Chabrier was soon on friendly terms with the dancers, drank manzanilla, and looked the gypsy girls straight in the eye, clapping his hands when the Andalusian girls waggled their hips, and crying in ecstasy 'Olé, Olé!' "

The rhapsody was first performed at a Lamoureux concert in Paris on November 4, 1883.

The themes include a *jota*—

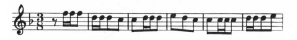

—and a *malagueña*—

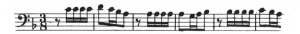

ESPRESSIVO. Italian, "with expression, with feeling." Abbreviated *espr.*

ÉTUDE. French, "study, exercise." This musical term may describe compositions specifically written as exercises designed to develop technical ability in the use of the fingers, or more elaborate pieces that require such technical achievements. Piano études, for example, may include the playing of scales and arpeggios in parallel and contrary motion with both hands, and octaves, sixths, thirds, and chord-playing; studies for the violin will emphasize similar finger dexterity for the left hand, and bowing with the right hand and arm.

ÉTUDES SYMPHONIQUES (*Symphonic Studies*). Composition for solo piano, Op. 13, by Schumann; composed in 1834, first published in 1837, and in a revised edition in 1852. Schumann originally intended to call the work the *Davidsbündler-Etüden:* i.e. studies, orchestral in character, of the characters Florestan and Eusebius in his imaginary *League of David* (*Davidsbündler*). The new title shows that his aim was to create a work of great breadth and technique, exploited in bravura style.

The composition is primarily a series of variations on a theme said to have been composed "by an amateur."

The amateur was Baron von Fricken, of Asch, father of Ernestine von Fricken, to whom Schumann was engaged for a time. In fact, the third and ninth of the eleven studies are not variations

Scene 1 of Eugene Onegin *at the Moscow Bolshoi Theater*

on the theme, but separate compositions. In the final edition five studies originally written for the work are omitted, and in the rondo-finale the principal theme is only a fragment.

The theme was based on a motif from Marschner's opera *Der Templer und die Jüdin* (*The Templar and the Jewess,* after Scott's novel *Ivanhoe*). In the opera, the theme is accompanied by the words "Who is the right honorable knight?"

Schumann is thought to have intended this in homage to his friend, Sir William Sterndale Bennett (the English composer to whom the work is dedicated), and his knightly countrymen.

EUGENE ONEGIN. Musical dramatic work by Tchaikovsky, completed in 1879. The composer was careful not to call the work an opera, preferring the title "lyrical scenes." Tchaikovsky, who wrote the libretto himself from Pushkin's poem of the same name, tried to use the original text to the greatest possible extent, but musical considerations forced him to write new verses for many sections. This free handling of a classic at first prevented the work from becoming popular in Russia.

A few days after he had come across the poem Tchaikovsky wrote to his brother Modeste: "You have no idea how crazy I am about this subject. . . . I am not blind to its defects; I know well enough the work gives little scope for operatic treatment, and will be deficient in stage effects. But the wealth of poetry, the human quality and simplicity of the subject, joined to Pushkin's inspired verses, will compensate for what it lacks in other respects."

The opera was begun in Russia and completed at San Remo. One afternoon in the spring of 1878, when Tchaikovsky was living alone at Brilov, the estate of his benefactress, Mme. von Meck, he played through *Eugene Onegin* to himself. He said later: "The author was the sole listener. I am half ashamed of what I am going to confide to you in secret: the audience was moved to tears, and paid the composer a thousand compliments. If only future audiences have the same feelings toward this music as the composer has!"

Tchaikovsky could not bear to think of Pushkin's poem on youth and love being performed by corpulent middle-aged singers, and therefore arranged for the work to be acted by the pupils of the Moscow Conservatory. The performance took place on March 29, 1879. Tchaikovsky was greatly pleased with it, but neither the public nor the press showed any interest or understanding. The reason was partly that the performers were amateurs, and partly that it was unusual for the action of an opera to take place in contemporary Russia and in modern dress. Nor did the music attract audiences of that age. It was a long time before this psychologically acute and richly varied opera received its true deserts.

Time: *1850*

Place: *Mme. Larina's estate and St. Petersburg*

Scene 1: *The garden of Mme. Larina's estate*

Mme. Larina (mezzo-soprano) has two daughters, Tatiana (soprano) and Olga (contralto), the former of a serious dreamy nature, the second rather frivolous. Two young noblemen, the lighthearted Lensky (tenor) and his friend, Eugene Onegin (baritone), arrive on a visit. Onegin is a man of the world, a cool and experienced Don Juan, while Lensky is straightforward and candid. Lensky makes eager love to his fiancée, Olga. As soon as Tatiana sets eyes on Onegin, she realizes that she has found her ideal man.

Scene 2: *Tatiana's bedroom*

Tatiana's old nurse, Filipievna (mezzo-soprano), tells her that she cannot choose for herself, but must marry the man selected by her parents. Tatiana confesses that she is violently in love, and, when she is alone, gives way to her feelings. In a letter to Onegin she declares her love for him.

(This is the famous "letter scene," a masterpiece of musical portrayal and artistic abbreviation, in which Tchaikovsky concentrates the experiences and emotions of a whole night into a scene of about twenty minutes.)

Scene 3: *In the garden*

Peasant girls are picking berries and singing. Tatiana waits for Onegin by a stream. He comes because she has written to him, but the little country maid does not interest him. He is not fitted for marriage, he says, but he will willingly be a brother to her *(Onegin's Aria):*

Could I pursue the common fashion
Of such as live a simple life,
Remain indifferent to passion,
Content with children, home and wife!
Ah, then you may be sure
'Tis you I'd choose to share my joys and woes.

Scene 4: *A ballroom in Mme. Larina's house*

Tatiana's birthday is being celebrated by a ball.

Onegin, who is bored in this provincial environment, flirts with Olga, and Lensky becomes jealous. A Frenchman, Triquet, sings a couplet (this song was the only successful number at the première in Moscow). Lensky can no longer bear to see how warm the friendship between Olga and Onegin has become. He insults Onegin, who replies by challenging him to a duel.

Scene 3 of **Eugene Onegin** *at the Metropolitan. George London in the title role and Lucine Amara as Tatiana*

Scene 6 of Eugene Onegin *at the Frankfurt Opera in 1957*

Scene 5: *The countryside*

Lensky is the first to make his appearance at the appointed place. He describes in a song how deeply he loves Olga and how uneasy he is about the future.

What can I look for, from this morning?
In vain I try to read its warning,
Impenetrable mystery.
No matter—it is God's decree.
The fatal shot to death may call me,
Or yet perhaps may pass me by!
So be it! Providence on high determines
All that shall befall me.
Blessed be God who made the light.

Onegin arrives. Although both understand the foolhardiness of fighting, the matter must be settled. Lensky is killed by Onegin's bullet.

Scene 6: *The palace of Prince Gremin at St. Petersburg*

Several years have passed. Tatiana is married to a middle-aged nobleman, Prince Gremin. They are giving a ball, and an elegant company is dancing a polonaise.

Onegin comes to the ball. All the years since the duel he has spent in wandering abroad, continuously tortured by pangs of conscience. Now he meets again his old acquaintance, Prince Gremin, and is presented to his wife, who does not seem to recognize him. The Prince tells his friend how he found Tatiana, and how she became the shining star of his life.

Scene 7: *A reception chamber in Prince Gremin's palace*

Onegin has asked to talk with Tatiana. He now realizes that he loves her and tells her so. She confesses that she still loves him, but she will not leave the husband to whom she has promised fidelity. She tears herself away from Onegin, who is left alone in his despair.

EUPHONIUM. Name used in Great Britain for the B flat tenor tuba. See *Wind Instruments.*

EURIDICE. The title of two settings of the Greek myth of Orpheus and Eurydice, the one by Jacopo Peri having been considered for a long time to be the first produced opera (1600). However, Giulio Caccini's *Dafne* had been performed in Florence in 1597, while his *Euridice* was heard after Peri's, in 1602. The confusion possibly arose because Caccini had succeeded in interpolating several of his own numbers in Peri's work. The two were close rivals.

EURYANTHE. Opera by Carl Maria von Weber, with libretto by Helmina von Chézy, completed on October 19, 1823, and first performed six days later.

Shortly after the great success of *Der Freischütz* in 1821, Weber received a request from the Kärntnerthor Theater in Vienna to compose an opera to Frau von Chézy's libretto. The manuscript consisted of an incoherent potpourri of romantic inventions: beautiful and crafty women, noble and heroic knights, dastardly villains, sinister specters, and a hero who makes a wager with the villain on his beloved faithfulness.

The action is based on an old French tale, and takes place in central France about 1100. Euryanthe of Savoy and the knight Adolar are in love. Despite her promise never to divulge to anyone that Adolar's sister Emma killed herself, she tells her confidante, Eglantine; the latter, in league with Count Lysiart who is jealous of Adolar, makes Adolar believe that Euryanthe has forsaken him, bringing forward as proof the fact that the secret of Emma's death has been given away. The story ends with punishment of the plotters and the reunion of the lovers, but not before a whole series of entanglements, including the appearance of Emma's ghost, has taken place.

That Weber could bring himself to compose music to such a text is due solely to his attachment to anything romantic. He was well aware of the libretto's defects, and expressed his dissatisfaction by always referring to the writer as "that woman Chézy." (She also wrote *Rosamunde* which Schubert set to music, and which was equally hopeless as a stage work.) Weber's music for *Euryanthe* contains some of his most beautiful work, and it is entirely owing to the defects of the libretto that the opera is rarely performed; nowadays the overture alone survives.

The festive note of chivalry in the *Euryanthe* music set the pattern for much of the content of Wagner's early stage works, and Weber's use

A scene from Act I of Euryanthe *as performed by the Stuttgart Opera*

of characteristic musical motifs for each of the characters in the opera was of great importance for the development of the leitmotiv technique. This technique, as employed in Wagner's *Lohengrin,* for example, is broadly speaking the same as that used in *Euryanthe.*

The overture begins with Adolar's *Ich bau' auf Gott und meine Euryanthe* (*I Trust in God and My Euryanthe*)—which Weber used as a kind of motto while he was composing the work —followed by a number of other motifs from the opera. It is, in fact, a summing up of the whole work.

EURYTHMICS. From Greek *eu,* "well," and *rhythmos,* "measured motion." The art of expressing music in gestures, the physical movements reflecting the musical notation. It was invented in the early 1900s by Emile Jaques-Dalcroze (1865–1950), professor of harmony at the Geneva Conservatory. See *Jaques-Dalcroze, Émile.*

EUTERPE. The Muse of lyric poetry in Greek mythology. Because music was sung, Euterpe came to be considered the Muse of music, which

EUTERPE

otherwise had no designated patroness among the nine Muses—possibly because music was pervasive among all the arts in ancient Greece.

EVANS, Geraint. Welsh baritone (1922–). After World War II Evans became a member of the Covent Garden company. He has appeared in Europe; made his American opera debut with the San Francisco Opera in 1959; and has regularly been a member of the Glyndebourne Opera company, both at Glyndebourne and at the Edinburgh Festival.

EVANS, Gillian (Gil). Canadian jazz arranger (1912–). Evans was arranger for the Ennis and Thornhill bands until 1948 when he became a free-lance arranger and leader. He has made several recordings with trumpeter Miles Davis.

EXPOSITION. The initial presentation, or statement, of thematic material, particularly in the sonata form and in the fugue. See *Sonata Form; Fugue; Music, Elements of.*

EXPRESSIONISM. A term (taken from the pictorial arts) to describe the music written during 1910–20 by Schönberg and his followers. The expressionists were concerned with the exploration in their music of subjective and psychological (often abnormal) states. See *Music Through the Ages.*

EXSULTATE, JUBILATE. Motet for soprano solo and orchestra, K. 165, by Mozart. The work was composed for the famous castrato singer Venancio Rauzzini, who, according to H. Abert, "had every virtue, sang like an angel, and was an excellent actor."

The work, which is really a dramatic solo cantata, was first performed on January 17, 1773. Although the words are taken from the Bible, the music is operatic, and the whole work, as Alfred Einstein says, "is simply a miniature concerto with an Allegro, an Andante, and a Presto or Vivace, hardly inferior, in brilliance or 'tenderness,' to a true instrumental concerto."

Ex - ul - ta - te,   ju - bi - la - te, o vos

FACCIO, Franco. Italian composer and conductor (1840–1891). One of the foremost opera conductors of Italy, he was chosen by Verdi to conduct the European première of *Aïda* and the world première of *Otello,* both at La Scala. His *Amleto* was the first opera for which Boito wrote a libretto based on Shakespeare.

FADO. Portuguese popular music, sung to guitar accompaniment and usually mournful in tone. Fado is not folk music and is characteristic only of music in cities and larger towns.

FAIR AT SOROCHINTZY, THE. Opera in three acts by Mussorgsky with libretto, based on Gogol, by the composer. This work, which Mussorgsky left unfinished at his death, was first produced in St. Petersburg in a version prepared by Liadov. Later versions by Sakhnovsky and Cui were produced in 1913 and 1917. The first American production, in a version by Nicholas Tcherepnin, was given by the Metropolitan Opera in 1930. The plot concerns the conflict of a peasant and his wife over which of two suitors their daughter should marry.

FAITH, Percy. Canadian conductor and composer (1908–). Faith is known for his radio, television, and recording performances, and as composer of musical backgrounds and arrangements. He began his professional career as a pianist, conducted for the Canadian Broadcasting Corporation, and has been a musical director for Columbia Records since 1950.

Manuel de Falla, a drawing by Pablo Picasso

FALCON, Cornélie. French soprano (1812–1897). Though she lost her voice after a relatively short career, her fame was so great that her name is still used to designate certain dramatic soprano roles. From 1832 to 1838, she created roles in many important operas, among them Rachel in *La Juive* and Valentine in *Les Huguenots.*

FALL, Leo. Austrian composer (1873–1925). Fall was renowned as a composer of gay operettas, of which he wrote about twenty, including the world success *The Dollar Princess* (1907). He scored other successes with *The Merry Peasant* (1907), *The Girl in the Train* (1908), *The Rose of Stamboul* (1916), and *Madame Pompadour* (1922).

FALLA, Manuel de. Spanish composer (1876–1946). Falla was a born musician and became an excellent pianist at an early age, although he had little instruction in music and did not attend his first symphony concert until he was seventeen. The music of Grieg and Beethoven, which he then heard for the first time, so fascinated him that from that moment his only ambition was to become a composer.

The Fair at Sorochintzy *at La Scala, Milan*

The only way a Spanish composer could earn money in those days was to write *zarzuelas,* or Spanish operettas. Falla wrote two, with no success, and then came into contact with the composer Felipe Pedrell, who infected him with his musical nationalism and religious fervor. Though Falla did not use folk tunes in his music, as Pedrell did, he made the traditional music of Spain, which long had been neglected, his natural medium of expression.

In 1904 Falla won the Academy of Art prize for the best musical work for the theater by a Spanish composer, with his beautiful, although not very original, two-act opera *La Vida Breve (Life Is Short),* in which the Andalusian style of music mingles with reminiscences of the *drame lyrique* of Massenet. After winning another first prize as a pianist, he taught in Madrid for two years. Then in 1907 he realized his great ambition—to go to Paris; intending to stay a week, he ended by remaining seven years.

Falla had little to live on in Paris, but it was the richest period of his life. Though he became a close friend of Debussy, Ravel, and Dukas, he did not become a French impressionist—he was too much of a Spaniard for that—but he improved his harmony and style and developed his orchestral ideas.

The outbreak of war in 1914 drove him home, where he at once established himself as the leading Spanish composer with his *Nights in the Gardens of Spain,* three symphonic impressions for piano and orchestra. He settled in Granada in a house close to the Alhambra.

His ballet pantomime *El Amor Brujo (Love the Sorcerer)* was written in 1915, and in 1917 he composed the work which, when revised for the Russian Ballet in 1919, became one of the ballet's greatest successes, *The Three-Cornered Hat.* These three works show Falla's supremacy as a composer. In them he gives the richest, truest, most versatile portrayal of Andalusian nature and life.

He now came to a decisive point in his career. If he had wished he could have continued in the same style and been certain of success everywhere. But his high ideals would not permit him to repeat himself; neither would he restrict himself to musical descriptions of his own region nor keep to music of his own time. In a strange series of compositions he departed farther and farther from his original idiom—from picturesque, colorful Andalusia into the cold proud

A scene from Falla's Atlàntida *at the Berlin State Opera, 1962*

Spanish province of Castile. His music was no longer fascinatingly Andalusian, sensuous and impressionistic; it now breathed the air of the Spanish highlands, cool, clear, and rich in contrasts.

His interest in historical Castilian music led to his puppet-opera *Master Peter's Puppet Show,* in which he put to music a scene from Cervantes' *Don Quixote;* and in the little song scena *Psyche* (1924), for mezzo-soprano and chamber orchestra, he tried to re-create a court concert given for King Philip V and Queen Isabella about 1730.

Bad health dogged Manuel de Falla all his life, and toward the end seriously hampered his work. In 1928 he started on a great dramatic cantata, *Atlàntida,* which was not yet completed when he left Granada for political reasons and went to Argentina, where he died in 1946. This work, completed by Falla's friend, Ernesto Halffter, finally was presented at La Scala in Milan in June, 1962; the following September an abridged version was given by the Metropolitan Opera at a concert during the opening week of Philharmonic Hall in New York's Lincoln Center.

Falla always emphasized that his aim was to write genuine Spanish music without using actual folk song. The only exception to this rule was *Seven Spanish Popular Songs* (1914). Otherwise he "borrowed" only two snatches of melody in *The Three-Cornered Hat,* one in his Concerto for Harpsichord, and two in *Master Peter's Puppet Show.*

The "Spanish" atmosphere of Falla's music is partly due to his use of church modes, especially in the "Andalusian" (A-G-F-E) or "Oriental" form (with G sharp). Otherwise his music is tonal, although very free, with some polytonality. Much of the special character of Falla's music lies in his mastery of Spanish rhythm, which often takes the form of polyrhythmics.

Best-known works:

OPERA

La Vida Breve, 2 Acts (1904)
Master Peter's Puppet Show, 1 Act (1922)

BALLETS

El Amor Brujo (Love the Sorcerer) (1915)
The Three-Cornered Hat (El sombrero de tres picos) (1919)

CHORAL

Atlàntida, scenic cantata in a prologue and 3 parts, for soloists, chorus, and orchestra (posthumously completed by Ernesto Halffter) (1928–46)

ORCHESTRAL

Nights in the Gardens of Spain (Noches en los jardines de España) (1909–15), piano and orchestra
Concerto for Harpsichord (1923–26)

PIANO

4 Pièces Espagnoles (1907–08)

SONGS

7 Canciones populares españolas (Blas de Laserne)

Victor Maurel, Verdi's first Falstaff, 1893

FALLOT, Guy. French cellist (1929–). Fallot studied cello with Paul Burger, at the Lausanne and Paris conservatories, and has won First Sonata Prize at the International Concours in Geneva, the Prix Piatigorsky, and other awards. He has since toured throughout Europe and in Asia, Africa, Australia and New Zealand, and North America. He made his first transcontinental concert tour with his pianist sister, Monique Fallot, in 1957, and performed again in the United States in 1960.

FALSETTO. From Italian *falso,* "false." Artificial manner of singing in which the larynx is forced to produce notes above its normal pitch. See *Yodeling.*

FALSTAFF. Opera in three acts, composed in 1893 by Giuseppe Verdi, with libretto by Arrigo Boito (adapted from Shakespeare). Verdi had written one comic opera *(Un giorno di Regno)* during the unhappy period of his life (1883–40) in which in the course of a couple of years he lost his wife and his two children. It was not a success, and he had adhered thereafter to tragic subjects. Indeed, the general opinion was that light music was outside his capabilities, and Rossini had spoken to this effect: "Verdi is a composer of a serious and melancholy disposition. Somber and thoughtful ideas pour out of his natural disposition with abundance and spontaneity, and are on that very account most precious, and I rate them most highly. But I doubt whether he can write even a semiserious opera like *Linda,* much less a comedy like *L'Elisir d'Amore."*

It can be seen from Verdi's correspondence that he was somewhat irritated by this statement, and promised himself to prove that it was untrue. The opportunity presented itself when Boito proposed that Verdi should write the music for his *Falstaff.* The composer pointed out his "great age" (he was seventy-eight) and made many other objections, but the excellent libretto tempted him, and there is no doubt he felt the attraction of winning laurels in this new sphere. At any rate, he accepted Boito's invitation "for amusement." he worked slowly— only two hours a day—and as late as 1891, when he had been working on the opera for a year, he wrote: "To come to *Falstaff,* all projects for the future seem to me folly, absolute folly! I will expound myself. I am engaged in writing

Act II of Falstaff, *as performed at the Glyndebourne Festival*

Falstaff to pass the time, without any preconceived ideas or plans; I repeat, to pass the time! Nothing else."

Nevertheless, the work advanced steadily; in 1892 it was finished, and the first performance, on February 9, 1893, at La Scala in Milan, caused a storm of enthusiasm. Performances at the other principal opera houses of Europe at once followed.

Falstaff has all Verdi's old melodiousness. The tunes merge into one another, and the dividing line between arias and recitatives is so small that the music flows like a continuous arioso—not Wagner's "endless melody," but rather an infinity of melodies, festoons of notes in constant life and movement, light, airy, buoyant, gay. Hardly a single section can be taken out of its context for concert performance, and so concise and rapid is the composition that the whole opera takes only two hours to perform. The balance between the vocal and the instrumental is kept so exactly that the opera is like a witty play on notes, a sort of scenic chamber music.

Time: *About 1400*   Place: *Windsor*

ACT I

Scene 1: *The Garter Inn*

Dr. Caius (tenor) is quarreling with Sir John Falstaff (baritone), who is said to have lamed his horse and cudgeled his servants. But Dr. Caius gets only abuse in return. Falstaff has written love letters to Mistresses Meg Page and Alice Ford. When his servants Bardolph (tenor) and Pistol (bass) refuse to deliver them to the ladies, Falstaff sends the missives by the page Robin and makes a great speech about honor to his servants, before kicking them through the door.

Scene 2: *In front of Ford's house*

Mistress Page (soprano) and Mistress Quickly (contralto) meet Mistress Ford (soprano) and her daughter Nanetta (soprano). The two ladies have both received identical notes from Falstaff and now they agree on taking a merry revenge on the fat old carouser. They depart to arrange the details.

Falstaff's servants have betrayed their master's plans to Ford (baritone). Fenton (tenor) offers to give him his deserts.

The young pair, Nanetta and Fenton, have a tender *tête-à-tête* during which they sing the little folk song which they use as a "signal" between them.

The ladies return and take counsel with Nanetta how they shall punish Falstaff. Ford discusses the same with Bardolph and Pistol.

ACT II

Scene 1: *The inn*

Falstaff is, as usual, mulling over a tankard of sack.

Bardolph announces that a lady wishes to speak with the gentleman and Mistress Quickly greets him with much ceremony as "Reverence":

Re-ve-ren - za!

In reply to his letter to Mistress Ford she has brought an invitation to a rendezvous between two and three o'clock the same day, and presents it with the characteristic, sprightly, and constantly repeated

dal-le due al-le tre

Ford enters with a bottle of wine. He introduces himself as "Fountain" and asks Falstaff to help him to win the favor of a lady—namely, Mistress Ford. If Falstaff manages to conquer her first, Fountain will find it easier later. Falstaff at once agrees to this. Ford is told about the agreed rendezvous, and is thunderstruck. After Falstaff has smartened himself up, the two gentlemen go out arm in arm.

Scene 2: *A room in Ford's house*

The four ladies come in together, and Mistress Quickly tells of her visit to Falstaff. Nanetta laments that her father wants her to marry Dr. Caius, but her mother promises to help her. Two servants bring in a large clothes basket, and Mistress Ford is left alone.

Falstaff arrives and makes violent love to Mistress Ford, but she manages to hold him at arm's length. Then Mistress Quickly rushes in to say that Mistress Page is on her way in. Falstaff, concealed behind a large screen, hears Mistress Page tell how insanely jealous Ford is. Then in comes the master of the house

himself, together with Dr. Caius, Fenton, Bardolph, and Pistol. Ford first looks into the basket for his rival, and then with the others begins to search the house. Falstaff creeps into the basket, and Nanetta and Fenton station themselves behind the screen. The men and the ladies return. They think they hear a kiss behind the screen, which falls over, and the lovers run away. Bardolph cries out that Falstaff is making off, and the men rush out to get hold of him. Nanetta comes in with Ford's servant, who takes away the basket and Falstaff in it.

ACT III

Scene 1: *Outside The Garter Inn*

Falstaff is in a vile temper. His adventure with Mistress Ford has ended in his being thrown into the river with all Ford's dirty clothes. He tries to comfort himself for his misfortune with a hot drink, while he sings his immortal song about the misery of the world.

Mistress Quickly comes in with another note—an invitation to a meeting in the park at midnight; Falstaff is to come disguised as "the black hunter Herne." The two enter the inn to arrange the details.

Ford, who is now aware that his wife is only making sport of Falstaff, combines with his friends and all the ladies to teach Falstaff a lesson. All are to meet disguised in Windsor Park and set upon Falstaff. Ford also has another plan: he is determined that Dr. Caius shall marry Nanetta, and proposes that Caius shall disguise himself as a monk. Nanetta is to be dressed in white, and if in the course of the night Caius comes to him with Nanetta, Ford will give them his paternal blessing. Fortunately Mistress Quickly overhears this sinister plan and warns Nanetta.

Scene 2: *Windsor Park*

In the moonlight Fenton—disguised as the fairy king, Oberon—calls to his beloved with a song, which

Act III, Scene 1 of Falstaff *at the Metropolitan Opera in the 1940s*

ends with their signal. Nanetta appears attired as the fairy queen, Titania.

Sul fil d'un sof-fio e-te-si-o Scor-re-te a-gi-li

   From secret caves and bowers
   Emerge, your locks entwining
   With fronds of fern and flowers . . .

Fenton is about to embrace her, but Mistress Ford stops him and puts on him a monk's cowl. Instead of Nanetta, Bardolph is going to appear in a white dress to cheat Dr. Caius.

As the clock strikes twelve Falstaff comes in, dressed as Herne the hunter with antlers on his head. He is soon joined by Mistress Ford, whom he greets with tenderness. Then Mistress Page cries out that "the wild army" is on the way, and the ladies flee, while Falstaff throws himself down underneath a large oak. Nanetta as fairy queen appears with a large train of "supernatural" beings. Falstaff is discovered, and because the "fairies" believe he has concealed himself there to see things which ought to be hidden from humans, he is condemned, tortured, and tormented. Finally, he obtains forgiveness for his misdeeds.

Two masked and disguised bridal couples appear. Ford gives his blessing, but discovers too late that he has agreed to Nanetta's union with Fenton and that Dr. Caius' "bride" is Bardolph. Dr. Caius is very angry, but as he and Ford and Falstaff have all been made sport of by the merry wives of Windsor, they decide to take it in good part, and in the lively closing fugue all agree that life is a joke and all human beings are fools.

FANDANGO. A Spanish folk dance in 3/4 or 6/8 time, danced to the accompaniment of singing, castanets, and, often, guitar. An old fandango melody was used by Gluck in his ballet *Don Juan* (1761) and by Mozart in *The Marriage of Figaro* (1786). Rimsky-Korsakov ends his *Capriccio Espagnol* with a fandango *astunano*.

FANFARE. Bugle call as originally used for military and hunting purposes and based on the tones of the triad. It often occurs as a motif in serious music (*e.g.* Beethoven's *Eroica* Symphony and *Leonora* Overtures No. 2 and No. 3; Dukas' *La Peri*).

FANTAISIE-IMPROMPTU. Composition for piano, in C sharp minor, Op. 66, by Chopin, first published after his death and against his expressed wishes. Arthur Hedley has pointed out that *Fantaisie-Impromptu* has a remarkable resemblance to an impromptu by Moscheles published in 1834, at the same time as Chopin was

writing his work. According to the custom of the period, however, Chopin could have used Moscheles' motif and published the composition, provided that he stated in a footnote that the motif was by Moscheles. The reason for not publishing the work would therefore appear to be that Chopin did not rate the composition very highly.

The theme in the middle part has been used as a popular song entitled *I'm Always Chasing Rainbows*.

FANTASIA. In earlier days this term signified a polyphonic composition similar to the toccata. Later it was used both for works in which a conventional form was not strictly adhered to, and for works in free form. Examples are Schubert's *Wanderer Fantasie,* which is also a large, free sonata composition, and Schumann's small *Fantasiestücke* with poetic titles.

Fantasia was also the title of an ambitious color cartoon film made by Walt Disney in 1941. See *Film Musicals*.

FANTASIA IN C. Op. 17, for piano, by Schumann, dedicated to Liszt. Walter Dahms calls this work "the swan-song of love, romance and passion," and Schumann himself wrote to Clara Wieck in 1839: "You will only be able to understand the *Fantasia* if you recall that unhappy summer of 1837, when I had to renounce you; now I have no longer any reason to compose in such a melancholy way."

An appeal had been launched for contributions to the Beethoven monument in Bonn, and the *Fantasia* was intended to arouse enthusiasm for the cause. Schumann had originally thought of calling the three movements *Ruins, Trophies,* and *Palms,* but he chose the present title on the advice of his publisher and inscribed the work with the verse by Schlegel which follows.

   Through all the tones that vibrate
   About earth's mingled dream,
   One whispering note is sounding
   For ears attent to hear.

Part I. The opening theme begins fortissimo, accompanied by quick figures in the bass.

There is an interlude in C minor, somewhat quieter, but still gloomy and bearing the title "In the style of a legend."

The theme of the Witches' Sabbath, used by Berlioz in the last section of his Fantastic Symphony, *also inspired Romantic painters*

Part II. *Maestoso.* This introduces a glorious theme in E flat major, in rich chords.

Part III. This brings the work to a peaceful and logical conclusion.

FANTASIESTÜCKE *(Fantasy Pieces).* Eight short compositions for piano, Op. 12, by Schumann, composed in 1837. These small works are autobiographical, connected as they are with Schumann's fight to win Clara Wieck.

Schumann wrote to Clara Wieck of this last piece: "While I was writing this I thought that everything would be resolved in a happy marriage, but at the end I began to be anxious about you again, so that now the death-bells and the marriage-bells sound together."

FANTASTIC SYMPHONY *(Symphonie fantastique).* Composition, with the subtitle *Episode in the Life of an Artist,* by Hector Berlioz (Op. 14). The work was written in the spring of 1830 and dedicated to Nicholas I of Russia. The first performance took place on December 5 of the same year.

In this epoch-making work, which introduced program music to the nineteenth century, Berlioz described his fervent love for the Irish actress Henrietta Smithson, who in 1827 had Paris at her feet over her interpretations of Ophelia and Juliet in Shakespeare's plays. On April 16, 1830, Berlioz wrote about the creation of the symphony to his friend Humbert Ferrand:

Since last I wrote I have undergone the most terrible sufferings. My ship has stranded cruelly, but now it is afloat again. Terrible realities . . . have brought about my recovery . . . I have confirmed my decision with a work with which I am entirely satisfied; and this is its subject:

"Episode in the Life of an Artist" (Large fantastic symphony in five parts).
1. A short adagio followed by an allegro section (waves of passion, aimless reveries, senseless passion, devotion, jealousy, rage, fear, etc.).
2. Scene in the country (adagio, thoughts on love and hope, overshadowed by dark premonitions).
3. A ball (brilliant and enchanting music).
4. March to the scaffold (wild and unreal music).
5. Dreams of a Witches' Sabbath.

Here you see, dear friend, how I have welded together my romance, or rather my story, and you will easily be able to recognize its hero. . . . I picture an artist equipped with a lively imagination, seeing for the first time his ideal woman. Her form is always before his eyes, accompanied by a musical motif of the same grace and nobility that he attributes to his beloved. This double *idée fixe* pursues him constantly; that is why the main theme in the allegro of the first part recurs in all the other parts.

He begins to hope that his love is being returned. One day in the country, he hears in the distance two herdsmen blowing cattle calls to each other. This rustic duet puts him into a wonderful state of reverie. "The melody" occurs again for a moment among the adagio themes.

He attends a ball, but the festivities leave him cold; he is still possessed by his *idée fixe* and the melody makes his heart throb in the middle of the grand waltz.

In a fit of desperation he takes opium. But instead of killing him the poison evokes a fearful vision: he believes that he has killed his beloved, that he has been condemned to death and is being executed. March to the scaffold. The melody returns, as a last thought of love, interrupted by the fall of the axe.

He sees himself surrounded by a horde of ugly witches and devils that have gathered to celebrate their Sabbath. The melody returns again, but instead of being full of beauty and grace it now seems common and trivial—the beloved, who has arrived for the burial of her victim, is seen to be only a common hussy. The ceremony commences. The bells toll, the whole devilish congregation kneels, a choir sings . . . *Dies Irae*, repeated by two other choirs in a ghastly parody; lastly the rondo, in which the whole congregation participates, and which, on reaching its climax, becomes mingled with the *Dies Irae* as the vision disappears.

Here you see, dear friend, the plan for this mighty symphony. I have just finished writing it.

Berlioz later wrote two new versions of this program. The only important alterations are that the order is varied (the second and third parts changing places), and that the *whole* work is said to describe an opium dream.

The revolutionary characteristics of the symphony are two: it follows a detailed program, and it introduces a leitmotiv (the *idée fixe*), which recurs in all the movements and expresses always the same definite concept. It was partly this *idée fixe* of Berlioz that led Wagner to adopt his leitmotiv technique.

I. *Largo, Allegro agitato e appassionato assai (Dreams, Passions).* This movement is introduced by a motif in the violins, largo, which Berlioz had taken from a youthful work, a song to his beloved "Estella." The theme is now made to personify his new love, Henrietta Smithson. He wrote in his memoirs: "The melody of that song, which I burned . . . before I left Paris, came cautiously back to memory when in 1829 I sat down to write my Symphonic fantastique. I thought it appropriate to express the overwhelming sadness that a young mind feels when an unhappy love begins to torment it."

The *idée fixe* occurs for the first time in the violins:

II. *Allegro non troppo (A Ball).* This is a waltz in the grand style, very delicately orchestrated; besides the strings, there are only two harps, two flutes, two clarinets, one oboe, and four horns.

III. *Adagio (Scene in the Fields).* This movement begins with a dialogue between English horn and oboe, followed by a quiet melody for violins and flutes in thirds that are developed and varied together with a variant of the *idée fixe*. In the end the English horn

Three scenes from the ballet, Symphonie fantastique, *choreographed by Leonid Massine, with décor by Christian Bérard, produced by the Ballets Russes de Monte Carlo*

occurs again, but in place of an answer by the oboe there is a violent thunderstorm (drum rolls) which forms the transition to the rhythmic drum strokes that introduce the fourth part.

IV. *Allegretto non troppo (March to the Scaffold).* The main theme is a rhythmically displaced descending G minor scale, adorned with contrapuntal figures, drum rolls, and fanfares.

V. *Larghetto, Allegro (Witches' Sabbath).* From the start the *idée fixe* is heard in an ugly, twisted caricature. Later the Gregorian *Dies Irae* comes in, first on bassoons, later on cornets and horn, constantly accompanied by bells. The wild witches' dance in fugue form ends the work.

Leonid Massine created a ballet to the *Symphonie fantastique* with that title, and Frederick Ashton's *Apparitions* closely resembles the program of the symphony, although it has different music.

FAREWELL SYMPHONY. Haydn's Symphony No. 45, in F sharp minor, composed in the autumn of 1772, while the composer was staying at Prince Esterházy's remote castle in the midst of a marsh by Lake Neuziedl in Hungary. Several accounts of the origin of the work exist, but, according to Dies and Griesinger, Haydn himself is said to have related this story: The Prince's private orchestra, with

The Esterházy Palace in Eisenstadt, where Haydn conducted the Prince's orchestra

Haydn as director, had spent the whole summer at the castle, and everybody was longing to go home to the little border town of Eisenstadt. But the Prince continually postponed the journey. In their distress the musicians asked Haydn to use his influence with the Prince. He decided to present the matter in his own way, and quickly composed a symphony in five movements, in the last of which the musicians one by one stopped playing, blew out the candles on their music stands, took their instruments under their arms and left. The Prince saw the point of Haydn's joke and let the musicians go home the next day.

In a half-forgotten book, *Anedotti piacevoli e interessanti,* by an Italian musician, Giacomo Ferrari, published in London in 1830, the author, who knew Haydn personally, says that Esterházy had become dissatisfied with his musicians and ordered Haydn to dismiss them all, with the exception of the first violin and the harpsichordist. Though distressed by having to ruin the livelihood of so many people, Haydn was compelled to obey, but made his protest in the form of this symphony. According to this version, he succeeded in saving the orchestra.

Often only the last two movements are played. After thirty-one bars of the last movement the first oboe and the second horn stop playing, pick up their music and leave the platform. Soon afterward the bassoonist and then the second oboist do the same; and one after another the musicians disappear until only two string players are left in their places. These, in Kretzschmar's words, "with great effort and many sleepy repetitions bring the symphony to a close, as if they were saying, 'We can't stand any more either!' "

FARINA, Carlo. Italian violinist and composer of the seventeenth century. He is known in history as the first violin virtuoso, and his compositions show that he developed the use of *staccato* and *pizzicato* effects, if he did not actually invent them. He also was one of the originators of the solo sonata.

FARINELLI (Carlo Broschi). Italian male soprano (1705–1782). He was the most famous of the *castrati* and one of the great singers of history. Trained by the composer and teacher, Niccolò Porpora, he became a master of im-

Prince Paul Anton Esterházy, Haydn's patron

FARINELLI

provisation as well as a singer with a beautiful voice and a dazzling technique. However it was not so much his brilliance as his powers of expression that roused audiences to sometimes hysterical enthusiasm.

After conquering Italy and Vienna, he became the idol of London for three years and, as a member of Porpora's rival company, almost brought about the ruin of Handel and his company. In 1737, he left England and went to Spain, where he remained as court singer for twenty-two years. So great was his power over Philip V, who suffered from a melancholia that only Farinelli's singing could relieve, that he was endowed with an opera company of his own in Madrid, in which he performed with his most famous contemporaries in operas by Porpora, Hasse, Pergolesi, and Scarlatti. Though his position at the Spanish court lasted for two reigns, it did not continue for a third, and he was dismissed with a large pension by Carlos III in 1759. His final years were passed in a luxurious palace near Bologna. See *Castrati.*

FARKAS, Ferenc. Hungarian composer (1905–). A pupil of Respighi, and the author

of many distinguished essays on music, he has been a professor at the Academy of Dramatic Art in Budapest since 1948. Although he has composed many works in almost all forms, he is best known for his film music and for incidental music to plays of Shakespeare.

FARLOW, Talmadge ("Tal"). American jazz guitarist (1921–). Farlow has played with Red Norvo and Artie Shaw and is acknowledged to be one of the outstanding guitarists on the jazz scene.

FARMER, Arthur S. American jazz trumpeter (1928–). Art Farmer has been associated with the Benny Carter and Lionel Hampton bands, among others, and performs frequently as a free-lance artist.

FARNABY, Giles. British composer (*c.* 1560– *c.* 1600). Little is known of Farnaby's life except that he made his home in London in 1586 and that he completed his studies at Oxford in 1592. In 1598 he published a collection of *Canzonets to Fowre Voyces,* but his chief claim

GERALDINE FARRAR

to fame rests on his virginal music, more than fifty pieces of which are to be found in the *Fitzwilliam Virginal Book*. Though not of the same stature as his contemporaries Byrd, Gibbons, and Bull, he made important contributions to the foundation of keyboard technique.

FARRAR, Geraldine. American soprano (1882–). After coaching with Lilli Lehmann, she made her debut with the Berlin Hofoper in 1901. After singing there and with the Paris Opéra-Comique, she made her triumphal debut at the Metropolitan Opera in 1906. She remained one of the most glamorous stars in opera until she retired in 1922. She sang many roles, of which Madame Butterfly and Carmen were the most popular. She made her debut as Juliette, and her farewell as Zaza, and created the roles of the Goose Girl in *Königskinder* and the title role in *Suor Angelica*. She sang in the American premières of many operas, including *The Damnation of Faust*, *Ariane et Barbe-bleue* (Dukas), and *Madame Sans-Gêne*. Among her other roles were Tosca, Manon, Louise, Thaïs, and Mignon. She also starred in several motion pictures and, after her retirement from opera, continued to sing in concerts for some years.

FARRELL, Eileen. American soprano (1920–). Miss Farrell made her professional debut in 1941 on the radio. She has sung with the Bach Aria Group as well as the principal symphony orchestras in the United States. She was primarily known as a concert artist until 1955 when her famous performance of the title role in Cherubini's *Medea* established her as an operatic soprano. Her formal debut was with the San Francisco Opera in *Il Trovatore*. She has toured throughout South America and Europe, appearing at the Casals Festival in Puerto Rico, Covent Garden, La Scala, and the Festival of Two Worlds in Spoleto.

Since her debut at the Metropolitan Opera in 1960, as Alceste in a revival of Gluck's opera, she has been acclaimed as a great American prima donna in the leading roles of *Andrea Chénier, La Gioconda, La Forza del Destino*, and *Cavalleria Rusticana*. Among her many famous recordings are arias and duets from Italian, French, German, and American operas, great scenes from Wagner operas, a complete performance of Berg's *Wozzeck* with the New York Philharmonic Symphony under Mitropoulos, and several jazz albums.

EILEEN FARRELL

FARWELL, Arthur. American composer (1872–1952). One of his teachers was the composer Humperdinck. He was an authority on music of the American Indians and used it as a basis for some of his own music. Among his academic posts were those of head of the music department at the University of California, and professor of theory at Michigan State College. He was music critic for *Musical America* from 1909 to 1913. His compositions include music dramas designed for school productions, chamber music, violin sonatas, a setting for tenor of *The Hound of Heaven,* and several symphonic works, of which the best known are *The Gods of the Mountain* and *Mountain Song.*

FASANO, Renato. Italian conductor (1920–). Fasano is known throughout the world as director of the singularly successful Italian chamber orchestra *I Virtuosi di Roma.* He has also been director of the Conservatory Cagliari and principal conductor of the concerts of the Conservatory Benedetto Marcello in Venice. Fasano is also the editor of a series of early Italian music, most of it never published before, issued by Ricordi of Milan.

FAULL, Ellen. American soprano. After voice lessons in high school she studied at the Curtis Institute of Music, Philadelphia. She made her debut as Donna Anna in the New York City Opera production of Mozart's *Don Giovanni.* This was followed by engagements as soloist with the Philadelphia Orchestra and the Boston, Chicago, and Pittsburgh symphony orchestras, and in numerous roles with the New York City and San Francisco opera companies. She has also sung at the Hollywood Bowl and at Chicago's Grant Park.

FAURÉ, Gabriel. French composer (1845–1924). At the age of nineteen he began to study music at the École Niedermeyer, where Saint-Saëns was one of his teachers. He left the school in 1866 to become church organist at Rennes; four years later he returned to Paris where he successively held posts as organist at St. Sulpice and St. Honoré, and as choirmaster at the Madeleine. In 1896 he was appointed professor of composition at the Conservatory, becoming director there from 1905 to 1920. Then increasing deafness forced him to resign. His pupils at the Conservatory included Ravel, Florent

GABRIEL FAURÉ

Schmitt, Georges Enesco, and Nadia Boulanger. In 1922 he was promoted to the highest rank in the Legion of Honor.

Fauré made his first appearance as a composer with a group of songs in 1865, and it is in this field that he has won his greatest fame. The exquisite beauty of his songs, with their purity of style, their poetic sensibility, and their melodic freshness earned him the title of the "French Schumann." Attention has frequently been drawn to the mingling in Fauré's art of a typical French grace and clarity with the spirit of classical Greek art. Thus Julien Tiersot wrote: ". . . it is not enough to recognize in him a Greek musician revived in our twentieth century: it is the spirit of Hellenism, as well as its forms, which is reborn in him. . . . He, too, thrusts himself beyond the spheres to bring back pure beauty."

Fauré's consummate artistry was also apparent in his piano music and chamber music, in which his subtle harmonic innovations, his classical elegance, and impeccable sensibility combine to produce compositions that are among

A scene from Fauré's Pénélope, *at the Teatro Colón in Buenos Aires*

the most treasured items in the repertoires of chamber music players. Fauré was less successful in the larger musical forms, his intimate art being unsuited to the breadth and vigor of the symphony or opera, but his Requiem (1887) is still frequently performed and, like his lyrical drama, the opera *Pénélope* (1913), contains many beautiful passages.

The originality and the modernity of Fauré's form and harmonic language have often been recognized. Thus André Coeuroy said that he "suggested twenty years before Debussy the syntax of the new century," and Vuillermoz wrote: "He created an altogether modern, logical, well-thought-out style, never sacrificing to passing fashions, but steadily tending toward greater serenity and simplicity. The easy grace of his art is deceptive: never did a creative artist present us with subtler and more powerful achievements."

Best-known works:

ORCHESTRAL

Ballade, for piano and orchestra, Op. 19 (1881)
Requiem, for soloists, chorus, orchestra and organ, Op. 48 (1887)
Masques et Bergamasques Suite, Op. 112 (1920)

CHAMBER MUSIC

Sonata No. 1 in A major for piano and violin, Op. 13 (1876)
Piano Quartet No. 1 in C minor, Op. 15 (1879)
Berceuse, Op. 16, violin and piano (1880)

Elégie in C minor, Op. 24, cello and piano (1883)
Piano Quartet No. 2 in G minor, Op. 45 (1886)
Papillon, Op. 77, cello and piano (1898)
Sicilienne, Op. 78, cello and piano (1898)
Quintet for Piano and Strings, No. 2, Op. 115 (1921)

PIANO

Romance sans paroles, No. 3, Op. 17 (1863)
Nocturnes (13):
  No. 3, A flat major, Op. 33 (1883)
  No. 6, D major, Op. 63 (1894)
Theme and Variations, C minor, Op. 73 (1897)
Preludes (9), Op. 103 (1911)

SONGS

Après un rêve (Bussine), Op. 7 (1865)
Automne (Silvestre), Op. 18 (1884)
Clair de lune (Verlaine), Op. 46 (1887)
En prière (Bordese) (1890)
En sourdine (Verlaine), Op. 58 (1890)
L'Horizon chimérique (de Mirmont), Op. 118 (1922)
Les Berceux (Prudhomme), Op. 23 (1882)
Le Secret (Silvestre), Op. 23 (1882)
Les Roses d'Ispahan (Leconte de Lisle), Op. 39 (1884)
Nell (Leconte de Lisle), Op. 18 (1880)
Nocturne (Villiers de L'Isle Adam), Op. 43 (1886)

FAURE, Jean-Baptiste. French baritone (1830–1914). After singing in the chorus at the Théâtre Italien in Paris, he graduated to secondary roles at the Opéra-Comique, where he eventually rose to fame. At the Opéra, he was the leading baritone and one of the greatest stars in French opera for seventeen years. He also appeared for seventeen years at Covent Garden in London. His performance as Mephistopheles in *Faust,* together with that of Nilsson as Marguerite, had much to do with the great success of the opera, which had first been a failure. He created the title role in Thomas' *Hamlet* and those of Nelusko in Meyerbeer's *L'Africaine* and Posa in Verdi's *Don Carlos.* He also was the composer of many songs, of which one, *Les Rameaux,* remains familiar throughout the world, as it is often sung in churches at Easter services.

FAUST. Opera in five acts, by Gounod, with libretto adapted from Goethe's *Faust* by Jules Barbier and Michel Carré. Gounod's first version was an operetta with spoken dialogue composed especially for the Paris Théâtre Lyrique where it was first performed in 1859. This was so successful that Gounod felt that the work could satisfy the more stringent requirements of the Paris Opéra; he therefore rewrote it as a grand opera, which had its first performance in 1869. *Faust* became one of the most frequently performed works in the Opéra repertoire, and has since swept the world.

At its first hearing no one thought Gounod's music melodious or easy to understand, and he created almost as great a stir as Wagner. Three years after the first performance of *Faust,* a critic of good repute in Paris wrote: "It is a misfortune for Gounod that he admires certain extravagant parts of Beethoven's last quartets. It is this turbid spring that has produced the inferior composers of modern Germany, people like Liszt, Wagner, Schumann. . . . If Gounod has really adopted the doctrine of the endless melody, the melody of the primeval forest and of the sundown . . . then he is irrevocably lost."

After the première of *Faust,* Gounod wrote: "What first wins the favor of the public is the obvious which lies on the surface, but it is that which lies under the surface that makes a work live and establishes it. It takes time to discover and comprehend the endless details which go to make a drama."

Several passages were added to the opera later. Valentine's prayer, which is heard in the overture, was written for the performance in London in 1864, and the ballet in the fifth act was written for opera performance in 1869. The Soldiers' Chorus was originally written for *Ivan the Terrible,* an opera which Gounod never completed.

An English critic wrote about the Garden

JEAN-BAPTISTE FAURE

Scene: "It is one of those inspirations that might have come from the dew of the summer twilight, from the scene of flowers, from the sound of water in the fountains. The short adagio, where the two declare their love, is so luxuriously beautiful and tender that nothing can surpass it."

Time: *Late Middle Ages*

Place: *Germany*

ACT I

Scene: *Faust's study. Easter Sunday*

Faust (tenor), an old man, sits at his writing table in deep contemplation. He realizes that his life has been wasted. Though he has accumulated knowledge, he has lost the things of greatest value to a human being—youth, beauty, and love. Life is no longer of any value to him, but as he raises a poisoned goblet to his lips, the sound of maidens singing comes to him through the window. He puts the goblet down. He no longer wishes to die, and decides to resort to necromancy to obtain what he longs for. He invokes Satan.

The Devil, calling himself Mephistopheles (bass-baritone), appears immediately. His face is demonic and he limps, but he has the appearance of a nobleman with a feather in his cap, a rapier at his side, and a

cloak over his shoulder. He offers Faust riches and power, but Faust wants youth. That, too, Mephistopheles can offer him—on conditions. On Earth he will be Faust's obedient servant, but after death—in Hell—Faust is to belong to him. Faust shudders and draws back in horror, but when Mephistopheles conjures up for him the image of a young and beautiful maiden, he gives way and signs the compact which Mephistopheles lays before him. Mephistopheles gives him a goblet, and as Faust drains it he is instantly transformed into a young and handsome cavalier. Accompanied by Mephistopheles, he goes out into the world to taste again the joys of life.

ACT II

Scene: *The market place*

The market place is full of townsfolk, men and women, young girls and students, and soldiers departing for the wars. They sing and dance.

Valentine (baritone), captain of the soldiers, has been given a picture of the Madonna by his sister Marguerite to keep him from harm, and he beseeches the Holy Virgin to protect the girl. A young student, Siebel (mezzo-soprano), who loves Marguerite, promises to look after her. The song of another young man, Brander (bass), is interrupted by the sudden appearance of Mephistopheles, who describes the dance round the Golden Calf led by Satan.

Clear the way for the Calf of Gold!
In his pomp and pride adore him.

Mephistopheles tells the fortunes of those about him. Brander will soon die. The flowers which Siebel will gather for Marguerite will wither at his touch. Mephistopheles spits out in disdain the wine given him by Brander. He can give them something better: he strikes the inn sign, which depicts a cask, and sparkling wine gushes from it. Filling his goblet, he proposes the health of the beautiful Marguerite; Valentine draws his sword, but it is shattered in mid-air, and he and his friends know that they are face to face with the Devil. Mephistopheles describes a magic circle round himself with the point of his sword, and their weapons are of no avail against him; but when they advance on him with the cross-shaped hilts upraised, he has to give way before the holy symbol. When the dancing begins again, Faust insists that Mephistopheles shall let him meet the maiden he has promised him.

Marguerite (soprano) enters. Faust offers to escort her home, but she bashfully refuses. He is disappointed, but Mephistopheles assures him that she will soon be his.

ACT III

Scene: *Marguerite's garden*

Siebel enters to gather flowers for Marguerite. He sings a charming little love song, *Gentle flowers in*

Top: *Act II of* Faust *at the Szeged (Hungary) National Theater.* Center: *Act III, Scene 2, at the National Theater in Sofia.* Bottom: *The Walpurgis Night scene at the Paris Opéra*

the dew, but even as he sings, the flowers in his hand begin to fade. Mephistopheles' prophecy has come true! But with a happy thought Siebel dips his fingers in holy water, and the flowers revive.

Siebel departs, and Faust and Mephistopheles enter. The latter laughs disdainfully when he sees Siebel's poor gift. He knows what will interest the maiden more, and goes out to fetch it. Faust is charmed by the neat simplicity of the garden and gives expression to his pleasure in the cavatina:

All hail, thou dwelling pure and lowly!
Home of an angel fair and holy,
All mortal fair excelling!

Mephistopheles comes back with a casket full of jewels which he places beside Siebel's flowers. He and Faust then hide in order to spy on her reactions.

Marguerite enters. She cannot help thinking about the young man who spoke to her in the market place. She seats herself at her spinning wheel, and sings the song of the *King of Thule.*

O'er the sea in Thule of old
Reign'd a King who was true-hearted,
Who, in remembrance of one departed,
Treasur'd up a goblet of gold!

Marguerite sees the flowers and picks them up, but then notices the casket and takes it into her hands. Dazzled by the beautiful jewels, she lets the flowers fall to the ground. She puts on a necklace, and looking at herself in a mirror which she finds in the casket, she thinks that she is more beautiful than a king's daughter. This aria is the famous *Jewel Song:*

Ah! the joy past compare
These jewels bright to wear!

She is surprised by her aunt, Martha (contralto), who assures her that the jewels must be from some noble suitor. Faust and Mephistopheles enter. Martha immediately becomes enamored of Mephistopheles, who brings her news of her husband's death.

Marguerite tells Faust of her loneliness. She once had a little sister to look after, and then her life was worth living. Now her sister is dead and her brother has gone to the war, and she has no one to keep her company. Faust is so touched that he decides to spare her, but Mephistopheles invokes the powers of night and commands them to inflame the pure soul of

The final scene of Faust *as performed at the Metropolitan Opera in the 1890s*

Marguerite. Marguerite opens her window and sings of her yearning for love. Faust hastens to her and she opens the door to admit him. Mephistopheles laughs scornfully.

ACT IV

Scene 1: *A church*

Women enter the church to pray. Marguerite comes in and kneels, but the congregation shuns her because it has become known that she is unmarried and is to have a child. In her despair, she turns to God.

Mephistopheles, shielding himself behind a column from the cross above the altar, embodying her bad conscience, reproaches her for what she has done. For her sin there is but one punishment—perdition. The church choir begins a chant of worship, but the voice of Mephistopheles rings in her ears: "Remember the days when you went into this church with an unstained heart. Now you are doomed." And suddenly the Fiend stands before her, black and threatening. With a cry of horror Marguerite swoons.

Scene 2: *Outside Marguerite's house*

The victorious soldiers return. Valentine is about to enter the house when Siebel stops him to tell him about Marguerite. He pleads with him to be merciful, but Valentine tears himself free and rushes in.

Night falls, and Mephistopheles, who has forced Faust to accompany him, enters and sings a mocking serenade to Marguerite.

"Catarina, while you play at sleeping,
You contrive to hear,
Thro' the lattice slyly peeping,
That your love is near."

But instead of the maiden, Valentine appears and demands to know who has seduced his sister. Mephistopheles indicates Faust. They fight a duel, in which Faust is aided by the evil power of Mephistopheles; Valentine, throwing away the picture of the Virgin which his sister had given him, is mortally wounded. The two culprits escape while a crowd gathers about the fallen man. Marguerite kneels beside her brother, but with his last breath he curses her.

ACT V

Scene 1: (Often omitted) *On the summit of the Brocken*

It is Walpurgis Night, the night before the first of May, when the witches gather on the summit of the Brocken to worship Satan. Mephistopheles has taken Faust with him, and he shows him many of the most beautiful courtesans of history performing a ballet. But Faust cannot forget Marguerite. In a vision he sees her with a red ring round her neck, and demands to be taken to her.

Scene 2: *Marguerite's prison cell*

Marguerite has lost her reason and has killed her baby. She is now waiting to be led to the gallows. While the guard sleeps, Faust and Mephistopheles enter. Faust tries to free her, while Mephistopheles keeps watch. Faust bids Marguerite make haste, but she only speaks of the beautiful time when they first met.

Suddenly Mephistopheles reappears, saying that they must depart. When Marguerite sees the Evil One, she shrinks back and, praying to God for protection, falls dead. Mephistopheles cries out that she is damned, but a heavenly chorus answers, "Saved!"

A host of angels carries Marguerite up to Heaven. Faust, in despair, follows her with his eyes, then falls on his knees in prayer. Mephistopheles is turned away by the shining sword of an archangel.

FAUST SYMPHONY. Composition for orchestra and (in the last movement) chorus and tenor, composed in 1854–55 (revised 1857) by Franz Liszt. The first performance, at a festival in Weimar in honor of Goethe and Schiller in September, 1857, was conducted by the composer himself. The symphony is dedicated to Berlioz, as an expression of gratitude to the creator of the program symphony, forerunner of the symphonic poem.

Liszt's *Faust* Symphony is outwardly a program symphony, but it can equally well be described as three symphonic poems, although continuity is preserved by the use of common thematic material. Liszt used his themes much in the manner of Wagner's leitmotiv.

FAYRFAX, Robert. English composer (1464–1521). His six Masses and two versions of the Magnificat, together with various motets and instrumental pieces, make him one of England's earliest known composers. Many consider him one of the best and most original that England has produced.

FEATHER, Leonard. British-American composer, critic, and jazz musicologist (1914–). Feather has attained fame as a composer, arranger, and, perhaps principally, as a writer on the subject of jazz. Born and educated in England, he came to the United States in 1935. For a time he was Count Basie's arranger; he wrote more than two hundred selections. Between 1950 and 1952 he conducted jazz programs for Voice of America, and organized the only jazz concerts ever presented at the Metropolitan Opera House. In addition to writing many articles on the subject of jazz, he is the author

Act II of Fedora *at La Scala, showing Fedora's mansion in Paris. This was the production mounted for Maria Callas in 1956*

of *Inside Bebop* (1949), The *Encyclopedia of Jazz* (1955), *The Book of Jazz* (1957), and *The New Yearbook of Jazz* (1958).

FEDORA. Tragic opera in three acts by Umberto Giordano, with libretto by Arturo Colautti, after a drama by Sardou. First produced at Milan in 1898, the opera is set in Russia and France in the late nineteenth century. The story tells of Princess Fedora who, after vowing vengeance on the murderer of her betrothed, falls in love with him, and, powerless to stop the pursuit of him and his family which she herself has set in motion, finally commits suicide.

FEE, Roger Dexter. American singer and educator (1918–). Fee is director of the Lamont School of Music at the University of Denver. He received his musical education at the American Conservatory of Music and made opera and oratorio appearances with Midwestern symphony orchestras. He previously served on the faculties of Illinois Wesleyan and Drake universities.

FERGUSON, Maynard. Canadian jazz trumpeter and leader (1928–). After heading his own band, Ferguson became known to American audiences as a member of the Jimmy Dorsey, Charlie Barnet, and Stan Kenton bands. He now leads his own large orchestra.

FERMATA. Italian "pause"; signified by ⌒ above a note.

FERRABOSCO, Alfonso. Italian composer (1543–1588). He was the best known of a large family of musicians, some of whom settled in England. He himself spent some years there and was known to have been a secret agent of some sort. He was a friendly rival of William Byrd and composed many madrigals, motets, and pieces for the lute.

FERRANTE AND TEICHER. American duo piano team. Arthur Ferrante and Louis Teicher first met, when they were six years old, as students at the Juilliard School of Music. They began their association at that time, later studied with Carl Friedberg and other teachers at Juil-

Kathleen Ferrier as Orfeo in the Gluck opera

liard, and taught theory and composition there after graduation. Since 1947 they have devoted their time to concertizing, appearing across the country, frequently on radio and television, and making many recordings. They are very well known for their arrangements and performances of popular songs and the lighter classics.

FERRAS, Christian. French violinist (1933–). Before he was twenty-five years old, Christian Ferras had played as soloist with the most important symphony orchestras of Europe. He won first prize at the Paris Conservatory when he was thirteen, captured the first prize at the international Marguerite Long Competition at Scheveningen in 1948, and played with Menuhin and Szigeti at the Strasbourg Festival in 1950. Together with Jean Barbizet he formed a sonata team. Ferras made his United States debut with the Boston Symphony Orchestra in 1959, earning highest praise from the critics for his polished and mature interpretation of the Brahms Violin Concerto.

FERRIER, Kathleen. English contralto (1912–1953). As a girl she had no intention of adopting music as a career. She was a good pianist, however, and in 1928 she won a musical competition arranged by the *Daily Express*. She was first heard publicly as a singer in 1937 when, for a bet, she entered the contralto class of a music competition in which she was already competing as a pianist. She won first prize in both classes.

Roy Henderson became her teacher, and *Messiah* at Westminster Abbey in 1943 was her first important appearance. She toured the country entertaining troops and workers during the war, and gradually built up a high reputation.

In 1946 Kathleen Ferrier sang the chief role in Benjamin Britten's *Rape of Lucretia* (written with her in mind), and the next year made a great impression in the title role of Gluck's *Orfeo* at Glyndebourne. At the first Edinburgh Festival in 1947 she sang in Mahler's *Das Lied von der Erde* conducted by Bruno Walter, who immediately became her greatest admirer. He invited her to sing in the same work in New York and in Salzburg (1949), and she also sang in Amsterdam, Vienna, and Milan.

She appeared as Orfeo at Covent Garden in February, 1953, and this proved to be her last performance. Suffering from a very painful illness, she died in October of that year.

Kathleen Ferrier's range was, broadly speaking, from F below middle C to high A, covering two octaves, and her voice was wonderfully rich, powerful, and beautifully rounded.

FESTIVAL OVERTURE 1812. Composition for orchestra, Op. 49, by Tchaikovsky, written in 1880 and commemorating the bitter Russian struggle which in 1812 broke the power of Napoleon and brought about his retreat from Moscow.

In a letter to Mme. von Meck, Tchaikovsky described the overture as "very noisy" and having "no great artistic value," adding that it was composed "without much enthusiasm." This statement is perhaps to be attributed to the facts that the overture was a commissioned work, and that Tchaikovsky nourished a great admiration for Napoleon.

Tchaikovsky made use in the overture of the Imperial Russian national anthem, fragments of Cossack songs, and folk tunes from the Novgorod district. In the battle scenes there occur strains from the *Marseillaise* and the *Tsarist* hymn, with the latter triumphant at the end. A long drum roll, like the thunder of cannon, proclaims the victory of the Russians, and bells chime out the joyful news.

The work was to have been first performed at the consecration of the Cathedral of Our Saviour in Moscow. Everything had been impressively planned. A gigantic orchestra, with a vast number of percussion instruments, was to be placed outside the cathedral; a battery of guns was to be fired by means of electric wires connected to the conductor's stand; and all the church bells in Moscow were to chime toward the end of the overture. This plan was never put into effect, and the overture received its first performance two years later at the opening of an exhibition in Moscow, without the effects. It has, however, been performed in the United States with bombs and giant fireworks.

FESTIVALS. Annual music festivals and summer series are an important, established part of musical life in many countries. A list of the best-known festivals follows.

Aaron Copland conducting at the Ojai Festival

FESTIVALS AND SUMMER CONCERTS
IN NORTH AMERICA

Ann Arbor May Festival, University of Michigan, Ann Arbor, Mich.

Aspen Festival, Aspen, Colo. Izler Solomon, musical director. June to September.

Bennington Composers' Conference and Chamber Music, Middlebury College, Middlebury, Vt. August.

Berea Bach Festival, Baldwin-Wallace Conservatory, Berea, Ohio. May.

Berkshire Festival, Tanglewood, Lenox, Mass. Boston Symphony, Erich Leinsdorf, conductor. July and August.

Bethlehem Bach Festival, Bethlehem, Pa. Ifor Jones, director. May.

Boston Arts Festival. June.

Brevard Music Festival, Brevard, N. C. James Christian Pfohl, director. August.

Caramoor Music Festival, Katonah, N. Y. Alfred Wallenstein, musical director. June.

Carmel Bach Festival, Carmel, Calif. July.

Casals Festival, San Juan, Puerto Rico. Pablo Casals, director. June.

Central City Festival, Central City, Colo. Emerson Buckley, musical director. June and July.

Chautauqua Institution, Chautauqua, N. Y. Walter Hendl, conductor; John Daggett Howell, opera director. June to August.

Cincinnati May Festival.

Cincinnati Summer Opera. Fausto Cleva, musical director. June and July.

Cleveland Summer Pops Concerts, Louis Lane, conductor. July and August.

Coonamessett September Festival, Woods Hole, Mass.

Esplanade Concerts, Boston, Mass. Boston Symphony, Arthur Fiedler, conductor. July and August.

Grant Park Summer Concerts, Chicago.

Hollywood Bowl Concerts, Hollywood, Calif. Los Angeles Philharmonic.

La Jolla Festival, La Jolla, Calif. June to August.

Los Angeles Music Festival, UCLA. Franz Waxman, conductor. June.

Marlboro Music Festival, Marlboro School of Music, Marlboro, Vt. Rudolf Serkin, artistic director. July and August.

Montreal Festival, Quebec, Canada.

Music Under the Stars, Milwaukee. John Anello, musical director. July and August.

Naumburg Symphony Concerts on the Mall, Central Park, New York City. May to September.

Newport Jazz Festival, Newport, R. I.

Ojai Festival, Ojai, Calif. May.

Peninsula Music Festival, Fish Creek, Wis. Thor Johnson, conductor. August.

Ravinia Festival, Ravinia Park, Ill. Chicago Symphony. Walter Hendl, artistic director. June to August.

Red Rocks Music Festival, Denver, Colo. Denver Symphony, Saul Caston, conductor. July and August.

Redlands Festival, Redlands, Calif. July and August.

Robin Hood Dell Concerts, Philadelphia. June to August.

Santa Barbara Festival, Santa Barbara, Calif. June.

Santa Fe Opera, Santa Fe, N. M. John Crosby, musical director. June to August.

Stadium Concerts, Lewisohn Stadium, New York City. June to August.

A concert at the Lucerne Festival directed by
Paul Sacher

Stratford Festival, Stratford, Ontario, Canada. July to
September.
Vancouver International Festival, Vancouver, British
Columbia. Nicholas Goldschmidt, artistic director.
July and August.

MUSIC FESTIVALS IN OTHER COUNTRIES
(Mostly held during the summer)

Austria: Bregenz, Graz, Salzburg, Vienna (Festival
Weeks).
Belgium: Ghent.
Czechoslovakia: Prague.
Denmark: Copenhagen.
Finland: Helsinki.
France: Aix-en-Provence, Arles, Besançon, Bordeaux,
Strasbourg.
Germany: Ansbach (Bach Festival), Augsburg, Bay-
reuth (Wagner Festival), Bonn (Beethoven Fes-
tival), Darmstadt, Donaueschingen, Düsseldorf,
Munich, Wiesbaden, Würzburg.
Great Britain: Aldeburgh, Bath, Edinburgh, Glynde-
bourne (Opera Festival), Norwich.
Greece: Athens.
Iran: Teheran.
Ireland: Dublin.

Israel: Haifa, Jerusalem, Tel Aviv.
Italy: Florence (Maggio Musicale Fiorentino), Perugia,
Rome (Baths of Caracalla, Santa Cecilia Concerts),
Spoleto (Festival of Two Worlds), Venice (Inter-
national Festival of Contemporary Music), Verona.
Japan: Osaka, Tokyo (East-West Music Encounter).
Lebanon: Baalbeck.
Monaco: Monte Carlo.
The Netherlands: Amsterdam, The Hague, Rotterdam,
Scheveningen, Utrecht (Holland Festival).
Norway: Bergen.
Spain: Granada, Santander, Seville.
Sweden: Stockholm.
Switzerland: Lausanne, Lucerne, Zurich.
Venezuela: Caracas.
Yugoslavia: Dubrovnik, Ljubljana, Split.

FÊTES. See *Debussy.*

FÊTES GALANTES. Six songs with accompaniment (published in two sets) by Debussy,
being settings of poems by Verlaine from his
collection of the same name. Debussy also set
other poems in the collection (*Pantomime* and

A scene from Jedermann, *Hugo von Hofmannsthal's
version of* Everyman. *This production has been an
annual event at the Salzburg Festival since its inception
in the 1920s*

Mandoline), but included only the following six under the title *Fêtes Galantes:*

Series I (1892):
1. *En Sourdine (In Secret).*
2. *Fantoches (Puppets).*
3. *Clair de Lune (Moonlight).*

Series II (1904):
1. *Les Ingénus (Young Lovers).*
2. *Le Faune (The Faun).*
3. *Colloque Sentimental (Sentimental Dialogue).*

Verlaine's poems ironically depict the elegant life of the eighteenth century as mirrored in the paintings of Watteau and Fragonard, and Debussy expressed both this atmosphere and the poet's satire in masterly fashion.

FÉTIS, François Joseph. Belgian composer and historian (1784–1871). A professor at the Paris Conservatory and later director of the Brussels Conservatory, he composed many operas and sacred works. However, his real importance was as the author of many works on musical theory and two histories, *Biographie universelle des musiciens* and *Histoire générale de la musique,* which, though often inaccurate, have been an indispensible reference for generations of scholars and students.

FEUERMANN, Emanuel. Polish cellist (1902–1942). After cello lessons with his father and Anton Walter, Feuermann gave a series of recitals at the age of eleven. In 1918 he became a cello teacher at the Cologne Conservatory, and in 1929 he went to teach in Berlin. He moved from Vienna to the United States in 1938. He was a frequent recitalist and soloist with orchestra, and was well known as a member of leading chamber music trios (with Heifetz, Primrose, and Artur Rubinstein).

FÉVRIER, Henri. French composer (1875–1957). A pupil of Massenet and Fauré, he composed chamber music, songs, and nine operas, one of which, *Monna Vanna* (1909), was widely produced and is still performed occasionally in Paris. Monna Vanna was one of the famous characterizations of **Mary Garden,** who also sang in Février's *Gismonda.*

FEYER, George. Hungarian-American pianist (1908–). A student of Dohnányi, Székely, and Kodály, at the Budapest Conservatory, Feyer

EMANUEL FEUERMANN

started his professional career as a concert pianist and shifted to the popular field. Playing popular music with a classical touch and vice versa, he appeared throughout Europe before arriving in the United States in 1951. Since then he has toured widely, appeared on television, and made many popular recordings.

FIBICH, Zdenek. Czech composer (1850–1900). From the age of ten Fibich studied music at Vienna, Leipzig, Mannheim, and Paris. After a term as conductor at the Prague National Theater, he returned to his native town of Šeboriče to devote himself to composition.

His six hundred works include operas, melodramas (in which he specialized), incidental music, symphonies, overtures, chamber music, 350 pieces for piano, songs, etc. Almost none of these are known today outside of Czechoslovakia, and the only work that is often heard is Jan Kubelik's transcription for violin and piano of *Poème* (from Fibich's idyl *In the Dusk,* 1893). Most of his music was directly inspired by poetry and by fairy tales of a fantastic nature, and in his melodramas he was strongly influenced by the musico-dramatic principles of Wagner.

An etching from the famous series, Prisons, *by Gian-Battista Piranesi, which vividly evokes the somber dungeon and fortress in* Fidelio

FIDELIO. The only opera composed by Beethoven. The plot is based on an actual experience of the author, Jean N. Bouilly, during the French Revolution. Bouilly wrote a libretto of his story for the composer Pierre Gaveaux, and this work was performed in Paris in 1798. The libretto was revised for Beethoven by the secretary of the court theater, Joseph Sonnleitner, who altered the title from *Leonora, or Married Love* (which Beethoven preferred) to *Fidelio*.

The work was performed for the first time on November 20, 1805, at the Theater an der Wien. As Napoleon had occupied Vienna a week before, the audience consisted mainly of French soldiers, and Beethoven withdrew the work after its third performance. Reduced from three to two acts, the opera was performed again on March 29, 1806, but the composer again withdrew it after the fifth performance. Eight years passed before the work was next performed. Three singers at the court opera were to have a benefit, and chose *Fidelio*. Beethoven undertook to revise the music again, and G. F. Treitsche improved the text. The performance was a great success, and from that date the work has been in the repertoire of all the great opera houses.

The form is that of a German *singspiel* (singing play), with music and spoken dialogue. The work has often been criticized on the grounds that Beethoven did not think dramatically, but musically; that when he did attempt the dramatic, the result was merely symphonic; and that his treatment of the human voice betrays his "instrumental" attitude. Nevertheless, the music is full of character, vivid, and energetic.

The taxing role of Leonora-Fidelio has been sung by many of the great dramatic sopranos of history, including Milder-Hauptmann (who was the first), Schröder-Devrient, Sontag, Malibran, Viardot-García, Tietjens, Ternina, Brandt, Lilli Lehmann, Lotte Lehmann, Flagstad, and Nilsson. See *Leonora Overtures*.

Time: *About 1600*

Place: *A state prison in Spain*

ACT I

The tyrannical Don Pizarro (baritone) is the governor of a state prison. The chief jailer Rocco (bass) possesses a young daughter, Marcellina (soprano), who is loved by a guard, Jaquino (tenor), but she prefers the young Fidelio (soprano), whom her father has just taken into his service. Fidelio is actually Leonora, a noble lady in disguise, who is searching for her husband Don Florestan (tenor). She believes that he is being kept a prisoner by some enemy, and her search has led her to Don Pizarro's prison.

Scene 1: *A room in the prison*

The scene opens with a lively quarrel between Marcellina and Jaquino. He proposes again to her, but she refuses him, telling him outright that she loves Fidelio. Rocco sides with her against Jaquino.

Fidelio returns from an errand in the town. Rocco, believing that Fidelio loves Marcellina, promises to help them. In a quartet, a warm and spirited canon, the four describe their feelings. Fidelio makes friends with Rocco, who promises to explain the work of the prison.

Scene 2: *The prison courtyard*

Don Pizarro has received a letter from a friend in Madrid telling him that the Minister of Justice, Don Fernando, is on his way to inspect the prison. An enemy of Pizarro, whom he has imprisoned illegally, is languishing in a deep dungeon, and the governor decides that he must be disposed of before the inspecting minister arrives. Pizarro tries to persuade Rocco to kill the prisoner. The old man refuses, but agrees to dig the grave. Pizarro resolves to murder the prisoner himself. Fidelio, who has heard the conversation, suspects that the unknown prisoner is her husband.

Ab-scheu-licher! Wo eilst du hin,   was hast du vor?

Foul murderer! What brought you here?
What would you do?
Lives there a fiend in Hell so cruel?

In order to verify her suspicion she makes Rocco let the prisoners out into the courtyard, but her husband is not among them. Pizarro arrives and furiously orders the prisoners back to their cells.

Rocco and Fidelio go down to the secret prisoner's dungeon to dig his grave.

ACT II

Scene 1: *The dungeon*

Don Florestan, lying in the darkness, chained to the wall, and emaciated from the treatment he has suffered, in a feverish vision sees his wife Leonora as an angel of salvation.

Gott! Welch Dunkel hier!   Oh grauenvolle Stille

Oh God! what everlasting darkness.
Murky stillness presses round about me.

Rocco and Fidelio enter and start to dig. To her horror Fidelio recognizes her husband, but dares not reveal who she is. Pizarro enters, and as he is about to stab Florestan, Fidelio rushes forward crying, "Kill his wife first." As Pizarro is about to kill them both, a trumpet sounds. The minister, Don Fernando, has arrived. Pizarro and Rocco hasten up the stairs, and Leonora and Florestan join in a jubilant duet.

Fidelio, Act I, Scene 1, and Act II, Scene 1, at La Scala

The final scene of Fidelio *in Wieland Wagner's production at Stuttgart*

Scene 2: *In the prison courtyard*

Don Fernando (bass) sets free all the prisoners and condemns Don Pizzaro to the dungeons. Rocco introduces Don Florestan and his wife and recounts the latter's brave conduct. Marcellina, in despair, is consoled by Jaquino. The opera ends with a chorus of praise for Leonora.

FIEDLER, Arthur. American conductor (1894–). Arthur Fiedler's leadership of the Boston Pops Orchestra concerts has made him an outstanding favorite in the United States and abroad. The son of Emanuel Fiedler, a violinist who played with the Boston Symphony Orchestra for twenty-five years, Fiedler studied at the Royal Academy of Music in Berlin. He was a pupil of Arno Kleffel, Rudolf Krasselt, Willy Hess, and Ernö Dohnányi, and made his debut as a violinist in Berlin at the age of seventeen. Returning to the United States at the outbreak of World War I, he was accepted as a violinist with the Boston Symphony Orchestra, then under the leadership of Dr. Karl Muck, and has remained with this musical institution ever since.

In 1929, he founded the Esplanade Concerts with a group of Boston Symphony Orchestra musicians, offering open-air, admission-free concerts. These concerts continue after more than thirty years, and are financed jointly by the Boston Symphony Orchestra and by public donations.

In 1930, Fiedler was appointed conductor of the famed Boston Pops Concerts, which were founded in 1885. He has brought distinction and great popularity to these concerts. In addition to his activities in Boston, Fiedler has been guest conductor of principal orchestras in the United States and Canada.

FIELD, John. Irish composer and pianist (1782–1837). A precursor of Chopin, he developed the lyric manner of piano playing. He originated the Nocturne form and wrote many works in that genre, as well as piano concertos and chamber music.

FIELDS, GRACIE. English singer and actress (1898–). One of the most popular entertainers in the world, she worked her way to the top via music halls and revue companies, and then became a film star. She entertained millions of troops and factory workers during the second World War and since has played to her adoring public on radio, television, in motion pictures, and revues. She now appears only infrequently, as she lives most of the time on Capri, where she operates a popular restaurant and marina.

FIFTH. Interval embracing five degrees of the diatonic scale; also the fifth note of a scale from lower *do*. See *Music, Elements of.*

FIGNER, Nikolai. Russian tenor (1857–1918). The leading tenor of the Maryinsky Theater in St. Petersburg, he created the role of Herman in Tchaikovsky's *Pique-Dame* in 1890. He also was celebrated as Lensky in *Eugene Onegin* and, particularly, as Otello in Verdi's opera. One of his most popular performances was as Don José to his wife's Carmen, and his only opera appearance outside Russia was opposite her in *La Favorita,* at Covent Garden in London in 1887.

FIGNER, Medea Mei-. Italian soprano (1859–1952). After a successful career in Italy and Spain, she married the Russian tenor Nikolai Figner and managed to adapt herself so well to a new country and a strange language that she became a great favorite at the Maryinsky Theater in St. Petersburg, where she often appeared with her husband and was considered unsurpassed as Carmen. She lived in Paris after the Revolution and died there at the age of ninety-three.

MEDEA MEI-FIGNER

FIGURED BASS. A system of notation originally used for harpsichord or organ music at the end of the sixteenth century. The bass part was written with a fixed code of figures under the notes indicating which chords could be used as a basis for improvised accompaniment to the other instruments or to vocal parts. Figured-bass playing required great skill, experience, ingenuity, and imagination.

Johann Sebastian Bach wrote: "Figured bass is the most perfect musical basis. It is played in such a way that the left hand plays the prescribed notes, while the right hand resorts to consonances and dissonances, so that a beautiful harmony is produced to the honor of God and a redeeming ease for the soul. Like all other music, figured bass must pay tribute to God and create well-being for the spirit. If this is ignored, the result is not real music, but a devilish noise."

ARTHUR FIEDLER

FILLE AUX CHEVEUX DE LIN, LA (*The Girl with the Flaxen Hair*). Prelude for piano by Debussy, No. 8 of his first collection (1910). The composition is based on Leconte de Lisle's *Scottish Poem,* the first stanza of which, freely translated, runs: "The young girl with the flaxen hair and the cherry lips sits amidst the clover in the flowering meadow, and sings all day. In the bright summer sun, Love sings, too, and takes part in the game."

Film Music and Musicals

THERE are two broad categories of film scores: those that are suited to their purpose; and those few that, in addition, have been successful in concert versions and are of independent musical interest.

Before the invention of sound motion pictures, scores to accompany films were more often arranged or improvised than specifically composed. The hack pianist who played during the showing of a silent film drew upon a large repertory of program pieces. Certain music publishers and film companies issued albums of piano selections with appropriate pieces labeled *The Chase, Love Scene in Moonlight, Terror, A Mother's Anguish,* etc. From the earliest days of films, well-known composers have done work for the medium. Saint-Saëns composed a score to accompany a silent film on the assassination of the Duke de Guise. Richard Strauss arranged a score for a silent film version of *Der Rosenkavalier,* which included a number of scenes not contained in the opera. Elaborate scores for silent films were composed by, among others, Florent Schmitt and Ildebrando Pizzetti. Other composers wrote scores meant to accompany filmed sequences in ballets (Satie's *Relâche,* Milhaud's *Le Boeuf sur le Toit,* and Antheil's *Ballet mecanique*) or merely to accompany a given mood in any film, such as Schoenberg's *Music for a Movie Scene.* Satie was one of the first distinguished composers to become seriously interested in film music, and some of the finest scores for sound films have been composed by his followers, particularly Honegger *(Mayerling* and *Pygmalion)* and Auric (*À nous la liberté, La Belle et la bête, La Symphonie pastorale, Moulin Rouge,* etc.).

Prokofiev's music for Eisenstein's *Alexander Nevsky* has become part of the concert repertory, as has his *Lieutenant Kije* score. Even so, these works are recognizable as film music. The purpose of a film score remains the same, whatever means the composer employs to fulfill it: that is, to heighten and accentuate mood and drama without intruding upon the viewer with something that he will be forced to listen to as "music." Since the development of sound films, the technique for scoring has been to dub in the music and other sound effects. The musicians play on cues while the film is run off on a movie screen or television monitor. Musical clichés and stock effects are an inevitable result of this musical method, and a score may command attention simply because its composer has succeeded in avoiding them.

Occasionally, music extracted from a film achieves independent popularity, such as Max Steiner's score for *Gone with the Wind* (probably the most famous of all film scores) and Addinsell's *Warsaw Concerto* from the film *Dangerous Moonlight.* Recently, the score from *Never on Sunday* by the Greek composer Monos Hadjidakis has had a huge record sale, as did Walton's score for *Henry V.*

The comedy stars Charles Chaplin and Jackie Gleason have composed or arranged scores for their own films. Since the perfection of sound techniques, most successful composers throughout the world have written for films. In England, the deans of music, Vaughan Williams and Bax, have been recruited for films, as have Bliss, Lambert, Berkeley, Gerhard, Holst, Ireland, and Fricker. England has developed several composers whose work is almost exclusively for films: William Alwyn, Alan Rawsthorne, Benjamin Frankel, Brian Easdale, Gordon Jacob, Ian Whyte. The German Hanns Eisler (who experimented with serial music in films) and the Italians Roman Vlad, Nino Rota, and Renzo Rossellini have made reputations as film composers. Japan and India, with their expanding film industries, are developing new composers for the medium; and it is to be expected that in future, electronic music will be more frequently used in films.

Though the greatest activity in film music has been in Hollywood, some of the most significant American scores have been composed for documentary films, particularly those by Virgil Thomson *(The Plough That Broke the Plains* and *The Louisiana Story),* which have become familiar in concert versions. Others are Blitzstein's *Native Land* and Kubik's *The Memphis Belle.* Among the most celebrated of film scores are those of Aaron Copland, who after *Our Town, Of Mice and Men,* and the Academy Award-winning score for *The Heiress,* did not compose for films again until recently, when he did the score for *Something Wild.* Another famous film score is that of Bernard Herrmann for Orson Welles' *Citizen Kane.* In recent years, Elmer Bernstein has become one of the most admired of film composers. Veterans of the medium, each of whom has done important

work, are Jean Wiéner, Maurice Jaubert, Ernst Toch, Alexander Tansman, Erich Korngold, Max Steiner, Victor Young, Franz Waxman, Miklos Roza, Alfred Newman, Dmitri Tiomkin, and Boris Morros.

Standard classics were often employed to accompany silent films, and have been used occasionally as background music in sound films such as *Brief Encounter,* which introduced Rachmaninoff's Second Piano Concerto to a whole new public. Walt Disney's cartoon feature, *Fantasia,* was a unique attempt to dramatize music of the great composers. Other films with stories involving musicians have employed famous performers like Artur Rubinstein on the sound tracks; and there was a successful use of opera arias in Grace Moore's hit of the 1930s, *One Night of Love,* in Mario Lanza's *The Great Caruso,* the Deanna Durbin films, and other films that have starred notable singers such as Lily Pons and Ezio Pinza.

Opera and ballet films have been few and

Aaron Copland conducting his score for Something Wild. *The film is shown, in this instance, on closed-circuit television, although most film scores are dubbed in with the composer-conductor viewing the film on a full-size movie screen*

A scene from the Pabst production of Kurt Weill's Driegroschen Oper, *one of the first "serious" musical films in sound*

Al Jolson in The Jazz Singer *marked the advent of musical films in 1927*

generally unsuccessful. One of the first starred Chaliapin in a semi-operatic *Don Quichotte* that was composed for the film by Jacques Ibert. One of the best was an early sound version of the Brecht-Weill *Dreigroschen Oper*. The Italians have filmed many operas, but they cannot be called successful as films. The Russians have been much more successful with film versions of *Eugene Onegin* and other operas. The English production of *The Tales of Hoffmann* was at least partially effective. One of the first and still one of the best of ballet films was the French-made *Ballerina,* while the most popular has been *The Red Shoes*. Others have been Gene

A scene from Gold Diggers of 1923, *a "silent" musical (which was probably just as well) starring Louise Fazenda* (right), *and a number of "vamps" attired in the latest fashions*

Kelly's *Invitation to the Dance* and Roland Petit's *Black Tights*. The frankly documentary approach to filmed versions of opera and ballet has produced permanent records of classics in the repertories of the Bolshoi Ballet and the Royal Ballet of England, as well as of the modern works of Martha Graham. The director Paul Czinner has filmed actual stage performances of *Don Giovanni* and *Der Rosenkavalier,* with results that at least pleased opera fans. However, the desired compromise between the wandering focus of the camera and that of the stage, which is essentially static, has yet to be achieved.

The film musical is another matter and one that has seen many developments. The Hollywood musical films of the 1930s, those of the *Big Broadcast* and *Gold Diggers* variety, were good-natured, spontaneous, and truly of the medium, although they may sometimes have been very simple and occasionally vulgar. The more pretentious films that followed, such as *The Goldwyn Follies,* were certainly more ambitious but now seem less entertaining. The operetta films, such as those starring Jeanette MacDonald and Nelson Eddy, were greatly popular for a time, as were the genuinely entertaining films of Ginger Rogers and Fred Astaire. Later original film musicals such as *Cover Girl, Meet Me in St. Louis, State Fair, Singin' in the Rain,* and *Funny Face* had elements that suggested the development of the film musical as a distinct form. But since 1957, with the exception of Lerner's and Loewe's *Gigi* (1958), film producers have confined themselves to adaptations of Broadway musicals, with the result that most of the great musical stars of films have returned to Broadway, gone into television or night-club work, or changed to straight roles in films.

Film adaptations of Broadway musicals have failed, on the whole, to add anything to the originals, and often have taken much away. Most of them have lost stature when transferred to the screen, for they tend to be overproduced, with a loss of conviction and immediacy.

It is still possible that, once they have adjusted to the changes brought about by television, film producers will discover a cinematic approach to the musical and even, perhaps, to a new form of music drama that will result in something approaching a true cinematic opera.

The following list of American film musicals stops at 1952; since then, most Hollywood offerings have been screen adaptations of Broadway shows. It is to be hoped, however, that soon the film industry will be able to present the public with original musicals of the caliber of *Seven Brides for Seven Brothers,* the original *State Fair, Singin' in the Rain,* and, of course, the delightful *Gigi.* All of these were created especially for the screen, and all of them achieved the high standards of the best Broadway show, while at the same time managing to take full advantage of the limitless possibilities of motion-picture techniques.

These girls from The Broadway Melody *of 1929 are obviously going to get somewhere*

Film Musicals in America

MAJOR AMERICAN FILM MUSICALS, 1927–1952

1927

THE JAZZ SINGER; Al Jolson, May McAvoy. The first full-length feature with a synchronized sound track, utilizing previously introduced songs.

1928

THE SINGING FOOL; Al Jolson, Betty Bronson. The first all-talking, all-singing musical film.

Original Songs: De Sylva, Brown, and Henderson; Dave Dreyer (lyrics: Billy Rose, Al Jolson).

Old Songs: De Sylva, Brown, and Henderson.

1929

THE BROADWAY MELODY; Charles King, Anita Page, Bessie Love. Winner of the Academy Award for the best film of 1929; also the first in the MGM series of four *Broadway Melodies.*

Original Songs: Nacio Herb Brown (lyrics: Arthur Freed); Willard Robinson.

Old Song: George M. Cohan.

A scene from The Red Shoes, *with Leonid Massine, Robert Helpmann, and Moira Shearer*

A great moment from Gold Diggers of Broadway: *the "diggers" have just descended into the mine, and the precious stones are displayed stage front*

GOLD DIGGERS OF BROADWAY; Nancy Welford, Conway Tearle, Winnie Lightner, Ann Pennington, Lilyan Tashman, Nick Lucas. First in the Warner Brothers series of five *Gold Diggers* films.

Original Songs: Joe Burke (lyrics: Al Dubin).

SUNNY SIDE UP; Janet Gaynor, Charles Farrell, Joe E. Brown, El Brendel.

Original Songs: De Sylva, Brown, and Henderson.

THE LOVE PARADE; Maurice Chevalier, Jeanette MacDonald, Lupino Lane, Lillian Roth.

Original Songs: Victor Schertzinger (lyrics: Clifford Grey).

1930

MONTE CARLO; Jeanette MacDonald, Jack Buchanan, Zazu Pitts.

Original Songs: Richard Whiting; W. Franke Harling (lyrics: Leo Robin).

1932

THE BIG BROADCAST; Bing Crosby, Leila Hyams, Stuart Erwin, Burns and Allen, Boswell Sisters, Mills Brothers, Arthur Tracy, Kate Smith, Cab Calloway's orchestra, Vincent Lopez' orchestra. First in the Paramount series of four *Big Broadcast* films.

Original Songs: Ralph Rainger (lyrics: Leo Robin); James Monaco (lyrics: Edgar Leslie).

Old Songs: Benny Carter; Oscar Rosbach (lyrics: Joyce Kilmer); Harry Barris (lyrics: Arthur Freed); Harold Arlen (lyrics: Ted Koehler); B. J. La Rocca; Harry Akst (lyrics: Sam Lewis, Joseph Young).

ONE HOUR WITH YOU; Maurice Chevalier, Jeanette MacDonald, Genevieve Tobin, Charles Ruggles, Roland Young.

Original Songs: Oscar Straus; Richard Whiting (lyrics: Leo Robin).

LOVE ME TONIGHT; Maurice Chevalier, Jeanette MacDonald, Charles Ruggles, Myrna Loy.

Original Songs: Richard Rodgers (lyrics: Lorenz Hart).

1933

FLYING DOWN TO RIO; Dolores Del Rio, Gene Raymond, Fred Astaire, Ginger Rogers.

Original Songs: Vincent Youmans (lyrics: Gus Kahn, Edward Eliscu).

FOOTLIGHT PARADE; James Cagney, Joan Blondell, Ruby Keeler, Dick Powell, Guy Kibbee.

Original Songs: Sammy Fain (lyrics: Irving Kahal); Harry Warren (lyrics: Al Dubin).

42ND STREET; Warner Baxter, Bebe Daniels, George Brent, Ruby Keeler, Dick Powell, Guy Kibbee, Ginger Rogers, Una Merkel, Clarence Nordstrom.

Original Songs: Harry Warren (lyrics: Al Dubin).

GOLD DIGGERS OF 1933; Warren William, Joan Blondell, Aline McMahon, Ruby Keeler, Dick Powell, Ginger Rogers.

Original Songs: Harry Warren (lyrics: Al Dubin).

HALLELUJAH I'M A BUM; Al Jolson, Madge Evans, Frank Morgan, Harry Langdon, Chester Conklin.

Original Songs: Richard Rodgers (lyrics: Lorenz Hart).

ROMAN SCANDALS; Eddie Cantor, Ruth Etting, Gloria Stuart, David Manners, Edward Arnold.

Original Songs: Harry Warren (lyrics: Al Dubin).

1934

ONE NIGHT OF LOVE; Grace Moore, Tullio Carminati. Except for the title song, score consisted of operatic arias.

Original Song: Victor Schertzinger (lyrics: Gus Kahn).

THE CAT AND THE FIDDLE (based on the stage musical of the same name); Ramon Novarro, Jeanette MacDonald, Frank Morgan, Vivienne Segal.

Original Stage Score: Jerome Kern (lyrics: Otto Harbach).

THE GAY DIVORCÉE (based on the stage musical *Gay Divorce*); Fred Astaire, Ginger Rogers, Alice Brady, Edward Everett Horton.

Original Stage Score: Cole Porter.

Original Songs: Harry Revel (lyrics: Mack Gordon); Con Conrad (lyrics: Herb Magidson).

1935

THE BROADWAY MELODY OF 1936; Robert Taylor, Eleanor Powell, Jack Benny, Frances Langford, Una Merkel, June Knight.

Original Songs: Nacio Herb Brown (lyrics: Arthur Freed).

A spectacular night-club number in The Broadway Melody of 1936. *Eleanor Parker is seen in white tails and tie*

GOLD DIGGERS OF 1935; Dick Powell, Gloria Stuart, Adolphe Menjou, Alice Brady, Glenda Farrell, Winifred Shaw.

Original Songs: Harry Warren (lyrics: Al Dubin).

MISSISSIPPI; Bing Crosby, Joan Bennett, W. C. Fields, Queenie Smith.

Original Songs: Richard Rodgers (lyrics: Lorenz Hart).

Old Song: Stephen Foster.

NAUGHTY MARIETTA (based on the operetta of the same name); Jeanette MacDonald, Nelson Eddy, Frank Morgan, Joseph Cawthorn, Elsa Lanchester.

Original Stage Score: Victor Herbert (lyrics: Rida Johnson Young, Gus Kahn).

Original Song: Herbert Stohart (lyrics: Gus Kahn).

ROBERTA (based on the stage musical of the same name); Irene Dunne, Fred Astaire, Ginger Rogers, Randolph Scott, Helen Westley.

Original Stage Score: Jerome Kern (lyrics: Otto Harbach).

Original Songs: Jerome Kern (lyrics: Dorothy Fields, Jimmy McHugh).

TOP HAT; Fred Astaire, Ginger Rogers, Edward Everett Horton, Erik Rhodes, Eric Blore, Helen Broderick.

Original Songs: Irving Berlin.

1936

BORN TO DANCE; Eleanor Powell, James Stewart, Virginia Bruce, Una Merkel, Sid Silvers, Buddy Ebsen, Frances Langford, the Foursome.

Original Songs: Cole Porter.

FOLLOW THE FLEET; Fred Astaire, Ginger Rogers, Harriet Hilliard, Randolph Scott, Lucille Ball.

Original Songs: Irving Berlin.

PENNIES FROM HEAVEN; Bing Crosby, Madge Evans, Edith Fellows, Louis Armstrong.

Original Songs: Arthur Johnson (lyrics: Johnny Burke).

SHOW BOAT (based on the stage musical of the same name); Irene Dunne, Allan Jones, Helen Morgan, Charles Winninger, Paul Robeson, Helen Westley, Hattie McDaniel.

Original Stage Score: Jerome Kern (lyrics: Oscar Hammerstein II, P. G. Wodehouse).

Original Songs: Jerome Kern (lyrics: Oscar Hammerstein II).

SWING TIME; Fred Astaire, Ginger Rogers, Victor Moore, Helen Broderick.

Original Songs: Jerome Kern (lyrics: Dorothy Fields).

THE GREAT ZIEGFELD; William Powell, Louise Rainer, Myrna Loy, Frank Morgan, Virginia Bruce, Fanny Brice, Ray Bolger. Winner of the Academy Award for the best film of 1936.

Original Songs: Walter Donaldson (lyrics: Harold Adamson).

Old Songs: Joseph Meyer (lyrics: B. G. De Sylva); Irving Berlin; Maurice Yvain (lyrics: Channing Pollock).

1937

A DAMSEL IN DISTRESS; Fred Astaire, Joan Fontaine, Burns and Allen, Ray Noble.

Original Songs: George Gershwin (lyrics: Ira Gershwin).

Fanny Brice looking very soignée in The Great Ziegfeld

Jeanette MacDonald glows in The Firefly *when she dances the fandango on a very large table*

THE FIREFLY (based on the operetta of the same name); Jeanette MacDonald, Allan Jones, Warren William.

Original Stage Score: Rudolf Friml (lyrics: Otto Harbach).

Original Songs: Rudolf Friml (lyrics: Gus Kahn, Robert Wright, George Forrest).

HIGH, WIDE, AND HANDSOME; Irene Dunne, Randolph Scott, Charles Bickford, Dorothy Lamour.

Original Songs: Jerome Kern (lyrics: Oscar Hammerstein II).

ON THE AVENUE; Dick Powell, Alice Faye, Madeleine Carroll, Ritz Brothers.

Original Songs: Irving Berlin.

ROSALIE; Eleanor Powell, Nelson Eddy, Frank Morgan, Ray Bolger.

Original Songs: Cole Porter.

SHALL WE DANCE; Fred Astaire, Ginger Rogers, Edward Everett Horton, Eric Blore, Harriet Hoctor.

Original Songs: George Gershwin (lyrics: Ira Gershwin).

SNOW WHITE AND THE SEVEN DWARFS; The first full-length animated cartoon.

Original Songs: Larry Morey; Frank Churchill.

WAKE UP AND LIVE; Walter Winchell, Ben Bernie, Alice Faye, Jack Haley, Patsy Kelly.

Original Songs: Harry Revel (lyrics: Mack Gordon).

1938

THE GOLDWYN FOLLIES; Adolphe Menjou, Kenny Baker, Ella Logan, Andrea Leeds, Helen Jepson, Phil Baker, Bobby Clark, Vera Zorina, Ritz Brothers.

Original Songs: George Gershwin (lyrics: Ira Gershwin); Vernon Duke (lyrics: Ira Gershwin); Ray Golden; Sid Kuller.

ALEXANDER'S RAGTIME BAND; Tyrone Power, Alice Faye, Don Ameche, Jack Haley, Ethel Merman.

Original Songs: Irving Berlin.

Old Songs: Irving Berlin and others.

CAREFREE; Fred Astaire, Ginger Rogers, Jack Carson, Ralph Bellamy.

Original Songs: Irving Berlin.

REBECCA OF SUNNYBROOK FARM; Shirley Temple, Jack Haley, Gloria Stuart, Bill Robinson, Raymond Scott Quartet.

Original Songs: Harry Revel (lyrics: Mack Gordon); Samuel Pokrass (lyrics: Jack Yellen); Sidney Mitchell; Lew Pollack; Raymond Scott.

1939

THE STORY OF VERNON AND IRENE CASTLE; Fred Astaire, Ginger Rogers, Edna May Oliver; Lew Fields. The score was composed of numerous early songs with one original number.

Original Song: Con Conrad; Harry Ruby (lyrics: Bert Kalmar).

George Balanchine choreographed this ballet sequence in The Goldwyn Follies. *Vera Zorina is about to emerge from the pool*

BABES IN ARMS (based on the stage musical of the same name); Judy Garland, Mickey Rooney, Douglas McPhail, Betty Jaynes, June Preisser.

Original Stage Score: Richard Rodgers (lyrics: Lorenz Hart).

Original Songs: Nacio Herb Brown (lyrics: Arthur Freed); Roger Edens.

Old Songs: Harold Arlen (lyrics: E. Y. Harburg); Gus Arnheim; Abe Lyman; Arthur Freed.

THE WIZARD OF OZ; Judy Garland, Ray Bolger, Jack Haley, Bert Lahr, Frank Morgan, Billie Burke, Margaret Hamilton.

Original Songs: Harold Arlen (lyrics: E. Y. Harburg).

1940

FANTASIA; Deems Taylor introduces eight classic selections.

By Johann Sebastian Bach:
Toccata and Fugue in D Minor

By Peter Ilyich Tchaikovsky:
The Nutcracker Suite

By Paul Dukas:
The Sorcerer's Apprentice

By Igor Stravinsky:
The Rite of Spring

By Ludwig van Beethoven:
Pastoral Symphony

By Amilcare Ponchielli:
Dance of the Hours

By Modest Mussorgsky:
Night on Bald Mountain

By Franz Schubert; lyrics: Rachel Field:
Ave Maria

Judy Garland and Mickey Rooney as they appeared in Babes in Arms *(1939)*

PINOCCHIO; the voices of Dickie Jones, Cliff Edwards, Christian Rub, Walter Catlett, Charles Judels, Evelyn Venable.

Original Songs: Leigh Harline (lyrics: Ned Washington).

ROAD TO SINGAPORE; Bing Crosby, Bob Hope, Dorothy Lamour. First in the Paramount series of seven *Road* films.

Original Songs: James Monaco (lyrics: Johnny Burke); Victor Schertzinger (lyrics: Johnny Burke).

1941

YOU'LL NEVER GET RICH; Fred Astaire, Rita Hayworth, Robert Benchley.

Original Songs: Cole Porter.

SUN VALLEY SERENADE; Sonja Henie, John Payne, Milton Berle, Glenn Miller's orchestra, Lynn Bari.

Original Songs: Harry Warren (lyrics: Mack Gordon).

BLUES IN THE NIGHT; Priscilla Lane, Richard Whorf, Jack Carson, Lloyd Nolan.

Original Songs: Harold Arlen (lyrics: Johnny Mercer).

1942

HOLIDAY INN; Bing Crosby, Fred Astaire, Marjorie Reynolds.

Original Songs: Irving Berlin.
Old Songs: Irving Berlin.

YANKEE DOODLE DANDY; James Cagney (winner of Academy Award for best performance of 1942), Joan Leslie, Walter Huston, Rosemary DeCamp, Jeanne Cagney. Film biography of George M. Cohan, whose old songs constituted the score.

Original Song: M. K. Jerome (lyrics: Jack Scholl).
Old Songs: George M. Cohan; Richard Rodgers (lyrics: Lorenz Hart).

YOU WERE NEVER LOVELIER; Fred Astaire, Rita Hayworth, Adolphe Menjou, Xavier Cugat's orchestra.

Original Songs: Jerome Kern (lyrics: Johnny Mercer).

Ethel Waters and Eddie Anderson were starred in
Cabin in the Sky *(1943)*

1943

CABIN IN THE SKY (based on the stage musical of the same name); Ethel Waters, Eddie "Rochester" Anderson, Rex Ingram, Duke Ellington's orchestra, Lena Horne.

Original Stage Score: Vernon Duke (lyrics: John Latouche, Ted Fetter).
Original Songs: Harold Arlen (lyrics: E. Y. Harburg).
Old Songs: Fred Dabney (lyrics: Lew Brown).

HIGHER AND HIGHER (based on the stage musical of the same name); Frank Sinatra, Michele Morgan, Jack Haley, Leon Errol, Paul and Grace Hartman, Mel Tormé, Marcy McGuire.

Original Stage Score: Richard Rodgers (lyrics: Lorenz Hart).
Original Songs: Jimmy McHugh (lyrics: Harold Adamson).

GIRL CRAZY (based on the stage musical of the same name); Judy Garland, Mickey Rooney, Nancy Walker, Tommy Dorsey's orchestra, June Allyson.

Original Stage Score: George Gershwin (lyrics: Ira Gershwin).
Old Song: George Gershwin (lyrics: Ira Gershwin).

THIS IS THE ARMY (based on the stage musical of the same name); Irving Berlin, George Murphy, Joan Leslie, Gertrude Niesen, Kate Smith, heading an all-star cast.

Original Stage Score: Irving Berlin.
Original Songs: Irving Berlin.
Old Song: Irving Berlin.

1944

CAN'T HELP SINGING; Deanna Durbin, Robert Paige, Akim Tamiroff, David Bruce.

Original Songs: Jerome Kern (lyrics: E. Y. Harburg).

COVER GIRL; Rita Hayworth, Gene Kelly, Phil Silvers.

Original Songs: Jerome Kern (lyrics: Ira Gershwin; Ira Gershwin and E. Y. Harburg).

GOING MY WAY; Bing Crosby (winner of the Academy Award for the best performance of 1944), Risë Stevens, Barry Fitzgerald. Winner of the Academy Award for the best film of 1944.

Original Songs: Jimmy Van Heusen (lyrics: Johnny Burke).
Old Song: J. R. Shannon.

MEET ME IN ST. LOUIS; Judy Garland, Margaret O'Brien, Tom Drake, Mary Astor.

Original Songs: Hugh Martin; Ralph Blane.
Old Song: Kerry Mills (lyrics: Andrew B. Sterling).

UP IN ARMS; Danny Kaye, Dinah Shore, Dana Andrews.

Original Songs: Harold Arlen (lyrics: Ted Koehler).

1945

ANCHORS AWEIGH; Frank Sinatra, Gene Kelly, Kathryn Grayson, José Iturbi.

Original Songs: Jule Styne (lyrics: Sammy Kahn); Sammy Fain (lyrics: Ralph Freed).

STATE FAIR; Jeanne Crain, Dick Haymes, Dana Andrews, Vivian Blaine, Charles Winninger, Fay Bainter. The only original film score by Rodgers and Hammerstein.
Original Songs: Richard Rodgers (lyrics: Oscar Hammerstein II).

WHERE DO WE GO FROM HERE? Fred MacMurray, June Haver, Joan Leslie.
Original Songs: Kurt Weill (lyrics: Ira Gershwin).

1946

THE JOLSON STORY; Larry Parks, the voice of Al Jolson, Evelyn Keyes, William Demarest, Bill Goodwin. The score comprised numerous songs introduced by Al Jolson and one original song:
By Saul Chaplin, Al Jolson, Jan Ivanovici.

CENTENNIAL SUMMER; Jeanne Crain, Linda Darnell, Cornel Wilde, William Eythe, Larry Stevens, Walter Brennan, Constance Bennett.
Original Songs: Jerome Kern (lyrics: Leo Robin, Oscar Hammerstein II).

THE HARVEY GIRLS; Judy Garland, John Hodiak, Angela Lansbury, Ray Bolger, Virginia O'Brien.
Original Songs: Harry Warren (lyrics: Johnny Mercer).

ZIEGFELD FOLLIES; William Powell, Fred Astaire, Lucille Bremer, Fanny Brice, Judy Garland, Kathryn Grayson, Lena Horne, Gene Kelly, Victor Moore, James Melton, Red Skelton, Esther Williams.
Original Songs: Roger Edens (lyrics: Ralph Freed, Earl Brent); Harry Warren (lyrics: Arthur Freed); Kay Thompson, Roger Edens; Hugh Martin, Ralph Blane.
Old Songs: George Gershwin (lyrics: Ira Gershwin); Philip Brahams (lyrics: Douglas Furber).

1947

GOOD NEWS (based on the stage musical of the same name); June Allyson, Peter Lawford, Joan McCracken, Mel Tormé, Patricia Marshall.
Original Stage Score: DeSylva, Brown, and Henderson.
Original Songs: Roger Edens (lyrics: Betty Comden, Adolph Green); Hugh Martin, Ralph Blane.

MOTHER WORE TIGHTS; Betty Grable, Dan Dailey.
Original Songs: Josef Myrow (lyrics: Mack Gordon).
Old Song: Harry Warren (lyrics: Mack Gordon).

THE PERILS OF PAULINE; Betty Hutton, John Lund, Constance Collier.
Original Songs: Frank Loesser; Raymond Walker (lyrics: Mack Gordon).

THE SHOCKING MISS PILGRIM; Betty Grable, Dick Haymes, Ann Revere, Gene Lockhart.
Original Songs: George Gershwin (lyrics: Ira Gershwin).

1948

THE PIRATE; Judy Garland, Gene Kelly.
Original Songs: Cole Porter.

EASTER PARADE; Judy Garland, Fred Astaire, Peter Lawford, Ann Miller.

Original Songs: Irving Berlin.
Old Songs: Irving Berlin.

1949

IN THE GOOD OLD SUMMERTIME; Judy Garland, Van Johnson, S. Z. Sakall.
Original Song: Fred Spielman (lyrics: Janice Torre).
Old Songs: Leo Friedman (lyrics: Beth Slater Whitson); Harry von Tilzer (lyrics: Junie McCree); Lewis Muir (lyrics: William Tracy, Ballard McDonald); Jean Lenox, Harry Sutton; Harold Arlen (lyrics: E. Y. Harburg).

ON THE TOWN (based on the stage musical of the same name); Gene Kelly, Frank Sinatra, Betty Garrett, Ann Miller, Jules Munshin, Vera-Ellen.
Original Stage Score: Leonard Bernstein (lyrics: Betty Comden, Adolph Green).
Original Songs: Leonard Bernstein (lyrics: Betty Comden, Adolph Green).

1950

ANNIE GET YOUR GUN (based on the stage musical of the same name); Betty Hutton, Howard Keel, Louis Calhern, Edward Arnold.
Original Stage Score: Irving Berlin.

THREE LITTLE WORDS; Fred Astaire, Red Skelton, Vera-Ellen, Arlene Dahl. Based on the lives of Kalmar and Ruby, whose old songs supplied the score.
Old Songs: Harry Ruby (lyrics: Bert Kalmar).

1951

AN AMERICAN IN PARIS; Gene Kelly, Leslie Caron, Oscar Levant, Georges Guetary, Nina Foch. Winner of the Academy Award for the best film of 1951.
Old Songs: George Gershwin (lyrics: Ira Gershwin; E. Ray Goetz, B. G. DeSylva).

THE GREAT CARUSO; Mario Lanza, Ann Blyth, Dorothy Kirsten, Jarmila Novotna, Blanche Thebom. The score contains operatic arias and one original song.
Original Song: Juveninto Rosas (lyrics: Paul Francis Webster).

ROYAL WEDDING; Fred Astaire, Jane Powell, Peter Lawford, Sarah Churchill.
Original Songs: Burton Lane (lyrics: Alan Jay Lerner).

1952

SINGIN' IN THE RAIN; Gene Kelly, Donald O'Connor, Debbie Reynolds, Jean Hagen.
Original Songs: Nacio Herb Brown (lyrics: Arthur Freed); Roger Edens (lyrics: Betty Comden, Adolph Green).
Old Songs: Nacio Herb Brown (lyrics: Arthur Freed); Al Goodhart (lyrics: Arthur Freed, Al Hoffman).

Supplementary Entry
1954

SEVEN BRIDES FOR SEVEN BROTHERS; Howard Keel, Jane Powell, Russ Tamblyn, Jeff Richards, Jacques D'Amboise, Marc Platt, Tommy Rall, Matt Mattox, Julie Newmar.
Original Songs: Gene de Paul (lyrics: Johnny Mercer).

FINCK, Henry T. American music critic (1854–1926). He was for 43 years the music critic of the New York *Evening Post* and wrote studies of Wagner, Strauss, Chopin, Grieg, Massenet, and Paderewski.

FINE. Italian, "end."

FINE, Irving G. American composer (1915–1962). A pupil of Walter Piston and Nadia Boulanger, Fine received his M.S. from Harvard University in 1938, and later studied in Europe. He was appointed assistant professor of music at Harvard University in 1947 and went to Brandeis University in 1950 as professor of music. He also taught at the Berkshire Music Center in Tanglewood. His compositions include works for orchestra, chorus, chamber ensembles, and piano. He also wrote some amusing *Children's Songs for Grownups.*

FINE, Vivian. American composer (1913–). Vivian Fine studied composition with Roger Sessions and composes in a modern style, revealing a preference for linear counterpoint. She has written works for piano and ballet, and was commissioned by the Rothschild Foundation to compose the ballets *The Life Expectancy of a Rose* and *Alcestis,* which were performed by Martha Graham.

FINE ARTS QUARTET, THE. Leonard Sorkin and Abram Loft, violinists; Irving Ilmer, violist; and George Sopkin, cellist. This string quartet came into being in 1946 as the featured attraction of a weekly radio program. The ensemble has made many concert tours of North America, and visited Europe twice, appeared in films and on television, and made a number of recordings. Since 1955 the Fine Arts Quartet has been in residence at the University of Wisconsin. Their repertory includes many contemporary as well as standard chamber works.

FINGAL'S CAVE (The Hebrides). Overture by Mendelssohn. The composer and his friend Klingermann visited Scotland and the Hebrides in 1829. Klingermann wrote of their visit to Fingal's Cave, a famous beauty spot in the island of Staffa: "We came there by boat and climbed over the mouth of the cave, with the tossing sea right below us. Never has greener water entered a more extraordinary cave. The stone pillars in the cave remind one of the pipes of a great organ—dark—and with a strange echo."

Mendelssohn wrote to his sister on August 7: "So that you may realize what an exceptional impression the Hebrides have made on me, I send you the enclosed, which came to me during my visit there."

The "enclosed" was what later became the first ten bars of the overture. When Mendelssohn came home and was asked about the Hebrides he is said to have replied: "That cannot be told in words, only played." In 1830 he wrote of the overture: "I do not regard it as complete in its present form. The middle passage is bad, it smells more of counterpoint than of waves, seagulls, and salt fish."

The overture received its final form in 1832, and was performed in London the following year. Wagner said that it "placed Mendelssohn among the foremost musical landscape painters."

FINGERING. The placing of the fingers on a fingerboard or keys. In scores, figures are written above the notes to indicate which finger is to be used, the numbers from one to five corresponding to the thumb and four fingers. Fingering is not only a technical but an artistic matter, as it is very important to the quality of the tone and the phrasing.

FINLANDIA. Symphonic poem, Op. 26, No. 7 (1899), by Sibelius. *Finlandia* was created at a time when Finland was suffering under Russian oppression. Several newspapers and maga-

Fingal's Cave, Staffa, the Inner Hebrides, Scotland

A scene from The Firebird *performed by The Royal Ballet*

zines had been banned, and in order to help the suffering journalists and their families, "Press Days" were organized in Helsinki in 1899, with elaborate entertainments in the form of theatrical performances, soirees, and concerts. These functions culminated in a gala performance at the Svenska Theater in Helsinki, November 4, 1899, at which the main items were six tableaux, depicting scenes from Finland's mythology and history. Sibelius had composed an overture for each tableau, accompaniments to the songs, and a tone poem to conclude the entertainment. This last work was given the name *Suomi* (the Finnish name for Finland).

Neither the critics nor the public realized at the time the full significance of the music, but a year later, when Sibelius had revised it and given it the title of *Finlandia,* it aroused tremendous enthusiasm. So great was the patriotic fervor displayed whenever it was played that the Russian authorities forbade all performances of the work in Finland.

Many years later Sibelius related: "It was a long time before *Finlandia* was performed under its present title. It was presented in Scandinavia as *Suomi;* in Germany it was called *Vaterland,* and in France *La Patrie.* In the Russian empire it could only be played under a title which would give no hint of its patriotic nature; when I was a guest conductor at Reval and Riga in 1904, I had to call it *Impromptu.*"

It was generally believed that *Finlandia* was based on Finnish folk tunes, but this Sibelius denied.

FINNEY, Ross Lee. American composer and educator (1906–). Finney has been composer-in-residence at the University of Michigan since 1948. He studied with Nadia Boulanger and Alban Berg, and has served on the faculties of Smith, Mt. Holyoke, and Darmouth colleges. He was a Guggenheim Fellow in 1939 and has composed many works for orchestra, piano, and string ensembles.

FINZI, Gerald. British composer (1901–56). Educated privately under Sir Edward Bairstow and R. O. Morris, Gerald Finzi was professor of composition at the Royal Academy of Music from 1930 to 1933. He composed a violin concerto, a piano concerto, the *Severn Rhapsody,* and a *Requiem da camera,* but was most noted for his songs and song cycles. He was particularly successful in setting poems by Thomas Hardy. His work is respected by musicians for its sincerity and musicianship, but gained little public recognition.

FIORAVANTI, Valentino. Italian composer (1764–1837). He composed more than seventy-five operas, many of them great successes in their time. The best known is *Le cantatrici villane* (1799), which has been rediscovered in modern times. He was essentially a composer of comic operas but in later life, when he was *maestro di cappella* at the Vatican, he composed a good deal of church music. His son, **Vincenzo** (1799–1877), also composed many operas with similar success.

FIREBIRD, THE (*L'Oiseau de Feu*). Ballet by Stravinsky. The idea of creating a ballet on the Russian fairy tale of the firebird came from Sergei Diaghilev, whose Ballets Russes charmed all Paris from 1906. Diaghilev originally intended Liadov to write the music, but he could never find the time, and the work was given to the young Stravinsky. It was completed in the spring of 1910, and the first performance at the Paris Opéra by Diaghilev's company was an overwhelming success.

The Firebird was Stravinsky's first big work and brought him immediate fame. Arranged as a suite, the music soon became one of the most popular concert numbers of our time, and to this day many consider this Stravinsky's most beautiful work. The reason is perhaps that at this date Stravinsky was still writing in the traditional manner, using methods of expression familiar to the public from the works of his Russian predecessors.

Alexander Golovine's décor used at the première of The Firebird *in 1910. Stravinsky has called it "a Persian carpet"*

The Firebird is completely of the school of Rimsky-Korsakov and presents the same magnificent and fascinating orchestral colors. The insinuating and intoxicating Oriental melodies and harmonies of Borodin and his refined chromaticism are echoed in the themes which describe Kastchei and his world. In the *Dance of the Firebird* there is the poetry of Scriabin, and in the finale the tonal clarity of Glinka and Mussorgsky.

But Stravinsky consciously and consistently used his masters' styles in his own way. The hero, the noble and upright Russian prince, is drawn in clear melodies and natural, uncomplicated rhythms, the more elaborate mode of expression being reserved for the supernatural elements.

In the garden of the castle of the wicked magician Kastchei, a tree full of golden apples shines in the moonlight. Suddenly innumerable flames shoot upward. This is the Firebird, which shows itself and then disappears. Young Prince Ivan pursues and catches it. The bird begs for its freedom, and pulls out a feather which it gives to the prince. He frees it, and it flies away rejoicing. Thirteen young princesses come running out of the castle, and one of them exchanges tender glances with Ivan. She signals to her friends to dance, and the dance ends with the prince embracing her. When day dawns the young princesses have reluctantly to return to the castle. In spite of their warning, Ivan decides to follow them.

The moment he opens the gate innumerable bells and gongs begin to sound. Crowds of demons, ghouls, witches, and monsters stream out of the dark castle in a burning red light. They whirl round at breakneck speed, and suddenly fall on their faces as Kastchei appears. The magician, catching sight of Ivan, advances on him to change him to a pillar of stone. Ivan is protected by the Firebird's feather and Kastchei is unable to cast his spell. Ivan calls on the Firebird for help. An irresistible magic streams from the bird's feathers, and Kastchei and his followers are forced to dance until they fall exhausted. Thereupon the bird lulls them to sleep with a cradle song.

Ivan enters the castle and returns with an egg containing the magician's soul. Hurling it to the ground, he destroys Kastchei's power forever.

The finale is the wedding procession of Ivan and his princess.

The Royal Fireworks, from a print

FIREWORKS MUSIC. Orchestral suite by Handel, composed for a fete held in April, 1749, at the command of George II, to celebrate the Peace of Aachen (October 7, 1748).

As a setting for the fete, the King had ordered the construction of an enormous "machine" in Green Park, in the form of a Doric temple one hundred feet high and four hundred feet wide, containing huge figures representing Peace accompanied by Neptune and Mars, with the King himself on the same scale, giving peace to Britannia. The whole was topped by a gigantic sun, beside which was built a gallery for one hundred musicians.

At a public dress rehearsal in Vauxhall Gardens, 12,000 people were present; traffic was held up for three hours by the crowds, and several people were injured. The fete itself was a fiasco: the temple caught fire during the fireworks display, and the crowd panicked.

Handel's *Music for the Royal Fireworks* was not published until 1786. It was scored for three trumpets, three kettledrums, three horns, three oboes, two bassoons, serpents, string instruments, and drums. (At the performance, each trumpet and horn part was played by three musicians, and in addition twenty-four oboists and twelve bassoonists took part.) One of the six movements is the melodious "largo alla Siciliana" entitled *La Paix* (Peace):

FIRKUSNY, Rudolf. Czech-American pianist (1912–). Firkusny, a student of Janáček, Suk, and Artur Schnabel, had to escape twice from his native country before settling in the United

The dance of Kastchei from The Firebird, *performed by The Royal Ballet*

States. His career had already received a promising start when he was forced to leave Czechoslovakia because of the Nazi occupation. He had visited the United States some years prior to this, and now he returned to America for a concert tour. He toured South America in 1943 and returned to Europe in 1946. During the Prague Festival of 1946 he emerged as a top-flight pianist. When the Communists took over Czechoslovakia, Firkusny decided to make his home permanently in the United States, and since 1949 he has successfully toured this country, giving concerts with most of the major orchestras. Firkusny has given much attention to contemporary music, being the first to perform concertos by Martinu, Hanson, and Menotti.

FISCHER, Annie. Hungarian pianist (1914–). She studied at the Franz Liszt Music Academy in Budapest with Arnold Szekely and Ernö Dohnányi. At the age of eight she made her concert debut there, and four years later she played Mozart and Schumann concertos in Zurich. In 1933 she won first prize in the first International Liszt Contest in Budapest. Thereafter she has concertized with numerous European orchestras under the most famous conductors of the present day.

FISCHER, Edwin. Swiss pianist (1886–1960). After beginning his studies at Basle, Fischer became a pupil (and, later, for nine years, a teacher) at Stern's Conservatory in Berlin. From 1914 he was a teacher of music for foreigners at the Potsdam Institute, where he exercised a decided influence over young concert pianists from all over the world.

Fischer became famous as a concert pianist

during the first World War. His interpretations of the great classical masters had a strong personal stamp, his style being admirably sure and grand. Fischer also conducted his own chamber music orchestra at Lübeck and Munich. He later returned to Switzerland to teach selected pupils.

Fischer has published a study on J. S. Bach, was the first pianist to record in its entirety *The Well-Tempered Clavier,* and he was chosen featured soloist at the great Bach festivals of Strasbourg and Vienna in 1950.

A critic wrote about Fischer: "Under the hands of an artist of such phenomenal gifts the most difficult works seem easy, and the longest program appears to be too short. The secret of Fischer's interpretations lies in their simplicity. It seems as if there is no interpreter at work: the music flows by itself, free of all technical obstacles. In Fischer lives a form of music-making which gives to every performance the atmosphere of spontaneous improvisation."

FISCHER, Emil. German baritone (1838–1914). A versatile singer, he was a star of the

DIETRICH FISCHER-DIESKAU

Dresden Opera and then of the Metropolitan Opera, where he was the greatly admired Hans Sachs in the American première of *Die Meistersinger* in 1886. Other roles that he was the first to sing in America are King Marke in *Tristan und Isolde* (1886); The Wanderer in *Siegfried* (1887); Hagen in *Die Götterdämmerung* (1888); and Wotan in *Das Rheingold* (1889).

FISCHER-DIESKAU, Dietrich. German baritone (1925–). His extraordinarily sensitive and mature interpretations of German lieder have made Fischer-Dieskau famous all over the world. Ever since his appearance on the international scene in 1950, he has been considered the top-ranking German recitalist. He has been equally successful on the opera stage and since 1958, Fischer-Dieskau has been on the roster of the Berlin State Opera, where he has been most successful in such operas as Verdi's *Falstaff* and Hindemith's *Mathis der Maler*. His unusual and versatile talent has also asserted itself in various roles in Mozart, Wagner, and Strauss operas. Fischer-Dieskau first appeared in the United States in 1955. He has given several American recital tours, appeared with major symphony orchestras, and through his many and amazingly varied recordings has gained an enormous following.

FISHER, Eddie. American popular singer and actor (1928–). Eddie Fisher became a television and film star after engagements in night clubs and resorts. His professional career began in Philadelphia in 1942 and, in 1949, he won national popularity touring with Eddie Cantor. Since then he has appeared frequently on television and in films.

FISTOULARI, Anatole. Russian-English conductor (1907–). A child prodigy, Fistoulari conducted Tchaikovsky's Sixth Symphony from memory at the Opera House, Kiev, when he was seven years old, and later toured Russia and Germany as a child conductor. After completing his musical education, he conducted for Chaliapin's season at the Théâtre Châtelet in Paris in 1933, remaining with the singer for three years. Some years later Massine engaged him as conductor for the Monte Carlo Ballet, with which he toured Europe and America.

Fistoulari then settled in London, conducting many well-known British orchestras, and in 1943–44 was principal conductor of the London Philharmonic Orchestra. In 1946 he founded the London International Orchestra. He became a British citizen in 1948.

FITELBERG, Jerzy. Polish-American composer (1903–1951). The son of Gregor Fitelberg, a well-known conductor and composer, he lived in Paris for seven years before coming to America. As a composer, he was strongly influenced by Stravinsky. His second and fourth string quartets won Elizabeth Sprague Coolidge prizes, and his other works include two piano and two violin concertos, a concerto for strings, two suites for orchestra, a cello concerto, a quintet for piano and woodwinds, a piano sonata, and other chamber pieces.

FITZGERALD, Ella. American jazz singer (1918–). Discovered at an amateur competition in Harlem in 1934, she later appeared as vocalist with Chick Webb's celebrated band. She at once gained great popularity, and after Webb's death took over the leadership of the band for a time. She has since continued to appear as a singer, touring America and Europe. She has fans all over the world who regard her as one of the greatest exponents of jazz singing and has made many recordings.

FIVE, The (*Les Cinq*). The name given to a group of nineteenth-century Russian composers who attempted to establish a genuinely national school of composition. The group comprised Balakirev, Borodin, Cui, Mussorgsky, and Rimsky-Korsakov. See individual entries under each of the composers mentioned.

FIZDALE, Robert. American pianist (1920–). Having studied at the Juilliard School of Music with Ernest Hutchinson, he formed a duo-piano team with Arthur Gold, and they made their debut at Town Hall in New York in 1946. They have played with the New York Philharmonic Orchestra under Mitropoulos and Bernstein, and have appeared with leading orchestras in the United States and abroad. In 1960, they received the Ingram-Merrill Foundation Award for study of Schubert four-hand literature. See *Gold, Arthur.*

FLAGELLO, Ezio. American bass (1931–). Flagello studied at the Manhattan School of

Kirsten Flagstad as Isolde

Music and, in Italy, at the University of Perugia. He was a Fulbright Scholar in 1955, and made his European debut in Rome in 1956, and his American debut with the Metropolitan Opera in 1957. Since then, he has established himself as an important *basso cantante.*

FLAGEOLET. A woodwind instrument similar to the recorder, with four finger holes in the front, and two thumb holes on the underside in the rear. See *Wind Instruments.*

FLAGSTAD, Kirsten. Norwegian dramatic soprano (1895–1962). She intended to be a pianist, but a friend of the family offered to train her voice, and at the age of eighteen she made her debut in opera as the little girl, Nuri, in d'Albert's *Tiefland.* She became famous throughout the Scandinavian countries, but it was twenty years before she was discovered by the rest of the world.

Then in the summer of 1933 at Bayreuth, where she was a soloist in Beethoven's Ninth Symphony, conducted by Richard Strauss, she was heard by a talent scout from the Metropolitan Opera, New York, who arranged for her to have an audition with its director, Gatti-

KIRSTEN FLAGSTAD

Casazza. The Metropolitan was seeking a replacement for Freda Leider, who had resigned, and Flagstad was engaged for one season.

No one fully realized the quality of her voice until the first rehearsal, when she astonished everyone in the theater; the conductor, Artur Bodansky, dropped his baton in stupefaction, and an aide was sent rushing to Gatti's office to bring him in to hear his "discovery."

The day after her debut, the well-known New York critic Lawrence Gilman wrote: "Mme. Flagstad is that rara avis in the Wagnerian woods—a singer with voice, with looks, with youth. The voice itself is both lovely and puissant. In its deep register it is movingly warm and rich and expressive. . . . The upper voice is powerful and true and does not harden under stress. The singing that we heard yesterday is that of a musician with taste and brains and sensibility, with poetic and dramatic insight."

Three days later Kirsten Flagstad appeared in *Tristan und Isolde* and received an even greater ovation. She became at one bound one of the greatest attractions in the history of the Metropolitan: nine performances of *Tristan und Isolde* brought the theater an income of $150,000. Without showing the least sign of fatigue she sang one great Wagner role after another, many without rehearsal. She became its cornerstone for the next few years. As a mark

of honor to its great new Wagnerian star, it opened its next season with *Die Walküre*—the first time in thirty-five years that the season had opened with a German opera. The next Metropolitan season opened with *Tristan und Isolde*.

In 1935, when Gatti-Casazza left the Metropolitan after being its principal director for twenty-seven years, he said: "My first gift to the Metropolitan was Caruso. My last is Kirsten Flagstad."

In 1936 Kirsten Flagstad sang at Covent Garden, London, and her Isolde was received with tremendous enthusiasm. In September of the same year, she had Vienna at her feet; her conductor, Weingartner, said afterward: "Kirsten Flagstad is the only Wagnerian singer I have conducted who sings absolutely flawlessly. She never holds a note longer than the composer intended, but respects measures and rests."

After touring the United States and Canada, she made a concert tour of Australia in 1936. She appeared at the extra World's Fair season at the Metropolitan. In 1941 she went home to German-occupied Norway to be with her sick husband. She remained in virtual retirement during the war, but from 1947 appeared again on the concert platform and opera stage in London, Amsterdam, Brussels, Paris, Milan, Barcelona, Buenos Aires, the United States, South America, and Havana. In 1949 and 1950, she took part in the Salzburg Festival, and in 1952 and 1953 she sang Dido at the Mermaid Theatre, London.

Kirsten Flagstad was able to learn a part very quickly; she learned Eurydice in Offenbach's *Orpheus in the Underworld* in one night, Desdemona in *Otello* in a week, Kundry in *Parsifal* in less than a week, and the First Lady in *The Magic Flute* in twenty-four hours. On the stage, she was always completely at her ease, and her absolutely flawless musical ear and exceptional sense of rhythm made it unnecessary for her to watch the conductor continuously. Of her magnificent voice she once said, "I never coddled it. I was never careful about the weather, and I almost never worried about colds." She retired after a series of farewell performances in 1953, but continued to make recordings until three years before her death. These final discs demonstrate that her voice had lost none of its former luster; if anything, it seemed to have gained in warmth and timbre.

Flagstad was probably the greatest Wagnerian singer, and perhaps the greatest dramatic soprano, of our generation. No other singer of her day, or of the present, can match the firm, glowing tones which Flagstad sang so effortlessly and so thrillingly.

FLANAGAN, William. American composer and critic (1926–). Flanagan studied with Burrill Phillips and Bernard Rogers at the Eastman School of Music, at the Berkshire Music Center with Arthur Honegger, Samuel Barber, and Aaron Copland, and in New York City with David Diamond. He has composed an opera, and orchestral, chamber, piano, choral, and film music, but is best known for his lyrical songs.

FLAT. The sign ♭, which is placed before a note to indicate that it is to be lowered by a half tone. See *Music, Elements of*.

FLEDERMAUS, DIE (*The Bat*). Operetta in three acts by Johann Strauss the Younger. The composer's third stage work, it is often called "the queen of operettas." The plot was drawn from a German comedy which had been rewritten by Offenbach's librettists Meilhac and Halévy for the vaudeville *Reveillon*. Steiner, the director of the Theater an der Wien, bought the vaudeville, but hesitated for some time to present it, since it was so specifically Parisian. It was then suggested that the work should be rearranged as an operetta with music by Strauss, and lyric writers Karl Haffner and Richard Genée worked on the adaptation.

The music was composed at the turn of the year 1873. Ernst Decsey wrote: "Strauss threw himself into the work with all the enthusiasm of a man in love. He did not leave his villa in Hetzendorfer Strasse, and in the course of six weeks, or to be precise forty-two nights, he composed the whole score. They were veritably nights of rapture."

The operetta had a cold reception at its première at the Theater an der Wien on April 5, 1874, and was withdrawn after only sixteen performances. But shortly afterward it had a

The second act of Die Fledermaus *in the Metropolitan Opera production*

tremendous success in Berlin, where it was performed over one hundred times, and on its next production in Vienna the previous verdict was reversed. During the next twenty years it was performed all over the world, from Bombay to Chicago, from Odessa to Melbourne. In 1894 it was included in the repertoires of serious opera houses. By 1940 it had had approximately twenty thousand performances throughout the world.

The action takes place at a spa; the time is the end of the nineteenth century.

The wealthy Gabriel von Eisenstein (tenor), having become involved in a libel action, has been given a short prison sentence. Before reporting at the prison, Eisenstein goes to a ball given by Prince Orlofsky (contralto), who has sent him an invitation through a mutual friend, Dr. Falke (baritone). Falke has a bone to pick with Eisenstein. During the previous carnival season the two had gone to a ball, Falke wearing the costume of a bat. They had got drunk, and Eisenstein had made Falke ridiculous by forcing him to appear in public in broad daylight not only considerably "under the influence" but clad in his ludicrous "bat" outfit.

Eisenstein has no idea that Falke is now contemplating revenge. He takes leave of his wife, Rosalinde (soprano), telling her that he is to begin his prison sentence that evening. As the parlormaid, Adele (soprano), has asked for the evening off (her sister Ida, a dancer, is going to smuggle her into Orlofsky's ball), the farewell takes the form of a trio, a witty operatic parody, in which they express hypocritical sorrow at their parting.

When Rosalinde is alone, one of her former admirers, the singing teacher Alfred (tenor), comes to visit her. To Rosalinde's amazement, he makes himself completely at home, even donning Eisenstein's dressing gown. Thus the complications begin. The prison gover-

Eisenstein leaves for jail: Left to right; *Roberta Peters as Adele, Theodor Uppman as Eisenstein, and Hilde Gueden as Rosalinde*

nor, Frank (baritone), arrives to collect his distinguished prisoner, and Alfred, afraid of compromising Rosalinde, has to submit to being mistaken for Eisenstein and accompany the governor.

Except Alfred, now languishing in prison, they all meet at Prince Orlofsky's ball. Eisenstein, introduced as the "Marquis of Renard," recognizes the parlormaid Adele by the dress of his wife's that she is wearing, but dares not reveal his true identity.

Meanwhile, Dr. Falke has told Rosalinde that her husband has gone to the ball and not to prison, and she decides to go to the ball also. Masked, she is presented as "a Hungarian Countess." Eisenstein immediately begins to flirt with her, and she succeeds in persuading him to give her his valuable watch, which she intends to produce later as proof of his infidelity. The whole gay party joins in a song of praise for champagne.

The prison governor Frank is also present at the ball, under the false name of the Chevalier Chagrin, and the "Marquis of Renard" strikes up a friendship with his "compatriot."

Orlofsky invites the guests to dance, and the waltz strikes up:

Frank makes a move to leave the party. Eisenstein realizes that he must hasten to report at the prison. So the new-found friends stagger off together.

At the prison the drunken jailer Frosch (speaking part) knows that his chief will most probably arrive with a hangover.

"But why should I worry?" Frosch asks himself, gazing deep into his glass. Frank and Eisenstein come reeling in. After much drunken confusion the situation is cleared, and Eisenstein and Frank tell each other their real names. But Frank has become sober enough to remember that he personally conducted Eisenstein to the prison the previous evening. Frosch also confirms that Eisenstein is properly ensconced in his cell.

Dr. Falke now puts his plan of revenge into operation, and brings Rosalinde with him to the prison office, where the whole matter is cleared up.

When Eisenstein learns that Alfred was arrested in his home and in his wife's company late in the evening, he demands an explanation. But when Rosalinde holds up his own watch and waves it before his nose, he can only laugh and admit that he flirted with his own wife for a whole night in the belief that she was somebody else. But the law must take its course, and he has to change places with Alfred and serve his sentence.

FLEISCHER, Editha. German soprano (1898–). From 1926 to 1936 she was one of the most valuable singers at the Metropolitan Opera, where she sang in the German, French, and Italian repertories. In 1931, she sang Hänsel in Humperdinck's *Hänsel und Gretel* in the first complete radio broadcast from the Metropolitan. Though she often sang dramatic roles, her real fame was as a soubrette, and she was un-rivaled in her time as Zerlina in *Don Giovanni,* Sophie in *Der Rosenkavalier,* Marcellina in *Fidelio,* and similar roles.

FLEISHER, Edwin A. American music patron (1877–1959). In 1909, he founded the Symphony Club in Philadelphia, an organization for training orchestral musicians. He began to collect scores for the club and eventually formed one of the most important music libraries in the world, which he presented to the Philadelphia Free Library in 1929.

FLEISHER, Leon. American pianist (1923–). Leon Fleisher gave his first recital at seven and a few years later became a pupil of Artur Schnabel. In 1943 he made his official debut with the San Francisco Symphony Orchestra and was immediately recognized as an outstanding talent.

Appearances followed throughout the United States. In 1952 Fleisher won the Belgian International Music Competition after competing with seventy young pianists from all over the world. Fleisher remained in Europe until 1954 for a triumphal tour. He is considered one of the outstanding American pianists of the younger generation.

FLESCH, Carl. Hungarian violinist and teacher (1873–1944). One of the celebrated musicians of his time, he performed throughout Europe and America, edited definitive versions of many classics, wrote a treatise on violin-playing that has become a standard work on the subject, and was the teacher of many famous violinists.

FLISSLER, Eileen. American pianist (1929–). A graduate of the Curtis Institute of Music, she has twice toured around the world, performing in numerous capital cities. Her second world-wide tour was as soloist with the Little Orchestra. More than a million copies of her music-appreciation recordings have been sold.

FLISSLER, Joyce. American violinist (1931–). Her concert and recital career burst into prominence on the occasion of an exceptionally successful Moscow recital debut in November, 1960.

FLOTHUIS, Marius. Dutch composer (1914–).

FRIEDRICH VON FLOTOW

One of the foremost musicians of his country, he also is a leading critic and writer on musical subjects. His best-known composition outside Holland is a flute concerto. His other works include symphonic and chamber music, a cantata for chorus and orchestra, piano pieces, and songs.

FLOTOW, Friedrich von. German composer (1812–83). The son of a nobleman, he was intended for a diplomatic career, but at sixteen started to study music while staying in Paris. He wrote several ballets and some twenty operas, of which the only one played today is *Martha.* This work is in the French *opéra-comique* style of the time, with simple and tuneful arias—which, however, often border on the sentimental. See *Martha.*

FLOWER, Sir Newman. English author and publisher (1879–). The owner of a leading English publishing firm, he formed a significant collection of music portraits and manuscripts and became an authority on Handel, as well as the author of books on Handel, Schubert, and Sir Arthur Sullivan.

CARLISLE FLOYD

FLOYD, Carlisle. American composer (1926–). Floyd took his earliest piano instruction from his mother. He was a scholarship student at Converse College, where he studied with Ernst Bacon, and received his degree in piano from Syracuse University in 1946. He joined the faculty of Florida State University where he still teaches. Floyd has written the operas, *Slow Dusk, Susannah* (1946), *Wuthering Heights* (1958), and *The Passion of Jonathan Wade* (1962). He was a Guggenheim Fellow in 1956.

Susannah and *Wuthering Heights,* performed by the New York City Opera, have added stature to American serious opera. *Susannah* won the New York Music Critics' Circle award in 1956, and was chosen to travel to the 1958 Brussels World Fair to represent American musical theater. It had its first performance at Florida State University in 1955, and its New York première the following year at the City Center under the baton of Erich Leinsdorf. Based on the Biblical story of Susanna and the Elders, the opera has a modern setting in the Tennessee mountain country. It is the tale of a beautiful girl wrongly suspected, then condemned by her neighbors, who finally is seduced by an evangelist. Susannah's lovely lyric aria *Ain't It a Pretty Night?* and the revival scene, in which the preacher's exhortations are heard against the background of the hymn-singing of the congregation, are the high spots of the two-act, ten-scene opera.

Floyd's unusual dramatic and melodic gifts were further developed and consolidated in *Wuthering Heights,* for which he wrote his own libretto based on the Emily Brontë classic. It received its première at the Santa Fe Opera in 1958, and its New York première by the New York City Opera the following year. It is one of the most powerful American operas. His most recent opera, for which, again, he wrote his own story and libretto, is *The Passion of Jonathan Wade,* produced by the New York City Opera at the City Center in 1962. An ambitious work with a Civil War setting, it was well received but has not yet duplicated the success of his earlier operas.

Other works by Floyd are *Lost Eden* (a suite for two pianos); a piano sonata; *Pilgrimage* (1955) for low voice and piano (or orchestra); and *The Mystery,* for voice and orchestra (1961).

FLUTE. See *Wind Instruments*.

FLYING DUTCHMAN, THE (*Der Fliegende Holländer*). Opera in three acts by Richard Wagner. This is one of Wagner's earlier works; he conceived the idea for it in 1839, while on a voyage from Pillau, East Prussia, to London, in flight from his creditors in Riga. Wagner described the voyage thus: "It lasted three and a half weeks and was full of excitement. Three times we were overtaken by violent storms, and on one occasion the captain had to seek refuge in a Norwegian bay. . . .

"The legend of the 'Flying Dutchman,' as I heard it told by the sailors, formed a vivid picture in my imagination. I felt as if I had myself experienced life among pirates."

In seamen's legend the Flying Dutchman was an impious Dutch skipper who set sail on a Good Friday to show his contempt for the Christian belief in God. As punishment he was condemned to roam the seas without rest until the Day of Judgment. To meet him on the seas meant misfortune. Heine made use of the legend, and Wagner borrowed the material for his opera from him.

In Wagner's opera the Dutchman has one chance of receiving God's forgiveness. This is the first time we meet the idea of "redemption" which played such an important part in Wagner's later works. The Dutchman is allowed to land every seventh year; if he meets a woman who promises fidelity to him and keeps her vow, he will be redeemed.

Because of financial difficulties, Wagner was forced to sell his libretto to the Paris Opéra, which commissioned a French composer, Pierre Dietsch, to write the music. This version was performed, unsuccessfully, in 1842 as *Le Vaisseau fantôme*. This did not prevent Wagner from composing his own opera, which had its première under his direction at the Dresden Court Opera on January 2, 1843. The role of Senta was sung by the great actress-singer Wilhelmine Schröder-Devrient. However, the real success of the opera began with its revival at Dresden in 1865.

The Flying Dutchman was Wagner's first step away from the normal opera form toward music drama. He wrote, thirty years later: "To the best of my knowledge there is no such striking transformation in such a short time in any other artist's life as that between *Rienzi* and the *Dutchman*."

George London as the Dutchman, Bayreuth, 1961

Act I of The Flying Dutchman *in Wieland Wagner's Bayreuth production of 1961*

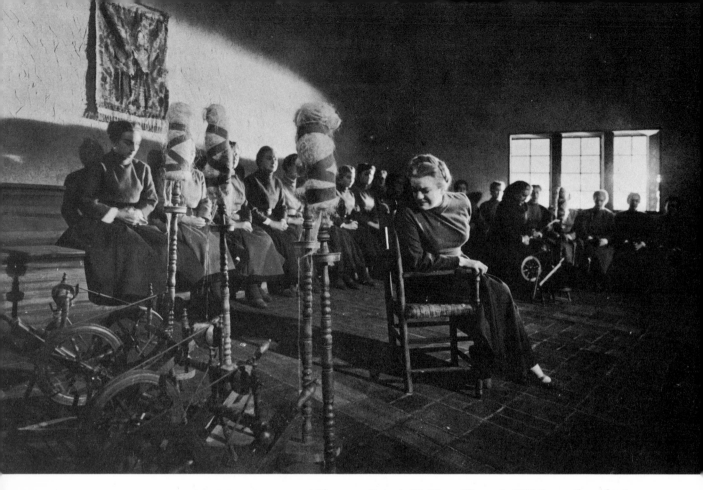

Senta's Ballad in Act II. Astrid Varnay as Senta in Wolfgang Wagner's 1955 Bayreuth production

Rienzi was only just ready when the *The Flying Dutchman* was nearing its completion.

The overture, which was written last, contains some of the motifs of the opera: first, the Dutchman's leitmotiv, which was supposed to be identical with a Hebridean folk tune and gives a realistic picture of the Captain's ceaseless wandering at sea; and secondly, the "redemption" motif.

Time: *18th century*

Place: *The coast of Norway*

ACT I

Scene: *An outer harbor*

The Norwegian skipper Daland (bass) has sought shelter in the harbor from a storm which has driven him fifty miles away from home. He hands over the watch to the Mate (tenor), who whiles away the time with a song. He has fallen asleep when a strange dark vessel glides into the harbor. A man, muffled in a black cloak, his face as pale as death, comes ashore. It is the Flying Dutchman.

After the recitative *Die Frist ist um (The term is o'er)* he sings the well-known aria lamenting his hard fate:

Oft into ocean's gaping maw,
Headlong I cast me in despair;
Alas! my death, I found it not!

Daland comes up from his cabin and sees the strange ship and its captain. He learns that the stranger is Dutch and has voyaged far afield. Daland invites him to come to his home, and in return the stranger gives him a chest full of gold and diamonds. Daland relates that he has a daughter, and the stranger asks to marry her. Delighted at getting such a rich son-in-law, Daland accepts the offer. The two captains weigh anchor and set sail for Daland's home.

ACT II

Scene: *A room in Daland's house*

A group of women are spinning, supervised by Mary (contralto), who has been the nurse of Daland's daughter Senta (soprano). Senta's thoughts are occupied by the legend of the unfortunate Flying Dutchman, who is shown in an old picture hanging on the wall. When Mary refuses to sing the song about the Dutchman, Senta sings the ballad about the unfortunate mariner who can only be saved from eternal damnation if he finds a faithful woman.

Jo-ho,   oo-ho-o-ho, jo-o-hoe,

Jo-ho-hoe! Jo-ho-hoe! Jo-ho-hoe! Jo-hoe!
Saw ye the ship on ocean main,
Blood-red her sails and black her mast,
On highest board with features pale,
Her captain stands in storm and blast!
Hwee! The tempest howls! Jo-ho-hey! Jo-ho-hey!
Hwee! The billows foam! Jo-ho-hey! Jo-ho-hey!
Hwee! Like a bird on the wing,
O'er the seas without rest he must roam!

As Senta reveals her inmost desire, to be the woman who will save the Flying Dutchman, her lover, the hunter Erik (tenor), arrives and is dismayed to hear her wish. When he says that Daland's ship is in sight, the women rush out to welcome it.

Erik tells Senta of a dream he has had; he saw Daland coming home with a stranger who is to marry Senta—it was the man whose picture hangs above the doorway. Senta is exultant; she is willing to sacrifice herself for him. Erik is appalled and leaves her. The door opens and a pale figure stands before her.

Daland appears behind him. He relates his meeting with the stranger, saying that he is rich and wishes to marry Senta. At first the stranger does not dare to believe that Senta will be his and will be faithful to him. Daland is very happy over the outcome and plans to celebrate the engagement.

ACT III

Scene: *The harbor*

The ships of Daland and the Dutchman lie moored to the quay. The women bring food and drink to Daland's sailors, who welcome them with joy. They sing and dance. The stranger's ship lies dark and silent. When the Norwegians try to persuade the Dutchmen to join in the feast, the gloomy crew sing a sinister song.

Erik reproaches Senta with having deceived him. Senta replies that she never seriously promised herself to Erik, and adds that his pain is as nothing compared with the sufferings of the stranger.

The stranger, seeing Senta with Erik, thinks that she has broken her vow. But as she has not yet made her vow before God, she will be spared the damnation that strikes those who have been unfaithful to him. With that he reveals who he really is, orders his men to make the vessel ready to sail, and goes aboard.

Senta, crying that she has always known who he is and that she will not fail him, throws herself into the sea. The Dutchman's ship strikes a rock and sinks. The figures of the Dutchman and Senta rise up from the sea to Heaven.

FOLDES, Andor. Hungarian-American pianist (1913–). Foldes began taking piano lessons at the age of five with his mother, and later studied with Ernö Dohnányi at the Franz Liszt Music Academy in Budapest. At nineteen he won first prize at the International Liszt Competition, and subsequently embarked on his first extensive concert tour of the Continent. He traveled extensively all over Europe until 1939, when he came to the United States. His American debut took place over the NBC radio network, and since then, Foldes has appeared as soloist with many American orchestras, including the New York Philharmonic, the Los Angeles Symphony, and the National Symphony orchestras.

Foldes has gained a reputation above all as a player of Beethoven, as well as an interpreter of the music of Bartók. His book *Keys to the Keyboard* has been published in nine languages.

FOLÍA. Portuguese, "folly." This was originally the name of a Portuguese carnival dance, performed at prodigious speed, with castanets, to animated music. The dance was performed by men only, but some of them were dressed in women's clothes. The name is now applied to one particular melody to which the Folía was danced and which has been popular for over 450 years.

The first occurrence of the Folía tune is in a guitar arrangement by Juan Ponce, about the year 1500. The tune had achieved such popularity in Spain by the seventeenth century that it was introduced as a social dance, in 3/4 time, something like a sarabande. Later it spread northward, appearing as a theme with variations of the nature of a chaconne or passacaglia, and became, without doubt, one of the most widely used melodies in Europe.

The entire Folía air consists of one tiny motif, which is repeated nine times in varying degrees within a fifth. Many composers have used the air as a basis for works, most of which have taken the form of an air with variations. The best-known Folías are: Farinelli, Folía for violin (1649); Corelli, Folía for violin, Op. 5, No. 12 (1700); R. Keiser, *Der Lächerliche Prinz Jodelet* (1726); *Vivaldi,* Sonata for two violins and cello (1737); J. S. Bach, *Peasant Cantata* (1742); Scarlatti, *Variazioni sulla Follia di Spagna;* Gretry, *L'Amant Jaloux* (opera, 1778); Cherubini, *L'Hôtellerie Portugaise* (opera, 1798); Liszt, Spanish Rhapsody for piano (1873); and Rachmaninoff, Variations on a Theme by Corelli, Op. 42 (1932).

FOLK MUSIC

TRADITIONAL GROUP EXPRESSION

FOLK MUSIC is an oral expression by a group of people of their time and place; it mirrors their culture. It differs from art music in that art music is composed and written down by an individual according to accepted rules of notation, while folk music is an oral tradition, usually the contribution of untaught persons. Many folk songs were, however, written originally. Folk songs in America were spread to a great extent by the early shape-note song books, such as *Christian Harmony, The Sacred Harp,* and others. Songs once communicated by and learned from books usually followed an oral tradition from that point.

Other early printed songs were the broadsides, originally British. They were songs about current events, especially hangings. They were written before the criminal was to be hanged, printed on one side of a big sheet of paper (hence "broadside"), and hawked at the execution. One of the most famous of these is a song now known as *Sam Hall*. It was originally written on the occasion of the hanging of one Jack Hall, a chimney-sweep, and told of his defiance of decency and morality. It was then taken up by the current defiers of various times and adapted to their purposes, and thus became the song we know today:

> Oh my name it is Sam Hall, it is Sam Hall.
> Oh my name it is Sam Hall, it is Sam Hall.
> Oh my name it is Sam Hall,
> And I hate you one and all,
> You're a bunch of ——— all,
> Damn your eyes.

> Oh I killed a man 'tis said, so 'tis said.
> Oh I killed a man 'tis said, so 'tis said.
> Oh I killed a man 'tis said,
> And I left him there for dead,
> With a bullet through his head,
> Damn his eyes.

This one is a little different from most broadsides, in that they usually pointed a moral. *Captain Kidd,* a close relative of *Sam Hall* in tune and stanza form, illustrates this. A song written for William Kidd's execution on May 9, 1701, it pictures him as a repentant sinner.

> Oh my name is Robert Kidd, as I sailed
> Oh my name is Robert Kidd, as I sailed
> Oh my name is Robert Kidd,
> God's laws I did forbid,
> And so wickedly I did,
> As I sailed.

Broadside ballads did not really become what we would call folk songs until they had had time to settle and be changed as people sang them.

Change is an integral part of the oral tradition. As can be seen in the ballads mentioned, even the names of the persons who served as the subjects for the songs were changed. Folk songs evolve out of a common store of melodies and stories. Alan Lomax says, "A folk song is actually a continuum of performances, each one varying in great or slight degree, and thus it grows as it lives, acquiring fresh material or losing bits of the old, and spawning variant forms, which continue to evolve. Every conceivable cultural, social, and psychological factor can come to bear upon this process. In the folk songs of the West, for instance, there has been a continual interplay between the written and the oral streams of culture—the former fixed eternally in print, the latter living mainly in the bodies of a community of carriers and subject to slips of memory and to group emotion" (*The Folk Songs of North America,* p. 28).

This process of evolution is an important characteristic of folk music. A particular song may be discarded for others, but it will be found *in* others in many ways. For example, the Negro style of singing is largely one of improvisation. In this style, a line or chant or moan may give way to another within the same song. This change may have such an effect as to change completely the mood or even the content of the song. Nevertheless, the original subject matter is still there to work with, and the singing of one song provides the impetus to make up another. Most folk songs retain their wholeness for a long, long time, with change coming more gradually and in smaller ways than is the case with the Negro habit of improvisation.

Another thing that sets folk music aside from art music is that it is not designed to impress the ear of the listener. Folk songs attain polish and are given ornamentation when they are sung, not for an audience, but for the singer himself. Personal ornamentation consists of a singer's own warbles, slides, grunts, yodels, or whatever goes into his style of singing, and he considers these his signature. Usually personal ornamentation is limited somewhat by local style.

GROUPS OF FOLK-MUSIC STYLES

Alan Lomax, in an article on "Folk Song Style" in *American Anthropologist,* divides all folk music (except most music of the Soviet Union, eastern Asia, and the Pacific) into ten groups. These are: the American Indian, Pygmoid, African, Australian, Melanesian, Polynesian, Malayan, Eurasian, Old European, and Modern European. The African, Eurasian, Old European, and Modern European groups are the most important in American folk music, most of which can be related to one or more of these four groups. Distinctive idioms and patterns of rhythm and melody, as well as specific tunes, have been found to be shared by widely separated peoples.

African folk music is identified by extreme reliance on the group for song and by a preponderance of complicated harmonic and rhythmic structure. "Singers leap into falsetto, insert bass part, grunt, shout, yell. Voices blend easily.

Ben Shahn's painting, Pretty Girl Milking a Cow, *takes its title from the well-known folk song of the same name. Collection Edgar Kaufmann, Jr., New York*

African tribal drummers with their instruments

The body is always in motion; the music is danced. Facial expression is lively and animated."

The Eurasian group includes Ireland, parts of the British Isles and France, Spain south of the Pyrenees, parts of Italy, the Moslem areas of Yugoslavia and Albania, southern Greece, Turkey, Arab Africa, the Near and Middle East, Pakistan, parts of India, Indonesia, China, Korea, and most of Japan. The singing in this group is solo, or poor unison, with songs accompanied for the most part. "Control and individualism are the key descriptive terms here. Co-operative music-making is achieved only by groups of adepts, and in some areas, such as China, was virtually nonexistent until recently." A falsetto voice is common, even among male singers, and suits long and complicated melodic lines. The tone of the accompanying instruments usually matches that of the singer.

The group classified as Old European includes the Hebrides, Wales, the west and north of England, Scandinavia, Brittany, Pyrenean France, Spain north of the Pyrenees, northeastern Portugal, Switzerland, most of Austria, Germany, Italy north of the Appenines, Czechoslovakia, western Yugoslavia, northern Greece, parts of Bulgaria and Romania, Lithuania,

White Russia, the Ukraine, and the Caucasus. The music is choral, with the style freer and more relaxed than the Eurasian. Singers use a deeper pitch than the falsetto tones used in Eurasia. While the Eurasian group expresses frustration in its singing, the Old European singers are relaxed: they sing with a rounded tone, sometimes with a liquid yodeling effect. "Old European tunes tend to be comparatively simple and unornamented. Blended unison is normal and many forms of polyphony exist."

Modern European includes the folk music of lowland Scotland, eastern and southern England, western and central France, central Spain, central Italy, Hungary, central Bulgaria, Romania, and colonial America. This group represents a combination of Old European and Eurasian. Almost all American folk songs, except those of the Negroes, belong in this group. It is characterized by solo songs and harsh unison on the refrains and choruses. "The whole area has a stronger interest in text than in tune, in sense than in emotional content. This is the land of the narrative ballad, the quatrain, the lightly ironic lyrical love songs, which have come to characterize the folk songs of Europe. It is also the area which most strongly influenced the development of folk songs in the colonies of North and South America, perhaps because the witty, intellectualized Modern European ballads and songs could move into new cultures more readily than the vague and dreamy choral songs of Old Europe, or the highly charged, highly elaborate and melancholy music of the south."

AMERICAN FOLK MUSIC

Lomax says in his book *The Folk Songs of North America* that "the first function of music, especially of folk music, is to produce a feeling of security for the listener. . . . To the traveler, a line from a familiar song may bring back all the familiar emotions of home, for music is a magical summing up of the patterns of family, of love, of conflict, and of work, which give a community its special feel and which shape the personalities of its members." This is why the early settlers brought their old songs with them to the new land. Some songs (mostly those that had a place in the village ceremonies of the Old World) did not last, and some did, undergoing changes in the process of becoming a part of the new land, changing their form and content.

Many songs were changed for religious reasons. The new colonies were Calvinist and very strict concerning pleasures of the flesh. An example of censorship of an Old World ballad when it was sung in America is *Foggy, Foggy Dew.* The American version has the tone of a repentant sinner, and the last verse leaves the bachelor still a bachelor, forever reminded of his wrong.

It must be understood that in the days when there was no television, no radio or movies, almost no books except the Bible, the only entertainment was music; dancing, at least in the early colonies, was forbidden. That left singing. And sing they did. They sang mostly religious songs, since most secular songs were not considered respectable. Nevertheless, they had fun, because in those days religious songs were sung in a fast and lively style. Secular songs, called "devil's ditties," were adapted to their own religious purposes.

In spite of the lively musical tradition, these people led narrow lives, and they required whoever lived with them to live the same. Those who wanted to live differently moved away from the first colonies, now settled and staid, to the frontier. The religious songs of these people underwent a striking change. Instead of singing them as dance tunes, they began to sing them like dirges. "Surge singing" became common. This form of singing arose from the pioneers' lack of psalters and hymnals. The leader of the congregation would call out in an abbreviated fashion the words and the melody for a couple of lines.

Then the congregation would sing it after him. Later, with the advent of shape-note singing and the glut of courses in this form of polyphonic singing, surge-singing disappeared in all but a few communities in Kentucky.

Shape-note, or sol-fa, singing is described in an *Easy Instructor,* published in 1798 in Philadelphia, as "a New Method of Teaching Sacred Harmony, containing the rudiments of music on an improved plan, wherein the naming and timing of the notes are familiarized to the weakest capacity." The notes were written on the staff as usual in four-part harmony, but instead of relying on the position of the note, the singer could tell from its shape what to sing. There were four shapes: triangle, circle, square, and diamond.

Up to this time all group singing on the frontier had been done in harsh unison, with everyone following the single melodic line. Shape-note singing revolutionized religious music by introducing harmony, or polyphony. Going to singing school became one of the most popular pastimes among frontier folk. Many books of shape-note harmony were sold and went a long way toward spreading different songs to different people, to contribute to the melting pot of American folk music.

Secular Songs

Life on the frontier was mostly hard work, with little time for fun. But every so often young people would gather, usually after some group project such as a molasses stir or a barn-raising,

LEADBELLY

La Llara, a classical Venezuelan folk dance

CAT IRON

PETE SEEGER

for relaxation. Since dancing was forbidden by their strict religion, the "play-party" game developed. (Later, these too were outlawed by the elders, but they were good for a time.) Usually, the words of the song described the action of the game. No instruments were played, as they also were forbidden, and all the accompaniment to the game was voice. One that has lasted is *Skip to My Lou*. It was a circle dance, with one of the dancers in the center. Usually the verses describe either the one in the center, or his or her thoughts. ("Fly in the buttermilk, shoo fly, shoo," or "Lost my partner, what'll I do?")

Other young people's songs were courting songs. Usually if a group were together at a corn-shucking bee or a church social, they would sing little songs, first the boys and then the girls, to test the mettle, so to speak, of the group opposite. *Paper of Pins* fits into this category, as does *Lolly Toodum,* the story of a girl who wanted to get married.

There were serious songs about love too. As a matter of fact, some communities referred to all secular songs as love songs. The love song in America usually follows the English tradition, which told about such people as Lord Lovel, little Musgrave (changed to Matty Graves or Magrave or other similar names), Lady Margaret and Sweet William, or Barbara Allen:

In Scarlet Town, where I was born
There was a fair maid dwellin'.
She made the boys cry well-a-day
Her name was Barb'ry Allen.

'Twas in the merry month of May
When roses they were swellin',
Sweet William on his death bed lay,
'Twas for love of Bar'bry Allen.

He sends for her; she comes to tell him that she still smarts at the memory of him toasting all the girls in town but her. He answers:

Oh yes I ken, I ken it well,
In the place where I was dwellin'
I gave a toast to the ladies all;
I gave my love to Barb'ry Allen.

She leaves and he dies. While walking in the fields, she hears his knell, and herself takes sick and dies of remorse. The last verse is not uncommon:

They buried her in the old churchyard;
Sweet William's grave was nigh her.
And out of his grew a red, red rose
And out of hers, a briar.

They grew and grew in the old churchyard;
Till they couldn't grow no higher,
And there they tied a true lover's knot,
The red rose and the briar.

The characters previously mentioned represent common ballad plots. There are about fourteen of these basic plots, each one existing in hundreds of variant forms. *Barbara Allen* is one of these.

As the frontier pushed west, the songs changed. The new land was harder to tame and less rewarding. Instead of shying away from their hardships, the pioneers made fun of them. They sang ironic songs telling how they loved the way they lived, and describing it in detail. A broad sort of humor arose, a humor of overstatement, the humor of Paul Bunyan. Some songs told of great men who were strong, brave, who feared nothing and could do anything. The pioneers also brought with them murder ballads, songs about killers and robbers.

The women too had their favorite songs. Frontier life was perhaps harder on the woman than on the man. It is no wonder that she preferred to sing songs of running away, of killing her husband, or morbid songs such as "The grave will decay you and turn you to dust; there's not one boy in a million a poor girl can trust." A favorite was *Black Jack Davy*. In this the wife runs off with a romantic gypsy figure (in some versions he is called Gypsy Davy or the Gypsy Laddy) and doesn't come back to her husband in spite of his pleading. She also sang "Pretty Polly" songs, about young girls who ran off with their lovers but were killed by them. There is a parallel here between these songs and the men's songs in which bad men—the famous gunmen who had shed all responsibility to society—were hanged. They show a wishful escapism—a desire to be free as the characters in the songs—coupled with acceptance of the rules and rigors of their way of life.

Songs of the Roving Trades

Men of "roving trades" sang their songs as they traveled from one section of the country to another. Canalers, rivermen, wagoners, railroad men, trail-herd cowboys, lumberjacks, gold seekers, and miners all had their own songs. Some were songs they had picked up and adapted to their own purposes, sometimes changing only a name, other times keeping only the tune and writing completely new lyrics. The lumberjacks, for instance, sang an adaptation of *The Cowboy's Lament,* also known as *The Streets of Laredo,* the famous song of another rambling trade, that of the cowboys.

These songs were mostly ballads, but they were different from the old love ballads. They were known as the "Come-all-ye" ballads, be-

cause so many of them began: "Come all ye young fellers" (or sailors, or cowboys). Their style was less subtle than that of the love ballads; instead of telling much of the story in dialogue (as in *Barbara Allen*), they were more closely allied to the broadsides—direct narrative, with dates and places named, and the importance of certain events often emphasized through exaggeration. Often the moral was stated outright, as a bit of advice from the singer to all the "young fellers" who had been called together to listen to his tale.

Many of their ballads told the story of their particular hero. The ballad of the railroad engineers' hero, Casey Jones, begins: "Come all ye rounders that want to hear/ The story of a brave engineer." Paul Bunyan was the lumberjacks' work giant, and John Henry was and still is the greatest of the railroading heroes.

Work Songs

There is a distinction between "roving songs" and work songs. Each of the roving trades had their store of folklore, their heroes and memorable events. They also sang the old love ballads, usually while traveling, after they had left a community where they had had, perhaps, a brief

BURL IVES

romance and a spree, and were feeling the loneliness of their way of life. The work songs, however, were sung while they did the actual work, and were designed to make the work go more quickly and smoothly. The rhythm and verse form was based on the length of the job to be done and on the rhythm of the work. The richest sources of these types of songs are the sailors' sea chanties and Negro prison songs.

The style of the work songs generally followed this form: the leader would sing the first line to set the pace of the work, then the others would join in the refrain. Usually the swing of a sledge hammer or the all-together pull on a rope came at the end of each line. If the job was not finished by the time the usual verses were done with, the leader was depended on to make up new ones to fill out the time. A good song leader was well appreciated both by the men and by the boss.

The lines of these songs did not hang together to make a story; they were a vehicle for short comments about the work at hand, the desire for female companionship or for a drink, and the low pay and the boss or captain. Since the captain realized the value of this form of outlet, references to himself or to bad working conditions were tolerated.

An example of a Negro prison song that shows this bitterness toward the captain is *Take This Hammer*. On the downswing of the hammer after "Take it to the captain," there seems no doubt that the workers wanted to hit the captain, rather than the stone, and escape. The leader gave his men a rest on the third "captain" by drawing out that word:

> Take this hammer, whaugh!
> Take it to the captain, whaugh!
> Take this hammer, whaugh!
> Take it to the captain, whaugh!
> Take this hammer, whaugh!
> Take it to the ca-aa-aptain . . . whaugh!
> Tell him I'm gone, whaugh!
> You can tell him I'm gone, whaugh!

The "whaugh!" was a grunt, with each hammer blow.

Topical Songs—Songs of Social Comment

The coming of industrialization, and the workingman's subsequent concern with bettering his working conditions, gave birth to a new kind of protest song.

The "Come-all-ye" song proved a good vehicle for union propaganda:

> Come all of you good workers,
> Good news to you I'll tell,
> Of how the good old union
> Has come in here to dwell.
>
> Which side are you on?
> Which side are you on?

Though the factory workers of today still have their heroes in song, in some songs that were concerned with the workingman's economic plight the hardworking, skilled craftsman has become an object of ridicule under the conditions of mass production. Specialized labor at the conveyor belt is monotonous, no longer an object worthy of attainment and of glorification.

Woody Guthrie's talking blues told what he saw as he traveled the country back and forth in the hard times of the thirties. He didn't like what he saw, so these songs were a vehicle for acid social comment. Alan Lomax says that the "talking blues is, ultimately, of Negro derivation. . . . Speaking in rhythm over a sung accompaniment is a common device among Negro preachers and blues singers (Leadbelly, for instance), and some early records exist of Negroes 'talking' a story over, or to, their guitars. The talking blues, however, with its delayed climax and its double or triple cracker on the end of the jokes, is a modern, white-folk creation," well suited to their "taste for darn fool ditties and for crazy, surrealist, and rather cynical humor" (Alan Lomax, *The Folk Songs of North America*).

Joan Baez, the youngest, and perhaps most brilliant, of today's folk singers

OSCAR BRAND

Topical songs are still being composed today by modern folk singers, for example Ernie Myers' *Pop Goes the Missile,* which is not a talking blues, but is sung to the tune of *Pop Goes the Weasel.*

Negro Songs

When the African slaves arrived in America, they could not read and were not Christians, but they very quickly acquired a smattering of Judeo-Christian folklore. They found that many stories in the Old Testament bore a striking resemblance to their own history; for example the Jews' captivity in Egypt. One of the most famous Negro spirituals, *Go Down, Moses,* is concerned with this captivity.

The African Negroes were accustomed to speaking with their gods as one might speak to another man. When they came to America and adopted the Christian deity as their own, they continued this practice.

The Negroes tended to be optimistic about life, which was fortunate, since, after they were freed, they found themselves no better off than before. The industrial revolution came to the South, bringing with it city life and city ways. No longer confined to plantations, the former slaves moved to the cities. There they could see more things and sing about them. Their new songs migrated with them up the Mississippi to St. Louis, to Chicago, to take the train or boat east and north.

The new song was the blues. It was bitter satire, social comment, about woman trouble and death. It rapidly developed, taking on its special form, the most common being the twelve-bar blues. It took something close to 4/4 time for a verse, and followed this chord progression: tonic, four bars; subdominant seventh, two bars; tonic, two bars; dominant seventh, one bar; subdominant seventh, one bar; tonic, one bar. There are variations among singers, but none is so different from the accepted standard as to be unrecognizable.

The words are in the form of conversation. The blues singer talks to himself, telling himself where he's been, how he feels, why he feels that way, what he's going to do about it. Mostly, the blues concerns itself with feeling.

Two Styles of Folk Song

The Negro and white styles of folk singing began as two widely divergent cultural phenomena. Compare the African style, in the section on groups of folk-music styles, with the Eurasian and the Modern European styles, both of which had a great influence on the white folk singers in America.

The Negroes, both in Africa and in America, engage in much group singing, with complicated harmonic and rhythmic structure. Body movements and extreme facial mobility accompany their musical expression. The singing voice is usually set at the person's normal speaking pitch. Many of their songs, particularly the blues, tell of personal experience, and are more concerned with feeling, or mood, than with content. Since the background of Negro music is based on song as a community affair, no Negro in a group hesitates to sing out and contribute his voice at a musical gathering. Much Negro music is pure improvisation; therefore new songs are born and old may die overnight.

The whites in America, because of their heritage from Eurasia and modern Europe, tend more toward solo than group singing. Until the advent of the shape-note songbooks in the late eighteenth century, no harmony was used in folk group singing, and even today, with harmony, the result of amateur folk choral singing is usually cacophony. The white solo ballad singer often sings in a tight, high voice, with face composed, and little body movement, except that needed to play his instrument. (This is particularly noticeable today among the singers of such sections of the country as the Appalachian Mountains, which have formed a cultural pocket where change from the old European songs and style of singing comes about slowly.) The white solo singer tells a tale, not of himself but of someone else, and sets store by remembering the content of a song so as to be an honest and accurate storyteller. Any audience he has is usually silent rather than participating. He most often sings only for himself, his family, or his friends, and any public display of his talents is generally a source of embarrassment to him.

Today, the two styles are merging, one influencing the other. This has been slowly happening since the two have been living side by side. The whites have adopted many Negro spirituals. The shouting Baptists of today are both whites and Negroes, and their songs and approach to religion are an outgrowth of the Negro's religion and spirituals. The Negro's blues are becoming more literary. (They used to be composed mostly of the repetition of one line, and gave forth a mood more than anything else. Now they tell a little more of a story.) And the white audience is losing its inhibitions, joining in the refrains with enthusiasm (folk singers have achieved particular popularity with college students), while the Negro has emerged as a solo entertainer for an abstaining (in other words, nonparticipating) audience.

FOMIN, Evstigney Ipatovich. Russian composer (1761–1800). A conductor at theaters in Moscow, he was the first Russian opera composer. His works, strongly Italian in style, are forgotten today but were very successful in their time. Though they were nationalistic in subject, their music was conventional, and it was not until a half-century later that Russia produced its own style in opera. Fomin's opera, *Melnik,* a comedy, held the stage for many years, and another, *Boyeslav,* had a libretto by the Empress Catherine II. One of his lesser operas was called *The Americans.*

FOOTE, Arthur. American composer, pianist, and organist (1853–1937). After receiving the first M.A. degree ever given in music in the United States from Harvard University, Arthur Foote embarked on a long career as organist and teacher. He was also a prolific composer. Of his works, written in the tradition of German romanticism, the Suite for Strings in E major is best known for its abundant lyricism and fine contrapuntal structure.

FOR HE'S A JOLLY GOOD FELLOW. An English party song, expressing approval of and general liking for a member of the company. The tune is very old. As a French nursery song, it was originally known as *Malbrouck s'en vat-en guerre,* with words telling of the Duke of Marlborough going to war.

The original words are said to have been written in 1709, but the author is unknown. Marie Antoinette sang *Malbrouck* as a cradle song, Beaumarchais introduced it into *Le Mariage de Figaro* in 1784, and Beethoven used it in his *Wellington's Victory,* or *Battle Symphony.*

FORD FOUNDATION. Endowed by the Ford motorcar family, this is one of the wealthiest and most influential of private foundations. Its scope is wide and its activities are many. In recent years, funds have been allotted to singers

THEODORE BIKEL

and instrumentalists with which to commission works from composers; orchestras have received money for training programs; and opera companies have been enabled to produce contemporary works. The many productions of American operas by the New York City Opera Company were made possible by the Ford Foundation. Grants also have been made to the Chicago Lyric and San Francisco operas as well as to the Metropolitan Opera.

FORM. Many attempts have been made to define musical form, and a distinction has often been drawn between outer and inner form. By outer form is meant the formal structure and the general formal principles used by the composer as the foundation on which he builds his work (sonata, fugue, variation, etc.). But such formal structures are not ready-made molds into which he merely has to pour his inspiration. It is the composer's constructive ability and his capacity for consecutive musical thinking that give his composition an inner form which has its source in his own personality and character. This inner form (often referred to as form *in* music) is not tangible. Once the composer has selected his outer form or ground plan, he has at his disposal all the theoretical principles of music and the technical principles of composition as tools with which to build up the inner form of his work.

"Of course, one may not go beyond fundamental principles of form. But it is most important to realize that these structural elements are only the outward expression of something internal, something hidden and spiritual, for the urge to create unity out of diversity is the essence of composition" (Roland-Manuel).

MUSICAL FORMS

Much music finds its forms in folk music, with the result that its phrases and periods are largely characterized by the strict regularity of popular song and dance, and have little of the irregularity of daily speech.

Roughly speaking, musical forms can be divided into six groups: two-part form (simple binary); three-part form (simple ternary); compound binary form (sonata); rondo; variation; and fugue.

The Two-part or Simple Binary Form

This is one of the simplest and most ancient of

EVSTIGNEY IPATOVICH FOMIN

musical forms. It is also known as A-B form. It reached its peak in the seventeenth and eighteenth centuries, when it was the chief form in all the dance movements (allemande, sarabande, gavotte, bourrée, etc.) which formed part of contemporary suites. The form was not greatly used after the middle of the eighteenth century.

It is clearly divided into two parts. The first begins in the tonic key and ends with a distinct cadence, in major on the dominant, in minor on a relative key. The second section begins in the dominant (relative key) and ends on the tonic.

	A			B	
T		D	D		T

We see that simple binary form, despite its division into two, represents a stylistic and structural unity. The two halves are not independent; B follows as a necessary supplement to A (B takes up the dominant and leads it back to the tonic). The musical material of simple binary form thus contains little contrast, and is, therefore, more suitable for smaller pieces.

Examples are: Purcell, Minuet; Bach, *Little Organ Book;* Handel, the minuets; Scarlatti, *Pastorale de Ballo;* and Couperin, *Le Moucheron* and *La Commère.*

The Three-part or Simple Ternary Form

This form, also known as A-B-A form, has been in use throughout the last two centuries, and is frequently used today. The first section begins and ends in the tonic key; the second section opens in a new key (the dominant or another relative key); and the third section is a recapitulation of the first.

	A			B			A	
T		T	D		D	T		T

Contrasting material is usually used in the second section. Each section in itself presents a closed har-

MAUREEN FORRESTER

monic unity. The form is sectional in contrast to simple binary, which is a typical continuous form.

The three-part form is found in French chansons of the sixteenth century, and came clearly to the fore in the *da capo* arias of *c.* 1700. The form is used in the following way in the minuets of Haydn and Mozart:

MINUET

A	B	A
Minuet section	Trio section	Minuet section
A B	A B	A B

The trio section forms a clear contrast to the minuet section which is played before and after it. Note that the individual sections are in two-part form; thus, while the larger form is three-part, its sections are still in two-part form. Such a building up from smaller parts to larger (the latter in a different form from the former) is often found in longer compositions.

The three-part form is to be found in many piano pieces from the romantic period, such as: Schumann, *Novelettes;* Chopin, Nocturnes; and Brahms, Fantasias.

For explanation of the sonata, rondo, variation, and fugue forms, see the respective headings.

FORRESTER, Maureen. Canadian contralto (1930–). Having sung in church and school choirs since childhood, Miss Forrester studied with Bernard Diamant in Montreal, and made her recital debut there in 1953. Since then, she has toured throughout Canada and the United States as a soloist with leading symphony orchestras, and appeared with the New York

Philharmonic, Philadelphia, and Cleveland orchestras in 1960. She has given recitals in Europe and appeared in several music festivals there. She won the Ladies Morning Musical Scholarship (1952) and Le Club Social Award (1953), in Montreal, and in 1957 toured Europe under the sponsorship of Jeunesses Musicales, making her debut in Paris at the Salle Gaveau.

FORSTER, Joseph. Austrian composer (1845–1917). He composed ballets, a symphony, and three operas, one of which, *Die Rose von Pontevedra,* won an important prize in 1893.

FORTE. Italian, "strongly," "loudly." Usually abbreviated to *f.* The superlative form of this adverb, *fortissimo,* means "very loud" (abbreviation *ff*). The abbreviation *fff* (for *forte fortissimo,* "very very loud") is sometimes used. See *Music, Elements of.*

FORTNER Wolfgang. German composer (1907–). Fortner was one of the first composers to find a way out of Germany's post World War II stupor. As one of the most noted musical educators, he joined the staff of Darmstadt's annual International Holiday Courses for Contemporary Music in 1946. In this capacity he has opened the eyes of a whole generation of young musicians to the works of modern music not available during the Hitler regime. Fortner's own style of composition was long influenced by Paul Hindemith, but after 1945 he came to his own style of twelve-tone music by way of free atonality. His compositions include works for orchestra, chamber music, piano, and voice. The operas *Der Wald* and *Die Bluthochzeit* (after Garcia Lorca) and the *Symphony 1947* are among his most impressive works. He has also composed concertos and choral works.

Fortner has taught extensively at Germany's important musical academies. At present he heads the composition department at the Hochschule für Musik in Freiburg, Breisgau. He has also appeared as conductor of orchestras and choruses. His most important pupil to date is Hans Werner Henze.

FORZA DEL DESTINO, LA (*The Force of Destiny*). Opera in four acts by Verdi, libretto by Piave based on a play by the Duque de Rivas. First produced in St. Petersburg on November 10, 1862; American première at the New York

Academy of Music on February 24, 1865. Verdi revised the opera in 1869. Though a complicated and cumbersome plot weakened the effect of this work, it has become one of the most popular of Verdi's secondary operas and contains much music that ranks with his best. Therese Tietjens sang in the English première, and in the first production at the Metropolitan Opera in 1918 Rosa Ponselle made her sensational debut opposite Caruso. More recently, the role of Leonora has been sung with great success by Rethberg, Milanov, Callas, Tebaldi, and Farrell. The story concerns the accidental shooting of Leonora's father by her lover and the eventual vengeance of her brother, who kills her after he has found her in the convent where she has taken refuge.

FOSS, Lukas. American composer, conductor, and pianist (1922–). Lukas Foss, born in Berlin, began music lessons at a very early age, and at the age of eleven was admitted to the Paris Conservatory, where he studied for four years. He was later a pupil at the Curtis Institute, Philadelphia, and studied under Hindemith and Koussevitzky.

A number of his minor works were performed in 1939, and in 1943 his orchestral work *The Prairie* was played by the Boston Symphony Orchestra with Koussevitzky conducting. Foss thus became the youngest composer to have a work performed by this famous orchestra.

Marion Bauer writes of *The Prairie:* "A new expression of an old faith drawn from the native soil. . . . And thus he developed a work in ora-

A scene from Sam Wanamaker's controversial production of La forza del destino *at Covent Garden, 1962*

torio style based on the American soil and spirit."

Lukas Foss has conducted many of America's leading orchestras, and has received several prizes, including the 1950 award offered by the American Academy in Rome.

Since 1953, Lukas Foss has been a professor of composition at the University of California, Los Angeles. He has frequently appeared as conductor and soloist with American and European orchestras. In the fall of 1963, he will become the new conductor of the Buffalo Symphony.

Best-known works:

The Prairie (1941–42), for chorus, four soloists, orchestra.
Song of Anguish (1945), for baritone solo and orchestra.
Song of Songs (1946), for soprano solo and orchestra.
String Quartet in G major (1947).
The Jumping Frog (1949), one-act opera, based on the Mark Twain story.

LUKAS FOSS

Second Piano Concerto (1951–53).
A Parable of Death (1953).
Psalms (1957), cantata for chorus and orchestra.
Symphony of Chorales (1958).
Time Cycle (1961), for soprano and orchestra.

FOSTER, Sidney. American pianist (1919–). Foster was graduated from the Curtis Institute of Music in 1938, and made his debut in 1941 with the New York Philharmonic Orchestra as the first winner of the Leventritt Award. He has since made many appearances throughout the United States in recitals and as soloist with leading symphony orchestras.

FOSTER, Stephen Collins. American composer (1826–64). Foster was the first American composer whose tunes became generally popular in Europe. Life in America at the time of Foster's childhood was in many ways hard and rough, and his father, a colonel, had, like the rest of the family, more feeling for the stern realities of life than for the charms of music.

At an early age Foster revealed a vigorous melodic talent, which he developed by frequent visits to Negro religious services, by listening to Negro music, and by playing a guitar belonging to his sister. He was given a sound education, in which the musical side was completely neglected. This greatly hampered his development, and obstructed the free unfolding of his creative imagination. Besides these difficulties, he sadly lacked self-confidence, and had no "money sense"—a fact which allowed his publishers to exploit him unscrupulously.

Prompted by the military traditions of his family, he thought for a time of entering the Navy, but he changed his mind and, on leaving school, began work as an accountant in Cincinnati. He had written his first composition, a waltz, at the age of thirteen and in 1844 he published his first song, *Open Thy Lattice, Love.* He founded a club in Cincinnati which met several times a week to sing the favorite tunes of the day, and for these gatherings he composed *Old Uncle Ned* and *Lou'siana Belle.*

A publisher undertook to bring them out, on condition that the composer resign his claim to a royalty on sales. Foster, quite ignorant of such matters, agreed, and within a very short time the songs had earned $10,000 for the publisher. Foster's next songs, *Way Down South* and *Oh, Susanna!,* won fantastic popularity and swept America. Encouraged by this success, he left his job and went to live in Allegheny City where he devoted himself to composition. Although the stream of songs which he composed included such favorites as *Old Folks at Home, My Old Kentucky Home,* and *Old Black Joe* and made him the most popular song writer in America, the sales of his songs brought him a yearly income of only about $800. These simple, ingenuous songs with their typical homely sentimentality and unpretentious melodies are now regarded as a part of American folk music, and have given Foster a unique position in the history of music.

His unhappy family life brought about a tragic ending to Foster's brilliant career. After his divorce in 1860 he succumbed to long drinking bouts, which led to his death on January 10, 1864.

Best-known songs:

> *Beautiful Dreamer* (1864)
> *Camptown Races* (1850)
> *Come Where My Love Lies Dreaming* (1855)
> *Jeanie with the Light Brown Hair* (1854)
> *Lou'siana Belle* (1847)
> *Massa's in de Cold, Cold Ground* (1852)
> *My Old Kentucky Home* (1853)
> *Oh, Susanna!* (1848)
> *Old Black Joe* (1860)
> *Old Dog Tray* (1853)
> *Old Folks at Home* (1851)
> *Ring, Ring de Banjo* (1851)

FOUNTAINS OF ROME *(Fontane di Roma).* Orchestral suite by Respighi, written in 1917.

The first movement depicts morning at the fountain of Valle Giulia with the herd boys passing by with their cattle and disappearing into the morning mist.

The second movement describes tritons and naiads rejoicing at the Triton fountain at morn in a wild dance under the cascades of water.

The third movement portrays the Trevi fountain at high noon. A peaceful singing theme is suddenly interrupted by fanfares, and Neptune passes by in his chariot drawn by sea horses, followed by sirens, tritons, and naiads.

The fourth movement pictures sunset at the fountain in the Villa Medici. A quiet, gentle melody is heard above the splashing of the water. The sound of bells intermingles with the song of the birds, and then all dies away in the stillness of night.

FOURNIER, Pierre. French cellist (1906–). Known the world over for his effortless per-

The famous portrait of Stephen Foster painted by his contemporary, Thomas Hicks

The Trevi Fountain, *one of the fountains Respighi depicted in* Fountains of Rome

Jean Françaix and Wolfgang Fortner

formances on the cello as well as his great musicianship, Fournier began his career under a severe handicap. Stricken by polio in his youth, he had to give up his first love, the piano, and chose the cello as his permanent instrument. Educated at the Paris Conservatory, he started out as a member of several orchestras and chamber music ensembles before embarking on his career as a soloist. By the end of the 1930s he was known throughout Europe. The second World War interrupted his career, and he devoted considerable time and effort to teaching at the Paris Conservatory where he became a professor in 1941.

After the war he immediately took up concertizing, playing concerts in France and England. He came to the United States in 1948, and his success in this country was undisputed from the beginning. He also toured South America and played at the famous European music festivals. He was made a Chevalier of the Legion of Honor in 1953 for his distinguished achievements.

FOURTH. Interval embracing four degrees of the diatonic scale; also the fourth note of a scale from lower *do*. See *Music, Elements of.*

FRAGER, Malcolm. American pianist (1935–). He studied with Evelyn Rubinstein, Carl Madliner, and Carl Friedberg. His first public appearance was at the Baldwin Town Hall in St. Louis in 1941, and he made his New York debut at Town Hall in 1952. He appeared with the New York Philharmonic Orchestra in 1960, and has made tours throughout the United States and abroad. He won second prize at the Geneva International Competition in 1955, the Michaels Memorial Music Award in 1956, the Career Award of the National Society of Arts and Letters, Los Angeles, in 1958, the Leventritt Competition, New York, in 1959, and first prize at the Queen Elizabeth Competition in Brussels in 1960. He was graduated magna cum laude from Columbia University in 1957.

FRANÇAIX, Jean. French composer (1912–). He is known especially for his delightful ballets *Beach, Scuola di Ballo, Les Malheurs de Sophie,* and *Le Roi Nu,* but his orchestral compositions have the same simple and elegant style. These include a concertino, piano concerto, quadruple concerto, and serenade. As a French author has said: "Gay, lively, and charming—a cool severity which reveals a meditative mind—such is Jean Françaix's music."

When he was requested to write a long composition on the Revelation of St. John, he replied that he would be willing to do it if the music could be "gentle, French and gay." But in fact the mighty oratorio *Apocalypse* (1947) is both magnificent and inspiring. Françaix was a pupil of Nadia Boulanger.

FRANCESCA DA RIMINI. Fantasy (after Dante) for large orchestra, Op. 32, by Tchaikovsky. In July, 1876, Tchaikovsky wrote home from Paris to his brother Modeste: "Early this morning I read the fifth canto of Dante's *Inferno,* and I was at once seized by the idea of writing a symphonic poem about Francesca da Rimini."

In October he wrote from Moscow: "I have just finished the composition of a new work— the symphonic fantasia *Francesca da Rimini.* I have worked at it *con amore,* and believe my love has been successful. The Whirlwind might perhaps correspond better with Doré's picture: it has not turned out quite as I wanted. However, an accurate estimate of the work is impossible until it is orchestrated and played."

The fantasy was finished in November, and in the following March the first performance was conducted by Nicholas Rubinstein in Moscow.

Saint-Saëns has compared Tchaikovsky's with Liszt's version of the same subject: "One of the finest and most sensitive of men has here suddenly let loose a whirlwind that shows as little compassion for his hearers as Satan for sinners. . . . Francesca is more appealing and more Italian in character in Liszt than in the great Slav master. But Tchaikovsky's design is clearer, and his is the better work from the musical point of view. However, the works can easily stand side by side; both are worthy of Dante."

The explanatory preface in the score runs: "Dante is on his way down into the second circle of Hell, where dwell the souls who have given themselves to the lusts of the flesh. Their punishment consists in being exposed for all time in eternal darkness to the most frightful storms, as in life they let themselves be driven by the storms of passion. Among the sufferers Dante discovers Francesca da Rimini, who relates her story."

Then follows a quotation from Canto 5 of the *Inferno,* telling how Francesca da Rimini, daughter of Guido Vecchio di Polenta, was married for political reasons to the deformed Gianciotto, son of Malatesta da Verrucchio, lord of Rimini; how she fell in love with his handsome younger brother Paolo, who became her lover; and how her husband, surprising them together, stabbed them both to death.

The music first describes the frightful sight that meets Dante at the entrance to the second circle of Hell. Then the first section pictures such figures as Semiramis, Dido, Cleopatra, and Helen of Troy. Eventually a clarinet recitative is heard, merging into a song describing the two lovers, Francesca and Paolo. Gradually a tone of anxiety appears more and more insistently, blaring fanfares on the brass reminding us that we are among the condemned.

Dante's story of Francesca and Paolo has also been the subject of several operas, notably those by Goetz (1877), Rachmaninoff (1906), and Zandonai (1914—libretto after a play by D'Annunzio). Henry Hadley composed a symphonic poem with the same title.

FRANCESCATTI, Zino. French violinist (1905–). Francescatti received his musical training from his parents, and made his debut in Marseilles in 1915. For a time he devoted himself to legal studies, but in 1927 he again took up the violin, and, after performing in various Paris orchestras, began his international career with tours in Europe and North Africa. He has since given concerts all over the world, and is regarded as one of the elite of violin virtuosos.

Francescatti has stated that the artistic personalities he esteems most highly are Brahms, Cézanne, and William Faulkner. Of musical works he is most fond of Bach's *The Well-Tempered Clavier,* which he considers "represents the most perfect form of musical inspiration." In his own career he is proud of having recorded the whole of Beethoven's Violin Concerto without pausing.

FRANCHETTI, Baron Alberto. Italian composer (1860–1942). Known as the Meyerbeer of modern Italy, he was a wealthy man who devoted himself to the composition of operas. He was a skillful technician, particularly in the handling of mass effects, and two of his operas, *Asrael* (1888) and *Germania* (1902), had wide success during his lifetime.

A scene from Francesca da Rimini, *the ballet version with Tchaikovsky's music and choreography by David Lichine. Performed by the Ballets Russes de Monte Carlo*

César Franck

(DECEMBER 10, 1822 – NOVEMBER 8, 1890)

FRANCK became a musician through his father's choice. He so ardently desired his two sons to be child virtuosos that, almost before they could walk, they were made to play, César the piano and Joseph the violin. When César was eleven, his father considered him mature enough to make a tour of Belgium, but it was not a success, and his father decided to move from César's birthplace, Liège, to Paris so that César might receive better teaching at the Conservatory. He was first sent to the best teacher of musical theory in Paris, Anton

CÉSAR FRANCK

Reicha, and in 1837 was admitted to the Conservatory.

The following year Franck gave evidence of his skill in playing at sight. At a piano competition he found the music given him so easy that he hit upon the idea of transposing the piece a third lower, and played the composition with bravura in the new key. But the result was not what he had expected. The director of the Conservatory, the aged Cherubini, was so indignant at the young man's breach of the rules that he refused to give him the first prize. On the other hand, the performance was so remarkable that a *grand prix d'honneur,* an award never made before, or since, by the Conservatory at such a competition, was created for him. Just as the greatest prize of all, the Prix de Rome, seemed to be within his reach, his father took him away from the Conservatory with the intention of making him, young as he was, begin a career as a virtuoso. But again his concert tours of Belgium were not attended with much success.

Five years later Franck finished his first big composition, the Biblical oratorio *Ruth.* This was not well received and was said by many to be a plagiarism; it was twenty years before it was performed the second time.

In February, 1848, Franck was married in Notre-Dame-de-Lorette, where he had been appointed organist four years earlier. The marriage took place in the middle of the Revolution of 1848 and the bridal procession had to climb over the barricades on their way to the church. Though poor, the couple were happy—especially César, who had at last escaped from his father's authority to a home of his own.

His life now fell into a routine and he went to work systematically. He drew up a timetable daily, in which the greater part of it had to be devoted to giving lessons to earn his daily bread.

He began at 5:30 A.M., but allowed himself two hours a day for "thinking" (which meant composing), reading good literature, and making a close study of the works of the great masters.

In 1851 he started working on an opera, *Le Valet de Ferme,* but the strain was such that he fell ill and had to give up composition for a time. By now Franck was an organist of outstanding merit, and in 1858 he was appointed organist at the newly built church of Sainte-Clotilde, which had one of the best organs in Paris. Here he could both display his outstanding talent and develop his unique contrapuntal technique—and so prepare himself for the great compositions which were soon to come. As an organist Franck was famous for his daring and imaginative improvisations. When Liszt heard him improvise he came out of the church deeply moved. "It was like hearing Johann Sebastian Bach extemporizing at his organ," he declared.

In 1872 Franck became professor of organ playing at the Paris Conservatory. His lovable nature, his modesty and his naïve trustfulness made "le père Franck" the idol of his many students, who included d'Indy, Pierné, Duparc, Chausson, and others. But he remained unknown as a composer; since he could not afford to present his large-scale works to the public, there were few beyond his circle of admiring pupils who knew and understood his music.

Franck worked on his magnum opus, *The Beatitudes* (based on the Sermon on the Mount) for ten years. When it was finished he decided to play it at his home before the leading musicians and critics of Paris. The Minister of Culture, the directors of the Conservatory and the Opéra, the reviewers, and the composer's friends were invited. But the day before the concert Franck unfortunately injured his hand so that he was unable to play the piano himself, and one of his pupils, Vincent d'Indy, had to take his place. On the eve of the concert the Minister sent a message that he was unable to come, and both the directors refused the invitation. Only a few of the critics were present, and they soon left one by one. The whole performance was a failure. Franck had hoped much from his work, but even his friends saw that it was too long for one evening and told him so. He was greatly disappointed, but not embittered.

It was not until fourteen years later that the whole of *The Beatitudes* was again performed

A detail from a portrait of César Franck

in public; then it was a success and established Franck as a great composer. But by then he had been dead for three years.

In 1887, eight years after the unsuccessful performance of *The Beatitudes,* Franck's friends arranged a subscription concert of his works. But although the program included such a work as his *Symphonic Variations,* the performers were underrehearsed and the evening was not a success. His admirers were bitter at the failure, and at the subsequent failure in 1889 of the now-famous Symphony in D minor. Even the members of the orchestra objected to it.

One reason why it was difficult for César Franck's compositions to gain acceptance was that he could not write opera—which was still the only form of music that counted in Paris. Franck's saintly personality manifested itself rather in his five symphonic poems and in his charming, even seraphic, oratorio, *The Beatitudes.* Yet he attained perhaps his richest expression in his Symphony in D minor (1886–88), his Quartet, and his Violin Sonata. The last-named became the favorite piece of Ysaÿe, who played it all over Europe. The String Quartet, performed for the first time in public in Paris in 1890, was an instantaneous success. Vincent d'Indy described the occasion: "The

CÉSAR FRANCK

and the whole composition is somewhat wanting in perspective.

Most of Franck's later works give evidence of his prolific musical inventiveness in their interesting treatment of motifs, contrapuntal skill, and combination of themes. He used all the devices of musical technique with easy naturalness and without in any way limiting his musical freedom of movement. His own compositions are the best examples of the principle of "a singing counterpoint" which he emphasized for all his pupils.

Franck had been an organist throughout his life, and in an almost unbroken series of organ compositions he gave evidence of his deep love and intimate knowledge of the instrument. His piano compositions, however, were written in two periods separated by nearly forty years. In the first his compositions were virtuoso pieces now long forgotten, but in the second he created two of the most beautiful works for piano ever produced in France. He wrote them, at the age of sixty-two, because he thought that the repertoire of the French pianists needed renewal. These were his *Prelude, Chorale and Fugue,* and *Prelude, Aria and Finale.*

FRANCK'S BEST-KNOWN WORKS

ORCHESTRAL

Symphony, D minor (1886–88)
Redemption, symphonic poem (1871)
Le Chasseur Maudit, symphonic poem (1882)
Variations Symphoniques (piano and orchestra) (1885)
Psyché, symphonic poem (1887–88)
   1. *Sommeil de Psyché*
   2. *Psyché enlevée par les zéphyrs*
   3. *Le jardin d'Eros*
   4. *Psyché et Eros*

CHAMBER MUSIC

Quartet in D major (strings) (1889)
Quintet, F minor (piano and strings) (1878–79)
Sonata, A major (violin and piano) (1886)

PIANO

Prélude, Choral et Fugue (1884)
Prélude, Aria et Finale (1886–87)

ORGAN

Grande Pièce Symphonique, Op. 17 (1860–62)
Pastorale, Op. 19 (1860–62)
Pièce Héroïque, B minor (1878)
3 Chorals (1890)
   1. E major
   2. B minor
   3. A minor

hall shook with applause the like of which is seldom heard. People rose to their feet, called for the composer, clapped, and screamed. Franck could not believe that the applause was for his music; he thought it was for the performers. Not until they persuaded him onto the platform, where he stood smiling, confused, and embarrassed, did he believe it. And on the day after this first success (he was then 68), he said to us with childish pride: 'There you are! The public is beginning to understand me!' "

A month later Franck was knocked down by an omnibus. His injuries led to a severe attack of pleurisy a few months afterward, and he died shortly afterward, leaving a legacy of beautiful and original compositions, and the musical inspiration he had provided for his pupils.

César Franck's most productive period came after his fiftieth year, and he wrote his greatest works in the last years of his life. In youth a disciple of Beethoven, he developed his own individual style only by very slow degrees. Like Wagner he developed a style so strongly chromatic that a listener might at times find himself in doubt as to the key. Yet his mild melodiousness—akin to the French *opéra comique*—gives his compositions a peculiar, almost naïve grace. It was difficult for the saintly Franck to give expression to evil, and for this reason some parts of *The Beatitudes,* in which the character of Satan is an important one, are noticeably weak,

SONGS

Nocturne (de Foucaud) (1884)
Panis Angelicus (from *Messe Solennelle*) (1872)
La Procession (Brizeux) (1888)
La Vierge à la crèche (Daudet) Duet (1888)

Symphony in D Minor

Franck's only symphony was begun when he was sixty-four, and performed in public for the first time the year before he died. Like most of Franck's works, it met with little understanding at first. Gounod said that it was an affirmation of incompetence pushed to dogmatic lengths, and another of the honorable professors at the Conservatory wrote, "Is this a symphony? Have you ever heard a symphony with a theme for cor anglais? Has Haydn or Beethoven ever done anything like that?"

The extreme conservatism of the Paris Conservatory was strongly opposed to Franck's symphony, in which he took "daring liberties"—with harmony in particular, and also with the formal organization of his materials. But in spite of this opposition, and although Bizet and Saint-Saëns had written symphonies before him, Franck has since been recognized as the founder of the French symphonic school.

César Franck's symphony is based on a pregnant three-note motif, which plays a decisive part throughout. It is almost identically the same motif as the well-known *Muss es sein?* in Beethoven's String Quartet, Op. 135, the main motif in Liszt's *Les Préludes,* and Wagner's "destiny" motif in *Die Walküre.*

The movements are:

I. Lento—Allegro non troppo.

II. Allegretto.

III. Finale—Allegro non troppo.

Symphonic Variations

This composition for piano and orchestra (1885) was not well received when first performed in 1886, but it is now one of César Franck's most frequently played works.

The term "variations" is used in a wider meaning than usual. Indeed, the symphonic treatment of several themes has caused the work to be called a piano concerto in one movement. Formally, the work consists of an introduction, a sprightly first, and slow second movement, and a lively finale. The introductory motif is sounded by the bass strings and answered by the piano in the following theme:

After a comparatively short dialogue, the orchestra brings in still another motif, which becomes important in the further development of the composition:

A scene from the ballet based on Franck's Variations Symphoniques, *with choreography by Frederic Ashton. Performed by The Royal Ballet*

FRANÇOIS, Samson. French pianist (1924–). François studied at the Nice Conservatory and, at the instigation of Alfred Cortot, enrolled in the École Normale de Musique in Paris. He later studied at the Paris Conservatory under Marguerite Long and Jacques Fevrier. He has given recitals in the United States and abroad with leading conductors and orchestras. He made his New York debut in 1947 under the baton of Leonard Bernstein.

FRANK, Claude. German-American pianist (1925–). Frank studied at Columbia University with Artur Schnabel. He made his debut at Town Hall in New York in 1950. Since 1953, he has been a faculty member and assistant to Rudolf Serkin at the Marlboro School of Music in Vermont. He has made numerous appearances with major symphony orchestras and in recitals in the United States and Europe.

FRANZ, Robert (*real name* **Knauth**). German composer (1815–1892). An organist and conductor who also edited works of Bach and Handel, he gained the support and admiration of Schumann and Liszt in 1843 when his first set of songs was published. In 1868, deafness forced him to give up composing. Altogether, he composed 257 songs, many of them masterpieces of the lieder repertory that are still performed extensively but are not as popular as they used to be.

FRAU OHNE SCHATTEN, DIE *(The Woman Without a Shadow).* Opera in three acts by Richard Strauss, libretto by Hugo von Hofmannsthal. First performed in Vienna in 1919; first United States performance by the San Francisco Opera in 1958.

This work is the fourth opera created by the talents of Strauss and Von Hofmannsthal, and it is probably the crowning achievement of the long and fruitful collaboration. Von Hoffmannsthal's book is a fantastic mixture of Oriental legend and Jungian symbolism, and Strauss' music is wrought with sumptuous colors and magnificent orchestration. *Die Frau ohne Schatten* is, unfortunately, very long (over three hours) and unbelievably taxing for the singers, which mitigates against frequent performances. The plot, briefly, is this:

The Emperor of the Southeastern Isles has married a supernatural being. Unless she can cast a shadow (and in so doing, bear mortal children) within a specified time, the Emperor will be turned to stone. Aided by her demoniacal Nurse, the Empress descends to the realm of mortals and attempts to gain the shadow of the Dyer's Wife. After many trials the Empress comes to the realization that to barter happiness and life at the expense of others' happiness is fruitless. Confronted by her husband in petrified form she refuses to rob the Dyer's Wife of her natural heritage of fruitfulness and life. By her unselfish act the Empress is made mortal, the Emperor restored to life, and all praise the power of love, life, and fecundity.

FRECCIA, Massimo. Italian conductor (1906–). Freccia began his musical studies at the Florence Conservatory and completed them in Vienna under Franz Schalk. In the 1930s he conducted the Budapest Philharmonic Orchestra. At Lewisohn Stadium in New York he made guest appearances in 1938–40. He held permanent appointments with the Havana Philharmonic Orchestra and the New Orleans Philharmonic-Symphony Orchestra (1944–52), and from 1952 to 1959 he was conductor of the Baltimore Symphony Orchestra.

FREEMAN, Lawrence ("Bud"). American jazz saxophonist (1906–). Freeman has been identified with the field of jazz in the United States, Europe, and South America since the 1920s. He has been a member of the Roger Wolfe Kahn, Ben Pollock, and Red Nichols bands,

Act III of Die Frau ohne Schatten; *the Emperor is restored to life. Vienna State Opera production, 1955*

played with Ray Noble, Tommy Dorsey, and Benny Goodman, toured South America with Joe Bushkin, and recorded with Bobby Hackett and Louis Armstrong.

FREEMAN, Russell D. American jazz pianist (1926—). He studied classical music and played with Shorty Rogers and Chet Baker. He has recorded with Baker and Jimmy Giuffre. He is thought of as a "West Coast" pianist.

FREISCHÜTZ, DER (literally, The *Free Shooter,* but usually translated more appropriately as *The Magic Bullet*). Opera in three acts by Weber, with libretto adopted by Friedrich Kind from Apel's and Laun's *Gespensterbuch (Book of Ghosts).* The libretto was delivered to Weber in March, 1817, and in the summer of the same year he began to write the music, but it was not until four years later, on June 18, 1821, that the opera was first performed. This was in Berlin, with Weber himself conducting, and the opera was greeted with thunderous applause. The following year, a performance in Vienna with Schröder-Devrient as Agathe began a craze for the opera that swept Europe. It had its first American performance in 1825. In 1826, Weber went to London for the production of his last opera, *Oberon,* at Covent Garden and was much pleased by a performance there of *Der Freischütz* with John Braham and Mary Anne Patton. Though *Der Freischütz* still holds the stage in Germany and Austria, it has not been given in America since 1929.

Der Freischütz represents the triumph of German romantic opera. Both France and Italy had earlier produced such operas, and many older German operas had contained much that was romantic. But no earlier German composer had concentrated the whole essence of romanticism into a single work. Admittedly it is not an opera by the strictest definition, since the music passages are connected by spoken dialogue, but into these three short acts is gathered the whole of the romantic passion for the days of old, with their fairy tales and folk songs.

The very spirit of nature is caught in the forest scenes, with the hunting horns and sounds of the chase, in pictures of village life with its dancing and prize shooting. Also truly romantic is the contrast between the good cheer and gaiety safe indoors at the inn, the woodland poetry of happy folk, and the sinister and mysterious

A nineteenth-century production of Der Freischütz

Wolf's Glen, the picturesquely villainous Caspar, and the terrifying figure of Zamiel. In the words of E. J. Dent: "To us of today the scene in the Wolf's Glen where the magic bullets are cast is still marvelously exciting, with its crescendo of horrors vividly illustrated by continuous music, interrupted only by fragments of spoken dialogue that seem the more horrible because they are not sung."

Weber's descriptions of nature possess a unique wealth of nuances of light and shade; his orchestration has a depth and perspective never before achieved. Weber said that he experienced every landscape as music.

As a result, the *Freischütz* overture speaks more directly to the imagination perhaps than any earlier work. After an eight-bar introduction, it first expresses (on horns accompanied by strings) the ineffable stillness of the scene deep in the woods (the only motif in the overture which does not occur in the opera). Then a sinister note suddenly breaks in—the arrival of Zamiel. The entirely novel effect of double-bass pizzicato and string tremolo is so striking that one commentator has said that "in this bar romantic opera was born." Then follow the motifs of the Wolf's Glen scene. The opera's most beautiful figure next enters the picture in a "maidenly" clarinet song, and the overture ends with a gay and lilting melody resembling a folk song.

The Wolf's Glen scene in Act II, Scene 2, of Der Freischütz *at the 1957 Florence May Festival*

Place: *Bohemia*   Time: *About 1650*

ACT I

Scene: *A forest shooting range*

There has been a shooting competition in the forest, and the farmer Kilian (baritone) has won the prize. The young huntsman Max (tenor) is usually the winner, but on this occasion, no one knows why, he has missed the mark every time.

The whole company has gathered at the inn. Kilian and the other farmers make fun of Max, and a fight breaks out between them. The forest ranger Kuno (bass) separates them. He bids Max be of good cheer: next day he is to fire one trial shot before the Prince, and if successful he will win both the post of forest guard and Kuno's daughter Agathe.

Max sings an aria describing life in the forest:

Durch die Wäl-der, durch die Au-en zog ich leicht-

Through the woodlands, through the meadows,
  Once I took my careless way;
Bird or beast that caught my fancy
  Fell at once an easy prey.
Then, when evening shadows deepen'd,
  Homeward happy I returned . . .

Formerly his aim was always sure but now his shots always miss the target—he does not know what is wrong and is in despair. His friend Caspar (bass), the hunter, tries to cheer him with a drinking song. Caspar is an abandoned fellow who has sold his soul to the Devil's envoy, "the Black Huntsman" Zamiel (speaking part). Caspar gives Max a "magic bullet," cast at midnight under the invocation of the Devil, which always hits its mark. By way of proof, Max shoots down an eagle which he would never have been able to hit with an ordinary bullet. Caspar persuades Max to meet him in the forest in the Wolf's Glen at night, to make more "magic bullets," explaining that Max can obtain seven bullets if he is willing to sell his soul. Blinded by his love, Max agrees, and Caspar gives vent to his exultation in a diabolical aria.

ACT II

Scene 1: *A room in the ranger's house*

Agathe and Annchen (sopranos) are waiting for Max. Agathe is full of evil forebodings, and Annchen tries to brighten her with a song about a happy hunter lad. When Agathe is left alone, fear and hope alternate in her aria *(Agathe's Prayer):*

Lei - se, lei - se, from - me Wei - se, schwing

Softly sighs the voice of ev'ning,
  Stealing thro' yon willow grove;
While the stars, like guardian spirits,
  Set their nightly watch above!
Through the dark blue vault of ether
  Silence reigns with soothing pow'r,
But a storm o'er yonder mountain
  Darkly brooding seems to low'r. . . .

Max comes in and proudly displays his eagle. He cannot stay long—he must fetch a stag which has been shot in the forest. When he says that it lies in the notorious Wolf's Glen, Agathe is terrified.

Scene 2: *The Wolf's Glen*

It is black night. Caspar is preparing to cast the bullets, and is awaiting his victim. In the meantime he tells Zamiel, the evil one, of the success of his plan, and in return is promised that he may replace Zamiel as the Black Huntsman for three years, if he can drive Max into Zamiel's power. On his way through the woods, Max seems to see his dead mother and Agathe, who vainly try to hold him back. Arriving at the Wolf's Glen, he calls upon Zamiel. While the bullets are being cast, a storm roars through the forest, and horrible creatures and spirits appear.

ACT III

Scene 1: *Next morning, in the forest*

The sun is shining brightly after the storm. At the shooting match Max has hit impossible targets. He asks Caspar for one more bullet: he must keep the last one for the trial shot before the Prince. But Caspar has already fired all his bullets, so Max has only one more left—and Zamiel can direct the last bullet toward any target that he determines.

Scene 2: *Agathe's room*

Agathe sings to drive away her fear. Her friends, arriving to dress her for the shooting meeting, sing a ditty in folk-song style, *The Maiden's Garland.* Then they all set out for the Prince's camp deep in the forest.

Scene 3: *Before the Prince's tent*

A choir of huntsmen sings a gay hunting song. Agathe comes through the woods with her spiritual adviser, a pious Hermit (bass). Prince Ottokar (baritone) orders Max to fire his test shot, indicating a white dove as the target. Agathe cries out "Don't shoot, Max! I am the dove." The dove flies away to a tree, into which Caspar has climbed. Max fires, and Agathe sinks to the ground, unconscious. But it is Caspar who has been hit and, falling from the tree, he dies and his body is thrown into the Wolf's Glen. The Prince demands an explanation, and Max confesses his guilt in casting the "magic bullets." The Prince is about to punish him when the Hermit comes forward and declares that only those who are themselves blameless may blame others. The Prince then agrees that Max shall receive both his betrothed and the post of forest guardian at the end of a year, on condition that he leads a good life during that time. A choir gives thanks to the Almighty.

The final scene of Der Freischütz, *at the Munich State Opera*

FREITAS BRANCO, Luís. Portuguese composer (1890–1955). A distinguished teacher, critic, and musicologist, he was probaly the most important contemporary composer in Portugal. His works include much church music, a choral symphony based on Byron's *Manfred,* five other symphonies, a violin concerto, two violin sonatas and one for cello, many songs and piano pieces, and arrangements for solo voices and chorus of Portuguese folk songs.

FREMSTAD, Olive (*real name* **Anna Olivia Nayan Fremstadt**). Swedish-American soprano (1872–1951). One of the great singers of her time, she was a child-prodigy pianist and began singing in church choirs in Minnesota, where she was brought from Sweden when she was twelve. She earned money as a pianist while she studied voice in New York and then, at the age of nineteen, went to Berlin for coaching with Lilli Lehmann. At twenty-three, she made her opera debut in Cologne, singing the mezzo role of Azucena in *Il Trovatore.* Under Lilli Lehmann's guidance, she became a dramatic soprano. After many European engagements, she made her debut at the Metropolitan Opera in 1903 and was immediately recognized as the greatest Wagnerian soprano since Mme. Lehmann herself. In 1907, she sang the title role in the American première of Strauss' *Salome.* Her greatest role was Isolde and she also sang Carmen, Gluck's Armide, and other French and Italian roles. Her opera career ended in 1915 but she continued to sing in concerts until 1920. She is remembered for her beauty as well as for her singing, which, according to contemporary accounts, was much like Flagstad's in warmth, security, and tonal expression.

FRENCH HORN. Brass wind instrument. The old French horn, having natural tones, was provided with a set of ten or twelve crooks, which the performer added as required to lengthen the tube and so lower the pitch. In the modern French horn (usually called simply the "horn") the same effect is obtained with valves. See *Wind Instruments.*

FRESCOBALDI, Girolamo. Italian composer and organist (1583–1643). Frescobaldi had already won such fame as an organist that when he was appointed organist at St. Peter's, Rome, at the age of twenty-five, a crowd of thirty thousand came to hear his first concert. He was especially celebrated as an improviser, and as a composer he specialized in variation works and capriccios. Although his works can be said to belong to the infancy of organ composition, they are still often played. Alfredo Casella has said that his great distinction was to produce "a truly instrumental music free from vocal tyranny."

GIROLAMO FRESCOBALDI

Olive Fremstad as Venus in Tannhäuser

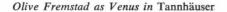

Best-known works:

ORGAN

Aria detta la Frescobaldi (harpsichord or organ)
Canzona dopo l'Epistola (*Fiori musicali*, 1635)
Canzona, F major (harpsichord and strings) (1637)
Gagliarde, No. 2 (harpsichord and orchestra)
Toccata per l'elevazione (*Fiori musicali*, 1635)

FREZZOLINI, Erminia. Italian soprano (1818–1884). The daughter of a famous basso buffo, she became one of Verdi's favorite singers and was celebrated, for her beauty as well as for her singing, in Europe and America. She created the soprano roles in two Verdi operas at La Scala in Milan—*I Lombardi* and *Giovanna D'Arco.* In 1855, she sang Gilda in *Rigoletto* in the American première at the Academy of Music in New York and two years later in the French première in Paris. She also sang Leonora in *Il Trovatore* at the French première in 1855.

FRICKER, Peter Racine. British composer (1920–). Since 1951, Fricker has been head of the music department of Morley College,

London. He composes in a dissonant idiom influenced by Bartók and the twelve-tone system. He has written two symphonies, two piano concertos, two violin concertos, and chamber and choral music. His works have been performed throughout the world.

FRICSAY, Ferenc. Hungarian conductor (1914–1963). Fricsay became known to the musical world through a fortunate circumstance: he was asked to substitute for Otto Klemperer during the Salzburg Festival of 1947. His great talent and ability had such an impact that he was immediately engaged for concerts and opera. He took over the RIAS Symphony Orchestra in West Berlin and transformed it into one of the finest orchestras in Europe.

Simultaneously he was chief conductor at the Berlin State Opera and traveled as a guest conductor throughout Europe. In 1956 he was appointed general music director of the Bavarian State Opera in Munich, a post which he held for two years. Fricsay also appeared as guest conductor of the Boston Symphony and the Houston Symphony orchestras.

FERENC FRICSAY

POVLA FRIJSH

His often highly controversial interpretations originated from his extraordinary sense of orchestral color and his strong intellectual capacity.

FRIEDBERG, Carl. German-American pianist and teacher (1872–1955). He was a pupil of, among others, Clara Schumann and became a noted virtuoso in Europe and America. For many years, he was a professor of piano at the Juilliard School in New York, where he taught many of the finest American pianists of the present generation.

FRIEDMAN, Ignaz. Polish pianist (1882–1948). A famous interpreter of Beethoven, Schumann, and particularly Chopin, he gave more than 2,800 concerts in almost every country of the world. Among his most famous appearances were those in Beethoven trios, with Huberman and Casals. He was a Leschetizky pupil and composed many piano pieces.

FRIJSH, Povla. Danish-American soprano (1885–1960). A pianist in her youth, she went to Paris to study singing and became widely known as a recitalist, appearing with such eminent musicians as Alfred Cortot and Pablo Casals. She made her New York recital debut in

1915 and won the highest esteem of her contemporaries. Her lieder interpretations—from Schubert and Schumann to Poulenc, Milhaud, and contemporary American songs—were admired throughout her American career, in which she was active until 1947.

FRIML, Carl Rudolf. Czech-American composer (1884–). Friml studied at the Prague Conservatory, where one of his teachers was Dvořák. He first went to New York in 1904 with Jan Kubelik, acting as the great violinist's accompanist for five years, and also giving performances as a concert pianist. After returning to his own country for a short time, he settled in America before the first World War. He has written numerous compositions for the piano, violin, and cello, but his greatest success has been in field of light opera.

Friml was the great operetta composer of the 1920s, his twenty-seven musical comedies including *Katinka* (1915), *Rose Marie* (1924), *The Vagabond King* (1925), and *The Three Musketeers* (1928). All were full of good tunes, skillfully orchestrated, and Friml set a pattern for musical plays which endured until the style of *Oklahoma!* ushered in a different type of musical show.

FRISKIN, James. Scottish pianist (1886–). Known widely as a Bach expert, Friskin has been a recitalist of note and a member of the faculty of the Juilliard School of Music in New York.

FRUGONI, Orazio. Swiss-American pianist (1921–). Frugoni began his piano studies when nine years old, was graduated from the Verdi Conservatory in Milan, and received further instruction from Alfredo Casella. In 1945 he won the Prix de Virtuosité at the Geneva Conservatory. In addition to frequent concert and recital appearances in Europe, he played regularly over the Swiss radio. He has resided in the United States since 1947. Besides continuing his yearly European concert tours and making appearances in this country, Frugoni is professor of piano at the Eastman School of Music in Rochester, New York.

FUCHS, Joseph. American violinist (1905–). Joseph Fuchs' career had an early and promising start. He became concertmaster of the Cleve-

land Orchestra at the age of twenty-one, and soon thereafter embarked on a career as a soloist. Fuchs appeared with many major symphony orchestras and was acclaimed everywhere as a virtuoso of the first rank. However, an operation necessitated by a long-neglected childhood injury forced him to give up the violin for four years.

In 1943 he made a remarkable comeback, and was soon recognized as one of the foremost violinists of the United States. After the war he traveled widely in Europe and South America as a soloist with many orchestras and chamber music organizations. Fuchs has constantly furthered the cause of contemporary music, and he has introduced many American and foreign works. He has often appeared in duo performances with his sister, Lillian Fuchs, an accomplished violist.

FUGUE (Latin *fuga,* "flight"). The fugue is the most exacting of all musical forms, but offers great scope for individaul exploitation. Its name indicates the way in which the voices or parts "flee" from each other.

The fugue begins with the so-called exposition, in which there is presented a subject or theme which is introduced by the first voice and serves as the basis for the whole fugue. One after another the remaining voices take up the subject. Thus, if the fugue has five voices, the subject will appear five times in the exposition; if it has two voices, the subject appears only twice. The later voices do not repeat the melody note for note, but enter a fifth higher or a fourth lower. If we take a four-part fugue, calling the voices soprano, contralto, tenor, and bass, and assume that a subject in C begins on *do,* the exposition may be illustrated thus:

Soprano: Subject in C, countersubject......................
Contralto: Subject in G, countersubject..................
Tenor: Subject in C, countersubject...............
Bass: Subject in G, countersubject...........

All voices enter with the subject. Once the first voice has introduced it and it has been taken up by the second voice, the first voice sings a countersubject, with which it continues after the other voices have entered with the subject. When all the voices have sung the subject, the exposition terminates.

The rest of the fugue is not so strictly bound by rules as the exposition. This is usually followed by an "episode," a freer section often based on short motifs derived from the subject or countersubject. Thereafter the subject reappears in a fresh aspect, another episode follows, the subject again, etc. There is no rule limiting the number of episodes or treatments of the subject. This depends entirely on the composer's ability to achieve variety and effective contrasts; to this end he may increase the time value of the notes of the subject (augmentation) or make the time value of the notes smaller (diminution), introduce rhythmic changes, combine the subject with the countersubject, and so on.

Sometimes *stretto* (Italian, "squeezed together") is introduced as an added effect, but this is not obligatory. In this case the entrances follow more sharply on each other's heels, so that before one voice has finished with the subject the second voice breaks in with it. This increase in intensity makes a natural approach to the conclusion, in which the subject is again clearly and distinctly emphasized. If more than one subject is developed one speaks of double, triple, or quadruple fugues.

J. S. Bach is considered the greatest master of fugal composition. His last works (*Musical Offering; The Art of the Fugue*) explore the whole range of contrapuntal construction. Monumental choral fugues can be found in the works of Handel. Beethoven in his later works used fugues for the purpose of dramatic intensification. The fugue has also often been employed as a conclusion for sets of variations.

The other imitative forms are in general based on the same principles as the fugue. The fugato is the most closely allied to the fugue; this is often not an independent composition, however, but a passage in fugal style in a larger, nonfugal work.

FULEIHAN, Anis. American composer and pianist (1903–), born in Cyprus, Fuleihan came to the United States in 1915 and became a pupil of Alberto Jonas in New York. After World War I he extensively toured in the United States and the Middle East. For some years he lived in Cairo, returning to the United States in 1928. He then served on the staff of G. Schirmer for several years.

He was appointed professor of music at Indiana University in 1947, and became director of the Beirut Conservatory in 1953.

Fuleihan has written works for piano (including two concertos), a concerto for theremin and orchestra, string quartets, songs, and choral compositions.

FURIANT. A traditional dance of Bohemia in 3/4 time. It has been used by Czech composers in symphonic works as a scherzo movement, and Smetana used it for one of the best-known sections of his opera, *The Bartered Bride.*

FÜRSCH-MADI, Emmy. French soprano (1847–1894). She made her name in Paris, London, New Orleans, and at the Academy of Music in New York. During the opening season of the Metropolitan Opera in 1883–84, she was a principal singer and was Laura in *La Gioconda* at its American première. Her most famous role was Donna Anna in *Don Giovanni.*

FURTWÄNGLER, Wilhelm. German conductor (1886–1954). The son of a Berlin professor of archaeology, he began studying music when he was eight years old. He composed a piano quintet when he was fifteen and not long afterward conducted an overture of his own composition. For a time he toyed with the idea of becoming a composer, but when he was twenty his talent as a conductor was established

WILHELM FURTWÄNGLER

by a concert at which, besides a work of his own, he presented Bruckner's Ninth Symphony.

From the post of choir conductor at Breslau he went to Zurich in 1906, and there conducted all kinds of music, including *The Merry Widow*. Of these performances he said: "I conducted Lehár's celebrated operetta as seriously as if it had been Wagner's 'Götterdämmerung.'"

After studying under Felix Mottl at Munich, he became court conductor at Mannheim in 1915, and guest conductor at several of the larger German cities. He was appointed to the famous Vienna Tonkünstler Orchestra in 1919, and when Richard Strauss retired from his position as conductor of the Berlin State Opera in 1920, Furtwängler was his natural successor. When Nikisch died in 1922, Furtwängler took over his position as conductor of the Leipzig Gewandhaus and of the Berlin Philharmonic orchestras.

Furtwängler conducted in the United States

Johann Fux, from Fedi's Il parnasso

for the first time in 1925. His sensationally successful debut led to further engagements with the New York Philharmonic Orchestra in 1926 and 1927. Furtwängler's unique position as the leading and most internationally renowned conductor who freely spoke his mind led to severe clashes with the Nazis in 1934, in the course of which he resigned all his posts. In 1935 the Nazi government made concessions and Furtwängler returned to the Berlin Philharmonic Orchestra. This, however, remained what has been called an "uneasy peace." He conducted in Germany all through the second World War, went to Switzerland in 1945, and returned in 1946 as chief conductor of the Berlin and Vienna Philharmonic orchestras. With both orchestras he toured widely and made many recordings.

Furtwängler's particular fondness for the masters of German classical and romantic music found expression in his unsurpassed interpretations of the works of Brahms and Beethoven. He published his penetrating thoughts on music in several monographs (Brahms, Bruckner, and a book on conducting). His compositions include a *Te Deum,* a piano concerto, two symphonies, and chamber music.

FUSCHI, Olegna. American pianist (1934—). Olegna Fuschi graduated in 1958 from the Juilliard School of Music where she was a pupil of Rosina Lhevinne, and she studied with Lillian Steuber in California. She made her New York debut at Town Hall in 1959, and has since had orchestral and recital engagements in the United States, South America, and Europe. In 1958, she received the Josef Lhevinne Memorial Award and the Concert Artists Guild Award, and in the following year, she won the Prix de Jacques Durand in Paris and the first prize of the International Recording Festival.

FUX, Johann Joseph. Austrian composer and organist (1660–1741). He was choirmaster of St. Stephen's Cathedral in Vienna and later of the Austrian court, where he was greatly favored. Of his 405 compositions that survive, most are church music. His opera *Constanza e fortezza* was performed in Prague in 1723, and his *Missa canonica* is considered a masterpiece by scholars. He was one of the great masters of counterpoint and wrote in Latin the famous treatise on that subject, *Gradus ad Parnassum.*

Supposed portrait of Franchino Gafori, attributed to Leonardo da Vinci. Ambrosiana, Milan

GABRIELI, Andrea. Italian organist and composer (1520–1586). He was organist at San Marco in Venice and a prolific composer of instrumental music, motets, and madrigals. Among his pupils were his nephew, Giovanni Gabrieli, and Hans Leo Hassler.

GABRIELI, Giovanni. Italian composer and organist (1557–1612). Like his uncle Andrea Gabrieli, with whom he studied, he was also an organist at San Marco in Venice. Considered the master of the Venetian school, he wrote both vocal and instrumental music, such of it characterized by antiphonal effects and a new exploitation of instrumental color. His later works represented a revolutionary departure from Renaissance style and profoundly affected future music through their influence on Claudio Monteverdi and Heinrich Schütz.

GABRILOWITSCH, Ossip. Russian-American pianist and conductor (1878–1936), born Ossip Gabrilovich. After studying at the St. Petersburg Conservatory with Anton Rubinstein, Liadov, and Glazunov, Gabrilowitsch studied piano with Leschetizky in Vienna. After 1896 he often toured Europe successfully, making his United States debut in 1900. This was followed by many American appearances. At the conclusion of the first World War he came to live in the United States and was named conductor of the Detroit Symphony Orchestra. He was later co-conductor of the Philadelphia Orchestra with Leopold Stokowski. He was the husband of soprano Clara Clemens, Mark Twain's daughter.

GADE, Niels Wilhelm. Danish composer and conductor (1817–1890). The son of an instrument maker, he studied violin, giving his first concert in Copenhagen at sixteen, and later studied composition. His overture *Echoes of Ossian* (1840) was his first major success, and his First Symphony (1841) was performed by Mendelssohn at a Gewandhaus concert in 1843. He later became a friend of Mendelssohn's, conducting Gewandhaus concerts during Mendelssohn's absence from Leipzig and was hired as a replacement for Mendelssohn upon the latter's death. He returned to Denmark at the outbreak of the Schleswig-Holstein war in 1848 and in 1850 became chief conductor of the Copenhagen Musical Society.

GADSKI, Johanna. German soprano (1872–1932). She studied voice with Schroeder-Chaloupka and made her debut in Berlin in 1889. Her American debut was as Elsa in *Lohengrin* with the Damrosch Opera Company in 1895. From 1898–1904 and from 1907–17 she sang with the Metropolitan Opera and was particularly admired for her Brünnhilde and Isolde.

GAFORI, Franchino. Italian theorist (1451–1522). He lived in several north Italian cities before settling at the Sforza court in Milan, where he was also singer and choirmaster at the Duomo, and later founded his own school. Among his numerous and influential writings were *Theorica Musicae* (1492) and *Practica Musicae* (1494).

GALILEI, Vincenzo. Italian composer and writer on music (1520–1591). Father of Galileo Galilei, the astronomer, Galilei was a member of the Florentine Camerata, the group responsible for the beginning of opera. His research on Greek music was of importance for their theories of music, and in 1581 he published his *Dialogue about Ancient and Modern Music*.

GALINDO, Blas. Mexican Indian composer (1910–). He studied with Chávez in Mexico and with Copland at the Berkshire Music Center. He has written ballets, orchestral works, and chamber music.

GALLI-CURCI, Amelita. Italian-born coloratura soprano (1882–). She studied piano, composition, and theory at the Milan Conservatory and became a teacher there. As a singer, however, she taught herself from the records of other great singers. She made her debut in 1909 at the Teatro Costanzi in Rome as Gilda in *Rigoletto,* and the result of her sensational success was a protracted tour of several years in Spain, Russia, and South America. Her Gilda in Chicago in 1916 brought her a standing engagement at the Chicago Opera for five years. In 1920 she went to the Metropolitan Opera, where she sang leading roles for ten years.

The possessor of an exceptionally high voice and of great technical perfection, she was at her best in lyrical parts. She retired from opera in the mid-1930s.

GALLI-MARIÉ, Célestine. French dramatic mezzo-soprano (1840–1905). She made her debut at Strasbourg in 1859 and later created the roles of Mignon (1866) and Carmen (1875).

GALLO, Fortune. Italian-born impresario (1878–). Active in America from 1895, he sponsored bands, ballet, opera, etc., and founded the San Carlo Opera Company (1909).

GALLUS, Jacobus. Slovenian composer (1550–1591) whose real name was Jacob Händl. A prolific writer, he worked as Kapellmeister at Olmütz and later at Prague.

GALOP. A quick dance for couples in 2/4 time, in fashion from 1820 until about 1900. The dance was executed with many variations of steps and hopping movements.

GALUPPI, Baldassare. Italian opera composer (1706–1785). A prolific composer, he was noted for his comic operas and for the development of the ensemble finale.

GAMELAN. The orchestra of Java or Bali, consisting of numerous gongs, bells, a flute, a fiddle, metallophones, xylophones, and drums.

GANZ, Rudolph. American pianist, conductor, and educator (1877–). Rudolph Ganz was born in Switzerland, but has been active on the American musical scene ever since his arrival in the United States in the fall of 1900. He is

Vincenzo Galilei, a detail from Fedi's Il parnasso

AMELITA GALLI-CURCI

RAYA GARBOUSOVA

MARY GARDEN

president emeritus of Chicago Musical College, having served this institution as head of the piano department, as director, and as president from 1934–54. He continues to serve as professor of piano. Ganz was a pupil of Busoni and has appeared widely as pianist and conductor. He was the permanent conductor of the St. Louis Symphony from 1921 to 1927, and has appeared as conductor and soloist with the New York Philharmonic and many other American orchestras. On the occasion of his eightieth birthday in 1957, the Rudolph Ganz Recital Hall was dedicated as one of Chicago's important concert halls.

GARBOUSOVA, Raya. Russian-American cellist (1906–). Born in Tiflis, Raya Garbousova began piano studies in the State Conservatory at the age of nine, and shortly thereafter began to learn the cello. She made several concert tours of Russia in her youth and also performed in major European cities. She came to the United States in 1934 and has since appeared in recitals and as soloist with the New York Philharmonic Orchestra and other leading organizations.

GARCIA, Manuel del Popolo Vicente. Spanish tenor and vocal teacher (1775–1832). Although also known during his lifetime as a composer, Garcia is remembered primarily as an extraordinarily successful singer and teacher. In 1825 he founded an opera troupe which toured the United States and Mexico. Among his pupils were his two daughters, Maria Malibran and Pauline Viardot-Garcia. His son Manuel Patricio Rodriguez Garcia (1805–1906), also a vocal teacher, invented the laryngoscope and was the teacher of Jenny Lind.

GARDEN, Mary. Scottish-born soprano (1877–). She was taken to America by her parents as a child, and lived in Chicopee, Massachusetts, Hartford, Connecticut, and from 1888 in Chicago. She began to learn the violin at six years of age; at twelve she played in a concert, and four years later appeared in amateur Gilbert and Sullivan performances. She went to Paris in 1896 to study singing, and gained her first notable success at the Opéra-Comique in April, 1900, substituting for the leading soprano in the title role of Charpentier's *Louise,* and playing the part for one hundred nights. Subsequently, she undertook engagements in Brussels and London, and created the chief soprano roles in Pierné's *La Fille de Tabarin* (1901), Debussy's *Pelléas et Mélisande* (1902), and Léroux's *La*

Reine Fiamette (1903). Her success in these roles and others, such as Carmen, Thaïs, and Salome, was attributable, for the most part, to her dramatic ability. She became associated with the Chicago Opera Company in 1910 and managed the 1921–22 season. Her voice, though imperfect, had a singular appeal, and her dynamic, imperious personality was unique. In 1952 she wrote (with Louis Biancolli) *Mary Garden's Story,* her autobiography.

GARLAND, Judy. American film star and singer (1922–). She made her stage debut at five, and ten years later had begun a highly successful film career. A nervous breakdown in 1950 threatened her career, but her London Palladium appearance two years later re-established her position. One of her most successful songs was *Over the Rainbow,* which she launched at the age of seventeen in the film *The Wizard of Oz.*

GARNER, Erroll. American jazz pianist (1921–). Garner is regarded as one of the most eminent jazz pianists, in spite of the fact that he cannot read a single note of music. When he was about three years old he played by ear from records, and at the age of seven he had a permanent feature spot on the Pittsburgh radio.

Garner has named Les Brown, Duke Elling-

GIULIO GATTI-CASAZZA

ton, and the late Fats Waller as his favorite musicians. About his musical credo he wrote: "I strive for relaxation all the time. My music must convey a mood. I try to get satisfying chord effects. . . . But above all, I want it to relax the listener and make him feel good. . . . I play just as I feel. I may suddenly find a chord which starts me off, and away I go. I am not in the least concerned about the result."

Garner's style of playing is immediately recognizable and has been characterized as "a relaxed but gay embroidery of the melody, where the right hand wanders hauntingly in the wake of the beat of the left."

Garner is a prolific composer, and has recorded a number of his own works. His recording of his *Play, Piano, Play* received the Grand Prix du Disque as the best jazz record of 1951.

GATTI-CASAZZA, Giulio. Italian impresario (1868–1940). He was general director of the Metropolitan Opera during 1908–35. He brought Arturo Toscanini with him from La Scala, thereby inaugurating a particularly bright chapter in the Metropolitan's history. During his tenure all departments of the house were vastly improved, 110 new works were presented, many old ones were revived, and American operas were for the first time given a hearing.

ERROLL GARNER

GAUDEAMUS IGITUR. An internationally famous students' song. The medieval German melody, by an unknown composer, was given its present form about 1788. The Latin words as sung today were written in 1781 by C. W. Kindleben, who based them partly on a thirteenth-century penitential psalm. Brahms used the tune as a theme in his *Academic Festival Overture.*

Gaudeamus igitur, juvenes dum sumus!
Post jucundam juventutem, post molestam senectutem,
Nos habebit humus.

GAUTHIER, Eva. Canadian soprano (1885–1958). She studied in Canada and at the Paris Conservatory, making her debut at Pavia in 1909. During her later period as a concert singer, she performed many contemporary works and studied Javanese and Malayan folk songs.

GAVOTTE. A dance form. Of French origin, it was mentioned as early as 1588, when it was already a dance in 4/4 *alla breve* time with an upbeat. In suites it was usually placed before or after the sarabande. The gavotte was originally divided into two parts, but later passed through a development similar to the minuet; either two gavottes were joined together, with the first repeated after the second (A-B-A), or a musette was joined to a gavotte in the same fashion (gavotte-musette-gavotte).

GAY, John. English poet and playwright (1685–1732). Gay is probably best known for having written the words of *The Beggar's Opera* to the popular tunes of his day. See *Beggar's Opera, The.*

GEBRAUCHSMUSIK. A term meaning roughly "music for use" applied to a movement started by Paul Hindemith and others in post-World War I Germany. Rather than writing music for the virtuoso performer to play before a paying audience, the composer was to write music which the amateur could perform (in his home or at informal community gatherings). The pieces therefore tended to be relatively short, relatively simple, and for small ensembles.

GEDDA, Nicolai. Swedish tenor (1925–). Gedda received his earliest musical education from his father, a member of the original Don Cossacks Choir and later leader of the choir of the Russian Orthodox Church in Stockholm. He completed his musical studies at the Stockholm Conservatory and made his operatic debut at the Royal Opera in Stockholm in 1953. After various appearances in leading European opera houses, he made his Metropolitan Opera debut in 1957, and since then has been a member of that company. He has concertized in the United States and Europe, has participated in the leading European music festivals, and has made many recordings.

GEIRINGER, Karl. German-born musicologist (1899–). He studied with Guido Adler and Kurt Sachs and has written in German and English on a wide variety of subjects. In 1941 he became a professor at Boston University and in 1955 was elected president of the American Musicological Society.

GEMINIANI, Francesco. Italian violinist and composer (1687–1762). Geminiani studied with Corelli and Alessandro Scarlatti. Among other theoretical works he wrote *The Art of Playing on the Violin* (1730), the first pub-

FRANCESCO GEMINIANI

lished violin method; many of its rules are valid to this day. A leading virtuoso of his time, he concertized in Italy, England, and Ireland. He composed many sonatas and concertos, and other works.

GERHARDT, Elena. German-born mezzo-soprano (1883–1961). Elena Gerhardt received her musical education at Leipzig Conservatory, and made her debut in 1903. Her long, fruitful artistic association with Artur Nikisch began at this time.

She was first heard in London during 1906 and six years later in New York, and her artistry and technique gained for her an international reputation as a singer of lieder. She began to teach at the Leipzig Conservatory in 1929, and in 1934 she held a special class in musical interpretation at the Guildhall School of Music, London. In 1933 she settled there, fulfilling concert engagements and teaching privately. Her autobiography, *Recital,* was published in 1953.

GERMAN, Sir Edward. British composer (1862–1936). In his youth Edward German Jones taught himself the violin while arranging and composing the music for a local band that he had organized. He entered the Royal Academy of Music in 1880, studying organ and violin. After playing the violin in orchestras for about a year he was appointed musical director at the Globe Theatre, London, where he first attracted attention with his incidental music for a production of *Richard III.* The three dances from his second theatrical composition, the music for *Henry VIII* (1892), caught the ear of the public and have continued to be general favorites, rivaled only by his *Nell Gwynn* dances (1900).

GERMAN REQUIEM (*Ein deutsches Requiem*). Composition for soloists, choir, and orchestra, Op. 45, by Brahms, composed 1857–68. The text has no connection with the Latin Requiem Mass; rather than setting the standard liturgical words, Brahms has created his text by piecing together sentences and paragraphs from various sections of the Bible; for example, from Psalms 39 and 84, from Corinthians, etc. It is thought that a direct stimulus of the work was the death of the composer's mother, although he had certainly begun the work before her death in 1865.

A friend related that Brahms carried a large

ELENA GERHARDT

concordance up to his home on a mountain near Zurich, in order to find the right scriptural passages. He sent the first and second parts of the work to Clara Schumann in 1865, with the following message: "If it is not already too late, please do not show the chorus to Joachim—it is the weakest part of the *Requiem.* As the whole thing may well be consumed by flames before you come to Baden, read only the fine words with which it begins. A chorus in F sharp without violins, but accompanied by harp and other fine things. . . . I have made up the text out of Biblical passages. . . . Perhaps you don't like a German text as well as the Latin one? I hope I shall succeed in fusing it into a whole."

The work falls naturally into two large divisions. The first, comprising parts 1–3, is marked by sorrow and lamentation, while the second (parts 4–7) leads the thoughts to the Resurrection and heavenly bliss.

Part 2, a solemn funeral procession in triple meter, is the oldest part of the work. It is based on sketches made in 1854 for a two-piano sonata, other parts of which eventually became the D minor Piano Concerto.

Part 5 is based on an ancient German burial custom, the backward call *(Wiederruf),* according to which a high voice at the graveside sang a psalm, which was supposed to be the last farewell of the departed. German church hymnals contain numerous psalms of this kind.

George Gershwin

(SEPTEMBER 26, 1898 — JULY 11, 1937)

THE second of four children, Brooklyn-born George Gershwin led the life of a typical New York youngster; in his own words, "music never really interested me. I spent most of my time with the boys in the street, skating, and in general making a nuisance of myself." But the arrival in the Gershwin household of a piano originally intended for the use of brother Ira soon aroused the interest of George, much to Ira's relief. In addition to his outdoor activities, he began taking piano lessons, and made astounding progress. By the time he was thirteen, George became a star pupil of an excellent teacher, Charles Hambitzer. He also studied briefly with Ernest Hutcheson, and took composition lessons from Edward Kilenyi, Sr. and Rubin Goldmark. Many years later, when al-

GEORGE GERSHWIN

ready a successful composer, he studied counterpoint with Henry Cowell and Wallingford Riegger.

George's academic education eventually took second place to his music; and he left school in May, 1914, to join the publishing house of Jerome H. Remick & Company, where he became one of Tin Pan Alley's youngest "piano pounders" (the term used for pianists who accompanied singers as they demonstrated the publishers' latest output for prospective performers). George often felt that he was capable of writing better songs than the ones he was helping to demonstrate, a particularly frustrating situation since his own efforts were being turned down by his employers. In 1916, however, his first song, *When You Want 'Em You Can't Get 'Em, When You've Got 'Em You Don't Want 'Em* (with words by Murray Roth) was accepted by a rival publisher, who paid George all of five dollars for it!

During this period, George thought more and more in terms of writing for the theater; and, in fact, managed to sell a song for *The Passing Show of 1916,* for which most of the score had been composed by Sigmund Romberg. The world of the musical theater fascinated him, and he quit the music publishing field to work as a free-lance accompanist. Among his first jobs was that of rehearsal pianist for an elaborate revue, *Miss 1917,* with music by Victor Herbert and Jerome Kern, the latter of whom was Gershwin's great idol. In later years, Gershwin said: "Kern was the first composer who made me conscious that most popular music was of inferior quality and that musical-comedy music was made of better material. I followed Kern's work and studied each song that he composed. I paid him the tribute of frank imitation and many things

I wrote at this period sounded as though Kern had written them himself."

Through this engagement, Gershwin came to the attention of the leading publisher of theater music, Max Dreyfus, who offered him a position as staff composer. Soon Gershwin's songs were being interpolated in various scores by other composers; and on May 26, 1919, *La, La Lucille,* the first Broadway show with an all-Gershwin score, had its première.

In the same year, Gershwin wrote his first great song hit, *Swanee,* with lyrics by Irving Caesar. It was an ideal number for Al Jolson, who sang it to enormous acclaim in a revue called *Sinbad;* a quarter of a century later, *Swanee* was featured in the biographical film *The Jolson Story,* and again became a nationwide hit.

From 1920 until 1924, Gershwin was occupied with turning out songs for five annual editions of *George White's Scandals.* Two lasting hits came out of this series, the joyous *I'll Build a Stairway to Paradise* (1922), and the first important Gershwin ballad, *Somebody Loves Me* (1924).

In 1924 Gershwin, on commission from Paul Whiteman, completed, in a period of three weeks, his first concert work—the world-famous *Rhapsody in Blue* for piano and orchestra. The work was orchestrated by Ferde Grofé, and Gershwin was soloist with Whiteman's orchestra in its première performance at New York's Aeolian Hall on the afternoon of February 12, 1924. Among the many distinguished musicians present at that memorable concert were Jascha Heifetz, Sergei Rachmaninoff, Leopold Godowsky, Walter Damrosch, Ernest Bloch, Willem Mengelberg, Leopold Stokowski, Fritz Kreisler, and Victor Herbert. (Herbert's *Suite of Serenades* also had its première at this concert, just three months prior to the composer's death.) The audience was wildly enthusiastic about *Rhapsody in Blue;* and the critics, with minor exceptions, agreed that here was a fresh and exciting talent with a great future.

Late the following year, Gershwin was again soloist in his second serious work, the *Concerto in F,* commissioned by Walter Damrosch, who conducted the work with the New York Symphony Society at Carnegie Hall on December 3, 1925. Like the *Rhapsody,* it was well received. It was hailed as representing a considerable advance in Gershwin's compositional technique,

George Gershwin conducting

and proved that he was a serious and competent enough musician.

A visit to Paris in 1928 inspired him to write a third orchestral piece, *An American in Paris,* a vivid musical description of the many moods of the City of Light. Walter Damrosch and the New York Symphony Society performed it at Carnegie Hall for a delighted audience in December of that year.

But Gershwin had by no means deserted his first love—the world of the theater. He and his brother Ira had been busily turning out dozens of wonderful songs for the Broadway musicals *Lady, Be Good; Tip Toes; Song of the Flame* (the latter two shows opening on Broadway the same month in which the *Concerto in F* had its première); *Oh, Kay!;* and *Funny Face.* Maurice Ravel, visiting New York during the run of *Funny Face,* saw the show and was quite enchanted with its score.

Constantly in search of new ideas, Gershwin began to weary of the conventional type of musical comedy for which he had been writing songs. In 1930, New York welcomed *Strike Up the Band,* the first of three satirical musicals that represented a great advance musically and lyrically over anything the Gershwins had done in the theater before. The second of these, *Of Thee I Sing,* produced on Broadway in 1931, won the 1932 Pulitzer Prize as the best play of the season, and achieved the longest run any Gershwin show has ever had. The third in the series, *Let 'Em Eat Cake,* a sequel to *Of Thee I Sing,* employing the same principal characters and cast, came in 1933, but did not do well commercially.

It had long been Gershwin's ambition to write an opera. As early as 1926, he had been impressed by DuBose Heyward's novel *Porgy* as a possibility for a libretto. Many commitments prevented him from finding the time to devote to so large an undertaking until 1934, when he began collaboration on the opera with Heyward and with Ira Gershwin, who assisted on many of the lyrics. In October 1935, the Theatre Guild produced *Porgy and Bess,* which ran on Broadway for 124 performances—a modest run by Broadway standards, but astounding by operatic ones. *Porgy and Bess* has since returned to Broadway for longer runs and has toured the world several times to tremendous acclaim.

In 1931 the Gershwins wrote the songs for the Janet Gaynor-Charles Farrell film *Delicious,* significant only because the score contained a section of what was later to be known as the *Second Rhapsody.* This work was given its concert première in January, 1932, by the Boston Symphony Orchestra under Serge Koussevitzky, with Gershwin as soloist.

During the middle 1930s, the Gershwins returned to Hollywood to turn out some of their best songs for the Fred Astaire films *Shall We Dance?* and *A Damsel in Distress.* A third film, *The Goldwyn Follies,* was well under way when George began to complain of severe headaches. An operation disclosed a tumor in his brain. He died in Hollywood at thirty-eight, never knowing that he had just been elected an honorary member of the Academy of Saint Cecilia in Rome—Italy's highest award to foreign composers.

Coming at the peak of his career, Gershwin's death was an incredible shock not only to his family and friends, but also to his countless admirers in many parts of the world. As the outstanding composer of a new and exciting kind of both popular and serious music that combined warmth, humor, and sophistication, he had become a national hero. Occupied as he constantly was with his many activities, he still frequently found time to give constructive advice and encouragement to aspiring young composers, and he had also developed into a highly gifted painter. Gershwin loved nothing more than to play his own music, which he did superbly. Whether on the concert stage, or during intervals between rehearsal sessions of his musical shows, or at private gatherings, his willingness and engaging zest as a performer never failed to convey itself to his equally delighted audiences. The writer John O'Hara expressed the sentiments of all Gershwin devotees when he wrote, "George Gershwin died on July 11, 1937, but I don't have to believe it if I don't want to."

George and Ira Gershwin in Hollywood, 1937

Best-known works:

OPERA

Porgy and Bess (3 acts, 9 scenes) (1935)
  Act: 1: *Summertime; A Woman Is a Sometime Thing; My Man's Gone Now*
  Act 2: *I Got Plenty o' Nuttin'; Bess, You Is My Woman Now; It Ain't Necessarily So; I Loves You, Porgy*
  Act 3: *There's a Boat Dat's Leavin' Soon for New York; Oh, Where's My Bess; I'm on My Way*

ORCHESTRAL

Rhapsody in Blue (piano and orchestra) (1924)
Concerto in F (piano and orchestra) (1925)
An American in Paris (1928)
Second Rhapsody (piano and orchestra) (1932)
Cuban Overture (1932)

PIANO

Three Preludes (1926)
  B flat major
  C sharp minor
  E flat major

MUSICAL COMEDIES

Lady, Be Good (1924)
  Fascinating Rhythm; Oh, Lady Be Good!
Tip-Toes (1925)
  Looking for a Boy; That Certain Feeling
Oh, Kay! (1926)
  Clap Yo' Hands; Do Do Do; Someone To Watch Over Me
Funny Face (1927)
  Funny Face; My One and Only; 'S Wonderful
Strike Up the Band (1927, revised 1930)
  I've Got a Crush on You; Soon; Strike Up the Band!
Show Girl (1929)
  Liza
Girl Crazy (1930)
  Bidin' My Time; But Not for Me; Embraceable You; I Got Rhythm
Of Thee I Sing (1931)
  Of Thee I Sing; Wintergreen for President; Who Cares?

FILM MUSIC

Shall We Dance? (1937)
  They Can't Take That Away from Me
A Damsel in Distress (1937)
  A Foggy Day; Nice Work If You Can Get It
The Goldwyn Follies (1938)
  Love Is Here To Stay; Love Walked In

SONGS

Swanee (1919)
The Man I Love (1924)

GERSHWIN, Ira. American lyricist (1896–). Ira Gershwin, one of the outstanding lyricists on the American scene, wrote the words for most of the songs, musical shows, and motion-picture scores composed by his brother George. This partnership reached its zenith of production in *Porgy and Bess,* and was responsible for the many contributions to the American musical comedy and drama listed in the foregoing biographical sketch on George Gershwin.

Ira Gershwin, however, did not limit his efforts solely to collaboration with his brother. He was also the lyricist for many other musical shows and motion pictures.

GERSTER, Etelka. Hungarian dramatic soprano (1855–1920). She made her debut in Venice in 1876 as Gilda in *Rigoletto* and her American debut at the New York Academy of Music in 1878 as Amina in *La Sonnambula*. She sang in New York again from 1880–83 and in 1887.

GERVILLE-RÉACHE, Jeanne. French dramatic contralto (1882–1915). A pupil of Mme. Viardot-Garcia, she made her debut at the Opéra-Comique in Paris in 1900 and created the role of Geneviève in *Pelléas et Mélisande* (1902). From 1907–10 she sang with the Manhattan Opera Company in New York and from 1911–12 with the Chicago Opera Company.

GESENSWAY, Louis. American composer and violinist (1906–). He became a violinist in the Philadelphia Orchestra in 1926. His system of "color harmony" has won wide respect among contemporaries. Among his compositions are *Suite for Strings and Percussion* (1935), a Flute Concerto, other orchestral works and chamber music, largely using woodwinds.

GESUALDO, Don Carlo. Italian composer (*c.* 1560–1614). Of noble birth, Gesualdo was a skilled lutenist. He composed six books of madrigals, sacred songs for five, six, and seven voices, and *Responsoria* for six voices. Many of his later madrigals are remarkable for their bold treatment of dissonance and high degree of chromaticism. A recent revival of Gesualdo has come about mainly through the efforts of the author, Aldous Huxley, and the arrangements made by Igor Stravinsky of a number of works.

Gesualdo murdered his wife because she

Don Carlo Gesualdo, a detail from a fresco in the Capuchin Monastery in Gesualdo, Italy

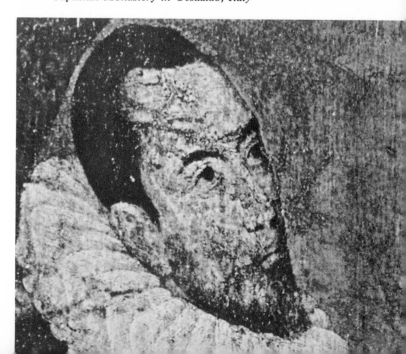

was unfaithful; however, since he was the Prince of Venosa, his punishment was merely a form of religious penance.

GEVAERT, Françoise Auguste. Belgian composer (1828–1908). He spent much time abroad but returned to Brussels to head the Conservatory. He composed twelve operas, three cantatas, other choral works, and songs.

GEWANDHAUS. A famous concert hall in Leipzig. The word means "warehouse," and the name is taken from the old market building where the clothes merchants and tradesmen of Leipzig formerly stored their goods. This was appropriated in 1781 by the then mayor, Karl Wilhelm Müller, and eleven other distinguished

Top: *The old Gewandhaus auditorium.* Bottom: *The present auditorium*

citizens, for their concerts, these twelve worthies forming the first Gewandhaus Orchestra.

The first public concert in Leipzig had been held in a private house in 1743; later, the Three Swans Inn was employed as concert hall. This was succeeded by the Gewandhaus, where concerts were held until 1885, when a modern building, comprising a large hall for orchestral concerts and a smaller one for chamber music, was erected. Under the leadership of Mendelssohn 1835–43, the Gewandhaus concerts were important musical events, and his successors, Gade, Hiller, Rietz, Reinecke, and Nikisch, maintained its reputation as Europe's most distinguished musical institution.

The orchestra, which until 1763 numbered only sixteen players, gradually became (especially under Mendelssohn's leadership) one of the best in Europe. For many years twenty concerts were given during each winter season, in addition to two welfare concerts, one for the orchestra's pension fund and one for people in distressed circumstances.

GHEDINI, Giorgio Federico. Italian composer (1892–). Since 1941 he has been a teacher at the Milan Conservatory; in 1951 he was appointed its director.

Among the older composers he esteems most highly are Andrea and Giovanni Gabrieli, Frescobaldi, Vivaldi, Bach, Mozart, Beethoven, Rossini, and Verdi. Contemporary composers who have influenced him most are Stravinsky and Bartók.

According to Domenico de Paoli, Ghedini's later works (after 1940) show "an always lively musical imagination, an extremely sure technique which never goes out of the way for the sake of audacity, yet is not bound by any preconceived theory, and a critical sense ever on guard against the slightest weakness. Ghedini is not a neo-classicist: he uses neither folk music nor the twelve-tone technique. . . . But he is always on the move, he cannot bear the beaten track."

Best-known works:

Partita (orchestra), composed in 1926; movements —Entrata, Corrente, Siciliana, Bourrée I and II, Giga.

Architettura (orchestra), composed in 1940.

Concerto Spirituale, *De l'Incarnazione del Verbo Divino,* composed in 1943. A composition for two sopranos, women's choir, and small orchestra, after Jacopone da Todi.

A scene from Gianni Schicchi *at the Metropolitan Opera*

Sette Ricercari (for violin, cello, and piano), composed in 1943.

Concerto dell' Albatro (violin, cello, piano, and small orchestra, with a speaking voice), composed 1944. Words from *Moby Dick,* by Herman Melville.

GIANNINI, Dusolina. American soprano (1902–). She studied with Marcella Sembrich, making her concert debut at Carnegie Hall in 1925 and her opera debut two years later in Hamburg. Her first appearance at the Metropolitan Opera was as Aïda in 1936. She created the role of Hester in her brother Vittorio Giannini's opera *The Scarlet Letter* (Hamburg, 1938).

GIANNINI, Vittorio. American composer, conductor, and teacher (1903–). Giannini studied at the Royal Conservatory, Milan; the Juilliard School of Music, New York; and after winning the Grand Prix de Rome, at the American Academy for four years. He has served on the faculties of the Manhattan School of Music, the Juilliard School, and the Curtis Institute.

Among his more important works are the operas *The Taming of the Shrew* and *Beauty and the Beast, Frescobaldiana* for orchestra, Concerto for Trumpet, *Canticle for Christmas,* Prelude and Fugue for Strings, and four symphonies. He is a gifted lyricist; his style closely relates to the mainstream of late Romantic music, especially German, and, to a distinctly lesser degree, contemporary trends in composition.

GIANNI SCHICCHI. One-act comic opera by Puccini; libretto by Giovacchino Forzano. It had its world première in New York in 1918 at the Metropolitan Opera House as part of the trilogy including *Il Tabarro (The Cloak)* and *Suor Angelica (Sister Angelica).* It is based on a true story of a citizen of medieval Florence.

Scene: *The bedroom of wealthy Buoso Donati, recently deceased*

Buoso's relatives are gathered around his bedside, pretending grief. Upset by a rumor that Buoso has left his fortune to a monastery, they search the room for his will and discover that the rumor is correct. Rinuccio (tenor), in love with Gianni Schicchi's daughter Lauretta (soprano), suggests that Schicchi (baritone), a clever Tuscan peasant who has made good in Florence, might be able to think of a ruse to change the will. Schicchi is at first reluctant to help the greedy relatives but is moved by Lauretta's love for Rinuccio. Making sure that no one outside the room knows of Buoso's death, he decides to impersonate the dying man so that he can dictate a new will. While Rinuccio goes in search of the notary, the relatives quarrel about which of them is entitled to which share of the property. Each tries to bribe Schicchi to leave him the best part. When the notary arrives, Schicchi dictates the will, and after leaving a few minor items to each of the relatives, leaves the bulk of Buoso's estate to himself. Since it is a serious criminal offense in Florence to impersonate a dead man, the relatives are powerless to stop Schicchi's

WALTER GIESEKING

action, and they rush in anger from the house, taking with them as many of Buoso's belongings as they can carry. Schicchi then gives his share of Buoso's estate to Lauretta as a dowry, thus enabling the lovers to marry. Rinuccio and Lauretta embrace, and Schicchi turns to ask the audience if he has not indeed put Buoso's money to good use.

GIBBONS, Orlando. English composer (1583–1625). The son and brother of musicians, he was a boy chorister at King's College, Cambridge, and at the age of twenty-one became organist of the Chapel Royal. He was also for the last two years of his life organist of Westminster Abbey.

Gibbons composed much church music (services, anthems, and hymn tunes), madrigals and motets, keyboard and instrumental music. His polyphonic works are among the finest composed by Englishmen; they include the anthems *Hosanna, Lift Up Your Heads* and *O Clap Your Hands.* His "chorus and verse" anthems anticipate those of Blow and Purcell.

Though renowned for his variety of style, "his prevailing tone is grave and solemn, as though with him the madrigal caught some echo from the Church service; he has keen feeling for expressive melody and harmonic beauty of sound" (Sir Henry Hadow).

GIBBS, Terry. American jazz instrumentalist (1924–). Gibbs plays the vibraphone in bop style. He has played with Tommy Dorsey, Buddy Rich, Woody Herman, and Benny Goodman, and has headed his own groups.

GIDEON, Miriam. American composer (1906–). She studied composition with Lazare Saminsky and Roger Sessions and received a master's degree from Columbia University in 1946. She has written chamber music, piano pieces, and orchestral works. In 1948, she was awarded the Bloch Prize. She has been on the faculty of Brooklyn College and of City College.

GIESEKING, Walter Wilhelm. German pianist (1895–1956). His German parents lived on the French Riviera, and Gieseking was born in Lyons. His father, who was a doctor, had been an all-around amateur musician as a student, and the son early showed signs of having inherited his musical talents. He received his first piano lessons when he was four years of age, but for the next ten years studied on his own initiative; he also had violin lessons for five years. He studied at the Hanover Conservatory under Karl Leimer, 1911–15. One of his first achievements was a series of concerts at which he played from memory all Beethoven's thirty-two piano sonatas. His official debut was in Berlin in 1920; he afterward played in all parts of the world.

Gieseking's large hands could play twelfths without difficulty. He did not practice new works at the instrument, but learned them by reading the score—even in railway compartments while traveling.

His interpretations were strictly objective, with precisely accurate tempo, but the expression was poetic and sensitive. Alfredo Casella's words in 1927 remained true for almost thirty years: "I look upon Gieseking as one of the most perfect and arresting figures given to the world of music in recent years."

Gieseking composed many works for the piano, several songs, and a quintet for piano and wind instruments.

He was best known and most admired for his singularly sensitive interpretations of impressionistic music, particularly the works of Debussy. After Gieseking's death in 1956 a critic wrote: "His interpretation of French music was something totally new in the history of piano playing. One would have been liable to believe in witchcraft had one not been aware of the deep humanity of his art. . . . From his hands emerged miracles of sound, musical visions which delighted the ear."

GIGLI, Beniamino. Italian tenor (1890–1957). Even as a small boy Gigli had a sensational singing voice as a member of the church choir in his native town, Recanati. After leaving school he worked in his father's shop for five years, and when his voice changed he took work in the evenings at a photographer's to earn extra money to pay for singing lessons. Ultimately he entered the St. Cecilia Conservatory in competition with twenty-six other applicants.

Gigli had his first real triumph in 1914, when he was twenty-four, at an international competition in Parma at which 105 singers from many countries competed. One of the judges found "top marks" inadequate as a standard for Gigli's performance, and wrote instead: "At last we have found THE tenor!"

In the same year Gigli made his debut as Enzo in Ponchielli's *La Gioconda,* and in 1915 he had a great success as Faust in Boito's *Mephistopheles* in Bologna. He now became known over the whole of Italy, and was invited to sing at all the great opera houses. Toscanini asked him to sing Faust at La Scala, Milan, in 1918.

Gigli toured abroad for the first time in 1920, first as guest artist in Buenos Aires and later at the Metropolitan Opera, New York. The following year he received a permanent engagement at the Metropolitan. His recently deceased countryman Caruso had been the great attraction at the Metropolitan for eighteen consecutive years, and for a long time Gigli had to endure being called "Caruso II." To this he would often reply: "I would rather be called Gigli I than Caruso II."

During his twelve seasons at the Metropolitan he was the highest-paid singer in the world. The operas of Verdi and Puccini were his most popular vehicles.

The economic crisis of the early 1930s forced the Metropolitan to cut salaries, but Gigli would not agree to a reduction and left America after a bitter quarrel with the Metropolitan directors. (He was earning about $100,000 a year at that time.) In the following years he gave concerts all over Europe, and made only casual visits to America. At this time he also played leading parts in several films.

Every year he financed an opera season in Recanati; he also defrayed the expenses of the musical training of many talented young people, and many stories are told of his munificent generosity.

GIGUE. See *Jig.*

GILBERT, Henry Franklin B. American composer (1868–1928). A pupil of MacDowell, Gilbert made use of the folk idiom of America, incorporating Negro, American Indian, and Creole melodies into his works.

GILBERT, Sir William Schwenck. English playwright (1836–1911). Gilbert was the elder partner of Arthur Sullivan and a man of many occupations and wide interests. He was in turn a civil servant, a counselor-at-law, an officer in the militia, a writer of popular verses *(Fun),* drama criticism *(Illustrated Times),* and theatrical burlesques, a dramatist, and a stage producer.

He thus had a wide background on which to draw for his librettos, but these would have been nothing without his special brand of humor, a

BENIAMINO GIGLI

way of turning everything topsy-turvy in order to show up the faults and inconsistencies in both persons and institutions. He was a clever versifier, equally at home in madrigal-style love lyrics or the patter songs of which he was the inventor.

In private life he was often caustic and irascible, but he could be very generous toward those in poverty and distress. Gilbert died in a gallant attempt to save a young woman from drowning. See *Sullivan, Sir Arthur*.

GILELS, Emil. Russian pianist (1916–). Emil Gilels burst upon the American musical scene late in 1955 and immediately established himself as one of the leading pianists of our time. As early as 1932 Artur Rubinstein recognized his phenomenal talent. In an interview in the *Saturday Review,* Rubinstein is quoted as saying: "If he ever comes here I might as well pack my bags and go." Gilels was educated in his native Odessa and at the Moscow Conservatory. In 1936 he won second prize in a contest in Vienna and in 1938 first prize at the renowned Ysaye Competition in Brussels.

He joined the faculty of the Moscow Conservatory and has ever since been one of its leading teachers. Gilels was repeatedly sent abroad by the Soviet Government. His American debut

EMIL GILELS

took place in Philadelphia after which he toured the nation as the first Soviet artist to appear in this country since 1921. Gilels is a pianist of extraordinary power and facility.

GILIBERT, Charles. French baritone (1866–1910). After successes in Brussels, he made his Metropolitan Opera debut in 1900 and sang there until 1903; then spent several seasons at the Manhattan Opera.

GILLESPIE, John Birks ("Dizzy"). American jazz trumpeter (1917–). Dizzy's first instrument was the trombone. In the 1930s he free-lanced with several groups, including Frank Fairfax's and Teddy Hill's. Predominantly influenced by Roy Eldridge at this point, he joined Cab Calloway's band (which at that time included Chu Berry and Cozy Cole) and began to work toward the development of his own original style. It was not until he joined Billy Eckstine's big band in 1944 that the general public began to notice him. By this time he had begun to originate the bop style, along with others. See *Jazz*.

GILLIS, Don. American composer (1912–). Gillis has principally devoted his talents to radio and television musical productions. He produced the Toscanini NBC Symphony Orchestra broadcasts. He has composed symphonies and other instrumental music.

GILLY, Dinh. Algerian-French baritone (1877–1940). Paris trained, he made his debut at the Opéra as Valentin in *Faust*. His Metropolitan debut was in 1910, and he was then engaged by Covent Garden. He was a particular favorite in London, and with his wife, singer Edith Furmedge, opened a singing school there.

GILMAN, Lawrence. American music critic (1878–1939). Self-taught in music, he served for many years as critic of the New York *Herald Tribune* and was author of the program notes for the New York Philharmonic and the Philadelphia Orchestra.

GILMORE, Patrick Sarsfield. American bandmaster (1829–1892). Gilmore was an extremely popular military bandleader active in the United States from about 1850. He organized three monster music festivals, in one of which he led an orchestra of 2,000 and a chorus of 20,000.

He even used cannon to provide strong accents. He claimed to have written *When Johnny Comes Marching Home.*

GINASTERA, Alberto. Argentinian composer (1916–). He resided in New York during 1946 and 1947 as the recipient of a Guggenheim fellowship. His music often has a nationalistic flavor which can be heard in the ballet suites *Panambí* and *Estancia,* and the *Argentinian Concerto* for piano and orchestra. Other works of his are the *Variaciónes Concertantes* for chamber orchestra, *Pampeana* No. 3 *(A Pastoral Symphony),* a string quartet, and the *Creole Faust* Overture.

GIOCONDA, LA. (*The Smiling One*). Opera based on Victor Hugo's play *Angelo, Tyrant of Padua,* by Amilcare Ponchielli, with libretto by Boito (written under the pseudonym of Tobia Gorrio), premièred at La Scala in 1876.

Time: *Seventeenth century*   Place: *Venice*

ACT I

Scene: *Before the Doge's Palace*

A beautiful streetsinger, La Gioconda (soprano), loves Enzo Grimaldi (tenor), a Genoese nobleman who has become a privateer for political reasons. Barnaba (baritone), a spy for the Inquisition, lusts after Gioconda, but she scorns him. In revenge he turns the crowd against her blind mother, La Cieca (contralto). However, the arrival of Alvise Badoero (bass), an official of the Inquisition, and his wife Laura (mezzo-soprano), save the old woman from being stoned. In gratitude La Cieca gives Laura her rosary.

Enzo and Laura had been betrothed, before he was exiled from Genoa, and they still love one another. Barnaba arranges an assignation between them, and then informs Laura's husband. Gioconda overhears the entire plot.

ACT II

Scene: *Enzo's ship*

Enzo and Laura reaffirm their love. Gioconda sneaks on board and is about to stab her rival when she notices her mother's rosary. Immensely moved, she spirits Laura from the ship and warns Enzo of Barnaba's treachery. Enzo sets fire to his ship to prevent Alvise from following Laura.

ACT III

Scene 1: *A room in Alvise's palazzo*

Convinced that Laura has been unfaithful, Alvise forces her to drink poison. He leaves, and Gioconda comes forth from a hiding place and gives Laura a sleeping potion, as a substitute.

Scene 2. *The ballroom of the palazzo*

Alvise is giving a masked ball. As entertainment, a ballet, *The Dance of the Hours,* is presented. Enzo enters, disguised, and attempts to kill Alvise, but is arrested. In despair, Gioconda offers herself to Barnaba if he will save her beloved. Barnaba agrees on condition that Gioconda's mother become his hostage.

ACT IV

Scene: *Gioconda's home on the Giudecca Canal*

Laura and Enzo are reunited and tell Gioconda of their undying gratitude. After they have departed she contemplates suicide. Barnaba appears to claim his reward, but Gioconda kills herself. She dies before Barnaba can tell her that he has just murdered her mother.

Act I of La Gioconda *at the 1956 Florence May Festival*

The last act of The Girl of the Golden West *at its Metropolitan première. In the noose: Enrico Caruso; protecting him: Emmy Destinn; pointing accusingly: Pasquale Amato*

GIOCOSO. Italian, "playful, joking."

GIORDANI, Tommaso. Italian composer (*c.* 1730–1806). His family formed a strolling opera company which traveled through Europe. In his later life he was active primarily in London and Dublin as conductor and composer, becoming an important force in Dublin music circles. He wrote some instrumental music and more than fifty operas, adaptations, and *pasticcios* in both English and Italian.

GIORDANO, Umberto. Italian composer of operas (1867–1948). The son of a workman, he studied music at Foggia and at the Naples Conservatory, and in 1888 composed a short opera *Marina,* which he entered in a competition. The prize was awarded to Mascagni's *Cavalleria Rusticana;* but the publisher (Sonzogno) who had organized the contest liked Giordano's entry and commissioned another opera from him, and from then on Giordano devoted himself to operatic work. Of his ten operas both *Andrea Chénier* (1896) and *Fedora* (1898) remain popular; *Madame Sans-Gêne* (1915) is occasionally revived in Italy.

An exponent of the Mascagni-Leoncavallo school, Giordano liked to use realistic, if theatrical, devices; *Fedora,* for instance, was the first opera in which a bicycle was brought onto the stage.

GIRL OF THE GOLDEN WEST, THE (*La Fanciulla del West*). An opera by Puccini. It had its première at the Metropolitan Opera in 1910. The libretto is set in California at the time of the Gold Rush, and is based on a play by David Belasco. It was revived at the Metropolitan in 1961, with Leontyne Price as Minnie.

GISELLE. Ballet in two acts, with music by Adolphe Adam; the original choreography was by Jean Coralli and Jules Perrot. The scenario, by Théophile Gautier, was based on a German legend recorded by Heine. The ballet, first produced in Paris in 1841, was first seen in London at Her Majesty's Theatre in 1842, and this perfect example of nineteenth-century Romanticism has remained continuously in the repertoire. Famous interpreters of the title role include: Pavlova, Karsavina, Markova, Fonteyn, Ulanova, and most recently, Maximova.

ACT I

In a Rhineland village the peasants are celebrating the wine harvest. Count Albrecht (disguised as Loys) is courting the village maiden Giselle, who returns his love. The jealous Hilarion, a gamekeeper, suspects Loys' identity. During the festivities Giselle, passionately fond of dancing, becomes so excited that her mother warns her of the fate of girls who dance to death before their wedding day: they turn into spirits called Wilis, who dance at night in the forest and lure men to destruction. But Giselle laughs at the prophecy.

The merrymaking is halted by the arrival of the Duke of Courland and his daughter, Princess Bathilde (to whom Albrecht is betrothed). Giselle's charming simplicity attracts Bathilde, and the girls confide to each other that they are betrothed. Hilarion, choosing the moment of his revenge, produces a sword and a cloak which he has found in Loys' cottage and unmasks Albrecht. Overwhelmed by her lover's cruel deception, Giselle becomes distracted. In her madness she stabs herself with Albrecht's sword, and dances until she falls lifeless.

ACT II

In a forest glade a cross marks the grave of Giselle. As midnight strikes, the restless Wilis appear, and at the command of their queen, Myrtha, begin their ghostly revels. They call Giselle from her grave and initiate her in the dance. Hilarion, lost in the woods, is pursued and driven to death in a lake. Then another victim appears—the mourning Albrecht, come to visit Giselle's tomb. The pitiless Queen of the Wilis condemns him to die from exhaustion through dancing. With Giselle he dances without respite, and helped by her encouragement survives till dawn. Then the power of the Wilis ceases, but the loving spirit of Giselle vanishes with the rest of them, and Albrecht is left lamenting.

GIUFFRE, James Peter (Jimmy). American jazz clarinetist and composer (1921–). Giuffre earned his Bachelor of Music degree at North Texas State Teachers' College in 1942 and studied composition with Dr. W. A. Violette in Los Angeles. His instruments are the saxophone and clarinet and he has composed many jazz instrumental selections including *Four Brothers* and *Four Mothers.*

GIULINI, Carlo Maria. Italian conductor (1914–). Giulini studied viola, composition, and conducting at the Saint Cecilia Academy of Rome. After World War II he appeared with the Saint Cecilia Orchestra; a year later he was named conductor of the Rome Radio Orchestra, and in 1950 was appointed music director of the Milan Radio. He made his first concert tour of Europe in 1951. Since 1953 he has conducted operas at La Scala, Milan, and at the Edinburgh, Glyndebourne, Holland, and Aix-en-Provence festivals. He has conducted the Israel Philharmonic Orchestra annually since 1956. In visits to the United States in 1956 and 1958 he was

Ekaterina Maximova in the Bolshoi Ballet's Giselle

guest conductor of the Chicago Symphony Orchestra.

GLANVILLE-HICKS, Peggy. Australian-American composer and critic (1912–). A pupil of Vaughan Williams, Gordon Jacob, Malcolm Sargent, Nadia Boulanger, and Egon Wellesz, Peggy Glanville-Hicks has written several stage works, among them *The Transposed Heads,* based on a novel by Thomas Mann, orchestral works (including *Three Gymnopédies* and *Sinfonia Pacifica*), choral works, film music, chamber music, and songs. Her opera, *Nausicaä,* with a libretto by Robert Graves, was given a highly successful world première at the 1961 Athens Festival. Recently Miss Glanville-Hicks was commissioned by the San Francisco Opera and the Ford Foundation to compose an opera which is to be set to Lawrence Durrell's play, *Sappho.*

GLASS HARMONICA. See *Harmonica (1).*

GLAZER, Frank. American pianist. Glazer has performed as soloist with the Boston Symphony, New York Philharmonic, Chicago, and Cincinnati Symphony orchestras, and in Europe; over radio and television in the United States and Europe; in recitals; and has made recordings.

GLAZUNOV, Alexander. Russian composer (1865–1936). A pupil of Rimsky-Korsakov, he

ALEXANDER GLAZUNOV

was only sixteen years old when he composed his first symphony, which caused a sensation on its first performance in St. Petersburg in 1882. In 1899 Glazunov became professor at the St. Petersburg School of Music, and was later its director. In later years, he produced his own works in Europe and America, but lived most of the time in Paris.

Glazunov was one of the most important and most productive of the younger Russian composers in whose music the language of Tchaikovsky is united with the national character of the new Russian school. His production embraces most types of music except opera, but he composed very little after the first World War and the Russian Revolution.

The Glazunov Quartet, formed in 1919, is recognized as one of Russia's best, and has given a number of concerts abroad.

Best-known works:

BALLET MUSIC

The Seasons, Op. 67 (1901)
Ruses d'Amour, Op. 61 (1899)
Raymonda, Op. 57 (1897)

ORCHESTRAL

Stenka Rasin, Op. 13, symphonic poem (1885)
From the Middle Ages, Op. 79, Suite (1903)
Violin Concerto in A minor, Op. 82 (1904)

GLEE. An eighteenth-century unaccompanied song for male voices, divided into several clearly defined sections, each expressing the mood or emotion of one part of the poem set. In the beginning its style was loosely polyphonic, suggesting that it was a descendant of the madrigal, but in the course of time it developed more in the harmonic style of the part song. The contents are not always as cheerful as the name implies.

In the latter half of the eighteenth century and thereafter, many societies devoted to the composition and performance of the glee were formed. Sir Arthur Sullivan, toward the end of the nineteenth century, made frequent use of a modified form of the glee in his famous comic operas.

GLENN, Evans ("Tyree"). American jazz trombonist (1912–). Glenn has been a member of the Benny Carter, Cab Calloway, Don Redman, and Duke Ellington bands, and has played on radio and television.

GLIÈRE, Reinhold Moritzovitch. Russian composer (1875–1956). Glière studied at the Moscow Conservatory with Taneiev, Arensky, and Ippolitov-Ivanov and was graduated in 1900. From 1920 until his death he was himself professor and leader of the composition class at the Conservatory; among his pupils were Khatchaturian, Miaskovsky, and Prokofiev.

When he was asked which composers have influenced him most, Glière replied: "My teacher Taneiev, Borodin, Rimsky-Korsakov, Bach, Schumann, and Grieg; the Russian people, who have composed wonderful emotional songs; and Rachmaninoff, Scriabin, Miaskovsky."

Glière began composing before the Revolution, but reached the height of his career after it.

The most important of his later works is the Azerbaijan opera *Shakh-Senem,* from a legend (1924, last edited 1934), and the Uzbekistan operas *Gulsara* (from folk motifs collected and written down by the Uzbekistan musicians Tokhtasyn Dsjalilov and Talib Sadykov, 1936), and *Leila and Medjun* (in cooperation with T. Sadykov, 1940).

Glière's music, abounding in clear emotional language and expressive melodies, is true to the realistic traditions of the Tchaikovsky–Rimsky-Korsakov school. These traditions form the basis of Glière's ballets *The Red Poppy* (1926–27, latest edition 1949) and *The Copper Rider* (after Pushkin, 1948–49), which have been successfully performed in Moscow, Leningrad, and other cities in the Soviet Union. *The Red Poppy* has been in the repertoire of nearly all Russian theaters since 1927; it is a realistic drama in which Soviet ideology plays a strong part. His best-known work in the West is the *Ilya Mourometz* Symphony, written in 1909–11.

GLINKA, Michael Ivanovitch. Russian composer (1804–1857). The son of a well-to-do landowner, Glinka was financially independent all his life. As a young man he became seriously ill, and later it was difficult for him to work for long periods. He received an excellent musical education, but always preserved his amateur status. He traveled a great deal, studied in Berlin, formed a friendship with Berlioz, and acquired a thorough knowledge of Italian and Spanish music (he showed his brilliant instrumental knowledge in two colorful orchestral Spanish sketches).

With his two operas *A Life for the Tsar* (1836; since the Revolution known as *Ivan Susanin*) and *Russlan and Ludmila* (1842), Glinka created the national trend in Russian music; Percy Scholes dubbed him "the father of the Russian national school, and one of the founders of the Romantic school and of the Romantic movement." Artistically, Glinka looked toward Western Europe, and his musical language was stamped by contemporary Italian modes of expression. But he tried to write music that would "make his countrymen feel at home," and he used in his operas—especially in the choruses—distinctive melodies which always bear the clear mark of their Russian origin.

Glinka's use of characteristic national musical features was of enormous importance in the evolution of Russian music. His great influence can be seen in the works of "The Five" and in those of Tchaikovsky and Stravinsky. "His works are the main source of Russian music," said Calvocoressi.

Berlioz wrote of Glinka's style of composition: "Glinka's talent is essentially supple and varied. His style has the rare advantage of being able to adapt itself . . . to the exigencies and

REINHOLD GLIÈRE

MICHAEL GLINKA

The celebration of the Glinka Centenary at the Maryinsky Theater during a performance of Russlan and Ludmila *in 1904*

character of the subject treated. Glinka can be simple and even naïve without ever condescending to employ a vulgar phrase. His melodies take unexpected turns, and are built on periods which charm by their very strangeness. He is a great harmonist, and uses the instruments with a care and an acquaintance with their most intimate

The Bolshoi production of Russlan and Ludmila

resources, which make his orchestra one of the most novel and vivacious modern orchestras one can hear."

Glinka's aesthetic views also played a great role outside Russia; Constant Lambert placed him second only to Liszt in historical importance in the nineteenth century. His influence is traceable as late as Stravinsky's *Le Sacre du Printemps* and Debussy's *Iberia*. What may be called French-Russian orchestration—in contrast to the Richard Strauss treatment—is a direct inheritance from Glinka, and it is not too much to say that the Russian ballet, and the whole direction of taste emanating from it, started with *Russlan and Ludmila.*

Best-known works:

OPERAS

A Life for the Tsar (retitled) *Ivan Susanin* in the U.S.S.R.), 4 Acts and Epilogue (1836)
   On the River's Farther Side
   Dances: *Polonaise, Krakoviak, Mazurka, Waltz*
   Susanin's aria: *Now I Am Far from All . . . .*
Russlan and Ludmila, 5 Acts (1842)
   Overture
   Act 2: Farlaf's Rondo: *The Happy Day Is Gone*
          Russlan's aria: *O Say, Ye Fields!*
   Act 3: Persian song: *The Evening Shadows*

ORCHESTRAL

Valse-Fantaisie (1839, revised 1856)
Jota Aragonesa
Kamarinskaya (Fantasia on 2 Russian folk songs)
   Wedding song
   Dance song

GLISSANDO. Derived from the French *glisser,* "to slide." A term indicating the execution of rapid scales by sliding over the keys or strings. In piano-playing the nail of the thumb or that of the middle finger is drawn rapidly across the keys. On the violin, viola, cello, and double bass the glissando is produced by sliding the finger along the string.

GLOCKENSPIEL. A xylophone-like percussion instrument consisting of a series of tuned steel plates which are struck with hammers to produce bell-like notes.

GLUCK, Alma. American soprano (1884–1938). She made her debut at the Metropolitan Opera in 1909 as Sophie in Massenet's *Werther.* Although a favorite with the opera public she gave up opera for the concert stage after three years. In 1914 she married Efrem Zimbalist.

Christoph Gluck

(JULY 2, 1714—NOVEMBER 15, 1787)

GLUCK was born in Weidenwang, a small Bohemian town in a frontier district where the population was half German and half Czech. He was the son of the gamekeeper to Prince Lobkowitz. At twelve, he was sent to a Jesuit school in Bohemia, where he had his first lessons in singing, violin, harpsichord, and organ, and studied the classics. At eighteen, he went to Prague for further study, and also learned the cello.

In 1736, under the protection of Prince Lobkowitz, he moved to Vienna, where he subsequently entered the service of the Italian Prince Melzi, whom he accompanied to Milan, where he was for four years a pupil of the composer Sammartini.

Gluck wrote his first opera, *Artaserse,* in 1741, at the age of twenty-seven. It was followed in quick succession by seven others, all testifying to his complete mastery of the Italian style, to which he felt himself bound for a long time to come.

On a journey with Prince Lobkowitz to London in 1745, he was immediately engaged at the Haymarket Theatre, where he staged two new works, *La Caduta de' giganti* and *Artamene.* The public gave these operas a lukewarm reception, but in London Gluck met Handel and had the opportunity of gaining an insight into his music that had a profound influence in the evolution of Gluck's own style. Handel's judgment of Gluck was harsh. "He knows no more counterpoint," he said, "than my cook."

Gluck joined Mingotti's itinerant opera company for a couple of years, visiting Copenhagen and Christiania (now Oslo), and then, in 1750, settled in Vienna. He was now thirty-five and his reputation as a musician was good, if not brilliant. In 1754 the Empress Maria Theresa was so delighted with his music to *Le Cinesi* that she appointed him conductor of her court orchestra. Gluck thus reached the height of his career overnight, so to speak; in 1756 he was made a papal knight and a member of the nobility.

As conductor of the court orchestra, Gluck studied French *opéra comique,* and this gave him a wider horizon and a more facile skill in musical expression. As the same time, he associated with eminent musicians who greatly influenced his aesthetic beliefs. The aim of his associates was a return from the overblown, florid

Gluck at the Clavier *by J. S. Duplessis.*
Kunsthistorisches Museum, Vienna

A scene from Alceste *at the Metropolitan Opera in 1941 with Marjorie Lawrence in the title role*

Italian style, then in vogue, to the natural simplicity of Greek art, and this became his object. He desired to abandon the unnatural, conventional, and intricate elements of Italian opera (and among these he included both polyphony and coloratura singing), and instead, as he said, "to reduce music to its proper function, that of seconding poetry by enforcing the expression of the sentiment."

His new outlook was expressed in his ballet *Don Juan* in 1761 and his opera *Orfeo ed Euridice* in the following year. Neither was a success, but he persevered in pursuit of his new principles and in his introduction to the opera *Alceste* (1767) he explained his aims for the reform of operatic style: "I resolved to avoid all those abuses which had crept into Italian opera through the mistaken vanity of singers and the unwise compliance of composers, which had rendered it wearisome and ridiculous, instead of being, as it once was, the grandest and most imposing stage of modern times . . . I have therefore been very careful never to interrupt a singer

in the heat of a dialogue in order to introduce a tedious ritornelle, nor to stop him in the middle of a piece either for the purpose of displaying the flexibility of his voice on some favorable vowel, or that the orchestra might give him time to take breath before a long-sustained note . . . I also thought that my chief endeavor should be to attain a grand simplicity, and consequently I have avoided making a parade of difficulties at the cost of clearness."

As neither *Alceste* nor *Paris and Helen* which followed in 1770, was appreciated in Vienna, Gluck decided to realize an old plan— to go to Paris and test the validity of his new ideas there. Parisian opera-goers were already familiar with the somewhat similar music of Lully and Rameau; and, moreover, Gluck, who was wise in the ways of the world, knew he could count on the support of the wife of the Dauphin, the Austrian Princess Marie Antoinette, who had been his pupil.

Gluck's calculations were right. The performance of his new opera *Iphigenia in Aulis* (1774) aroused immense interest in Paris, although approval was not unanimous. A few days after the first performance Marie Antoinette wrote to her sister in Vienna: "We can find nothing else to talk about. You can scarcely imagine what excitement reigns in all minds in regard to this event. . . . Everybody has taken sides, and they attack each other just as if it were a question of religion."

An open feud between supporters and opponents of Gluck was joined. The opposing camp, the champions of the Neapolitan opera, called the Italian composer Piccinni to Paris and commissioned him to compose music to the libretto of the opera *Roland* which Gluck contemplated writing. Piccinni was a capable musician, but his *Roland* was not a success, while Gluck scored a decisive victory for his new style with the operas from his Vienna period and his new compositions *Iphigenia in Tauris* and *Echo and Narcissus* (both 1779). Baron von Grimm, previously a warm admirer of the traditional Italian music, wrote: "I do not know whether this is melody, but perhaps it is something better. When I hear *Iphigenia* I feel that I am listening to Greek tragedy."

A. W. Lock has described the two rival styles: ". . . the one striving merely to please the ear with sensuous melody and to avoid complexity by use of simple harmonic background, and the other emphasizing dramatic expressiveness and the development of the instrumental accompaniment."

Gluck was not moved by a passion for reform, but by aesthetic considerations only. He was self-reliant and shrewd, a wise and cultured man, but his attitude to the problems which occupied him was a little detached—as is shown by his unconcerned composition of works in true Italian style between his reformed operas. A close friend thus described Gluck at this time: "Anyone seeing him in frock coat and wig would hardly have guessed that this was an eminent creative genius. He was not stout, but short and thickset, with a muscular body, round head, and broad face ruddy and pock-marked. His eyes were small, deep-set and bright, and full of expression. . . . A lover of truth, he called a spade a spade, a habit which drove the polished Parisians to despair. He was immune to flattery, except from persons whom he held in high esteem. . . . He was greedy at table, but he never overate or got drunk. He made no secret of his

desire for money, and close scrutiny would reveal a good deal of egotism in him, especially at table, where he always thought that he was privileged to have the tidbits." Ernest Newman wrote that "his personal character shows itself both in his music and in his physical structure. To the last he was a hardy, virile peasant, trained to rough and sturdy habits of life. In his face can be clearly seen those qualities that appear again in his music and in his correspondence: the head is thrown back proudly and confidently, the large and mobile mouth has an air of quick intelligence, and the eyes look straight and fearlessly upon the beholder."

After *Echo and Narcissus* Gluck wrote nothing of note. He retired to Vienna, and there died of apoplexy. Martin Cooper wrote that "at his death Gluck enjoyed an international reputation. The principles for which the last 25 years of his life had been a struggle were already accepted in whole or in part by the rising generation of operatic composers—Mozart, Salieri, Cherubini, and later Spontini and Beethoven. The hallmark of his music is a simple nobility, a natural grandeur more effective than any verbal propaganda in showing up the artificiality and aridity of the *opera seria*."

Alfred Einstein stressed the skill with which Gluck realized the characters of his operas: "Gluck saw into the nature of them all and portrayed them with elemental rhythms, virile austerity and a minimum of purely 'musical' music, straining his untiring energies in the at-

A scene from Iphigenia in Tauris *at the 1962 Salzburg Festival*

The Glyndebourne Festival Theatre, originally a country estate in Sussex

tainment of subtle dramatic interpretation. Strong in purpose, in Vienna and Paris alike he pursued his ideal. How far above the cheap plaster-antiques of his age stand his vivid conceptions and visions of these classic characters! How grand the scenes that Gluck succeeded for the first time in welding into a whole from solo, dance and chorus! What an art was his in accumulation, contrast and peroration! He had the power of creating an inner unity that replaced the unity of conventional form."

Although Gluck wrote nine symphonies, some chamber music, seven French *opéras comiques,* several ballets, and over thirty Italian operas, his seven "reformed" operas are all that matter, and these works have given him a place among the foremost composers in the history of operatic music. Even now, two centuries after the first night of *Orfeo,* that opera is still in the permanent repertoires of most opera houses, a mark of honor shared by no other opera of like age.

GLUCK'S BEST-KNOWN OPERAS

Orfeo ed Euridice, 3 Acts (Italian 1762, French 1774)
    Act 1: *Objêt de mon amour*
    Act 2: *Danse des furies*
            Dance of the Blessed Spirits
    Act 3: *J'ai perdu mon Euridice*

Alceste, 3 Acts (Italian 1767, French 1776)
    Overture
    Divinités du Styx
Paris and Helen, 5 Acts (1770)
    Act 1: *O del mio dolce ardor*
Iphigenia in Aulis, 3 Acts (1774)
    Overture
    Act 2: Ballet . . . . Gavotte
Armide, 5 Acts (1777)
    Act 4: Ballet . . . . Musette
Iphigenia in Tauris, 4 Acts (1779)

GLYNDEBOURNE. A privately owned and operated opera house, founded in 1934 by John Christie and his wife, the singer Audrey Mildmay, at their Glyndebourne (Sussex) home. Opera performances, which rank musically and artistically with the best in Europe, are given every summer under the direction of Carl Ebert and, until his death in 1951, under the conductorship of Fritz Busch.

During its first years Glyndebourne concentrated on the Mozart operas *The Marriage of Figaro, Don Giovanni, Così fan tutte,* and *The Magic Flute,* but later added Verdi's *Macbeth* and Donizetti's *Don Pasquale* to its repertory. The theater was closed during the war. When it reopened, Gluck's *Orfeo,* Richard Strauss' *Ariadne auf Naxos,* Rossini's *La Cenerentola,* and Mozart's *Idomeneo* were gradually added to the repertory. The company has performed at the Edinburgh Festival and lent its house to the English Opera Group for premières of Benjamin Britten's *The Rape of Lucretia* (1946) and *Albert Herring* (1947).

In the past ten years the repertory has been enlarged even further to include such works as *Der Rosenkavalier, Fidelio,* Gluck's *Alceste, Pelléas et Mélisande,* and such rarities as Monteverdi's *Coronation of Poppea* and Rossini's *Comte Ory.* Contemporary operas have been represented with Busoni's *Arlecchino,* Stravinsky's *Rake's Progress,* and Hans Werner Henze's *Elegy for Young Lovers.*

GOBBI, Tito. Italian baritone (1915–). In 1937 Gobbi won an international competition at Vienna, and he made his debut in Rome a year later as the elder Germont in *La Traviata.* He scored a great success both here and in guest appearances as Falstaff at La Scala, Milan, and in *Simon Boccanegra* at Rome immediately afterward. He was engaged by the Stockholm Opera in 1947–48, and afterward made his

Tito Gobbi in Verdi's Simon Boccanegra

BENJAMIN GODARD

debut as a concert singer in London. He has since toured in Africa and the United States. He made his Metropolitan Opera debut in January, 1956, as Scarpia in *Tosca.* Gobbi has appeared in several films, and has made numerous recordings.

GODARD, Benjamin. French composer (1849–1895). Godard was educated at the Brussels Conservatory, where Vieuxtemps was one of his teachers. He wrote compositions of almost every kind—operas, symphonies, chamber music, choral works, songs, etc.—all in a simple, gracious style. He was at one time a very popular composer of the Romantic school, his works showing a marked Schumann influence. Today he is remembered only for his songs *Chanson de Florian* and the popular *Berceuse* from the opera *Jocelyn* (1888).

GOD BLESS AMERICA. A patriotic song with melody and lyrics by Irving Berlin. Originally composed for Berlin's World War I show *Yip Yip, Yaphank,* it was revived for Kate Smith in 1938, and immediately became extremely popular.

LEOPOLD GODOWSKY

GODOWSKY, Leopold. Polish-American pianist and composer (1870–1938). Godowsky was an internationally famous piano virtuoso and a composer especially known for his arrangements and editions of piano masterworks. Sent to Berlin to study at the Hochschule für Musik at the age of fourteen, he left for the United States after a few months. He gave his first recital in Boston in 1884 and embarked on a career of recitals and appearances in the great music centers of the world. He remained in the forefront of piano recitalists until 1930, when illness caused his retirement. He served on the faculty of the New York College of Music in 1890 and in other teaching posts. He wrote numerous original pieces for piano in addition to transcriptions of works by Chopin, Schubert, Strauss, and others.

His son, Leopold Godowsky, Jr., an accomplished violinist, is co-inventor of the Technicolor process of photography and is married to Frances Gershwin, sister of George and Ira Gershwin.

GOD SAVE THE QUEEN (KING). National anthem of the United Kingdom and of the countries of the British Commonwealth. The tune is also used for the national anthems of Switzerland and Liechtenstein.

There have been conflicting opinions about the origin of the melody, and in fact seven different composers have been mentioned as its originator. The strongest claim is that of Dr. John Bull (1562–1628); a tune remarkably similar to *God Save the Queen* (although in the minor) occurs in one of his pieces for harpsichord, and it is known that the composer played this piece before James I.

Words written to the melody, besides the British version, are the Swiss *Rufst du, mein Vaterland* (German) or *O, Monts Indépendants* (French); the former Prussian *Heil dir im Siegerkranz;* and the American *My Country, 'Tis of Thee.*

GOEB, Roger. American composer and conductor (1914–). Following graduation from the University of Wisconsin, Goeb studied composition with Nadia Boulanger and Otto Luening, and received his Ph.D. from the University of Iowa in 1945. He served on the faculties of the Juilliard School and Columbia University, and received Guggenheim Fellowships in 1950 and 1952. He has composed four symphonies, numerous works for string and chamber orchestras, a violin concerto, and chamber music. *Prairie Song* for woodwind quintet is one of his most frequently heard pieces.

GOEHR, Walter. German-born conductor (1903–1960). A pupil of Schoenberg, he conducted many theater and radio orchestras in Germany until 1931, when he went to England as musical director of phonograph record companies and, later, conductor of the BBC Theatre Orchestra. A composer of much music for radio features, films, and stage plays, he was on the teaching staff at Morley College, London.

GOETHE, Johann Wolfgang von. German poet (1749–1832). Although his musical tastes favored the weaker composers of his time, his poems and dramas have been an important stimulus to major composers. Schubert, for example, set 59 Goethe poems, Hugo Wolf 51, and material from *Faust* has been used as the basis of works by, among others, Berlioz, Boito, Gounod, Wagner, Liszt, Mahler, Spohr, Busoni, and Schumann.

GOETSCHIUS, Percy. American music teacher and writer (1853–1943). Goetschius taught musical history and theory in Germany from 1876 to 1890. Then he returned to the United States, teaching at Syracuse University, the New England Conservatory of Music, and the Institute of Musical Art in New York. His books on musical theory (especially on form and counterpoint) were prominent in American music education in the first quarter of the twentieth century.

GOETZ, Hermann. German composer (1840–1876). After studying in Berlin with Hans von Bülow and Hugo Ulrich, he settled in Switzerland as an organist and music teacher. His opera, *The Taming of the Shrew,* was extremely successful and remained popular for many years.

GOGORZA, Emilio Edoardo de. Spanish-American baritone (1874–1949). A concert singer, he also taught voice at the Curtis Institute in Philadelphia. He was married to the famous soprano Emma Eames.

GOLD, Arthur. Canadian pianist (1919–). A member of the well-known piano duo of Gold and Fizdale, he trained at the Juilliard School of Music under Josef and Rosina Lhevinne and made his debut at Town Hall, New York, in 1946. See *Fizdale, Robert.*

GOLDBERG, Szymon. Polish-American violinist (1909–). A child prodigy, at the age of nine Goldberg was heard by Wanda Landowska, who advised his parents to send him to study with Carl Flesch in Berlin. At sixteen he was appointed concertmaster of the Dresden Philharmonic Orchestra. Four years later Wilhelm Furtwängler named him to the same post with the Berlin Philharmonic Orchestra. A few years later he began to devote himself entirely to tours as a recitalist and soloist with orchestras, and to make recordings.

Between 1930 and 1935, he formed and played in a trio with Emanuel Feuermann and Paul Hindemith, and between 1935 and 1940, a duo with Lili Kraus.

In 1948 he made his American recital debut and has since made ten concert tours of the United States. He has been artist-in-residence and one of the directors of the Aspen Festival and also conducts the Netherlands Chamber Orchestra.

GOLDBERG VARIATIONS. Composition for the harpsichord by Johann Sebastian Bach. It derives its name from the harpsichordist Johann Gottlieb Goldberg, a pupil of Bach in the service of Count Kayserling, the Russian envoy in Dresden. Kayserling was a great admirer of Bach and whenever he traveled to Leipzig took Goldberg with him to visit the great master. J. N. Forkel relates in his biography of Bach: "The Count was often ill and plagued by insomnia. At such times Goldberg, who resided at the Count's palace, was called upon to play all through the night. Once when visiting Leipzig the Count remarked to Bach that Goldberg needed some harpsichord pieces of a quiet but at the same time cheerful and lively character as a relaxation and encouragement for him during

SZYMON GOLDBERG

Richard and Edwin Franko Goldman

his sleepless nights. Bach thought he could best fulfill the request with a set of variations. Thereafter the Count always referred to the variations as his own; he never tired of listening to them, and when a sleepless night came he invariably said: 'Dear Goldberg, play one of my variations for me.' "

Bach certainly never received such generous payment for any other composition. Count Kayserling presented him with a golden goblet and 100 louis d'or (about $500).

The variations comprise the longest writing in all the classics for solo instrument. They were printed in 1742 with this description: "Exercise, consisting of an aria with different variations for the two-manual harpsichord, written for the entertainment and pleasure of lovers of this instrument."

The *Aria* is a sarabande which Bach had written some years previously in Anna Magdalena Bach's *Notenbuch*. The melody is a fine example of the elegant, ornamental art of the period. The basis for this gigantic set of variations, however, is not so much the melody of the *Aria* as its harmonic structure. The entire work could be called a series of improvisations on a bass line, improvisations which run their course through free forms employing the customary virtuoso technique of baroque keyboard playing as well as strictest canonic structures.

The *Goldberg Variations* are thus one of the most representative keyboard works of the eighteenth century.

GOLDEN COCKEREL, THE. See *Coq d'Or, Le.*

GOLDMAN, Edwin Franko. American band conductor and composer (1878–1956). He formed the world-famous Goldman Band in 1911 and conducted its many concerts at New York City parks and college campuses until his death. He studied at the National Conservatory of Music and between 1895 and 1905 was cornettist with the Metropolitan Opera orchestra. He composed more than one hundred marches, the best known being *On the Mall,* and other compositions for band and wind instruments. Upon his death, leadership of the Goldman Band was taken over by his son, Richard Franko Goldman.

GOLDMAN, Richard Franko. American band conductor, composer, and critic (1910–). Son of Edwin Franko Goldman, he succeeded, in 1956, to the leadership of the Goldman Band, whose open-air concerts in New York City parks have been a feature of the summer season since 1918. Goldman was graduated from Columbia University and lived in Europe for several years where he studied composition with Nadia Boulanger. In 1937, he became associate conductor of the Goldman Band. He has been visiting professor of music at Princeton and Columbia universities, and was chairman of the Department of Literature and Materials of Music at the Juilliard School. He received the 1961 Alice M. Ditson Award for outstanding contribution to American music.

GOLDMARK, Karl. Austro-Hungarian composer (1830–1915). Trained as a violinist and pianist, he settled in Vienna, where he supported himself by giving piano lessons, and, for a time, by writing music criticism. His first opera, *The Queen of Sheba* (1875), was very successful. He wrote four other operas, several concert overtures, symphonies, instrumental concertos, chamber music, piano pieces, choral works, and songs.

GOLDMARK, Rubin. American teacher and composer (1872–1936). Rubin Goldmark, a nephew of Karl Goldmark, studied with Joseffy,

Dvořák, and others. He was head of the composition department of the Juilliard School of Music from 1924 until his death. Among his pupils were Gershwin, Copland, Jacobi, Giannini, and Berezowsky. He composed numerous orchestral, instrumental, chamber, piano and vocal works.

GOLDOVSKY, Boris. Russian-American opera director, conductor, and pianist (1908–). Goldovsky studied at the Moscow Conservatory and then journeyed to Berlin to work with Artur Schnabel and Leonid Kreutzer. After graduating from the Liszt Academy of Music in Budapest, he came to the United States and studied conducting with Fritz Reiner at the Curtis Institute in Philadelphia. He became head of the opera departments at both the Berkshire Music Center and the New England Conservatory, and he directs the New England Opera Theater in Boston. He has staged many operas at Tanglewood, and he is musical director of the annual festival at Worcester, Massachusetts.

GOLLIWOG'S CAKE-WALK. See *Children's Corner Suite*.

GOLSCHMANN, Vladimir. Russian-American conductor (1893–). Golschmann had most of his training in Paris, where he was born. After some years as violinist with several orchestras, a French music lover sponsored a symphony orchestra for him and Golschmann introduced his own series of concerts which specialized in contemporary music. He rapidly became known through extensive guest appearances with several European orchestras.

Golschmann made his American debut in 1923. In 1931 he was appointed permanent conductor of the St. Louis Symphony Orchestra. He held this post for twenty-five seasons, retiring in 1955 to devote himself to guest appearances with American and European orchestras. He later became conductor of the Tulsa Philharmonic Orchestra.

GOLTZ, Christel. German soprano (1912–). Christel Goltz began her career as a dancer and member of the chorus at provincial German opera houses. In 1936 she was engaged at the Dresden State Opera, and she joined the Vienna State Opera in 1947. She has appeared throughout Europe and the United States in dramatic

Christel Goltz as Salome

parts such as Salome, Elektra, and Marie in *Wozzeck*.

GOMBERT, Nicolas. Flemish composer (*c.* 1490–1556). Almost nothing is known of his early life. He was probably a student of Josquin des Pres and was definitely a musician in the service of Charles V. He wrote masses, motets, and chansons in the Netherlands style. His work is characterized by a preference for uniform texture (within each line, infrequent rests; within each piece, constant number of voices) and for imitation, particularly close imitation.

GOMES, Antonio Carlos. Brazilian composer (1836–1896). During his lifetime his operas were extremely successful, but except in Italy and Brazil, they have since passed out of favor, although the overture to *Il Guarany* (1870) occasionally appears on concert programs.

GONDOLIERS, THE (or *The King of Barataria*). Twelfth of the Gilbert and Sullivan operas. In two acts, it was first performed at the Savoy Theatre, London, on December 7, 1889. Gilbert's satire was here aimed against ideas of what would today be called socialism. Though it has less plot than any other opera in the Gilbert and Sullivan series, and its characterization is superficial, the gaiety and charm of the piece have made it one of the most invigorating of the Savoy operas.

Sullivan wrote the long opening scene, which he probably never equaled for spontaneity and tone color, after a visit to Venice.

Time: *1750*   Place: *Venice*

ACT I

Scene: *The Piazzetta, Venice*

Two handsome gondoliers, Marco (tenor) and Giuseppe (baritone), are choosing their brides from among the *contadine* by a game of blindman's buff. Marco catches Gianetta (soprano), and Giuseppe Tessa (contralto). As they run off to get married a gondola glides up and from it step the Duke of Plaza-Toro (baritone), the Duchess (contralto), their daughter Casilda (soprano), and "His Grace's private drum" Luiz (tenor). The duke sings the famous, candidly autobiographical *In Enterprise of Martial Kind:*

In en-ter prise of mar-tial kind when there was

He explains to Casilda that she was married at the age of six months to the infant son of the King of Barataria, and is now queen, but no one knows the whereabouts of her husband, who was conveyed to Venice as a child by the Grand Inquisitor when the old King of Barataria became a bigoted Wesleyan Method-

Benny Goodman at the height of his fame

ist. Casilda, however, is in love with Luiz. Don Alhambra (bass), the Grand Inquisitor, enters and explains that he entrusted the young prince to a gondolier who had a son of the same age and unfortunately mixed up the two children. The only person who can tell the youths apart is the prince's foster mother Inez (who is Luiz's mother). When Giuseppe and Marco return with their brides, Don Alhambra informs them that one of them is the King of Barataria, and that until the mystery is unraveled they must reign jointly. The gondoliers depart, and the *contadine* wave a tearful farewell.

ACT II

Scene: *A pavilion in the Court of Barataria, three months later*

Marco and Giuseppe are discovered sitting on the royal throne, clad in magnificent robes, cleaning the royal crown and scepter. In a delightful song, *Of Happiness the Very Pith,* Giuseppe describes his day's work as a king. Marco, explaining that the only joy lacking is female society, sings one of the best-loved tunes of the opera, *Take a Pair of Sparkling Eyes:*

Take a pair of spark-ling eyes,— Hid-den

When the *contadine* run in, the kings declare a grand banquet and dance. Tessa and Gianetta are very upset when, on the arrival of Casilda and her family, Don Alhambra informs Marco and Giuseppe that one of them is married to Casilda.

Finally, Inez is found and brought in to solve the mystery. She confesses that when an attempt was made to steal the young prince, she substituted her own son, so that the child she now calls her son, Luiz, is in fact the King of Barataria. Casilda and Luiz are overjoyed, and Marco and Giuseppe and their brides greatly relieved.

GONSALVES, Paul. American jazz saxophonist (1920–). He has been a member of the Count Basie, Dizzy Gillespie, Tommy Dorsey, and Duke Ellington bands.

GOODMAN, Benny. American clarinetist and band-leader (1909–). Goodman could play the clarinet when he was ten years old, and as a young man played with several well-known bands—Ben Pollack's, Phil Napoleon's, Red Nichols', and others. In 1933 he formed his own orchestra in New York and appeared regularly in the radio feature *Let's Dance.*

During this period, with the brothers Fletcher and Horace Henderson working as arrangers for him, he developed a new, more elaborate style of jazz music for larger orchestras.

In January, 1938, Goodman and his band gave at Carnegie Hall the first swing concert to take place in a concert auditorium, and were received with thunderous applause.

An important feature of Goodman's musical activities has been the "band within a band," small select ensembles ranging from a trio to a septet with which Goodman has made many celebrated recordings of chamber jazz.

The Benny Goodman Trio, with Teddy Wilson as pianist and Gene Krupa as drummer, was especially famous. Goodman was one of the first to allow Negroes to play in a white orchestra, and it was he who launched Lionel Hampton, the vibraphone player, on his career.

Rex Harris writes of Goodman's clarinet playing: "In the early days he played with a warm, liquid tone, with a recognizable, though not exaggerated, roughness . . . but when he formed his large swing band in 1934 he began to concentrate on purity of tone and technique."

Goodman—who is considered one of the best clarinet players in the world—does not confine himself to dance music. He has recorded Mozart's Clarinet Quintet with the Budapest Quartet, and in 1938 made an extensive tour of America with two of the finest serious musicians of the time, Joseph Szigeti and Béla Bartók (the latter composed *Contrasts,* a trio for violin, clarinet, and piano, for the three of them). Goodman has also commissioned special works for clarinet by contemporary composers, among them Aaron Copland and Paul Hindemith.

In 1962 he took American jazz to the U.S.S.R. in a six-week tour under the Cultural Exchange plan with his band and vocalist Joya Sherrill, and was enthusiastically acclaimed by Soviet critics.

GOODRICH, Wallace. American conductor and organist (1871–1952). Director of the New England Conservatory until 1942, he was also at various times conductor of many groups including the Boston Opera, and organist for Trinity Church and the Boston Symphony. He composed an Ave Maria for chorus and orchestra.

GOOSSENS, Sir Eugene. British conductor and composer of Belgian origin (1893–1962). He belonged to a distinguished musical family, his grandfather and his father having, like himself, conducted the Carl Rosa Opera Company. His brother Leon is a famous oboist, and his sisters Sidonie and Maria are internationally known harpists. He was taught music from an early

EUGENE GOOSSENS

age, and studied at the Bruges Conservatory and the Royal Academy of Music.

He was first a violinist, but when in 1916 he was given the opportunity of conducting Stanford's opera *The Critic* he was so successful that he decided to adopt conducting as a career. Five years later he founded his own orchestra. In 1923 he came to the United States as conductor of the Rochester Philharmonic; in 1931 he succeeded Fritz Reiner as conductor of the Cincinnati Symphony. From 1947 to 1956 he was conductor of the Sydney Symphony and director of the New South Wales Conservatory in Australia. He was knighted in 1955. His compositions include the operas *Judith* and *Don Juan of Mañara,* ballets, many symphonic works, concertos and chamber music.

LOUIS MOREAU GOTTSCHALK

GLENN GOULD

GOOSSENS, Leon. British oboist (1897–). The brother of the eminent composer and conductor Eugene Goossens, he took his first oboe lesson at the age of ten. He later studied at the Royal College of Music, and at the age of sixteen was invited by Sir Henry Wood to act as temporary first oboe of the Queen's Hall Orchestra, being given the post permanently in the following year. He was badly wounded during the first World War. After a further period as principal oboe with various orchestras, Goossens decided to devote himself entirely to solo playing and teaching.

He was appointed professor of the oboe at the Royal College of Music in 1923 and at the Royal Academy of Music in the following year. He has appeared with the greatest success in most of the principal cities of the world. Numerous works have been written for him, and he is considered by many the greatest of living oboe players.

GOPAK (also *Hopak*). A lively Russian folk dance in 2/4 time.

GORDON, Joseph H. American jazz trumpeter (1928–). Gordon has headed his own group and been a member of the Charlie Parker, Lionel Hampton, Art Blakey, and Don Redman bands.

GORIN, Igor. Russian-American baritone (1908–). Gorin studied at the Vienna Conservatory for five years. Since his arrival in the United States in 1933, Gorin has won national recognition for his radio and television performances and for his appearances as recitalist, as soloist with orchestras, and at leading opera houses through the country. He has appeared annually in the part of Brigham Young in the music drama *All Faces West,* produced especially for him each summer since 1948 in Ogden, Utah. He has portrayed the elder Germont in *La Traviata* and the title role in *Rigoletto* with the NBC-TV Opera, toured Australia and New Zealand in 1959, and has made numerous recordings.

GORITZ, Otto. German baritone (1873–1929). After many successes in Germany, he made his Metropolitan Opera debut as Klingsor in the first *Parsifal* outside Bayreuth. He remained at the Metropolitan until 1924.

GÖTTERDÄMMERUNG. See *Opera* and *Ring of the Nibelung. The.*

GOTTSCHALK, Louis Moreau. American pianist and composer (1829–1869). Gottschalk was the first native-born American musician to achieve international prominence. A child piano prodigy, he went to Paris while in his teens to complete his education. His pianistic success in Paris was followed by triumphs in concert halls of Switzerland and Spain. He won the admiration of such eminent persons as Berlioz, Chopin, and the Queen of Spain. Thereafter he toured extensively in North and South America, where he usually performed nothing but his own compositions at his recitals. His *Cakewalk* (used, with other works, in the ballet score by Hershy Kay) and other piano pieces are still performed occasionally. He wrote two operas and various orchestral pieces. Gottschalk's autobiography, *Notes of a Pianist,* is brilliant and articulate.

GOULD, Glenn. Canadian pianist (1932–), born in Toronto. Gould was educated at the Royal Conservatory of Toronto, and graduated at the age of twelve. He made his first public orchestral appearance with the Toronto Symphony Orchestra when fourteen years old. His American debut, in Washington, D. C., in January, 1955, was acclaimed by critics, as was his New York debut a week later. Gould's worldwide fame was achieved primarily through his unorthodox recording of Bach's *Goldberg Variations.* He has since toured the United States, Europe, and the Soviet Union in recitals and appearances with major symphony orchestras. His dynamic personality has helped to make him one of the most colorful performers of the younger generation.

Gould is also a composer. His first major work, a string quartet, was commissioned and given its première by the Canadian Broadcasting Corporation.

GOULD, Morton. American composer and conductor (1913–). He began to play the piano at the age of four, and at six published his first composition, a waltz entitled *Just Six.* By the time he was twenty-one, he had acquired a varied academic and concert background as well as considerable experience in the fields of theater and radio. He has since achieved distinction as composer, arranger, pianist, and conductor, of both serious and popular music.

Best-known works:

Third Symphony (1947–48), first performed the same year
Fall River Legend (1948), ballet, first performed the same year
Concerto for Orchestra (1944–45), first performed 1945
Spirituals for Orchestra (1940), first performed 1941

Among his most famous works is the *Pavanne,* popular with symphony orchestras and dance bands alike.

GOUNOD, Charles. French composer (1818–1893). Born in Paris, Gounod was given piano lessons by his mother, who was a pianist by profession, and while still at school he made up his mind to be a musician. In 1836 he became a pupil at the Paris Conservatory, among his teachers were Reicha, Halévy, and Lesueur;

MORTON GOULD

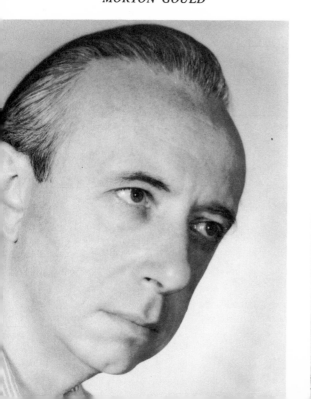

A drawing of Gounod by Dominique Ingres, dated 1859

he won the "petit" Prix de Rome in 1837 and two years later the Grand Prix.

As a center of music, Rome had little to offer at that time. What most impressed Gounod was Palestrina's music and the Sistine Chapel, and owing to his religious turn of mind the solemn, severe, and history-permeated atmosphere of Rome appealed greatly to him.

In 1843 he went to Berlin, and from there to Leipzig to visit Mendelssohn. He wrote in his memoirs: "Mendelssohn received me admirably. I use that word on purpose to indicate the good will with which a great man like him received a youngster who could be no more than a schoolboy to him. Mendelssohn gave himself up entirely to me for the four days I was in Leipzig. He asked me to play my latest works for him, and uttered words of appreciation and encouragement which I valued highly."

On this journey Gounod became acquainted with many of the great German compositions, and this influence gave his music a touch of gravity and depth which distinguished it from most French music of his day. On his return, he became organist and choirmaster at a Paris church. He was much occupied with theological studies and thought seriously of becoming a priest; but he finally decided to persevere as a composer, concentrating on opera. His greatest interest was certainly church music, but he had also a great longing for the theater, and, moreover, dramatic music was in vogue in France.

Gounod's first grand opera (Sapho) was presented to the public as early as 1851, but it was not a great success; he was more successful with a comic-opera version of Molière's Le Médecin Malgré Lui (1858). But Faust, which was played for the first time on March 19, 1859, at the Théâtre Lyrique, was his first real triumph, and the greatest success of his life. At first the public and the press were a little bewildered by the music, which seemed German and Wagnerian, but opinion soon changed, and Faust has since always shared with Carmen first place among French operas.

Gounod's later operas, Romeo and Juliet and Mireille, were also popular, but they did not equal Faust. His other operas are very seldom performed.

Gounod lived in England from 1870 to 1875; among his activities was the creation of what is now the Royal Choral Society. Toward the end of his life, his religious inclinations were manifested in such works as his oratorios La Rédemption, Angeli Custodes, Christus Factus Est, and Mors et Vita.

Although Gounod won his name as a composer of opera, he was in fact no dramatist. The dramatic element in his work is relatively weak. His vivid portrayal of Mephistopheles in Faust is an exception. On the other hand, he had melodious invention and lyric charm of a very rare order. The qualities that make his music live are its happy tunefulness; poetic, often elegant harmony; healthy, easily understood humor; and firm Germanic construction.

In the France of his day he was a pioneer, and his genius was to exercise a great influence on French music, evinced particularly by Massenet, but also even by Bizet and César Franck.

Best-known works:

OPERAS

Faust, 5 Acts (1859)
    Act 1: *Rien! en vain j'interroge*
    Act 2: *La Kermesse*
          Avant de quitter ces lieux
          Le veau d'or
          Valse: *Ainsi que la brise* (arranged for orchestra and, by Liszt, for piano)
    Act 3: *Faites-lui mes aveux (Flower Song)*
          Salut! Demeure chaste et pure (Cavatina)
          Ballade: *Il était un roi de Thule*
          Air des bijoux (Jewel Song)
          Il se fait tard (Love duet)
    Act 4: *Versez vos chagrins (When all was young)*
          Chœur des soldats (Soldiers' chorus)
          Serenade: *Vous qui faites l'endormie*
          Écoute-moi bien (Valentin's death)
    Act 5: Ballet music: *Nuit de Walpurgis*
          Alerte! Alerte! (Trio)

Mireille, 4 Acts (1864)
Overture
    Act 1: Valse: *O légère hirondelle*
    Act 3: *Anges du Paradis*

Romeo and Juliet, 5 Acts (1867)
    Act 1: *Ballade de la reine Mab*
          Valse: *Je veux vivre* (Juliet's Waltz Song)
    Act 2: *Lève-toi* (Romeo's cavatina)
    Act 5: *Salut, tombeau* (Tomb scene)

ORCHESTRAL

Funeral March of a Marionette (originally for piano)
Little Symphony for Wind Instruments, B minor

VOCAL

Ave Maria (Meditation on Bach's Prelude in C major from *The Well-Tempered Clavier;* numerous arrangements)

A scene from an Italian performance of Gounod's Mireille *in 1864*

GRAAS, John. American jazz instrumentalist and arranger (1924–). Graas has a strong classical background, having studied at the Berkshire Music Center and played with the Indianapolis Symphony Orchestra and the Cleveland Orchestra. He has been a member of the Claude Thornhill, Tex Beneke, and Shorty Rogers bands and has successfully adapted the French horn to jazz performances.

GRACE NOTES. Notes, printed in small type, indicating graces or musical ornaments. Their time value is usually not counted, being subtracted from adjacent notes, though large groups of grace notes can sometimes amount to the value of a single note, as in the cadenzas of Chopin and other romantic composers. In such cases the accent of the grace notes is not subject to the strict beat, but remains flexible. The chief grace notes are the acciaccatura, appoggiatura, mordent, turn, and trill. See *Music, Elements of.*

GRADUS AD PARNASSUM. A traditional title (meaning, "steps to Parnassus") for books of graded instruction, the most famous of which are J. J. Fux's book of counterpoint instruction (1725) and Muzio Clementi's piano studies for the development of finger dexterity (1817).

Debussy gives a humorous description of a child's struggles with these studies in *Dr. Gradus ad Parnassum,* No. 1 in the piano suite *Children's Corner.*

GRAF, Herbert. Austrian-born opera stage director (1904–). The son of Max Graf, noted critic, he studied with Guido Adler, receiving a Ph.D. from the University of Vienna in 1925. He was stage director in several European opera houses before coming to the United States in 1934 to produce opera for the Philadelphia Orchestra. He has been stage director at the Metropolitan Opera for many years, and recently acted as director of the Zurich Festival. He has written three books, the latest being *Producing Opera for America.*

GRAFFMAN, Gary. American pianist (1928–). His father, Vladimir Graffman, studied with Auer, Heifetz, and Elman and is a well-known violin teacher. Gary Graffman studied piano with his father, with Mrs. Harold Morris, and, at the Curtis Institute of Music in Philadelphia, with Isabelle Vengerova. He made his debut at the age of eight with the Philadelphia Symphonette under Fabien Sevitzky. In 1947 he appeared with the Philadelphia Orchestra three times. He received the Rachmaninoff Fund Special Award in 1948, the Leventritt Award the following year, and a Fulbright Scholarship in 1950. He has since toured Europe six times, performing as soloist with leading orchestras; toured South

PERCY GRAINGER

America; and has performed in recitals and with such leading orchestras in the United States as the New York Philharmonic, the Cleveland, and NBC Symphony orchestras. He has made a number of recordings.

GRAINGER, Percy Aldridge. Australian-American composer (1882–1961). Long resident in the United States, Grainger, a native of Melbourne, became an American citizen in 1914. A pupil of Busoni and a friend of Grieg, he was as a young man a well-known concert pianist. Grieg wrote about him in his diary: "I had to live to reach the age of 64 to hear Norwegian piano music rendered with so much understanding and genius. In his manner of playing folk dances and songs he breaks new ground. . . ."

Grainger specialized in the playing of Grieg's A minor Piano Concerto, and published an edition of it, with all the composer's own comments. He also helped make better known the music of Delius, Cyril Scott, and others.

As a composer Grainger devoted himself mostly to free adaptations of folk songs. Espe-

cially popular among his works are *Country Gardens* and *Shepherd's Hey*.

GRAMM, Donald. American bass-baritone (1927–). A graduate of Wisconsin College of Music (1941), Wisconsin Conservatory of Music (1944), and the Chicago Musical College, his operatic debut was made with the New York City Opera in 1952. Since then he has appeared with twenty-one major symphony orchestras in the United States, at Tanglewood—annually since 1953—and other festivals, and in various recitals and concerts. He received the Oliver Ditson Scholarship in 1945 and 1946, and the Paul Lavalle Award of the National Federation of Music Clubs in 1947.

GRANADOS Y CAMPINA, Enrique. Spanish composer (1867–1916). Granados received an excellent musical education, partly in Paris, and became an outstanding pianist, touring Europe with the violinist Jacques Thibaud and the cellist Pablo Casals. Their programs included many works composed by Granados on their travels. In Barcelona he founded the Classical Concert Society and a piano school, the Granados Academy.

His compositions include an opera and many piano pieces, the best known of the latter being his Spanish dances (partly based on the old Spanish *tonadillas*) and his *Goyescas,* inspired by Goya's paintings. There are a beauty and an intimate feeling in some of these pieces which remind one of Chopin and Grieg.

Granados rearranged several of the *Goyescas* as an opera with the same title. It was to have been performed in Paris, but the outbreak of war in 1914 prevented this. But *Goyescas* was performed at the Metropolitan Opera, New York, in 1916, and Granados came to America with his wife to attend the première. The performance was a triumph for Granados, and he and his wife boarded the British liner *Sussex* to return to Spain and their six children. The *Sussex* was torpedoed by a German submarine in the English Channel, and both Granados and his wife lost their lives.

Rhythm and harmony were not Granados' strong points; his specialties were rather melody and feeling. As G. Jean-Aubry says, "He created themes with the enduring character of folk tunes—without borrowing from folk music."

Pedro G. Morales sums up: "Granados'

personal touch is instantly recognizable, even in borrowed material. . . . Seldom has the soul of Spain been so vividly revealed in music as in the opening theme of *The Maiden and the Nightingale* (from *Goyescas*), an original tune which has almost a classical nature."

Best-known works:

OPERA

Goyescas, 3 Scenes (1916)
    Intermezzo (arranged for cello and piano)

PIANO

12 Danzas españolas, Op. 37 (1893)
Goyescas (1912)
    1. *Los requiebros*
    3. *El fandango del Candil*
    4. *Quejas o la Maja y el Ruiseñor (The Maiden and the Nightingale)*
10 Tonadillas al estilo antigue
    2. *El majo discheto*

GRANDJANY, Marcel. French harpist, composer, and teacher (1891–). Grandjany began the study of the harp at the age of eight. A student of Henriette Renie, he won the first prize of the Paris Conservatory before his fourteenth birthday. He made his debut with the Lamoureux Orchestra and gave his first harp recital in 1908. He served as organist and choirmaster at the Sacred Heart Basilica in Paris for several years. Since 1938, he has been head of the harp department at the Juilliard School of Music, and, since 1943, has been a member of the staff of the Montreal Conservatory. He has. written songs, piano music, and many selections for the harp.

GRANT PARK. See *Festivals.*

GRAU, Maurice. Opera impresario (1849–1907). From 1898–1903 the Metropolitan Opera was leased to Grau's opera company; previously he had organized other opera companies, sponsored artists' tours, etc.

GRAUN, Karl Heinrich. German composer (1704–1759). Graun began his career as a singer in Brunswick. From 1735 on he was employed by Frederick the Great, first as a singer, then as contractor for the court's Italian opera company, and finally as *Kapellmeister.* He wrote 28 operas, many harpsichord concertos, trio sonatas, etc., but is now probably best re-

ENRIQUE GRANADOS Y CAMPINA

membered for his sacred music. His Passion oratorio *Der Tod Jesus* was a particular favorite in Germany until the beginning of this century and was performed there annually for over a hundred years.

GRAVE. Italian, "heavy," "serious." See *Music, Elements of.*

GRAY, Cecil. British writer on music (1895–1951). He was music critic for the *Daily Telegraph* and the *Manchester Guardian;* wrote books on Gesualdo, Sibelius, Peter Warlock, and others; founded, with Philip Heseltine (Peter Warlock), a music magazine, *The Sackbut;* and was also a composer.

GRAYSON, Kathryn. American soprano and film actress (1924—). Among her successful and popular films have been *It Happened in Brooklyn, The Toast of New Orleans, Show Boat, Lovely to Look At,* and *The Grace Moore Story.*

GRECO, Armando ("Buddy"). American jazz singer, pianist, and arranger (1926—). Greco was associated with Benny Goodman for several years and has since become a popular singer.

GREEN, Benny. American jazz trombonist

(1923–). Green has played with Earl Hines and Charlie Ventura and leads his own quintet. He has made several records with Miles Davis and Sarah Vaughan.

GREEN, Ray. American composer (1909–). A student of Albert Elkus and Ernest Bloch, he has been chief of music for the Veterans Administration and executive secretary of the American Music Center. He has written for orchestra, band, chamber groups, etc.

GREEN, Urban ("Urbie"). American jazz trombonist (1926–). A professional musician at the age of sixteen, he played with Frankie Carle, Gene Krupa, and Woody Herman. He has recorded with Jonah Jones among others.

GREENBERG, Noah. American choral conductor (1919–). Greenberg studied with the composers Arnold Zemachson and Harold Brown. He is the founder and director of the New York Pro Musica, which made its first appearance in 1953. He was a Guggenheim Fellow in 1955 and is choral director at the Mannes College of Music. With W. H. Auden, he edited *An Elizabethan Songbook*.

GREENSLEEVES. A traditional English tune dating probably from the early sixteenth century. Various sets of words have been written to it. The tune is mentioned by Shakespeare and other writers of his time, and Pepys refers to it under the title of *The Blacksmith*. A beautiful flowing melody, it is the basis of Vaughan Williams' *Fantasia on Greensleeves*.

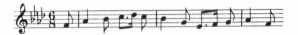

GREGORIAN CHANT. The body of monophonic music codified under the administration of Pope Gregory I (590–604) for use in Roman Catholic Church Masses and services. The term also includes later additions to this fixed repertory of liturgical melodies. See *Modes; Plainsong*.

GRETCHANINOV, Alexander. Russian-born composer (1864–1956). He studied piano in Moscow and composition with Rimsky-Korsakov at the St. Petersburg Conservatory. Leaving Russia in 1925, he took up residence in Paris, and in 1939 he came to the United States.

ALEXANDER GRETCHANINOV

ANDRÉ GRÉTRY

A scene from Grétry's Zémire et Azor (*based on* Beauty *and the* Beast) *at the 1955 Bath Festival*

Gretchaninov composed operas, oratorios, cantatas, symphonies, and chamber music, and was also a master of religious choral writing. He also composed many piano pieces and songs.

Curiously enough the work for which he is most widely known is his earliest and shortest composition, a cradle song which he wrote in his student days.

Best-known works:

SONGS

Berceuse (Cradle song), Op. 1, No. 5 (Lermontov)
The Captive, Op. 20, No. 4 (Pushkin)
Flowers Were Growing (from the opera *Dobrinya Nikitich*, 1903)
My Country, Op. 1, No. 4 (Tolstoy)
Night, Op. 5, No. 2 (Kursky)
Over the Steppe, Op. 5, No. 1 (Plescheev)
Snowflakes, Op. 47, No. 1 (Bryusov)

GRÉTRY, André Érnest Modeste. Belgian-French composer (1741–1813). He studied in Rome, then taught in Geneva, but finally moved to Paris on Voltaire's advice. His first Paris opera, *Le Huron* (1768), made him fashionable at once. This was followed by a long stream of extremely popular operas, some of which are revived from time to time.

Grétry was overwhelmed with marks of honor; streets bore his name, memorials were raised to him, and he received large sums of money from the court and the theaters. The Revolution put an end to this prosperity, but he preserved his popularity, passing the last years of his life at Rousseau's former house at Montmorency, near Paris.

The majority of Grétry's fifty operas are comic plays interspersed with songs. A master of simple tunefulness, he gave great importance to recitative. He had a considerable influence on the future development of comic opera, and on composers like Boieldieu, Auber, and Adam. Grétry is represented today chiefly by ballet music taken from his many theatrical works.

Best-known works:

OPERAS

Zémire et Azor, 4 Acts (1771)
  La Fauvette avec les petits
  Pantomime (or *Air de Ballet*)
Céphale et Procris, 3 Acts (1773)
  Ballet Suite: *Tambourin*
  Gavotte
L'Amant Jaloux, 3 Acts (1778)
  Tandis que tu sommeilles (Serenade)
Richard Coeur de Lion, 3 Acts (1784)
  O Richard, o mon roi

Edvard Grieg

(JUNE 15, 1843—SEPTEMBER 4, 1907)

ONE of Edvard Grieg's ancestors on his father's side (Alexander Grieg) came from Scotland. The composer's mother, a member of a family with long traditions in the Civil Service, was an excellent pianist; and from babyhood Edvard, who was born in Bergen, Norway, was familiar with the music of Mozart and Chopin. Mozart was his mother's favorite composer, a preference which the boy inherited. His musical tastes led his parents to ask the world-famous violin virtuoso Ole Bull (who was related to Grieg on the maternal side), when he visited them in 1858, what he thought of the musical abilities of the fifteen-year-old Edvard. Grieg

EDVARD GRIEG

later wrote: "I cannot imagine what Ole Bull saw in my childish attempts at music. But he became serious and spoke to my parents in a hushed voice. Whatever they discussed, it could not have been to my disadvantage, for suddenly Ole Bull stepped across to me and, shaking me by the shoulders in that special way of his, said, 'You are off to Leipzig, my boy, to become a musician!' "

Grieg studied at the Leipzig Conservatory for four years, with only a six-month break—caused by an inflammation of the lungs which left him with an impaired left lung for the remainder of his life. The next three years he spent partly at home, partly in Denmark, and partly on travels in Germany and Italy. In Norway he was influenced by Ole Bull's nationalism, and his stay in Denmark brought him into contact with Gade and other leading personalities in Scandinavian music. But of far greater significance was his association with his compatriot, the composer Rikard Nordraak, who had visions of a new kind of Norwegian music based on native folk tunes. Nordraak's undaunted spirit and self-assurance were in sharp contrast to Grieg's shy reserve, and his personality as a whole made a tremendous impression on Grieg. Nordraak taught him to have confidence in himself, and made him conscious of his gifts as a composer.

In 1867 Grieg married his cousin Nina Hagerup, a Danish singer "with a wonderful voice and an equally wonderful execution. To me she has become—that much I can safely say—the only true interpreter of my songs."

A letter from Liszt warmly praising his music brought Grieg a scholarship for studies in Italy, and he made Liszt's acquaintance in Rome. Back in Norway once more, Grieg stayed for a time in Christiania (Oslo) and then settled down in Bergen, where he began one of his greatest works, the music for *Peer Gynt,* written at the request of the playwright, Hendryk Ibsen. This occupied him almost two years, and the score was not completed until the autumn of 1875. In 1879, Grieg became known to the European musical world, when he played his Piano Concerto at the Gewandhaus in Leipzig. The Leipzig critics were lukewarm, but the public took the work to their hearts, and it has ever since been one of the most popular compositions of its kind.

Grieg next spent a few years as an orchestra conductor in Bergen, but he found permanent engagements irksome, and embarked on a series of concert tours. As conductor, solo pianist, and accompanist to his wife, he met with success wherever he went. The international publishing house of Peters, in Leipzig, gradually took over most of his works, which soon became known throughout the world.

Grieg often said that the concert tours proved a strain on him—"All physical and mental energy goes down the drain," he complained in one of his letters—and a yearning for the summers at home haunted him on all his travels.

He gave his first concert in London in 1888, and, with his wife, earned immediate popularity, returning in 1889 and 1896 and receiving an honorary Mus.D. from Cambridge. He made his first appearance in Berlin at the beginning of 1889, and toward the end of that year in Paris. In both cities "the apostle of Norwegian musical nationalism" met with immense success.

These tours made Grieg an international figure, and this had its effect on him as a composer. As early as 1877 he had indicated in private letters that his attitude was no longer so one-sidedly national as had been the case earlier. "No pursuit of nationalism! I will try to discard

A portrait of Grieg and his wife Nina by P. S. Kröger. National Museum, Stockholm

that notion and write straight from the core of my being—whether the result happens to be Norwegian or Chinese."

Twelve years later he declared: "In my more recent works I have been striving toward a wider, more universal view of my own individuality, a view which has been influenced by the great trends of our time—that is to say, the cosmopolitan trends."

During the last seven years of his life Grieg had to fight against steadily failing health. The celebration of his sixtieth birthday (1903) ranked among the happier events, and he was still able to compose—a small volume of piano pieces, *Moods,* Op. 73, dating from 1905, brought to a conclusion the series of his numerous lyrical compositions for piano. He had even planned to make a concert tour of England in the autumn of 1907, but his health steadily deteriorated during that summer and he had to enter a hospital at Bergen. Here he died on September 4 of that year, his ashes being placed

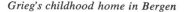

Grieg's childhood home in Bergen

in a cave hewn into the mountainside at his country home, called Troldhaugen, near Bergen.

Grieg was essentially a lyricist and poet in music. He said himself: "By painting in music Norwegian scenery, the life of the Norwegian people, Norwegian history, and Norwegian folk poems, I believe I am really able to achieve something."

And elsewhere: "Great musicians like Bach and Beethoven have built churches and temples in loftier regions. I wanted—as Ibsen put it in his last dramas—to build dwellings for people where they may feel at home and be happy."

Like Chopin and Schumann, he found his most natural form of expression not in works of large-scale construction, but in those of more modest dimensions filled with an atmosphere of intimate feeling.

Grieg composed as many as 150 songs, and indeed in all his music he is a singer creating enchanting melodies, patterned on the folk songs and dances of his native land, but bearing some quality which is his alone. Lawrence Gilman wrote in his analysis of Grieg's music: "Grieg has individuality—individuality that is seizing and indubitable. That, one feels, is his distinguishing possession. His accent is unmistakable. His speech may sway one, or it may not; but always the voice is the voice of Grieg. . . . Grieg is thrice-admirable in this: he wears no one's mantle: he borrows no man's speech."

Grieg with the young Percy Grainger, who became one of the foremost interpreters of his compositions

Grieg's grave at Troldhaugen, his country home

GRIEG'S BEST-KNOWN WORKS

INCIDENTAL MUSIC

Sigurd Jorsalfar (1872) (play by Björnson)
　The Norse People (*Norrönafolktet*) (male chorus)
　Homage March (orchestra)
Peer Gynt (1874–75) (play by Ibsen)

ORCHESTRAL

Piano Concerto, A minor, Op. 16 (1868)
Peer Gynt Suite No. 1, Op. 46 (1888)
Peer Gynt Suite No. 2, Op. 55 (1891)
(4) Norwegian Dances, Op. 35 (1881)
(4) Symphonic Dances, Op. 64 (1898)
The Elegaic Melodies, Op. 34 (1880–81)
Holberg Suite, Op. 40 (strings) (1884)
(2) Norwegian Melodies, Op. 53
Lyric Suite, Op. 54 (1891)

CHAMBER MUSIC

String Quartet, G minor, Op. 27
　Romance
Sonatas (violin and piano)
　No. 1, F major, Op. 8 (1865)
　No. 2, G major, Op. 13 (1867)
　No. 3, C minor, Op. 45 (1887)
Sonata (cello and piano), A minor, Op. 36

PIANO

Pictures of Folk Life, Op. 19 (1872)
Bridal Procession
Ballade, G minor, Op. 24 (1875)
Lyric Pieces (10 Books)

A scene from a Norwegian production of Peer Gynt

Grieg's house at Troldhaugen

Piano Concerto in A Minor, Op. 16

This was composed in the summer of 1868 during a holiday in Denmark, and was performed for the first time on April 3, 1869, in Copenhagen. The work was dedicated to the Norwegian pianist and composer Edmund Neupert, who was the soloist at the first performance.

Of his visit to Liszt in Rome during the spring of 1870, Grieg wrote: "Fortunately I had just received the manuscript of my concerto from Leipzig, and was thus able to take it with me. . . . I wondered whether he [Liszt] would really play my concerto straight off. I considered it an impossibility. Liszt took a different view. When he asked, 'Would you like to play it?' I hastened to tell him that I could not, as I had never practiced it. Liszt then picked up the manuscript, walked across to the piano, and, with his characteristic smile, said: 'Well then, I will show you that I cannot play it either.' And with this he started playing. . . .

"In the very last bars where the first note of the theme, G sharp, is changed to G in the orchestra . . . he suddenly stopped short, rose to his full height, left the piano and, with giant strides and one arm raised above his head, marched the whole length of the huge monastery hall, virtually roaring forth the theme. On reaching the above-mentioned G, he extended his arm in the imperious manner of a Caesar, and shouted: 'G, G, not G sharp! Terrific! That is as genuine as Swedish punch!'

"When it was all over, he said to me with strange intensity of feeling, as he handed me the book: 'Just you carry on as you have started; I assure you, you have the wherewithal for it; and don't allow yourself to become discouraged!' "

The concerto has always aroused either the wildest enthusiasm or the most damning criticism. Cherbuliez has drawn attention to its actual musical merits: "Grieg's concerto is outstanding above all because of its melodious and rhythmic independence, a quality which was achieved by the use of Norwegian folk music, especially in the last movement. . . . It has the advantage of concentrated thematic construction. In the first movement a certain relationship to the first movement of Schumann's Piano Concerto cannot be denied. But . . . the composition shows an imaginative quality arising from the abundance of secondary themes."

The movements are:

I. *Allegro molto moderato. Animato.*

II. *Adagio.*

III. *Allegro moderato molto e marcato.*

GRIFFES, Charles Tomlinson. American composer (1884–1920). He studied with Humperdinck and others in Berlin with the intention of becoming a concert pianist. A chance overhearing of Ravel's *Jeux d'eau* changed his direction toward composition. He returned to the United States in 1907 and supported himself by teaching at a boys' school while continuing to compose. Although German-trained, he was influenced by the new music from the French and Russian schools as well as by Oriental music. He composed piano music, songs, several orchestral works, and a few stage works. One of the most talented American composers of his period, he began to receive recognition shortly before his early death.

Best-known works:

ORCHESTRA

The Pleasure Dome of Kubla Khan (Coleridge) (1920)
Poem for Flute and Orchestra (1918)

PIANO

Four Roman Sketches, Op. 7 (1915–16)
   The White Peacock (also for orchestra)
   Nightfall
   The Fountain of Acquà Paolo
   Clouds (also for orchestra)
Sonata

GRISI, Giuditta. Italian mezzo-soprano (1805–

CHARLES TOMLINSON GRIFFES

Giuditta Grisi and the tenor Carradori in Pacini's opera, Ivanhoe

1840). She made her debut in Vienna in 1823 and later sang in Italy and in Paris at the Théâtre Italien under Rossini's management. Bellini wrote the part of Romeo in *I Capuleti ed i Montecchi* (1830) for her (her sister, Giulia, sang Juliet).

GRISI, Giulia. Italian soprano (1811–1869). After singing in Italy for several years, she made her Parisian debut in the title role of Rossini's *Semiramide* in 1832 at the Théâtre Italien. A phenomenal success, she continued to sing there and in London, retiring only in 1861. Bellini wrote the role of Juliet in *I Capuleti ed i Montecchi* (1830) for her. She often sang with the great tenor, Mario (whom she later married). The blending of their two voices—which, judging from contemporary accounts must have been among the greatest in an age noted for fabulous voices—inspired Heine to write of their singing, "the rose is the nightingale among flowers, the nightingale the rose among birds."

GRIST, Reri. American soprano. While a student she won the Marian Anderson, Queens College Orchestra Society, YMHA Young Artists, Sullivan, and Blanche Thebom awards. She was a soloist in churches, and in Bach's *Magnificat* at the Berkshire Festival. After ap-

Giulia Grisi, center, Giuditta Pasta, and the tenor Donzelli in Norma

pearances in musical theater and on television, she performed with the New York City, Santa Fe, and Cologne Opera companies. She was soloist in Mahler's Symphony No. 4, performed and recorded by the New York Philharmonic, Leonard Bernstein conducting. Igor Stravinsky chose her for the title role of his *Le Rossignol (The Nightingale),* which he conducted for the Washington Opera Society in 1960.

GROFÉ, Ferde. American composer and conductor (1892–). Grofé received his earliest musical education from his mother, and from his uncle, Julius Bierlich, and his grandfather, Bernhardt Bierlich, respectively concertmaster and first cellist in the Los Angeles Symphony Orchestra. He also studied with Homer Gunn and Herman Wasserman and received the degree of Mus.D. at Illinois Wesleyan University in 1946. A conductor of radio orchestras, he also appeared as guest conductor at the Hollywood Bowl, Carnegie Hall concerts, Robin Hood Dell, and Lewisohn Stadium. He is perhaps best known for his orchestral works, including *The Grand Canyon Suite, Mississippi Suite,* and *Hollywood Suite.*

GROSSMAN, Herbert. American conductor (1926–). Grossman was a boy soprano until his voice changed. He studied piano and trombone, and with Karol Rathaus and Curt Sachs at Queens College, and with Serge Koussevitzky, Leonard Bernstein, and Boris Goldovsky at Tanglewood. From 1947 to 1952 he was associate conductor of the Queens Choral Society. He joined the NBC Opera in 1949 and became full conductor with that company in 1956, conducting *The Marriage of Figaro* and *Madame Butterfly* on tour of the United States. He has conducted the New York City Opera, the Baltimore Symphony Orchestra, and several other opera and symphonic groups, and recorded with the Vienna Symphony Orchestra.

GROVE, Sir George. English writer on music (1820–1900). Known principally for his *Dictionary of Music and Musicians,* published in 1879–89 in four volumes, he began writing on music by contributing program notes for the Crystal Palace concerts (1856–96). He discovered (with Sir Arthur Sullivan) many unknown Schubert manuscripts, including the *Rosamunde* music, and was director of the Royal College of Music from its formation in 1882 until 1894. The fifth edition of Grove's *Dictionary,* published in 1954 in nine volumes, was edited by Eric Blom.

GRUEN, John. American composer and critic (1926–). Gruen studied composition in Milan and orchestration with Virgil Thomson in New York. He is known primarily as a composer of art songs, including *13 Ways of Looking at a Blackbird* (Wallace Stevens), *Pomes Penyeach* (James Joyce), and *Seven by cummings* (e.e. cummings), which are recorded. In 1959 he began concert reviewing for the New York *Herald Tribune.*

GRUENBERG, Louis. Russian-American composer and pianist (1884). He began his career in music as a pianist, and studied piano and composition with Busoni. He made his debut with the Berlin Philharmonic Orchestra in 1912. As a composer, he has been much influenced by jazz; this is reflected in his opera *The Emperor Jones* and in *Jazzberries,* a work for piano. His Violin Concerto is occasionally performed.

GRUMIAUX, Arthur. Belgian violinist (1921–). After appearances as a child prodigy in his native Belgium, Grumiaux was educated at the Conservatory of Charleroi. He subsequently attended the Brussels Conservatory, and also studied with Alfred Dubois and Georges Enesco. While still a student, he won the Prix Vieuxtemps and the Belgian Competition.

Grumiaux's professional career was interrupted by World War II, after which he emerged as one of the leading European soloists, playing with major symphony orchestras all over the Continent. He was invited to give recitals in the United States in 1952 and again in 1953.

FRANK GUARRERA

A violin by Giuseppe Bartolomeo Guarneri

GUADAGNINI. Family of famous violin-makers of Piacenza, Italy. Lorenzo (1695–1745), followed the examples of Stradivarius; his son Giovanni Battista (1711–1786) made instruments that are considered the best of the family's. He worked in Milan, Parma, and Turin. His descendents continued the tradition, although never so well, until the last of the family, Paolo, died in an Italian ship torpedoed in 1942.

GUARNERI. Italian family of violin-makers. The founder was Andrea (*c.* 1625–1698), a fellow pupil, with Stradivari, of Nicolo Amati. He worked at Cremona. His elder son, Pietro Giovanni (1655–1720), settled in Mantua and produced some magnificent instruments. Andrea's younger son, Giuseppe Giovanni Batista (1666–*c.* 1740), took over his father's workshop at Cremona. Giuseppe's son, Pietro (1695–1762), settled in Venice. The great master of the family was Giuseppe Bartolomeo (1698–1744), another son of Giuseppe Giovanni Batista. He was known as Giuseppe del Gesù, from the initials I.H.S. placed after his name on his labels. After Stradivari's instruments, his are the finest voilins for perfection of tone, though their form is less perfectly symmetrical and is infinitely varied. Paganini's violin was made by Giuseppe del Gesù.

GUARNIERI, Camargo. Brazilian composer and conductor (1907–). Next to his prolific colleague Villa-Lobos, Guarnieri is probably the most important Brazilian composer. He received his education in São Paulo and Paris. In 1940 he was appointed conductor of the Philharmonic Society and teacher at the São Paulo Conservatory. He has traveled widely and visited the United States in 1942, 1946, and 1947, conducting his own compositions. He is a founder-member of the Brazilian Academy of Music.

Guarnieri's works include several symphonies, smaller pieces for orchestra, two piano concertos, and numerous songs. His music is strongly influenced by Brazilian folklore.

GUARRERA, Frank. American baritone (1924–). After extensive studies at the Curtis Institute of Music, Guarrera made his operatic debut at the New York City Opera in the fall of 1947. Toscanini heard him sing in the preliminaries of the Metropolitan Auditions of the Air and engaged him to sing at the Boito Festival at La Scala. After his initial success (in Boito's *Nerone*), he stayed at La Scala to sing other baritone parts before returning to the United States to sign a contract with the Metropolitan Opera in December, 1948.

GUEDEN, Hilde. Austrian soprano (1917–). Hilde Gueden began her career as a singer of Viennese operettas, and won immediate success in *Goodbye, Goodbye*. When the Germans invaded Austria in 1938, she went to Switzerland and sang for two years at the Zurich Opera. Engagements in Munich and Rome followed. After the war, she sang at the Salzburg Festival, the Vienna State Opera, La Scala, and at festivals in Scotland, Holland, and England. In 1950 she was engaged to sing at the Metropolitan Opera in New York, and she remained on the roster of that institution for several years.

Hilde Gueden has been heard in a variety of modern operas. She has sung the leading female roles in Stravinsky's *The Rake's Progress* and in Blacher's *Romeo and Juliet*. She is primarily known, however, for her exquisite interpretations of Mozart and Verdi.

GUGGENHEIMER, Mrs. Charles S. American impresario (1881–). Mrs. Guggenheimer, with the assistance of Mrs. Arnold Volpe, founded the summer concert series at Lewisohn Stadium,

HILDE GUEDEN

New York City, in June, 1918. Affectionately known as "Minnie" by thousands of concertgoers, she has managed the concerts ever since with unusual dedication and flair.

GUI, Vittorio. Italian conductor (1885–). Having studied at the Liceo de Santa Cecilia, he made his first public apeparance at the age of twenty-two, when he conducted Ponchielli's *La Gioconda* at the Adriano Theater in Rome. He later conducted opera in Naples and Milan, and in 1928 became director of the Orchestra Stabile in Florence.

Gui conducted at the Italian season at Covent Garden in 1938–39, and had a great success at the Edinburgh Festival in 1948–49. He broadcast a series of twelve concerts with the BBC Symphony Orchestra in 1950.

He has won great respect for his sterling musicianship and imaginative interpretations, and for the precision and sparkle he obtains from an orchestra, especially in Mozart operas.

Gui has composed chamber music and cantatas, and has published several volumes of critical essays.

Yvette Guilbert by Toulouse-Lautrec

tive interpretations of folk songs. She made her American debut in 1896.

Guilbert's inquisitive mind, and keen artistic intuition, led her to discover many medieval songs and street cries, which, when sung in her inimitable manner, became extremely popular. One of her famous numbers was *La Fiacre,* which is well known today in Charles Trenet's rendition. Guilbert also made recordings (some of which are still in print), and acted in films. She wrote a delightful autobiography entitled, *Chanson de ma vie.*

GUION, David Wendel Fentress. American composer (1895–). He studied the piano in Vienna for three years, returning to the United States in 1915, when he published his first composition. As a composer Guion is entirely self-taught.

Guion is probably best known for his popular concert arrangement of *Home on the Range,* but he has also composed a great number of songs of the same type. He has been termed America's foremost authority on the folk music of the western and southern United States.

Guido d'Arezzo, from a twelfth-century manuscript

GUIDO D'AREZZO. Italian teacher and musical theorist (*c.* 990–1050). A Benedictine monk, Guido is celebrated for his popularization (and possibly invention) of notation reform. He developed the nomenclature *Ut, Re, Mi, Fa, Sol, La,* for the major hexachord (the first six notes of the major scale) from the first syllables of a then popular hymn, and he developed the four-line staff. He also invented the Guidonian Hand, a memory aid for singers.

GUILBERT, Yvette. French diseuse and folk-song singer (1867–1944). She made her debut as an actress in 1885 and as a café singer in 1890, and later became known for her distinc-

Guitar Course

THIS short course aims to teach the student to play from music a simple tune on the guitar, and to use a selection of chords. The student must, of course, be familiar with music notation. See *Music, Elements of*.

TUNING

If you have a piano, it is easy to tune a guitar. On the keyboard in the figure below, the notes have been marked which correspond to those produced by open strings on the guitar.

The same six notes are here written in standard musical notation:

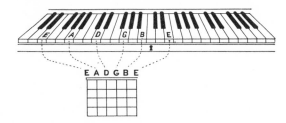

For simplification, guitar music is written an octave higher than it actually sounds, thus covering the full range in one clef. For the guitar, therefore, the six open string notes are written as follows:

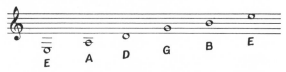

The guitar may also be tuned with the help of a pitch pipe with six notes, each corresponding to one of the open strings of the guitar.

A third method is as follows: Tune the E string (the thickest) by some other instrument; then press the string against the fifth fret, and tune the A string to the note thus produced. The other strings may be tuned

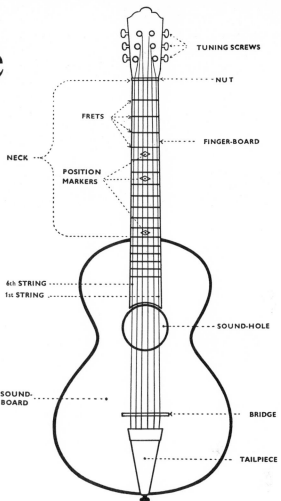

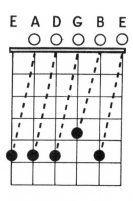

similarly, with the exception of the B string which should be tuned to the note produced by the G string pressed against the fourth fret.

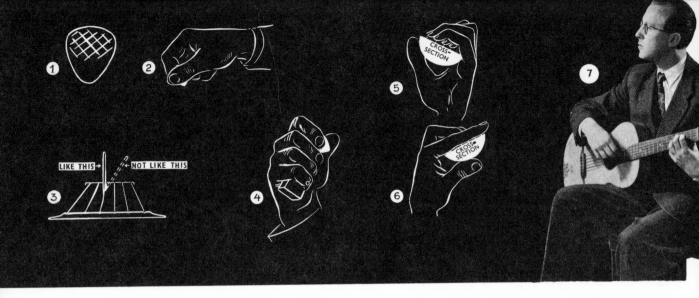

1. *Plectrum.*
2. *Plectrum held between the thumb and the index and middle fingers of the right hand.*
3. *Plectrum must be held perpendicular to the strings.*
4. *The right hand must be closed loosely enough to leave room for a matchbox.*
5. & 6. *How the fingers of the left hand grip the neck.*
7. *How to hold the guitar.*

PLAYING POSITION

The guitar is usually played in a sitting position. The chair must not be too high, because the guitar rests on the lap and a high chair will prove uncomfortable since the instrument will have a tendency to slide forward. This disadvantage can, however, be offset by resting one foot on a small stool.

The waist of the guitar is placed on the right thigh, the right forearm resting over the edge, just above the tailpiece, so that the guitar is pressed against the body. *No support should be given with the left hand.* The neck of the instrument should be horizontal or point slightly upward.

THE PLECTRUM

The plectrum should preferably be of tortoise shell, but one of celluloid can be used. It must not be too thick, yet not so thin as to be too pliable; a reasonably thick plectrum gives a richer tone. Neither should it be too pointed. Make a few scratches with a sharp knife, lengthwise and crosswise, to make the plectrum easier to hold. Be sure that there are no sharp edges near the point; smooth them off with a fine file. The plectrum may then be polished, if desired, by rubbing it against a piece of soft unpainted wood; this treatment makes it slide more smoothly over the strings.

RIGHT HAND

Hold the plectrum in the right hand between the thumb and the index and middle fingers, as indicated in figure 2. It must not protrude too far—it should, in fact, be hardly visible. Do not hold it too firmly, but try to let it roll on the fingertips, as it were. It should be twisted a little, but the plane of the plectrum should remain perpendicular to the strings (see figure 3). The plectrum must not penetrate too deeply between the strings, but should just brush them.

The wrist should be slightly bent to allow the hand to swing over the strings. The movement must not come from the elbow, and the forearm must remain stationary. The remaining fingers of the hand should also be bent inward, but not so far that they are pressed against the palm. Holding a matchbox in the hand when practicing (figure 4) helps to produce the correct position of the hand. The plectrum should strike the strings about six inches from the bridge: the nearer to the bridge, the sharper the tone. Avoid playing too loudly; the guitar is at its best when played quietly. If the instrument is played too violently, the strings rattle and the tone is lost.

LEFT HAND

It is no part of the function of this hand to support the neck of the instrument. The neck must not fall down between the thumb and the index finger (see figure 5). The thumb is only used to supply counter-pressure to that exerted by the fingers against the finger board. Bend the wrist well forward, and keep the upper arm against the body. The fingers should press the strings perpendicularly against the finger board, and immediately below the frets. This is very important in order to avoid rattling of the strings. (Remember to keep your fingernails cut short.) If two or more strings are to be depressed with one finger, this must be laid flat against the finger board (see figure 6). The handicap of short fingers can be largely overcome by a supple wrist, and difficulty in reaching the farther strings will disappear with practice.

In the instructions which follow, the fingers are numbered as shown in the diagram on page 553 (top, left). The thumb is not numbered; normally it is very rarely used, and it is indicated by the letter T.

The next diagram shows how the fingers of the left hand depress the strings.

Note that the first finger is only to be used for the first fret, the second finger only for the second fret, and the third finger only for the third fret.

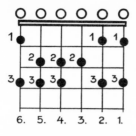

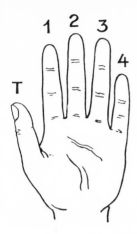

Left: Numbering of fingers, as used in the instructions. Above, right: How the fingers are used to depress the strings. (Strings are numbered at bottom.)

The diagram below shows the corresponding notes in normal notation. Remember to press the strings perpendicularly against the finger board, and practice this sequence over and over again.

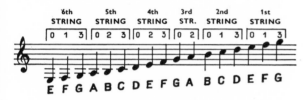

The figures over the notes show which fingers are to be used, and above the figures is given an indication of the appropriate strings. It will be seen that all these notes may be played on the lowest three frets.

PLAYING A TUNE

The student can now attempt a little tune. The fingering has been purposely omitted, since practice at playing from music, rather than from figures, is essential.

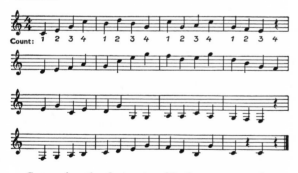

Comparing the first note with the sequence above, it is found to be C, and above it is the figure 3. This means that the third finger must be used to press the fifth string against the third fret. To produce the next note, E, the second finger presses the fourth string against the second fret.

Do not be tempted to write the fingering over the music. Practice one bar at a time, learning it by heart.

Each bar contains four quarter notes. As you play the notes, count aloud 1, 2, 3, 4, 1, 2, 3, 4, and so on. In the fourth, twelfth, and last bars a note or two are replaced by a rest. Rests must be counted in the same way as notes.

In the preceding tune, all the notes have equal value. In the next piece there are notes of different values:

All notes should be played on the down stroke. Play the first note in each bar with a little more accent than the others, as this helps to mark the rhythm.

Here is a little exercise in 3/4 time:

Down stroke: **⊓**   Up stroke: **V**

In 3/4 time we count three in a bar; notice that the tune begins on a "preliminary" note. Eighth notes are to be played with alternate down and up strokes. The other notes are played only on the down strokes. The note G, which appears in the sixth and seventh bars, is tied. This means that the two Gs together form *one* note, which should only be struck *once*.

Now a simple waltz in G can be attempted.

Practice similar simple tunes that can be found in community song books.

CHORDS

Symbols and diagrams are used instead of standard musical notation for chords. With their help any desired chord can be played.

Unless otherwise stated, each diagram represents that part of the finger board nearest the tuning screws. The vertical lines represent the strings, and the horizontal lines the frets. The black dots show where the fingertips should depress the strings. The numbers under the diagram indicate the fingering. The letter O above a string indicates that it should be played open— that is to say, not touched by any of the fingers of the left hand. An example is this chord in G (below, left):

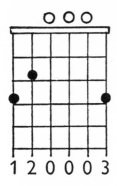

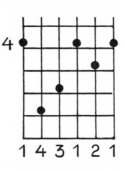

When the top of a diagram does not represent the end of the finger board, the number of the fret is indicated by a figure printed at the side. As an example the diagram of a chord in E is shown (above, right). The fret to the right of the number corresponds to the

fourth fret on the guitar. Later, when the pupil has become more skilled, diagrams are abandoned and symbols are used:

Major chords are indicated by a capital letter (C, G, D, etc.).

Minor chords are indicated by a capital letter and a small m (Cm, Gm, Dm, etc.).

Sevenths are indicated by capital letter and the number 7 (C7, G7, D7, etc.).

Sixths are indicated by capital letter and the number 6 (C6, G6, D6, etc.).

Major Sevenths are indicated by capital letter, the abbreviation maj., and the number 7 (Cmaj7, Gmaj7, etc.).

Minor Sevenths are indicated by capital letter, the small letter m, and the number 7 (Cm7, Gm7, etc.).

Minor Sixths are indicated by capital letter, the small letter m, and the number 6 (Cm6, Gm6, etc.).

Diminished Sevenths are indicated by the abbreviation dim., or by ÷ or ° (Cdim, C÷, or C°).

Augmented Fifths are indicated by the abbreviation aug. or by + (Caug. or C +).

Ninths are indicated by capital letter and the number 9 (C9, G9, D9, etc.).

It is important to remember to strike only those strings marked with a black dot or the letter O above the diagram.

It does not matter if the chord is simplified a little by playing only four strings instead of six. The chord does not sound quite so rich, but it is there all the same, and it is better to play cleanly on four strings than badly on six. After practice it will be possible to play cleanly on six strings as well.

Guitar Finger Board Chart

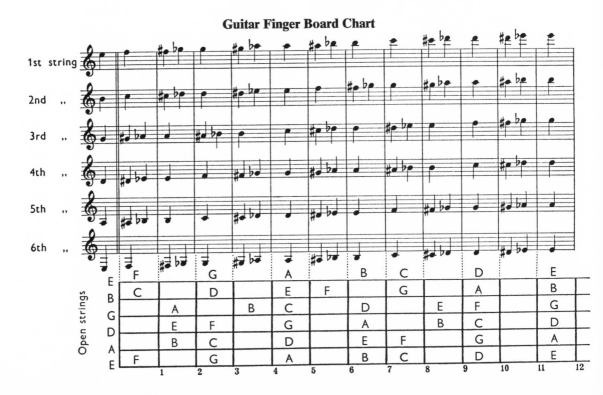

ACCOMPANIMENT

Let us now examine a simple guitar part written in standard symbol form.

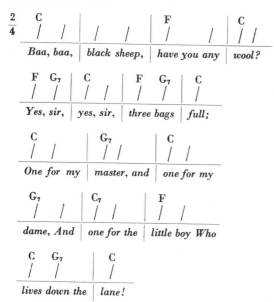

$\frac{2}{4}$ | C / / | / / | F / | C / / |

Baa, baa, | black sheep, | have you any | wool?

F G₇ | C | F G₇ | C
/ / | / / | / / | / /

Yes, sir, | yes, sir, | three bags | full;

C | G₇ | C
/ / | / / | / /

One for my | master, and | one for my

G₇ | C₇ | F
/ / | / / | / /

dame, And | one for the | little boy Who

C G₇ | C
/ / | / /

lives down the | lane!

The first chord is C, which is fingered as shown in the diagram on the right:

The first finger must press the second string against the first fret, the second finger must press the fourth string against the second fret, and the third and fourth fingers must press the fifth and sixth strings respectively against the third fret. The first and third strings are open (untouched).

Having placed the fingers, strike all the strings with the plectrum, and the result is a C major chord. Those who find it too difficult at first to play on all six strings may restrict themselves to the four strings on the right of the diagram.

Now strike four beats on the strings in the tempo of a comfortable walking pace, and sing "Baa, baa, black sheep" in the same tempo. Your starting note is given you by the second string.

In the third bar there are two beats on the chord of F (below, right); in the fourth, two beats on the chord of C.

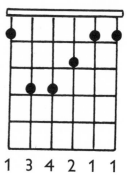

The F chord is more difficult than the chord of C, because the first finger has to depress the first and the second strings together. First place the second and third fingers; they must not lie flat over the strings, so bend the last joint of the fingers as much as possible. Then place the first finger between the first and the second strings. (Remember to keep the fingers well up to the frets.)

The fifth bar contains a new chord, G7 (below). This is an easy chord. In the thirteenth bar there is a C7 chord, but here the beginner may play the ordinary C chord.

Practice these three chords over and over again, and in time it will become easy to change from one to the other without fumbling. Do not play too loud: this is not a solo but the accompaniment to a song.

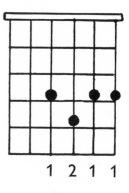

When the chords in the first position have been mastered, those higher up the finger board can be attempted. They are not more difficult—in fact, they are often easier. Farther up the finger board, the fingers are closer together.

It is not difficult to find material to enlarge one's repertoire. The piano music of popular dance numbers usually gives chord symbols. Band arrangements always show symbols for guitar, and many community songbooks include them.

REVIVED INTEREST IN GUITAR

After a flourishing period as a solo instrument at the beginning of the nineteenth century when such virtuosos as the Spaniards Aguado y Garcia and Sor and the Italians Carulli and Giuliani brought renown to the instrument, the guitar declined in importance and was chiefly used for song accompaniments. Toward the end of the century, however, the Spaniard Tárrega re-established it as a solo instrument, and in our time Andrés Segovia has shown that the guitar fully merits a place in the concert hall. In the early 1940s the Society of the Classic Guitar was founded in New York, and since 1946 it has issued its own journal, *The Guitar Review*.

Flamenco guitar music, performed by such masters as Sabicas and Montoya, also has gained much popularity.

DIAGRAMS FOR VARIOUS CHORDS

THE diagrams are grouped according to the different types of chord—major chords, minor chords, etc. The diagrams within each chord group are arranged according to the fingering required. In each fingering group the three positions lying nearest the nut are placed one under another. If, for example, you look at the three major chord diagrams in the second column from the left, you will notice that the fingering is the same for all three, the fingers being moved one fret down for each semitone. The diagram at the bottom illustrates a D sharp (E flat) major chord. If an E major chord with the same fingering is required, the fingers have to be moved down one fret.

By using the three diagrams in this way, it is possible to work out chords farther down the neck.

Note particularly:

a. A circle on a nut above a string indicates that the string is to be played open.

b. Strings without numbers are not to be played, e. g. in Sixths, third column from left, fourth string.

c. Several of the "fingering groups" do not have the same fingering in all three diagrams; the upper (or two upper) is different. If you use the fingering of the lower diagram in the upper (or two upper), one or more of your fingers will come above the nut. Thus, these upper diagrams have open strings, and sometimes different fingering. Use the fingering of the lowest diagram for chords farther down the neck.

d. In Augmented Fifths and Diminished Sevenths the semitone is indicated by the sharp sign only.

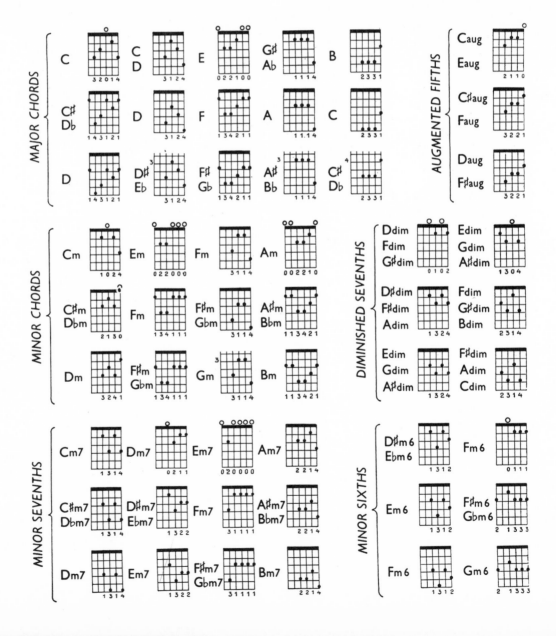

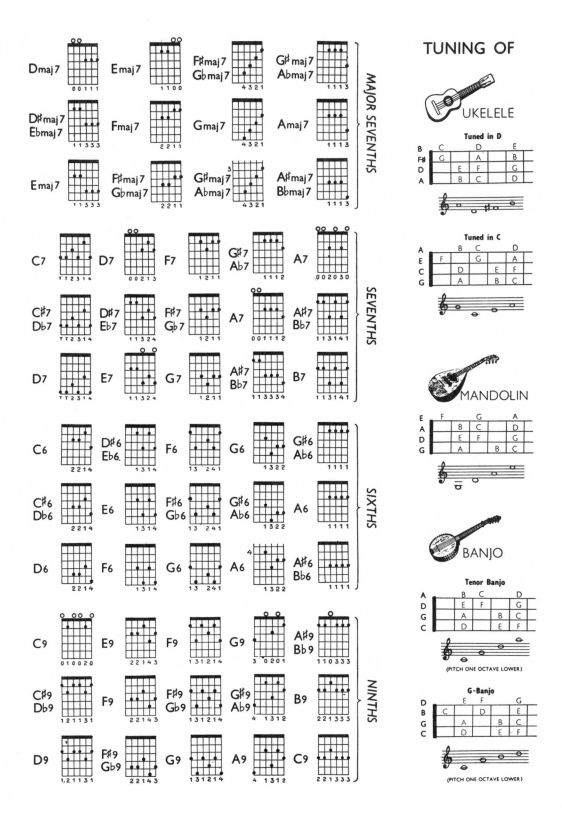

TUNING OF

UKELELE

Marie Gutheil-Schoder as Carmen

GULDA, Friedrich. Austrian pianist (1930–). He is equally at home in the realms of the Beethoven sonata and modern jazz. He was discovered after World War II at the International Competition at Geneva, and was immediately engaged by many major European orchestras. He appeared as soloist at music festivals in Prague and Vienna. His many recordings made him well known to American music lovers even before his debut at Carnegie Hall in 1950. Six years later he realized one of his greatest ambitions by playing at New York's Birdland and at the Newport Jazz Festival. Gulda has since performed all over the United States, Europe, and South America, as an interpreter of both classical music and jazz.

GULLIN, Lars. Swedish jazz saxophonist (1928–). A classical pianist and composer, Gullin has also won recognition as a jazz instrumentalist. He has recorded in Sweden with several American musicians, including Stan Getz and James Moody, and won a poll conducted by the American jazz magazine *Down Beat* in 1954.

GURRE-LIEDER. One of Arnold Schoenberg's first important compositions, the *Gurre-Lieder* was composed between March of 1900 and March of 1901. The orchestration, however, took ten years to score. This is not surprising considering the panoramic scope of the work which calls for an orchestra of over 150 players, three four-part male choruses, and eight-part mixed chorus numbering at least 100, five soloists, and one narrator (or "speaker"). The *Gurre-Lieder,* uncut, takes nearly two hours to perform.

The text is taken from a narrative poem by Jens Peter Jacobsen, a nineteenth-century Danish poet and botanist. The story of the *Gurre-Lieder,* in brief, is as follows:

> King Waldemar of Denmark, although married, is in love with the beautiful Tove, whom he visits in a castle in Gurre. The first part of the work is a series of songs for the lovers.
>
> In the second part, through the voice of the Wood-Dove it is learned that Waldemar's queen has had Tove murdered, and describes Waldemar's grief.
>
> In the third part, Waldemar curses God, and for this sin is compelled to ride eternally through the night sky with a retinue of ghostly hunters.
>
> The final part describes the hideous nocturnal ride as seen through the eyes of terrified peasants. The work ends with the sunrise and a beatific paean to sunlight, spring, nature, and love. This great peroration is performed by the full complement of choral and instrumental forces, and produces a shattering effect upon the listener.

The musical style of the *Gurre-Lieder* is most extraordinary as it combines a super-Wagnerian idiom that might be called the apotheosis of late Romanticism, with the beginnings of Schoenberg's experiments in chromaticism, atonality, and *sprechgesang*. Next to *Verklärte Nacht* and *Pelleas and Melisande* it is his most accessible work for the average concert audience. Unfortunately its elephantine proportions mitigate against frequent performances.

GUTHEIL-SCHODER, Marie. German mezzo-soprano (1874–1935). Trained in Weimar, she was active there until 1900, when she joined the Vienna Opera. She was appointed stage director of the Opera in 1926. Known for her performances of such dramatic roles as Carmen, Elektra, and Salome, she was also an early interpreter of Schönberg's music.

GUYS AND DOLLS. American musical comedy first presented in 1950, with book by Jo Swerling and Abe Burrows and score by Frank Loesser. It ran for more than 1,200 performances at Broadway's 46th Street Theater, and remains one of the most popular American musicals. Based on several short stories by Damon Runyon (principally *The Idyll of Sarah Brown*), the script is almost entirely written in the peculiar dialect so characteristic of that author, in which the various gamblers, loafers, and assorted riff-raff speak a highly stylized speech largely based on the elimination of contractions. These exotic specimens, who bear such names as Nicely-Nicely, Nathan Detroit, and Harry the Horse, are complemented perfectly by Loesser's musical score, capturing as it does the honky-tonk blues sound of Broadway. Some of the more popular tunes in the show are *I'll Know, A Bushel and a Peck, If I Were a Bell, My Time of Day, I've Never Been in Love Before, Take Back Your Mink,* and *Luck Be a Lady.*

GYPSY BARON, THE *(Der Zigeunerbaron).* Operetta composed in 1885 by Johann Strauss the Younger. On a visit to Budapest in 1883,

Strauss asked the poet Moritz Jokai for the text of a new operetta. Jokai suggested his short story *Saffi,* and Strauss commissioned Ignaz Schnitzer to write the libretto. The greater part of the music was composed before the words were written.

At the time, Strauss was yearning to break away from the typical operetta traditions and try his hand at true operatic style. Thus in *The Gypsy Baron* the waltz takes a far less dominant place than in the other Strauss operettas.

The main theme of the overture, which also forms the finale of the first act, was actually an idea for a Hungarian national anthem which Strauss entered in a competition held by the Hungarian Government in 1867. It won first prize, but as he was an Austrian his tune was never used.

Act I of The Gypsy Baron *in the Metropolitan Opera production.* **Left to right:** *Walter Slezak as Szupan, Laurel Hurley as Arsena, and Nicolai Gedda as Barinkay.*

Act III of The Gypsy Baron *in the Metropolitan Opera production.* Left to right: *Nicolai Gedda as Barinkay, Lisa Della Casa as Saffi, Regina Resnik as Czipra, and Alessio de Paolis as the Emperor of Austria*

The operetta had its first performance at the Theater an der Wien in 1885, and was a huge success.

The action takes place in Hungary, in the eighteenth century. The young Sandor Barinkay (tenor), descendant of a wealthy Hungarian family, returns unknown after the wars to his ancestral home. At his entrance he sings the waltz couplet *Yes, All in the World—I Know and Even More.*

In his absence, his estates have been appropriated by the rich pig-breeder Szupan (bass), whose beautiful daughter Arsena (soprano) attracts Barinkay's attention. But she is secretly in love with Ottokar (tenor), the son of Mirabella (contralto), who has brought her up.

An old gypsy woman, Czipra (contralto), who lives nearby with her daughter Saffi (soprano), recognizes Barinkay as the son of the old landowner and calls together all the gypsies, who proclaim Barinkay as the gypsy baron. He falls in love with Saffi, and is married to her in true gypsy style in his father's dilapidated castle.

Saffi has a dream in which she sees a treasure lying hidden in the castle. Barinkay orders an excavation to be made, and discovers his father's treasure beneath the walls (*The Treasure Waltz, Schatzwalzer*).

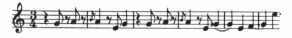

Szupan quarrels with Barinkay over the treasure. Soldiers, led by an officer, Homonay (tenor), arrive to enlist men for the wars. (*The Enlistment Song* is the main theme of the overture.) The pig-breeder and Ottokar are inclined to go with them. When Czipra discloses that Saffi is a daughter of the last Turkish governor, the Pasha of Temesvar, Barinkay also resolves to go to war, so as to be a worthy husband for her. His conduct in battle is heroic and, on his return, in reward for his bravery the property is restored to him and he is given a title. Szupan and Ottokar also return safely, and Arsena marries her beloved Ottokar.

GYPSY SONGS (*Zigeunerlieder*). Compositions for four voices and piano, Op. 103, by Brahms. It was undoubtedly Brahms' intention that this collection of songs should be music for "household use," in the tradition of the English and Dutch madrigals of the Renaissance period. The *Zigeunerlieder* were written at Thun in the summer of 1887, the year in which the Double Concerto was composed. The words, based on Hungarian folk songs, were put together by the composer's friend Hugo Conrat, a Viennese businessman. The melodies, on the other hand, are not folk tunes, as in the case of the *Hungarian Dances,* but Brahms' own original compositions. The tenor part is particularly demanding; it was intended for the opera singer Gustav Walter, who did much to make the songs known.

H

H. In German musical notation, H is used for the note called B in English notation.

The German B denotes the note called B flat in English notation. Formerly, in German notation B flat was indicated by the roman letter b, and B natural by the Gothic ♭; the resemblance of the latter to the roman h later led to the use of H as the symbol for B natural. Thus Bach's theme B-A-C-H in *The Art of the Fugue* is rendered in English notation B flat-A-C-B.

The German use of b for B flat led to the adoption of ♭ as the "flat sign" for all notes, and the Gothic ♭ was adapted to ♯ as the "natural" sign.

HAAS, Joseph. German composer (1879–1961). Haas studied with Max Reger and Karl Straube, and in 1911 was appointed composition teacher at the Stuttgart Conservatory. He later taught at the Institute of Church Music in Munich and at the Hochschule für Musik in Munich. His operas, church music, orchestral, instrumental, and choral works (among them the oratorio *Die heilige Elisabeth*) are well known in Germany, where he was an important influence on contemporary music.

HAAS, Monique. French pianist (1909–). A student at the Paris Conservatory with Lazare Lévy, and later with Robert Casadesus and Rudolf Serkin, Mme. Haas made her first public appearance in Paris in 1928. She toured Europe, Russia, Australia, South Africa, and the Middle East, playing recitals and appearing as soloist with leading orchestras and conductors. She received the Grand Prix du Disque for her interpretation of the Debussy *Études*. Mme. Haas is married to the composer Marcel Mihalovici.

HABA, Alois. Czech composer (1893–). After studying in Prague, Vienna, and Berlin, Haba became a teacher at the Prague Conservatory. One of the most independent composers of our time, he was the first to compose in a scale divided into microtones (intervals smaller than a half tone). He has made a thorough study of the use of 1/3, 1/4, 1/6, and 1/12 tones.

"Haba proposes an 'athematic' system of composition, in which the melodic line cannot be subdivided into phrases, motifs or periods. . . . This indefinite and vague melody, which Haba employs in his quartet in quarter tones, Opus 12, carries with it another complication:

MONIQUE HAAS

ALOIS HABA

that of never repeating itself, nor any of the fragments of which it is composed. Undoubtedly the procedure is convenient, and it is not to be wondered at that Haba has had numerous disciples" (Adolfo Salazar).

HABAÑERA. A Cuban dance, also found, and probably originating, in Spain. It takes its name from the city of Havana, and its punctuated 2/4 rhythm is reminiscent of the tango. Well-known habañera compositions are Yradier's *La Paloma* and *El Arreglito* (used as a basis for Bizet's famous Habañera in *Carmen*).

HABENECK, François Antoine. German-French composer, violinist, and conductor (1781–1849). He was first a violinist at the Paris Opéra, then one of its principal conductors for many years. For twenty-three years, he was a professor of violin at the Conservatory; for two decades he conducted the Société du Concerts du Conservatoire, which he founded and with which he introduced the symphonies of Beethoven to France. His compositions include concertos and other works for the violin, chamber music, and ballets.

HENRY HADLEY

HACKETT, Charles. American tenor (1893–1942). Hackett studied voice in Boston and later in Florence. He made his opera debut in Genoa, and sang at La Scala, Milan. His American debut was in the role of the Count in *The Barber of Seville,* with the Metropolitan Opera. He was a member of the Chicago Civic Opera from 1923 until 1933. He rejoined the Metropolitan Opera in 1934 and remained until 1939, when he became a teacher at the Juilliard School. His best roles were in the French repertory.

HACKETT, Robert Leo (Bobby). American jazz instrumentalist and band leader (1915–). Bobby Hackett has been one of the outstanding American jazz artists for more than twenty years. His instruments are trumpet, cornet, and guitar. He has been a featured player with the bands of Pee Wee Russell, Joe Marsala, Horace Heidt, Glenn Miller, and Glenn Gray; has made many recordings with Jackie Gleason; and has achieved national fame through his appearances on radio and television shows.

HADLEY, Henry Kimball. American composer and conductor (1871–1937). A pupil of George Chadwick at the New England Conservatory of Music, he later studied abroad. Orchestras that he conducted include the Seattle and San Francisco symphonies, the Manhattan Symphony, and the New York Philharmonic Orchestra, of which he was associate conductor. In 1933, he conducted the first concert of the Berkshire Festival, which he helped to establish. He composed choral music, four symphonies, tone poems, and other orchestral works. His opera, *Azora,* was produced by the Chicago Opera in 1917 and in 1918, another opera, *Bianca,* won the prize offered by the singer William Wade Hinshaw. The Metropolitan Opera produced his *Cleopatra's Night* in 1920. Though Hadley's works are almost unknown to audiences today, he was considered one of the important American composers of his time. As a conductor, he did much to promote the works of other American composers.

HAEFLIGER, Ernst. Swiss tenor (1919–). A pupil of the tenor Julius Patzak, he made his concert debut in 1942. Well known in oratorio, he introduced Frank Martin's *Le Vin herbé* and other contemporary works. He has been prominent in many European opera houses, particularly the Berlin Staatsoper, where he sang in Mozart and the lighter Italian operas. He has recorded the role of Florestan in *Fidelio,* Schubert and Brahms lieder, and other music. He sang the role of Tamino in Mozart's *The Magic Flute* at Glyndebourne. He made his North American debut in 1959 at the Vancouver Festival, and his first North American tour of the United States in 1960, in the course of which he appeared four times as soloist in Mahler's *Das Lied von der Erde* with the Cleveland Orchestra and recorded the same work under Bruno Walter's baton.

HAENDEL, Ida. Polish violinist (1923–). Ida Haendel showed her first sign of talent when she began to play simple pieces on her sister's violin, at the age of four. She studied at the Warsaw Conservatory, where she won a gold medal at the age of nine, and later with such masters of the violin as Szymon Goldberg, Carl Flesch, and Joseph Szigeti.

She has toured Europe and the United States, and her career has been a series of triumphs everywhere. "She has all the gifts of the violinist—beautiful tone, dazzling technique and perfect intonation," one critic has said.

Mayor Haffner of Salzburg

HAFFNER SYMPHONY. Mozart's Symphony No. 35, in D major, K. 385. In 1776 Mayor Haffner of Salzburg had ordered a serenade and a march for his daughter's wedding; these form the suite now known as the Haffner Serenade (K. 250). Six years later, when Mozart was living in Vienna, he received a message from his father that he must write a new serenade for the Mayor. Mozart replied: "You have no understanding how difficult it is to arrange such a work for orchestra. It is necessary for me to work at night—I cannot manage it any other way. . . . I will write as quickly as I can, and as well as haste will allow."

A year later, when Mozart glanced through his hasty piece, he was completely surprised at its quality, and decided to transform the serenade into a symphony. He discarded the introductory march and one of the minuets, and added parts for flute and clarinet in the first and last movements. The symphony was played in this form in Vienna in 1783. It is regarded as one of the most elegant and brilliant of all symphonies, and is one of Mozart's most often played works.

I. *Allegro con spirito.* This is completely dominated by the introductory theme (forte), with harsh leaping double octaves played by the whole orchestra in unison.

No real supporting themes occur; the rhythmic contours of the main theme are always in the foreground, often in canon and in complicated counterpoint. The symphony is representative of the early Viennese classical form in that the climax is already worked up in the first movement, a lessening of tension following in the later movements.

II. *Andante.* A tranquil and simple theme gradually dissolves into finely varied violin figurations.

III. A festive minuet, framing an extremely melodious trio.

IV. *Presto.* Mozart's direction was to play this as quickly as possible. The theme has an unmistakable likeness to Osmin's aria in *The Abduction from the Seraglio.*

HAGEMAN, Richard. Dutch-American composer (1882–). He came to America in 1906 as accompanist to Yvette Guilbert. He was a conductor at the Metropolitan Opera from 1912 to 1921. His opera *Caponsacchi* was produced at the Metropolitan in 1937. He also composed film scores and many songs, including the popular *Do Not Go, My Love.*

HAGEN, Betty-Jean. Canadian violinist (1931–). She studied with Alexander Nicol, at the Chicago Conservatory, at Toronto's Royal Conservatory, with Ivan Galamian, and at the Juilliard School. She has won Walter Naumburg, Harriet Cohen, and Leventritt awards, the Pathé-Marconi prize, and the Carl Flesch Medal. She has toured the United States and Europe as recitalist and as soloist with orchestras, including the New York Philharmonic, Cleveland, and Amsterdam Concertgebouw orchestras, and the Orchestre de la Suisse Romande in Geneva.

HAHN, Reynaldo. French conductor and composer (1875–1947). A pupil of Massenet at the Paris Conservatory when he was eleven years old, Hahn began his career as a composer with songs for piano accompaniment. The song *Si mes vers avaient des ailes (If My Words Only Had Wings),* which later became so popular, was written when he was only sixteen.

As a conductor, Hahn was known as a brilliant interpreter of Mozart's operas; he was guest conductor at Salzburg and, from 1945, conductor at the Paris Opéra.

HAIEFF, Alexei. Russian-American composer (1914–). Haieff received his early education in Manchuria. In 1931 he came to the United States and studied at the Juilliard School of Music with Rubin Goldmark, Frederick Jacobi, and Alexander Siloti. He studied composition with Nadia Boulanger in Paris during 1938–39, held two Guggenheim Fellowships (1946 and 1949) and a Fulbright Scholarship in Italy, and became a Fellow at the American Academy in Rome. There he became composer-in-residence in 1952–53.

Alexei Haieff is a composer of the Stravinsky heritage. His music consists of clear-cut melodic lines, full tonal harmonies, and interesting rhythmic patterns and jazzlike effects. His compositions include works for ballet, chamber groups, piano, and the voice. His orchestral works include two symphonies, the Violin Concerto (1948) and, most notably, the Piano Concerto (1952), which received the New York Music Critics' Circle Award for 1952.

HAIG, Alan W. (Al). American jazz pianist (1923–). Haig began his musical career playing with Coast Guard bands during the war; he then free-lanced around the Boston area and was

REYNALDO HAHN

briefly with Jerry Wald. He became an important member of the bop coterie that sprang up in New York, playing with Dizzy Gillespie, Charlie Parker, and others. He joined Chet Baker in 1954, and has made numerous recordings.

HAIL, COLUMBIA! American patriotic song. The tune is *The President's March,* written in 1789 as an inaugural march for George Washington by Philip Phile or Phylo, violinist and leader of a Philadelphia orchestra. The words were written to fit the music by Joseph Hopkinson in the summer of 1798, when England and France were at war and the Americans were disputing among themselves which side they should support. Hopkinson's intention was to write a song that might "get up an American spirit which should be independent of, and above, the interests, passion and policy of both belligerents, and look and feel exclusively for the Americans' own honor and rights."

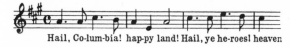

Hail, Co-lum-bia! hap-py land! Hail, ye he-roes! heaven

HAINES, Edmund Thomas. American composer and teacher (1914–). A graduate of the Kansas City Conservatory, he pursued graduate studies at the Eastman School of Music. He has served on the faculties of the University of Michigan and Sarah Lawrence College, and was a Guggenheim Fellow (1956–58). He has composed music for orchestra and piano, and works for chamber and choral groups.

HAITINK, Bernard. Dutch conductor (1929–). Haitink studied violin at the Amsterdam Conservatory and conducting with Felix Hupka and Ferdinand Leitner. In 1955 he was appointed permanent conductor of The Netherlands Radio Philharmonic Orchestra (Hilversum), and in the 1957 and 1958 Holland Festivals he led both his own orchestra and The Hague Residentie Orchestra. First guest conductor of the Amsterdam Concertgebouw Orchestra in the 1956–57 season, he conducted that orchestra on its tour of England in 1959 and on its tour of the United States and Canada in 1961. He has been guest conductor of the Los Angeles Philharmonic, Pasdeloup, Bavarian Radio (Munich), and other orchestras.

LASZLO HALASZ

HALASZ, Laszlo. Hungarian-American conductor (1905–). Halasz studied piano and conducting at the Budapest Conservatory, graduating in 1929. He toured Europe as a concert pianist and conducted the Budapest Opera, the Prague Opera, and the Vienna Opera and Volksoper. In 1936 he came to the United States, becoming a citizen in 1943. He was conductor of the St. Louis Grand Opera (1939–42) and the New York City Opera Company, where he conducted many operas of the contemporary repertory. Since 1951 he has conducted opera performances in the United States and Europe. He is musical director of the Empire State Music Festival, New York.

HALE, Philip. American music critic (1854–1934). Hale began his musical studies at an early age and, as a boy, played the organ in church. He was graduated from Yale University in 1876 and later studied music in Europe. From 1901 he edited the program notes of the Boston Symphony Orchestra and for many years was the brilliant and outspoken music critic of the Boston *Herald*.

HALÉVY, Jacques François. French opera composer (1799–1862). Though *La Juive (The Jewess)* is the only Halévy opera that is still performed in opera houses, he was one of the most prolific of French stage composers. After winning the Prix de Rome in 1819, he wrote several operas that were not produced, but he became successful in 1828 when Malibran sang in his *Clari. La Juive,* one of the landmarks in French opera, was produced in 1835. Halévy composed to order for three major Paris theaters and was often working simultaneously on serious and comic operas. During his entire career, he served in various teaching capacities at the Paris Conservatory. He composed almost forty operas in all as well as several ballets and cantatas. His daughter married Bizet, the great composer of *Carmen*; Bizet completed *Noé* (later *Le Déluge*), the opera that Halévy left unfinished at his death.

HALFFTER, Ernesto. Spanish composer (1905–). Halffter studied composition with Manuel de Falla and Adolfo Salazar. From 1934 to 1936 he was director of the Seville Conservatory. In 1936, at the outbreak of the Spanish Civil War, he moved to Lisbon. He has written an opera and chamber music, and he completed Falla's unfinished dramatic oratorio, *Atlàntida,* which was given as an opera at La Scala in Milan, and in 1962 was given its American première in concert form in New York at Philharmonic Hall, during the gala opening week of the new Lincoln Center.

HALFFTER, Rodolfo. Spanish-Mexican composer (1900–). The brother of Ernesto Halffter, he emigrated to Mexico in 1939, where he has written a ballet and a violin concerto showing neo-classic influence.

HALL, Edmond. American jazz clarinetist (1901–). Hall's career as a jazz clarinetist has brought him into association with many of the outstanding jazz musicians of the past five decades. He has played with Charlie Skeets, Claude Hopkins, Lucky Millinder, Red Allen, Teddy Wilson, and Eddie Condon, and has headed his own band.

HALLE, Adam de la. French troubadour (*c.* 1240–*c.* 1286). One of the most famous of the French poet-musicians of the twelfth and thirteenth centuries, he was a master of song writing. He wrote *Le Jeu de Robin et Marion,* a pastoral play incorporating popular songs of the time; and motets and chansons.

HALLÉ, Sir Charles. German-English pianist and conductor (1819–1895). The son of a church organist, Hallé performed in public at the age of four. In 1836 he went to Paris and became friendly with Chopin and Liszt. In 1848 he moved to England, settling in Manchester, where he conducted an orchestra, choruses, and opera. Hallé established subscription concerts in 1857 with his own orchestra, which is still in existence and has greatly influenced the musical life of England.

HALLELUJAH. Hebrew (Latin, *alleluia*), "the Lord be praised." Originally a cry of jubilation in Jewish religious ceremonies, it was inserted into the Catholic liturgy at an early date as part of the Mass for the Easter and Christmas festivals. The word is well known from Handel's oratorio *Messiah,* in which the *Hallelujah* Chorus forms a triumphant conclusion to the second part of the work. When this was first heard, at

JACQUES HALÉVY

Covent Garden in 1743, the King (George II) and the whole audience rose and stood throughout the chorus, and this custom has been maintained ever since.

Bach used the word in his cantata *Christ lag in Todesbanden,* and Mozart's *Alleluia* for soprano and orchestra from the motet *Exsultate, Jubilate* is also well known. The final chorus of Honegger's *King David* is a Hallelujah chorus.

HALVORSEN, Johan August. Norwegian composer (1864–1935). Halvorsen, who had been given violin lessons from a very early age, was one of Brodsky's pupils at Leipzig, and in 1888 became first violinist and leader of the Aberdeen Philharmonic Society. A year later he left for Helsinki, where he taught at the Conservatory, and from there he made various tours, including one to St. Petersburg, where he received lessons from Leopold Auer. On his return to Norway he settled in Bergen, where he married Grieg's niece, Annie.

Halvorsen's compositions are suffused with joy, a classical urge for clarity and purity, and a vigorous, healthy, unromantic delight in good work. He regarded his art as the most natural thing in the world, and his sincere nature loathed all forms of affectation. His simple outlook is aptly illustrated by this statement: "If the composer really feels what he has written strongly enough for it to have an effect on those who hear it, then he has fulfilled his aim."

His compositions include two symphonies, a violin concerto, the *Entry of the Boyards* march, and music to an Indian drama, *Vasantasena.*

HAMBOURG, Mark. Russian-British pianist and composer (1879–1960). Hambourg made his debut in Moscow at the age of eight and, when he was ten, performed in London. He made his first world tour in 1895 and his New York debut in 1898. His daughter Michal is a concert pianist of high quality, his brother Jan was a professional violinist, and his brother Boris was the cellist of the Hart House String Quartet in Toronto. Mark Hambourg composed many works for piano and was author of *How to Become a Pianist* and *From Piano to Forte,* his autobiography.

HAMERIK, Asger. Danish composer (1843–1923). He trained as a pianist with Von Bülow, who advised him to concentrate on composition. Later, he was a pupil and assistant of Berlioz, and for twenty-five years was a director of the Peabody Institute in Baltimore. He composed many orchestral works, including six symphonies, choral music, and four operas.

HAMILTON, Forestsorn ("Chico"). American jazz drummer (1921–). Hamilton started as a clarinetist and turned to the drums. He formed a band with his schoolmates Charles Mingus, Ernie Royal, and Illinois Jacquet, and later appeared with Count Basie and Lionel Hampton. He worked with Lena Horne for several years, was one of the organizers of the Gerry Mulligan Quartet, and currently heads his own quintet. He has appeared in films, including *The Road to Bali* and *Sweet Smell of Success.* He is responsible for several interesting innovations, such as the use of the cello as a jazz instrument.

HAMILTON, Ian Ellis. Scottish composer (1922–). He became known through awards by the Royal Philharmonic Society and the Koussevitzky Foundation. His most successful works have been a string quartet and a clarinet quintet. He also has composed concertos, piano works, symphonies, and a ballet.

HAMLIN, George. American tenor (1868–1923). He sang with the Philadelphia-Chicago Opera Company and was a noted lieder singer, introducing to America many of the songs of Richard Strauss.

HAMMERKLAVIER SONATA. Piano sonata in B major, Op. 106, by Beethoven (*Hammerklavier* was the German word for piano) Composed in 1818 and dedicated to Archduke Rudolph of Austria, this is considered one of Beethoven's finest works and one of the greatest of all compositions for the piano. Beethoven received in 1818 a grand piano as a gift from Thomas Broadwood in London, and began to compose his Op. 106 soon afterward. The work appeared with the designation *Grosse Sonate für das Hammerklavier*—to make it clear that it could not be played on the harpsichord.

Upon delivery of the manuscript, Beethoven wrote to his publisher: "Here you have a sonata which will keep the pianists busy and which will still be played after fifty years have gone by." The truth is that even today the *Hammerklavier* Sonata is among the most difficult pieces in the pianist's repertoire.

The work consists of the customary four movements of the classical sonata. The first movement is introduced by a violent "motto theme," followed by the short but lyrical first subject. Paul Bekker has called this movement "a titanic struggle."

The customary order is upset, however, as the composer puts the *Scherzo* in second place. The third movement, *Adagio,* is one of the most intensely moving pieces Beethoven ever created. Nohl has called it "a prayer" and Lenz speaks of it as "the greatest Adagio in all piano music."

The last movement, *Allegro risoluto,* is the exact opposite of the generally frivolous Finale. Beethoven uses, as he often does in his last period, a polyphonic form, the fugue, for the expression of intense dramatic action. The development of its fierce theme, which is based on a trill, is of extraordinary dramatic power. Max Reger has called this piece "a monster fugue," obviously referring to the enormous technical difficulty of this piece as well as to its spiritual content.

HAMMERSTEIN, Oscar. German-American impresario (1846–1919). He made his fortune through the invention of a device used in the manufacture of cigars and spent it on opera, which was his passion. In addition to producing and financing opera performances, he built several opera houses; the most successful of these was the Manhattan Opera House, where, from 1906 to 1910, he gave brilliant seasons, presenting altogether 463 performances of 49 operas. Among the works that he introduced to America were *Pelléas et Mélisande, Louise Thaïs, Sapho,* and *Elektra.* Some of the famous singers who made their American debuts under his direction were Mary Garden, Luisa Tetrazzini, Maurice Renaud, John McCormack, Alessandro Bonci, and Charles Dalmorès. In 1910, the Metropolitan Opera bought Hammerstein out, on condition that he refrain from producing opera in New York for ten years. Three years later, he attempted to violate the agreement after building the Lexington Avenue Opera House, but was restrained by a law suit that the Metropolitan brought against him. He also built opera houses in Philadelphia and in London, where, in 1911, he gave a season of opera that was a financial disaster.

HAMMERSTEIN, Oscar, II. American librettist (1895–1960). He was the grandson of the impresario Oscar Hammerstein and the son of William Hammerstein, a theatrical producer. After studying law, he entered the theatrical world in 1918 as a stage manager for his uncle, the producer Arthur Hammerstein. The first production with which he was associated was an Ed Wynn vehicle entitled *Summertime.* This was the beginning of one of the great careers in American theatrical history. By the time it ended, with Hammerstein's death in 1960, he had helped bring about a revolution in the American musical theater; his contributions during four decades included every advance in musical comedy and operetta techniques, from the stereotyped romantic "book" to the dramatically cogent and superbly integrated librettos of the later Rodgers and Hammerstein creations. Alone or in collaboration with others, Hammerstein wrote more than a thousand songs, thirty stage works, and many films. In 1920, he worked with Otto Harbach and Frank Mandel as librettist and lyric writer. His first hit, *Wildflower,* was produced in 1923, and a series of

OSCAR HAMMERSTEIN I

OSCAR HAMMERSTEIN II

successful Broadway musicals, by various composers, incorporating his books and lyrics followed: *Rose Marie* (1924), *Sunny* (1925), *Song of the Flame* (1925), *Desert Song* (1926), *Show Boat* (1927), *The New Moon* (1928), *Good Boy* (1928), *Rainbow* (1928), *Sweet Adeline* (1931), *Music in the Air* (1932), *May Wine* (1935), and *Carmen Jones* (1943).

Show Boat, written in collaboration with composer Jerome Kern, is the greatest of Hammerstein's earlier successes. Its original Broadway production ran for 572 performances; it had four revivals, and was filmed in three versions.

During the 1930s, Hammerstein contributed to motion pictures but his basic interest was in the theater. In 1943 he began the "perfect partnership" with composer Richard Rodgers. Their collaboration began with *Oklahoma!* (1943) and continued, until Hammerstein's death, with *Carousel* (1945), *Allegro* (1947), *South Pacific,* a Pulitzer Prize winner (1949), *The King*

and I (1951), *Me and Juliet* (1953), *Pipe Dream* (1955), *Flower Drum Song* (1958), and *The Sound of Music* (1959).

On the occasion of Hammerstein's sixty-fifth birthday, Richard Rodgers paid tribute to his associate, writing in The New York *Times:* "He's never been accused of being rude or dishonest or intolerant. His mind and his heart have given enormous pleasure and comfort to millions of people. There remains only one more thing to point out on Oscar's sixty-fifth birthday and that is that for the last sixty-five years he's been having an absolutely wonderful time himself."

HAMMOND, Joan Hood. New Zealand soprano (1912–). She studied at the Sydney Conservatory and was a violinist in the Sydney Philharmonic for three years before studying voice in Vienna and with Dino Borgioli in London, where she made her concert debut in Handel's *Messiah* in 1938. After her Covent Garden debut in 1948 as Leonora in *Il Trovatore,* she became prominent in the roles of Tosca, Aïda, and Butterfly. Her American debut was as Tosca with the New York City Opera Company.

HAMPTON, Lionel. American jazz instrumentalist (1913–). One of the most colorful and influential musicians of the swing era, Lionel Hampton plays the drums and piano in addition to his main instrument, the vibraphone. His career blossomed in 1936 when he met and recorded with Benny Goodman, and became a vibes player with Goodman's band. He made numerous recordings with Goodman and with pick-up bands of his own during the next four years, many of which are much prized by collectors, for they include virtually every prominent jazz musician then playing. In 1940 Hampton formed his own orchestra, and reached a position of paramount importance through his recording of *Flying Home.* Throughout the 1940s he remained commercially and musically successful; by the early 1950s, however, the band's emphasis on drive and excitement had led it away from jazz toward the field of rhythm and blues.

For all this, Lionel Hampton remains a dynamic and popular musical personality, and deserves full credit for introducing the vibraphone and vibraharp to jazz as featured solo instruments.

LIONEL HAMPTON

George Frideric Handel

(FEBRUARY 23, 1685 – APRIL 14, 1759)

HANDEL, who was baptized Georg Friedrich Händel, Anglicized his name after settling in England, spelling his second name incorrectly as Frideric instead of Frederic (k), and exchanging the "*ä*" in his surname for simple "*a*." He became a naturalized British subject in 1726.

Handel's forefathers had for generations been coppersmiths in Silesia, but his father broke with this tradition. He was a medical student and became the royal Saxon valet-physician; at the age of sixty he married Dorothea Taust, a clergyman's daughter, and they had one son, Georg Friedrich, who was born in Halle.

Even in his earliest years the boy showed such a pronounced and unusual talent for music that his father—who was not musical at all—had to agree much against his will to his son's receiving tuition in it. The Duke of Saxe-Weissenfels had heard the boy playing the organ, and it became known in court circles that it was his wish that he be given a musical education. Handel's first teacher was the organist at the Maria Church in Halle, Friedrich Wilhelm Zachau (1663–1721), an excellent musician of the North German school. It was not long before the young Handel became known publicly as both organist and composer. With Zachau, he also studied harpsichord, violin, and oboe, becoming a proficient performer on all three.

In Berlin, where he had been sent in 1696 to continue his studies, the Elector Friedrich heard the eleven-year-old boy play, and offered to pay for his further training in Italy. His father forbade it, probably because he did not wish his son to be forced into a life of court servitude, and on his father's death in 1697, young Handel made his way home to Halle and there attended school. In deference to his father's wishes he studied law at the University, but his interest in music won the day: in 1702 he obtained the post of organist at the Reformed Church in Halle,

and in the following year he gave up the study of law.

In search of a more thorough musical education, he left his post in 1703 and went to Hamburg, then one of the leading musical centers of Germany. The opera in Hamburg was run by the town and the townspeople—something quite unique at that time—and the manager was the then well-known composer and conductor Rein-

GEORGE FRIDERIC HANDEL

A scene from Handel's opera, Giulio Cesare *at the Munich Opera*

hard Keiser (1673–1739). Handel became a member of the opera orchestra and a pupil of Keiser, who besides being a composer of note was, during the forty years that he was attached to the Hamburg Opera, responsible for making it the leading opera house in Germany.

During his four years in Hamburg, Handel acquired technical knowledge and practical experience in everything that had to do with opera (his first works in this form were performed there), and at the same time profited greatly from acquaintanceship with such eminent musicians as Mattheson and Telemann. In 1707 Handel left for Italy, where he lived in Florence, Rome, Venice, and Naples, wrote several operas in the Italian style, oratorios, and cantatas, and came into contact with some of the greatest musicians of his time—men like Alessandro and Domenico Scarlatti, Antonio Lotti, Arcangelo Corelli, and Agostino Steffani.

After three years in Italy, he made his way back to Germany to take up the position of

orchestra leader to the Elector of Hanover. After six months he was granted a year's leave of absence to visit London, where his opera *Rinaldo* (1711) was performed. In 1712 he again applied for—and received—permission to go to London, and this time he settled down so comfortably there that, without asking permission, he stayed longer than the time granted him, losing his post in Hanover and earning the disfavor of the Elector as a result. However, he stood high in the favor of Queen Anne. When the Elector of Hanover succeeded to the throne in 1714 and came to England as George I, Handel's position was at first precarious, but his many patrons among the peerage brought about a reconciliation between him and the new king, although Handel was not given the same position at court as he had enjoyed in Hanover. On the other hand, he was appointed organist and orchestra leader to the immensely rich Duke of Chandos and lived at his palace at Canons for three years. His duties there afforded a good deal of spare time for composing, and he had an excellent orchestra and choir at his command.

In 1719 a so-called Royal Academy of Music was founded in London with the aim of producing Italian operas, and Handel was given a leading position in this undertaking. His tasks were not only to stage the operas, conduct the performances, and go over to the Continent to engage the singers, but also to compose the operas. It was exactly the right work for a man so active, energetic, and full of initiative as he, but at the same time it was a tiring, nerve-racking, and often unrewarding job. The Italian singers were uncontrollable, demanding, and vain, and all manner of intrigues, scenes, and scandals were daily occurrences. The sensations thus caused attracted attention, but detracted from the seriousness of the enterprise. Handel put all his energy into his work and obtained excellent artistic results from this difficult material, but he was almost as quick-tempered and impulsive himself. It has been said, for example, that he was once so angry with an unreasonable prima donna that he picked her up in his arms, held her over a window sill, and threatened to drop her into the street.

The operas which Handel wrote for the Academy were highly successful, and he became a popular figure. But in the long run the public became tired of the Italian theater with its intrigues and scandals; Handel had influential opponents, and the court was soon divided into two parties—for and against him. In 1728, as the crown to his misfortunes the first performance of *The Beggar's Opera* by Gay and Pepusch was given. With its popular ditties and folk tunes, its scorn for Italian opera, and its witty satire on the social life of the times, it was exactly what the people wanted. It was an unparalleled success, and for many years won the public away from any other form of musical entertainment. Within one year after *The Beggar's Opera* opened, it attracted so much patronage that the Academy was forced to close down for lack of public support.

Handel refused to acknowledge defeat; he went to Italy to find the newest works of the leading Italian composers, gathered together a new company of Italian singers, and reorganized the Academy. For a while he had the public with him, but his victory did not last for long. To competition from *The Beggar's Opera* was added that of a rival Italian company supported by the Prince of Wales, and in 1733 Handel had to close his theater for the second time.

He courageously produced Italian opera in London again the following year, this time at the newly built Covent Garden, and at first was successful. But by 1737 the battle was over; both his and the rival company were bankrupt, and Handel himself was financially ruined. At this time he suffered a paralytic stroke, and upon the advice of his physicians retired to Aix-la-Chapelle. Several months there brought about a recovery, and he was soon working hard composing operas for an Italian company. But he never again tried to take over the management of an operatic company.

The day of Italian opera in London was over. Handel found himself considering the oratorio with increasing preoccupation. Even on his first visit to Italy he had written two successful oratorios, and later he had composed the great work *Esther*.

In technique for the new medium, he was not lacking: his extensive experience writing for voices and instruments stood him in good stead, as did his dramatic experience, so necessary for the effective storytelling demanded by this new concept of unstaged musical drama. And Handel was a practical man—if opera could no longer pay, perhaps oratorio would.

His *Messiah* was written at a time of deep despair. Financially ruined, he had made up his mind to withdraw from all public activity and had even, in the spring of 1741, given his fare-

A contemporary drawing of the memorial concert for Handel in Westminster Abbey, 1759

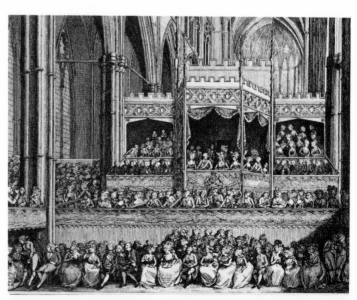

well concert. His forty-sixth—and last—opera, *Deidamia,* was performed only three times, and he was now fully aware that this chapter of his life was ended once and for all.

For some years his creditors could have sent him to the debtors' prison at any time. That they did not do so was due to his reputation for honor and honesty. They knew that he would do all he could to pay off his debts, and therefore wisely let him continue in freedom. His competitors unashamedly performed Handel's own operas to draw the public away from his theater, and arranged parties and entertainments on the days when his works were being performed. Yet at such a time he was able to produce his greatest work. But his *Messiah* established his greatness for all time, and conquered even his opponents. Even so, he had to fight for years to put his finances on a sound basis. He leased theaters for performances of his oratorios, gave concerts of organ music, and conducted; all the time he was also taking part, as before, in charity concerts.

But *Messiah* was a turning point. He now began to pay off his debts, although it was a long process. He had to write ten more oratorios,

among them *Samson* and *Judas Maccabaeus* before he could feel, in 1750, that he was financially sound again.

Jephtha (1751) was his last oratorio. While he was working on it he began to lose his sight, and after three painful eye operations he became completely blind. He patiently reconciled himself to the fact that his life as a composer was over, but he remained active in other fields to the last, playing his organ works from memory and later conducting from the organ performances of his oratorios. By now all opposition had completely vanished. His concerts were events which always drew a full house, and, since he lived as simple a life as ever, he could put aside considerable savings. On his death in London, he left an estate worth $100,000.

In his own lifetime, Handel achieved an impressive reputation, and was generally considered, as he is to this day, England's greatest composer after Purcell. Not only was he honored and respected during his lifetime, but he was accorded the honor of burial in Westminster Abbey.

Handel's talent is, of course, undisputed. But

Handel's Hercules, *performed at La Scala, Milan, in 1959*

this talent was accompanied by a strong streak of practicality and ambition. Handel was not an impractical dreamer or philosophical idealist. While he never sacrificed his own musical standards, he nevertheless was not one to miss an opportunity to satisfy royal, aristocratic, or public patronage, and he managed to combine a life of musical service to the great (the standard *modus operandi* of the day for a musician who made his living through his art) with a startlingly successful business career as a producer of opera and oratorio.

He was also a man of expediency. He was willing to write to order, and able to write fast. *Joshua,* for instance, was written in only three weeks; *Solomon* in five; *Samson* in four; and *The Messiah* in three! Little wonder, then, that Handel often "stole from himself," inserting into one work a movement previously written (and performed) for another. The detection of these transpositions is a musical parlor game, as well as the detection of sections of his works which have clearly been borrowed from those of other composers—a practice, incidentally, generally condoned and even accepted in his own time. Sheer exigency is the explanation: the time allowed for the preparation of a performance was often less than that required to copy out the orchestral parts.

Handel's style largely reflects that of his Italian, rather than his own German, contemporaries. His vocal writing, of course, is based on the Italian operatic conventions of his time, requiring the virtuoso technique possessed by the leading singers of the day. His instrumental works, particularly the Concerti Grossi, are written in the style of Vivaldi, Corelli, and Telemann. What is remarkable in his work are not the compositional innovations, but rather the individual merit and character he was able to achieve within the standard musical language of his day.

Born the same year as Bach, he represents the other side of the musical coin, the worldly, successful composer of immediately popular, seemingly uncomplicated, extroverted works. But in its accessibility lies the way to an understanding of his musical greatness.

Most of Handel's enormous output can be found in the ninety-seven volumes of manuscripts housed in the British Museum. The majority of the works are vocal (forty-six operas, thirty-two oratorios, and twenty-two cantatas),

Portrait of Handel by an unknown artist

but he also found time to write both large and small instrumental works. For many years the operas and instrumental works were overshadowed by the oratorios, especially in England, where they had a great influence on musical life.

THE OPERAS

Handel's operas were almost completely unknown until 1920, when six of them (*Rodelinda, Ottone, Giulio Cesare, Serse, Ezio,* and *Radamisto*) were performed in Germany and other countries, and made a deep impression. Clarity and purity of construction and dignity and nobility of composition were seen to be their characteristics. But they mark no epoch in operatic history; as Abdy Williams has written: "Handel took the opera as he found it and embellished it by his great genius. He was content to work on established forms, trusting for success to the employment of the best singers and instrumentalists that could be obtained."

A scene from Handel's oratorio Samson *staged at Covent Garden in 1959*

THE ORATORIOS

His oratorios, on the other hand, did open a new era. As Hugo Leichtentritt said: "The Handel oratorios are not ecclesiastical music, but grandiose dramas, the continuation of the Handel operas in another sphere. . . . They do not deal with a mere theatrical plot, involving individuals, but are rather concerned with whole nations in their relation to the divine laws, with events of national, even world-wide importance. . . . Biblical stories were chosen by Handel because of their universal validity, their elemental power, their grandiose simplicity. . . . Compared with the monumental Handel oratorio, the earlier Italian oratorio of Carissimi and his successors appears as a juvenile, undeveloped beginning or as a virtuoso show-piece; on the other hand, the entire oratorio of the 18th and 19th centuries rests on a Handelian foundation."

From the musical point of view it is the great choral passages which give the oratorios their power to uplift. Handel loved to paint with a broad brush. His effects are clear, but details are not his concern; he writes in the grand manner, and conquers with the wonderful simplicity of his melodies and his steady and powerful rhythm. He builds his works like gigantic temples, and bounds them with regularly arranged accented endings. He is not interested in surprises and has no need of the contrapuntal web of themes, but he uses again and again, as support, the pure major and minor keys. In this way his music gains peace, security, and impressive power.

The most famous of the oratorios is, of course, *The Messiah*. Grove's Dictionary, speaking of the surprising lack of success of its first London performance (only at subsequent performances, seven years later, did it capture its listeners), comments with remarkable restraint: "Since then there has been no dearth of performances."! There is scarcely an English-speaking city which, since that prophetic performance in 1750, has not enjoyed at least an annual Christmas-time rendition.

In recent years, however, there has been a movement among conductors and concert entrepreneurs to revive the lesser-known oratorios: in fact, a season rarely passes in New York without the performance of a "newly discovered" Handel oratorio. See *Messiah*.

INSTRUMENTAL WORKS

In recent years more and more of Handel's instrumental works have been rescued from obscurity. His famous twelve string Concerti Grossi, Op. 12 were written in the Italian style, and the interplay of the orchestra with the smaller instrumental groups is impressively used. The first movement is usually a stately overture, followed by four or five often quite short movements.

Handel also composed a number of concerti grossi for woodwinds and strings, concertos for solo instruments and orchestra, and a great deal of chamber music for two, three, or four instruments.

The oft-performed Viola Concerto in B minor is not an original work of Handel's but an arrangement by the viola-player Henri Casadesus (1879–1947).

ORGAN CONCERTOS

Handel was one of the greatest organists of his day. His playing always attracted an audience, and he often played in the intervals between the acts of his operas and sections of his oratorios. Many of his organ concertos are written in the half-improvisatory style of entr'acte music. Their wide variety encompasses a range from great pomp and solemnity to sly humor and grace.

ORCHESTRAL SUITES

Both Sir Hamilton Harty and Sir Thomas Beecham have revised and reorchestrated various instrumental works by Handel. One of Beecham's arrangements is of a passage from the opera *Il Pastor Fido,* under the title *The Faithful Shepherd.* Others are musical arrangements for modern ballets, such as *The Gods Go a-Begging,* written for Diaghilev in 1928, *The Origin of Design* (1932), and *The Great Elopement* (in the 1940s).

Handel did, however, leave two original suites—the *Water Music* and the *Music for the Royal Fireworks.*

HARPSICHORD WORKS

Handel composed several suites, two sonatas, a fantasy, some fugues, and a number of smaller pieces for harpsichord. He used to write small dances and similar pieces at odd moments so that he always had at hand many minuets, sarabandes, courants, and gigues which he could collect into suites, as occasion required. These works provide clear evidence of his great inventiveness and melodic ability.

The most frequently played of his harpsichord works are the Chaconne in G major, from the second set of suites (No. 2), and the air with variations from the Suite No. 5 in F major, which has become famous under the title of *The Harmonious Blacksmith.*

HANDEL'S BEST-KNOWN WORKS

OPERAS

Rinaldo (1711)
Teseo (1712)
Il Pastor Fido (1712; second version, 1734)
Floridante (1721)
Guilio Cesare (1723)
Rodelinda (1725)
Alessandro (1726)
Arianna (1733)
Alcina (1735)
Atalanta (1736)
Berenice (1737)
Serse (Xerxes) (1738)
Imeneo (1738–40)
Semele (1743)
Masque, *Acis and Galatea* (c. 1720)

ORCHESTRAL

6 Concerti Grossi, Op. 3, for winds and strings (known as *Haubois Concerti*) (1729?)
12 Concerti Grossi, Op. 12, for strings (1739)
17 Organ Concertos (1738; 1740)
Oboe Concerto (No. 3), G minor
Violin Concerto, B flat major
Water Music (c. 1717)
Music for the Royal Fireworks (1749)

INSTRUMENTAL CHAMBER MUSIC

6 Violin Sonatas (1724)
9 Flute (recorder) Sonatas (1724)
22 Trio Sonatas for 2 violins, oboes or flutes, and continuo (1696; 1733; 1738)

VOCAL CHAMBER MUSIC

77 Italian Cantatas (for solo voice or voices and instrumental accompaniment)
20 Italian Duets, with continuo (1707–08; 1741–45)

HARPSICHORD WORKS

17 Suites (or Lessons), in 2 vols. (1720; 1733)
2 Sonatas, each in C major
Various short dance movements, fugues, and other occasional pieces

ORATORIOS

Esther (1720; revised 1732)
Tolomeo (1728)
Deborah (1733)
Athalia (1733)
Israel in Egypt (1738)
Saul (1738)
Samson (1741)
The Messiah (1741)
Belshazzar (1744)
Hercules (1744)
Judas Maccabaeus (1746)
Occasional Oratorio (1746)
Joshua (1747)
Susanna (1748)
Solomon (1748)
Theodora (1749)
Jephtha (1751)

OTHER CHORAL WORKS

The Passion According to St. John (Ger. text) (1704)
Utrecht *Te Deum* and *Jubilate* (1713)
Chandos Anthems (1716–18)
Coronation Anthems (1727)
  Zadok the Priest
  The King Shall Rejoice
  My Heart Is Inditing
  Let Thy Hand Be Strengthened
Ode, *Alexander's Feast* (1736)
Funeral Anthem for Queen Caroline (1737)
Ode for St. Cecilia's Day (1739)
Cantata, *L'Allegro ed Il Penseroso* (1740)
Dettingen *Te Deum* (1743)

HANDY, William Christopher. American composer and trumpeter (1873–1958). Born in Florence, Ala., Handy's first musical experience was singing in his father's Methodist church. Although forbidden to play any instrument other than the church organ, he secretly bought himself a cornet and became a member of the local brass band. After some years spent in teaching, working in a steel mill, and playing in a quartet in Chicago and St. Louis, he became bandmaster and cornet soloist with Mahara's Minstrels with whom he toured the United States and Canada. He eventually acquired his own band, and settled in Memphis.

In 1909 he published the first of his celebrated blues compositions, the *Memphis Blues,* and in September, 1914, he wrote the *St. Louis Blues,* which became one of the most frequently recorded of all musical compositions. After that Handy composed, re-created, arranged, and edited many blues and popular songs, which have earned him the title of "The Father of the Blues." Sigmund Spaeth says of him: "If Handy did not actually create the Blues . . . he made them available to interpreters and listeners throughout the world, and for this his assumption of paternalism may well be excused. It is

W. C. HANDY

impossible to think of that highly individual type of music today without thinking of the name of W. C. Handy." See *Blues.*

HANNIKAINEN, Tauno. Finnish conductor (1896–). He belongs to a distinguished musical family and has toured as a cellist with his brothers in a family trio. As a conductor of many principal European and American symphony orchestras, he has done much to popularize the music of his compatriot, Sibelius.

HANON, Charles-Louis. French pianist and teacher (1820–1900). Hanon wrote many studies for the piano. His sixty progressive studies, *The Virtuoso Pianist,* became a widely employed piano instructional guide.

HÄNSEL UND GRETEL. Fairy-tale opera in two acts by Humperdinck, with libretto by Adelheid Wette, the composer's sister. The work was originally intended for the family circle, but Humperdinck persuaded the Royal Theater in Weimar to produce it at an afternoon performance at Christmas, 1893, with Richard Strauss conducting. It was such a success that other theaters in Germany also performed it, and soon it was being played all over the world.

Humperdinck was a student and intimate acquaintance of Wagner. His musical idiom is very much related to Wagner's technique of development and orchestration. Nevertheless Humperdinck has admirably succeeded in creating the atmosphere of a fairy tale, a subject matter quite different from Wagnerian mythology. The musical material used in *Hänsel und Gretel* was partly derived from Westphalian folk tunes.

ACT I

Scene 1: *At home in the cottage*

Gretel (soprano) is knitting, and Hänsel (mezzo-soprano) is binding brooms. Becoming hungry, they stop working and dance happily round a milk jug:

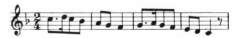

Their mother, Gertrude (mezzo-soprano), becoming angry, strikes out at them, but hits the milk jug. Furious, she sends the children out into the woods to pick berries.

Their father, the broom-maker Peter (baritone), returns home, having sold his wares in the town, bought some food, and gotten a little drunk. When he

A scene from Hänsel und Gretel *at La Scala, Milan*

HOWARD HANSON

hears that the children are out in the forest, he is afraid lest the witch at Ilsenstein should catch them. The mother also becomes anxious, and they go off together to search for the children.

Scene 2: *In the forest*

Hänsel picks berries while Gretel sits under a tree and sings the old song about the Sandman:

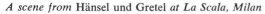

A cuckoo is heard. The children enjoy the berries, but as darkness begins to fall they become frightened and call for their mother and father. Tired and faint-hearted, they sit down. The Sandman comes and sprinkles sand in their eyes, and after they have sung the evening prayer, they fall asleep.

ACT II

Scene: *The witch's house*

The children are still asleep at dawn. The Dew Fairy appears in a bluebell and shakes dewdrops on them. Gretel wakes and rouses Hänsel. As the mist rises they turn round to find a house made of sweets and cake behind them. The children delightedly pick pieces off the house and eat them, then dance and sing.

The old witch (mezzo-soprano) comes out. She pretends to be kind to them, but when she throws a sling around Hänsel's neck he becomes afraid. He manages to escape and starts to run away with Gretel,

but the witch waves her magic wand and the children cannot move from the spot. Then the witch shuts Hänsel into a cage to fatten him up, and Gretel is forced to help in the house. Hänsel manages, however, to get out, and hides. The witch makes up the fire, and rides round the house on her broomstick.

The witch orders Gretel to look into the oven to see if the cakes are done. Gretel pretends to be slow-witted and asks the witch to show her how. As the witch bends to demonstrate, the children push her into the oven. Gretel, who has learned the witch's spell, waves the magic wand and at once all the be-witched children, who have been standing like a fence round the house, come to life again. They are all dancing for joy when Hänsel's and Gretel's parents discover them.

HANSLICK, Eduard. Austrian music critic (1825–1904). For many years, he was the most powerful critic in Europe. He also wrote many books on music, including a history of opera. Though he approved of Brahms and Schumann, he was the enemy of Wagner and Liszt. Wagner took revenge by making Hanslick the model for Beckmesser in *Die Meistersinger*.

HANSON, Howard. American composer (1896–). He attended Luther College, the Institute of Musical Art in New York, and Northwestern University. His career as an educator began at the College of the Pacific. In 1924, he became director of the Eastman School of Music in Rochester, N. Y., and has since developed it into one of the finest in America. He also founded and directs the American Music Festival, an important annual forum for contemporary composers, and conducts the Eastman Philharmonia Orchestra, which in 1962 made an extended tour of Europe, Russia, and the Middle East.

Since 1921, when he won the Prix de Rome, Dr. Hanson has been a prominent composer and is considered an exponent of the romantic school. When asked about his musical creed, he answered: "I believe in music as a tonal art which speaks directly to the ears of those who are sensitive. I believe its impact should be emotionally and spiritually direct. I am against the over-cerebration which too frequently results in emotional sterility. I have been called a conservative-modernist, a neo-romanticist, and even 'the American Sibelius'—none of which titles I particularly resent or applaud. I prefer to stand on the results of my music."

Best-known works:

Lament for Beowulf (chorus and orchestra): a setting of the Anglo-Saxon epic, archaic and primitive in character.

Merry Mount (opera): based on the psychological conflict between the Puritans and Cavaliers of early New England. Produced at the Metropolitan Opera House in 1934.

Cherubic Hymn (chorus and orchestra): a mystical and dramatic setting of a portion of the Greek Liturgy.

Drum Taps (chorus and orchestra): setting of three of the most striking of Walt Whitman's Civil War poems: *Beat, Beat Drums; By the Bivouac's Fitful Flame; To Thee, Old Cause.*

Four Symphonies: No. 1 (*Nordic*); No. 2 (*Romantic*); No. 3, written to celebrate the landing of the Swedes in Delaware; No. 4 (*Requiem*).

HARASIEWICZ, Adam. Polish pianist (1932–). Harasiewicz is one of the outstanding young pianists of today. In 1958 he represented his country at the Brussels World's Fair; previously he received first prizes in the Rzeszów Competition (1947) and the International Chopin Competition in Warsaw (1955). He studied at the Kraków Conservatory.

HARBACH, Otto. American lyricist and librettist (1873–1963). One of the most prolific

A scene from Howard Hanson's Merry Mount *at its Metropolitan Opera première*

and successful writers of American musical comedy, Harbach had a significant hand in over fifty Broadway musicals from 1908. His collaborators included the top composers in the field: Kern, Gershwin, Youmans, Friml, Romberg, and many others. Some of his better known works include *The Firefly* (1912), *Rose Marie* (1924), *No, No, Nanette* (1925), *The Desert Song* (1925), and *Roberta* (1933). His writing, which he jokingly referred to as "corny," is marked by the same sentiment and compassion which characterized his pupil, Oscar Hammerstein II. See *American Musical Theater.*

HARDELOT, Guy d'. Pseudonym of Mrs. Helen Rhodes, nee Guy, French composer of songs (1858–1936). She studied at the Paris Conservatory, and was acquainted with many French composers, especially Gounod and Massenet. She toured America in 1896 with the famous soprano Emma Calvé. After her marriage she made her home in London.

Her many popular songs include *Because* (perhaps the best remembered of all drawing-room ballads), *Three Green Bonnets,* and *I Know a Lovely Garden.* These were sung all over the world by Calvé, Melba, and other famous singers, and by thousands of amateurs.

HARMAN, Carter. American composer and music critic (1918–). Harman was a student of Roger Sessions at Princeton University, and after army service, continued his studies at Columbia University. Between 1947 and 1952 he was a music critic on the New York *Times* and, between 1952 and 1956, music editor of *Time* magazine. He has written an opera, *Charms for the Savage,* and a book, *A Popular History of Music from Gregorian Chant to Jazz.*

HARMONICA (1). Name of several instruments in which the source of sound is glass rubbed or struck; also called *musical glasses.* If a number of wine or water glasses are placed side by side, with a different amount of water in each, and a wet finger is rubbed lightly over their edges, notes of varying pitch are obtained, according to the amounts of water in the glasses. By adjusting the amounts of water, the glasses can be tuned so as to form a scale on which tunes can be played. Gluck performed on such an instrument in London in 1746.

The glass harmonica constructed by Ben-

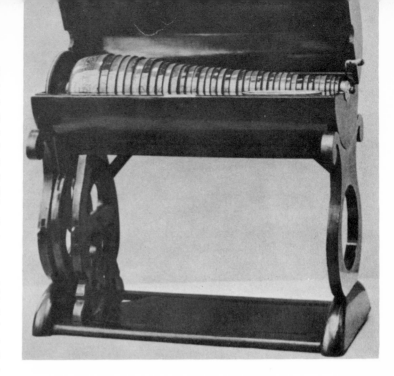

An eighteenth-century Czech glass harmonica

jamin Franklin in 1752 consisted of glass bowls of varying size fixed around a central axis. These were made to rotate by means of a pedal, and the player touched the polished surface of the bowls with moistened fingers. Mozart wrote a quintet for this instrument, accompanied by strings and wind instruments, and Mendelssohn conducted a performance of it at the Leipzig Gewandhaus.

The name harmonica is also given to a form of dulcimer in which strips of glass are struck with hammers.

HARMONICA (2). An instrument consisting of a narrow frame containing slots in each of which a small free metal reed vibrates laterally when the instrument is held to the lips and blown or sucked. The reeds are graduated in size to produce the notes of the scale, and half tones are sounded by drawing in the breath. In some models other shifts of key are obtained by pressing or pulling out a knob at the end of the frame.

A simple tune in chords can be played by moving the instrument from side to side across the mouth, but virtuosos of the harmonica (or mouth organ) combine this with movements of the hand and tongue to create beautiful single note effects. A world-famous contemporary harmonica player is Larry Adler.

HARMONICS (1). Overtones having a frequency which is a whole-number multiple of the frequency of the fundamental note. See *Timbre.*

HARMONICS (2). The harmonics of stringed instruments, sometimes called flageolet tones, which are high, thin, flutelike tones produced by holding the finger lightly on the string at a nodal point. Domenico Ferrari (1722–80) is said to have introduced the playing of harmonics, and Paganini further developed the technique.

HARMONIOUS BLACKSMITH, THE. Air with variations from Suite No. 5, by Handel. The piece was first given this name in 1820, a hundred years after its composition. There was living in Bath at that time a young man who kept a music shop and had previously been a blacksmith. He was called the harmonious blacksmith because he was always singing. And as it was usually this Handel tune that he sang, the name came to be transferred from the man to the melody.

Haydn's harpsichord, in the collection of the Museum der Gesellschaft der Musikfreunde, Vienna

By 1830 a legend had grown up that Handel had composed the tune while taking shelter from the rain in a smithy near Edgware. Before long it was "discovered" that the blacksmith's name was Powell, and in the end both his hammer and his anvil were "found." In 1879 these treasures of musical history were sold to a Mrs. Maskelyne. It was only in recent years that this story was exploded.

HARMONIUM. A small keyboard reed organ, the reeds being vibrated by wind from bellows worked by the player's feet. See *Organ.*

HARMONY. Any simultaneous combination of sounds is a harmony, though in a narrower sense the combination should be pleasing or agreeable. Harmony also applies not to single formations of sounds (chords), but to successions of chords and the relationship between them. It denotes the chordal or vertical structure of a composition in contrast to melody and counterpoint, which are part of horizontal structure. See *Music, Elements of.*

HAROLD IN ITALY. Symphony in four movements, with solo viola, Op. 16 (1834), by Berlioz, the composer's third symphony. In 1834 Berlioz was commissioned by Paganini to write a viola concerto, and chose as his program an episode from Byron's epic *Childe Harold*. Identifying himself with the hero of the poem, Berlioz based his symphony on his own experiences in the Abruzzi Mountains. The viola was meant to interpret Harold's (and Berlioz's) *joie de vivre* and melancholy, while the orchestra describes the Italian landscape and the colorful life of the people.

The four movements are very different in character, but the viola has a repeated motif which gives unity to the work. The program is indicated in the titles of the movements:

  I. *Harold in the Mountains.*
  II. *March and Evening Prayer of Pilgrims.*
  III. *Serenade of the Abruzzi Mountaineer to His Beloved.*
  IV. *Orgy of Brigands.*

HARP. See *Stringed Instruments.*

HARPSICHORD. A keyboard instrument, also called the cembalo or clavicembalo, in general use from the sixteenth through the eighteenth century, and undergoing a revival today. Its strings, instead of being struck, are plucked by plectra consisting of quills or, sometimes, leather points. There are two or more strings to each note, the number in use being varied by means of stops or pedals. Variation in the pressure of the fingers has very little effect.

The oldest surviving harpsichord originated in Rome in the 1520s. Most early harpsichords are Italian, and considered as furniture are beautiful works of art.

Many of the well-known composers of the Baroque period were celebrated virtuosos on this instrument. Its sound, variable by using up to eight stops, is sharp, clear, and of a sweeping festivity if played at full power. Many harpsichords are equipped with two or three keyboards, thus extending the range of technical possibilities.

The harpsichord is not only used as a solo instrument. Its function within the baroque orchestra is of fundamental importance. Under ideal conditions, baroque music should be played on the harpsichord. The same holds true for the accompaniments to recitatives of seventeenth- and eighteenth-century operas.

The harpsichord is no longer in general use, having been supplanted by the modern piano since the late eighteenth century. Nevertheless there are a number of excellent and internationally acclaimed harpsichordists. Wanda Landowska was first among these. The harpsichord has also been used, experimentally, in jazz.

HARRELL, Mack. American baritone (1909–1960). A graduate of the Juilliard School, he later taught there and at Southern Methodist University. He became distinguished as a lieder singer and joined the Metropolitan Opera in 1939. Two of his best roles were Amfortas in *Parsifal* and Dodon in *Le Coq d'Or*. He was Nick Shadow in Stravinsky's *The Rake's Progress* at the American première in 1953. With the New York Philharmonic, he sang in concert versions of *Wozzeck* and *Christophe Colomb.*

HARRIS, Roy Ellsworth. American composer (1898–). Harris was interested in music from childhood, but did not decide on a musical career until 1924. As early as 1935 Harris was regarded

ROY HARRIS

as one of the most original of American composers and a few years later he had become one of the most popular, his works being the most frequently performed. For some time Harris has been composer-in-residence at Cornell University.

Harris' music is markedly individual. He had created his own style long before he became acquainted with other modern composers. His rhythm and tempo are nonsymmetrical, his melody is influenced by sacred modes, and he has his own peculiar style of harmony. He has more in common with Sibelius and Stravinsky than with the more radical Schoenberg, Alban Berg, Hindemith, and Bartók, and he regards himself as a neo-classical composer. There is little humor or lightness in his music.

Harris himself says: "I believe that music has been steadily running downhill since Beethoven, because orchestral color has been exploited at the expense of all other elements of music. This sort of romantic attitude has governed man for more than two hundred years and has brought us to a sorry pass. . . . It really is an attitude of supreme egoism, wherein the individual assumes a *summum bonum* of all wisdom and beneficence in his own self. . . . The hope which carries me forth in my life-work is that of expressing in clear, organic, classic form the dominant emotional impulses which mold my life from day to day."

His compositions include seven symphonies, choral works, chamber music, and piano pieces. Best known among these works are Symphony No. 3 (1938) and Symphony No. 7 (1951).

HARRIS, Willard P. (Bill). American jazz trombonist (1916–). A prominent stylist, Harris has influenced many young musicians. He has played with Benny Goodman, Woody Herman, and Charlie Ventura, performed on tour with Jazz at the Philharmonic, headed his own groups and conducted a disk jockey program in Florida.

HARRISON, Guy Fraser. Anglo-American conductor (1894–). Harrison studied at Oxford and at the Royal College of Music. He became conductor of the Eastman Theater Orchestra in Rochester, New York, shortly after coming to this country in 1920. He conducted the Eastman Civic Orchestra until 1951, and was also associate conductor of the Rochester Philharmonic Orchestra. In 1951 he was appointed conductor of the Oklahoma City Symphony Orchestra.

LOU HARRISON

HARRISON, Lou. American composer (1917–). Harrison has studied with Henry Cowell and Arnold Schoenberg. He has taught at Mills College, the University of California at Los Angeles, Reed College in Portland, Oregon, and Black Mountain College in North Carolina. He was a music critic on the New York *Herald Tribune* from 1945 to 1948, and wrote articles for *Modern Music*. He has received grants from the American Academy of Arts and Letters, and the National Institute of Arts and Letters; Guggenheim Fellowships in 1952 and 1954; a Fromm Foundation award; and a commission from the Louisville Orchestra. He received a prize at the Roman International Composers Conference in 1954.

He has been interested in unorthodox and exotic sonorities, incorporating such sound sources as automobile brake drums, glass bowls, lengths of plumber's pipes, and flower pots in one or another of his works for percussion instruments. Gamelan influences are obvious in some of his important works, for example the Suite for Solo Violin, Solo Piano and Small Orchestra (1951) and *Canticle No. III* for percussion. Some of his compositions, for instance *Canticle No. I* and *Labyrinth No. 3,* both for percussion ensemble, display marked power, uncommon sensitivity to timbres, and a charming melodic gift. His works include orchestral and chamber music; choral music (most important is the *Mass*); an opera, *Rapunzel;* incidental and ballet music; and piano pieces.

HARSÁNYI, Tibor. Hungarian-French composer (1898–1954). A pupil of Kodály, he was first successful as a pianist and was a friend and disciple of Bartók. His works include two operas, ballets, songs, chamber music, orchestral and choral pieces, and pieces for violin, piano, and flute.

HARSHAW, Margaret. American soprano (1912–). After studying at the Juilliard School, she won the Auditions of the Air and made her debut at the Metropolitan Opera in 1942. She performed leading mezzo-soprano and contralto roles until she became a dramatic soprano in 1950. Since then, she has been a prominent interpreter of the Wagner heroines at the Metropolitan, Covent Garden, the Bayreuth Festival, and with other leading opera companies. She also has given many recitals and has been soloist with most of the major American symphony orchestras.

HART, Lorenz. American lyricist (1895–1943). He and Richard Rodgers began their collaboration, which lasted until Hart's death, while they were students at Columbia University. They worked for seven years before having their first success, a small revue for the Theatre Guild, which was intended for only a single performance but ran for a year and a half. From then on, they went from success to success. The rare combination of Hart's lyrics with Rodgers' music resulted in many musical-comedy hits, including *A Connecticut Yankee, On Your Toes, Babes In Arms, The Boys From Syracuse, Pal Joey,* and *By Jupiter.* See *American Musical Theater; Richard Rodgers.*

HARTMANN, Arthur. Hungarian-American violinist (1881-1956). He was brought to America as a child and became a famous prodigy, performing most of the modern violin repertory before he was twelve. As an adult, he toured extensively and played in recitals with Debussy, whose friend he became.

HARTMANN, Carl. German tenor (1895–). His unusual height and handsome appearance made him famous as Siegfried and Tristan in German opera houses, and at the Metropolitan Opera, where he sang from 1937 to 1939.

HARTMANN, Karl Amadeus. German composer (1905–). Hartmann first studied with Josef Haas and Hermann Scherchen, and in 1941 with Anton von Webern, adopting the twelve-tone method. After the end of World War II, he organized a musical society, Musica Viva, in Munich. In 1953 he was elected president of the German section of the International Society for Contemporary Music. He has written an opera; six symphonies; a concerto for piano, wind instruments, and percussion; and numerous works for various instrumental combinations.

HARTMANN, Thomas de. Russian pianist and composer (1886–1956). He studied at the Moscow Conservatory with Arensky and Taneiev. Well known as a pianist, he also was a conductor and achieved some distinction as a painter. His compositions include many songs, an opera, several ballets, concertos for various instru-

Margaret Harshaw as Venus in Tannhäuser

ments, orchestral and piano works, and chamber music.

HARTY, Sir Herbert Hamilton. British conductor and composer (1879–1941). Harty was taught piano, viola, and counterpoint by his father and became organist at Magheracoll Church at the age of twelve.

He went to London in 1900 and rapidly became known as an admirable accompanist; works like his *Comedy Overture* (1907) won him recognition as a composer. After considerable experience as conductor with the London Symphony Orchestra, Harty was appointed conductor of the Hallé Orchestra in 1920, where he fully maintained the high standards and traditions established by Richter. He had a special interest in the works of Berlioz.

His works include *Ode to a Nightingale* for soprano and orchestra (1907), the symphonic poem *With the Wild Geese* (1910), the Violin Concerto in D minor (1909), *Irish Symphony* (rewritten in 1923), and orchestrations of pieces by Handel, notably a selection from the *Water Music.* Harty also wrote arrangements of Irish folk songs and settings of Irish poems, distinguished for their delicate charm. Lady Harty was the well-known soprano, Agnes Nicholls.

HÁRY JÁNOS. Orchestral suite by Zoltán Kodály, based on his music for a *singspiel* (ballad opera) of the same name, which had its first performance in 1926 in Budapest. The libretto was written by Paulini and Harsányi from Johann Garay's poem *The Discarded Soldier*. The score contains a cimbalom part.

The peasant Háry János has been a soldier, and now tries to compensate for the misery of his existence by telling boastful stories. His wild imaginings are a symbol of man's unfulfilled dreams; at the same time he is the poet, for the harmless cock-and-bull story is the father of all poetry. The *singspiel* tells of the wonderful feats performed by Háry: how he tames the wildest of horses, goes to war and makes Napoleon a prisoner, rescues a princess from the clutches of a dragon, and nevertheless remains faithful to his beloved and refuses all offers of reward.

The sections of the suite are:

    I. Prelude: The Fairy Tale Begins.
   II. Viennese Musical Clock.
  III. Song.
  IV. Battle and Defeat of Napoleon.
   V. Intermezzo.
 VI. Entrance of the Emperor and His Court.

Only once in the suite did Kodály make use of a truly Hungarian folk song (in the third movement); the Intermezzo contains the ancient *Recruiters' Dance* with trio, dating from the eighteenth century.

HASKIL, Clara. Rumanian pianist (1895–1960). Clara Haskil made her debut in Vienna at the age of seven. She then became a pupil of Alfred Cortot and Gabriel Fauré. When the great pianist Busoni heard her play, he was so impressed with her talent that he asked her to study with him in Berlin. In Europe, Clara Haskil soon became known for her immaculate and sensitive musicianship, both as a concert artist and as a performer of chamber music. She has played Beethoven sonatas with Enesco, Ysaye, and Casals. Today her recordings of Mozart's sonatas for violin and piano, with Arthur Grumiaux, belong to the finest examples of their kind.

Clara Haskil has made her name on the concert scene particularly as an interpreter of Bach, Mozart, and Beethoven. Her fame spread in the United States, particularly after her appearances with Leopold Stokowski and with the Boston Symphony Orchestra under Charles Munch in 1956.

HASSE, Faustina Bordoni. Italian soprano. (1700–1781). She was, with Francesca Cuzzoni, the most famous singer of her time, and

*Johann Adolph Hasse, a portrait
by Felicitas Hoffmann*

*Faustina Hasse-Bordoni, a portrait
by Felicitas Hoffmann*

Two scenes from the Juilliard School of Music production of Háry János

the furious rivalry between the two led to riots in London, where they were singing in Handel's company. Gifted with beauty and extraordinary vocal dexterity, she was for 34 years adored by audiences and the pet of princes in Italy, Austria, Germany, and England. She was the wife of the composer Hasse, to whom she was married for fifty-eight years.

HASSE, Johann Adolph. German composer (1699–1783). Though his music is almost completely unknown today, he was one of the most successful composers of his time. Altogether, he composed almost sixty operas in the Italian style and was the acknowledged master of the form before the advent of Gluck and Mozart.

HASSLER, Hans Leo. German composer (1564–1612). The son and brother of famous organists, he was himself an accomplished organist. One of the most interesting of the pre-Bach Baroque composers, he wrote many madrigals and other pieces in the Italian style, motets, masses, and various organ works.

HAUBIEL, Charles. American composer (1892–). Haubiel studied piano with Rudolph

Ganz and Josef and Rosina Lhevinne, and composition with Rosario Scalero. He has occupied various teaching posts. He was the recipient of the first prize at the 1928 Schubert Centennial Contest for his set of symphonic variations, *Karma.* He has written many compositions for various instrumental combinations.

HAUER, Josef Matthias. Austrian composer (1883–1959). Hauer began his musical studies while a public school teacher. Greatly interested in the mathematical construction of music, he developed his own system of composition. In 1912, he published the piano piece *Nomos,* which incorporated the beginnings of twelve-tone music and foreshadowed the Schoenberg system. See *Twelve-Tone Music.*

HAUFRECHT, Herbert. American composer (1909–). Haufrecht studied music first with his mother, then at the Cleveland Institute of Music with Herbert Elwell and Quincy Porter, and later with Rubin Goldmark at the Juilliard School. Folk music, including jazz, and children's music have been special areas of attention and experience for Haufrecht. Some of his compositions, while serious in purpose, incor-

MINNIE HAUK

porate folk idioms to some extent, for example, his *Square Set* for strings. He has written works for orchestra, chamber orchestra with narrator, strings, band, chorus, piano, and guitar; a music play; songs; and chamber music, notably *A Woodland Serenade* for wind quintet, a fresh and sensitive work.

HAUK, Minnie. (*real name* **Amalia Mignon Hauck**). American soprano (1852–1929). She made her debut at fourteen and became one of the most famous actress-singers of her time. At the New York Academy of Music, she sang Juliette in Gounod's opera and Manon in Massenet's opera at their American premières. One of the first great Carmens, she sang the role more than 600 times in four languages and was the first to sing it in England and America. In 1891, late in her career, she appeared at the Metropolitan Opera. She toured America with her own company, sang throughout Europe, and altogether performed in one hundred roles.

HAUSSERMAN, John. American composer (1909–). Hausserman studied at the Cincinnati Conservatory and later in Paris with Marcel Dupré and Le Flem. He has writtten three symphonies, chamber music, and a concerto for voice and orchestra.

HAUTZIG, Walter. Austrian-American pianist (1922–). Born in Vienna, where he studied at the State Academy of Music, he came to the United States in 1939. He was graduated from Curtis Institute in 1943 and made his recital debut the same year in New York's Town Hall. This recital won him the Town Hall Endowment Award. He has since made several tours of the United States, nine tours of Europe, six tours of Latin America, and two tours of the Orient; has appeared extensively in the Middle East; and has made recordings.

HAWKINS, Coleman. American jazz saxophonist (1904–). Hawkins originally played piano and cello, turning to the saxophone at the age of nine. He was the first famous tenor saxophonist in jazz, and for some time enjoyed unparalleled predominance on that instrument. He first recorded with Fletcher Henderson in 1923, and after free-lancing both in the United States and in England, formed his own nine-piece orchestra in 1939. He made the difficult transition from traditional jazz to bop, and led the orchestra which first recorded the new sound in 1944. See *Jazz.*

His full, fluid tone, for so long the most imitated in jazz, passed from popular favor with the advent of the lighter, more reedy sound of the "cool school," typified by Stan Getz. Nevertheless, musicians and the public alike join in acclaiming Hawkins' musicianship and lyric gift.

HAYASAKA, Fumio. Japanese composer (1914–). Hayasaka studied in Tokyo with Alexander Tcherepnin. In 1938 he won the Weingartner Prize. He is known in the United States for his scores to Japanese films, the most noted being *Rashomon.*

Franz Joseph Haydn

(MARCH 31, 1732—MAY 31, 1809)

FRANZ JOSEPH HAYDN was the son of a wheelwright in the small country town of Rohrau, forty miles from Vienna. The family had lived in the district for several generations, but is said to be of German origin. The second of twelve children, Joseph grew up in very poor circumstances. The greatest pleasure the children had in their daily life was singing, both parents being musical. In the evening the family would gather in the largest room of the cottage and sing to the father's harp accompaniment. Haydn said of his childhood: "Almighty God, whom I thank for all his numberless gifts, gave me such an aptitude for music that, when I was six years old, I could take my place in the church choir like a grown man and sing the Masses, and could also play a little on the clavier and violin."

When he was eight, his beautiful voice was discovered by George Reutter, choirmaster at the Cathedral of St. Stephen in Vienna, where he became a choirboy. His years at St. Stephen's were hard. At the choir school the boys received so little food that Haydn spoke of his time there as a "time of unbroken fasting." Nor did he receive much musical instruction; but he studied theory by himself and practiced the clavier. When his voice changed, at seventeen, he was turned out on the streets, and had to make a living by teaching music to children and taking part in small serenade ensembles.

Before long Haydn was lucky enough to make the acquaintance of the Italian composer and singing teacher Niccolo Porpora, who gave him employment as his servant and accompanist at his singing lessons. Haydn put up with his master's harshness since Porpora corrected his attempts at composition, taught him Italian, and gave him voice training.

He obtained his first independent post, as a member of Prince Fürnberg's chamber ensemble, in 1755, and four years later became *Kapellmeister* to Count Morzin. A few years before, he had fallen in love with a young girl who, however, had decided to become a nun. Haydn remained in contact with the family, and in 1760 he married the girl's elder sister, Maria Anna Keller, who was two years older than he. It was an unhappy marriage—as Haydn said, "It was all the same to her whether her husband was a shoemaker or an artist"—and became all the

Franz Joseph Haydn, a portrait by Longhi.
Brooklyn Museum, New York

more bitter to Haydn when his first love, Therese Keller, later left the nunnery.

In 1761 a turning point in his life was reached when he was appointed deputy *Kapellmeister* to Prince Paul Anton Esterházy, the most distinguished, wealthy, and powerful of Hungarian nobles. The Prince was a passionate music lover, and musical indeed was life at his palace in the small town of Eisenstadt, southeast of Vienna. As Werner, the *Kapellmeister,* was old and ailing, it was understood that Haydn should take over most of his work. Every week he had to direct two opera performances, two big concerts, and all the rehearsals of the twelve-piece orchestra (later considerably augmented) and the six singers, and administer and supervise the musicians, copyists, instruments, music library, etc. The next year, upon the death of Prince Paul Anton, his brother Nicholas, also an enlightened and enthusiastic musical amateur, succeeded him as Prince. In 1766, Haydn became *Kapellmeister,* in complete charge of all music for the Esterházy establishment. It was an ideal post: well-paid, well-appreciated, and offering complete artistic freedom. Haydn described his position thus: "My prince was satisfied with all my works; I was praised; as head of an orchestra

A bust of Haydn by A. Robatz

The church in Eisenstadt where Haydn is buried

I could experiment, observe what heightened the effect and what weakened it, and so could improve, expand, cut, take risks; I was cut off from the world, there was no one near me to torment me or make me doubt myself, and so I had to become original."

The position did, of course, have its drawbacks. Though Haydn enjoyed artistic liberty, he had little social freedom. He was one of the Prince's servants. True, in the course of time he became highly respected, but he remained a servant, dependent and bound. Handel, forty years earlier, had felt it impossible to relinquish his freedom for any length of time. But Haydn had a master who made his dependency relatively easy to bear, and in any case he was no rebel. He had been accustomed from childhood to defer to others, and apparently he felt it no indignity to accept the position of a servant.

Another drawback to his position was the location of the Esterházy residence at Eisenstadt, a tiny town cut off from the currents of artistic and musical life. When Prince Nicholas built a new castle out in the desolate marshes by the Neusiedler Lake, and spent most of the year there, Haydn was even more completely separated from the developments of the age. The products of his employment in the Esterházy retinue were five Masses, eleven operas, about sixty symphonies, forty string quartets, 125 trios for Prince Nicholas' favorite instrument, the viola di bordone (barytone), about thirty clavier sonatas, and many other works.

Prince Nicholas, who had been Haydn's employer for twenty-eight years, died in 1790. His successor disbanded the orchestra, but Haydn kept his salary and his title as leader of

A performance of Haydn's opera L'Incontro improviso *at Prince Esterházy's private theater*
The composer is seen at far left, conducting from the harpsichord

the Prince's musicians, without having any duties. He moved at once to Vienna, where at last he could meet admiring friends and colleagues, above all Mozart, with whom he had maintained a close friendship for some years.

Once he was finally free of the yoke, Haydn determined never to take such a position again, and refused the offer of an appointment to the Court of Naples. He had been a servant all his life; now he wanted to live a free man and see the world. While he had been shut up in the Esterházy palaces his name had spread across Europe; former members of his orchestra had made his compositions known everywhere, and publishers abroad had been bringing out many of his works without permission. His name was revered throughout the musical world, and he soon received, from the violinist and impresario Salomon, the offer of an extended concert engagement in London. He joyfully accepted. He would have to work hard—he contracted to write six symphonies and to direct twenty concerts—but hard work had no terrors for Haydn, and the financial terms were generous. He could not speak a word of English, and the trip was in every respect a leap into the unknown; but it was these exciting circumstances that attracted him and made him accept the English offer against the advice of his friends. Two months after the death of Prince Esterházy, and less than a fortnight after receiving Salomon's offer, Haydn was on his way to London.

This stay in England was from first to last triumphant. He was received enthusiastically, his music made the deepest impression, he won friends everywhere, he was received at Court and played frequently for the Prince of Wales, he became an honorary Doctor of Music of Oxford, and the financial results surpassed his expectations. In the midst of all the exacting social life and frequent public appearances, Haydn still found the time to compose. His twelve *London* symphonies show that his reception in London inspired him to give of his very best, for these are undeniable masterpieces.

While he was in London he attended one of the great Handel festivals, in which over a thousand instrumentalists and singers took part. Handel's oratorios made a deep impression on Haydn—he is reported to have said, on hearing the *Hallelujah Chorus,* "He is the master of us all"—and this encounter with Handel's music had great importance for his later work.

Haydn's tomb at Eisenstadt

After a stay of eighteen months (January, 1791, to June, 1792) Haydn returned to Vienna, but he no longer felt completely at home there. Mozart was dead, and one of his closest friends, Marianne von Genziger, died soon afterward. He was therefore very willing to accept another invitation to London, and arrived there in February, 1794, for another stay of eighteen months. It was suggested that he should settle permanently in London, and he even received an offer from the Royal Family to live at the palace. It was a temptation: Haydn had as many good friends in London as in Vienna, and was much more of a celebrity there. But he decided against it; life in London was too strenuous for him, for he was beginning to feel older and to realize that he had to husband his strength. In England he could not have attained any higher position; indeed, if he had stayed he would have had to strive hard to keep the position he had won. He preferred to return to the quieter life of Vienna, where much less attention was paid to him and where no demands were made on him. Moreover, there was now a new head of the Esterházy family, and the new Prince asked Haydn to come back and take over the direction of his orchestra again. Haydn accepted.

He spent the winters in Vienna and only the summer months at Eisenstadt, and his work for Esterházy was limited to the composition of some church music. Haydn thus had time for other things, and soon after his return he addressed himself to the great work to which Handel's music had inspired him—the oratorio *The Creation,* to a text adapted from Milton, translated by Baron van Swieten.

The years 1796 to 1798, when he was writing *The Creation,* were perhaps the happiest of Haydn's life. He was deeply religious, and his sense of the greatness of his task gave him a feeling of uplifting joy. "I fell on my knees each day and begged God to give me strength to accomplish the work successfully."

All his other compositions had been composed for immediate use and for a known audience. *The Creation* expressed his thanks to God for what life had given him, and he was overjoyed when it was a triumph, was repeated several times immediately after the first performance, and was produced over and over again in all countries. The success gave him the impetus to compose another similar work, *The Seasons,* to words by Van Swieten. This was finished in

A performance of Haydn's opera, Il Mondo della Luna *at the 1959 Holland Festival*

two years, and was almost as great a success as *The Creation.*

Haydn was now seventy, and began gradually to withdraw from public life. He still conducted now and then—for the last time in 1803, when he conducted *The Seven Words of Our Saviour on the Cross,* which he had written eighteen years before for the Cathedral of Cadiz. In the last five years of his life, he failed visibly, finally becoming so weak that he had to give up composition altogether. He was able to complete only two movements of his final quartet, one of a projected group of six. It is touching to learn that, to comfort himself, it was his habit often to play his *Emperor's Hymn,* the Austrian national anthem he had written in 1797, inspired by the patriotic enthusiasm of the English crowds singing *God Save the King.*

As late as March 27, 1808, he was able to attend a performance of *The Creation.* A year later, on May 11, 1809, he was shaken when the French bombarded Vienna and a shell fell near his home. He died twenty days later.

Haydn was a simple, plain, and easily contented man, extremely conscientious, loyal, sober, and sane, but also natural, candid, and vigorous. He prized ordered conditions, peace, quiet, and harmony. His fresh humor and sound peasant wit saved him from stiffening into conservatism. Haydn was most certainly not without warmth, as witness his relationship with Mozart. In spite of the difference in their ages (Mozart was twenty-four years younger), there developed a warm friendship between the two great composers, and Haydn was always eager to assert Mozart's incomparable genius and to expatiate upon the beauty of his music. His opinion of the younger man was expressed in his famous statement to Mozart's father, Leopold: "I tell you before God, as an honest man, that your son is the greatest composer I know, either personally or by name; he has taste, and moreover the greatest science in composition."

In an outburst of affection he wrote to one of his commissioners: "If only I could stamp into the soul of every music lover the same deep

A contemporary engraving of Franz Joseph Haydn

understanding and profound feeling which I experience regarding the inimitable work of this great master! ... I became furious when I think that this one and only Mozart has not yet been engaged at a Royal Court! Do pardon this deviation of mine: I love this man too much."

Though full of graceful deference toward his princely masters, Haydn could be obstinate when necessary. He always bravely defended the interests of his musicians, and took fatherly care of them. It was not without reason that they called him Papa Haydn.

Haydn was an extremely devout, and also extremely systematic man. His own account of his working method gives a fascinating insight into the source of his inspiration and accomplishment: "I get up early, and as soon as I have dressed I go down on my knees and pray God and the Blessed Virgin that I may have another successful day. Then when I've had some breakfast I sit down at the clavier and begin my search. If I hit on an idea quickly, it goes ahead easily

and without much trouble. But if I can't get on, I know that I must have forfeited God's grace by some fault of mine, and then I pray once more for grace until I feel I'm forgiven."

If Haydn compliantly adapted himself to the social conditions in which he lived, he was, as an artist, entirely independent. "The free arts and the beautiful science of composition will not endure mechanical fetters," he wrote in 1779. "Both the mind and the soul must have their freedom." Granted that he was no revolutionary but an "evolutionist," his steady, free, and natural growth nonetheless led him far from his starting point and resulted in something completely new and individual. Taking his point of departure partly from the baroque choral works and the Italian style of opera which he had learned to know in youth, and partly from the early sonata form, he developed the new form, the symphony, to the point where Beethoven could take over and in his turn develop it.

Throughout his long life, he was open to new ideas and interested in every novelty. He learned from everything, not least from the symphonies of his friend Mozart. In his music, therefore, this lover of ordered peace and quiet became bold, original, and unrestrainedly inventive, although his unusually logical and systematic nature led him to attach special importance to clear and definite form. Martin Bernstein has explained Haydn's historical importance: "He has been called the 'father of the symphony' and the 'father of the string quartet,' but both forms existed long before Haydn. Nor did he invent any new form. His real importance is that he crystallised these forms for all time, and by making constant use of them showed the world their musical possibilities."

W. Oliver Strunk writes in the same vein: "While Haydn had been at work, a new kind of music had grown from tentative beginnings to conscious maturity; his own music had itself passed through every stage in that growth, now following in a path cleared by others, now leading the way. With the possible exception of Handel, no great composer was ever more prolific; with the possible exception of Beethoven, no great composer ever maintained so fresh an outlook. Keeping pace with contemporary developments and more often anticipating them, Haydn ended even more progressively than he had begun."

In the last years of his life Haydn wrote in a

letter to a group of amateurs who had written to thank him for his music: "Often, as I struggled with obstacles of all kinds opposed to my works . . . an inner voice whispered to me: There are so few happy and contented men here below— on every hand care and sorrow pursue them— perhaps your work may some day be a source from which men laden with anxieties and burdened with affairs may derive a few moments of rest and refreshment. This, then, was a powerful motive for persevering, this the reason why I can even now look back with profound satisfaction on what I have accomplished in my art through uninterrupted effort and application over a long succession of years."

The cataloguing of Haydn's enormous output is beset with difficulties. Since the second World War, the able and devoted young musicologist H. C. Robbins-Landon has done much important work in this field. Many works attributed to him—some even published as his in his lifetime—were not written by him; many others are of doubtful origin, and a large number of his compositions have been lost. An exact total of his works, therefore, cannot be given.

There are between 104 and 140 symphonies, thirteen piano concertos, three to seven violin concertos, eighty-three string quartets (including quartet arrangements of *The Seven Words*), about thirty piano trios, fifty-two piano sonatas, thirteen operas, ten cantatas and oratorios, and twelve Masses. He also wrote puppet operas and *singspiele,* divertimenti, overtures, concertos for various instruments, and many smaller works such as songs.

His most important compositions were his instrumental works. Haydn himself thought highly of his own operas until he heard Mozart's; then he realized that dramatic music was not his field.

Of his instrumental compositions, several of his concertos are regularly played (concertos for piano, cello, and trumpet), a few of his piano trios are popular, and the piano sonatas are steadily gaining ground; but it is the string quartets and symphonies that are of chief interest. Of these two forms Haydn is the great master. Regarding his earliest compositions in these forms, it must be remembered that in Haydn's day there was no real difference between orchestral and chamber music. Trios were written for orchestra, and symphonies for three, four, or five instruments. Thus the titles mean very little. The chief distinction is that the orchestral works often have a continuo, and an accompanying clavier part, while the chamber works do not.

Thus among Haydn's works attributable to 1755–56—Op. 1 and 2, with six string quartets in each—we find his First Symphony (Op. 1, No. 5). Similarly, Nos. 3 and 5 of Op. 2 were sextets for two horns, and all were originally divertimenti. With the exception of the symphony they were in five movements, with a minuet before and after a slow middle movement, and quick movements at the beginning and end.

Haydn's death mask

The Haydn Monument in Vienna

HAYDN'S BEST-KNOWN WORKS

ORCHESTRAL

Symphonies (104):
No. 45, F sharp minor (1772), *Farewell*
No. 49, F minor (1768), *La Passione*
No. 53, D major (1773), *Imperial*
No. 73, D major (1781), *La Chasse*
Paris symphonies (Nos. 82–87):
No. 83, G minor (1785), *La Poule*
No. 86, D major, Op. 52, No. 2 (1786)
No. 88, G major, Op. 56, No. 2 (1786)
No. 91, E flat major, Op. 66, No. 3 (1788)
No. 92, G major, Op. 66, No. 2 (1788), *Oxford*
London symphonies (Nos. 93–104):
No. 93, D major, Op. 83, No. 2 (1791–92)
No. 94, G major, Op. 80, No. 1 (1791), *Surprise*
No. 96, D major, Op. 77, No. 2 (1791), *Miracle*
No. 97, C major, Op. 83, No. 1 (1791–92)
No. 98, B flat major, Op. 82, No. 2 (1792)
No. 99, E flat major, Op. 98, No. 3 (1793)
No. 100, G major, Op. 90 (1794), *Military*
No. 101, D major, Op. 95, No. 2 (1794), *Clock*
No. 102, B flat major, Op. 98, No. 2 (1794–95)
No. 103, E flat major, Op. 95, No. 1 (1795),
    Drum-Roll
No. 104, D major, Op. 98, No. 1 (1795), *London*
Toy Symphony (1788)
German Dances (*Deutsche Tänze*) (1792)
Sinfonia concertante, B flat major, Op. 84 (1792)
Piano Concerto, D major, Op. 21 (1784)
Violin Concerto, C major, "No. 1" (1765)
Cello Concerto, D major, Op. 101 (1783)
Trumpet Concerto, E flat major (1796)

CHAMBER MUSIC

String Quartets:
B flat major, Op. 1, No. 1 (1755), *Hunt*
F major, Op. 3, No. 5 (1765), *Serenade*
E flat major, Op. 33, No. 2 (1781), *The Joke*
C major, Op. 33, No. 3 (1781), *The Bird*
D major, Op. 50, No. 6 (1784–87), *The Frog*
B flat major, Op. 64, No. 3
D major, Op. 64, No. 5 (1790), *The Lark*
E flat major, Op. 64, No. 6
G minor, Op. 74, No. 3 (1793), *The Rider*
D minor, Op. 76, No. 2 (1797–98), *Fifths*
C major, Op. 76, No. 3 (1797–98), *Emperor*
B flat major, Op. 76, No. 4 (1797–98), *The Sunrise*
D major, Op. 76, No. 5 (1797–98)
String Trio, D major, Op. 32, No. 1 (c. 1760)
Piano Trios:
D major, Op. 63 (1790)
G major, Op. 73, No. 2 (1795)
F sharp minor, Op. 73, No. 3 (c. 1795)
E flat major, Op. 75, No. 3 (c. 1795)

HARPSICHORD OR PIANO

Fantasy, C major, Op. 58 (1789)
Sonatas:
No. 20, C minor (1771)
No. 37, D major (1780)
Variations, F minor, Op. 83 (1793)

These works are simple in the extreme. The melodies are mostly repeated broken chords, played almost exclusively on the violins. The other parts play a formal accompaniment, and the development of the motifs is very naïve. This is typical homophonic music, approximating in form the old binary dance form. The first movement begins and finishes in the main key (tonic), while the middle section glides over into the neighboring key (dominant) before returning to the main key.

These facile and cheerful compositions were completely in the style of the time, and show no individual features apart from suggestions of Haydn's own gay melody and rhythm. Nevertheless, they represent the beginning of the development that led to the masterpieces which Haydn wrote thirty to forty years later.

The turning point in his career is marked by the publication of the *Russian* quartets (Op. 33) in 1781. In the *Paris* symphonies (1786), the *Oxford* Symphony (1788), and the two sets of quartets written in 1789 and 1790, Haydn reached full maturity.

MASSES

Paukenmesse (Kettledrum Mass; Missa in tempori belli), C major (1796)
Nelsonmesse (Nelson Mass), D minor (1798)
Theresienmesse (Theresa Mass), B flat major (1799)

ORATORIOS

The Creation (Die Schöpfung) (1798)
The Seasons (Die Jahreszeiten) (1801)
The Seven Words (Die Sieben Worte) (Written 1785 for orchestra with recitative; arranged for voices by Haydn, 1796; also arranged as string quartets)

SONGS

My Mother Bids Me Bind My Hair (Hunter) (1794)
She Never Told Her Love (Shakespeare) (1798)
Austrian National Hymn (included in the *Emperor* Quartet) (Austrian version: *Gott erhalte Franz den Kaiser;* German version: *Deutschland über alles*)

SYMPHONIES

The supreme importance of Haydn in the history of the symphony is threefold:

He introduced thematic material which distinguishes itself from the dull formulas generally used at this time. Haydn's themes are melodious, often inspired by folk music, and full of humorous inventions and innovations.

He shifted the emphasis within the sonata form more and more from the exposition to the development section, thus setting off the spark which kept the sonata form alive and fascinating to composers for a century.

By making the minuet an obligatory movement he established the four-movement symphony.

Haydn always used the sonata form in the first movement, and often in the last movement; otherwise the last movement is often a rondo, but never the minuet or gigue of his predecessors. In the slow movement he often introduced variations—a novelty in the symphony—while the minuet is developed more and more into a vigorous, humorous composition, though always retaining the minuet form.

Haydn regarded the majority of his symphonies as occasional works. They were all written to order, very often within a relatively short time limit for a definite audience, at a definite place, and for a definite occasion. The demand for them was so great that in the thirty-six years between the first and last symphony (1759–1795) Haydn produced as many as 104.

In his later years Haydn wrote, it is believed, for an orchestra of forty players, and, as the concert halls of those days were comparatively small, his music must have been a revelation of orchestral color and light to his contemporaries. In fact, it was regarded by many as "scandalously noisy." One of his innovations was to abandon the old practice of filling out the harmonies from the clavier. As far as Haydn was concerned the clavier gradually became superfluous, although this did not prevent him from conducting his symphonies to the end of his life from his place at the clavier.

Sir Hubert Parry wrote of Haydn: "He . . . found out new ways of contrasting and combining the tones of different members of his orchestra, and getting a fuller and richer effect out of the mass of them when they were playing. In the actual style of the music, too, he made great advances; in his hands, symphonies became by degrees more vigorous and, at the same time, more really musical."

The last twenty-two of Haydn's symphonies are the most frequently played, and of these the *Paris* symphonies, *Oxford* Symphony, and *London* symphonies are most popular. (See *London, Oxford, Paris.*) The youthful works *Le Matin* (No. 6), *Le Midi* (No. 7), and *Le Soir* (No. 8) are occasionally played.

No. 26, Christmas

This got its name through a misunderstanding; its proper title is the *Lamentatione,* after the slow movement, which uses a Gregorian melody, *The Lament of Jeremiah,* often played at Easter.

No. 28

This symphony has attracted attention because the first movement develops a theme very similar to the opening motif in Beethoven's Fifth Symphony—the familiar three repeated eighth notes.

No. 45, Farewell Symphony. See *Farewell Symphony*.

No. 48, Maria Theresa

The work has this name because it was played to the Empress when she was on a visit to Prince Esterházy in 1773.

No. 63, La Roxolane

This symphony gained its name from a French song which appears in variations in the second movement. The first movement was originally an overture for Goldoni's play *Il Mondo della Luna.*

Cover for Songs with Piano Accompaniment

No. 73, La Chasse

This work is so called because Haydn himself gave the name to the last movement; this movement was originally a prelude for the third act of Haydn's opera *La fedeltà premiata,* the other movements being added to it later.

The symphonies after 1782 show the influence of Mozart, especially in the frequent chromatic melodies.

QUARTETS

In five of the six quartets of Op. 3 (1756–65) the number of movements had already been reduced to four, and Haydn invariably kept to this number in all his later quartets, thereby establishing the four-movement form (with a slow movement and a minuet between two quick movements), which has remained ever since the form of the string quartet and the symphony.

Op. 3, No. 5

The second movement is the beautiful little piece which under the name of *Serenade* has become perhaps the most popular of Haydn's lesser works.

Homer Ulrich points out the great development between the first eighteen quartets and the next six in Op. 9 (about 1769), and stresses that "the themes of Op. 9 are no longer so firmly tied to the tonic triad, but are full of imaginative little melodic bits."

Six Quartets, Op. 17

In these quartets, written in 1771, Haydn created brilliant movements with virtuosolike parts for the first violin; these were clearly written directly for the first violinist at Esterházy, the excellent player Luigi Tomasini.

Six Quartets, Op. 20

But still more important are the innovations introduced the following year in the six quartets of Op. 20, the so-called *Solo* or the *Great* quartets, in which Haydn no longer concentrated the melody in the violins, but gave the viola and cello melodically important parts. In fact he changed from purely homophonic to polyphonic music; this was the beginning of the genuine quartet style, in which all the instruments have equal rights and each part is individually written. Ulrich draws attention to the first bars of Op. 20, No. 2, where the cello has the theme, while the first violin is not heard, and comments: "This simple fact is world-shaking when one realizes how completely the first violin had dominated in the first thirty quartets. . . . The final movements of three of the quartets (Op. 20, Nos. 2, 5, and 6) are four-voice fugues. . . . Seen as fugues *per se,* they mark a return of the contrapuntal element to instrumental music."

Six Quartets, Op. 33

Dedicated to the Grand Duke Paul of Russia, these quartets are often called the *Russian,* also sometimes the *Maiden* quartets, and sometimes the *Scherzo* quartets because the minuets (in contrast to Haydn's usual practice) are called *scherzi.* These mark a further important development in Haydn's style. He had given

independence to the individual instruments by writing contrapuntally; now he gave them unity by elaboration of the motif or theme. Haydn had certainly used thematic development in earlier compositions, but never so consciously and consistently. From now on development of the theme became essential; all four parts were still given equal value as far as possible, but all the parts were permeated with thematic material. Likewise Haydn's melodies changed their character and came to consist of richly contrasting motifs, split into small individual sections, then gathered, set against each other and worked over together, with contrapuntal devices. This is the most important feature of the new quartets.

The "completely new and special manner" in which Haydn claimed that Op. 33 was written was, then, the union of the homophonic melody of his own age with polyphonic elements from the past, brought together into an organic unity in what we now call the quartet style. At the same time the sonata form, as we know it today, came into existence.

The movements of the new form are:

I. Allegro movements in sonata-allegro form, with a clear development section.

II. Slow movement, usually in three parts, with a contrasting middle section in place of the development, sometimes also sonata or variation form.

III. Minuet movement, in three parts: minuet section, trio, and minuet section repeated. In the course of time Haydn gave new content to the minuet, increased the tempo, and made it into a really humorous movement. (Movements II and III are in reverse order in most of the older quartets.)

IV. Rondo movement, form A-B-A-C-A-D-A or similar, with continually repeated refrain, sometimes rondo-sonata.

This is the main plan in Haydn's quartets, but no composer has ever been freer or more unorthodox in his forms. Haydn was always finding new permutations and combinations.

Of the six quartets in Op. 33 two have nicknames: No. 2 is called *The Joke,* from the droll treatment of the melody in the presto conclusion of the finale; and the light and merry No. 3 is called *The Bird,* from the violin duet in the scherzo trio.

Six Quartets, Op. 50

These were written in 1786 for King Frederick William of Prussia. As the king was a capable cellist and an eager chamber music player, these works contain pleasing, effective, and richly developed cello parts. They are the first of the eighteen quartets influenced by Mozart. The influence is especially apparent in the very frequent use of chromatic melodic lines. After Mozart's death, Haydn returned to his former diatonic method.

Up to Op. 50 Haydn has always used roughly the same plan for his first movements:

1. Exposition of two not especially different groups of themes, with one group most often in the main key, the other in a contrasting key.

2. Development of the themes (very simple to begin with), particularly of the first group of themes.

3. Re-exposition and recapitulation of first section, but now with both groups in the main key.

From Op. 50 onward the careful recapitulation of the first section is dropped, and the re-exposition is developed into a concluding coda.

The slow movement in No. 5 has been called *The Dream,* while No. 6 has received the name of *The Frog* from its last movement. Op. 51, *The Seven Words,* is really an orchestral piece arranged for string quartet.

Op. 54 (three quartets) and Op. 55 (three quartets)

These were written in 1788–90, and their vigor and spontaneity, with an exceptionally varied scale of feeling, give us the impression of meeting the older quartets in an amplified form. Though full of surprises, because Haydn was by now continually employing his artistic means in new ways, they embody no innovations with regard to form.

Op. 55, No. 2

This quartet has received the name *The Razor.* The story goes that the English publisher Bland, who had come to Eisenstadt to obtain the publishing rights of some of Haydn's compositions, entered Haydn's room one morning while the composer was shaving himself with a wretchedly poor razor. In his desperation Haydn exclaimed: "I would give my best quartet for a good razor!" Bland rushed back to his room and returned with a pair of excellent English razors and thus obtained the publishing rights of the quartet.

The later quartets bring no further developments in form. Haydn had now reached a solution that opened up the richest possibilities of both variety and unity, and the exploitation of these fully occupied him in later years.

Six Quartets, Op. 64

These contain his most popular quartets, No. 5 being the famous *Lark Quartet.*

Op. 71 (three quartets) and Op. 74 (three quartets)

These came in 1793. The last has been given the name *The Rider* from its first theme.

Six Quartets, Op. 76

Three of these quartets, composed in 1798, have nicknames: No. 2 is called the *Fifths Quartet,* from the descending fifths of the opening movement, the minuet being the famous *Witch Minuet.*

No. 3 is called the *Emperor Quartet,* the second movement being a sequence of variations on the Austrian national anthem. Haydn, inspired by England's *God Save the King,* had composed the anthem in 1797.

No. 4 is *The Sunrise,* from the feeling of rising and growth in the main motif.

Two Quartets, Op. 77

After his journeys to London, probably in 1799, Haydn wrote these two great quartets, which represent the peak of his art. They were first intended for flute and piano, but later transcribed for string quartet. After that he wrote only two movements of his last quartet, but could not manage to complete the work as planned. Though he was then seventy-one, the composition is as fresh and vigorous as the work of a young man.

Haydn's harpsichord, in the room in which he died

HAYDN, Johann Michael. German composer, known as Michael Haydn (1737–1806). Though he was in his own time, as he has been ever since, overshadowed by his famous brother, Franz Joseph, he composed some music of fine quality. His personality and the circumstances of his life provided a marked contrast to those of his brother. Michael Haydn remained a provincial, rough-mannered and devout but much respected. Michael Haydn believed that, given the same advantages, he would have been as successful a composer as his brother, but he did not permit envy to interfere with their mutually respectful relationship. For most of his life, he was organist and music director to the Archbishop of Salzburg. One of his Masses was presented in Vienna with the Empress Maria Theresa performing the soprano part. His works include several operas, many symphonies and other instrumental works, and more than 300 religious works. Ironically, some of these were for many years attributed to Franz Joseph Haydn and only recently have musicologists given Michael Haydn his due.

MICHAEL HAYDN

HAYDN VARIATIONS. Compositions by Brahms: Op. 56a (for orchestra) and Op. 56b (for two pianos). At the house of his friend Pohl, the biographer of Haydn, Brahms found in 1870 a number of unpublished works by Haydn, among them six divertimenti for oboes, horn, bassoons, and serpent (an obsolete instrument, which Brahms replaced by the double bassoon). The first of them contained a theme called *St. Anthony Chorale* (it is not known whether the melody was Haydn's own), and this forms the theme of Brahms' *Haydn Variations*.

He completed the Variations in the summer of 1873 during a sojourn at Tutzing in Bavaria. Clara Schumann stated after a performance in Leipzig in the following year: "The Variations are unbelievable! I do not know what to admire most—the characterization in each single variation, the magnificent interchange of grace, power and depth, or the effective orchestration. What architecture! What an ascent, right to the end! This is in Beethoven's spirit from first to last."

The theme occupies five bars:

It is first played straightforwardly, and then treated in nine variations. The last variation, designated *Finale,* is built up as a passacaglia; a simplified version of the theme repeated eighteen times forms the bass for this section. Then comes the splendid chorale in full orchestra.

HAYES, Clancy. American jazz singer and banjo player. A member of a musical family, he became a professional at eighteen. He had a wide reputation as a singer in San Francisco and Los Angeles in the 1930s and joined Lu Watters' Yerba Band in 1938. He has also worked with Bunk Johnson and Bob Scobey, and has made several records.

HAYES, ROLAND. American tenor (1887–). Hayes is noted for his interpretations of Negro spirituals and lieder. He was an early pupil of W. A. Calhoun and of Jennie Robinson at Fisk University, and later pursued his musical studies in Europe. From 1916 on, he concertized in the United States and abroad, and appeared with leading symphony orchestras in the principal music centers of the world.

HEAD, Michael. English composer, singer, and pianist (1900–). A professor of piano at the Royal Academy of Music, he is well known for his many songs to texts by famous English poets, which have become popular with present-day singers and audiences. Some of his songs are conspicuous for melodic appeal and others for their elaborate and subtle accompaniments. For many years, Head gave recitals at which he accompanied himself in his own songs and those of other composers.

HEATH, Percy. American jazz bassist (1923–). Heath attended the Granoff School of Music, Philadelphia, and found his first job with a local trio. He appeared with the Howard McGhee sextet, performed at the Paris Jazz Festival, and played with Miles Davis, Fats Navarro, and Dizzy Gillespie. He is best known as a member of the Modern Jazz Quartet.

HEATH, Ted. British band leader (1902–). Out of a job during the Depression, he joined other unemployed musicians playing in the London streets. One day while he was playing outside a big hotel, the hotel's band leader, Jack Hylton, rushed out and asked him to substitute for an absent trombonist. He was immediately successful, and later played with other leading English orchestras. Heath next formed his own all-star band, which became well known on the radio in 1945. His Sunday "swing sessions" at the London Palladium packed the house to the limit of its capacity, and he was a great attraction at the Hammersmith Palais de Danse. Ted Heath and his band are now regular broadcasters and one of the most popular swing bands. They toured the United States in 1956. Heath composed the music for the hit songs *Lovely Week-End* and *Gonna Love That Guy*.

HEBRIDES OVERTURE. See *Fingal's Cave*.

HECHT, Joshua. American bass-baritone. Hecht became a student and protégé of Rosa Ponselle after appearing as a soloist with the U. S. Army Field Band. First singing with the Baltimore Opera, he has been enacting a wide variety of principal roles, including several distinguished contemporary works, with the New York City Opera since 1955. He has also appeared with the Pittsburgh, Philadelphia, New Orleans, and NBC-TV opera companies, and in

ROLAND HAYES

the festivals of Central City, Chautauqua, and Puerto Rico. He joined the San Francisco Opera in the fall of 1961.

HEFTI, Neal. American jazz trumpeter, arranger, and leader (1922–). Hefti has played with and arranged for an imposing collection of jazz groups since he began with Bob Astor in 1941, including those of Woody Herman, Charlie Ventura, and Count Basie. He has written many famous tunes; *Bubbles, Plymouth Rock, Why Not?*, and others are still played. He has also done much popular music work, leading bands and working in television.

HEIDEN, Bernhard. German-American composer and teacher (1910–). He grew up in a musical atmosphere and composed his first pieces at the age of six. From 1929 to 1933 he studied in Berlin with Hindemith, who is the main influence in his work. He emigrated to America in 1935, and in 1945 studied musicology with Donald Grout at Cornell University. He became head of the composition department at Indiana University in 1946. His compositions include orchestral and choral works, chamber music, and piano sonatas.

HEIDENRÖSLEIN *(Wayside Rose)*. Song by Schubert, composed in 1815, to the words of Goethe's poem.

Sah ein Knab'ein Rös-lein stehn, Röslein auf der Hei-den

Once a boy a wild rose spied,
In the hedgerow growing,
Fresh in all her youthful pride;
When her beauties he descried
Joy in his heart was glowing.
Little wild rose, wild rose red,
In the hedgerow growing.

The German-Danish composer C. E. F. Weyse had put Goethe's poem to music as early as 1794, and in 1827 Heinrich Werner composed for it another melody which became very popular:

HEIDSIECK, Eric. French pianist (1936–). Son of the French champagne magnate, Heidsieck was encouraged to study, when he was six, by Alfred Cortot. He made his recital debut at

JASCHA HEIFETZ

Rheims at the age of nine and first appeared in London six years later. He won the 1959 first prize of the French Academy of Recording, and made his first North American concert tour during the 1960-61 season.

HEIFETZ, Jascha. Russian-American violinist (1901–). Heifetz was given violin lessons by his violinist father at the age of three, and at seven he gave a public performance of Mendelssohn's concerto. In the same year Leopold Auer chanced to hear him play, and arranged for him to enter the St. Petersburg Conservatory. Auer was a brilliant teacher, and Heifetz made such progress that six years later he was able to play with the Berlin Philharmonic Orchestra under Artur Nikisch.

When the first World War broke out, Auer took his pupils Heifetz, Toscha Seidel, and Max Rosen to Norway, and from there Heifetz traveled to the United States. In the succeeding years he built up through many world-wide tours a reputation as one of the greatest violinists— if not the greatest—of the day. He made his American debut at Carnegie Hall in 1917, and became a naturalized American citizen in 1925.

Heifetz was at one time reproached for a certain lack of warmth in his art, but in the course of time his playing gained in intensity and feeling. While, therefore, his first performances were praised for his phenomenal technique and assurance, his later concerts gave equal evidence of a beautifully rich and expressive tone.

HEINE, Heinrich. German poet and critic. (1797–1856). The great poet, who was also a brilliant journalist, often wrote pieces on music for French and German journals. Few poets have inspired as much great music as he did. Songs set to his texts have been composed by, among others, Schubert, Schumann, Franz, Brahms, Liszt, Wolf, Bruckner, Grieg, Mendelssohn, Borodin, Tchaikovsky, Mussorgsky, Rimsky-Korsakov, Rachmaninoff, and Mac-Dowell. Wagner's *The Flying Dutchman* and the famous ballet *Giselle* were based on poems by Heine.

HEINEFETTER, Sabine, Maria, Kathinka, Fatima, Eva, and **Nanette.** Six sisters who were concert and opera singers in the early nineteenth century. The best known were Sabine and Maria, both of whom died insane.

HEINZE, Sir Bernard Thomas. Australian conductor (1894–). Heinze studied with Vincent d'Indy in Paris and at the Royal College of Music in London. In 1926 he was appointed professor of music at the University of Melbourne. Between 1933 and 1949, he conducted the Melbourne Symphony Orchestra, and in 1956 he became director of the State Conservatory in Sydney.

HELDENLEBEN, EIN (*A Hero's Life*). Symphonic poem for full orchestra, Op. 40, by Richard Strauss. It was composed in 1898 and first performed the following year, the composer conducting.

The score contains only headings of the six parts into which the work is divided, giving no other indications that can serve as a program.

1. The hero.
2. The hero's adversaries.
3. The hero's courtship.
4. The hero's battlefield.
5. The hero's works of peace.
6. The hero's release from the world.

Although the work can be interpreted as a general portrayal of the life of a hero, it is quite certain that Strauss had himself in mind. One proof of this is afforded by the fifth part, in which he uses many themes from his previous works.

HELICON. Name of a type of bass tuba. See *Wind Instruments.*

HELLER, Stephen. French pianist and composer (1813–1888). Heller studied in Vienna with Anton Halm. In 1838 he went to Paris, where he became the friend of Berlioz, Chopin, and Liszt. Highly successful as a pianist, he was judged by some critics to be superior to Chopin. He composed small piano pieces in a romantic salon style which became very popular. In all, he wrote several hundred piano pieces.

HELM, Everett. American composer, critic, and musicologist (1913–). A graduate of Carleton College, Minnesota, where he was assistant college organist, and of Harvard University, Helm studied composition in Europe with Malipiero and Vaughan Williams, and musicology with Alfred Einstein. He taught music on the college level from 1933 until 1944, and served as theater and music officer under the United States Military Government from 1948

Frieda Hempel as Marguerite of Valois in Les Huguenots, *the role in which she made her Metropolitan debut*

to 1950. In 1952 he became European correspondent for *Musical America,* and its editor-in-chief in 1962. He returned as head of their European bureau in 1963. His compositions include an opera, a ballet, choral pieces, and two piano concertos.

HEMPEL, Frieda. German coloratura soprano (1885–1955). She became a star of the Berlin Hofoper in 1905 and in 1911 sang the Marschallin in *Der Rosenkavalier* at its first Berlin performance, a few months after the Dresden première. In 1913, she sang the role in the American première at the Metropolitan, where she had made her debut the year before as Marguerite in *Les Huguenots.* She was greatly popular in a variety of roles, including Eva in *Die Meistersinger,* Pamina in *The Magic Flute,* Rosina in *The Barber of Seville,* Marie in *The Daughter of the Regiment,* and Lucia.

SKITCH HENDERSON

FLETCHER HENDERSON

Her concert career continued for a decade after she retired from opera. In 1920, she gave a series of recitals to celebrate the hundredth anniversary of Jenny Lind's birth.

HENDERSON, Cedric ("Skitch"). American composer, conductor, and pianist (1918–). Henderson studied at the Juilliard School and with Albert Coates, Arnold Schoenberg, Frederick Prausnitz, and Fritz Reiner. He became an arranger, composer, and pianist in films, and for singers such as Bing Crosby and Frank Sinatra. After World War II, he devoted his principal efforts to radio and television work and was made musical director of the National Broadcasting Company. He made his New York debut in 1953 with the New York Philharmredth Orchestra and, since then, has been guest conductor of many major orchestras in the United States and England.

HENDERSON, Fletcher. American jazz pianist, arranger, and composer (1898–1952). After graduation from Atlanta University, Henderson came to New York in 1920 to continue his studies in chemistry, and took a part-time job as pianist with W. C. Handy. Soon he was working as pianist with a record company, and eventually he was leading the small group which accompanied Ethel Waters.

From 1923 to 1939 he led his own band, which became extremely popular, and with which he accompanied several of the best-known blues singers, including Bessie Smith. Many of the members of the band were outstanding jazz soloists.

Henderson constantly experimented with the band's possibilities, and his arrangements had a great influence on the development of jazz during the latter half of the 1930s. He is considered to have been one of the best arrangers of jazz music in the world. Benny Goodman used Henderson's arrangements after 1935, and in 1939 engaged him as full-time arranger. Goodman was undoubtedly greatly indebted to Henderson for his success with his swing style. See *Jazz.*

HENDERSON, Ray. American composer (1896–). See *De Sylva, Brown, and Henderson.*

HENDERSON, William James. American music critic and composer (1855–1937). A graduate of Princeton University in 1876, Henderson studied piano and voice but was chiefly self-taught in theory. He wrote many librettos of light operas. From 1887 to 1902 he was music critic of the New York *Times,* and for thirty-five years, until his death, music critic for the New York *Sun.* He lectured extensively on musical history and the development of vocal art.

HENDL, Walter. American pianist and conductor (1917–). Hendl began to study music when he was sixteen. Three years later he received a scholarship from the Curtis Institute of Music, where he studied piano with David Saperton and conducting with Fritz Reiner. For two years he taught at Sarah Lawrence College and studied conducting with Serge Koussevitzky at Tanglewood.

After his discharge from the Army at the end of World War II, Hendl appeared as soloist and conductor with the Pittsburgh Symphony Orchestra and as guest conductor with the CBS Symphony and the Boston Pops orchestras. He was subsequently engaged by Artur Rodzinski as assistant conductor of the New York Philharmonic-Symphony Orchestra, where he remained

for four seasons, frequently substituting for Mr. Rodzinski.

In 1949 he was appointed principal conductor of the Dallas Symphony Orchestra, and in 1953 was given the position of musical director of the Chautauqua Symphony Orchestra. He is presently associate conductor of the Chicago Symphony Orchestra.

HENKEMANS, Hans. Dutch composer and pianist (1913–). Henkemans is a composer of note and also holds the degree of Doctor of Medicine. He studied piano with Bernard van der Sigtenhorst-Meyer and composition with Willem Pijper. He made his debut at the age of nineteen, performing his own piano concerto. His works include a symphony, two piano concertos, a violin concerto, string quartets, songs, and choruses.

HENRIOT-SCHWEITZER, Nicole. French pianist (1924–). One of the best-known French pianists, Nicole Henriot-Schweitzer studied with Marguerite Ong at the Paris Conservatory, and made her debut with the Pasdeloup Orchestra at the age of fifteen. She was soon engaged for

WALTER HENDL

NICOLE HENRIOT-SCHWEITZER

recitals and concerts with major symphony orchestras. During World War II she was connected with the French Resistance movement. After the war she played in London and, in 1947, was invited to come to the United States. Her concerts with the New York Philharmonic and the Boston Symphony orchestras were triumphantly successful. She has since played throughout Europe and the United States, and appeared at the Prague, Salzburg, and many other festivals.

HENRY V. King of England (1387–1422). The hero of Agincourt, he reigned from 1413 to 1422 and was conspicuously musical, keeping many musicians at court. A Gloria and Sanctus known as "Roy Henry" are believed to be of his composition.

HENRY VIII. King of England (1491–1547). He is known to have composed numerous vocal works during his reign of thirty-eight years, of which only a few part-songs, a motet, and some viol pieces survive.

HENSCHEL, Sir George. German-English composer, conductor, and singer (1850–1934).

Henry VIII, a portrait by Hans Holbein the Younger in the Galleria Corsini, Rome

Henschel, who was of Polish descent, appeared in public as a pianist at the age of twelve and as a bass singer at sixteen. Famous as a lieder singer to his own accompaniment, he was a lifelong friend of Brahms. A student at the Leipzig Conservatory, he made his home in England from 1877. Upon the foundation of the Boston Symphony Orchestra in 1881 he became its first conductor; during the same year he married the soprano Lillian June Bailey (1860–1901), with whom he gave popular vocal recitals in Europe and America until her death.

Henschel founded the first London Symphony Orchestra in 1886 and conducted it for nine years. He was also the first conductor of the Scottish Orchestra (1893–1895). He became a British subject in 1890, married another American singer, Amy E. Louis, in 1907, and was knighted in 1914.

HENSEL, Fanny (Cécile). German pianist and composer (1805–1847). Sister of Felix Mendelssohn, she received her musical education at home. She married the painter Hensel in 1829, shortly before the death of her brother. She published four books of songs and a collection of piano pieces.

HENSEL, Heinrich. German tenor (1878–1935). A famous Parsifal, he appeared at Bayreuth, Covent Garden, and the Metropolitan Opera, where he made his debut as Lohengrin in 1911.

HENZE, Hans Werner. German composer (1926–). A student of Wolfgang Fortner and René Leibowitz, Henze was recognized as an exceptional talent at the Darmstadt Holiday Courses in the summer of 1946 and has become one of the most controversial figures in contemporary European music. Although Henze has extensively used the twelve-tone system, he refuses to be dominated by its purely structural aspects. He is gifted with an enormous flair for orchestral color and does not avoid occasional naturalistic effects. His profound interest in folklore is noticeable in such works as *König Hirsch* (1956), *Neapolitan Songs* (1957), and *Nachtstücke und Arien* (1957). Henze has composed operas (notably *Der Prinz von Hambourg* and *Elegy for Young Lovers),* symphonies, concertos, chamber music, piano music, and a variety of smaller orchestral pieces.

HERBERT, Victor. Irish-American composer of operettas (1859–1924). Born in Dublin, Victor Herbert was taken to the Continent by his widowed mother when he was seven, for musical training. She remarried and the family settled in Stuttgart, where Victor studied cello at the conservatory. After further study and experience with various orchestras, he became cellist with the Stuttgart orchestra, for which he wrote several symphonic works.

In 1886 the Metropolitan Opera Company, searching for new singers in Europe, offered a contract to the soprano Theresa Foerster, who was engaged to Herbert. She accepted with the provision that her fiancé be given a contract as cellist with the Metropolitan's orchestra. Their future secured, they married and came to America.

Herbert's first musical comedy, *Prince Ananias,* was written in 1892; its success was not sufficient to persuade Herbert to give up his other work, and he took over the leadership of a military band, composed a new cello concerto, and later also became leader of a symphony orchestra. But his second musical comedy, *The Wizard of the Nile,* was an enormous success, and with his other musicals, thirty in all, made him tremendously popular in the United States and celebrated all over the world. His most popular musical comedies, which contain songs that are still played today, were written between 1898 and 1913. These include *The Fortune Teller, Babes in Toyland, Mlle. Modiste, Naughty Marietta, Sweethearts,* and *The Red Mill.* Each was proof of his romantic talent. After *Sweethearts* in 1913, his career, though financially successful, showed a decline in popularity. Public taste was changing and the romantic operetta in the Viennese tradition began to lose its appeal in the years after the first World War. His later operettas, although they had respectable runs, are now chiefly remembered only for occasional songs—*I Might Be Your Once in a While,* from *Angel Face; When You're Away,* from *The Only Girl; Thine Alone* from *Eileen* (which he considered his finest score); *A Kiss in the Dark* from *Orange Blossoms.* He also wrote two grand operas, neither very well received, scores for several editions of the Ziegfeld Follies, and many individual songs.

HERMAN, Woodrow Charles ("Woody"). American jazz clarinetist and leader (1913–).

Louis Joseph Ferdinand Hérold, a lithograph by J. Dupin

A member of well-known bands in the 1930s (those of Harry Sosnik, Gus Arnheim, and Isham Jones), Herman formed his own band in 1937. His ability to adapt to changing trends and styles in popular music has kept him prominent in the entertainment world since then. He introduced Stravinsky's *Ebony Concerto,* written for him, at Carnegie Hall in 1937 and has been an outstanding recording artist. He has composed many songs, including *Woodchopper's Ball* and *Blues on Parade.*

HÉROLD, Louis Joseph Ferdinand. French composer and pianist (1791–1833). Ferdinand Hérold studied at the Paris Conservatory. Later an accompanist at the Théâtre-Italien, he wrote ballets and piano pieces. He wrote more than twenty operas, produced at the Opéra-Comique between 1816 and 1833; the best known of these were *Zampa* and *Le pré aux clercs.*

HERRMANN, Bernard. American composer (1911–). Prominent as a radio conductor, he has composed an opera, *Wuthering Heights;* a cantata, *Moby Dick;* film scores; a string quartet, a symphony, and a violin concerto.

HERTZ, Alfred. German-American conductor (1872–1942). Hertz studied at the Raff Conservatory, and held several positions as an opera conductor in Germany. In 1902 he was engaged as conductor of German repertory at New York's Metropolitan Opera. The next year, against the wishes of the Wagner family, he conducted the first American performance of *Parsifal,* with the result that he was denied permission to conduct Wagner in Germany. In 1915 he was engaged as conductor of the San Francisco Symphony Orchestra, a position he held until 1930. He organized the summer series of concerts at the Hollywood Bowl in 1922, and conducted more than a hundred performances there.

HERZ, Herman. German-American conductor (1908–). Herz has been musical director of the Duluth Symphony Orchestra since 1950. He trained at the State Academy of Music in Munich, held positions at the Munich Opera and the Municipal Theater in St. Gall, Switzerland, and conducted ballet in Berlin and on tour. Between 1936 and 1947, he lived in Johannesburg, South Africa, where he conducted opera, ballet, and symphony. He came to the United States in 1947, taught at the Berkshire Music Center, and directed opera on television until his appointment to the Duluth Symphony Orchestra.

HESELTINE, Philip. See *Warlock, Peter.*

DAME MYRA HESS

HESS, Dame Myra. British pianist (1890–). A student at the Guildhall School of Music before the age of eight and later a pupil of Tobias Matthay at the Royal Academy of Music, she made her debut in London when seventeen years old, and soon won fame as an interpreter of Bach, Mozart, Beethoven, Schumann, Brahms, and Scarlatti. She has toured in England, Europe, and the United States, giving recitals and concerts with the greatest orchestras. She appeared with Toscanini by his special request.

In 1941 she was created a Dame of the Order of the British Empire, and received the Royal Philharmonic Society's gold medal. In the next few years she was given honorary degrees by the Universities of Cambridge, London, Manchester, St. Andrews, Durham, Reading, and Leeds.

Following a concert in 1952 the New York *Herald Tribune* music critic wrote: "Myra Hess is quite clearly one of the great ones. . . . Simply, she has great musical wisdom. Her knowledge of music as a language, from without as from within, has reached that stage so rarely reached, where wisdom like the distilled essence of all those things once learned, bestows the final freedom, eloquence and authority. . . . What she evokes from each composer is at once a revelation of their quality and a tribute to her own personality."

Lawrence Gilman called her "a poet, sensitive and exquisite, finely touched and richly gifted, and an interpreter of the sacerdotal kind—dedicated and absorbed and self-effacing."

HESS, Willy. German violinist (1859–1939). A pupil of Joachim and at one time concertmaster of the Boston Symphony, he was famed as a soloist in a wide repertory and as leader of several string quartets. His instrument was a famous Guadagnini.

HEUBERGER, Richard. Austrian composer and critic (1850–1914). He was for some years an influential critic in the journals of Vienna and Munich. Beginning his career as a conductor, he turned to composing and achieved a great success with his operetta *Der Opernball* (1898). He also composed five other operettas, four operas, and two ballets.

HIBBLER, Albert. American jazz singer (1915–). Despite the handicap of blindness, Hibbler has become a well-known and popular vocalist. He has sung with Duke Ellington and headed his own band. His unique singing style has been described by Duke Ellington as "tonal pantomime."

HIDALGO, Elvira de. Spanish soprano (1901–). She sang coloratura roles at the Metropolitan Opera in 1910 and again in 1924. She also sang at Covent Garden and many other opera houses in Europe. Her importance today rests on the fact that she was the teacher of Maria Callas.

HIGGINSON, Henry Lee. American music patron (1834–1919). Henry Lee Higginson is best known to the music world as the founder of the Boston Symphony Orchestra. A student of voice and piano in his early twenties, he became a banker in Boston, and in 1881 assumed the responsibility of providing a substantial portion of the annual budget of the orchestra then in formation. The Boston Symphony Orchestra, then consisting of sixty-seven musicians, gave its first concert on October 22, 1881, and, in 1885, the summer series of pops concerts was inaugurated. In October, 1900, the orchestra moved to its permanent home, Symphony Hall. Higginson retained guidance of the organization until shortly before his death.

HILDEGARDE. American singer (1906–). The daughter of a Milwaukee delicatessen-store proprietor, Hildegarde Loretta Sell became one of the world's most glamorous entertainers. In 1929, when she was trying to earn a living as a pianist, she met Anna Sosenko, a music student, and three or four years later they formed a partnership which lasted for many years. After a precarious start in Paris, they decided that Hildegarde should adopt a completely new personality and technique. Dressed like a mannequin, she sang sophisticated European songs in a pink and gold spotlight at night clubs and cabarets, where, gliding from table to table, she would greet celebrities like old friends. She first became famous at the London Ritz in the 1930s and, on her return to the United States, with the help of adroit publicity she was soon earning fabulous sums in night clubs.

Irving Berlin has called her "the greatest artist and stylist of song in the profession today."

HILL, Edward Burlingame. American composer (1872–1960). Hill came from a distinguished family of educators. He pursued his academic studies at Harvard University and studied music with John Knowles Paine. He joined the faculty of Harvard as an instructor in music in 1908 and retired in 1940, having served as chairman of the music department. Among his compositions, which are strongly influenced by the French impressionist school, are symphonies, sonatas, and string and piano quartets. He is the author of *Modern French Music.*

HILL, Richard S. American music librarian (1901–1961). Trained at Oxford and Cornell universities, he was for twenty-one years head of the Reference Section of the Music Division in the Library of Congress.

HILL, Urelli Corelli. American violinist (1802–1875). A pupil of Spohr, he helped to found the New York Philharmonic Society and played in the orchestra for thirty years. At the end of his life, he played in theater orchestras.

HILLER, Johann Adam. German composer and conductor (1728–1804). Though his works are hardly known today, he was of great importance in the development of German opera, having originated the form known as the *singspiel,* which reached its apex with Mozart's *Magic Flute.* Hiller (whose real name was Hüller) succeeded Bach at the Thomasschule in Leipzig, where he established the famous Gewandhaus concerts. He was a great partisan of Handel's music and edited many of his works and those of other composers. He wrote many books on music, as well as eleven *singspiele* (the most successful was *Die Jagd*), and various ballets and cantatas.

HILLER VARIATIONS. (*Variations and Fugue on a Merry Theme by J. A. Hiller*), Op. 100, by Max Reger. This composition, finished in 1907, was first performed in Cologne. In a letter dated 1904 Reger wrote: "... I have found a beautiful theme of his [Hiller's], which simply asks for variations; I am going to make the most ethereal forms grow out of this 'Mozartian' theme, and hope to make it into something first-rate."

Indeed, in this work Reger gave full rein to his ingenuity and outstanding technical adroitness, as well as to his sparkling sense of humor. Reger's theme was taken from Hiller's comic *opera Der Ärntekranz.*

The theme, *Andante grazioso,* is:

There are eleven variations and a final fugue in the work, which is regarded as one of Reger's best orchestral compositions. Max Hehemann writes: "When the double fugue piles the sound masses on top of one another, and then the main theme finally eclipses the confusion of sound, the joyous cry rings out: It is good to be alive!"

HILLIS, Margaret. American choral conductor (1921–). She studied composition at Indiana University and then became assistant to Robert Shaw. Since 1951, she has conducted many fine concerts with her own choral group and with other organizations, performing old and new choral works, and opera in concert form.

HILSBERG, Alexander. Polish-American conductor and violinist (1900–1961). He began his career in Russia, where he studied with Auer. In 1923, he came to America and, in 1926, joined the Philadelphia Orchestra, of which he later became concertmaster and then associate conductor. He also was conductor of the Curtis Institute's symphony orchestra and, in 1953, became director of the New Orleans Symphony.

HINCKLEY, Allen Carter. American bass (1877–1954). He began with the Bostonians, a famous company of light-opera performers, and then went abroad to seek a career in opera. With the Hamburg Opera, he became established as a Wagnerian bass. After appearances in other European theaters, including Covent Garden, he joined the Metropolitan Opera in 1908, making his debut under Toscanini's direction as Hagen in *Die Götterdämmerung.*

Two scenes from Hindemith's opera, The Harmony of the World, *at the Munich State Opera*

HINDEMITH, Paul. German-American composer (1895–). Paul Hindemith showed unusual musical ability at an early age: he was an excellent violinist at thirteen, and seven years later became the leader of the Frankfurt Opera orchestra. While following his serious studies at the Frankfurt Conservatory he obtained more general practice and experience by playing in movie houses, theater orchestras, and dance bands. In 1922 he founded the well-known Amar String Quartet, in which he played the viola. At about the same time, he became one of the organizers of the Donaueschingen Chamber Music Festival, one of the most important and influential festivals of contemporary music in the twentieth century, which has been active in introducing and supporting new compositions, new composers, and new techniques for over forty years.

Hindemith has stated his views on technique very definitely: "The basis of all worth-while composition must be, of course, inspiration and worth-while musical ideas; after that comes technique. There seems to be an impression that there is today too much technique. It is my impression that there is not nearly enough technique. To be a composer, in the modern sense, requires years of daily intimacy with music of all kinds, not merely the process of playing it, or hearing it, but that of investigating and studying. When a composer writes, he must be able to do so without any consciousness of technique. A great novelist or dramatist surely never thinks of grammar, or syntax, or rhetoric."

Hindemith also came to the conclusion that the music of our time was too abstract, and that it was necessary to discover forms which music lovers could really enjoy. He decided that a composer of today should not write freely in order "to express his personality" or, as he put it in 1927: "In our time a composer ought really to write only when he knows to what end he is writing. The time when one composed merely for the sake of composing is gone forever."

And in 1952, in the introduction to his book, *A Composer's World,* he stated further: "Music, as we practice it, is, in spite of its trend toward abstraction, a form of communication between the author and the consumer of his music."

As early as 1928 he wrote in the introduction to one of his works: "This music is written neither for the concert hall nor for artists; the idea is only to provide interesting new practice material for those who play for a small circle who are of the same mind. Because of this there is no great technical burden laid on the performer."

Hindemith has always been essentially a practical composer. This is nowhere better demonstrated than in his innumerable examples of *Gebrauchsmusik,* literally, "music for use." These works, many of them it must be admitted more interesting for the performer than the listener, include a large collection of sonatas for instruments which have a limited repertoire, such as the double-bass, English horn, tuba, French horn, trumpet, etc. He has also written concertos for unusual chamber combinations and orchestra, again with the intention of extending the literature available to players of these instruments.

Hindemith's compositional practice is essentially polyphonic, in a sense a present day evocation of the approach of Bach. His early works, which exhibited a tendency toward atonality, were apt to be dry, dissonant, impersonal, almost too "intellectual." Since the 1930s, however, his writing has taken on a warmer cast, mixing a contemporary romanticism with the sterner stuff of the neo-Baroque.

Although his musical thinking is still primarily contrapuntal, his harmonic usage has taken on a warmth as well as theoretical

PAUL HINDEMITH

firmness, based on his acoustical conclusions expounded in *The Craft of Musical Composition*. These theories, while admitting dissonances deemed unthinkable, even immoral, by the standards of traditional harmonic usage, still translate back to the fundamental harmonic sounds and patterns of earlier practice. His works are strongly based in tonality, although the limits of tonal usage have been stretched to admit of more remote sounds than were formerly thought possible.

Hindemith's orchestration, and writing for instruments generally (with the possible exception of the piano), is always felicitous, a result, doubtless, of his own wide performing experience as a violinist and violist, as well as his ability to play several other orchestral instruments. Unfortunately, however, in many cases the music does not utilize the timbre of the given instruments to the fullest advantage, with a resultant lack of color and sonority. One sometimes has the impression that the music is conceived in the abstract and only later assigned to specific instruments. A noteworthy exception is the opera *Mathis der Maler* (1934); the orchestral suite of this opera is probably the best known of Hindemith's works.

The early 1930s were a difficult time for Hindemith. He had been in charge of composition at several of the largest music schools, was regarded as the foremost composer of his generation, and had a brilliant reputation as a viola player. But in the Nazi state his music was blacklisted; it was labeled "degenerate art," and its performance was forbidden.

Hindemith left Germany for the United States in 1938 and in 1940 became professor of composition at Yale University. During the next ten years, his fame as a musical educator spread throughout the country. Many young American composers studied with him during this period.

Some of his best-known works were composed during this time, among others *Ludus Tonalis,* subtitled "contrapuntal, tonal and piano technical studies."

This work consists of twelve fugues with a musical link after each, a prelude, and a postlude which is its exact converse. Hindemith here tried to create a sort of modern parallel to Bach's *Well-Tempered Clavier,* presenting the possibilities of the twelve tones of the chromatic scale. The work is, in a way, a practical illustration of his *The Craft of Musical Composi-*

tion, a two-volume composition textbook based entirely on the laws of acoustics. In this book Hindemith rejects the old harmony system, but nevertheless refuses to adopt the mechanical division of the scale. He recognizes no musical laws except the natural ones, and maintains, for example, that no chord can be deemed ungrammatical if the composer considers it essential. He is also the author of a concentrated course in *Traditional Harmony,* in two volumes, and of *Elementary Training for Musicians.*

Hindemith returned to Europe in 1953 after a short appointment at Harvard University. He lives in Switzerland and is professor of composition at the University of Zurich. He frequently appears as conductor or soloist performing his own works with many European orchestras.

Best-known works:

OPERAS

Cardillac (1926)
Neues vom Tage (1929)
Mathis der Maler (1934)
The Harmony of the World (1957)
The Long Christmas Dinner (1960)

BALLET

Nobilissima Visione (1937)

ORCHESTRA

Concerto for Orchestra (1925)
Philharmonic Concerto (1932)
Symphonic Dances (1937)
Nobilissima Visione (Suite) (1938)
Concerto for Violin and Orchestra (1940)
Concerto for Cello and Orchestra (1940)
Symphony *Mathis der Maler* (1934)
Symphony in E flat (1940)
The Four Temperaments, for piano and string orchestra (1940)
Symphonic Metamorphosis on Themes by Weber (1943)
Sinfonia Serena (1946)
Symphony, *The Harmony of the World* (1951)

CHAMBER ORCHESTRA

Five *Kammermusiker,* Concertos for Wind Instruments, Piano, Violin, Cello and Viola, Op. 36, Nos. 1–5 (1924–28)
Concert Music for Viola and Chamber Orchestra, Op. 48 (1930)
Concert Music for Piano, Brass Instruments and Harp, Op. 49 (1930)
Concert Music for Strings and Brass Instruments, Op. 50 (1931)
Der Schwanendreher (viola and orchestra) (1935)

CHORUS

Apparebit Repentina Dies (1947)
6 Chansons (a cappella) (1939)
Requiem, *When Lilacs Last in the Door-yard Bloom'd* (1946)

CHAMBER MUSIC
String Trio, Op. 34 (1924)
Six string quartets (1919–45)
Sonatas for all string and brass instruments with piano
Kleine Kammermusik, Op. 24, No. 2 (1922)

PIANO
Suite 1922 (1922)
Three piano sonatas (1936)
Ludus Tonalis (1942)

HINES, Earl ("Fatha"). American jazz pianist and leader (1905–). The son of musical parents, Hines was already performing professionally while still in high school. After an engagement in the Louis Armstrong band, he organized his own band in 1928, with which he continued for twenty years. Since 1951 he has led small groups. His influence on the evolution of jazz piano has been great, and included among the alumni of his band are such well-known personalities as Dizzy Gillespie, Charlie Parker, Billy Eckstine, and Sarah Vaughan.

HINES, Jerome. American bass (1921–). Since 1946 Hines has been associated with the Metropolitan Opera in New York as a leading bass. His career began in 1940 with the Los Angeles Light Opera Company. Later appearances with the San Francisco Opera (1941), the San Carlo Opera (1942), the Opera Association of the Golden West (1943), the New Orleans Opera (1945), and the Central City Opera (1946) brought him recognition. He won the Caruso Award in 1946. He is especially well known for his portrayals of Mephistopheles in Gounod's *Faust* and of Boris Godunov.

HINRICHS, Gustav. German-American conductor (1850–1942). He was assistant conductor to Theodore Thomas with the American Opera Company and founded and conducted a company of his own in Philadelphia, with which he toured extensively. He conducted the American premières of several famous operas, including *Cavalleria Rusticana, Pagliacci,* and *Manon Lescaut.* In 1904, he conducted at the Metropolitan Opera.

HINSHAW, William Wade. American baritone (1867–1947). A prominent educator as well as a singer, he was Dean of Music at Valparaiso University and President of the Chicago Conservatory. He appeared in opera with the Henry Savage Company, the Metropolitan, and several European companies. His most important roles were in the Wagner repertory. At the Metropolitan, he sang in the première of Parker's *Mona.* In 1918, he offered a prize for a short opera, which was won by Hadley's *Bianca.* His son Carl served in the House of Representatives as Congressman from California.

HINTON, Milton. American jazz bassist (1910–). After appearances in Chicago, he became a member of the Cab Calloway band in 1936 and remained a prominent member of that aggregation for fifteen years. He has since played with Joe Bushkin, Jackie Gleason, Louis Armstrong, Teddy Wilson, and Benny Goodman, and has been a CBS staff musician.

HISTOIRE DU SOLDAT, L' *(The Soldier's Tale).* A story in eight parts to be told, acted, and danced, with music by Stravinsky, and text by Ramuz. Composed in 1918, it was published in 1920. Stravinsky has described the origin of the work. In the autumn of 1917 he was living in Geneva. Together with other artist friends in equally difficult situations created by the war—

JEROME HINES

A performance of L'Histoire du soldat *at the Hamburg State Opera in 1946*

the author Ramuz, the conductor Ansermet, and the painter Auberjonois—he conceived an original way of earning money; they would start a theatrical tour of a piece with the fewest possible performers. Ramuz was to write the play and Stravinsky the music, Ansermet was to conduct and Auberjonois to design the costumes and décor. They soon managed to find a backer, and set to work. The subject was taken from a collection of Russian folk stories and legends, but its content was of general interest.

The first performance in 1918 in Lausanne caused great interest, but the projected tour had to be abandoned on account of the influenza epidemic which was at the time ravaging Europe. The music was later arranged as a concert suite.

In *L'Histoire du soldat* modern music and the experimental theater were brought together in intimate conjunction for the first time. The work was epoch-making, not only by reason of its

plan, but also because of its artistic attitude, its abundance of ideas, its brilliant technique, and its fearless use of its material.

L'Histoire du soldat is a symbolic account of the defeat of the human element in the gamble of life. The story is recited by a narrator to a series of mimed scenes, accompanied by music for a small chamber orchestra of six instruments (clarinet, bassoon, cornet, trombone, violin, double bass) and percussion. The eight parts are:

1. Soldier's March.
2. The Soldier's Violin—Music at the Brook—Pastorale.
3. Royal March.
4. Little Concerto.
5. Three Dances: Tango, Waltz, Ragtime.
6. The Devil's Dance.
7. Grand Chorale.
8. Triumphal March of the Devil.

1. The soldier, on leave, sets out for his home, full

of longing to see his sweetheart and his mother. But the way is long, and he stops for a rest.

2. He sits beside a brook, playing his violin. The Devil, in the shape of a little withered old man, sneaks up behind him. He first lies watching, and listening to the music, then approaches the soldier from behind and tries to take the violin. At first the soldier will not give it up, but when he is offered in exchange a book with the promise of gold and power, he lets the violin go, and accepts the little man's invitation to stay with him for three days.

The three days become three years, and when the soldier finally comes home even his mother does not recognize him, and his sweetheart has long been married to another. Furiously he attacks the Evil One, who is now a big fat cattle-dealer. But the Devil escapes, and the soldier discovers the value of the book he was given: it gives him all the riches of the earth and all the knowledge of the world, but it cannot give him love.

The Devil comes to him again as a sweet but false old woman. She carries the violin, but when the soldier tries to play it, it is dumb. He tears the book to pieces; the spell is broken, and he is a soldier again. He goes to the castle of a king who has proclaimed that whoever can heal the sick princess shall have her as his wife.

3. In the courtyard of the palace he again meets the Devil, who this time appears as an elegant and famous virtuoso, and who carries the soldier's violin. They play cards. The Devil wins every time, but drinks so much that he rolls under the table. The soldier immediately seizes the violin.

4. He plays triumphantly over the unconscious body of the Evil One. He sees that his music will cure the princess, and wedding bells and happiness beckon.

5. The soldier comes to the princess, who is lying in bed. He plays so passionately that she rises and begins to dance. The Devil creeps in in the disguise of a huge animal with great clawed feet.

6. But the soldier knows what to do: he begins to play again, and the Devil has to dance. He tries desperately to hold his feet still with his hands, but cannot prevent them from dancing. In the end he falls flat and is thrown out.

7. But the soldier is not happy, for thoughts of his mother make him homesick. He and the princess set off for his mother's home. But at the crossroads the blood-red prince of Hell is waiting with the violin.

8. The Devil plays in triumph, and the soldier has to follow him. In vain the princess calls his name; the Devil drives him before him.

HISTORY OF MUSIC. See *Music Through the Ages.*

HIVELY, Wells. American composer (1902–). Best known of Hively's works are *Summer Holiday (Rive Gauche)* and *Tres Himnos,* both for orchestra.

H.M.S. PINAFORE (or *The Lass That Loved a Sailor).* Fourth of the Gilbert and Sullivan operas, first performed at the Opéra Comique, London, May 25, 1878. The partnership's first great success, this opera firmly established the new English comic opera tradition begun in *Trial by Jury.* This "tight little, bright little" piece about the Royal Navy appealed not only to the hearts of all Englishmen, but to Americans as well, and no less than six pirated versions of the opera appeared in the United States simultaneously with the first London run.

The work was not an instantaneous success, but when Sullivan played selections from the opera at a promenade concert the tunes caught the public imagination, and the catch phrase "What, *never?* Well, hardly ever!" was soon heard all over London. The object of Gilbert's satire is social snobbery, and in particular the fallacy of theories of equality. The plot is stereotyped and the denouement absurd, but there is a captivating tunefulness, spontaneity, and wit in the tunes and lyrics, as exemplified in the gay, sparkling chorus which opens the opera.

ACT I

Scene: *The deck of H.M.S. Pinafore off Portsmouth*

Little Buttercup (contralto), a bumboat woman, "the rosiest, the roundest, and the reddest beauty in all Spithead," comes aboard as the sailors are busy scrubbing the decks for the expected arrival of Sir Joseph Porter, First Lord of the Admiralty, and sings her merry little waltz ditty *I'm Called Little Buttercup.* A young sailor, Ralph Rackstraw (tenor), is in love with the Captain's daughter Josephine (soprano), who, however, is to be betrothed to Sir Joseph Porter. The latter duly arrives, attended by "his sisters and his cousins and his aunts," and announces himself in two celebrated songs: *I Am the Monarch of the Sea* and *When I Was a Lad:*

When I was a lad I serv'd a term as of-fice

Ralph plans to elope with Josephine, but the plot is overheard by the boatswain Dick Deadeye.

ACT II

Scene: *On deck at night*

Captain Corcoran (baritone) is singing *Fair Moon, To Thee I Sing,* when Little Buttercup approaches and reveals her affection for him. The captain repulses her because of the difference in rank between them, but she hints that "things are seldom what they seem." Sir Joseph complains that Josephine does not respond to his suit. Dick Deadeye reveals the elopement plan, and he and the captain lie in wait for the elopers, "carefully on tiptoe stealing." In the excitement of the capture the captain swears "a big, big D," which is overheard by Sir Joseph. For this depravity the captain is ordered to his cabin.

Little Buttercup discloses that the captain and Ralph had been accidentally exchanged while they were babies, whereupon Sir Joseph makes Ralph captain, and reduces Corcoran to able seaman. Since it is now out of the question for one of his exalted station to marry the daughter of a seaman, Sir Joseph consents to the marriage of Ralph and Josephine, while the former captain consoles himself with Little Buttercup. The crew finish the opera with *It's Greatly to His Credit That He Is an Englishman.*

HOCKET. A device used in medieval counterpoint before the development of true *staccato* and *legato* effects. Literally, a hocket was a rest between notes.

HODGES, John Cornelius ("Rabbit"). American jazz saxophonist (1906–). Hodges played with Duke Ellington from 1928 to 1951. He and Benny Carter have been acknowledged as the most famous saxophonists of the 1930s. He has made numerous recordings, and his sweet, melodic style has been widely imitated.

HOFFMAN, Irwin. American conductor (1924–). Hoffman, after graduation from the Juilliard School of Music, where he studied violin with Mischa Mischakoff, studied with Serge Koussevitzky at Tanglewood for three years. He made his orchestral debut at the age of seventeen, leading the Philadelphia Orchestra at Robin Hood Dell. In 1949–50 he was musical director for the Martha Graham Dance Company, conducting over one hundred performances. He became conductor of the Vancouver Symphony Orchestra in 1952, a post he retains, and has been guest conductor at Grant Park (Chicago) and of the St. Louis Symphony and Toronto and Vancouver CBC orchestras.

He has also composed two string quartets and a violin sonata. He is married to the violinist Esther Glazer.

HOFFMANN, E(rnst) T(heodore) A(madeus). German novelist and composer (1776–1822). The famous author of the fantastic tales on which Offenbach based his opera, *The Tales of Hoffman,* was also an important figure in music. He composed instrumental music, incidental music to dramas, and several operas, one of which, *Undine,* has been produced in modern times. As an astute music critic, he wrote for journals in Leipzig and Berlin.

HOFMANN, Josef. Polish-American pianist and composer (1876–1957). Hofmann, who composed under the name Michael Dvorsky, was born into a family of exceptional musical talent, and began to play the piano at the age of four under the tutelage of his father, Casimir Hofmann. He made his first public appearance at the age of six, and at nine made his debut with the Berlin Philharmonic Orchestra. This was followed by an extensive tour of Scandinavia and visits to leading European cities. At eleven he performed at the Metropolitan Opera with great success. He pursued his studies with Moskowski and Anton Rubinstein and concertized widely throughout the world. He served as director of the Curtis Institute of Music, in Philadelphia, from 1926 to 1938. He was regarded, especially by musicians, as one of the world's greatest pianists.

HOFMANNSTHAL, Hugo von. Austrian poet and dramatist (1874–1929). Though he is much admired in German-speaking countries for his plays and poetry, he is known elsewhere chiefly for his play *Jedermann (Everyman)* and for the superb librettos he wrote for Richard Strauss, of which the best known are *Elektra, Der Rosenkavalier, Ariadne auf Naxos, Arabella,* and *Die Frau ohne Schatten.*

E. T. A. HOFFMANN

JOSEF HOFMANN

HUGO VON HOFMANNSTHAL

HOIBY, Lee. American composer (1926–). Hoiby studied piano with Egon Petri at Mills College and composition with Gian-Carlo Menotti at the Curtis Institute of Music. He has been a Fulbright and Guggenheim Fellow and has won National Institute of Arts and Letters and Louisville Student awards. He has written two operas, *The Scarf* (one act), performed by the New York City Opera in 1959, and *Beatrice* (three acts), and composed orchestral pieces.

HOLBERG SUITE. Composition by Grieg, the Norwegian title being *Fra Holbergs Tid (From Holberg's Time)*. The work was written in 1884 for the celebration of the bicentenary of the birth of the Norwegian-Danish author Ludvig Holberg, and Grieg evidently tried to give it the style and form of the seventeenth century. He often referred to the work as a "be-wigged piece."

The composition was originally written for piano, but in February, 1885, Grieg decided to arrange it for string orchestra: "I have arranged the wretched Holberg Suite for string orchestra. Maybe it will sound quite well. The final movement (rigaudon) I have arranged for solo violin and solo viola, and then introduced a great deal of pizzicati in the rest of the orchestra."

Hubert Foss commented: "The work abounds in magnificent string effects . . . it is Grieg's most carefully elaborated piece of orchestration, despite the fact that it is confined to strings."

The suite has six movements:

I. *Prelude.*
II. *Sarabande.*
III. *Gavotte.*

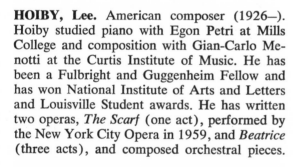

IV. *Musette.*
V. *Air.*

VI. *Rigaudon.*

HOLDE, Artur. German-American music critic (1885–1962). Holde studied at the University of Berlin with Max Friedländer and Herman Kretzschmar. He was conductor at the Frankfurt Synagogue from 1910 to 1936. In 1937 he came to the United States and was choirmaster at the Hebrew Tabernacle in New York City from 1937 to 1943. He was music critic of the German publication *Aufbau* in New York.

HOLLANDER, Lorin. American pianist (1944–). Lorin Hollander's father, Max Hollander, was concertmaster of the NBC

Symphony Orchestra. Lorin began to study music at the age of five, later became a pupil of Edward Steuermann, and at eleven entered the Juilliard School of Music and made his debut with the National Orchestral Association, Leon Barzin conducting, at Carnegie Hall. Later he regularly played over NBC radio. During his concert tour of the United States he was a soloist at Lewisohn Stadium, made his Grant Park debut with the Chicago Symphony Orchestra, and made five appearances with the New York Philharmonic Orchestra and three with the National Symphony Orchestra. He has recorded works by several composers.

HOLLIDAY, Billie ("Lady Day"). American jazz singer (1915–1959). Billie Holliday first earned wide attention as a result of recordings made with the Teddy Wilson Orchestra in the 1930s. She was also featured vocalist with the Benny Goodman, Count Basie, and Artie Shaw orchestras, and made tours of the United States and Europe as a soloist and with Jazz Club USA. *Lady Sings the Blues* is her autobiography.

HOLLYWOOD BOWL. A huge outdoor concert hall near Los Angeles, California. Hills rising from a sloping floor provide a natural amphitheater with excellent acoustical properties. Thousands flock here each summer to listen to concerts given by the Los Angeles Philharmonic Orchestra under internationally famous guest conductors.

HOLMBOE, Vagn. Danish composer (1909—). He began as a painter, and has done considerable research in folk music, which has influenced the style but not the content of his music. Now the outstanding Scandinavian composer, his works include ten chamber concertos, six symphonies, two violin sonatas, an opera, and a ballet.

HOLST, Gustav. British composer (1874–1934). Holst was descended from a Swedish family which had settled in England in 1807. He began to compose almost as soon as he could hold a pen, and acquired considerable experience in his early years as a village organist and as a

The Hollywood Bowl

conductor of choral societies. At the age of nineteen he entered the Royal College of Music, where he spent five years studying composition with Sir Charles Stanford.

On the completion of his studies he joined the Carl Rosa Opera Company as trombonist, subsequently playing for several years with the Scottish Orchestra. From 1906 he was director of music at St. Paul's Girls School, London, and he also taught at Morley College.

He became teacher of composition at the Royal College of Music in 1919. An inspiring teacher and a man of strong ideals, Holst overworked, and after a nervous breakdown in 1924 spent the rest of his life in seclusion, devoting himself to composition.

Holst wrote a large number of works in a highly individual style, and won a place as one of the foremost British composers of his day. For a time he was much influenced by Hindu philosophy, and during this period composed two operas, *Sitra* and *Savitri,* and four sets of choral hymns from the *Rig-Veda.* Turning from this style he wrote *The Planets* (1915), a brilliant and impressive suite of tone poems for large orchestra which is perhaps the best known and most popular of his works. Holst further strengthened his reputation with *The Hymn of Jesus* (1917), the opera *The Perfect Fool* (1921), and other large choral works.

In 1930 he published a set of *Twelve Songs* to words by Humbert Wolfe which, with their individual type of declamation and with a harmonic accompaniment reduced to the bare essentials, reflected a new austerity of style. The orchestral *Egdon Heath* displayed this same quality, and in his later years Holst became increasingly occupied with "linear" writing, a direction which led inevitable to polytonality. An example of this later work is his concerto for two violins and orchestra (1930).

In his earlier works Holst was sometimes reproached with eclecticism, but, as his friend Vaughan Williams said, "Holst's weaknesses are the defects of his qualities—occasionally his magnificent technique masters him and the end gets lost in the means. Sometimes he spoils the noble simplicity of his work by an unnecessary piece of elaboration; at other times the very individuality of his thought which requires such a personal technique causes a flaw in his work. . . . But as time goes on these discrepancies get fewer and fewer, his style gets maturer,

GUSTAV HOLST

simpler and more individual, and this individuality shows through all his music; whether it is in the most extreme harmonic and rhythmical thought of *The Planets* or the absolute simplicity of the *Four Carols,* his signature is plain on every page."

Best-known works:

OPERAS

Savitri, 1 Act (1916)
The Perfect Fool, Op. 39, 1 Act (1923)
    Ballet music

ORCHESTRAL

St. Paul's Suite (strings), Op. 29, No. 2 (1913)
The Planets Suite, Op. 32 (1916)
   1. *Mars, the Bringer of War*
   2. *Venus, the Bringer of Peace*
   3. *Mercury, the Winged Messenger*
   4. *Jupiter, the Bringer of Jollity*
   5. *Saturn, the Bringer of Old Age*
   6. *Uranus, the Magician*
   7. *Neptune, the Mystic*
The Hymn of Jesus (with chorus), Op. 37 (1917)

SONGS

This Have I Done for My True Love, Op. 34a, No. 1
I Vow to Thee, My Country (Spring-Rice)

HOLY CITY, THE. Song by Stephen Adams, to words by Fred Weatherly, composed in 1892. It became one of the most popular songs of its time throughout the English-speaking world, and retains an established place in the vocal and choral repertoire.

HOME, SWEET HOME. Song by Sir Henry Bishop to words by John Howard Payne (1791–1852). As a young man Payne went to London to make his way as an actor and dramatist. His greatest success was the opera *Clari, the Maid of Milan,* with music composed by Bishop. Among the songs in *Clari* was *Home, Sweet Home,* which was publicly performed for the first time in London in 1823. Bishop had previously used the melody in another opera, and the tune had originally appeared as *Sicilian Air* in a collection of folk songs which he had pushed. This led to a natural misunderstanding, and *Home, Sweet Home* was presumed to be a folk tune. Bishop had to go to court to prove that he had composed the tune himself. The deciding factor was his confession that a Sicilian tune had been lacking from his collection of folk songs, and he had composed one to fill the gap.

The song's popularity increased rapidly. It was used in the singing lesson in Rossini's *Barber of Seville,* and became a favorite item in the repertoires of Jenny Lind and Adelina Patti.

Mid plea-sures and pal-a-ces,   Though we may roam

LOUISE HOMER

HOMER, Louise. American contralto (1874–1947). She was one of the foremost opera stars of her day and became known throughout the world from her recordings with Caruso. She was a student at the New England Conservatory of Sidney Homer, later a well-known pianist and song composer (1864–1953), whom she married in 1895. Her debut, as Leonora in *La Favorita,* took place in Vichy in 1898. After singing at Covent Garden, she made her debut at the Metropolitan in 1900 as Amneris in *Aïda.* She remained a Metropolitan star until 1919, after which she sang with the Chicago Opera.

HOMOPHONY. From Greek *homoios,* "similar, alike," and *phone,* "sound, voice." A term for music in which one voice, usually the treble, carries the melody, while the others accompany in chords: the converse of polyphony, in which all voices are independent.

HONEGGER, Arthur. Swiss composer (1892–1955). His parents were Swiss, but he lived in Le Havre, where the boy was born and received his education. He said that he was attracted to composition as a career by hearing two of Bach's

ARTHUR HONEGGER

cantatas at the age of eleven. He studied for four years at the Zurich Conservatory and from the age of nineteen at the Paris Conservatory, where he came into contact with Milhaud and the other members of "Les Six." See *Six, Les.*

He was a teacher at the École Normale, Paris. In 1946 he gained the Schweitzerisches Tonkünstlerverein's prize for composition, and in 1948 was made an honorary doctor of Zurich University. He was elected President of the International Authors and Composers Association in 1949.

Although a member of "Les Six," Honegger did not always see eye to eye with the other members of the group or with their spokesman, Jean Cocteau. He was by no means an iconoclast; he admired Wagner as "a continuer of the classical in music"; and he did not "patronize music-hall or fairground music, but, on the contrary, favored chamber music and symphonies in their most serious and rigorous forms."

"Seriousness and austerity are dominant elements in his music, but in addition he possesses a keen sense of dramatic values, a strong penchant for realism, and a rare feeling for striking instrumental effects, which enabled him, to a greater extent than most of his colleagues, to make a direct and powerful impression upon the general public" (Gilbert Chase).

These qualities were first fully shown in his dramatic psalm *Le Roi David (King David),* which brought him world fame in 1921. Before this success Honegger had already attracted attention with *Nigamon's Song* (1919) on an Indian motif, the charming *Pastorale d'été (Summer Pastorale)* (1920), and the intensely contrapuntal, hard, and violent "mimic symphony" *Horace victorieux* (1921). This last work "marks the freeing of his personality as a composer. In this athletic symphony he shows himself in the fullness of his power. We can see a clear reaction against the types of expression

Honegger's Joan of Arc at the Stake, *performed at the Hamburg Opera*

which imitators of Stravinsky had made fashionable" (Roland-Manuel).

Honegger's "portrait of a locomotive," *Pacific 231,* was a striking success in 1923, and in 1925 he wrote the Biblical opera *Judith,* which many regard as a purer and more powerful and mature work than *Le Roi David,* of which it is a kind of parallel.

In these works he carried out the principles he had expressed in 1919: "I attach great importance to musical architecture, which I should never want to see sacrificed for reasons of a literary or pictorial order. My model is Bach. . . . I do not seek, as do certain anti-Impressionists, the return to harmonic simplicity. I find on the contrary that we should use the harmonic materials created by the school which preceded us, but in a different way—as the base of lines and rhythms."

In the chamber music written in his youth he shows sound polyphonic technique, and the same lively counterpoint is to be found in his Concertino for piano and orchestra (1924), which, incidentally, is one of the few works in which Honegger uses jazzlike syncopation. His musical description of a football game, *Rugby* (1928), was a popular work in the style of *Pacific 231.*

Among the more important of his later works may be mentioned his symphonies, especially the Second, for strings and trumpet (1941), and the Third, subtitled the *Liturgical,* written in 1946. Charles Munch, who conducted the first performance of the Third Symphony, says that Honegger here raises the question of man's relationship to God.

However, Honegger reached his peak in dramatic works in the grand manner, using orchestra, choir, and soloists. Cocteau's opera *Antigone* shows him as a powerful dramatist, the music being completely subordinated to an overriding rhythm; *Les Cris du monde* exposes man's fate in a mechanized world; while the ballet *Semiramis* is a strong, colorful, and superbly orchestrated work. Honegger also, surprisingly enough, wrote some operettas: *The Tale of King Pausole* (1934) showed him to be a witty parodist, and the amusing *Les Petites Cardinal,* which he wrote in cooperation with Jacques Ibert, was a great success at Offenbach's old theater, the Bouffes Parisiens, in 1938.

Of far greater significance is another dramatic work written in the same year and as enthusiastically received as was *King David* seventeen years earlier—the mystery play *Joan of Arc at the Stake,* to words by Claudel. Both in the stage performance at the Paris Opéra in 1950 and in radio productions, the intensity and violent, lifelike, and dramatic effects of this oratorio made a deep impression.

Darius Milhaud wrote early in Honegger's career: "He is one of those on whom we may rely to keep the traditions of absolute music alive . . . of music that needs for its full expression nothing but the guidance of his inspiration and his patiently acquired and unfailing craftsmanship."

A quarter of a century later René Dumesnil wrote these words about Honegger: "From his first works up to 'Joan of Arc at the Stake' and the 'Liturgical Symphony,' Honegger has constantly reached greater heights and constantly renewed himself. His work not only stands in the forefront of today's music—but it seems that it will record for posterity all that our time has to offer."

Best-known works:
  Three quartets.
  Five symphonies.
  Antigone (1927), tragic opera, libretto by Cocteau.
  Les Cris du monde (Cries of the World) (1931), for soloists, chorus, and orchestra.
  Semiramis (1934), ballet by Valéry.
  Jeanne d'Arc au bûcher (Joan of Arc at the Stake) (1938), oratorio, words by Claudel.

Honegger has also composed ballets; incidental, radio, and film music; other choral and orchestral works; chamber and instrumental music, including piano pieces; and about fifty songs.

A scene from Honegger's Judith

HOOGSTRAATEN, Willem van. Dutch conductor (1884–). His career began as a violinist and he gave recitals with the famous pianist, Elly Ney, to whom he was then married. His conducting career began in Germany and Holland and he came into prominence as conductor of the Mozart festival in Salzburg. He came to America in 1923 and became a fixture of the concerts at the Lewisohn Stadium. For many years, he was the permanent conductor of the Portland Symphony Orchestra. His specialty was the music of Brahms.

HOPAK. See *Gopak.*

HOPKINSON, Francis. American composer and statesman; a signer of the Declaration of Independence (1737–1791). Hopkinson was a lawyer who was greatly interested in music. He was the composer of what is said to be the first piece of music written by a native American, *Ode to Music,* composed in 1754. He is also credited with the first original American song, *My Days Have Been So Wondrous Free,* written in 1759 and dedicated to George Washington.

HORA. A kind of dance. Originally Hebrew, it has become a standard form, like gopak or gigue.

HORENSTEIN, Jascha. Russian-born conductor (1899–). Horenstein studied at the Vienna Academy and, in 1923, made his debut conducting the Vienna Symphony Orchestra. From 1925 to 1928 he was conductor of the Berlin Symphony Orchestra, and from 1929 until 1933 he directed the Düsseldorf Opera. He came to the United States in 1941, and has appeared with the New York Philharmonic and other orchestras. In 1956 he conducted the London Symphony Orchestra at the Johannesburg Festival in Mahler's Second Symphony.

HORN. See *French Horn.*

HORNE, Lena. American jazz and popular singer (1918–). In 1937 Lena Horne performed regularly in the Noble Sissle Show at the Cotton Club, and she was vocalist with Charlie Barnet's orchestra until 1940. She has since made a number of blues records with Duke Ellington and with Teddy Wilson's orchestra. She toured

LENA HORNE

Europe in 1947, 1950, and 1955. Lena Horne has become one of today's leading blues singers, with a noticeable likeness in style to that of her great predecessor, Ethel Waters. She has appeared in a number of films, including *Harlem on Parade* (1942), *Stormy Weather* (1943), *As Thousands Cheer* (1943), *Broadway Rhythm* (1943), *Two Girls and a Sailor* (1944), *Cabin in the Sky* (1944), and *Words and Music* (1948).

HOROWITZ, Vladimir. Russian-American pianist (1904–). Horowitz entered the Conservatory in Kiev at the age of twelve, and experienced his first success when a famous soprano sang three of his compositions with himself as accompanist. The Revolution cost his family their home and fortune, and Horowitz was obliged to give concerts in Kharkov for payment in the form of food and clothing. In 1924–25 he gave twenty-five different concerts in Leningrad and Moscow; later he went to Germany and created a sensation in Berlin. In Paris Horowitz was persuaded by an impresario to accompany him

VLADIMIR HOROWITZ

not to be dull is "to be true to one's own deepest impulses and aspirations."

Paderewski called him the greatest of the younger pianists, and Henri Prunières once wrote: "He has all the technical gifts in addition to exquisite musical sensitiveness. He excels in the interpretation of Bach and Liszt, but he can play Ravel and Debussy to perfection."

HORSZOWSKI, Mieczyslaw. Polish-American pianist (1892–). A student at the Lvov Conservatory and later a pupil of Theodor Leschetizky in Vienna, he is head of the piano faculty, with Rudolf Serkin, at the Curtis Institute of Music. Horszowski made his first public appearance in Warsaw at the age of nine, toured Europe extensively, and gave many recitals with Casals. He came to New York in 1940 and has concertized widely. He is a regular soloist each year at the Casals Festival in Puerto Rico, a well-known member of chamber music and sonata ensembles, and appears as a soloist with orchestras. He has recorded with Joseph Szigeti, Pablo Casals, Alexander Schneider, and other first-rank musicians.

HANS HOTTER

to the United States, where he has resided ever since.

Horowitz has constantly driven himself toward perfection and has permitted only a limited number of his recordings to be issued. He has always confined himself to a few public appearances each year and recently has given no concerts at all, preferring to restrict himself to study and recording. His field of study is wide and he maintains that "it is impossible to understand the significance of a composition without knowing the composer's other works."

Horowitz has no liking for the concert hall and always feels ill at ease when confronted by a large audience. "I would rather play just for a few friends." He relates that his father-in-law, Arturo Toscanini, once said to him: "They criticize us for not playing 'classically,' by which they mean it must not be too fast, too slow, too loud, or too soft. That leads to dullness."

Horowitz suggests that the one certain way

HOTTER, Hans. Austrian baritone (1909–). A thorough musician, he abandoned a career as a conductor when he discovered the quality of his vocal endowment. He has been a star of the Munich and Vienna State operas and of the Salzburg Festival. His Metropolitan debut was in 1950 in the title role of *The Flying Dutchman,* one of his finest characterizations. He sang roles in the world premières of three Strauss operas: *Friedenstag* (1938); *Capriccio* (1942); and *Die Liebe der Danae* (1952). As a lieder singer, he has been considered one of the greatest of his time. Critics have hailed his performance of Schubert's cycle *Die Winterreise* (which he has recorded three times) as the finest within memory.

HOVHANESS, Alan. American composer (1911–). Hovhaness studied with Converse at the New England Conservatory of Music, and at Tanglewood, on scholarship, with Martinu. He has received an award from the National Institute of Arts and Letters, two awards from the Guggenheim Foundation, and commissions from the Fromm Foundation, Bethsabee de Rothschild Foundation, and Louisville Orchestra (Concerto No. 7 for Orchestra).

Hovhaness is a very prolific composer. His works comprise orchestral and choral compositions, instrumental and chamber music, and film, ballet, and other incidental music. Some of his works are frequently performed; they reflect an intensely personal style which often incorporates Near Eastern melodic color and Occidental techniques. Important orchestral works by him include Concerto No. 1 for Orchestra *(Arevakal), The Mysterious Mountain,* Prelude and Quadruple Fugue, and Concerto No. 7. *The Flowering Peach* Suite, *Khaldis,* the Piano Concerto, *Is There Survival* Ballet Suite, *Out of the Depths* (violin and piano), and the Alleluia and Fugue, Op. 40b, are among his outstanding works for various instrumental combinations.

HOWARD, John Tasker. American composer and writer (1890–). Among Howard's most notable contributions are *Our American Music, Our Contemporary Composers,* and books on Stephen Foster and Ethelbert Nevin.

HOWE, Mary. American composer (1882–). Mary Howe was graduated from the Peabody Conservatory of Music. She began her professional career as a pianist, and turned to composing in 1920. Since then she has written many orchestral works (notably *Stars* and *Sand*), choral compositions, chamber music, instrumental solos, and songs, which have been performed by leading orchestras, groups, and prominent soloists. She is a member of the Board of Directors of the National Symphony Orchestra, in Washington, D. C.

HSIEN-MING, Lee. Chinese pianist (1918–). Lee Hsien-Ming studied in China and later in Paris, and has toured Europe. She is married to the composer Alexander Tcherepnin.

HUBAY, Jenö. Hungarian violinist and composer (1858–1937). Hubay received his first musical education from his father, a composer and violinist, and made his first appearance as a soloist when he was only eleven. After study under such famous violinists as Joachim and Vieuxtemps, he began his international career in Germany when he was eighteen. He later formed a string quartet which was soon recognized as one of the best in Europe. From 1882 to 1886 Hubay was professor of the violin at the Brussels Conservatory. He then accepted the same post at the Budapest Conservatory.

The possessor of a highly developed technique, beautiful tone, and fine musical feeling, Hubay was one of the leading figures of the Hungarian violin school. Szigeti, Stefi Geyer, and Telmányi were among his pupils.

As a composer Hubay was very productive.

ALAN HOVHANESS

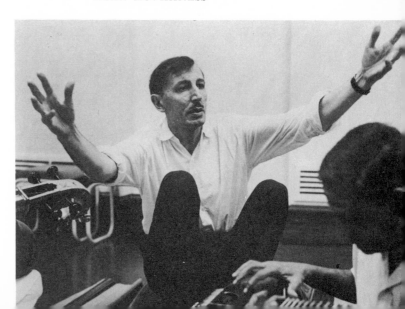

A scene from a nineteenth-century performance of Les Huguenots *at the Paris Opéra*

He wrote six operas, four symphonies, four violin concertos, and other works.

Best-known works:

VIOLIN AND PIANO

Hungarian Czardas Scenes
 No. 4, Op. 32 (*Hejre Kati*)
 No. 5, Op. 33 (*Waves of Balaton*)
Intermezzo (from the opera *The Violin Maker of Cremona*, 1894)
The Zephyr, Op. 5

HUBERMAN, Bronislaw. Polish violinist (1882–1947). Huberman's early studies were at the Warsaw Conservatory. In 1892, he was taken to Berlin, where he studied with Joachim. He made several public appearances at the age of eleven and was engaged by Adelina Patti to appear with her at her farewell concert in Vienna in 1895. He made many world tours, came to the United States in 1940, and returned to Europe after the war.

HUCBALD. Flemish composer and music theorist (*c.* 840–*c.* 930). A monk and director of a singing school, Hucbald designed a musical staff of which each line represented one string of a musical instrument.

HUCKO, Michael A. ("Peanuts"). American jazz clarinetist (1918–). Hucko has been with Joe Marsala, Charlie Spivak, Ray McKinley, and Benny Goodman, and now devotes himself principally to radio and television performances.

HUEHN, Julius. American baritone (1910–). After graduating from the Juilliard School, he made his debut at the Metropolitan Opera as the Herald in *Lohengrin* in 1935. For the next decade, he was prominent in the Wagner repertory there and with the opera companies of San Francisco, Chicago, and Cincinnati. Since 1945, he has been teaching at various universities.

HUGHES, Edwin. American pianist and teacher (1884–). A pupil of Joseffy and Leschetizky, he gave many concerts in Europe and America and played two-piano recitals with his wife, Jewel Bethany. He conducted master classes throughout America and edited many standard piano works. He also was secretary of the National Music Council.

HUGUENOTS, LES. Opera by Meyerbeer, with libretto by Scribe. Generally considered Meyerbeer's masterpiece, *Les Huguenots* was one of the most frequently given of all operas until 1910, when Meyerbeer's popularity began to decline. First produced at the Paris Opéra in 1836, it served as a vehicle for many all-star casts and was successfully revived, after long neglect, in 1962 at La Scala, when two of the stars were Joan Sutherland and Giulietta Simionato.

The complicated plot concerns the struggle between Catholics and Protestants, and the conciliatory efforts of Marguerite de Valois. The chief concern is the ill-fated love between Raoul, a Huguenot nobleman, and Valentine, the daughter of a Catholic nobleman. Act V, which depicts the Massacre of St. Bartholomew's Day, was usually omitted in performance.

HUME, Paul. American music critic (1915–). Hume studied at the University of Chicago and took private lessons in piano, organ, and voice. He has been organist, choirmaster, and baritone soloist at various churches in Chicago and Washington, and has given many song recitals. In 1946 he became music editor and critic of the Washington *Post*. In 1950 he wrote an unfavorable review of a song recital by Margaret Truman which evoked a famous letter of condemnation from her father, then President. The letter is now part of the collection in the Truman Museum at Independence, Missouri.

HUMORESQUES. Compositions for piano, Op. 101, by Dvořák. They are a set of eight light pieces, composed in 1894. Written in America just after Dvořák had decided to return home, they express his happiness at this prospect.

The best known of the *Humoresques* is the ever-popular No. 7, one of the most widely celebrated of all musical compositions, which has been arranged for almost every instrument and combination of instruments.

HUMPERDINCK, Englebert. German composer (1854–1921). After studying at the Cologne Conservatory and the Royal Music School in Munich, and winning several important prizes, he went to Italy; there he met Wagner, who became the important direct influence on his work. Wagner took him to Bayreuth to assist in the production of *Parsifal,* and it is believed that Humperdinck composed a few bars to fill out a transition that was too short for the scenery change. From 1885 to 1887, he taught theory at the Barcelona Conservatory and continued his own attempts at composition. Though he had attracted attention with a *Humoresque* for orchestra in 1880, his success as a composer did not come until 1893, when his opera *Hänsel und Gretel* was produced in Weimar. This work made him world famous, and he was never able to duplicate its success with an opera of similar quality, though his fifth opera, *Königskinder,* produced by the Metropolitan Opera in 1910, had a vogue for a time, chiefly because of the performance of Geraldine Farrar. He composed incidental music for *The Miracle* and for several Shakespearian plays, as well as for *Lysistrata* and *The Blue Bird.*

Humperdinck, about 1890

HUMPHREY, Doris. See *Modern Dance.*

HUNEKER, James Gibbons. American music critic and writer (1860–1921). Huneker studied piano with Georges Matthis and Rafael Joseffy, later teaching for a time under Joseffy at the National Conservatory of Music, New York. He became, successively, music critic of the Philadelphia *Press,* the New York *Times,* and the New York *World.* He wrote a number of books, discussing music, art, and literature.

HUNGARIAN DANCES. Compositions for piano by Brahms. Book I (Nos. 1–5) and Book II (Nos. 6–10) were published in 1869, and Book III (Nos. 11–16) and Book IV (Nos. 17–21) in 1880. They were all written for four hands, but Brahms himself arranged several of the dances for two hands.

Brahms had always been keenly interested in folk music, especially Hungarian, and typical Hungarian features mark several of the rondos in his instrumental concertos and his chamber music works. He had become acquainted with many of these dances in his youth, when he accompanied Reményi, the Hungarian violin virtuoso, at his concerts. He wrote down some of them on his travels in Hungary, but also used other sources.

Brahms offered the dances to Simrock, the publisher, "as genuine gypsy children," and they were described on the title page as "arranged" by Brahms. But it is fairly certain that at least three of the dances were his own original compositions. In spite of the careful declaration on the title page, immediately after their publication in 1869, Brahms was publicly accused of having stolen both the melodies and the arrangements. Reményi claimed that he had composed most of the melodies when he and Brahms were working together. But it appeared that the tunes had come out in popular Hungarian collections many years before.

Brahms played the Hungarian dances in the solo arrangement for the first time at a concert in Budapest in 1867. To his amazement they were a failure on that occasion, the Hungarians claiming that the piano was not the right medium for their national music. One publisher rejected the collection—an action he bitterly regretted later. The 1869 edition is for four hands, without opus number; Brahms did not number them among his compositions because he regarded himself as a mere arranger.

Even so, it is entirely due to Brahms that these melodies have become common property. The technical simplicity of the edition for four hands contributed to their popularity; the later edition for two hands is considerably more difficult.

In using the title *Hungarian Dances,* Brahms, like Liszt with his *Hungarian Rhapsodies,* made the mistake of confusing Hungarian with gypsy melodies. These dances are pure gypsy music. True Hungarian folk music was brought to light for the first time in this century by Béla Bartók and Zoltán Kodály.

No. 5:

No. 6:

THE HUNGARIAN QUARTET

HUNGARIAN QUARTET. Zoltán Szekely and Michael Kuttner, violins; Denés Koromzay, viola; and Gabriel Magyar, cello. The quartet made its debut in Budapest in 1935 and in a few years achieved high stature in Europe. Early in its career the members of the ensemble emigrated to Holland, where they stayed until 1950. In that year the ensemble became quartet-in-residence at the University of Southern California. Their recording of the seventeen Beethoven quartets won the Grand Prix du Disque, and their interpretations of the Bartók quartets are widely known. In 1958 the Hungarian Quartet played 125 concerts in a highly successful European tour.

HUNGARIAN RHAPSODIES. Compositions for piano by Liszt. Between 1851 and 1855 Liszt composed fifteen Hungarian Rhapsodies for piano, and between 1879 and 1886 five more were produced. The twentieth Rhapsody was never printed, but the manuscript is preserved in the Liszt museum at Weimar.

When the Rhapsodies were first published, they provoked a storm of enthusiasm, both because, musically speaking, they represented something new, and because of the widespread sympathy for the Hungarian fight for freedom against the Austrians and Russians.

Liszt made the Rhapsodies sound Hungarian by using characteristic abrupt tempo changes. These striking changes derive from Hungarian dance forms: the slow, melancholy *lassú* and the quick, impassioned *friss*. The special harmonic traits, and such other peculiarities as syncopation and sudden leaps into a higher key, show, however, more affinity with gypsy music than with Hungarian folk music.

In order to obtain closer acquaintance with Hungarian gypsy music, Liszt lived for a time with the gypsies at Raiding. He later wrote: "We were living with them—right among them. We slept together with them under the open starry sky, played with their children and chatted with the old folk. We listened to their music in the glow of the campfire. . . ."

Liszt's book *The Gypsies and Their Music in Hungary* (1859) caused bad feeling among his Hungarian countrymen because—as in his Rhapsodies—he gave the entire credit for all Hungarian folk music to the gypsies and completely ignored the contribution of the Hungarians themselves. Since then the field work of Béla Bartók and Zoltán Kodály has shown that Hungary possesses genuine national folk music of a totally different character from what Liszt and Brahms called Hungarian.

Six of the Hungarian Rhapsodies are also to be found in an orchestral version but numbered differently. No. 14 becomes No. 1; No. 12 is No. 2; No. 6 is No. 3; No. 2 is No. 4; No. 5 remains the same; No. 9 is No. 6.

No. 2 is the best known of the rhapsodies:

Blind Beggar Playing the Hurdy-Gurdy by Georges de la Tour, in the Museum at Nantes

HUNT, Walter ("Peewee"). American jazz trombonist (1907–). The son of musical parents, Hunt was graduated from the Cincinnati Conservatory of Music in 1929. He played with the Glen Gray Casa Loma Orchestra until 1942. After war service, he formed his own group. He is noted for his humorous playing of Dixieland music.

HURDY-GURDY. A stringed instrument in which the strings are bowed by a rosined wheel turned with one hand, and stopped by keys operated with the other. See *Stringed Instruments*.

HURLEY, Laurel. American coloratura soprano (1927–). Laurel Hurley won three National Federation of Music Clubs awards in her teens and then toured the United States in a leading role in a Shubert revival of Romberg's

LAUREL HURLEY

and concerts. Educated in Russian schools, he came to the United States in 1905 and began his career as manager of the weekly concerts at the Hippodrome in New York City. In 1914 he became a naturalized American citizen.

Since then he has brought outstanding artists and groups from abroad to perform in the United States. Among them are Anna Pavlova, Feodor Chaliapin, Isadora Duncan, the Russian Ballet, the Old Vic, the Sadler's Wells Ballet, the Moiseyev Folk Ballet, and the Théâtre National Populaire. He is the recipient of the French Legion of Honor Award. His autobiography is entitled *Impresario.*

HUSA, Karel. Czech-American composer (1921–). After study in Prague, Husa went to Paris in 1946 for further study with Arthur Honegger and Nadia Boulanger. In 1954 he was appointed a member of the music faculty at Cornell University. He has composed chamber and orchestral works.

HÜSCH, Gerhard. German baritone (1901–). Famous for his Papageno in Beecham's recording of *The Magic Flute,* and for recordings for the Hugo Wolf Society, he has been a star of

GERHARD HÜSCH

The Student Prince. She made her operatic debut in 1950 in Hartford. She coached with Sergius Kagen of the Juilliard School of Music in 1951, and the same year made her Town Hall recital debut in New York City as a Naumburg Award winner. She was then engaged by the New York City Opera, where in five spring and fall seasons she sang leading roles in twenty-two operas. She has been a member of the Metropolitan Opera company since 1955, singing such roles as Olympia in *Tales of Hoffmann,* the Queen of the Night in *The Magic Flute,* Susanna in *The Marriage of Figaro,* and Musetta in *La Bohème.* She has sung on television, with the American Opera Society, and at festivals and summer series, and has made recordings.

HUROK, Sol. Russian-American impresario (1888–). Sol Hurok is acknowledged as one of the world's outstanding impresarios of ballets the Berlin and Vienna State Operas; at Bayreuth he sang Wolfram in *Tannhäuser* under Toscanini.

HUSH-A-BYE, BABY. This cradle song, composed by Effie I. Canning in 1886 to the nursery-rhyme words, caused a great sensation in contemporary American popular music. George Jackson launched the song in Europe toward the end of the 1890s. It is often called *Rock-a-Bye, Baby*.

HUSS, Henry Holden. American composer and pianist (1862–1953). A descendant of Jan Huss, he studied at the Munich Conservatory and became well known as a pianist. He also gave many recitals with his wife, the soprano Hildegard Hoffmann. His compositions include choral works, concertos for piano and violin, and chamber music.

HUTCHESON, Ernest. Australian-American pianist and educator (1871–1951). He studied piano in Australia with Max Vogrich and played concerts at an early age. He was sent to the Leipzig Conservatory to study with Reinecke, and was graduated in 1890. He performed his own piano concerto in 1898 with the Berlin Philharmonic Orchestra. He came to the United States in 1900 and was head of the piano department at the Peabody Conservatory in Baltimore until 1912. From 1924 until 1937 he was dean of the Juilliard School of Music in New York. In 1937, he was appointed its president and held that post until 1945.

HUTTON, Betty. American singer and film actress (1921–). Betty Hutton owes her accomplishments—as singer, tap-dancer, and acrobat—to her mother's early training. She scored a sensational success on Broadway as a revue actress, and in 1942 went to Hollywood to take part in a song-and-dance film. She was soon a star. During the second World War she entertained the American Army in Europe, and in 1945 she appeared for a time at a fashionable Chicago night club. The most successful of her later films was *Annie Get Your Gun* (1951). Since 1952 she has appeared frequently on television and in night clubs.

HYMNS. From Greek *hymnos,* "a poem". In the early days of Christianity the term was used for any song in praise or adoration of God, but it was later restricted to a song with specially written words not taken from the Scriptures, thus distinguishing it from a Psalm.

LATIN HYMNS

St. Ambrose (*c.* 340–397), Bishop of Milan, is credited with the foundation of the hymnody of the Catholic Church, and his example was followed by St. Benedict and other monastic leaders, until the hymn became accepted in Divine Service. These early hymns, which date from a period when music was purely melodic, soon acquired their own plainsong melodies, many of which have survived into modern hymnbooks, though nowadays either harmonized for four parts or provided with an organ accompaniment.

The composition of hymns in the polyphonic style dates from the thirteenth century; the most famous collection is Palestrina's great work *Hymni totius anni (Hymns for the Whole Year)* published in 1589. The masterly contrapuntal treatment and expressive harmonies of these hymns produce effects of indescribable beauty. The English composers Tallis and Byrd also wrote excellent hymn tunes in this style during the sixteenth century.

THE CHORALE

Martin Luther (1483–1546), the reformer and founder of Protestantism, introduced vernacular hymns into the German Church in support of his principle that the congregation should take a full part in the service. The first Lutheran hymnbook appeared at Wittenberg in 1524; it contained only eight hymns, but there soon followed other collections. Many Lutheran hymns, such as *A Mighty Fortress* (by Luther himself), *Now Thank We All Our God,* and *O Sacred Head Now Wounded,* are still to be found in modern Protestant hymnbooks. J. S. Bach wrote many incomparable settings for the German chorales, in the eighteenth century.

THE ENGLISH HYMN

The hymn was admitted as a part of the English service by a decree of Elizabeth I, and in 1623 James I gave George Wither a patent permitting him to have *Hymns and Songs of the Church* bound with the Psalter. But the hymn was not generally accepted as having a rightful place in divine services until nearly a hundred years later. Isaac Watt's first hymnal appeared in 1709, soon followed in 1737 by John Wesley's hymnbook, published in Georgia. Congregational singing was an important feature of the Methodist movement, and the extensive use of hymns by the Wesleys prompted other nonconformist sects to follow suit. The eighteenth century was thus a period of prolific hymn production, unfortunately not always of a high standard, as the tunes were often spoiled by florid elaborations and frivolous mannerisms.

The Oxford (High Church) Movement of the latter half of the nineteenth century stimulated interest in plainsong and in the chorale, and hymns from the Latin and German with their original melodies became more common in the hymnbooks. The standard of church music rose, and composers like W. H. Monk, Dykes, and Stainer produced hymn tunes of genuine musical value. Many of the most popular English hymn tunes date from this period. In *Hymns Ancient and Modern,* which appeared in 1861, and *The English Hymnal* of 1906 an attempt was made to avoid the worst excesses of Victorian sentimentality and to introduce more vigorous plainsong and folk-song tunes. The same aim was successfully pursued in *The Oxford Hymn Book* and in *Songs of Praise.*

A feature of American hymn-singing in the latter part of the nineteenth century was the gospel hymn, brought into prominence by the evangelist Moody and his collaborator Sankey in their *Sacred Songs and Solos.* The texts of many of these hymns reflected the doctrine of "salvation by grace," and have been made familiar all over the world by the Salvation Army.

THE METRICAL PSALM

Still the most popular form of congregational singing in Presbyterian churches, the metrical psalm antedated the modern hymn by two centuries. It was the invention of the Calvinists of Geneva, and was introduced into the stricter Protestant communions from there. Many English Protestants who fled to Geneva during the persecutions of the sixteenth century were influenced by the French Psalter. The first collection published in England was that of Sternhold and Hopkins (1562); later psalm books were those of Este (1592), Playford (1677), and Tate and Brady (1696). Many of the metrical psalm tunes were given new words by Anglican hymn-writers, but some were borrowed with the same words, for *Hymns Ancient and Modern* and other hymnbooks.

Hymn Singing, *an engraving by Hogarth*

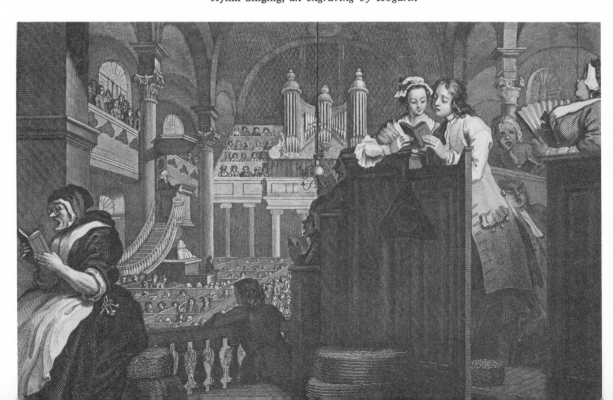

I

IBERIA. A suite of twelve pieces for piano by Isaac Albéniz, published between 1906 and 1909. Each piece depicts some place or scene in Spain; they are, as J. B. Trend wrote, "inspired by the rhythms, harmonies and turns of phrase of Spanish popular music, particularly the songs and dances of Andalusia." The most celebrated pieces are *Triana, Evocación, El Puerto, El Corpus en Sevilla,* and *El Albaicin,* all of them displaying a wealth of harmonic, rhythmic, and sonorous effects.

Georges Jean-Aubry has written: "*Iberia* marks the summit of the art of Albéniz. . . . One finds here all that emotion and culture can desire. The composer here reached a sureness of touch and grasped an originality of technique which demand attention and which have no ulterior object. . . . Albéniz has all the power of the poet—ease and richness of style, beauty and originality of imagery, and a rare sense of suggestion.

Goya's Majas on a Balcony, *Metropolitan Museum of Art, New York*

"A list of the themes alone of *Iberia* would suffice to show their richness in melody and the variety of their rhythm. But more wonderful than the beauty of their themes is their suppleness and fluidity; their langorous intonation, or their heat and energy. That in which Albéniz is inimitable is the atmosphere he creates around a theme, the scenery with which he surrounds the 'melodic personage'—a word, a song or a murmured confession. The method of Albéniz . . . is almost inscrutable. It obeys only subtle and personal laws. An expressive counterpoint, always ductile and full of movement, supports his themes, plays with them or crosses them. The parts seem at times inextricably intermingled, and then suddenly all is again resolved in lucidity."

Some of the pieces were later transcribed for orchestra by Arbós, and have gained great popularity in this form.

IBÉRIA. Orchestral suite by Debussy, first part of his trilogy *Images (Pictures),* associated with folk dances from various countries. *Ibéria* was composed in 1908, *Rondes de printemps* (based on French folk motifs) in 1909, and *Gigues* (based on English motifs) in 1913. Today the three pieces are seldom performed together, but *Ibéria* is often played alone.

The suite, as its name suggests, was written in honor of Spain. Debussy visited Spain only on a single day's trip to San Sebastian, but he "knew Spain from books and paintings and from songs and dances sung and danced by native Spaniards" (Falla).

The suite consists of three movements:

1. *Par les rues et par les chemins* (In the streets and byways).
2. *Les parfums de la nuit* (The fragrance of the night).
3. *Le matin d'un jour de fête* (The morning of a festival day).

Before the first performance on February 20, 1910, Debussy told the program editor: "It is no use asking me for any anecdotes about this work. There is no story linked with it, and whether or not the public will be interested in the work depends entirely on the music."

According to Falla, at the first performance of *Ibéria* Debussy said that his object "was not to write Spanish music, but rather to translate into music the impressions which Spain had awakened in him." And Falla continues: "I hasten to add that he has done this in a wonderful manner. The village theme, which is the basic theme of the work—a kind of *sevillana*—seems to float in a transparent atmosphere of glittering light. The intoxicating spell of Andalusian nights, the joy of the fiesta when the people dance through the streets to the strains of a *banda guitarras* and *bandurrias*—all this whirls about in the air, rises and falls."

Debussy, on his day in San Sebastian, went to see a bullfight, according to Falla, who believes that he there found his inspiration for the last movement of *Ibéria*. Falla adds that he wrote "better and more truly Spanish music than many Spanish composers who know their fatherland only too well."

IBERT, Jacques. French composer (1890–1962). Ibert won the Prix de Rome in 1919 and only two years later, with the publication of his *Ballade de la geôle de Reading* to Oscar Wilde's poem, became one of the foremost composers of his generation. In 1947 this work was revised and performed as a ballet. His next great work was the orchestral suite *Ports of Call (Escales)*.

In the witty opera *Angélique,* or *Wife for Sale,* occur for the first time what are perhaps Ibert's most characteristic qualities—his brilliant humor, rapierlike wit, charm, and originality. The same qualities are encountered again in his string quartet, which also shows his amazing mastery of technique.

In his lively and sentimental opera *Le Roi d'Yvetot,* Ibert has given a picture of fairy-tale France where the amusing and pathetic are to be found side by side. In collaboration with Honegger he wrote *L'Aiglon* (after Rostand) and the opera *Les Petites Cardinal.* In *Diane de Poitiers* (1934), a sort of ballet-opera, he has cleverly used some of the gems of old French polyphony, framed in his own sparklingly clear music. Of his smaller compositions a number of piano pieces, including *Le Petit âne blanc* and *Divertissement,* have gained wide popularity.

Ibert himself regarded as his chief works:

Ports of Call (Escales) (1920–22), for orchestra, first performed 1924.
Angélique (1925), opera, first performed 1926.
Saxophone Concerto (1934), first performed the same year.
String Quartet (1937–42), first performed 1943.
The Knight-Errant (1936), ballet, first performed 1950.

Ibert defined his musical creed thus: "To

JACQUES IBERT

be able to choose. To work conscientiously. To write only what I understand and what satisfies my imagination.

"My music is the direct expression of my thoughts. I write with an open mind, and wish people to listen to my music in the same way."

Regarding the piano piece *Le Petit âne blanc* Ibert gave this characteristic explanation: "I had not determined beforehand to write about a little white donkey—I always try to free my music from any description or design. But once while on a cruise I visited Tunisia, which is the homeland of the little white donkey, and I wrote the piece there. It was its color and rhythm which afterward prompted me to call it *Le Petit âne blanc.* The aim of music is to recall an impression rather than be directly descriptive. And the composer should limit his borrowings from the outside world to those elements which awaken his creative ability."

Ibert was director of the Académie Française in Rome from 1937 to 1961.

IDOMENEO. Opera in three acts by Mozart, K. 366, one of his most important *opera seria* works. The full title is *Idomeneo, Re di Creta, ossia Ilia ed Idamante (Idomeneus, King of Crete, or Ilia and Idamante).* The text was written by the court chaplain Varesco, and the first performance took place on January 29, 1781, in Munich.

The opera was received with great enthusiasm in Mozart's time, but in later years it has not maintained its position and is now very rarely performed. This is due partly to its lifeless libretto and partly to a decline of interest in *opera seria.* The music is not completely convincing as a dramatic whole, though some of the individual numbers have become established favorites in the concert hall.

The overture, which is often played, is shot through with the drama of the opera.

ILLICA, Luigi. Italian dramatist and librettist (1857–1919). One of the most successful librettists of his time, he did his best work with Giuseppe Giacosa as his collaborator. Together, they wrote the librettos for Puccini's three most popular works: *Tosca, La Bohème,* and *Madame Butterfly.* Among the librettos that Illica wrote alone are those for Giordano's *Andrea Chénier* and *Siberia;* Catalani's *La Wally;* Franchetti's

Cristoforo Colombo, Mascagni's *Le Maschere, Iris,* and *Isabeau;* and others for Alfano, Montemezzi, and Gnecchi. He and Giacosa also wrote the libretto for Puccini's *Manon Lescaut.*

IMBRIE, Andrew. American composer (1921–). Imbrie studied piano with Leo Ornstein for twelve years, and after studying with Nadia Boulanger at Fontainebleau for a short time, earned degrees at Princeton University and the University of California at Berkeley (where he now teaches); he worked with Roger Sessions at both institutions. In 1947 he was a Prix de Rome winner, and in 1959 he received the Walter W. Naumburg Recording Prize. He has composed orchestral, choral, piano, and chamber music (including three quartets, the first of which won the New York Music Critics' Circle Award for chamber music in 1944).

IMPRESSIONISM. In music a style of composition intimately connected with the works of Claude Debussy. The term originated in France late in the nineteenth century simultaneously

Act II of Idomeneo *at Glyndebourne, designed by Oliver Messel*

with the style of painting identified by the same name and a similar movement in literature. Painters such as Cézanne, Renoir, Degas, and Monet sought to paint without photographic exactitude. Their primary concern was to capture on their canvases the atmosphere surrounding their objects, their relation to light and shadow, and their place within the ever-changing color scheme of nature.

The goals of the French musicians were much the same. Debussy's works, for example, bear such titles as *Clair de lune (Moonlight), La Mer (The Sea), Nuages (Clouds), Reflets dans l'eau (Reflections in the Water)* and *Jardins sous la pluie (Gardens in the Rain).*

Impressionism is closely linked with the phenomena of nature, thus forming an intentional contrast to the emotional style of Richard Wagner's music which completely dominated musical thinking at the end of the nineteenth century.

The famous Spanish poet José Ortega y Gasset expresses the following opinion: "After Wagner, music had to be freed from personal feelings and cleansed until it achieved an exemplary objectivity. This was Debussy's great mission. Thanks to him, it became possible to listen to music in peace, without tears or fainting fits. . . . Debussy freed music from the human element, and it is for this reason that he marks a new era."

Technically speaking this was achieved by: (a) The introduction into Western music of Oriental elements such as pentatonic as well as whole-tone scales and their harmonic consequences (augmented triads, seventh and ninth chords based on major thirds, etc.); and (b) The use of a harmonic vocabulary basically not so different from the chromatic language of Wagner's *Tristan und Isolde* but avoiding the conclusiveness of established harmonic progressions and their cadential endings.

Many composers were influenced by impressionism, notably Ravel, Satie, and Dukas in France, Delius in England, the Spaniards Albéniz and Falla, and the Hungarian Kodály. See *Music Through the Ages.*

IMPROMPTU. Latin, *in promptu,* "in readiness." Since the 1820s a term for small piano pieces of a character that suggests improvisation. There are many examples in the works of Schubert, Schumann, and Chopin.

Above: *Curtain designed by Giorgio de Chirico for* L'Incoronazione di Poppea. Below: *production at La Scala*

IMPROVISATION. The art of composing directly on an instrument at a performance, that is, playing music not written down beforehand but proceeding straight from the imagination of the player. In the earliest days all music was improvised. The art has been retained in church music as a feature of organ playing, and it has experienced a renaissance in the jazz music of our age.

INCORONAZIONE DI POPPEA, L' (*The Coronation of Poppaea*). Monteverdi's last opera, with libretto by Francesco Busenello. The story is about the Roman emperor Nero's love for Poppaea, the wife of one of his generals. Nero exiles the general and divorces his own wife in order to marry Poppaea. The work is one of the first great dramatic achievements in opera, and has been successfully revived, both in concert and stage versions, today.

VINCENT D'INDY

INDIA, Sigismondo d'. Italian composer (*c.* 1582–*c.* 1627). Though he is of lesser importance than his great contemporary, Monteverdi, he was one of the pioneers in the Italian art of song. His madrigals, monodies, church music, and works for the stage were composed in the conventional polyphonic forms but contained innovations in harmony and true originality of melody. His work was done at the courts of the Duke of Savoy and the Duke of Modena. Late in his life, he composed for the Julian Chapel in Rome.

INDIAN LOVE LYRICS. Four very popular songs by Amy Woodforde-Finden to verses by Laurence Hope. In these songs she demonstrated exceptional talent in the creation of atmosphere; with their tunefulness and suitability for amateur voices, this gained for them world-wide popularity. The four songs are: *Pale Hands I Loved (The Kashmiri Love Song), Less Than the Dust, Temple Bells,* and *Till I Wait.*

INDY, Vincent d'. French composer (1851–1931). Born into a noble family, his talents were encouraged by his parents and, particularly, by his remarkable grandmother. He was something of a prodigy and grew into a dedicated composer with a fine musical intellect and a sympathetic

personality. The great influences on his work were first Berlioz and later Franck, who became his teacher. After traveling in Germany, he became a passionate Wagnerian. However, through the influence of his friends and, indirectly, of Wagner himself, he determined to compose as a French nationalist and turned to the study of the folk music of his country. He built a home in the Cévennes, where he found the inspiration for his masterpiece, the *Symphony on a French Mountain Air* for piano and orchestra, Op. 25, which is the only one of his many compositions that has become a staple of the repertory. As the real director (under Franck) of the Société Nationale de Musique, he exerted a vigorous and profound influence on French musicians. He also helped to found and directed a private conservatory, the Schola Cantorum. His opera, *Fervaal,* designed to be the great nationalist opera of France, was much admired at its première but, though it has been revived occasionally, has failed to gain real popularity.

Though d'Indy composed ambitiously and energetically in almost all forms, his influence was eclipsed by that of Debussy, and he has remained a neglected and underrated composer, though his great services to French music, as teacher and conductor, have long been acknowledged. He composed twelve operas (six of which were produced), many choral works, songs, piano pieces, much chamber music, and a variety of orchestral works, including overtures, symphonies, and the *Istar* symphonic variations, which exhibits his mastery of form and orchestration and remains, after his Op. 25, the best known of his works.

Best-known works:

ORCHESTRAL

Symphony on a French Mountain Air, G major, Op. 25, No. 1 (*Symphonie cévenole*) (piano and orchestra) (1886)
Introduction from the opera *Fervaal* (1897)
La Forêt enchantée, symphonic ballad
Istar, symphonic variations

INGEGNERI, Marc Antonio. Italian composer (*c.* 1542–1592). He was choirmaster of the Cathedral of Cremona, where he was a teacher of Monteverdi. His church music remained unknown until some of it was discovered to have been confused with that of Palestrina, though it is markedly different in harmony.

INGHELBRECHT, Désiré-Émile. French composer and conductor (1880–). He was a friend of Debussy in the composer's later days and excels in conducting his works. He has written chamber music, vocal works, and ballet music, and has arranged works for orchestra by Albéniz and Couperin.

INTERMEZZO. Opera by Richard Strauss, composed to his own libretto. First produced in Dresden, November 4, 1924. The principal characters are modeled on Strauss and his wife, and the plot supposedly is based on an actual misunderstanding that took place between them. Strauss dubbed this opera "a domestic comedy." It is concerned with the difficulties ensuing between a husband and wife when a love letter is received by the husband from a woman who intended it for another. The American première took place, in a concert version, in 1963.

INTERMEZZO. This term is normally used nowadays for short character pieces, usually for piano; but it may also signify a short orchestral piece inserted in the middle of an opera, for example the intermezzo in *Cavalleria Rusticana*. In sixteenth-century Italy the word denoted a song or madrigal inserted between the acts of a play. By the eighteenth century the intermezzo had become a light and merry farce played in the middle of a serious opera, and as such it was the source of *opera buffa*. An example of such an intermezzo is Pergolesi's *La Serva padrona (The Maid Mistress)*, 1733.

INTERNATIONALE, THE. The official Socialist and Communist song, composed in 1888 by Adolphe Degeyter to words written by Eugène Pottier, a Lille woodworker, during the Paris Commune of 1871. It was the official anthem of the Soviet Union from 1917 to 1944.

Hanni Steffak and Herman Prey in Strauss' Intermezzo *at the Munich State Opera*

INTERPRETATION. The word used to denote the personal aspect of a musical performance. It designates those elements of tone, tempo, and phrasing that are the performer's own.

INTERVAL. The difference in pitch between two notes. See *Music, Elements of.*

IN THE STEPPES OF CENTRAL ASIA. Symphonic poem by Borodin, composed in 1880, originally commissioned for a representation of tableaux vivants given in honor of the twenty-fifth anniversary of the reign of Tsar Alexander II. It shows the composer's gifts for rich harmony and a charmingly natural combination of themes. This description is printed in the score: "Across the steppes of Central Asia a peaceful Russian song is heard. In the distance the sounds of camels and horses and the strains of a haunting Oriental melody are heard. Protected by Russian arms, the caravan moves safely and untroubled on its long journey through the endless wastes. The Russian and Asiatic melodies merge in a harmony that dies away like an echo across the plain."

The clarinet plays the Russian melody and the English horn the Asiatic, and these are later played simultaneously in varying places. Pizzicato double basses illustrate the trotting of the horses, and the long high notes on the strings express the monotony of the endless horizon of the steppes.

IN THE STILL OF THE NIGHT. Slow foxtrot from the film *Rosalie* (1937), with words and music by Cole Porter. This composition is considered to be among Porter's best, and one critic places it in the same category as such famous examples of modern American songwriting as Irving Berlin's *Always,* Gershwin's *Summertime,* and Jerome Kern's *Smoke Gets in Your Eyes.*

INTROITUS. A psalm used to introduce the Mass. It is sung before the *Gloria Patri,* and repeated after it, set to music from Gregorian chant. There are introits for every ecclesiastical day, and the first words of the various psalms supply the Latin names for the days.

INVENTIONS. Thirty keyboard pieces by J. S. Bach, written about 1720, when he was conductor of the orchestra at the small Court at Köthen. They were intended as exercises for

A painting by the nineteenth-century Russian artist, Vassili Veretshchagin: Kirghiz Yurts [*Mongolian tents*] *by the Chu River, a typical landscape of the Kirghiz steppes in Central Asia*

his son Wilhelm Friedemann Bach. Later Bach collected them together in one book, calling the fifteen two-part pieces "inventions" and the fifteen three-part pieces "sinfonias." The word "inventions" was later adopted as the title of the whole collection.

"The term 'inventions' for such pieces did not, as was once believed, originate with Bach, but was borrowed from an unknown composer whose works Bach once copied for his sons. Bach could just as well have called his compositions 'preludes'. . . .

"The *Inventions* were not written for the harpsichord but for the clavichord—the domestic keyboard instrument of that time" (Albert Schweitzer).

INVITATION TO THE DANCE (*Aufforderung zum Tanz*). Concert waltz for piano by Weber. It was composed in Dresden in the summer of 1819, while the composer was working on *Der Freischütz,* and was given the title of *Rondo brilliant* and dedicated to the composer's wife. In 1841 it was revised for orchestra by Berlioz, who used it as ballet music in a performance of *Der Freischütz,* and in 1896 Felix Weingartner reorchestrated the work.

Weber's composition came into existence when the waltz as a dance was still scarcely known, and it certainly inspired such later world-famous composers of waltzes as Joseph Lanner and Johann Strauss the Elder. H. E. Jacob maintained, however, that the rhythm of Weber's composition was not, as had been thought, completely new. He pointed out that Beethoven's friend, the pianist Hummel, for example, had written waltzes in quick time; what was new about Weber's *Invitation* was that it was not only a dance, but a piece of program music.

Weber takes us by the arm into a candlelit ballroom. The dancers are men in silk waistcoats and dark blue coats, and beribboned ladies in puffed sleeves and cashmere shawls scented with lavender.

The composer sketched the program on the score: A gentleman approaches a lady and invites her to dance with him. She answers shyly and evasively. He presses his request more

Vaslav Nijinsky and Tamara Karsavina in Le Spectre de la Rose *based on* Invitation to the Dance

earnestly, and after much persuasion she gives in and they swing happily into the dance.

Le Spectre de la Rose, the famous ballet set to this music (in the Berlioz version) by Michel Fokine was, as danced by Nijinsky and Karsavina, a staple of the *Ballets Russes* repertory.

IOLANTHE, or *The Peer and the Peri.* Seventh of the Gilbert and Sullivan operas, first performed at the Savoy Theatre, London, on November 25, 1882, as an "entirely new and original fairy opera." In this, the first opera written for the new Savoy Theatre erected by D'Oyly Carte for the exclusive performance of Gilbert and Sullivan works, Gilbert again satirizes an English institution—in this instance, the House of Lords—though the lyrics are directed at all pretense and unearned privilege. The mixture of the fairy world with the House of Peers creates a typical topsy-turvy "Gilbertian" situation. Sullivan's music is in the Mendelssohn style, and occasionally has an evocative magical quality very similar to that of *A Midsummer Night's Dream.* Deems Taylor considers the score "one of the most spontaneous and ingratiating that Sullivan ever wrote."

Act III of Iphigenia in Aulis *at the Berlin State Opera, 1955*

IPHIGENIA IN AULIS *(Iphigénie en Aulide).*
Opera in three acts by Gluck, with libretto by
du Roullet based on Racine's tragedy, first performed in Paris in 1774.

The overture closely reflects the atmosphere
of the opera. A quiet introductory theme, striking the tragic keynote of the work, soon changes
to an allegro section with motifs of a stately
monumental character, interrupted by a beautifully lyrical melody which has become one of
Gluck's most famous themes.

Since Gluck made the overture continue
uninterruptedly into the music of the opening
scene, a conclusion had to be written for concert
use, and the overture was revised by both Mozart
and Wagner. Wagner's version, being more
suitable for modern instruments, is more often
performed than Mozart's.

The scene of the opera is laid in Aulis during the
siege of Troy. The goddess Artemis demands that the
Greek King Agamemnon should sacrifice his daughter
to her so that the Greek fleet can reach Troy in safety.
Although Iphigenia is about to marry the young hero
Achilles, she decides to sacrifice herself for her people.
Her heroism makes such an impression on the goddess
that she withdraws her claim and promises the Greeks
a safe crossing to Troy.

IPHIGENIA IN TAURIS *(Iphigénie en Tau-
ride).* Opera in four acts by Gluck, with libretto
by François Guilliard, first performed in Paris
in 1779. The story is a continuation of *Iphigenia in Aulis,* the intervening events being later
described in Richard Strauss' *Elektra.* The famous "opera war" between followers of Gluck
and Piccinni was climaxed when both composed
operas on this subject. Piccinni's work, produced
two years after Gluck's, was obviously inferior,

and its première was ruined when the prima donna fell down drunk during the performance.

The overture is an early example of program music, the quiet introductory andante being called *Calm,* and the succeeding allegro section having these comments on the score: *Storm—Hail and Rain—Iphigenia—The Storm Abates—The Storm Ceases.* The strong influence of Rameau, who was one of the first to describe impressions of Nature by means of the orchestra, is noticeable here.

The scene of the opera is Tauris after the siege of Troy. Iphigenia has been made high priestess in Artemis' temple, and a barbaric law demands that she should sacrifice to the goddess every stranger who enters the land. When her brother Orestes, who is a Greek, is driven ashore by a storm Iphigenia has the task of sacrificing him. She fights desperately to save his life, and finally succeeds after a series of bloody and dramatic incidents.

IPPOLITOV-IVANOV, Michael. Russian composer (1859–1935). A product of the St. Petersburg Conservatory, where Rimsky-Korsakov taught him composition, he became director of the Tiflis School of Music and later professor at the Moscow Conservatory. At both places he was also a conductor of concerts and operas.

He remained in Russia after the Revolution, composing many songs and marches dedicated to the Soviet leaders, among them *Song to Stalin*

Act II of Iphigenia in Tauris *at the Munich State Opera in 1959*

and the *Voroshilov March,* which was very popular in the Red Army. The Communists awarded him many prizes and high distinctions.

Ippolitov-Ivanov wrote interesting recollections of fifty years of Russian music (1934). During his stay at Tiflis, he came into contact with Georgian and Armenian folk music, which inspired him to write his best-known work, the famous *Caucasian Sketches.* He spent many years in the Caucasus transcribing the strange, exotic melodies of its inhabitants, and wrote an authoritative book on their songs. His other works include operas, orchestral pieces, chamber music, and songs. Rosa Newmarch has described his style as "essentially lyrical, straightforward and agreeably melodious."

IRELAND, John. English composer (1879–). Ireland's early musical development was slow, but it was conscientiously thorough. He entered the Royal College of Music when he was fourteen and did not leave until he was twenty-one. During the next seven years he wrote much, but his penchant for self-criticism caused him to leave nearly all of it unpublished. In 1908, however, he won the Cobbett prize for a one-move-

JOHN IRELAND

ment chamber work with his Fantasy Trio in A minor, and the following year saw the publication of his Sonata in D minor for violin and piano. It is characteristic of the composer that these works were both issued later in revised versions. In 1913 Ireland produced his first important orchestral work, *The Forgotten Rite.* It is, however, in the field of chamber music that he has had his greatest success.

Best-known works:
Sonata in A minor for violin and piano (1916).
Trio No. 3, for violin, cello, and piano (1936).
Concerto for piano and orchestra (1930).
A London Overture (orchestra) (1937).
The Forgotten Rite (orchestra) (1913).
Symphonic Rhapsody *Mai-Dun* (orchestra) (1920).
Legend for piano and orchestra (1933).

IRVING, Robert. English conductor (1913–). Irving was a classical scholar at Oxford, but from and early age he had decided on a musical career. He completed his studies at the Royal College of Music, London, as conductor, pianist, and cellist. After serving in the Royal Air Force in World War II, he joined the British Broadcasting Corporation in Glasgow in 1945, conducting regular symphonic broadcasts with the BBC Scottish Orchestra until 1948, when he joined the Sadler's Wells Ballet Company. He has been one of the principal conductors of the Royal Ballet. Since 1959, he has been the conductor of the New York City Ballet.

ISAAC, Heinrich. Finnish composer (*c.* 1450–1517). At twenty-one Isaac became organist at the court of Lorenzo de' Medici in Florence; he remained in Florence for twenty-five years and thereafter traveled intermittently. He wrote both church and secular music—music of genius—in every form known in his time, including songs, motets, hymns, and masses.

I.S.C.M. (International Society for Contemporary Music). Founded in 1922 in Salzburg, this organization with headquarters in London has branches in every country. Its object is to arrange annual international music festivals at which works by contemporary composers are produced. Edward J. Dent was the first president of the society, and was largely responsible for its formation.

ISOUARD, Nicolo. Maltese pianist and composer (1775–1818). A talented and prolific opera composer and a pianist popular in society, he began composing in the Italian style, using the name Nicolo because of family objection to his career. Later, he became a master of the French *opéra comique,* producing thirty-nine works that were less original than highly competent, but very popular in their time. Among them are *Joconde* and *Les Rendezvous bourgeois.* His popularity gave way to that of Boieldieu and Méhul, and none of his operas has survived the test of time.

ISTEL, Edgar. German composer and musicologist (1880–1948). He was the author of many books, including a study of Wagner, treatises on the opera, and biographies of Paganini and Cornelius. As an editor, he was responsible for editions of Hoffmann's tales and Rousseau's opera, *Pygmalion.* He composed six operas, songs, choral music, and incidental music for plays, and taught and lectured in Germany, Spain, England, and the United States, where he lived during the last ten years of his life.

ISTOMIN, Eugene. American pianist (1925–). A pupil of Kariena Siloti, Rudolf Serkin, and Mieczyslaw Horszowski, Eugene Istomin is one of the many successful graduates of the Curtis Institute of Music. His career began when he received the Leventritt Award in 1943, which afforded him the opportunity of appearing as soloist with the New York Philharmonic and other leading orchestras. Istomin has been closely connected with the Casals Festivals in France and Puerto Rico, appearing as soloist as well as participant in chamber music concerts. Casals has predicted for him "a great career." He is fulfilling the prediction. Istomin has toured the United States, Europe, and the Far East, and is one of the best known of the younger American pianists.

ITALIAN CONCERTO. Composition for solo harpsichord by J. S. Bach. The formal title of the work is *Concerto in the Italian manner . . . for two-manual harpsichord.* The naming of the instrument is worthy of note: Bach undoubtedly felt that this work, like the *French Overture* and the *Goldberg Variations,* could only be interpreted on a two-manual harpsichord.

The *Italian Concerto* and the *French Overture* both belong to the second part of Bach's

NICOLO ISOUARD

Clavierübung, which was issued in 1735. Bach himself said: "The *Clavierübung* is composed of a Prelude, Allemande, Courante, Sarabande, Gigue, Minuet, and other fancies, as recreation for music lovers."

In this piece for the solo harpsichord Bach utilized the baroque solo concerto form and technique, with its rondolike alternation between *tutti* (full orchestra, represented here by both manuals played together) and *solo* (solo instrument, the upper manual). He is said to have received his inspiration for the work by one of Georg Muffat's famous five-part string suites, *Florigium primum,* which appeared in 1695. Albert Schweitzer is of the opinion that the themes of the *Italian Concerto* and *Florigium primum* are "so strikingly alike that there is no question of a pure coincidence."

ITALIAN SYMPHONY. Mendelssohn's Fourth Symphony, in A major, Op. 90, inspired by his visit to Italy in 1831 and completed in 1833. The London Philharmonic Society paid him 100 guineas for this symphony and the *Fingal's Cave* and *Trumpet* overtures.

Perhaps the most frequently played of Mendelssohn's symphonies, this work enchants by its gay charm and suggestions of Italian sun and joy of life. But its completion represented a hard task; and Mendelssohn several times doubted

JOSÉ ITURBI

if he could ever finish it; he suffered, he said, "the bitterest moments I have ever endured or could have imagined" during its composition.

The symphony has four movements. The first, *allegro vivace,* is full of tuneful gaiety; the second, *andante con moto,* has been christened the *Pilgrims' March;* the third is marked *con moto moderato;* and the last movement is a saltarello *(presto).*

ITALIENISCHES LIEDERBUCH *(Italian Song Book).* Settings for solo voice by Hugo Wolf of forty-six poems in tthe Italian style by Heyse, published in two separate volumes in 1890 and 1896. They were originally written with piano accompaniment, but many of them were later orchestrated by Wolf himself and others by Reger. A striking feature of these songs is the perfect balance Wolf achieves between words and music. Commenting on the fact that the second set of songs was written in five weeks, Ernest Newman wrote: "It is evident that he must have worked at white heat. . . . He made no sketches: his brooding upon a poem would at the right time result in a quasi-cataleptic state in which the poem generated, as it were, its own music, full-born in an hour or two, complete in form and in virtually every point of detail."

ITURBI, José. Spanish pianist and conductor (1895–). The son of a gas-worker who tuned pianos in his spare time, Iturbi took to the piano as a child and first performed in public at the age of seven. He was the pianist at Valencia's first movie theater; there he was discovered by a journalist who organized a fund to finance his further training. He studied in Barcelona and at the Paris Conservatory, but had to take posts as a night-club pianist in Paris and Zurich to earn a living. He was discovered again at Zurich, and was appointed piano professor at the Geneva Conservatory. Since then his career as a concert pianist has been brilliant.

As a conductor he achieved such success on his first appearance in Mexico that he was engaged for a further eleven concerts. Later he conducted the New York Philharmonic, the Philadelphia Orchestra, and several other famous orchestras in the United States and abroad. He has toured all the principal cities of the United States, South America, Africa, and the East Indies.

IVANOVICI. Romanian composer (1848–1905). He was a military band master and composed waltzes, one of which, *Danube Waves,* made him famous. It became a popular hit when, as *The Anniversary Song,* it was introduced by Al Jolson on the sound track of the film, *The Jolson Story.* Ironically, most of the facts concerning Ivanovici, including his first name, appear to have vanished from the records.

IVES, Burl. American ballad singer (1909–). Descended from seventeenth-century English and Scottish emigrants who pioneered as farmers and preachers, Burl Ives learned many old folk songs and ballads from his mother and grandmother during his childhood. Later, on leaving college, he explored the United States with a banjo, continually adding to his store of songs. Since then he has exchanged his banjo for a guitar, and the skillful presentation of his songs—now humorous, now poignant—has made him one of America's most popular entertainers.

Ives' unique knowledge of American folk songs was recognized when the *Encyclopaedia Britannica* asked him to record 120 songs in a set of six albums entitled *Historical America in Song* for use in schools. Ives has appeared in many motion pictures *(So Dear to My Heart, Sierra, East of Eden, The Power and the Prize, This Is the Army, Knickerbocker Holiday,* and *Show Boat)* and scored an outstanding success on the Broadway legitimate stage in Tennessee Williams' *Cat on a Hot Tin Roof.*

He is author of the *Burl Ives Song Book, The Book of Irish Songs,* and his autobiography, *Wayfaring Stranger.*

IVES, Charles. American composer (1874–1954). Charles Ives' first music teacher was his father, an accomplished musician and active bandmaster in his native Danbury, Conn. The elder Ives, while giving the boy a thorough conventional grounding in music theory, encouraged free musical thinking in the son; experimenting with music in quarter-tones, simultaneous performances of several different pieces, in different keys, and other unorthodox musical ideas.

Young Charles continued his musical studies at Yale University, working with Horatio Parker, and supporting himself as a church organist. Upon graduation, he decided with Yankee shrewdness, to enter a business, pursuing music in his leisure time. He chose insurance, then a new, promising, and idealistic field, and ultimately became one of this country's most successful insurance executives.

Composing on weekends, in the evening, and during vacations, he completed an impressive number of works, most of them composed during the years 1906–1917. An independent, taciturn New Englander, possessed of a dry wit and a thoroughly individual angle from which he viewed the world of men and its activities, he rarely attended concerts or involved himself in contemporary musical affairs. In fact, he did not even attempt to arrange performances of his own works, and did not hear many of them until long after they had been composed.

This self-imposed musical isolation had its advantages: by not distracting himself with the ideas, techniques, conventions, and traditional strictures of others, his imagination could run free, and he produced music so thoroughly original and prophetic that it was only by the 1940s that the rest of the musical community caught up with him. And this twenty and more years after he had retired from both insurance and composition!

Ives' best-known works include his orchestral essays *Central Park in the Dark, The Unanswered Question,* and the *Orchestral Set No. 1, Three Places in New England,* which includes the evocative *The Housatonic at Stockbridge;* the *Concord Sonata* for piano; the *Harvest Home Chorales,* for chorus, brass choir, string bass, and organ; the stirring *General William Booth's Entrance into Heaven,* based on the Salvation Army hymn, *Are You Washed in the Blood of the Lamb,* for chorus and brass band; and the collection *114 Songs.*

Ives' music is characterized by its use of tone clusters, chromatic dissonance, polytonality, atonality, irregular rhythms, polyrhythms, stereophonic distribution of several performing groups in the hall, and a strong dose of transformed American folk songs, Civil War band tunes, and revival hymns. As unorthodox in its notation as in its sounds, the music is difficult to read and difficult to perform. Ives himself was rather casual about performance problems. He did not insist that his works be played exactly as he had written them (or indeed, played at all); he merely observed that the music had demanded to be written in a certain way, and it did not matter very much if no one could ever perform it.

Ives stands as a maverick in the historical line-up of American composers. Influenced by none of his predecessors, except of course his father, and the anonymous composers of the popular tunes of his youth, he in turn had very little direct influence on his successors. A few adventurous souls managed to find their way to him at his Danbury farm, or to ferret out those

CHARLES IVES

compositions which had been privately published. By the 1930s, there were occasional performances of his works, accompanied by cries of "belated recognition," and the final accolade appeared in 1947, when he received the Pulitzer Prize for music. Of his contemporaries, Carl Ruggles and Wallingford Riegger represent a parallel line of development; among the younger composers, Henry Cowell and Henry Brant reflect his influence. Brant is noted for his experimental, nonharmonic combinations of sounds and stereophonic groupings; Cowell, whose book on Ives is standard, for his devotion to tone clusters.

Best-known works:

ORCHESTRAL

Symphony No. 1 (1896)
Symphony No. 2 (1897–1902)
Symphony No. 3 (1901–04)
Symphony No. 4 (1910–16)
The Unanswered Question (before 1908)

Maria Ivogün as Zerbinetta

Three Outdoor Scenes (1898–1911)
  1. *Hallowe'en*
  2. *The Pond*
  3. *Central Park in the Dark*
A Symphony: Holidays (1904–13)
  1. *Washington's Birthday*
  2. *Decoration Day*
  3. *Fourth of July*
  4. *Thanksgiving and/or Forefather's Day*
Orchestral Set No. 1: Three Places in New England
  1. *Boston Common*
  2. *Putnam's Camp*
  3. *The Housatonic at Stockbridge*
Universal Symphony (unfinished) (1911–16; 1927–28)

CHAMBER MUSIC

String Quartet No. 1, *A Revival Service* (1896)
String Quartet No. 2. (1907–13)

INSTRUMENTAL MUSIC

Sonata No. 1 (violin and piano) (1903–08)
Sonata No. 2 (violin and piano) (1903–10)
Sonata No. 3 (violin and piano) (1902–14)
Sonata No. 4 (violin and piano) (1914–15)
Piano Sonata No. 1 (1902–09)
Piano Sonata No. 2 (*Concord*) (1909–15)
  1. *Emerson*
  2. *Hawthorne*
  3. *The Alcotts*
  4. *Thoreau*
Some Southpaw Pitching (piano) (1908)
The Anti-Abolitionist Riots (piano) (c. 1908)
Variations on a National Hymn (*America*) (organ) (1891)

CHORAL WORKS

Sixty-Seventh Psalm (1898)
Three Harvest Home Chorales (1898–1912)
General William Booth's Entrance into Heaven (1914)

SONGS

Ann Street
Charlie Rutledge
The Children's Hour
Ich Grolle Nicht
In Flanders Fields
Serenity
Songs My Mother Taught Me

IVOGÜN, Maria (Inge von Günther). German coloratura soprano (1891–). Her mother was a well-known singer and she was a protégée of Bruno Walter, who introduced her at a Mozart festival in Munich. Her greatest success was as Zerbinetta in Strauss' *Ariadne auf Naxos,* one of the most brilliant and demanding of all coloratura roles. She appeared mostly in Munich and in London at Covent Garden, as well as in America with the Chicago Opera. Other roles in which she became celebrated were Gilda in *Rigoletto* and Constanza in *The Abduction from the Seraglio.*

MAHALIA JACKSON

JACCHINI, Giuseppe Maria. Italian composer (?–1727). His instrumental music helped the concerto form to develop by increasing the importance of the solo instrument, particularly the cello.

JACHET DA MANTOVA. Italian composer (?–c. 1559). He was choirmaster of Mantua Cathedral and composed motets that were an important influence on Palestrina's music.

JACKSON, Greig S. ("Chubby"). American jazz bassist (1918–). Jackson came to prominence during his association with the Woody Herman band and played with Charlie Barnet, Raymond Scott, Jan Savitt, and others. He has headed his own band and toured Scandinavia with his own quintet.

JACKSON, Mahalia. American singer (1911–). Mahalia Jackson is known for her rich, full-voiced renditions of sacred music, spirituals, and blues. Daughter of a clergyman, she sang in his choir at an early age. Working in Chicago as a hotel maid, she organized a quartet which appeared at various Baptist churches. In 1945, she began to attract national attention through her recordings, and in 1952 made a successful Euro-

pean tour. She has appeared in several concerts at Carnegie Hall, and at the Newport Jazz Festival.

JACKSON, Milton ("Bags"). American jazz vibraharpist and pianist (1923–). After studying at Michigan State University, Jackson, a "bop" vibraharpist, joined the Dizzy Gillespie band and came to New York. Since 1946 he has played with Thelonious Monk, Woody Herman, and principally with the Modern Jazz Quartet. He is generally conceded at present to be the major jazz performer on his instrument.

JACOB, Gordon. British composer (1895–). Jacob began to compose when he was ten, and had his first orchestral work performed when he was fifteen. During the first World War he was badly wounded and was a prisoner of war in Germany for two years; after the armistice he became a journalist. He did not begin to study music seriously until he was twenty-five. From 1924 to 1954 he was professor of theory, composition, and orchestration at the Royal College of Music, London. He has written an excellent book on orchestration, *Orchestral Technique* (1936).

Best-known works:

> Concerto for Oboe and Strings (1933)
> Variations for Orchestra (1935–36)
> Quintet for Clarinet and Strings (1940)
> Symphony No. 2, in C major (1944–45)
> Concerto for Bassoon and Strings (1946)
> Symphonic Suite (1948–49)

JACOBI, Frederick. American composer, conductor, and teacher (1891–1952). Jacobi studied with Ernest Bloch, Rafael Joseffy, Rubin Goldmark, and, at the Berlin Hochschule für Musik, Paul Juon. He was an assistant conductor of the Metropolitan Opera from 1913 to 1917. Then he went to the Southwest to study Pueblo Indian music; many of his compositions employ American Indian themes. Another group of his works is based on Jewish motifs. He wrote an opera, *The Prodigal Son;* choral and orchestral works, including two symphonies; concertos; chamber and instrumental music (notably the Ballade for violin and piano, 1942); pieces for piano and organ; and about a dozen songs. Many distinguished American composers have been his pupils at the Juilliard School of Music, where he taught composition after 1935.

JACOPO DA BOLOGNA. Italian composer (fourteenth century). One of the earliest and most important of the Italian Ars Nova composers, his motets, madrigals, and instrumental pieces had a great influence on musical development in Italy.

JACQUET, Illinois. American jazz saxophonist (1921–). Jacquet has been a member of the Lionel Hampton, Cab Calloway, and Count Basie bands. He has made several tours with his own group, and is credited with establishing a style of jazz saxophone which is widely imitated.

JADLOWKER, Hermann. Latvian tenor (1879–1953). A noted opera singer and cantor, he was a star of the Berlin and Vienna court operas. At the Metropolitan Opera, where he appeared for three seasons, he sang Italian, French, and German roles, and was the King's Son in Humperdinck's *Königskinder* at the world première in 1910.

JAGEL, Frederick. American tenor (1897–). Jagel's parents were both pianists. He studied in Milan and made his debut at the Metropolitan Opera as Rhadames in *Aïda* in 1927. He was a leading tenor there for twenty years in a wide range of roles and also sang for four seasons with the San Francisco Opera.

JAMAL, Ahmad. American jazz pianist (1920–). Jamal was born in Pittsburgh. He headed his own group in Chicago and appeared in New York on tour. He now heads the Ahmad Jamal Trio, through which he has become a major jazz influence. Not only pianists but instrumentalists of all types have commented on his superb musicianship and revolutionary approach to jazz.

JAMES, Harry. American trumpeter and band leader (1916–). His first fifteen years were spent with the circus for which his father was band leader. Later he began to play with various dance orchestras in Texas, joining Ben Pollack's band in 1935, and Benny Goodman's band two years later.

James was the most famous trumpet soloist of Goodman's successful swing period. On Goodman's advice, he formed his own orchestra in 1939, giving it a sweeter character, and specializing in sumptuous arrangements. James has made a large number of recordings, and appeared in many films.

JAMES, Philipp. American composer, conductor, and teacher (1890–). A student of Rubin Goldmark and Rosario Scalero, James was musical director of Victor Herbert operettas in New York between 1911 and 1916. He was choirmaster of St. Mark's Church in the Bouwerie, New York, and conducted the Brooklyn Orchestral Society. From 1933 until 1955 he was head of the department of music at New York University and is now professor emeritus. He has composed symphonies, and other orchestral, choral, and organ works.

JANÁČEK, Leoš. Czech composer (1854–1928). Janáček's is one of the leading names in modern Czech music, particularly in the sphere of opera, in which he was a worthy successor to Smetana. His most important compositions were written after 1910, when his style took a radical turn and he became one of the foremost modernists. Leoš Janáček was a choirboy at the Augustine monastery at Brno, where he was given a sound musical training, and later pursued his studies at the Prague Organ School, and in Leipzig and Vienna. He was appointed director

LEOŠ JANÁČEK

of the Brno Philharmonic Orchestra, and then professor at the Prague Conservatory.

Fame as a composer came to him late in life. His masterpiece *Jeji Pastorkyna (Her Foster Daughter)*, better known as *Jenufa*, was given a few performances at Brno in 1904, and then fell into almost complete oblivion. But when the work was revived twelve years later in Prague it was a great success; it was performed in New York in 1924. Janáček followed up his success with other dramatic works—*Katya Kabanová, The Makropoulos Secret, The Cunning Little Vixen,* and *The House of the Dead* (based on the novel of Dostoevsky). Interest in these operas has increased steadily in recent years and productions of them in European opera houses have become more frequent. So far, only *Jenufa* and *Katya Kabanová* have been heard in America.

Janáček was very fond of passionate, tragic situations, and his tonal language is more akin to the Russian than the Western style. In his rich rhythmical and orchestral coloring he often makes use of strange chordal relationships and small melodic motifs.

He has also written pieces for orchestra, chamber and choral music, and instrumental works.

A scene from Janáček's The Cunning Little Vixen *at Weisbaden*

JANEQUIN, Clément. French composer (*c.* 1472–*c.* 1560). Though he composed masses and motets, his importance is as one of the originators of program music. He composed many instrumental pieces with titles such as *The Song of the Birds, The Battle,* and *The Hunt.*

JANIGRO, Antonio. Italian cellist (1918–). Janigro studied at the Milan Conservatory and at the École Normale de Musique, in Paris, with Alexanian. He has toured Europe, South America, Africa, and Asia with I Solisti di Zagreb. In 1939 he was appointed professor at the Zagreb Conservatory.

JANIS, Byron. American pianist (1927–). Janis played his first piano recital when he was nine years old. Advised to continue his studies, he enrolled at the Chatham Square Music School, and was later guided by Vladimir Horowitz. In 1942 Janis won a decisive success playing with the NBC Symphony Orchestra. He made his recital debut at Carnegie Hall in 1948 and was praised as an exceptional talent. Janis has since toured the United States, South America, and Europe.

JANIS, Conrad. American jazz trombonist (1928–). A versatile actor and musician, he has headed his own band and frequently appeared with it on television. He is coauthor of the book *They All Played Ragtime.*

JANISSARY MUSIC. The military bands of the Janissaries, the bodyguard of the Sultan of Turkey, made extensive use of such instruments as drums, cymbals, and triangles. After the wars between Austria and Turkey in the seventeenth century, military bands were formed in the West on the Turkish model, the pipers and drummers being equipped with all the typical Turkish instruments—large and small drums, kettledrums, cymbals, triangles, piccolos, trumpets, jingle bells, and glockenspiel. One curious instrument was the Turkish crescent, or "Jingling Johnny," a stick upon which hung bells with horse tails in the regimental colors, surmounted by a crescent.

Such instruments were also used in serious music when an Eastern or "Turkish" coloring (*alla turca*) was desired. Examples are to be found in Gluck's *Iphigenia in Tauris* (the dance of the Scythians) and Mozart's *The Abduction from the Seraglio.*

JANSSEN, Herbert. German baritone (1895–). A noted lieder singer and opera star, he performed many Wagner and Strauss roles in Berlin, Bayreuth, Vienna, Paris, London, San Francisco, and New York, where he was a member of the Metropolitan Opera from 1939 to 1950. He was best known as Wolfram in *Tannhäuser,* Amfortas in *Parsifal,* and in the title role of *The Flying Dutchman.*

JANSSEN, Werner. American conductor and composer (1900–). A graduate of Dartmouth College (1921), Janssen studied with Frederick Converse in Boston and composed operettas at an early age. Between 1930 and 1934, he attended the American Academy in Rome and was recipient of the Prix de Rome. He made his debut as a conductor in that city. He has conducted the New York Philharmonic and the Philadelphia, Cleveland, Chicago, Detroit, Portland (Ore.), St. Louis, Rochester (N. Y.), Baltimore, and Los Angeles symphony orchestras, as well as almost every prominent European and South American symphony orchestra. In 1940, he organized the Janssen Symphony Orchestra in Hollywood, which appeared in concerts and broadcasts and made many recordings.

JAQUES-DALCROZE, Émile. Austrian dance theorist (1865–1950). He founded the system of rhythmic exercises known as eurythmics and his theories of bodily movement have had much influence on the world of music and dance. In 1910 he founded a school at Hellerau, near Dresden, and he has written many books on the subject of dance. He was professor of harmony at the Geneva Conservatory. See *Eurythmics.*

JARDINS SOUS LA PLUIE *(Gardens in the Rain).* Composition for piano by Debussy. It is the last of the three pieces in the collection *Estampes* (Engravings), published in Paris in 1903. It is, however, of earlier date, having been sketched out in 1894.

Kajsa Rootzén describes it as follows: "The piece is in the form of a brilliant toccata with sharply drawn melodic contours. In the midst of the rustling, dripping and splashing of the rain, themes taken from two French nursery rhymes are clearly heard: *Do, do, l'enfant, do (Sleep, My Child, Sleep)* and *Nous n'irons plus au bois (No More Shall We Go into the Woods).* It is these playfully inserted snatches of melody

Herbert Janssen as Wolfram in Tannhäuser

which lend their special charm to this delicate sound picture."

JARNACH, Philip. French composer (1892–). Jarnach trained chiefly in Paris and studied with Busoni. He completed the latter's unfinished opera *Dr. Faustus.* He has written mostly chamber music.

JÄRNEFELT, Armas. Finnish conductor and composer (1869–1958). After studying in Berlin with Busoni and in Paris with Massenet, he held minor posts in German opera houses, finally returning to Helsinki as conductor of the orchestra there. While conductor of the Helsinki Opera he was instrumental in introducing Wagner's works to Finland. As chief conductor of the Stockholm Opera (1907–32) he became one of the leading figures in Swedish musical life.

Järnefelt composed orchestral and choral pieces, and some chamber and piano music, most of it with a national tinge. His *Praeludium* for orchestra is well known all over the world.

JARNOVIC, Ivan (Giovanni Giornovichi). Italian violinist and composer of Croatian descent (*c.* 1740–1804). One of the famous violin virtuosos of his time, he performed with enormous success throughout Europe before settling in Russia. He composed sixteen violin concertos and a number of chamber music works. His grandson, Pierre Jarnovic, was a French cellist and composer of some repute.

JAZZ

INDIGENOUS AMERICAN MUSICAL FORM

JAZZ is an indigenous American folk music resulting from the fusion of African rhythms with European concepts of harmony and melody.

The importation of slaves to the United States began in 1619. As the American society expanded it became apparent that the use of slaves was more fitted to the sprawling plantation system of the South than to the urban mercantilism of the North. It was, then, in the Southern states of Mississippi, Louisiana, Florida, Tennessee, Alabama, and the Carolinas that the fusion of African culture with the miscellany of English, Irish, French, and Spanish cultures occurred.

The heart of jazz is its rhythmic complexity, refined in Africa and infused into European harmony

This joining of cultural and ethnic strains occurred on many levels. Musically, it manifested itself by the expression of the complex rhythms of a primitive culture through the use of modern instruments belonging to a relatively advanced society. However, along with the guitar, cornet, trombone, clarinet, tuba, drums, double bass, and piano, the human voice and makeshift instruments such as kazoos, washboards, bottles, jugs, and tubs were pressed into the service of human expression. Much of the music performed by the Negro people was closely related melodically and rhythmically to the physical movement associated with some particular work pattern. We hear of levee songs, sea chanties, railroad songs, prison songs, and above all, songs of protest and despair. See *Folk Music*. Play songs, vendor chants, and the various dance steps as well were often rooted in the workaday activity of the slaves.

The heritage of each African slave varied according to his tribal ancestry. In general all tribes exhibited some degree of rhythmic facility, and in some cases they revealed a primitive development in antiphonal chanting (voices singing in counterpoint). In the various areas of his new environment, the African heard for the first time voices or instruments moving in vertical blocks of sound, which we know as harmony. The Lutheran hymns, French marches, and Scotch-Irish folk songs all revealed to the slave this commonplace aspect of all Western music. More important, this harmony was based upon a strange and new scale, the cornerstone of all Western music since the Renaissance—the diatonic major scale. Since much of the tonal development of African pitch was based upon quarter-tone scales quite beyond our half-tone unit, confusion about certain tones of the diatonic scale (particularly the third, fifth, and seventh) resulted in the creation of a tonal idiom

A cellar barroom on Basin Street, typical of those frequented by the pioneers of jazz, is shown in this scene from the film New Orleans

which came to be known as the blues. Specific aspects of this evolving Negro music were represented at first by folk blues, gospel music, spirituals, and stomps; later boogiewoogie, struts, rags, one-steps, and finally jazz evolved. During this slow evolution one basic characteristic has always been present—a fundamental pulse of quarter notes joined with a harmonic fabric moving in some slower unit (half notes, whole notes, etc.) and a melodic line moving in some quicker unit (eighth notes, sixteenth notes, etc.). The blues idiom lies deep in the life of the Negro people. The recordings of such great folk singers as Huddie Ledbetter ("Leadbelly"), Big Bill Broonzy, and "Blind Lemon" Jefferson document the moving history of the days of slavery and the Reconstruction. Representing a joining of the simple I-IV-V harmony of the church hymn and the improvised line, the blues remains an active and vital source of inspiration to the jazz musician. See *Blues*.

NEW ORLEANS

Although various confluent forces met throughout the South, they focused particularly in the cosmopolitan city of New Orleans. Here the dynamic melting of the African, English, French, and Spanish cultures represented in microcosm a vast sociological process prevalent throughout the South and, by the middle of the nineteenth century, in large sections of the Midwest, Chicago, and New York.

In New Orleans, by 1880, the basic format of the jazz ensemble had developed. This format was built upon the instrumental structure of the French marching bands (two cornets, clarinet, trombone, tuba, and drums.) The first jazz bands played in sporting houses, gin mills, and barrel houses, at weddings, funerals, and the Mardi Gras. Tales still persist of now-fabled aggregations: the Original Zenith Brass Band, Buddy Bolden's Ragtime Band, and the Olympia Band, the Eagle Band, Bunk Johnson's Original Superior Band, the Original Dixieland Jass Band. With the closing in 1917 of Storyville, the "sporting district" of New Orleans, a general exodus of individuals and ensembles moved up the Mississippi River to Natchez, Vicksburg, Memphis, Cairo, St. Louis, East St. Louis, Hannibal, Fort Madison, Rock Island, and Davenport. From this exodus many ensembles of shifting personnel appeared, the most important being the Creole

BUNK JOHNSON

Jazz Band led by Joe "King" Oliver and featuring young Louis Armstrong as second cornetist. Other personnel at one time or another included clarinetists Jimmy Noone, Johnny Dodds, and Barney Bigard, trombonists Honoré Dutry and "Kid" Ory, and drummer "Baby" Dodds. The Creole Jazz Band captured the imagination of the Chicago public (particularly the Chicago musicians), and through the presence of the dynamic genius of Armstrong established a revolutionary concept of jazz which led away from the rigid ensemble format of the early New Orleans bands toward emphasis of the role of the virtuoso improviser—still the cornerstone of present-day jazz. Armstrong emerges as the central figure of the New Orleans period, and by establishing new levels of virtuosity and emotional expression set the primary goals for all future jazzmen.

One other New Orleans figure whose contribution ranks close to Armstrong's is Ferdinand "Jelly Roll" Morton—pianist, raconteur, and apochryphal figure of the 1920s. Morton consolidated the two fundamental trends in the pianism of his day: barrel-house, blues, and boogiewoogie on one hand, and the great rag tradition which flowered in the Midwest (St. Louis and Sedalia, Missouri) and the East (Philadelphia and New York) on the other. Morton was one of the first to realize that the future of jazz piano must result from joining the feeling of the blues with the technical skills of

ragtime. This consolidation was later carried on by Earl "Fatha" Hines and Thomas "Fats" Waller; however, Morton remains the initial catalyst in the process.

Barrel-house piano refers to a strident blues style played in the raucous bars of New Orleans. Employing eight- and twelve-bar forms, this style established the "gutty" feeling of all jazz piano.

Boogiewoogie was a unique pianistic development without precedent in the classical literature of that instrument. This style was characterized by a two-voice architecture: an ostinato (repeated figure) appearing in the left hand which supported an improvised line in the right.

Ragtime was notated keyboard music with elaborate structural and technical qualities, generally without improvisation. Borrowed in form from the classical military march, and employing the technical virtuosity of a Chopin scherzo, this style became the precursor of all succeeding swing-bass piano.

CHICAGO

The Chicago period of jazz (1922–32) was significant for the emergence of the white musician as an innovator in the new music. It has long been the contention of certain jazz authorities that the Negro musician possesses a special rhythmic gift that makes him superior as a performer of jazz. From the scientific standpoint this is an indefensible position; however, there is no doubt of the leading position of the Negro musician in jazz, even today. This position of leadership can be traced to the cultural history of the Negroes, who possess the vitality and exuberance found everywhere in a people deprived of status and material reward, who must look within themselves for their satisfactions.

Previously the Original Dixieland Jass Band and the New Orleans Rhythm Kings, both white ensembles, had traveled north to Chicago and New York to reveal an enthusiasm and a reasonably serious concern for the values of the new art form, if not always a high level of musicianship. George Brunis and Leon Rappolo in particular exhibited the musical and technical skills which were to influence the young Chicago musicians. As the Chicagoans became more familiar with the professional routines of these ensembles they formed groups of their own, at first emulating their predecessors, later developing style qualities ever since associated with the raucous abandon documented in the novels of Scott Fitzgerald. These groups also acted as an incubator for many of the leading instrumentalists of the swing era in the 1930s.

Some of the legendary names associated with this period include the following: *clarinet:* Benny Goodman, Frank Teschemacher, "Pee Wee" Russell; *saxophone:* "Bud" Freeman, Frank Trumbauer; *cornet (trumpet):* "Bix" Beiderbecke, "Muggsy" Spanier, Jimmy McPartland, "Red" Nichols; *piano:* Joe Sullivan, Jess Stacy; *drums:* Gene Krupa, George Wettling, Davy Tough; *banjo (guitar):* Eddie Condon, Eddie Lang; *trombone:* Floyd O'Brien, Jack Teagarden, and "Miff" Mole.

The musical catalyst of this period was Beiderbecke, the organizing genius Teschemacher. The groups variously called The Austin High Gang, The Chicago Rhythm Kings, The Blue Friars, The Wolverines, and the Mound City Blue Blowers, at one time or another made a series of recordings documenting the frenetic enthusiasm of the "Jazz Age." By the early 1930s much of this activity had ceased, as tragic death and the appearance of the big commercial dance bands stilled the leading voices of the period. In general, the music of the Chicago school, in contrast to that of New Orleans, was characterized by quicker tempos, the innovation of the tenor saxophone, the emergence of the piano as a fundamental jazz instrument, and the appearance of the improviser as the major figure of jazz.

NEW YORK

Since jazz consciously adapts itself to its surrounding milieu, we find that the three basic trends in New York jazz of the 1920s stem from three important aspects of the entertainment industry—the bars, the dance halls, and the night clubs. From the bars came ragtime piano, "stride" piano, Harlem piano; from the dance halls came the great bands; from the cabarets, the blues singers. The development of rag and barrel-house piano in the South and Midwest was more than matched by a lusty East Coast school representing a composite of minstrel, rag-blues, and what was known as "raggin' the classics." In the South it had been Morton, King Porter, and Tony Jackson; in the Midwest rag pianists Scott Joplin, Thomas Turpin, and James Scott, as well as the boogiewoogie pianists Jimmy Yancey, Clarence Lofton

King Oliver's band in 1923. Oliver is in the center with trumpet, and clarinetist Johnny Dodds is on his left

Louis Armstrong and Billie Holliday in the film New Orleans

("Cripple Clarence"), Rufus Perryman ("Speckled Red"), Maceo Merriweather ("Big Maceo"), and Clarence Smith ("Pine Top") had forged new levels of feeling and skill. In New York early rag pianists like Eubie Blake, "Lucky" Roberts, and James P. Johnson established a line of descent destined to influence all jazz piano for the next decade. These men were the leaders of a style variously called "Harlem" piano due to its geographical center, or "stride" piano because of the rapid swing bass motion of the left hand. Willie "The Lion" Smith and Thomas "Fats" Waller emerged in the 1930s as the central figures leading directly to the great Art Tatum of the succeeding decade.

In the dance halls such as Roseland and the Savoy in New York, the big bands moved from the simple polyphony of the earlier groups toward a three-section (brass, reeds, and rhythm) arrangement, with the use of these instruments playing in ensemble units. This trend, led by composer-arrangers Fletcher Henderson, Don Redman, and Duke Ellington, established the format of the big bands of the next thirty years. Ellington in particular created entirely new concepts of sonority, voicing, and ensemble playing which firmly placed the jazz orchestra in the forefront of the jazz art. Other orchestras of importance included "Chick" Webb's band (featuring singer Ella Fitzgerald) and McKinney's Cotton Pickers.

In the cabarets, the vocal tradition dating back to both religious and secular sources was continued by quasi-jazz performers such as Ethel Waters and by jazz singers Bessie Smith and Sippie Wallace, in direct line of descent from the great "Ma" Rainey. Billie Holliday in the 1940s probably represented the last link in this great tradition.

EARL HINES

HARRY JAMES

LIONEL HAMPTON

SWING

The swing era (1932–40) was the era of the big bands. Individual virtuosi like tenor saxophonists Coleman Hawkins and Ben Webster, clarinetist Benny Goodman, alto saxophonist Benny Carter, and trumpeter Roy Eldridge, no longer worked with informal "jam" groups, but rather in the section of a ten- to sixteen-piece band. The big breakthrough in popularity came with the appearance of the Benny Goodman orchestra. Goodman, the central figure of the swing era, turned to writers like Henderson, Redman, and Jimmy Mundy for arrangements; he also welded together an aggregation which played with a precision hitherto unknown in large ensembles. More important, due to the all-white personnel of the band, Goodman was able to achieve an "exposure" via radio, hotels, ballrooms, and recordings that was impossible for the Negro bands of the period. Further, in the performances of the trio and quartet which accompanied the band, the color bar was completely destroyed even in strongly segregated areas of the country. The popularity of the Goodman band produced a unique joining of an artistic effort with nationwide acceptance—something never quite equaled before or since in jazz.

In addition to the large ensembles featuring leader-clarinetist Goodman, trumpeter Harry James, pianist Jess Stacy, and drummer Gene Krupa, the two small chamber groups were formed: a trio featuring Goodman, Krupa, and pianist Teddy Wilson; and a quartet consisting of the aforementioned trio plus vibraphonist Lionel Hampton. Other bands of a quasi-jazz character employing jazz techniques in some modified form included those of Tommy and Jimmy Dorsey, Artie Shaw, Les Brown, Charlie Barnet, and Glenn Miller. Important Negro bands of the period were the Andy Kirk orchestra, featuring Mary Lou Williams, the first woman to be a world-famous instrumentalist-pianist; Jimmy Lunceford's orchestra; pianist Earl Hines and his orchestra, and finally the Count Basie band which had evolved out of the Benny Moten orchestra of Kansas City. Hines deserves particular mention as an important figure in the historical development of jazz piano; with "Fats" Waller, he played a leading role in releasing the piano from the clichés of ragtime by adapting the more expressive trumpet style of Armstrong to the keyboard.

Important soloists of the period include the following: *piano:* Teddy Wilson, Earl Hines, Art Tatum, Mary Lou Williams; *clarinet:* Benny Goodman, Artie Shaw; *alto saxophone:* Benny Carter; *tenor saxophone:* Coleman Hawkins, Ben Webster; *trombone:* Trummy Young; *trumpet:* Roy Eldridge, Harry James, Bunny Berigan, Charlie Shavers; *vibraphone-xylophone:* Lionel

DIZZY GILLESPIE

COUNT BASIE

Hampton, Red Norvo; *drums:* Gene Krupa, Jo Jones, Buddy Rich, Sid Catlett, Cozy Cole; *vocalists:* Billie Holliday, Ella Fitzgerald, Mildred Bailey, and Frank Sinatra.

THE TRANSITION YEARS

An art form sometimes exhausts the available techniques of a period and must disappear "underground" for a while in order to evolve new tools and resources. This describes the position of jazz at the end of the swing era. The rhythmic and harmonic tools of swing had been exploited by virtuosi such as Hawkins, Tatum, Wilson, Eldridge, and Goodman. Toward the end of the 1930s new voices, expressing new rhythmic and harmonic inflections, began to be heard. Charlie Christian playing the electrified guitar, Lester Young expressing new melodic concepts of improvisation on the tenor saxophone, Jimmy Blanton exploring unknown worlds on the double bass, Jo Jones modifying the rhythmic exploitation of the drums—all of these explorations anticipated and presaged what came to be known as the "bop revolution."

EARLY PROGRESSIVE (BOP)

The term "bop" was a phonetic expletive describing the short wrenched phrases of this new music.

The advent of bop meant many things. The big-band era ended and the personnel split up into smaller groups. The time-honored swing-bass, moving in quarter-note, octave chord, or tenth-chord displacements in the left hand, disappeared from the scene. The tempo spectrum was extended greatly, and more complex harmonic materials utilizing post-impressionist idioms derived from Stravinsky, Hindemith, and the contemporary Russian school of composition, were developed. Virtuoso levels were raised in the improvised line to include the thirty-second- and the sixty-fourth-note values. There was a general return to small-group polyphony, and a resurgence of the traditional twelve-bar blues as a primary source of texture and idiom. Perhaps most significant, the Negro musician became the major innovator in jazz, and jazz ceased to be a functional dance music, but became instead a music simply to be listened to.

The leading figures of the early progressive period were alto saxophonist Charlie Parker, trumpeter "Dizzy" Gillespie, and pianists "Bud" Powell and Thelonious Monk. Centered in New York in various clubs on Fifty-second Street and in Harlem, the new style seemed on first hearing to be strange, strident, having no apparent relation to previous jazz styles. As a

THELONIOUS MONK

MAX ROACH

COZY COLE

result these innovations escaped the attention of an American public busy with the popular escapist entertainment of the wartime period.

What had occurred was finally revealed in the polished arrangements of the Stan Kenton orchestra and the George Shearing quintet. Both groups leaped to almost immediate national popularity as they utilized the new bop concepts in somewhat modified form. The "second herd" and "third herd" of band leader Woody Herman, as well as the ill-fated big band of Dizzy Gillespie, also strove for some permanent balance of artistic achievement and commercial popularity, but the economic structure of the big bands had reached such complexity that few groups were able to remain together for sufficient time to achieve any artistic purpose. One especially serious blow to the big bands was the gradual closing of the large dance halls and hotel ballrooms throughout the country.

As the decade of the 1940s closed, many people in the jazz ranks began to feel the pressure of a basic conflict within the art form. On one hand, jazz had suddenly reached popularity not as a functional folk music to be danced to, but rather as a serious art form demanding the attention usually reserved for a Beethoven quartet. On the other hand, the revolutionary achievements of Parker, Gillespie, and Powell seemed to have exhausted the human limits of the art form, leaving room only for refinements by lesser figures. To many musicians it appeared that in particular Charlie Parker had summed up the essence of all jazz, and only imitation remained as a serious challenge.

THE WEST COAST MOVEMENT

Strangely enough, a partial answer to this question came in the form of a new regional style emanating from California, which became known as "West Coast." Several factors contributed to this new development. The motion-picture studios in Los Angeles brought together the largest concentration of top-flight nonclassical musicians in America. The Stan Kenton orchestra, too, had for some years made its home base in California, providing a similar concentration of some of the finest writing and improvising talents in the country at the time. Unlike the East Coast jazz scene, which was dominated by Negro performers, the West Coast movement was essentially an all-white resurgence. The aspect of the movement cannot be dismissed as a simple problem of discrimination among the performers; for all practical purposes this did not exist. But on a much deeper cultural level there was a basic conflict of tradition and environ-mental background, which created divergent attitudes both socially and aesthetically. The Negro performer gravitated toward the established groups in the East and avoided the hostile West Coast area, dominated in part by the then Jim Crow motion-picture studios.

The appellation "West Coast" is difficult to define in musical terms. If there was a "West Coast sound," it certainly became identified with the arranging innovations of Philadelphia-born Gerry Mulligan. While playing with the Stan Kenton band Mulligan had led a revolt against traditional big-band scoring techniques by reducing the personnel to nine or ten men and avoiding the older concept of "section" writing. By "dovetailing" (meshing the brass and reeds and employing an open sound of fourths and fifths instead of the traditional thirds) a new "sound" was created and popularized through recordings by the Miles Davis "Ninette," the Mulligan "Tenette," Shorty Rogers' "Giants," and the Dave Pell "Octette."

Quite apart from this mainstream trend was the phenomenal success of the Dave Brubeck Quartet, featuring alto saxophonist Paul Desmond. Adapting a modified "theme and variations" approach, the group featured a contrapuntal interplay between piano and saxophone,

The Jimmy Giuffre Three: Giuffre, Jim Hall, and Bob Brookmeyer

GEORGE SHEARING

avoiding in general the traditional concept of the virtuoso "blowing" line. Although a large segment of the Brubeck audience through the years can rightfully be considered "fringe," there is no doubt that this quartet spearheaded the expanding concert and festival developments of the 1950s.

A group of equal popularity but more musical significance was the Gerry Mulligan Quartet, featuring leader-baritone saxophonist Mulligan and trumpeter Chet Baker. Also employing a contrapuntal approach, but without the intrusive presence of the piano, this group achieved a polyphonic beauty never before heard in jazz. Another West Coast chamber group, which explored the use of flute and cello, was the Chico Hamilton Quintet.

THE EAST COAST (1948–1955)

Before and during the West Coast activity, which lasted roughly from 1950 to 1954, a serious consolidation of the early bop innovations continued in New York, led by such outstanding figures as the following: *piano:* Horace Silver, John Lewis, Oscar Peterson, Lennie Tristano; *tenor sax:* Stan Getz, Wardell Gray; *alto sax:* Sonny Stitt, Lee Konitz; *baritone sax:* Serge Chaloff; *trumpet:* Miles Davis, Clifford

JULIAN "CANNONBALL" ADDERLEY

JOHNNY HODGES

Brown; *trombone:* J. J. Johnson; *bass:* Charlie Mingus, Oscar Pettiford, Ray Brown; *drums:* Art Blakey, Kenny Clark, and Max Roach.

The important groups emerging from this period followed three basic trends:

1. *The "Hard" Groups* (The Jazz Messengers, Miles Davis Quintet, Horace Silver Quintet, and Max Roach–Clifford Brown Quintet). The term "hard" used to describe these groups refers to the biting rhythmic character of the "rear" line (bass, piano, drums) supporting equally incisive trumpet or saxophone soloists comprising the "front" line. All of these groups were patterned on the Parker-Gillespie Quintet of the early 1940s. Each featured unison "heads" or melodic lines interspersed with horn or piano solos. In a sense this is a traditional format dating back to the early marching bands of New Orleans.

2. *The Chamber Groups* (The Modern Jazz Quartet, Lennie Tristano Quintet, and Red Norvo Trio). Each of these groups chose a different course of activity. The Modern Jazz Quartet, by far the most successful musically and commercially of all the chamber groups,

explored the joining of jazz feeling or content with classical form. Tristano's interest lay in the evolving harmonic system to hitherto unexplored regions. The Norvo trio featured the contrapuntal interplay of xylophone, guitar, and bass similar to that found in the Mulligan quartet.

3. *The Experimental Groups* (The Charles Mingus Jazz Workshop, Cecil Taylor Trio, Teddy Charles—Bob Prince Composer's Workshop, William Russo, John Coltrane, and Ornette Coleman). Charles Mingus has worked with small combinations exploring atonality and various onomatopoeic devices. Pianist Cecil Taylor also functions within an atonal framework, but without any recognizable success in jazz terms. Composers Teddy Charles and Bob Prince have been the most successful of those working with "extended form" (forms exceeding the normal thirty-two-bar length

Helen Jepson in the title role of Thaïs

of most traditional jazz material. Composer William Russo has met the problem of projecting jazz into classical form by developing a compositional skill extending to the symphony orchestra. His *Titans* was performed by the New York Philharmonic Orchestra in 1960. Tenor Saxophonist John Coltrane has explored the revolutionary idea of building an improvised line from isolated "vertical" extensions of each chord, rather than by connecting the chords through the traditional "horizontal" line.

Alto saxophonist Ornette Coleman who appeared on the jazz scene in 1960, dramatically presented an unqualified statement of both atonality and extended form which bore little or no relation to any previous styles or idioms. Coleman symbolizes the present dilemma of jazz—whether to continue along the time-honored path of diatonic symmetrical harmony, or to enter the thorny areas of atonality and extended form.

Jazz improvisation involves diatonic harmony moving in a quarter-note pulse. Historically, the theory and practice of improvisation can be traced back to the Renaissance. Traditionally, all improvisation offers two alternatives: (1) *theme and variations:* melodic exposition based upon the orderly development of a stated theme through diminution, augmentation, imitation, inversion, etc., and (2) *figured bass:* melodic exposition in which one abandons the stated theme and builds an entirely new melodic line, based upon the chords or harmonic underpinning of the composition. In general the history of jazz improvisation has centered about the use of figured bass, with only occasional use of theme and variations.

JEANNE D'ARC AU BÛCHER *(Joan of Arc at the Stake).* Scenic oratorio by Arthur Honegger with a text by Paul Claudel, composed 1934–35 and first performed in Basel, Switzerland, in 1938. This work belongs to the most important musical creations of the twentieth century. Honegger combines elements of oratorio, opera, and legitimate theater with a musical language of extreme diversity. The very large chorus dominates soloists and speaker. An exceptionally large orchestra (which includes electrical instruments) gives the composer the possibility of portraying the dramatic action by means of the most unusual modern orchestration.

The final scene of Jeanne d'Arc au Bûcher *with Olga Villi in the title role and Vittorio Gassman as the Friar. Teatro Massimo Bellini, Catania*

The action revolves around Joan of Arc at the stake prior to her death in the flames. The events leading to her execution come to life in scenes of intense dramatic power: the "voices" which call her to the liberation of France, the crowning of the French king at Rheims after her victory over the English, the adoration of her people at this moment and their wrath after her conviction as a witch, the bigotry of court and clergy (portrayed as a card game), and again the "voices" which eventually dominate the music as Joan is consumed by the flames.

Jeanne d'Arc au Bûcher was first performed as an oratorio. The first stage performance took place in Zurich in 1942. A French critic wrote of this work: "Orchestra, solos, and even the recitation seem to be borne by the breadth of this music. There is no let-up, no breathing spell during these seventy minutes. The source of inspiration never dries out. . . . One leaves intensely moved by the power of this work."

JEFFERSON, "Blind Lemon." American jazz and folk singer and guitarist (*c.* 1883–*c.* 1930). Jefferson is important for the great influence he had on blues singers Huddie Ledbetter ("Leadbelly") and Josh White. They recorded together during the mid-1920s.

JELINEK, Hanns. Austrian composer (1901–). A pupil of Franz Schmidt at the Vienna Academy of Music, he has composed many choral, symphonic, and chamber works in a style influenced by polyphonic music of the past and jazz music of the present.

JEPSON, Helen. American soprano (1905–). Daughter of a musical family, Helen Jepson sang in choir groups in her earliest years and went on to study at the Curtis Institute and with Mary Garden in Paris. She sang leading roles with the Metropolitan Opera from 1934 to 1943 and also appeared with the Chicago Civic Opera.

JERGER, Alfred. German baritone (1889–). A leading performer in Germany and Austria and in London at Covent Garden, he has sung many roles, among them Mandryka in Richard Strauss' *Arabella,* which he sang at the première in Dresden in 1933.

JERITZA, Maria (Mizzi Jedlitzka). Czech soprano (1887–). One of the great prima donnas of her time, she was a strong singer, an effective actress, and a powerful personality. As Tosca, one of her most famous roles, she was said to have pleased Puccini more than any other singer. Her first big success was in the title role at the première of Richard Strauss' *Ariadne auf Naxos* in Stuttgart in 1916. From then on she was a star, appearing in German, Italian, and French operas, as well as in operettas, at the Vienna Staatsoper and many other great theaters. She was the outstanding personality at the Metropolitan Opera from 1921 to 1932 and returned as a guest in 1951 to sing Rosalinde in *Die Fledermaus.*

Mme. Jeritza also created the role of the Kaiserin in Richard Strauss' *Die Frau ohne Schatten* and sang the leading roles in the American premières of *Die tote Stadt, Die aegyptische Helena, Turandot,* and *Jenufa.*

JEUNESSES MUSICALES. This organization was created in Belgium in 1940 and shortly thereafter established in France. After World War II it became a forum for young people of many different countries for the purpose of getting together for the better understanding of one another's cultures. International symphony orchestras were formed from among the participants, directed by well-known conductors. Gradually the emphasis of the Jeunesses Musicales' annual conventions began to shift more to the performance and analysis of contemporary works. Composers of international reputation were invited to discuss their works and works by others of their nationality. Nine Western European countries and Canada have been host to conventions of the Jeunesses Musicales' which has affiliated organizations all over the world.

JEWEL SONG. See *Faust.*

JEWELS OF THE MADONNA, THE. Three-act opera by the Italian composer Ermanno Wolf-Ferrari. The Intermezzo is occasionally performed at Pops concerts.

JIG, French, *gigue.* Originally the name of a stringed instrument, it was given from the sixteenth century to an Irish folk dance, which probably took the name from the instrument used to accompany it. The dance spread to England and Scotland during Elizabethan times, becoming very popular both for dancing and as a chamber music form. It is said to have been introduced into France by Charles II.

The jig formed a quick section of the suite, and because of its lively tempo soon became the accepted finale. In the usual binary form, it was in some form of animated triple time, usually 6/8 or 12/8, less often 3/4 or 3/8. See *Scottish Dances.*

JINGLE BELLS. Song by American composer J. S. Pierpoint, written in 1857, and a winter favorite ever since. There was at one time an English version, *Dashing Through the Snow,* with a different tune for the chorus.

JIRÁK, Karel. Czech composer (1891–). The author of an important book on musical forms, he has been a conductor and director of musical programs for the Czech radio. In 1947, he joined the faculty of Roosevelt College in Chicago. His many compositions include five symphonies, an opera, chamber music, piano pieces, and several song cycles.

MARIA JERITZA

JOACHIM, Joseph. Hungarian violinist (1831–1907). He was one of the greatest violinists of his age and, with Paganini, Ole Bull, and Sarasate, remains one of the legendary virtuosos of the century. He made his debut at seven and at twelve went to Leipzig, where Mendelssohn immediately realized his abilities, accompanied him at his first concert, and took him as a pupil at the Conservatory. At thirteen Joachim first visited England, where he remained the most popular of all violinists for more than sixty years.

In 1853, he became concertmaster to the King of Hanover and in 1863 married the contralto Amalie Weiss, from whom he was divorced twenty years later. He left his post in Hanover in 1866, and became director of the Berlin Hochschule für Musik, where he influenced many pupils later celebrated in the musical world and founded the world-famous Joachim Quartet.

A modest man, Joachim was heaped with honors by the courts and universities of Europe. He was a close friend of Brahms and had a great influence on some of the latter's works. The Violin Concerto, Op. 77, is dedicated to Joachim and was first performed by him after he had advised Brahms on composing for the violin. Joachim's own compositions—violin concertos, overtures, and songs—much influenced by Schumann and Brahms, are seldom heard today.

JOÃO IV. King of Portugal (1604–1656). As Duke of Bragança, he formed a magnificent library of music, which was later destroyed in the Lisbon earthquake of 1755. As King (1640–56), he wrote treatises on music and composed many church works, some of which are still sung in the churches of Portugal.

JOB. This ballet, or "masque for dancing" as it was entitled, was based by Geoffrey Keynes on William Blake's illustrations of the Book of Job. The music, composed by Vaughan Williams, was first heard in a concert version at the Norwich Music Festival of 1930. After this performance the music critic of the London *Times* wrote: "The music, in its acceptance of form and its rejection of formalism, is of a piece with Blake. It contains tunes of such a simple beauty that one seems to have known them always, but their lines lead on into a realm of

Job, *by William Blake*

musical thought that one enters for the first time. The Saraband of the Children of God, Job's Dream, and the Pavane and Galliard of the ultimate vision are salient instances."

The first stage presentation of the work, with choreography by Ninette de Valois, was given by the Camargo Society in 1931.

Blake's vision of the Book of Job is arranged in eight scenes.

JOBIN, Raoul. Canadian tenor (1910–). After winning the Metropolitan Auditions of the Air, he joined the Metropolitan Opera in 1940 and for eight seasons sang the principal tenor roles in the French repertory, and in revivals of *Pelléas et Mélisande, Louise, Daughter of the Regiment, Tales of Hoffmann, Lakmé,* and in the world première of Menotti's *The Island God.*

JOCHUM, Eugen. German conductor (1902–). Jochum studied at the Augsburg Conservatory and the Musical Academy in Munich. He began his conducting career in München-Gladbach. Between 1926 and 1929 he served as chief conductor in the opera houses of Kiel, Mannheim, and Duisberg. In the ensuing years he toured with the Berlin Philharmonic Orchestra and, in 1934, succeeded Karl Muck as chief conductor of the Hamburg Philharmonic Orchestra. He made his first American appearance in 1958 with the Los Angeles Symphony Orchestra. In 1960 he was appointed co-conductor (with Bernard Haitink) of the Concertgebouw Orchestra in Amsterdam, Holland.

Edward Johnson in the title role of Peter Ibbetson

JOHANNESEN, Grant. American pianist (1921–). After graduation from the McCune School of Music in 1941, Johannesen continued his studies with Robert Casadesus and Nadia Boulanger at the Fontainebleau Academy, later studying with Egon Petri. His first New York recital took place at Times Hall in 1944. He has appeared at many music festivals, in recital, and as soloist with foremost orchestras in the United States and Europe. He was soloist with the New York Philharmonic Orchestra during its 1956 European tour, concertized for the first time in South America in 1952, and toured Australia and the Far East in 1960. He won first prize at the International Piano Competition in Ostend, Belgium (1949), and The Harriet Cohen International Award (1958).

JOHANSEN, David Monrad. Norwegian composer and critic (1888–). Johansen studied with Humperdinck in Berlin; then he returned to Norway where he taught and wrote music. He wrote orchestral, instrumental, and chamber music, songs, and large-scale choral works (notably *Voluspå*) in a style influenced by romanticism, nationalism, and impressionism.

JOHN BROWN'S BODY. Popular American marching and community song. The composer of the tune is unknown, but it is said to have been first sung (to different words) at parties in Charleston, South Carolina. The tune was taken over by revivalist preachers for their meetings.

Recruits from the Southern states introduced it in the Union Army, and the Federal soldiers stationed at Fort Warren, near Boston, in 1861, made up to fit the tune doggerel verses poking fun at their sergeant, a certain John Brown. These soon became associated with the anti-slavery hero John Brown, leader of the raid on Harpers Ferry, and the song spread through the North as the marching song of the Union Army in the Civil War.

The poet and feminist Julia Ward Howe wrote to fit this tune the fine *Battle Hymn of the Republic*.

JOHNSON, Edward. Canadian tenor and operatic impresario (1881–1959). He studied at the University of Toronto, appeared in light opera in New York in 1907, and then went to Italy for further study. There he appeared in opera under the name of Eduardo di Giovanni. He joined the Metropolitan Opera in 1922, and in 1935 he was appointed general manager of that company, succeeding Herbert Witherspoon. He served in this position until 1950.

JOHNSON, Hunter. American composer (1906–). Johnson studied at the University of North Carolina and at the Eastman School of Music, from which he was graduated in 1929. He was head of the department of composition at the University of Michigan from 1929 to 1933. He received the Prix de Rome in 1933. He has written orchestral works, a ballet, and chamber music.

JOHNSON, James ("Osie"). American jazz drummer and arranger (1923–). Johnson has played with several groups, including those of Earl Hines, Dorothy Donegan, and Tony Scott. He was an arranger for Dinah Washington, and his jazz works have been recorded by Benny Goodman and Frank Wess.

JOHNSON, James L. ("J. J."). American jazz trombonist (1924–). A "bop" stylist, he played with Benny Carter, Count Basie, Woody Herman, and Oscar Pettiford, and toured with Kai

Winding as a member of the team of "Jay and Kai." He has recorded frequently as head of his own group and also with Miles Davis, Chubby Jackson, Charlie Parker, and Winding. Probably the major influence on the modern jazz trombone, he has taken the instrument in a new direction; his tone has none of the bite, or "growl," of the traditional trombone sound, but instead is extremely pure and smooth. "J. J." is widely imitated, but few musicians have the virtuoso technique to equal him.

JOHNSON, Lockrem. American composer (1924–). Johnson received his training at the Cornish School of Music in Spokane, Washington, and at the University of Washington. He has served on the faculty of the University of Washington. In 1952 he held a Guggenheim Fellowship. He has composed a chamber opera, six piano sonatas, violin sonatas, a ballet, and choral music.

JOHNSON, Thor. American conductor (1913–). Johnson has been active on the American musical scene since his teens. In high school he organized a symphony orchestra, the first of many under his direction. As a student at the University of North Carolina he served as associate conductor of the North Carolina Symphony Orchestra. With a master's degree in music from the University of Michigan he went to Europe to study with such famous conductors as Felix Weingartner and Bruno Walter.

He joined the faculty of the University of Michigan in 1937, and during the next few years became the conductor of several orchestras and music festivals in the South and Midwest. During World War II he organized and conducted an orchestra at an army base in England.

He was appointed conductor of the Juilliard Symphony Orchestra in 1946, and in 1947 he became musical director and conductor of the Cincinnati Symphony Orchestra, a post he retained for eleven years. He has furthered contemporary music by commissioning composers to write scores for orchestra, and has instructed and advised hundreds of young musicians in matters pertaining to their careers.

In 1957 Johnson resigned as musical director at Cincinnati to become conductor of the Northwestern University Symphony Orchestra.

JOHNSON, William ("Bunk"). American jazz trumpeter (1879–1949). One of the outstanding pioneers of New Orleans jazz, Johnson started his career as a professional musician at the age of fourteen, and at sixteen joined Buddy Bolden's famous orchestra. In 1899 he left Bolden and played for a couple of years with the band of a traveling circus. His heyday was from 1911 to 1914, when he was chief performer in the elite Eagle Band. In 1914 he retired in order to become a music teacher, but later played for several years with various orchestras.

In 1942 a group of jazz enthusiasts, having decided to make records with an orchestra of veteran New Orleans musicians, sought him out. They found him living in extreme poverty, and they had to buy him a set of false teeth before recording could begin. These records, on which Johnson played, among other tunes, his own *Franklin Street Blues,* show that he was still a first-rate musician. Johnson later made a comeback, forming his own orchestra and touring the United States with it until his death.

JOIO, Norman Dello. See *Dello Joio, Norman.*

JOLIVET, André. French composer (1905–). In 1936, he founded, with Messiaen, Lesur, and Baudrier, the musical group called Young France. In 1945, he became musical director of the Comédie Française.

THOR JOHNSON

Jolivet began by following Schoenberg's atonalism, but has developed toward a more understandable musical speech. In a statement in 1949 on twelve-tone music he said that none of the Parisian atonalists had been able to answer the question: "what is the decisive criterion whereby you are able, *merely by hearing* an atonal work, to say whether it is good or bad? I must confess that I think that music is created to be heard with the ear and sung with the voice. Instead of giving myself up to the cheap intellectual amusement of putting together notes which have value only for the eye, I prefer to divert myself with crossword puzzles."

Jolivet has named as his chief works:

> String Quartet No. 1 (1934)
> *Mana,* for piano (1935)
> Five Ritual Dances (1939)
> *The Soldier's Three Complaints* (1940)
> Concerto for Ondes Martenot (an electrical instrument) (1947)

He has also composed *Suite Transocéane* (1955) for the Louisville Orchestra, and other instrumental music.

JOLSON, Al. American singer and actor (1886–1950). Born in St. Petersburg, Russia, Jolson was brought to the United States as a small boy by his father, who was a cantor in a synagogue. The boy's interest was always in the theater, and when still in his teens he was already singing, dancing, and clowning in burlesque and vaudeville and developing the mannerisms which came to characterize him. His Southern accent was borrowed from a Negro playmate; his appearance in blackface derived from the tradition of the minstrel shows; and he was already going down on one knee to sing when he appeared in his first Broadway production, *La Belle Paree,* in 1911. *Vera Violetta* in the same year brought him stardom, and he went on to enormous success in a series of musical extravaganzas featuring his voice and personality against lavish backgrounds, with scores by Romberg and others, and many interpolated songs—Gershwin's first big hit, *Swanee,* was introduced in *Sinbad* (1918). *Robinson Crusoe, Jr.* (1916) set the pattern; others were *Bombo* (1921), *Big Boy* (1925), *The Wonder Bar* (1931). His last

ANDRÉ JOLIVET

AL JOLSON

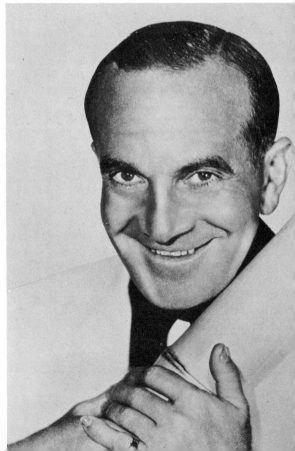

Broadway appearance was in 1940, in *Hold onto Your Hats,* by Lane and Harburg.

Meanwhile, sound motion pictures had been developed. Jolson was starred in the first film musical, *The Jazz Singer,* in 1927, and his fame, already nation-wide from the tours of his shows, now became world-wide. Among his other musical films—largely built, like the Broadway shows, to display his inimitable talents—were *The Singing Fool* (1928), *Mammy* (1930), *Hallelujah, I'm a Bum* (1933), *Swanee River* (1940), *Rhapsody in Blue* (1945), *Burlesque* (1945), and *Jolson Sings Again* (1950).

During the second World War Jolson gave all his time to entertaining soldiers at the battle fronts, and when the Korean War began he again toured the front. He died while on leave in San Francisco. In the film about his life, *The Jolson Story,* Jolson is portrayed by Larry Parks, but the songs are his own recordings.

JOMMELLI, Niccolò. Italian composer (1714–1774). He was one of the most prolific and successful of the opera composers of the Neapolitan school, which was founded by Alessandro Scarlatti. Jommelli advanced the art to the point at which it was then revitalized and revolutionized by Gluck and Mozart. His florid arias became the vehicles for the great singers of the eighteenth century, including the famous *castrati.* Only Hasse rivaled him in energy and popularity. Of his seventy operas, none has survived in the modern repertory, though some of his church music is performed, particularly the *Miserere* for two voices, which was his last work. Many of his operas had texts by Metastasio.

JONAS, Maryla. Polish pianist (1911–1959). Maryla Jonas appeared as a child prodigy in Warsaw at the age of nine, and studied with Paderewski, Sauer, and Turczynski. She toured Europe from 1926 until 1933. After the Nazi invasion of Poland in 1939, she escaped to Rio de Janeiro, where she gave a series of concerts. She appeared at Carnegie Hall in 1946 in a successful debut recital and, thereafter, continued to appear in recitals and as soloist with orchestras in the United States and Europe.

JONES, Allan. American singer and film actor (1907–). Educated at the University of Syracuse and N.Y.U., Jones later studied in London

NICCOLÒ JOMMELLI

under Clara Novello Davies and Sir Henry Wood. He began his career as an opera singer, and in 1935 entered films, his greatest success being *Firefly,* in which he sang the ever-popular *Donkey Serenade.* Others of his films are *A Night at the Opera, Show Boat, A Day at the Races, The Great Victor Herbert,* and *The Boys from Syracuse.*

JONES, Alton. American pianist and teacher (1899–). Jones is a graduate of Drake University and the Institute of Musical Art in New York. He made his debut at London's Aeolian Hall in 1925 and was soloist with the New York Philharmonic Orchestra. Since 1921 he has been on the staff of the Juilliard School of Music, where he is chairman of the piano faculty.

JONES, Charles. Canadian-American composer (1910–). Jones studied composition at the Juilliard School of Music and with Aaron Copland at Tanglewood. Thereafter he taught at Mills College and was twice guest conductor of the San Francisco Symphony Orchestra. He has composed orchestral, chamber, and instrumental works, and a ballet.

The final scene from Jonny Spielt Auf *at the Metropolitan in 1929. Lawrence Tibbett is seen as Jonny*

JONES, Henry (Hank). American jazz pianist (1918–). A "modern" jazz stylist, he has played with "Hot Lips" Paige, Coleman Hawkins, and Howard McGhee, and has toured with Jazz at the Philharmonic. He was accompanist for Billy Eckstine and Ella Fitzgerald, and has recorded with Stan Getz, Lester Young, and Charlie Parker.

JONES, Jonah. American jazz trumpeter (1909–). Jones joined the band of a Mississippi River paddle steamer in 1929 and later played with the Jimmy Lunceford, Stuff Smith, and other prominent jazz bands. In 1954, after an appearance at the Paris Jazz Festival, he formed his own group, which has created a distinctive muted jazz style.

JONES, Jonathan ("Jo"). American jazz drummer (1911–). Jones is known in jazz circles for his light and unique style. He has recorded with Harry James, Teddy Wilson, Lionel Hampton, Mildred Bailey, and Billie Holliday, and played with the Charlie Ventura and Ben Webster groups.

JONES, Quincy D. American jazz trumpeter, pianist, and arranger (1933–). Jones studied trumpet at Schillinger House in Boston before joining Lionel Hampton. He has recorded many of his jazz compositions and worked as arranger for Ray Anthony. After spending several years in France, he returned to the United States to form a highly successful big band.

JONES, Robert. English composer of the early seventeenth century. He wrote airs for the lute and many madrigals of a distinctive character, such as *Oriana seeming to wink at folly* (for six voices), *Sing, merry birds* (for four voices), and *Come, doleful owl* (for five voices). Another composer of the same name lived in the previous century and was one of the court musicians to Henry VIII. He composed a Mass and a Magnificat, and a song *Who shall have my fayr lady.*

JONES, Sidney. English composer (1861–1946). A conductor of opera in London and the provinces, he composed nine operettas, of which the first, *The Geisha,* was almost as great a success as Gilbert and Sullivan's *The Mikado,* which it resembled. His *The Girl From Utah* also was very popular in England and America.

JONES, Thaddeus J. (Thad). American jazz trumpeter (1923–). Before joining the Count Basie band, he was a member of a family trio and played with Billy Mitchell and Larry Steele. He has earned much praise as a soloist.

JONGEN, Joseph. Belgian composer and teacher (1873–1953). Jongen studied at the Liège Conservatory and later taught there. He won the Prix de Rome in 1897, and other prizes. He was a concert and church organist and also pianist in a chamber music ensemble. He was director of the Brussels Conservatory from 1925 to 1939. He composed concertos; orchestral, choral, and chamber music; piano, organ and other instrumental pieces; an opera; and a ballet.

JONNY SPIELT AUF *(Johnny Strikes Up).* Jazz opera in two acts with music and words by Ernst Křenek, first performed in Leipzig, 1927, and since produced all over the world.

The first jazz opera ever composed, it was the subject of controversy everywhere. An appreciation by Hugo R. Fleischmann included this: "All that attracts our generation found a place in

Jonny—films, broadcasting, the loudspeaker, jazz, the foxtrot, luxury hotels and express trains. . . . Above all, Křenek was the first serious composer who dared to make use of American dance forms, which every musically educated person had previously regarded as blasphemous. . . ."

Křenek himself said that he had written the opera in order to "interpret the rhythms and atmosphere of modern life in this age of technical science." The opera brought him immediate prosperity. His publisher relates: "The opera was translated into eighteen languages. Its melodies were thumped out on the radio, played on café violins, and whistled in the streets. When the Austrian Tobacco Monopoly manufactured a new cigarette, they called it *Jonny*. And on top of it all there came a vociferous Prussian lawyer from Berlin, who bought the film rights for Warner Brothers. The film was never made, but the check was all right. The whole thing was fantastic. . . ."

JOPLIN, Scott. American jazz pianist and composer (1868–1917). Joplin was one of the earliest and finest of the ragtime pianists, and his *Maple Leaf Rag,* written in 1893, is still occasionally heard.

JORDÁ, Enrique. Spanish conductor (1911–). At present the permanent conductor of the San Francisco Symphony Orchestra, Jordá became well known through his musical activities in his own country and guest engagements with leading European symphony orchestras. He was principal conductor of the Madrid Symphony Orchestra from 1943 to 1945 and musical director of the Capetown (South Africa) Symphony Orchestra. His appointment to the San Francisco Symphony Orchestra in 1954 followed guest engagements in 1952 and 1953.

JORDAN, Irene. American soprano (1919–). She began as a mezzo at the Metropolitan Opera in 1946 and after some years became a soprano, first coloratura, and later dramatic. She has sung with the Chicago, New York City, and Covent Garden companies and made many appearances with major symphony orchestras, and in concert performances of several unusual operas.

JORDAN, Irving Sydney ("Duke"). American jazz pianist (1922–). His career began with Steve Pulliam's Manhattan Sextet in 1939. After free-lancing with various groups for a number of years, gradually improving his technique and musicianship, Jordan was heard by Charlie Parker and immediately engaged. One of the earliest bop pianists, he also worked with Stan Getz, Roy Eldridge, Oscar Pettiford, and others, and has written several fine tunes, the best-known of which is probably *Jordu.*

JÖRN, Karl. Latvian tenor (1876–1948). At the Metropolitan Opera, where he sang from 1909 to 1914, he was Hans in *The Bartered Bride* and the Italian Singer in *Der Rosenkavalier,* in their American premières. He also sang Wagnerian roles.

JOSEFFY, Rafael. Hungarian pianist (1852–1915). Beginning his piano studies at the age of eight, Joseffy attended the Leipzig Conservatory and continued as a student of Liszt and Tausig. He made his American debut in New York in 1879 at a symphony concert under Leopold Damrosch. He settled permanently in New York and became well known as a teacher, virtuoso, and as an editor of piano works.

JOSQUIN DES PRÉS (*also* **Després** or **Des Préz**). French composer (*c.* 1440–1521). Josquin was a pupil of Okegham and spent a number of years in Italy, first as a chorister at Milan Cathedral, and subsequently as choirmaster at the courts of the Sforzas in Milan and the dukes of Ferrara. In 1509 he settled in Condé sur

JOSQUIN DES PRÉS

MARCEL JOURNET

l'Escaut and became head of the musical college, a post he held until his death.

Josquin was a prolific composer of both sacred and secular music (mostly choral). His greatest works are probably the masses, *Ave Maris Stellis* and *De Beata Vergine;* his numerous chansons and motets are also of great musical importance.

The contrapuntal techniques of the previous generation finds its culmination in his music. Josquin absorbed these and imbued them with humanism and an elevated form of artistic expression. In spite of his technical mastery, his music is never dry or mannered. Martin Luther said of Josquin: "He is the master of the notes, others are mastered by them."

JOSTEN, Werner. German-American composer (1885–1963). Josten studied with Rudolph Siegel and Emile Jaques-Dalcroze in Europe. He became assistant conductor at the Munich Opera in 1918. In 1921 he settled in the United States, becoming a professor of music at Smith College. He wrote ballets; choral, orchestral, chamber, and instrumental works; and songs.

JOTA. A dance in three-quarter time that is native to the provinces of Aragon and Navarre in northern Spain.

JOUBERT, John. South African composer (1927–). He composes in a modern idiom that

retains tonality and form. His works include a ballet, *The Legend of Princess Vlai,* chamber music, piano pieces, songs, and several symphonic pieces.

JOURNET, Marcel. French bass (1867–1933). His beautiful voice and impeccable style are evident in the recording he made as Méphistophélès in the first complete phonograph version of *Faust.* Although over sixty at the time, his vocal powers were unimpaired. His career began at the Monnaie in Brussels and continued at the Paris Opéra, Covent Garden in London, and the Metropolitan Opera, where he was one of the stars of its "golden age." In later years, he sang with Mary Garden and the Chicago Opera, and for almost twenty years was a regular member of La Scala in Milan.

JOYCE, Eileen. Australian pianist (1912–). Eileen Joyce's father was a miner, and she was born in a tent on a Tasmanian mining location. Her parents could not afford to give her music lessons, but she saved the little money she earned for piano lessons.

After three years' study she made her London debut at the Queen's Hall under Sir Henry Wood, playing a Prokofiev concerto in her first Promenade Concert. Three years' further study with Tobias Matthay and Artur Schnabel followed, and she embarked on her strikingly successful professional career.

JUCH, Emma. American soprano of Austrian parentage (1865–1939). After her debut at sixteen in London, she became a leading singer at the New York Academy of Music and with the American Opera Company, performing many roles in operas by Meyerbeer, Verdi, Mozart, and Wagner. In 1889 she began a three-year tour of the United States with her own company, after which she became a prominent concert singer.

JUDSON, Arthur. American concert manager (1881–). Arthur Judson has achieved eminence in the field of music as performing artist, educator, and concert manager. In 1900, after successful appearances as violinist and conductor, he was appointed dean of the Conservatory of Music of Denison University. After some years with the publication *Musical America,* he assumed the management of the Philadelphia

Orchestra in 1915. In 1922 he joined the New York Philharmonic Orchestra in the same capacity, a post which he occupied until 1956.

His concert management bureau in New York City was merged, in 1930, with several others, into Columbia Concerts Corporation, with Mr. Judson at its helm. Today, known as Judson, O'Neil and Judd, it is prominent in the field of concert management throughout the world.

JUILLIARD, Augustus D. American music patron (1836–1919). Juilliard was a prominent industrialist who left a large part of his estate for the furtherance of music in the United States. The Juilliard Foundation conceived and maintains the Juilliard School of Music.

JUILLIARD QUARTET. Robert Mann and Isidore Cohen, violins; Raphael Hillyer, viola; and Claus Adam, cello. The quartet was founded in 1946 by William Schuman, then president of the Juilliard School of Music, with the aid of the Juilliard Foundation, as the school's quartet-in-residence. The ensemble has toured the United States and Canada, Europe, Russia, the Middle East, and the Far East. It has made many recordings, including the Bartók and Schoenberg quartets and other chamber music. The quartet has appeared at the Salzburg, Vienna, Berlin, Budapest (1958 Bartók Festival), and Edinburgh festivals in Europe, and at Tanglewood, Ojai, and the first Inter-American Music Festival, Washington, D. C., in the United States.

JUILLIARD SCHOOL OF MUSIC. The history of the Juilliard School of Music begins with the founding, in 1905, of The Institute of Musical Art by Frank Damrosch and James Loeb. Fifteen years later the Juilliard Foundation was established through a legacy of Augustus D. Juilliard, and its income was devoted to the establishment of the Juilliard Graduate School in 1924. Since 1926, the Institute and the Graduate School have been operated together as the Juilliard School of Music, and were formally amalgamated in 1946.

John Erskine was president of the school from 1928 to 1937, Ernest Hutcheson from 1937 to 1945, and William Schuman from 1945 to 1962. Peter Mennin assumed the presidency in 1962, succeeding William Schuman who was appointed president of Lincoln Center for the Performing Arts. The objective of all its admin-

istrators has been the development of a professional school in the highest sense, which transcends the merely vocational, and which looks upon training in music or dance not only as a means to a career, but as the basis of a liberal education through formal instruction and the interrelating of shared artistic experience.

The curriculum is divided into three areas: major study of voice, piano, composition, conducting, organ, orchestral instrument, or dance; performance in large or small ensembles; and study in the literature and materials of music. The student may also elect a concurrent course of academic studies. The course leading to the award of the diploma of the school normally takes four years; the Bachelor of Science degree usually follows five years of study. Graduate study is also offered in the fields enumerated

Juilliard Quartet

A model of the new Juilliard School to be built at Lincoln Center

above. Private instruction in the student's chosen instrument or specialty is the core of the Juilliard curriculum.

The Juilliard School is housed in a spacious, six-story building at 122nd Street on Claremont Avenue adjacent to Riverside Drive, in New York City. It has a faculty of more than one hundred and thirty members. Its facilities include twenty-five classrooms, forty-one teaching studios, four large rehearsal rooms, and numerous practice rooms. The concert hall seats one thousand and has a fully equipped stage and large orchestra pit. The more intimate recital hall seats three hundred. The School's library comprises a collection of approximately 5,000 books on music and dance, 4,000 books on non-musical studies, and 20,000 music scores.

The Juilliard School plans to move to the Lincoln Center for the Performing Arts, New York City.

JULLIEN, Louis Antoine. French conductor (1812–1860). A great popular entertainer, he was most successful in England, where he conducted mammoth orchestras in the famous Quadrilles which he composed or compiled for special occasions. Though not a musician of particular talent, he did much to make music more available and more appreciated by the public, and introduced many works to England. His attempts at producing opera and other ventures ruined him financially.

JUPITER SYMPHONY. Mozart's last symphony, in C major, K. 551. It was completed on August 10, 1788, and is the last of the three great symphonies (the others were the E flat major and G minor) which Mozart composed that summer between June 26 and August 10. It was possibly the English music publisher J. B. Cramer who gave the symphony its nickname, but Percy Scholes cannot find the name in use before 1821. Sir Donald Tovey maintained that no work of Mozart's should have been given the name of a Roman god, since his music more closely resembles the classical Greek ideal.

Every key had its special meaning for Mozart, and C major was the key for ceremonial or festive occasions, for pomp and splendor. This symphony is full of broad effects and, as in so many other of his works in this key, Mozart calls for a large orchestra with trumpets and kettledrums. The *Jupiter* is transparently clear and elegant, on classically clean lines, powerful but without heaviness.

I. *Allegro vivace*. The opening theme expresses a feeling of victory and triumph. The dualism of Mozart's thematic work, which is distinguished by a forceful opening followed by a continuation of melodious character, is notable here. In spite of the supporting theme's charming character the feeling of triumph remains throughout the movement.

An inexhaustible richness of variation is unfolded with contrapuntal mastery, and there also occurs the theme from a light comic opera tune he had earlier composed for the words "You are a bit dense, my dear Pompeo, go and study the ways of the world."

II. *Andante cantabile*. This is an elegiac movement but its poise and breadth are in exact accordance with the basic feeling of the symphony.

III. *Menuetto*. This has a calm controlled character. The opening motif, which carries the whole movement, begins pianissimo, but soon develops into a marked rhythmic buoyancy, wherein it is varied both contrapuntally and chromatically. The airy trio forms an idyllic interlude.

IV. *Allegro molto*. This finale is regarded as one of Mozart's great technical masterpieces. The movement is remarkable for its ingenious counterpoint and its heroic, monumental character. F. H. Törnblom writes: "It is not surprising that the finale of the Jupiter Symphony has aroused much discussion, for if there is anything which bears witness to the spirit's triumph over matter, it is this masterpiece. . . . It is an Olympian Mozart, with a transfiguring light over his countenance, who meets us in the Jupiter Symphony."

The whole movement is based on five quite short and simple themes varied and played against one another. All five themes make their appearance in different variations in the great coda which closes the work.

JURINAC, Sena. Yugoslavian soprano (1921–). Sena Jurinac received her musical education at the Zagreb Musical Academy, and made her debut as Mimi in *La Bohème* at the Zagreb Opera in 1942. She has been with the Vienna State Opera since her first appearance there in 1945. She is especially renowned for her roles in Mozart, Richard Strauss, and Wagner operas. She has been closely associated with the Glyndebourne Opera, where she began to sing in 1949. Her only appearances in America have been with the San Francisco Opera in 1959, when she sang Madame Butterfly, Eva in *Die Meistersinger,* and Donna Anna in *Don Giovanni.*

DMITRI KABALEVSKY

Clamecy is one of his most important works, and he has composed several symphonies. In 1950 Kabalevsky completed his third opera, *Taras' Family,* with a subject from the second World War (after Boris Gorbatov's novel *The Inflexible).*

Kabalevsky seeks a melodic, expressive, and clear musical language; strictly developed form and carefully worked out detail are characteristic of his instrumental music.

Kabalevsky considers his chief works to be the Violin Concerto (1948), first performed in 1948, and the Cello Concerto (1949), first performed in 1949. Other well-known works of his include *Comedians,* Op. 26 (orchestra); Piano Concerto No. 3; twenty-four Preludes for piano, Op. 38; and the overture to *The Master of Clamecy,* known as the *Colas Breugnon* Overture (the opera libretto is based on Romain Rolland's novel of that name).

Kabalevsky is a teacher of composition at the Moscow Conservatory and director of the music section of the Institute of Art History in the Academy of Science.

KADOSA, Paul. Hungarian composer (1903–). A follower of Bartók, he has fused Magyar folk music with his neo-classic style. An excellent pianist, he has composed many piano works, as

K. (occasionally, K.V.). Abbreviation for Köchel-Verzeichnis (Köchel listing), found in connection with the titles of works by W. A. Mozart. Although Mozart occasionally attempted to catalogue his own compositions, Ludwig von Köchel (1800–77) made the first complete and chronological listing of all of Mozart's works then known. The Köchel Catalogue, revised by Alfred Einstein in 1937 and again in 1947, is considered the only authentic source material on Mozart's works. Each piece is indicated in the Köchel Catalogue with its appropriate chronological number and accompanied by an extensive account of the history of its origin. For the precise identification of a specific Mozart work (for example, Symphony No. 40, G minor), the mentioning of its Köchel number (K. 550) is of supreme importance.

KABALEVSKY, Dmitri Borisovitch. Russian composer (1904–). He studied composition under Miaskovsky at the Moscow Conservatory and has composed in almost all forms, including instructional piano music, children's songs, and music for films, radio, and stage plays. His Violin Concerto (1948), written for the thirtieth anniversary of the Communist Youth Federation, was awarded a Stalin Prize, as was his Second Quartet. The opera *The Master of*

MAURICIO KAGEL

well as choral, orchestral, and chamber music. He is best known for his concertos for piano, violin, and viola.

KAGEL, Mauricio. Argentine composer and pianist (1931–). Kagel received his education in Buenos Aires. In 1956 he was appointed coach and conductor of the Argentine Chamber Opera and the Teatro Colón. At the same time he conducted on the Argentine radio and served as musical consultant to the University of Buenos Aires.

Since 1957 Kagel has lived in Cologne, Germany, and devotes himself to the study of electronic music. His compositions include chamber music and works for chorus and piano. His *Transición I* was produced in collaboration with the Westdeutscher Rundfunk in Cologne, and *Transición II,* written for piano, percussion, and magnetic tape, was first performed at Darmstadt in 1959. The percussion is executed on the strings of the piano, and the metal and wooden parts of the instrument are also utilized for new effects. Kagel has also conducted the Rhenish Chamber Orchestra. See *Electronic Music.*

KAHN, Eric Itor. German-American pianist and composer (1905–1956). Kahn studied at the Hoch Conservatory in Frankfurt. In 1938, he toured as accompanist to Casals in France and North Africa. In 1941, he emigrated to the United States where he organized the Albeneri Trio with Alexander Schneider, violinist, and Benar Heifetz, cellist. He was awarded the Coolidge Medal in 1948 for his services to chamber music. He wrote several chamber works and piano pieces, adopting the twelve-tone method of composition. See *Twelve-Tone Music.*

KAHN, Norman ("Tiny"). American jazz drummer and arranger (1924–1953). Kahn took up the drums at the age of fifteen, and was soon free-lancing around the New York area. He worked with George Auld, Boyd Raeburn, Chubby Jackson, and Stan Getz, and did a daily radio show, playing vibraphone. One of the first of the "modern" drummers, he exercised a great influence on jazz.

KAHN, Otto. German-American financier and music patron (1867–1934). He was chief patron of the Metropolitan Opera for many years and president of its board of directors.

KALINNIKOV, Basil. Russian composer (1866–1901). A brilliant music student, he was forced to live in great poverty, which ruined his health and curtailed his career as conductor of the Italian Opera in Moscow. His Symphony No. 1 in G minor became an international success before his death and is still in the repertory. He also composed a Second Symphony, songs, chamber music, and choral works.

KALLIR, Lilian. American pianist, born in Prague of Austrian parents. Lillian Kallir studied piano with Hermann de Grab and Isabelle Vengerova, chamber music with William Kroll, and violin, theory, and composition with Hugo Kauder. While in her teens she won a National Music League award, resulting in a number of coast-to-coast tours in the United States, and the American Artists Award of the Brooklyn Institute of Arts and Sciences. She has appeared annually in Europe since 1954, toured Great Britain in 1958 with the Leipzig Gewandhaus Orchestra, and appeared as soloist three times with the Berlin Philharmonic Orchestra under Herbert von Karajan in 1959. She has made annual recital tours in the United States and has also been heard here on television and as soloist with the New York Philharmonic and other orchestras.

KÁLMÁN, Emmerich. Hungarian composer of operettas (1882–1953). After training at the Budapest Musical Academy, Kálmán began to compose and soon won an audience for his catchy tunes and fiery rhythms. A music critic has described his operettas as "a kind of offshoot from the Viennese operetta with a dash of gypsy music." His most popular works were *The Gypsy Princess* and *Countess Maritza.* Kálmán wrote: "In a symphony it is possible to simulate a creative ability which one does not really possess. But even the simplest melody, the slightest waltz, must be really created and must have in it a spark that goes straight to the heart."

Kálmán lived in Vienna for many years. Then in the 1930s he appeared as a conductor in many European cities, settling in Paris for a time in 1938, and finally, in 1940, moving to America.

Best-known operettas:

Sári (1912)
The Gypsy Princess (Die Czardasfürstin) (1915)
Countess Maritza (Gräfin Maritza) (1924)
The Circus Princess (Die Zirkusprinzessin) (1926)

Gertrude Kappel as Brünnhilde

KALOMIRIS, Manolis. Greek composer (1883–1962). One of the most influential forces in Greek music, he wrote many books and through his music attempted to create a national music for Greece. Many of his works are based on folk songs and his operas have utilized national legends. He composed orchestral works, chamber music, several operas, and many arrangements of Greek folk songs.

KAMIEŃSKI, Maciej. Polish composer (1734–1821). He was the first Polish opera composer. Though written in the Italian style, his first opera, *Misery Contented,* produced in Warsaw in 1778, raised a nationalist furor.

KAMINSKI, Heinrich. German composer (1886–1946). Because of official Nazi disapproval during Kaminski's lifetime, the quality of his choral music, songs, and chamber music has been recognized only since his death. Since the second World War, his work has had some influence on younger German composers, who have been attracted to his neo-Baroque style and his revitalized use of medieval forms. His first opera, *Jürg Jenatsch,* was produced by the Dresden Opera in 1928, and his second, *Das Spiel von König Aphelius,* was produced posthumously at Göttingen in 1951.

KAMINSKY, Max. American jazz trumpeter (1908–). Kaminsky remains one of the most popular Dixieland-style trumpet players. He has played with Red Nichols, Frank Teschemacher, George Wettling, Tommy Dorsey, Artie Shaw, Eddie Condon, Sidney Bechet, Bud Freeman, and a host of other famous musicians, often leading his own groups, and making many recordings.

KAPELL, William. American pianist (1922–1953). Kapell studied with Olga Samaroff at the Philadelphia Conservatory of Music and made his New York debut in 1941. He appeared with all major American orchestras and toured Europe. He met his death in an airplane crash while returning from a concert tour of Australia.

WILLIAM KAPELL

KAPELLMEISTER. German, literally "chapel master"; choirmaster or orchestral conductor. The term *Kapellmeistermusik* means derivative or academically correct but uninspired music.

KAPPEL, Gertrude. German soprano (1884–). A leading Wagnerian soprano in Vienna, Munich, and at Covent Garden in London, she sang all the Brünnhildes in the *Ring* cycle, as well as Isolde, at the Metropolitan Opera from 1928 to 1935. She also appeared there as Elektra, and as the Marschallin in *Der Rosenkavalier.*

KARAJAN, Herbert von. Austrian conductor (1908–). Karajan's career began as opera conductor in Ulm (1917–33) and Aachen (1933–38). He studied at the Vienna Academy of Music, and was still in his twenties when he was invited to conduct the Vienna Symphony Orchestra and the Salzburg Opera. Before World War II he also conducted in Belgium, Holland, France, Italy, and Scandinavia. From 1938 to 1942 he was one of the principal conductors of the Berlin State Opera, and remained as conductor of the Opera Symphony Concerts for some time thereafter.

In 1948 he was appointed artistic director of the Gesellschaft der Musikfreunde in Vienna,

HERBERT VON KARAJAN

emerging as one of the leading European orchestra conductors. Numerous recordings with the Vienna Philharmonic Orchestra and the Philharmonia Orchestra of London made him well known all over the world.

In 1955, Karajan became director of the Berlin Philharmonic Orchestra, and in 1956 he was appointed general director of the Vienna State Opera. At the same time he was a principal conductor at La Scala, Milan, and a member of its board of directors, as well as conductor-in-chief of the Philharmonia Orchestra of London. He has conducted in Bayreuth and became director of the Salzburg Festival in 1957.

Karajan has visited the United States at the head of several European orchestras and was guest conductor of the New York Philharmonic Orchestra in 1958.

Karajan is, without doubt, the busiest conductor in Europe, controlling the principal musical organizations in the heart of the Continent. His style combines a phenomenal awareness of orchestral sound with utmost technical precision. His interpretations are determined by the smoothness of his remarkable technique, which conveys to every orchestra his highly personal conception of sound.

KARELIA SUITE. Composition for orchestra, Op. 11 (1893), by Jan Sibelius. The suite was written at the request of Finnish students to accompany tableaus of incidents in the history of Karelia (the mountain district on the Finnish-Russian border) performed at an entertainment in aid of cultural development in Eastern Finland. The suite comprises three of the eight sections which Sibelius composed for the occasion: Intermezzo, Ballad, and *Alla Marcia.*

KARG-ELERT, Sigfried. German organist and composer (1877–1933). Karg-Elert studied at the Leipzig Conservatory with Reinecke and Jadassohn and in 1919 was appointed to its faculty. He gave recitals in the United States in 1932, and was soon recognized as one of the foremost virtuosos of the organ. His compositions are in a brilliant style, inspired by baroque music but embellished with impressionistic devices.

KARPE, Kenneth Lee. American concert impresario (1930–). Karpe has introduced many jazz artists to the American concert public, including such figures as Thelonious Monk and Sonny Rollins. He has also been active in bringing Indian music to the American people, and has presented several concerts featuring Indian musicians.

KASSERN, Tadeusz. Polish composer (1904–1959). One of Poland's leading composers, he was also a diplomat and the cultural attaché at the Polish Consulate in New York. His compositions include a concerto for soprano, a symphonic poem in memory of Pilsudski, chamber music, piano pieces, and songs.

KASTENDIECK, Miles. American music critic (1905–). After serving on newspapers in New Haven and Brooklyn, he became music critic for the New York *Journal-American* in 1946 and has written for the *Christian Science Monitor* since 1945.

KASTLE, Leonard. American composer (1929–). A graduate of the Curtis Institute of Music, he has studied with Rosario Scalero, Gian-Carlo Menotti, and George Szell. Kastle is best known for his three-act opera, *Deseret,* which was given its première by the NBC-TV

MILTON KATIMS

Opera in 1961. Other works include a piano sonata, *A Whitman Reader,* for voice and orchestra, and *Three Whale Songs* from *Moby Dick,* which won the Baxter Prize offered by the Intercollegiate Music Council for the best work for male chorus in 1962. Kastle is currently working on a new opera, *The Pariahs,* which takes place on Nantucket Island during the great whaling days of the early 1800s.

Kastle's orchestration and his handling of the vocal line are both extremely skillful, and though he is not an "avant-garde" composer his works are complex in their construction without overriding the basic melodic scheme within his musical fabric.

KATCHEN, Julius. American pianist (1926–). Katchen studied with David Saperton and made his debut with the Philadelphia Orchestra in 1937. He is a graduate of Haverford College. In 1948, after a tour of Israel, he settled in Paris. He has since given many successful concerts in Europe.

KATIMS, Milton. American conductor and violist (1919–). A graduate of Columbia University, Katims was assistant conductor of the National Orchestral Association (1933–35), solo violist and assistant conductor of the WOR Orchestra, and soloist with the Wallenstein Sinfonietta (1935–43). He made his Carnegie Hall debut as guest conductor of the National Orchestral Association in 1936, and appeared frequently with the Budapest and New York string quartets throughout the United States and at the Library of Congress.

He was invited by Toscanini to join the NBC Symphony Orchestra as first violist in 1943, became a protégé of Toscanini, and conducted this orchestra on many nation-wide broadcasts. He has been guest conductor of prominent orchestras in the United States and abroad, and taught a master class in viola at the Juilliard School from 1946 to 1954.

In 1954 he was called to the podium of the Seattle Symphony Orchestra, where he now serves as conductor and musical director.

KAUFMAN, Louis. American violinist (1905–). Kaufman studied with Kneisel and has received the Loeb Prize (1927) and a Naumberg Award (1928). Since 1950 he has toured in Europe.

KAY, Hershy. American composer (1919–). Kay studied at the Curtis Institute with Felix Salmond, the cellist, and others. He has orchestrated and arranged the scores of Leonard Bernstein's *On the Town, Peter Pan,* and *Candide;* Walter Hendl's *Dark of the Moon;* and other musical comedies. Kay became associated with the dance in the 1940s, composing and arranging a number of ballets for Martha Graham and Pearl Primus.

In 1951 the New York City Ballet commissioned him to compose a work based on nineteenth-century minstrel tunes. Using music by Gottschalk as a departure, he wrote *Cakewalk.* A concert suite from this ballet score has often been performed by orchestras. This was followed by music for a classic ballet in the cowboy idiom, *Western Symphony,* and by *Stars and Stripes,* another ballet for the City Center. Kay completed the orchestration of Kurka's opera *The Good Soldier Schweik* after Kurka's death.

KAY, Ulysses. American composer (1917–). Kay attended the University of Arizona, studied at the Eastman School of Music with Howard Hanson and Bernard Rogers, and continued with Hindemith at Yale University and Tanglewood. After serving with the United States Navy, he went to Rome as a winner of the Rome Prize of the American Academy of Music and was granted a Fulbright Scholarship. He received a Gershwin Memorial Award (1947) and a grant from the National Institute of Arts and Letters. He has composed operas, orchestral and choral music, and chamber music in a neoclassical style.

KAYE, Danny. American comedian and singer (1913–). Danny Kaye's original style was well known to a limited but discriminating audience before his first appearance, in 1939, in the Broadway production *Straw Hat Revue.* Since then he has become one of America's leading comics. His voice varies from "opera bass" to "Irish tenor" and his phenomenal volubility can reach a speed of over 250 words per minute. His comedy consists of seemingly spontaneous quips, nonsense babble, and farcical songs, all presented with an uninhibited personal charm. He has scored outstanding successes with his appearances in the United States and abroad, through his many musical shows and films, and as ambassador at large for the United Nations

ULYSSES KAY

Children's Fund. He returned to Broadway with his one-man show in the spring of 1963.

KEILBERTH, Joseph. German conductor (1908–). One of Germany's foremost conductors, he is the director of the Hamburg Philharmonic and the Bamberg Symphony and has been director of the Dresden State Opera. He frequently conducts performances of the Hamburg State Opera and at the Bayreuth Festival.

KEISER, Reinhard. German composer (1674–1739). As director of the Hamburg Opera from 1703 to 1717, he was a powerful force in the musical life of Germany and a colorful personality. One of the earliest of dramatic composers, he produced more than a hundred stage works, many of which have been lost. Thirty-three authenticated operas of his composition exist today, of which the last, *Circe,* is perhaps the best known. He also wrote much church music and was one of the originators of the dramatic oratorio.

KÉLER, Béla. Hungarian violinist, band conductor, and composer of light music (1820–1882). Successively a law student and a farmer, he took up music in 1945, studying in Vienna, playing the violin at the Theater an der Wien, and composing dance music. He became conductor of the Lanner Band in Vienna. His dances and other light pieces, notably the *Lustspiel Overture,* achieved great popularity.

KELL, Reginald. English clarinetist (1906–). One of the great contemporary virtuosos of his instrument, he has performed, in concert and on recordings, with the great orchestras and chamber groups of the world.

KELLEY, Edgar Stillman. American composer and teacher (1857–1944). Kelley studied in Chicago and then attended the Stuttgart Conservatory. Upon his return to the United States he served as organist in Oakland and San Francisco, conducted performances of light opera in New York, and taught piano and theory in various schools, including the New York College of Music. He returned to Germany in 1902, and taught there until 1910, when he was appointed dean of composition at the Cincinnati Conservatory. He retained this position until his death. He wrote incidental, orchestral, chamber, and instrumental music; and songs.

KELLEY, Norman D. American tenor (1917–). Kelley has been a member of the Metropolitan

MICHAEL KELLY

CLARA LOUISE KELLOGG

Opera Company since 1956. He made his debut at Milan's La Scala in 1947 and has performed at the Opera Nacional, Mexico City, the Central City Opera, Colorado, the San Carlo Opera, New York, and the New York City Opera. He sang in the première performances of *The Good Soldier Schweik* (Kurka) and *Voyage to the Moon.* He studied at the Eastman School of Music.

KELLOGG, Clara Louise. American soprano (1842–1916). One of the famous opera stars of her time, she was one of the first great Aïdas in America. At the New York Academy of Music, where she sang for sixteen years, she appeared in many roles ranging from dramatic to coloratura. Her Marguerite in *Faust* was the first to be heard in New York. She also sang during many seasons at Her Majesty's and Drury Lane theaters in London and, from 1874 to 1876, toured America with her own company. In later years, she was a leading concert artist.

KELLY, Gene. American dancer and singer (1912–). Kelly intended to study law but by the time of his graduation from the University of Pittsburgh in 1933, he had determined to devote himself to dancing. He won a small dancing role in the Broadway show *Leave It to Me* in 1938, after which he attracted attention in Saroyan's *The Time of Your Life*. Soon afterward, he rose to stardom in the title role of the famous musical *Pal Joey*. He became a motion-picture star in 1942 and has remained at the pinnacle ever since, appearing in twenty-three films. Recently, he has starred in a television series and has directed several successful films.

KELLY, Michael. Irish tenor (1762–1826). Early in his career, he knew and worked with Mozart for four years and sang both Don Basilio and Don Curzio in the world première of *Le Nozze di Figaro* in Vienna on May 1, 1786. He became a star performer in London in 1787 and for many years appeared there at Drury Lane and the King's Theater (which he managed). He composed music for sixty stage works, some of them very successful in his day. His famous *Reminiscences,* which was ghost-written by Theodore Hook, appeared the year he died.

KELLY, Wynton. American jazz pianist (1931–). A well-known soloist, he has been a member of the Lester Young and Dizzy Gillespie groups, and for several years was Dinah Washington's accompanist. He now free-lances, playing club dates and making recordings with numerous small groups.

KEMBLE, Adelaide. English soprano (1814–1879). The daughter of Charles Kemble and sister of Fanny Kemble, she was a pupil of the famous diva, Giuditta Pasta. In 1841, she achieved a sensational success as Norma at Covent Garden in London, but two years later renounced her career in favor of marriage.

KEMPE, Rudolf. German conductor (1910–). He served as first oboist with the Dresden Gewandhaus Orchestra from 1929 to 1936. In 1949, he became director of music for the State Orchestra in Dresden, and from 1952 until 1958 served as director of the Munich Opera. He has conducted the German repertory at the Metropolitan Opera and at Covent Garden, and appeared as conductor at the Salzburg and Edinburgh festivals.

KEMPEN, Paul van. Dutch conductor (1893–1955). He was guest conductor of many major European orchestras and, before the war, permanent conductor of the Dresden Philharmonic.

He became well known in America through recordings.

KEMPFF, Wilhelm. German pianist and composer (1895–). Kempff studied with his father and made several tours of Germany and Scandinavia as a pianist, featuring improvisation as part of his programs. At the end of World War II, he made a world tour. He is widely known as one of the finest interpreters of Beethoven, and he has written several symphonies, an opera, and pieces for piano and organ.

KENNAN, Kent Wheeler. American composer (1913–). Kennan studied piano and organ before entering the University of Michigan, and he later studied at the Eastman School of Music and with Pizzetti at the Academy of St. Cecilia in Rome, In 1939 he became a member of the faculty of Kent State University in Ohio. After serving in the Pacific as a band leader for the United States Army during the war, he returned to teaching at the University of Texas. He has written a symphony and works for various solo instruments with orchestra, of which his *Night Soliloquy* for flute and orchestra is frequently heard.

RUDOLF KEMPE

KENT KENNAN

LOUIS KENTNER

KENNEDY-FRASER, Marjory. Scottish soprano (1857–1930). As recitalist, editor, collector, and lecturer, she became well known in England and America. She specialized in the folk songs of Scotland, the Hebrides, and Somerset.

KENTNER, Louis. Hungarian-British pianist (1905–). Kentner received his musical education from Anton Szekely, Leo Weiner, and Zoltán Kodály, with whom he studied composition at the Royal Academy of Music, Budapest. He was awarded a Chopin prize at Warsaw and a Liszt prize at Budapest.

He began his career as a concert artist at the age of fifteen, and since then has visited most European countries. He now resides in London, being a naturalized British subject. He has given first performances to many new works of British composers, among them William Walton's Violin Sonata (with Yehudi Menuhin) and concertos by Alan Rawsthorne and Michael Tippett.

He made a triumphant American recital debut in Town Hall, New York City, in 1957, and an equally successful debut as soloist with the New York Philharmonic Orchestra the following year. He has made two tours of America, appearing as recitalist and as soloist with the Philadelphia, Chicago Symphony, Los Angeles Philharmonic, Toronto Symphony, and other orchestras. He toured the Far East and South America in 1956.

Kentner has played under many of the great international conductors, including Bruno Walter, Sir Thomas Beecham, and Otto Klemperer. He has made many records, and played the *Warsaw Concerto* in the film *Dangerous Moonlight*. He is particularly known for his playing of Liszt and Schubert, but his musical interests are wide. On several occasions he has given performances of the complete cycle of Beethoven's thirty-two piano sonatas, and the forty-eight preludes and fugues of Bach's *The Well-Tempered Clavier*. He is in the first rank of the world's pianists.

Kentner has written three sonatinas for piano, published in 1940.

KENTON, Stanley Newcomb (Stan). American jazz leader, pianist, and arranger (1912–). Born in Wichita, Kansas, and raised in Los Angeles, Kenton studied with his mother and various private teachers and wrote his first arrangement in 1928. He joined Everett Hoagland in 1934 and free-lanced until 1941, when he formed his own band at Balboa Beach and made some recordings. The orchestra began to acquire a national reputation in 1943 through its distinctive sound, particularly in the reed section, and through such vocalists as June Christy, Gene

Howard, and Anita O'Day. Kenton shared arranging chores with Pete Rugolo until the group disbanded in 1947. In 1950 he toured with a forty-piece orchestra which had as a slogan "Innovations in Modern Music."

Kenton has introduced scores of fine musicians to the public, and his band's flawless and inventive arrangements, by himself and such men as Rugolo, Shorty Rogers, Bill Holman, and Gerry Mulligan, have provided a real contribution to the jazz world. Less important for his piano work than for his leading and arranging, Kenton is seldom heard in extended solos.

KEPPARD, Freddie. American jazz cornettist (1883–1932). Keppard was one of the leading trumpet players in New Orleans jazz. His highly individual style, marked by his fabulous skill in shading, was imitated by many of the leading trumpeters of the second jazz generation.

From about 1900 Keppard played in several well-known New Orleans bands, including the Olympia Band, and in 1913 went to California to join the Original Creole Orchestra. When this orchestra was dissolved in 1918 in Chicago, Keppard went to New York for a time, but soon returned to Chicago where he stayed for the rest of his life. There for a time he had his own orchestra, but also continued to play with a number of others, including Erskine Tate's.

Unfortunately, there are no recordings of Keppard's remarkable playing. When RCA Victor made him an offer, he refused on the ground that others would be able to appropriate his style by listening to his records.

KERN, Jerome. American composer (1885–1945). Jerome Kern was of German-Czech descent. He grew up in musical surroundings, learning to play the piano from his mother at an early age, and was a member of small orchestras both at home and at school. Even before leaving school he had written small compositions for amateur theatrical societies and bazaars.

After passing through the New York Conservatory, he pursued his studies in Europe. His ambition was to become a composer for the theater, and when he was engaged as "house composer" by Charles Frohman, an American theater man in London, he was given plenty of opportunity for studying the demands and possibilities of the stage. Nevertheless, he did not have an easy time on his return to New York, and he even worked as a demonstration pianist in a

STAN KENTON

JEROME KERN

large store. It was not until 1911 that he managed to edge his way into the Broadway theater world with the successful modernizing of an old show. His first great success came in 1914 with *They Didn't Believe Me* from the operetta *The Girl from Utah.*

Kern then went from strength to strength with a long series of operettas, his librettists including Guy Bolton and P. G. Wodehouse. In later years he also wrote a good deal of film music.

His greatest success was the music for Oscar Hammerstein II's dramatization of Edna Ferber's novel *Show Boat* (1927). John Tasker Howard says of this: "*Show Boat* was almost a folk opera, with folk music of Kern's composing. Seldom has any subject been treated with better taste, musical and dramatic, than in this unpretentious classic. Some have gone so far as to say that if there is ever to be an American school of opera, this is the model upon which it must be based."

Jerome Kern also wrote music of a more serious kind, including a symphonic version of the *Show Boat* music in 1941—*Scenario for Orchestra on Themes from "Show Boat"*—and a free symphonic work, *Portrait of Mark Twain,* in 1942.

He was one of the most popular and most successful composers of light music in the world, standing, together with Irving Berlin, in the very front rank of theatrical composers. His ingenious rhythms, his constantly surprising harmony, and his original tunes raise many of his best songs to a level far above the ordinary tune of the day. The tunes from *Show Boat* and *Cover Girl* belong with the finest popular music of our time. See *American Musical Theater.*

Of composers, Kern most admired Wagner, Puccini, and Tchaikovsky. He was very fond of old handicrafts—English furniture, Chinese porcelain, silversmiths' work, and rare books.

On the occasion of his death the following message from President Truman was read over the radio: "I am one of the many grateful millions who have played and listened to Jerome Kern's music. And I want to be one of his countrymen paying tribute to him today. His tunes will live in our voices and warm our hearts for many years to come, for they are one with those simple and sincere songs that are independent of time and fashion. . . ."

KERR, Harrison. American composer (1897–).

Kerr studied with Nadia Boulanger at the American Conservatory in Fontainebleau in 1921 and, returning to the United States, taught music in Cleveland and New York. He was later appointed executive secretary of the American Music Center. In 1949 he became dean of the College of Fine Arts at the University of Oklahoma, a position he still holds. He has written four symphonies, a violin concerto, two string quartets, and two piano sonatas, which have been performed throughout the world.

KESSEL, Barney. American jazz guitarist (1923–). Kessel has played with Charlie Barnet, Artie Shaw, and Frank De Vol, toured with Jazz at the Philharmonic, and was a member of the Oscar Peterson Trio. He has recorded extensively with Benny Carter, Billie Holliday, Roy Eldridge, and Lester Young.

KETELBEY, Albert William. Pseudonym of Wlliam Aston, English composer and conductor (1880–1959). Ketelbey studied in Birmingham and at the Trinity College of Music in London, and conducted the orchestra at several London theaters.

The motions made by the hands of a performer on the kettledrums

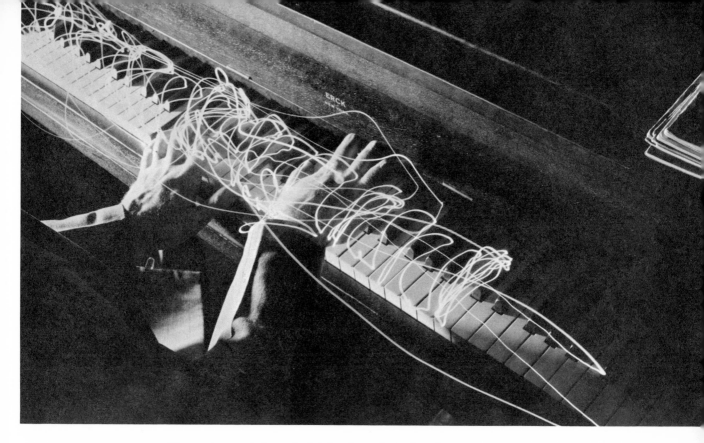

The motions made by a pianist's hands on the keyboard

Ketelbey's own favorites were his two symphonic suites *Three Fanciful Etchings* and *Sweet Romantic*.

KETTLEDRUM (or Timpany). The most important of the percussion instruments, it consists of a hemispherical shell of copper or an alloy, with a "head," usually made of calfskin, which is stretched across the top. The tension of this skin is controlled by screws. The kettledrum was introduced into the orchestra about 1670. See *Percussion*.

KEY (1). A system of tones. To say that a piece of music is in the key of C major, etc., indicates that it adheres to the note material relating to the scale in question, and that the tonic (keynote) of that scale is a governing factor in its musical structure. See *Music, Elements of*.

KEY (2). One of the levers on a piano, organ, etc., depressed by the fingers of the player to produce the tones. See *Keyboard*.

KEY, Francis Scott. American author of *The Star-Spangled Banner* (1779–1843). Key, a lawyer by profession, interceded for the release of an American physician being held prisoner by the British fleet during the war of 1812. He was detained aboard a British man-of-war while Fort McHenry was bombarded through the night of September 13-14, 1814. Seeing the American flag still flying in the morning, he was inspired to write the verses on the back of an envelope. The words were set to the tune of a then popular drinking song, *To Anacreon in Heaven*. See *Star-Spangled Banner, The*.

KEYBOARD. The row of levers on the piano, organ, accordion, celesta, etc., by which the fingers sound the notes. It received its present form in the middle of the fifteenth century. The modern piano keyboard usually has eighty-eight keys spanning seven and a quarter octaves. Bach's harpsichord had only five octaves.

KHACHATURIAN, Aram Ilyich. Russian composer (1903—). Khachaturian moved to Moscow in 1921, and entered the Gnessin School of Music, first in the cello class and after

1925 in the composition class. From 1929 to 1934 he studied at the Moscow Conservatory in Miaskovsky's composition class. He has since lived in Moscow.

Khachaturian's music bears the mark of Armenian folk music, and has its origins in Russian classical Orientalism, in principles worked out by Glinka, Balakirev, Borodin, and Rimsky-Korsakov. With its powerful rhythmic momentum, its dramatic contrasts, its dynamics and wealth of Oriental colorings, it makes a highly forceful impact. His talents are perhaps heard at their best in the ballet *Gayne,* from which he arranged two suites; his Piano Concerto, Violin Concerto, Cello Concerto, and *Masquerade Suite* are also much played. Khachaturian won the Stalin Prize for his Violin Concerto (1940), *Gayne* (1941), his Second Symphony (1943), which took as its theme "the wrath of the Soviet people waging a fight for humanity," and the music to the film *The Battle for Stalingrad.* He is the composer of the national anthem of the Armenian Soviet Socialist Republic.

Khachaturian has been given the title People's Artist of the Soviet Union and decorated with the Order of Lenin and the Order of the Red Workers' Flag. In 1947 he was elected deputy

ARAM KHACHATURIAN

to the Supreme Soviet of the Armenian Soviet Socialist Republic. In 1948, with Prokofiev and Shostakovitch, he was publicly rebuked by the Central Committee of the Communist Party for "formalist trends" and "bourgeois ideology," and undertook to mend his ways.

Best-known works:

Piano Concerto, composed and first performed in 1937
Poem for Stalin, composed and first performed in 1938
Violin Concerto, composed and first performed in 1940
Gayne (1941), ballet, first performed 1942 (includes the famous *Sabre Dance*)
Cello Concerto, composed and first performed in 1947
Symphony No. 2, composed and first performed 1943
Three arias for solo voice with orchestra (1947)
Music to the film *The Battle for Stalingrad* (1949)
Ode of Lamentation, in memory of Lenin, composed and first performed 1949
Poem Overture, composed and first performed 1950

KHOVANTCHINA. Next to *Boris Godunov,* Mussorgsky's most important opera. The orchestral introduction is often heard although the opera is infrequently staged in this country. The libretto deals with Russian political history in Peter the Great's time. The opera, composed between 1872 and 1880, was completed and orchestrated by Rimsky-Korsakov. This version had its first performance in St. Petersburg in 1886. It contains some of Mussorgsky's finest lyrical passages, but is less cogent and unitary, dramatically, than *Boris Godunov.*

KHRENNIKOV, Tikhon. Russian composer (1913–). Khrennikov studied at the Moscow Conservatory with Shebalin. His works include symphonies, a piano concerto, and operas. As secretary-general of the Union of Soviet Composers, he took part in denouncing Prokofiev and other musicians for "formalism" in 1948.

KIENZL, Wilhelm. Austrian composer (1857–1941). A native of Graz, he was encouraged by Liszt and influenced by Wagner, about whom he later wrote a monograph. His compositions include many songs, piano pieces, choral and orchestral works, in addition to nine operas, of which one, *Der Evangelimann,* was greatly successful for some years after its first production in Berlin in 1895.

KIEPURA, Jan. Polish tenor (1902–). His

A scene design for Khovantchina at the Bolshoi Theater in Moscow

opera career began in Warsaw in 1926 and continued in Vienna, Berlin, Milan, London, Paris, South America, and New York, where he sang at the Metropolitan Opera from 1937 to 1938 and 1941 to 1942. With his wife, Marta Eggerth, he has given many concert tours, and has starred in several motion pictures and on Broadway in a successful revival of *The Merry Widow.* His roles at the Metropolitan included Rudolfo in *La Bohème,* the Duke in *Rigoletto,* Don José in *Carmen,* and Des Grieux in *Manon.*

KINDERSCENEN *(Scenes of Childhood).* A collection of piano pieces by Schumann, forming his Op. 15. It was published in 1838. In a letter to his fiancée, Clara Wieck, the composer described how the work came into being: "I don't know whether or not it is an echo of what you once said to me—that sometimes you think I am like a child—anyway, I was suddenly inspired, and dashed off thirty quaint little pieces. I have chosen a dozen of these, and called them 'Scenes of Childhood.' I am sure you will enjoy them; but to do so, naturally you must forget that you are really a virtuoso."

Another letter written at the same time gives an indication of how greatly Schumann was inspired by Clara: "It is very curious, but if I write much to you, as I am doing now, I cannot compose. The music all goes out to you."

There are thirteen pieces in *Scenes of Childhood:*

1. *Von fremden Länder und Menschen* (Of foreign lands and peoples)
2. *Curiose Geschichte* (Strange story)
3. *Hasche-Mann* (Playing "tag")
4. *Bittendes Kind* (Child's petition)
5. *Glückes genug* (Quite happy)
6. *Wichtige Begebenheit* (Important event)
7. *Träumerei* (Reverie)
8. *Am Kamin* (At the fireside).
9. *Ritter vom Steckenpferd* (Knight of the hobby-horse)
10. *Fast zu ernst* (Almost too severe)
11. *Fürchtenmachen* (Frightening)
12. *Kind im Einschlummern* (Child falling asleep)
13. *Der Dichter spricht* (The poet speaks)

Schumann emphasized that the pieces were not written for children, but were an adult's appreciation of childhood composed for adults. He also explained that the titles were allotted afterward, as suggested by the atmosphere of the music.

The best known of the pieces is *Träumerei:*

KINDLER, Hans. Dutch-American conductor and cellist (1892–1949). Kindler studied cello and piano at the Rotterdam Conservatory, receiving first prize in both instruments upon his graduation in 1906. He continued his cello studies with Pablo Casals. He toured Europe and the United States as a cello virtuoso, settling in America. In 1931 he organized and conducted the National Symphony Orchestra in Washington, D. C., and held this post until his resignation in 1948.

KING, Wayne. American orchestra leader (1901–). King was a pioneer in broadcasting and became radio's most popular dance-band leader in the 1930s.

KIPNIS, Alexander. Russian-American bass singer (1891–). Even as a child Alexander Kipnis had a fine voice. His father, who wanted his son to go into business, only reluctantly agreed to send the boy to the Warsaw Conservatory, which recommended further training in Berlin.

When the first World War broke out Kipnis was interned. But a German colonel heard him sing and summoned his brother, who was an impresario, with the result that Kipnis was engaged for the Hamburg Opera.

He arrived in America in 1922 as a member of the Wagner Festival touring company, and sang all the leading bass roles in nine seasons at the Chicago Civic Opera. During this period he became an American citizen.

He later became the leading bass at the Berlin State Opera and was a perennial guest at Covent Garden and the Bayreuth and Salzburg festivals. In Vienna, too, he was immensely popular. He made his debut at the Metropolitan Opera in 1936 and during the next ten years gave notable performances in many roles, including Boris Godunov, Sarastro in *The Magic Flute,* Gurnemanz in *Parsifal,* and Arkel in *Pelléas et Mélisande*. His son Igor has become a well-known harpsichordist.

KIRCHGESSNER, Marianne. German harmonica virtuoso (1770–1809). Blind from the age of four, she became celebrated throughout Europe for her performances on the glass harmonica. It was for her that Mozart composed his Adagio for that instrument, and his Quintet for harmonica, flute, oboe, viola, and cello.

KIRCHNER, Leon. American composer (1919–). Kirchner grew up in California, where he studied piano as a child. At the University of California in Berkeley he studied theory with

Hans Kindler and Rudolf Firkusny

ALEXANDER KIPNIS

Elkus and Strickland and composition with Ernest Bloch. In 1942 he went to New York to study with Roger Sessions.

After serving with the armed forces during World War II, Kirchner returned to Berkeley for a Master's degree in music. In 1947 he was appointed to the faculty. He was granted a Guggenheim Fellowship in 1948, and in 1950 he was made an associate professor at the University of California at Los Angeles. In 1954, Kirchner became a professor at Mills College.

Kirchner's important orchestral works include his *Sinfonia*, first performed with the New York Philharmonic Orchestra in 1952; Toccata for Strings, Wind Instruments, and Percussion (1956); and a piano concerto which he first performed himself with the New York Philharmonic Orchestra in 1956. He has also written vocal compositions and chamber music.

KIRKBY-LUNN, Louise. English mezzo-soprano (1873–1930). Equally celebrated in concert, oratorio, and opera, she was a star at Covent Garden and with the Carl Rosa Company in London, and with the Henry Savage Company in America. Her most famous roles were Orfeo, Dalila, Amneris in *Aïda,* Fricka in *Die Walküre,* and Ortrud in *Lohengrin.* Her

RALPH KIRKPATRICK

last opera appearance was at Covent Garden in 1923, as Kundry in *Parsifal.*

KIRKPATRICK, John. American pianist (1905–). Kirkpatrick graduated from Princeton University in 1926, and studied in Paris with Isidor Philipp and Nadia Boulanger. He has appeared in recitals and in chamber music concerts in the United States, and is principally interested in American music. In 1939 he performed from memory the enormously difficult *Concord Sonata* by Charles Ives.

KIRKPATRICK, Ralph. American harpsichordist (1911–). Acclaimed by Carleton Sprague Smith as "the ablest harpsichordist in this country," Ralph Kirkpatrick is known throughout the world for his remarkable interpretations of eighteenth-century music. He studied with Wanda Landowska and Günter Ramin. His American debut in 1934 was an immediate success, and Kirkpatrick has since played recitals all over the world, appearing as soloist with many major symphony orchestras. His book on Domenico Scarlatti, published in 1953, has received wide acclaim. He is currently a professor of music at Yale University.

KIRSTEN, Dorothy. American soprano (1919–). Dorothy Kirsten studied at the Juilliard School of Music in New York, earning her tuition as a telephone operator. By 1938 she had frequently been engaged to sing over the radio,

Dorothy Kirsten as Manon in Puccini's Manon Lescaut

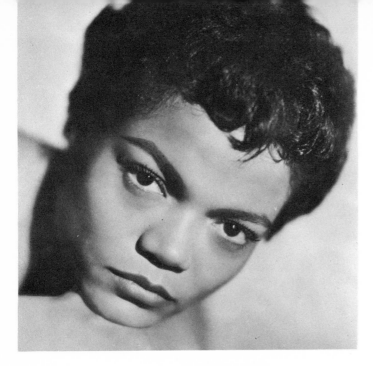

EARTHA KITT

and on one of these occasions Grace Moore heard her and offered to finance her career, and later coached her. Miss Kirsten studied in Europe, and returning to the United States in 1940, she made her debut with the Chicago Opera Company. She traveled widely, and was engaged by the New York City Opera in 1944 to sing major soprano roles.

Since 1945, when she made her debut as Mimi in *La Bohème,* she has been a leading soprano of the Metropolitan Opera and has been heard frequently over radio and television. She is one of the most successful American singers, and has appeared in several motion pictures, including *Mr. Music* and *The Great Caruso.*

KISS ME, KATE. Musical comedy by Cole Porter, with book by Sam and Bella Spewack and lyrics by the composer. First performed at the Majestic Theater, New York, in 1948, the show has since been seen all over the Western world.

A scene from the original Broadway production of Kiss Me, Kate

The action takes place before, during, and after an American company's performance of Shakespeare's *The Taming of the Shrew*—in the dressing rooms, on the stage, and in the corridor leading to the stage.

The plot of Shakespeare's comedy, in which the manly, forceful Petruchio tames the temperamental and beautiful Katherine, and Lucentio woos Katherine's younger sister Bianca, is paralleled in the private lives of the actors. Lois Lane (Bianca), in a knee-length dress and endlessly chewing gum, is continually trying to get hold of a dollar or two to extricate the small-time actor Bill Calhoun (Lucentio) from his financial difficulties. The stylish Lilli Vanessi (Katherine) carries on with a wealthy, middle-aged admirer, because Fred Graham (Petruchio), her divorced husband—who can never resist the flattery of the chorus girls—takes too long to discover that it is really Lilli whom he loves. Two amiable gangster types provide the crazy comedy.

KISTLER, Cyrill. German composer (1848–1907). A devoted Wagnerian, he was cited by Bernard Shaw as one of the most talented of composers. However, his many works, including several operas, orchestral pieces, songs, and choral music, have not survived the test of time.

KITT, Eartha. American singer and actress (1928–). Eartha Kitt left a job in a shirt factory to join Katherine Dunham's touring revue *Caribbean Rhapsody* in 1946. Leaving the company in Paris, she was singing in night clubs when she was noticed by Orson Welles, who cast her as Helen of Troy in his *Dr. Faustus* and dubbed her "the most exciting woman in the world." It was, however, her phenomenal success in *New Faces of 1952* that made her internationally famous.

Since then, Miss Kitt has enhanced her reputation as a singer and actress by her television, stage, and night-club appearances in the United States and Europe. She has made many popular recordings, and her films *New Faces* (1953), *Anna Lucasta* (1956), and *Accused* (1957) have also been much praised. Her autobiography is entitled *Thursday's Child*.

KLAFSKY, Katharina. Hungarian soprano (1855–1896). She began as a domestic servant and was sent by her employers for voice study. For some years, she sang secondary roles and then, for a few years before her death, was a star in Wagnerian roles at the Hamburg Opera, Covent Garden in London, and with the Damrosch Opera Company in America. One of her most famous roles was Fidelio.

KLAMI, Uuno. Finnish composer (1900–1961). A pupil of Ravel, he was best known for his *Kalevala* Suite. Among his many choral and symphonic works are two symphonies, violin and piano concertos, and the *King Lear* Overture. He also composed music for plays of Eugene O'Neill.

KLAVIER. German, "keyboard instrument."

KLEBE, Giselher. German composer (1925–). Klebe belongs to the new generation of German composers who became known through the efforts of such organizations as the Internationale Ferienkurse für Neue Musik in Darmstadt and the Donaueschingen Music Festival. He studied with Boris Blacher and Josef Rufer in Berlin. His compositions are written in the twelve-tone idiom. His most important works include *Die Zwitschermaschine* (inspired by a painting by Paul Klee), *Elegia Appassionata* for piano, violin, and cello (Op. 22), Symphony for Forty-two Strings (1951), Concerto for Violin, Violoncello and Orchestra (1954), and the opera *Die Räuber* (1957).

KLEIBER, Erich. Austrian conductor (1890–1956). Kleiber was one of the foremost opera conductors of his time. His career is intimately linked with two famous institutions, the Berlin

ERICH KLEIBER

State Opera and the Teatro Colón in Buenos Aires. Kleiber was director of the Berlin State Opera from 1923 to 1935, and during this period he first conducted operas by Křenek, Milhaud, and Alban Berg, among other contemporary works. He voluntarily left his Berlin post in protest against the policies of the Nazi government and went to Cuba where he formed an excellent orchestra. Subsequently Kleiber became an Argentinian citizen and was one of the most important conductors ever to head the Teatro Colón.

In 1950 Kleiber returned to Europe. During the next three years he was guest conductor at Covent Garden, London; then he went back to Berlin to become director of the State Opera for the second time. In 1956 he once again left this renowned opera house, this time after a bitter controversy with the East German Communist regime which controlled the State Opera.

KLEIN, Herman. English critic (1856–1934). He studied singing with Manuel García and was himself a singing teacher. He was music critic of *The Sunday Times* for twenty years and also wrote for the New York *Herald*. His many books, among them a life of Patti, are a valuable guide to the musical life of his time.

OTTO KLEMPERER

KLEIN, Jacques. Brazilian pianist (1930–). After studies with William Kapell and others, Klein in 1953 entered and won the Geneva International Competition. Soon thereafter he embarked on his first concert tour, making his orchestral debut with the Philharmonia Orchestra in London. Subsequently he made many concert and recital tours of Europe and South America, including solo appearances with the London Philharmonic, Vienna Symphony, Santa Cecilia (Rome), Mozarteum (Salzburg), and other orchestras. He made his United States debut in 1959 as soloist with the New York Philharmonic Orchestra.

KLEINSINGER, George. American composer (1914–). A graduate of the Juilliard School, he is best known for his *Tubby the Tuba* (1942), an entertaining and educational work in which the characters are represented by musical instruments. Among his other works are *archy and mehitabel* and *Peewee the Piccolo*. He also has composed choral and orchestral music, a string quartet, and the charming children's opera, *The Tree That Found Christmas*.

KLEMPERER, Otto. German conductor (1885–). Klemperer studied in Hamburg, Frankfurt, and Berlin. Gustav Mahler recognized the young musician's great talent and recommended him to the German Theater in Prague. Engagements elsewhere in Europe followed, and Klemperer soon became director of the Cologne Opera. He went from there to Berlin to become musical director of the Kroll Opera, and his activities in this post attracted wide attention. Not only did he perform the standard repertoire with a new purity of style, but he also became noted for his first performances of contemporary operas by Stravinsky, Křenek, Hindemith, Schoenberg, and others. In 1933, the Nazi government forced him to resign his post, and he came to the United States, where he had made a concert tour in 1925.

Klemperer was engaged as musical director of the Los Angeles Philharmonic Orchestra, and within a few seasons developed that orchestra into one of the finest musical organizations in the United States. He was guest conductor of many American and European orchestras.

Ill health forced him to curtail his activities for a number of years. Under the most trying conditions, he re-entered the lists as director of the Budapest Opera in 1947, resigning three years later. Klemperer has toured Europe and America since that time, appearing with the major symphony orchestras.

KLETZKI, Paul. Polish conductor and composer (1900–). Paul Kletzki studied composition in Poland and Berlin. He became known as a conductor comparatively late in his career. After engagements with the Israel Philharmonic Orchestra and various European orchestras, he was appointed musical director of the Liverpool Philharmonic Orchestra in 1954. His recordings made him well known in the United States, and in 1958 he became conductor of the Dallas Symphony Orchestra.

KLINDWORTH, Karl. German pianist and conductor (1830–1916). He began as a violinist and then became a piano pupil of Liszt. For a time, he was conductor of the Berlin Philharmonic and was prominent as manager, pianist, conductor, and teacher in the musical life of England and Germany. He is best known for his piano arrangements, particularly those of Wagner's *Ring* operas.

KLOSE, Margarete. German mezzo-soprano (1905–). She has been prominent, mainly in Strauss and Wagner roles, for many years at the Berlin Staatsoper and the Bayreuth festivals. She also has sung in London at Covent Garden and with the San Francisco Opera.

KNAPPERTSBUSCH, Hans. German conductor (1888–). In 1922 Knappertsbusch succeeded Bruno Walter as general music director of the Munich State Opera, a post he held until he resigned in 1938 following a controversy with Nazi authorities. After World War II he conducted at every music center of Europe, including the Bayreuth Festival.

KNEISEL, Franz. Romanian-American violinist (1865–1926). From 1885 until 1903, Kneisel was concertmaster and soloist with the Boston Symphony Orchestra. In 1887 he founded the Kneisel Quartet, which played with great success in the United States and Europe for thirty years. He was a professor of violin at the Institute of Musical Art in New York City.

KNOCH, Ernst. German conductor (1875–1959). He was Felix Mottl's assistant at the Karlsruhe Opera, then conducted at Bayreuth and other centers. On a world tour he conducted the first Australian performance of *Tristan und Isolde*. In 1914 he settled in the United States.

KNOTE, Heinrich. German tenor (1870–1953). He was a member of the court opera at Munich from 1892 until 1914, but obtained a leave of absence to sing elsewhere, and was a leading German tenor at the Metropolitan for several seasons. He later sang in Berlin, Würzburg, and again in Munich.

KOBBÉ, Gustav. American author (1857–1918). He wrote for many musical publications and was the author of the famous *Complete Opera Book,* as well as books on Wagner and his operas.

KOCHANSKI, Paul. Polish violinist (1887–1934). He was concertmaster of the Warsaw Philharmonic, studied with César Thomson in Berlin, and taught in Russia until 1921, when he came to the United States. He taught at the Juilliard School of Music from 1924, and concertized widely in the United States and Europe. He was a champion of modern music.

KÖCHEL, Ludwig von. See *K.*

KODÁLY, Zoltán. Hungarian composer (1882–). Kodály grew up in a small provincial town that afforded no facilities for serious musical studies. Although he played the violin, sang in the church choir, and also began to compose, it was not until he became a student at the University of Budapest, and at the same time enrolled himself as a pupil of the Conservatory, that his musical training began. Most of his student works, influenced by Brahms and later by Debussy, were destroyed by the composer.

Aware that the published "Hungarian" folk music did not give a true picture of the folk melodies of his homeland, Kodály began in 1905 to collect folk songs; on his extensive travels, spread over many years, he collected more than three thousand melodies. In 1906 he began a long association with Béla Bartók, becoming professor at the Budapest Conservatory in the same year. In 1919 he was appointed deputy director, and in 1946 president, of the Conservatory.

As a composer Kodály became known for his songs and chamber music, but he first gained the ear of the public with the choral work *Psalmus Hungaricus,* written in 1923 on the occasion of the golden jubilee of the union of the two towns Buda and Pest.

Shortly afterward Kodály showed another aspect of his genius in the splendidly gay and elegant music of the opera *Háry János,* which in the form of a suite has won universal popularity. He next showed his feeling for picturesque effects in a couple of finely instrumented dance suites, *Dances of Marosszék* and *Galànta Dances.*

ZOLTÁN KODÁLY

Kodály has subsequently confirmed his reputation as Hungary's most eminent composer, after Bartók, with a series of large choral and orchestral works. His Mass, with the somewhat misleading title *Missa Brevis* (originally an organ Mass, but in 1945 rewritten for orchestra), is frequently played, and his Concerto for Orchestra, his Orchestral Variations, and his *Kádár Kata,* a Transylvanian folk ballad for singers and light orchestra, have aroused great interest. Edwin Evans sums up Kodály's style: "Three strands are entwined in Kodály's music. The most prominent and therefore most easily recognizable is the national . . . Hungarian folk music. Next to that, and equally important, is that Kodály is a born lyrist, with a gift of melody. If one could imagine a modern Hungarian Schubert he would fit the description, except that he is more passionate. . . . The third strand is the leaning to the picturesque, which is given free play in *Háry János* and elsewhere. . . . He stands out as a tone-poet, imbued with lyrical feeling."

Best-known works:

ORCHESTRAL
Orchestral Suite from the opera *Háry János* (1926)
Dances of Marosszék (1930)
Galànta Dances (1933)
Concerto for Orchestra
Peacock Variations
Theater Overture (1927)
Symphony No. 1 (1961)

CHAMBER MUSIC
Duo for Cello and Violin, Op. 7 (1914)
Quartet No. 1, Op. 2 (1908)
Quartet No. 2, Op. 10 (1916–18)
Sonata for Cello, Op. 8 (1915)
Sonata for Cello and Piano, Op. 4 (1909–10)

PIANO
It Is Raining in the Village, Op. 11, No. 3 (1917–18)

CHORAL AND VOCAL
Psalmus Hungaricus (Psalm 55) (1923)
Jesus and the Traders (1934)
Missa Brevis (1945)
Te Deum (1936)

KOECHLIN, Charles. French composer and writer (1867–1951). A pupil of Massenet and Fauré, Koechlin published numerous works on musical theory, and was for many years president of the French section of I.S.C.M.

His own compositions in an individual harmonic and contrapuntal style were recognized and admired, though only a few of them were printed, and none became really popular. But he exercised a great influence on the younger generation of French composers.

Koechlin named as his chief works:

Sonatas for cello and piano, violin and piano, choir and piano, etc

Landscapes (1914), *Sea Pictures* (1916), *The Old Country House* (1920), all for piano

Four Symphonic Poems, based on Kipling's *Jungle Book*

Two Symphonies; a musical homage based on the name BACH

Doctor Fabricius, symphonic poem, first performed in 1949

He also wrote a short opera, ballets and incidental music, film scores, numerous choral and orchestral works and songs, and chamber and instrumental works.

KOGAN, Leonid. Russian violinist (1924–). Kogan studied the violin with his father, a photographer and amateur musician, and at the age of ten went to Moscow to work with Abram Yampolsky at the Moscow Conservatory. He graduated in 1948. He was appointed to the Conservatory faculty, and organized a concert trio with the pianist Emil Gilels and the cellist Mstislav Rostropovitch. He married a sister of Gilels, a violinist, and has often appeared with her in works for two violins. In 1951, he received the first prize at the International Competition in Brussels. In 1958 he made his American debut, and has played with major American symphony orchestras. He is in the first rank of the world's violinists.

KOHS, Ellis B. American composer (1916–). Kohs studied at several institutions, including the Juilliard School of Music. Among his teachers were Bernard Wagenaar, Hugo Leichtentritt, Roy Harris, Walter Piston, and Igor Stravinsky. He was awarded a Ditson Fellowship at Columbia University in 1946. His works include chamber, choral, orchestral, and piano music.

KOLISCH, Rudolf. Austrian-American violinist (1896–). Kolisch was introduced to chamber music in his childhood. During his student days he became a friend and associate of Arnold Schoenberg and participated in the concerts of the Schoenberg Society. In 1922 he organized the Vienna String Quartet, and five years later the Kolisch Quartet. This outstanding ensemble

LEONID KOGAN

was invited to the United States in 1935 to play in the Library of Congress, and subsequently settled in this country. It is justly famous for its brilliant interpretations of contemporary music (Schoenberg, Bartók, Berg, Webern), and has become quartet-in-residence at Michigan State University.

KOL NIDREI. Hebrew, "All Promises." One of the most sacred of Hebrew melodies, sung in the synagogue on the Day of Atonement. The German composer Max Bruch wrote a set of variations for cello and orchestra on this melody, first performed in Leipzig in 1881. In the first part of Bruch's work the cello introduces the tenderly beautiful melody, which is worked up into a number of variations, leading to the second part, in which Bruch makes the orchestra introduce a particularly moving melody, later taken up by the cello. The work has also been arranged for cello and piano.

KOLODIN, Irving. American music critic (1908–). Irving Kolodin is one of the most prominent American music critics, writers, and commentators. He studied at the Institute of Musical Art in New York City and in 1930 joined its faculty as an instructor in harmony

KIRIL KONDRASHIN

and theory. From 1932 until 1950 he was music critic of the New York *Sun,* and since then he has been music editor and associate editor of the *Saturday Review.* He has lectured at the Juilliard School and, from 1953 to 1959, was program annotator for the New York Philharmonic Orchestra. Among his books are *The Metropolitan Opera, The Kingdom of Swing* (with Benny Goodman), *The Critical Composer, Guide to Recorded Music, The Composer as Listener,* and *The Musical Life.*

KONDRASHIN, Kiril. Russian conductor (1914–). Born in Moscow, Kondrashin studied piano and conducting at the Moscow Conservatory. He has directed opera in Moscow and Leningrad and also made many appearances as guest conductor of orchestral concerts. He regularly makes guest appearances throughout the Soviet Union. He came to New York to conduct the Symphony of the Air with Van Cliburn as soloist, in the Tchaikovsky and Rachmaninoff concertos; he had conducted these works at the International Tchaikovsky Competition, which Cliburn won. He has recorded with Cliburn, Sviatoslav Richter, David Oistrakh, Emil Gilels, and Leonid Kogan.

KONITZ, Lee. American jazz saxophonist (1927–). After study at Roosevelt College, Chicago, he played with Claude Thornhill and Miles Davis. He has appeared with Lennie Tristano, toured Scandinavia, and was associated with Stan Kenton before heading his own group. He is one of the relatively few alto saxophonists who have not been content to follow in the footsteps of Charlie Parker. See *Jazz.*

KONYA, Sandor. Hungarian tenor. After making his reputation at La Scala and other leading opera houses of Europe, he sang with the San Francisco Opera and made his debut at the Metropolitan Opera as Lohengrin in 1961. One of today's outstanding tenors, he is equally successful in German and Italian roles.

KORJUS, Miliza. Polish coloratura soprano (1912–). Miliza Korjus grew up in Kiev, and acquired her first knowledge of singing from her father's large collection of recordings of operatic singers. At the age of seventeen she went to Latvia to try her luck as a concert singer, and after studying for a time at the Moscow Conservatory she made her name on a concert tour of Sweden and Finland. Having appeared in many operas and operettas, always with increasing popularity, she was given a Hollywood contract.

KORN, Peter Jona. German-American conductor and composer (1922–). Korn started to compose at the age of six, and at nine was accepted in a special composition class at the Berlin Hochschule für Musik. From 1933 to 1936 he attended school in England, studying with Edmund Rubbra, and made his conducting debut at the age of thirteen. For the next five years he lived in Palestine, studying composition with Stefan Wolpe at the Jerusalem Conservatory. He came to the United States in 1941 and was made a citizen in 1944. He studied with Ernst Toch and Arnold Schoenberg at the University of California, and in 1948 founded the New Orchestra of Los Angeles, which has built its reputation on the presentation of seldom-heard works.

KORN, Richard. American conductor (1908–). A graduate of Princeton (1928) and a student at the Juilliard School, Korn was a clarinetist with the National Symphony Orchestra in 1939 and 1940 and assistant conductor of the National Orchestral Association from 1940 to 1942. He won a fellowship in conducting with Koussevitzky in 1941, and was assistant conductor of the New York City Opera. He has appeared as guest conductor of symphony orchestras the world over. He is a prominent supporter of American music; the Orchestra of America, of which he is musical director, in its first two seasons (1959–60 and 1960–61) presented the works of fifty American composers.

KORNGOLD, Erich Wolfgang. Austrian composer (1897–1957). Korngold was a child prodigy who, at the age of thirteen, wrote a piano sonata that was played by Artur Schnabel. His one-act operas *Violanta* and *Der Ring des Polykrates* received their world premières under Bruno Walter in Munich in 1916. *Violanta* was also performed by the Metropolitan Opera in 1927. His opera *Die Tote Stadt* was first presented in Hamburg in 1920, and at the Metropolitan Opera in 1921, with Maria Jeritza in the chief role. Korngold modernized a number of Johann Strauss operettas and conducted them in Berlin and elsewhere. After 1934, he was active as a composer for motion pictures in Hollywood. He wrote incidental music for *Much Ado About Nothing,* and composed many orchestral and chamber music works, including the Violin Concerto in D major, Op. 35.

KÓSA, György. Hungarian composer and pianist (1897–). A pupil of Bartók and Dohnányi, he has been a noted accompanist and chamber-music player. His best-known works are oratorios, cantatas, and an opera-ballet, set to Biblical texts. Requiem Mass (1949) is Kósa's response to his country's sufferings in the war.

KOSHETZ, Nina. Russian soprano (1894–). She won fame first at the Moscow Imperial Opera, and then in joint recitals with Rachmaninoff. After appearances at the Paris Opéra, she joined the Chicago Civic Opera and became an outstanding concert artist. Recently, she has taught in Los Angeles and played prominent roles in motion pictures.

KOSMA, Josef. Hungarian composer (1905–). Long a citizen of Paris, he has composed symphonic music and many ballet and film scores. His songs, particularly those composed to texts by

Jacques Prévert, have won him great popularity.

KOSTELANETZ, André. Russian-American conductor (1901–). Kostelanetz was only twenty when he was appointed assistant conductor at the Imperial Opera, Petrograd. When, in 1922, the hunger and want that followed the Revolution made life there too difficult, Kostelanetz and his family came to America, where he found employment as accompanist for a number of well-known singers.

He studied American light music and was soon convinced that "popular music is also good music," and that "composers like Gershwin, Cole Porter, Rodgers, and Irving Berlin could and ought to be treated as seriously as Beethoven and Brahms." He made his American debut as a conductor in 1924 in early broadcasts from New York, and a few years later he was appointed permanent conductor of the Columbia Broadcasting System.

Kostelanetz won immense popularity with his original arrangements and "dehydrated classical music" or "middle music," as he called it: "I think it permissible to cut down large works to purely melodic passages." Long-drawn-out developments "are intended for musicians and only put off other people." As an example, Kos-

ANDRÉ KOSTELANETZ

telanetz managed to distill Tchaikovsky's overture to *Romeo and Juliet* from its normal sixteen minutes down to less than five.

He also gave his music a "new expression and sonority" by making use of variations of amplification in microphones. Kostelanetz has often appeared as guest conductor with the leading American and European symphony orchestras.

KOUSSEVITZKY, Serge Alexandrovitch. Russian-American conductor (1874–1951). Koussevitzky played at conducting orchestras as a child and, when he was seventeen, with only three rubles in his pocket left his home town for Moscow to study music. His only income while at the Philharmonic School was his fees as a double-bass player, which he thankfully accepted. After having passed the final examination with distinction in 1894, he gave solo concerts throughout Russia during the following ten years, and was considered one of the most able double-bass virtuosos.

Koussevitzky on the podium

Koussevitzky subsequently undertook concert tours in Germany, France, and England and became famous on his instrument. In 1905 he married the daughter of a Russian millionaire. When his father-in-law asked him what he would like for a wedding present he answered without hesitation, "A symphony orchestra!" His wish was granted, and he was given the money he needed to found an orchestra of seventy-five players.

He gave his first concerts in Moscow in 1907, conducting first performances of many works by younger Russian composers, including Scriabin and Stravinsky.

In 1910–14 he and his orchestra undertook three concert tours in hired steamboats, traveling thousands of miles down the Volga, and brought the music of Beethoven, Brahms, and Tchaikovsky to places which had never heard a symphonic orchestra before. The first tour alone cost him $125,000, but this did not deter him from his work of bringing music to the people.

For a short time after the Russian Revolution he was director of the Russian State Orchestra, but in 1920 he fled to Paris. "I left Russia because of Lenin and Trotsky," he said. "I had a million dollars and they took them from me!"

In Paris he started a publishing business to issue the works of the new Russian composers, and organized the brilliant Koussevitzky concerts which became the chief musical events of the Paris season.

When in 1924 he was asked to take over the moribund Boston Symphony Orchestra, he wrote: "I shall give Boston music it has never heard before!" His reorganization swiftly made the Boston one of the world's foremost orchestras.

Koussevitzky was a persevering advocate of a musical center where composers, serious students, and ordinary listeners could come to play, learn, and hear. His ambition was realized with the inauguration in 1938 of Tanglewood, in the Berkshire Mountains of Massachusetts, a combination of school, university, and concert hall which has been of great importance to the musical development of the United States. See *Berkshire Music Center.*

In 1943 the conductor founded in memory of his wife the Koussevitzky Music Foundation, which encourages young composers by commissioning works and making grants.

KRALL, Heidi. American soprano. Heidi Krall

HEIDI KRALL

LILI KRAUS

studied with Nevada van der Veer at the Cleveland Conservatory. She appeared in small opera companies, in Broadway musicals, and in a leading role in the London production of Menotti's *The Consul*. In 1953 she won the Metropolitan Auditions of the Air and began her membership with the Metropolitan Opera. She has since portrayed Elisabeth in *Tannhäuser* and Desdemona in *Otello* at the Berlin State Opera, sung at Lewisohn Stadium, Chautauqua, and Red Rocks (Denver), and has frequently appeared on television.

KRAMARZ-KROMMER (or Cramer), František. Bohemian composer and violinist (1759–1831). A violinist, choirmaster, and bandmaster, he became a favorite of the Emperor Francis II and composed about 150 works in the style of Haydn and Mozart that are now forgotten but were popular in his time.

KRAMER, A. Walter. American composer and critic (1890–). Kramer served on the staff of *Musical America* between 1910 and 1922, and after devoting himself to composing in Europe for several years, returned in 1929 to become editor-in-chief of that publication. He served as the first musical director for the Columbia Broadcasting System and in recent years has been active in music publishing. He has written

two symphonies, orchestral works, choruses, and instrumental pieces in addition to more than three hundred other compositions and one hundred songs which have been published.

KRASNER, Louis. Russian-American violinist (1903–). Krasner was brought to the United States as a small child. He was graduated from the New England Conservatory in Boston in 1923, and continued his studies abroad with Karl Flesch, Lucien Capet, and Otakar Sevčik. In 1934, he commissioned Alban Berg to write a violin concerto for him; Krasner played it for the first time at the Barcelona Festival of the International Society for Contemporary Music in 1936. He also performed the première of Schoenberg's Violin Concerto in 1940. He is professor of music at Syracuse University.

KRAUS, Lili. Hungarian-British pianist (1905–). Lili Kraus studied with Bartók, Kodály, and Artur Schnabel, and taught at the Vienna Conservatory for several years. She was detained by the Japanese in the Dutch East Indies during World War II. She became a British subject in 1948. She is noted for many fine performances with the violinist Szymon Goldberg, and has made several appearances in the United States with major symphony orchestras. She has made a long series of tours

FRITZ KREISLER

conducting in Philadelphia and New York. When Furtwängler relinquished his directorship of the Berlin State Opera, Krauss became his successor for a brief period, but he soon left to become director of the Bavarian State Opera in Munich.

Krauss was one of the important conductors of his time. Although he led famous performances of the Wagner operas at Bayreuth, he was most celebrated as an interpreter of Mozart and Richard Strauss. He was a close friend of Strauss and often conducted performances of his operas in which Viorica Ursuleac, who was Frau Krauss, sang the leading roles. Thus, Frau and Herr Krauss were prima donna and conductor at the world premières of Strauss' *Arabella, Capriccio, Die Liebe der Danaë,* and *Friedenstag,* which is dedicated to them. Frau Krauss often was accompanied in recitals by her husband.

KRAUSS, Gabrielle. Austrian soprano (1842–1906). She was a pupil of Mathilde Marchesi, who was probably the most famous singing teacher in history. Mme. Krauss first was a star of the Vienna Hofoper and then of the Paris Opéra, where she sang in the gala concert that opened the present opera house in 1875. Three nights later, she sang in the first regular performance, as Rachel in *La Juive.* When *Aïda* had its French première, she sang the title role. According to Mme. Marchesi in her *Memoirs,* Mme. Krauss was both a great actress and a great singer.

KREHBIEL, Henry Edward. American critic and author (1854–1923). He was for six years the music critic of the Cincinnati *Gazette* and then, in 1880, became the music critic of the New York *Herald,* a post he retained for 43 years. In addition, he was an authority on Negro music, active as a lecturer, and one of the earliest American champions of Wagner, Brahms, and Tchaikovsky. His position and influence in the musical life of New York were second to none, and many of the books he wrote are still of importance, including his study of Afro-American folk music, several works on opera, and his definitive edition of Thayer's *Life of Beethoven.*

KREIN, Alexander. Russian composer (1883–1951). He and his brother Grigory were the creators of a school of music based on Jewish

throughout Europe, Asia, Australia, Africa, and America, and is particularly well known for her interpretations of Mozart's music.

KRAUS, Otokar. Czech baritone (1911–). A leading figure in English opera, he has sung at Covent Garden in many Italian, German, and English operas. One of his most celebrated performances was as Caspar in *Der Freischütz* opposite Joan Sutherland. He created the roles of Diomede in Walton's *Troilus and Cressida* (1954) and King Fisher in Tippett's *The Midsummer Marriage* (1955). In 1951 in Venice, he created the role of Nick Shadow in Stravinsky's *The Rake's Progress.*

KRAUSS, Clemens. Austrian conductor (1893–1954). Krauss studied at the Vienna Conservatory. After being choir conductor at the theater in Brünn (Brno) and holding appointments in various German towns, he became director of the Vienna State Opera in 1929, and was one of the leading conductors at the Salzburg festivals. In 1929 he also visited the United States, sources in Russia. His best-known work outside Russia is his film music. He composed an opera, chamber and orchestral music, piano and instrumental pieces, songs and arrangements of Jewish folk music, and incidental music for plays produced in the Jewish theaters in Russia.

KREISLER, Fritz. Austrian violinist and composer (1875–1962). Kreisler's first teacher was his father, a well-known doctor, who had great difficulty in persuading his son to practice. The boy's talent, however, was so obvious that his father decided that he should enter the Vienna Conservatory, and after three years, when he was only ten, he won a gold medal. He was sent to Paris and studied under Massart and Delibes; two years later he was awarded the Premier Grand Prix.

He began his career as a concert violinist by voyaging with Liszt's pupil Moriz Rosenthal to America. The anticipated success, however, did not materialize, and his father made him study medicine. But he soon returned to Paris, this time to become a painter. Called home for military service, he went to the Military Academy and passed with high honors, but the life of a soldier did not suit his temperament, and he still dreamed of becoming a violinist. After eight weeks' practice in a cabin in the mountains he regained his technical skill, and in 1899 had a new debut in Berlin. On a second trip to America he had an enormous success, and after a few years he was counted among the world's foremost violinists.

Kreisler was wounded in the first World War. The income he derived from extensive tours of the United States he sent home to assist his countrymen; this practice was brought to an end when America entered the war, but for a long time he organized welfare work on a grand scale and provided over 1,500 needy artists in his homeland with the necessities of life.

When Austria became more settled, the government offered Kreisler a diplomatic post, which he declined. He toured the world many times, and in 1933 settled in America. In 1941 he was involved in a traffic accident which rendered him incapable of playing for several years. When he walked onto the platform at his first concert after the war, in Carnegie Hall in New York, the audience rose to its feet and applauded him for several minutes.

Kreisler always remained a Viennese at heart, and Strauss and Lanner are reborn in his music. The three Viennese melodies *Liebesleid (Love's Sorrow), Liebesfreud (Love's Joy),* and *Schöne Rosmarin (Fair Rosemary),* which he composed in youth, were first published as newly discovered compositions by Lanner which Kreisler claimed to have found and rescored for violin. Kreisler rescored many old compositions for his own use, and when he exhausted these began to compose "old" pieces for himself, still claiming that they were rescorings. When he later admitted his "fraud" a sharp controversy arose as to whether a composer has any right to use someone else's name. The majority, however, took it—as Kreisler himself said—"with good humor and friendliness." The work had been done so cleverly that it was impossible not to admire Kreisler's skill; one of his "rescorings" was even used as an example of style at a historical concert. Other works by him include many violin virtuoso pieces such as *Caprice Viennois* and *Tambourin Chinois,* and a string quartet.

As a violinist Kreisler's chief characteristic was the irresistible charm which derived from his soft and sensitive but always lively tone. In his later years his concerts almost exclusively featured his own works, and his repertoire of classical works was always rather restricted. His interpretations were highly individual; even his methods of fingering were completely his own.

KREISLERIANA. Eight fantasias for piano, Op. 16, by Schumann, composed and published in 1838 and revised in 1850. Schumann took the title from E. T. A. Hoffmann's book *Fantasiestücke in Callots Manier,* in which a conductor named Kreisler plays a leading part. Schumann explained to a French admirer: "The title can only be fully understood by a German. Kreisler is a figure in one of E. T. A. Hoffmann's stories—an eccentric, wild, but efficient conductor. You will really appreciate him."

But it was Schumann's longing for his fiancée, Clara Wieck, that was the real theme of this music. He wrote to her about *Kreisleriana:* "One of your ideas, and you are the main theme yourself."

Later he wrote of this work and *Kinderscenen:* "Play my *Kreisleriana* sometimes. In some of the sections you will find a completely wild passion, your life and mine together, and many of your features. In *Kinderscenen* everything is the reverse—gentle, and happy, like our future."

R. H. Schauffler has commented: *"Kreisleri-ana* discloses the depths of its creator's mind, almost untouched by the realities of the outside world. It brings us close in to his sudden surprising changes of mood—despair, brooding melancholy, uncontrollable outbursts of joy. . . ."

KREMER, Isa. Romanian soprano (1887–1950). Known chiefly as a ballad singer, she was an authority on folk music, particularly those of Yiddish and Hebrew origin, and sang in recitals for many years both in Europe and America.

KŘENEK, Ernst. Austrian-American composer (1900–). Křenek studied at the State Academies of Music in Vienna and Berlin. The work which made him world-famous was his jazz opera *Jonny Spielt Auf* (1927), for which he also wrote the libretto.

In his student days he learned a moderate modernism which was based on German post-Romantic polyphony, but under Artur Schnabel's influence his work soon developed in a new direction. At the beginning of the 1920s Křenek entered what he calls his "first atonal" period (chief product, his Symphony No. 2).

As Křenek became more and more interested in the problem of personal freedom, it played an increasing part in his music. His little "theatrical cantata" *Zwingburg* (1922) treats of the "tragic fate which is the destiny of man, who does not seem able to reach a really free state, because people either surrender to unbridled anarchy or are sacrificed to dictatorship."

In 1924 Křenek went to Paris, and certain French composers' ideas made a deep impression on him. "I came to the conclusion that the direction I had followed hitherto in my work, was untenable. In my new outlook music should satisfy a real need in the society for which it is written—it should be useful, entertaining, and practical." The outcome of this period was *Jonny Spielt Auf,* the libretto of which was only an extreme "expression of my continual concern with the idea of freedom, this time in relation to my experience abroad. Jonny and his America were symbols of the full life, of optimism and freedom." See *Jonny Spielt Auf*

Křenek had interested himself little in religious questions, but he now gradually turned again to the Catholic Church in which he had been reared. At the same time he worked intensely on the question of musical expression, especially on atonality. "I buried myself in the study of the works of Schoenberg, Berg, and Webern as if I were taking a beginner's course in composition." After long reflection and study he resolved "to keep to the twelve-tone technique." He admits that "the work was desperately difficult to begin with, and it advanced very slowly. It was as if I had forgotten how to compose." Doubt whether the twelve-tone technique was justified constantly recurred, but he over-

A scene design for Křenek's opera, Karl V, *at the Prague National Theater*

came it because he felt that "no other method of writing would ever satisfy me again." See *Twelve-Tone Music.*

Even then Křenek produced many smaller compositions and commissioned works in which he did not use the twelve-tone technique. "I was never completely sure if it was a legitimate practice, or if I had broken a promise. . . . When I composed such pieces it was not my intention to admit that the twelve-tone technique is suited only to special, exclusive works. But perhaps that is just what it is. History will give us the answer."

He came to the United States in 1937 and became a citizen in 1945. He taught composition at Vassar College from 1939 to 1942 and was dean of fine arts at Hamline University, St. Paul, from 1942 to 1947. Since 1947 he has lived in Los Angeles, appearing as lecturer in the United States and in Europe.

He has stated: "Looking back over the evolution of my musical style, I am not astonished that even benevolent observers became confused and vacillating in their faith. Whenever they thought I had comfortably settled down in some stylistic district, I was not at the expected place the next time."

He cites the following as his chief works:

Second Symphony (1922), first performed 1923. "The largest orchestral work I have written so far. Bold, somewhat somnambulistic, reaching out for new possibilities. An extraordinarily expressive intensity in the last movement."
Orpheus and Eurydice (1923), opera, first performed 1926. "Expressionistic attempt at opera in the grand style."
Karl V (1933), opera, first performed 1938. "An ambitious historical, philosophical, and religious interpretation. My first essay in the twelve-tone technique."
String Quartet No. 7 (1943–44), first performed 1944. "The best integration of constructive consequence and expressive vitality which I have achieved so far."
Fourth Symphony (1947), first performed 1947. "Application to the monumental symphonic style of fifteen years of experience in the twelve-tone technique."

Křenek has written many other works for orchestra, operas, ballets, incidental music, choral works (notably *Lamentations of Jeremiah,* Op. 93, in 1941), chamber music, songs, and instrumental music (including six piano sonatas).

KREUTZER, Konradin. German composer (1780–1849). He sang the tenor role in at least

ERNST KŘENEK

one of his own operas and was an opera conductor in Stuttgart and Vienna. Of his forty operas, only *Der Verschwender* is still performed.

KREUTZER, Rudolphe. French violinist and composer (1766–1831). He was the most famous of a large musical family. A brilliant virtuoso and composer of many operas, ballets, concertos, string quartets, and trios, his name endures in history because of the Beethoven sonata, which he never played, that is called the "Kreutzer," and for his set of forty Études that every advanced student has used for the study of technique.

KREUTZER SONATA. Beethoven's sonata for violin and piano, No. 9, in A major, Op. 47, composed in 1802–1803 in Vienna. The final movement was written before the first two movements, which were completed only immediately before the first performance in Vienna in 1803, when the violin virtuoso George Augustus Polgreen Bridgetower (*c.* 1780–1860) played the sonata, with Beethoven at the piano.

The *Kreutzer Sonata* was originally written for Bridgetower, who at that time was one of Beethoven's closest friends. He was a British subject and "a mulatto of somewhat obscure origin," his father having been an African. Beethoven therefore first called the composition *Sonata Mulattica.* For some unknown reason

JOSEF KRIPS

conductor of the State Opera and later professor at the Music Academy.

After the second World War, Krips began to rebuild the musical life of Vienna, reviving the Opera and conducting the Vienna Philharmonic Orchestra. From 1950 to 1954 he was conductor-in-chief of the London Symphony Orchestra.

In 1953, Krips was invited to direct the Cincinnati May Festival and in 1954 he became principal conductor of the Buffalo Philharmonic Orchestra. He is still frequently heard as guest conductor in London and Vienna.

KROLL, William. American violinist (1901–). Kroll studied in Berlin and at the Institute of Musical Art in New York. He became first violinist of the Coolidge String Quartet, and appeared with it at numerous chamber music festivals in the United States and in Europe. He organized the Kroll Quartet.

KRONOLD, Selma. Polish soprano (1866–1920). She was the first in America to sing Santuzza in *Cavalleria Rusticana,* Nedda in *Pagliacci,* and the title role in *Manon Lescaut.* She also sang at the Metropolitan Opera.

KRUEGER, Karl. American conductor (1894–). A student of philosophy and law, Krueger became a protégé of Arthur Nikisch and studied composition with Robert Fuchs. He conducted under Nikisch, Weingartner, and Schalk, and from 1919 to 1924 was assistant conductor of the Vienna State Opera. Returning to the United States, he took over the baton of the Seattle Symphony Orchestra. He has appeared as guest conductor with major symphony orchestras in the United States and Europe, expanded the Kansas City Philharmonic into a regional organization under the name of the Midlands Orchestra, and served as conductor of the Detroit Symphony Orchestra from 1943 through 1949.

KRUPA, Gene. American jazz drummer (1909–). One of the most famous of all jazz drummers, Gene Krupa worked with many groups, both large and small, during the 1920s and early 1930s. In 1935 he joined the Benny Goodman orchestra and immediately became a sensation; no picture of the swing era would be complete without him. His feature solo on the best-selling recordings of *Sing Sing Sing,* with the

their friendship was later broken off, and in 1804 the sonata was dedicated to the famous violin virtuoso Rodolphe Kreutzer.

Ferdinand Ries told how "on the day of the concert at half-past five Beethoven summoned me to his house, and said: 'Write out quickly this violin score for the first allegro!' " The piano score was marked only here and there. At eight o'clock that morning Bridgetower had to play the beautiful theme in F major with variations from Beethoven's handwritten music. The last allegro, in A major in 6/8 time, on the other hand, was very neatly written out, as it had been intended for an earlier sonata in A major (Op. 30). Beethoven later inserted the variations in that earlier sonata.

KRIPS, Josef. Austrian conductor (1902–). Krips studied under Weingartner, who engaged him as chorus master and assistant conductor at the Vienna Volksoper. He became conductor at Aussig in 1924 and went from there to Dortmund. For some years he was general music director of the Karlsruhe State Opera, but he returned in 1933 to Vienna where he was first

Goodman ensemble, made him famous overnight. In 1938 he left Goodman to found his own band, which played successfully together until 1943, and included Roy Eldridge on trumpet and vocalist Anita O'Day.

Krupa rejoined Goodman and free-lanced with Tommy Dorsey during the war, and led his own band again from 1944 to 1951. He toured with the Jazz at the Philharmonic troupe for a few years, leading his own trio between concerts. In March, 1954, he started his own drum school with Cozy Cole. His driving, vital beat and flashy showmanship are still to be enjoyed in night clubs or on television.

KRUSCENISKI (Krucenisca), Salomea. Polish-Italian soprano (1875–1953). She was the first (after Rosina Storchio, who sang in the unsuccessful première at La Scala) to sing the role of Madame Butterfly, and her performance in the première of the revised version at Brescia helped the opera to its sensational success all over the world. At La Scala, she was famous as Aïda, Salome, La Gioconda, and in Wagnerian roles. In 1915 at La Scala, she created the title role in Pizzetti's *Fedra*.

KUBELIK, Jan. Czech violinist (1880–1940). Jan Kubelik was accepted as a pupil at the Prague Conservatory at the age of twelve, and had immediate success there and in Vienna when he began his concert career. After a concert in London in June, 1904, with Hans Richter's orchestra, one critic wrote of him as "the new Paganini." On his first concert tour in America in 1902–03, he had similarly magnetized his listeners with his phenomenal technique and the warmth and passion of his playing. Many critics found his performances superficial, but with concert audiences his personality made up for any deficiencies in this respect.

Kubelik moved to the United States in 1935, appearing as soloist with an orchestra conducted by his son Rafael and giving radio concerts in Cincinnati and Chicago. Among Kubelik's compositions were six violin concertos.

SELMA KRONOLD

RAFAEL KUBELIK

Charles Kullman as Prince Shuisky in Boris Godunov

KUBELIK, Rafael. Czech conductor and composer (1914–). The son of the famous violinist Jan Kubelik, he had a thorough musical education and, after leaving the Prague Conservatory in 1934, accompanied his father on tours of Europe and America.

Kubelik was appointed acting conductor of the Czech Philharmonic Orchestra in 1936, and held this post until the Communists took control of the country. He moved to England in 1948, and a year later became conductor of the Amsterdam Concertgebouw Orchestra. In 1949 Kubelik made his American debut with the Chicago Symphony Orchestra, and was appointed musical director of that orchestra in 1950.

In 1953 he returned to Europe. He has been musical director of Covent Garden since October of 1955, and has appeared as guest conductor of major orchestras in Europe, South America, and the United States. He conducted the New York Philharmonic Orchestra during the 1957–58 season. He is considered one of the foremost interpreters of Slavic music, and has composed four operas, a symphony, concertos for cello and violin, string quartets, and other violin and piano music.

KUBIK, Gail. American composer (1914–). A graduate of the Eastman School of Music (1934), Kubik earned his master's degree at the American Conservatory, Chicago, and did graduate work at Harvard. Among his teachers were Walter Piston and Nadia Boulanger. He has served on the faculties of Monmouth College (Illinois), Dakota Wesleyan University, Columbia Teachers College, the University of Southern California, and the Academy of St. Cecilia in Rome. He received first prize in the Jascha Heifetz competition (1941); a Guggenheim Fellowship (1944); then the Prix de Rome (1950), and a Pulitzer Prize (1952). His works include symphonies, chamber music, band music, and incidental music for stage and screen.

KUHLAU, Daniel Frederick. German-Danish composer and flutist (1786–1832). A member of the Danish court orchestra, Kuhlau composed operatic, dramatic, and instrumental music; his piano sonatinas are well known to young pianists.

KUHNAU, Johann. German composer and organist (1660–1722). He was organist of St. Thomas', Leipzig, and became musical director of the University of Leipzig in 1700. The greatest pre-Bach composer of keyboard music, he is best known for his *Biblical Sonatas* and other works for clavier, although he also wrote church music.

KULLMAN, Charles. American tenor (1903–). Kullman studied in New Haven (his native city), at the Juilliard School of Music, and at the American Academy in Fontainebleau. After a brief period of teaching at Smith College, he joined the American Opera Company. In 1930 Kullman went to Europe, where he was engaged by Otto Klemperer to sing at the Kroll Opera. He later had roles at the Berlin State Opera, Covent Garden in London, and the Vienna State Opera, and appeared at the Bayreuth and Salzburg festivals. In 1935, he made his American debut at the Metropolitan Opera in New York, singing the role of Faust. He has been associated with that company ever since, and has scored major successes in a variety of leading tenor parts. In

1956, Kullman was appointed resident tenor at the Indiana University School of Music.

KUNZ, Erich. Austrian bass-baritone (1909–). Born in Vienna, Kunz studied at the Vienna Academy with Theo Lierhammer. After singing roles in small German opera companies, he appeared at Glyndebourne in 1936. From 1941 on, he sang leading parts at the Vienna State Opera, and has specialized in lighter Mozart roles, such as Figaro, at the Salzburg festivals. In 1943 he was the youngest artist at Bayreuth, appearing as Beckmesser in Wagner's *Die Meistersinger.* He is known for his dramatic as well as vocal talents, and is especially famous for his interpretations of such buffo parts as Leporello, Papageno, and Osmin. He made his American debut at New York's Metropolitan Opera in 1952. He has frequently been heard at the Edinburgh Festival and elsewhere in Europe in opera and in recital. He has made many recordings, including four albums of German student songs.

KUPFERMAN, Meyer. American composer (1926–). Although essentially self-taught in composition, Kupferman attended the High School of Music and Art, Queens College, and the Chatham Square Music School, all in New York City. Since 1951 he has been teaching at Sarah Lawrence College. In 1959 he won the La Guardia Memorial Award for outstanding achievement in the field of music.

His one-act opera *In a Garden* (with libretto by Gertrude Stein) was presented at the Edinburgh Festival by the After Dinner Opera Company, and toured in Europe under the auspices of the United States government's "Amerika Haus." *In a Garden* was later produced by the Phoenix Theater, New York, and at the Berkshire Festival. Best known of his other works are Little Symphony, Symphony No. 4, Lyric Symphony, and *Draagenfoot Girl,* a full-length children's opera. A major direction in Kupferman's recent work has been the synthesis of jazz and symphonic materials: Sonata on Jazz Elements (1958); *Blast of Silence,* a film score (1960); and other works.

KURENKO, Maria. Russian-American soprano (1889–). Her career began in Moscow and continued with the Los Angeles, Chicago, and Boston opera companies. A noted recitalist, particularly in pre-classic and ultra-modern music, she is a specialist in the songs of Tchaikovsky and Medtner.

KURKA, Robert. American composer (1921–1957). Kurka studied the violin with Kathleen Parlow and Hans Letz and received his M.A. degree from Columbia University in 1948. Although largely self-taught in composition, he studied briefly with Otto Luening and Darius Milhaud. From 1948 to 1951 he taught music

Johann Kuhnau conducting a concert in St. Thomas' Church, Leipzig

ROBERT KURKA

MELANIE KURT

at the College of the City of New York, and later at Queens College and Dartmouth College. He was co-winner of the Gershwin Memorial Award in 1950 and was a Guggenheim Fellow in 1952 and 1953. The year of his death he received the first Brandeis University Creative Awards Prize.

In 1952 the Little Orchestra Society gave the première of his suite from *The Good Soldier Schweik*. His opera of the same title was first performed, by the New York City Opera, in 1958. He composed two symphonies and other orchestral music, concertos, five string quartets and other chamber music, five violin sonatas, and piano and other pieces.

KURT, Melanie. Austrian soprano (1880–1941). A pupil of Lilli Lehmann, she made her reputation in Leipzig, Berlin, and at Covent Garden in London. At the Metropolitan Opera from 1915 to 1917, she sang Wagnerian roles, and the title roles in Beethoven's *Fidelio* and Gluck's *Iphigenia in Tauris*.

KURTZ, Efrem. Russian-American conductor (1900–). Kurtz studied at the University of Riga, the St. Petersburg Conservatory, and later in Berlin, under Nikisch. From 1921 to 1933 he conducted ballet in Europe, and toured with the Ballets Russes de Monte Carlo from 1933 until 1942. He came to the United States in 1943 and was engaged as conductor of the Kansas City Philharmonic Orchestra. In 1948 he became conductor of the Houston Symphony Orchestra, and in 1955 he was appointed principal conductor of the Liverpool Symphony Orchestra in England.

KURZ, Selma. Austrian coloratura soprano (1875–1933). One of the great stars of her time at the Vienna Hofoper, she sang in many performances under Mahler's direction. In London at Covent Garden she was much admired as Gilda in *Rigoletto* and Violetta in *La Traviata*. Her daughter, Desi Halban, is a successful concert singer.

KVAPIL, Jaroslav. Czech composer (1892–1958). A pupil of Janáček and Reger, he was a noted organist and choral conductor and a professor of composition at the Janáček Academy in Brno. His compositions include an opera, many symphonic works, of which the best known is his *Victory* Symphony, much chamber music, piano pieces, and songs.

LA. The sixth note of the diatonic scale according to the movable *do* in solfege (see Tonic Sol–Fa). In classic fixed-*do* solfege, *la* corresponds to A.

LABIA, Maria. Italian soprano (1880–1953). She began at the Stockholm Opera, where her sister, Fausta, was a popular favorite. Later, she sang Tosca with Hammerstein's company in New York and was a famous Salome at La Scala.

LABLACHE, Luigi. Italian bass of French and Irish parentage (1794–1858). After making his debut at eighteen, he sang in Naples and Sicily for five years before scoring a tremendous success in 1817 at La Scala as Dandini in *Cenerentola*. He then became the most famous basso of his time, going from triumph to triumph in St. Petersburg, London, and Paris, where, at the Théâtre Italien, he created the roles of Don Pasquale (1843), and Giorgio in *I Puritani* (1835). In 1827, he sang in Mozart's Requiem at Beethoven's funeral. In 1836, he gave singing lessons to Queen Victoria. He was an impressive actor despite his great girth, and he was equally successful in serious and *buffo* roles.

LABROCA, Mario. Italian composer (1896–). A pupil of Malipiero and Respighi and an asso-

Luigi Lablache as Dr. Dulcamara in L'Elisir d'Amore

ciate of Casella, he has been a well-known critic and an orchestra director of La Scala and of Radio Italiana. His compositions include chamber music, a symphony, and choral works.

LABUNSKI, Feliks Roderyk. Polish composer (1892–). Resident in America since 1936, he has written articles for many music journals. His compositions include choral music, songs, piano pieces, and orchestral and chamber works.

LACK, Fredell. American violinist. Fredell Lack made her debut recital in Oklahoma City at the age of eight. Three years later she was soloist with the Tulsa Symphony Orchestra. At the age of seventeen she was soloist with the St. Louis Symphony Orchestra under Vladimir Golschmann. Further studies were with Josephine Boudreaux, Louis Persinger, and at the Juilliard School of Music. Winner of National Federation of Music Clubs and American Artists' awards, she made her Town Hall debut in 1943. In 1947 she became concertmaster of the Little Orchestra Society, with which she was often soloist. She is founder and first violinist of the Lyric Art Quartet.

LACY, Michael Rophino. Irish librettist, actor, and violinist (1795–1867). After a career as a violin prodigy, he became an actor and made many adaptations of current operas for English productions, of which the most successful was his version of *Der Freischütz*.

LA FORGE, Frank. American pianist, composer, and teacher (1879–1953). La Forge's career started as a pianist. A student of Theodor Leschetizky, he toured Europe and the United States primarily as accompanist to such artists as Ernestine Schumann-Heink and Marcella Sembrich. He settled in New York in 1920 to teach voice. He was eminently successful as a musical educator and voice coach. Among his pupils were Lawrence Tibbett, Marian Anderson, and Richard Crooks.

LA HALLE, Adam de. See *Halle, Adam de la.*

LAINE, Frankie. American popular singer (1913–). Laine made his first informal appearance as a singer in the Merry Garden Ballroom in Chicago at the age of fifteen, but there followed years of struggle during and after the depression. By 1941 Frankie Laine had decided to abandon a singing career; he worked in a munitions factory and wrote songs in his spare time. He resumed singing in 1946 in a Hollywood night club, and in a few years achieved a phenomenal success. It was the recording of *That's My Desire* which brought him to the top.

LAJTHA, László. Hungarian composer, conductor, and folklorist (1892–). After graduating from the Royal Academy of Music in Budapest, Lajtha became associated with Bartók and Kódály in their folk music researches. During that time he also made a number of visits throughout Europe and familiarized himself with the new musical trends that were coming into being at that time, all of which he studied and absorbed. This study and his thorough knowledge of folk music, combined with a strong individual talent for composition, have all had equal importance in shaping his career.

In 1941 he founded a chamber orchestra, which he conducted until 1944, when he was appointed musical director of the Hungarian radio. Lajtha has published many studies of Hungarian and Transylvanian folk music, and his own works have been influenced by this music as well as by the music of Debussy and Bartók. He has composed in all forms, and his score for the film version of T. S. Eliot's *Murder in the Cathedral* won him wide praise in England and the United States.

LAKMÉ. Opera by Léo Delibes. It was first produced at the Opéra-Comique in Paris in 1883 with libretto by Edmund Gondinet and Philippe Gille. The title role, a demanding coloratura soprano part, is that of the daughter of a Brahman priest in love with a British officer. When her plans to marry him are doomed to failure, she takes her own life. Famous Lakmés have been Adelina Patti, Lily Pons, and Marie Van Zandt.

LALANDE, Michel Richard de. French composer and organist (1657–1726). Largely self-taught as a performer of several instruments, Lalande studied music under Chaperon. Eventually he became director of the royal chapel and chamber music for Louis XIV, serving the court for forty-five years. In this connection he wrote several ballets, intermezzos, and opera-ballets. His most important contribution was his

A scene from Lakmé *with Lily Pons in the title role*

synthesis of the French and Italian styles of Lully and Cavalli, which is most evident in his elaborate motets. These motets became the model for the Versailles style of French church music.

LALO, Édouard. French composer (1823–1892). For a long time Lalo had difficulty in making a name for himself as a composer, and he became so disheartened that he did not write a single note for seven years. The French public's lack of appreciation was due to the fact that at first Lalo composed chiefly chamber music, which attracted very few, and because his elaborate and richly colored works were regarded as "advanced" and difficult to understand.

His first success came when his *Divertissement* (taken from the ballet music to an unperformed opera, *Fiesque*) was given in 1872. His position was further strengthened by the enthusiastic reception accorded his Violin Concerto, performed by Sarasate in 1874. The following year Sarasate premièred the *Symphonie Espagnol* for violin and orchestra, and Lalo's reputation was ensured. Of all the works of this composer, it is the latter which has remained in the international repertoire and is frequently performed.

In the years that followed Lalo made the most of his special gift for creating local color, his brilliant orchestration, and his resilient and stirring rhythms, as expressed for instance in the Cello Concerto (1876), *Rapsodie Norvégienne* (1881), *Concerto Russe* (1883), and the Piano Concerto (1889).

Lalo also achieved fame as an opera composer,

but here again it was a hard-won victory. Almost insuperable difficulties had to be overcome before his great work *Le Roi d'Ys* was performed in 1888, but then, contrary to all expectations, it met with great success. This was not the case with his music for the ballet *Namouna* (1882), which was magnificently orchestrated and far outshone the musical content of many popular ballet scores in currency at that time. Lalo then made an orchestral suite of *Namouna*'s music, and this was greeted with the appreciation it so well deserved. It is now considered one of the masterpieces of nineteenth-century French music, and its "vital, warm and colorful pages, so novel in orchestral treatment,"

Édouard Lalo, an etching by Paul Mathey

Two designs for the 1941 revival of Le Roi d'Ys *at the Paris Opéra.* Top: *Act. I.* Bottom: *finale of Act III*

blazed the trail for French composers such as Debussy and Dukas. "Lalo was the real pioneer of the modern French school" (Henri Prunières).

Julien Tiersot wrote of Lalo: "The music of Lalo is essentially an aristocratic art. It is sculpture created with extreme delicacy, outlined without any visible effort, and brought into being . . . with the utmost naturalness."

Lalo's son, Pierre (1866–1943), was a distinguished writer on musical subjects. He was music critic of *Le Temps* for sixteen years and wrote articles for *Débats*.

LAMBERT, Alexander. Polish composer and pianist (1862–1929). A pupil of Bruckner, he composed many piano pieces and played in concerts with Sarasate and Joachim.

LAMBERT, Constant. English composer and conductor (1905–1951). Son of the Australian painter G. W. Lambert, he was educated at Christ's Hospital before going to the Royal College of Music. While still a student, aged twenty, he was commissioned by Diaghilev to write a ballet for that company: this was *Romeo and Juliet,* which was performed in 1926.

A few years later Lambert became conductor for the Sadler's Wells Ballet, and from 1938 to 1947 was its musical director. The artistic atmosphere in which he had grown up helped him to play an important part in the company's development.

Lambert's most successful composition is *Rio Grande,* for choir, piano, and orchestra, to a poem by Sacheverell Sitwell (1929). This is built on jazz rhythms, and there is—as Hubert Foss remarked—"something more than English in this music, a feeling of the south and its blazing sun."

There followed a piano concerto and two very demanding and serious compositions (the composer himself said that *Rio Grande* was sheer Hollywood by comparison). These were *Music for Orchestra,* which was performed at the I.S.C.M. festival in London in 1931, and *Summer's Last Will and Testament* (1936), for solo baritone, choir, and orchestra.

Constant Lambert was also an active critic. In his lively, provocative book, *Music Ho! A Study of Music in Decline* (1934), he gave expression to his very independent opinions on the music of our time.

LAMMERS, Gerda. German soprano (1919–). She has been acclaimed at the Metropolitan and throughout Europe for her singing of Elektra.

LAMOUREUX, Charles. French conductor (1834–1899). A conductor of great merit, Lamoureux is best remembered for the foundation of the Concerts Lamoureux, held annually in Paris from 1881. He was a stanch champion of Wagner and did much to promote works by contemporary French composers.

LAMPERTI, Francesco. Italian teacher (1813–1892). He was the most celebrated singing teacher of his time.

LANDAU, Siegfried. German-American conductor (1921–). A pupil of Pierre Monteux, he founded and became permanent conductor of the Brooklyn Philharmonia Orchestra, and has been musical director of the Chattanooga Opera since 1960. He has composed chamber, ballet, and orchestral works.

LÄNDLER. A type of slow waltz of southern Germany and Austria, of earlier origin than the waltz itself. See *Waltz.*

LANDON, H. C. Robbins. American musicologist (1926–). He has become an outstand-

WANDA LANDOWSKA

ing authority on Haydn, and the supervisor of the current project to publish a definitive edition of Haydn's works and to record them as well.

LANDORMY, Paul. French musicologist and critic (1869–1943). He was a professor of philosophy and studied singing with Pol Plançon before he became critic of *La Victoire* and the distinguished author of many books and articles on musical subjects.

LANDOWSKA, Wanda. Polish harpsichordist and pianist (1877–1959). After studying at the Warsaw Conservatory and the Berlin College of Music, she became established as a pianist. Her profound interest in neglected music of the past then prompted the decision to devote herself to the harpsichord. As a result, she brought about the rehabilitation of that instrument as a medium for musical expression and became one of the world's outstanding concert artists, as well as a musicologist of the front rank. She also was an expert composer and wrote many articles for leading music publications.

Mme. Landowska made her first appearance as a harpsichordist in 1903 and from that time toured extensively throughout Europe, Africa,

Wanda Landowska at the harpsichord

and America. She was responsible for the new attitude toward the keyboard music of Bach and for revived interest in that of Couperin, Scarlatti, Haydn, Mozart, and others. Works that were specially composed for her include Poulenc's *Concert champêtre* and De Falla's Harpsichord Concerto. In 1912, Pleyel built an instrument for her that she designed.

Between the two world wars, Mme. Landowska lived in a villa outside Paris, where she conducted classes and gave concerts in her garden studio. In 1940, she was forced to flee Paris, abandoning her library and unique collection of instruments. For the rest of her life she lived in America, maintaining her studio at Lakeville, Connecticut, where she made many of her definitive recordings, including Bach's *Well-tempered Clavier* and *Goldberg Variations*. She continued to perform in concerts for many years and often appeared as a pianist as well as a harpsichordist. She once said: "Ever since I embarked on my campaign for old music, it has been my aim to bring to light the fact that the so-called 'old music' is a living strength, often more 'modern' than modern music.

Mme. Landowska, who was a small, slight woman, brought immense scholarship to her interpretations. But she also played with an affecting clarity and vitality, with perfect rhythmic impulse, and with the confidence and communication of a rare technician who had a true affinity for the music at hand.

LANE, Gloria. American mezzo-soprano. In 1948 she won the Philadelphia *Inquirer*'s "Voice of Tomorrow" contest and appeared at Robin Hood Dell. Then she studied at Tanglewood with Boris Goldovsky. In 1950 she created the role of the Secretary in Menotti's *The Consul;* the following year she joined the New York City Opera and made guest appearances all over the United States. She has performed at the Empire State, Central City, and Glyndebourne festivals; the San Francisco Opera; Caracalla and the Opera, Rome; La Scala, Milan; Covent Garden, London; the Berlin State Opera; and in other European cities. She has sung with the NBC-TV Opera since 1956. Her portrayal of Carmen has won high praise for its vitality and fine singing.

LANG, Benjamin. American pianist, composer, and conductor (1837–1909). The son of Eastwood Lang, a noted piano teacher, he became prominent in Boston as a pianist and as conductor of the Apollo Club, Caecilia, and the Haydn and Handel Societies. He was one of the first to conduct Wagner's *Parsifal* in America.

LANG, Paul Henry. Hungarian-American musicologist and critic (1901–). Lang studied at the Academy of Music in Budapest, the University of Paris, and Cornell University. He became editor of *Musical Quarterly* and professor of musicology at Columbia University. In 1941 his important book *Music in Western Civilization* was published. He has been chief critic of the New York *Herald Tribune* since 1955.

LANGE, Francisco Curt. German-Uruguayan musicologist (1903–). One of the important figures in South American music, he has been active in behalf of modern composers, discovered many lost manuscripts, edited a leading music journal, and written many books and articles.

LANGE, Hans. German-American conductor (1884–1960). Lange made his debut as solo violinist in 1903 with the Berlin Philharmonic Orchestra. He became assistant conductor, then associate conductor of the New York Philharmonic Orchestra, was associate conductor of the Chicago Symphony Orchestra from 1936 to 1946, and conducted the Albuquerque Symphony Orchestra from 1950 to 1958.

LANGLAIS, Jean. French composer and organist (1907–). Langlais was born blind. His first musical studies were at the Paris Institut des Jeunes Aveugles and later at the Paris Conservatory with Dukas (composition) and Marcel Dupré (organ). He was organist at several Paris churches. In 1945 he became organist of Sainte-Clothilde, the church where César Franck had been organist. He is best known for his organ and church music, though he has composed in other forms.

LANGSTAFF, John. American baritone. Langstaff's vocal studies were mainly with Arthur Gerry, Edgar Schofield at the Juilliard School of Music, and Richard Bonelli at the Curtis Institute. After recovering from wounds received in World War II, he went to England, appearing in recital as soloist over B.B.C., and at the Stratford-on-Avon Shakespeare Festival, and recording folk songs with Gerald Moore as accompanist. He has appeared at children's concerts with the New York Philharmonic, Montreal and National (Washington, D. C.) symphony orchestras, the Little Orchestra and New York Oratorio Societies, and many other groups; in leading roles in Gilbert and Sullivan and other operas, serious and light; as recitalist and lecturer in nearly every state of the union, and over radio and television.

LANNER, Joseph. Austrian dance composer and orchestra leader (1801–1843). Even in his childhood Lanner showed distinct musical talent, and he was practically self-taught as both violinist and composer. He joined a dance orchestra when he was twelve, and by 1818 had formed his own ensemble which played for dancing and entertainment at popular amusement places. His viola player was Johann Strauss the Elder, then aged fifteen. The ensemble gradually expanded until Lanner was head of a large dance orchestra, with Strauss as deputy conductor.

Lanner began by arranging popular melodies and dances, but before long his program consisted mainly of his own compositions. Inspired by Weber's famous piano piece *Invitation to the*

Gloria Lane as Carmen

Dance, he aimed at raising the waltz to a higher level. He set the form of the Viennese waltz that we have come to know, evolving it from the Ländler. By broadening it and enriching its musical development, he gave to the waltz that combination of high spirit and sentiment considered now to be typically Viennese.

As a violinist Lanner had a soft, winning tone which reflected his genial disposition, though his playing lacked Strauss' emotional power and distinctive rhythm.

Lanner was often reckless enough to advertise the first performance of a waltz of which he still had not written a note on the morning of the concert. He never doubted that he would get the musical idea he needed. He simply assembled his musicians at home, and as soon as he had finished part of the waltz, his colleagues started to orchestrate it, while copyists wrote out the parts: it was like a music factory. Meanwhile, the composer worked on the next section of the piece. As new ideas came to him, he added them to the composition, and two hours later the waltz was finished. Rehearsals began, and in the evening the work was played in public.

After a time Strauss began to compose as well, and he left Lanner's orchestra to start his own in 1825. This was a severe blow to Lanner, who composed one of his most famous waltzes, *Trennungs Walzer (Parting)* on that occasion. Now the "waltz war" began between Lanner's and Strauss' orchestras. But the two leaders were never enemies, although they must have drifted apart. Competition forced them always to do their best, Lanner's simple, popular, sentimental vein contrasting with Strauss' buoyant brilliance.

Lanner never undertook tours abroad as Strauss did, but his popularity in Vienna was tremendous, and he became band leader for the 2nd Civic Regiment as well as conductor at the court balls. Altogether he wrote 207 works—polkas, galops, quadrilles, marches, as well as waltzes.

The idolatry aroused by Strauss and Lanner in Vienna was once described by the critic Hanslick: "It would be impossible to imagine the delirious enthusiasm aroused by the two . . . every time a new waltz was played the newspapers flew into raptures, and numberless articles were written about Lanner and Strauss which were both frivolous or serious, and at times of even greater length than those devoted to Bach and Mozart. The sweetly intoxicating three-quarter rhythm, which captured both the brain and the feet, put all serious music into the shade. Of course, it goes without saying that all of this served to make audiences unable to accept anything serious."

From 1832 Lanner was director for the evening entertainments at the Leopoldstadt theater. These performances, which included symphonic and operatic concerts, were of a high artistic standard and enjoyed a considerable reputation in the musical life of Vienna.

Lanner's son August (1834–55) followed in his father's footsteps. His daughter Katti was a dancer. She made her debut at the Vienna State Opera, and subsequently appeared at most of the leading European theaters. Her techniques and artistry must have been considerable as she was known as "the Taglioni of the North." After her retirement she became a famous teacher and *maîtresse de ballet*.

Best-known waltzes:

Pestherwalzer, Op. 93
Die Werber, Op. 103
Die Kosenden, Op. 128
Hofball-Tänze (Court Ball Waltzes), Op. 161
Steirische Tänze, Op. 165
Die Romantiker, Op. 167
Abendsterne, Op. 180
Die Mozartisten, Op. 196 (from Mozart operas)
Die Schönbrunner, Op. 200
Alt Wien Walzer (potpourri—arranged by Kemser)

LANZA, Mario. American tenor (1922–1959). Lanza, whose real name was Alfred Arnold Cocozza, was of Italian origin. His father, who was an invalid as a result of the first World War, was an enthusiastic admirer of Caruso and bought all the Caruso recordings he could find. In this way, Lanza heard operatic music from childhood, and at the age of ten knew the chief arias from over fifty operas.

After his discharge from the army in 1945, Mario Lanza toured extensively with the Bel Canto Trio, appeared in solo recitals and as soloist with several symphony orchestras, and then began a successful career at Hollywood.

Lanza's films include *The Great Caruso* (1952) and *Because You Are Mine* (1952).

LAPARRA, Raoul. French composer (1876–1943). Laparra studied at the Paris Conservatory with Massenet and Fauré. He won the Prix de Rome in 1903 for his cantata *Ulysse*. He was primarily a composer of operas (for which he was usually his own librettist), although he also wrote a number of instrumental works. His most famous opera is *La Habanera* (1908),

JOSEPH LANNER

which was given its American première in 1910 by the Boston Opera Company, and also performed by the Metropolitan Opera Company in 1923–24. Laparra's music is characterized by a strong feeling for the atmosphere and rhythms of Spain and the Basque region.

LA PRADE, Ernest. American composer and author (1889–). La Prade studied the violin at the Cincinnati College of Music and the Brussels Royal College of Music, and composition with the Belgian composer Joseph Jongen. He taught at the Cincinnati College and played in the Cincinnati Symphony from 1909 to 1912, and in the New York Symphony from 1919 to 1928. He has written a comic opera, songs, and other works. From 1950 to 1954 he was music supervisor of N.B.C.

LAREDO, Jaime. Bolivian violinist (1941–). Laredo studied violin in San Francisco with de Grassi and Houser, and in Cleveland with Gingold. In 1954 he was accepted at the Curtis Institute of Music where he studied under Ivan Galamian. He played his first recital when eight years old and made his Carnegie Hall debut at eighteen, after several recitals and a successful tour. He is the youngest winner of the Queen Elisabeth Award of the Belgian International Music Competition, which he received in 1959.

LARGO (1). Italian, "broad." A tempo indication, meaning in a broad, spacious, or very slow manner. It is also often used as a term for a piece of music of a serious, dignified character.

LARGO (2). Name by which one of Handel's most popular works is known. Handel's *Largo,* often heard in an instrumental arrangement, is really the aria *Ombra mai fu* from the beginning of Handel's opera *Xerxes.* See *Xerxes.*

LARGO AL FACTOTUM. See *Barber of Seville, The.*

LARSEN-TODSEN, Nanny. Swedish soprano (1884–). Larsen-Todsen began her career as a lyric soprano, but as her voice developed she was able to sing dramatic roles and specialized in the Wagnerian repertoire. At the height of her career she sang at most of the leading European opera houses, including the Bayreuth Festival and La Scala, and from 1925 to 1927 was a member of the Metropolitan Opera. She was considered one of the finest Wagnerian sopranos of her day.

LARSSON, Lars-Erik. Swedish composer and conductor (1908–). In his earlier works Larson showed himself to be a typical exponent of neo-classicism, but later he reverted to a conservatively romantic musical language. He has always insisted that music should speak for itself: "Listen to my music as music, and if you cannot understand it without explanation, then it is not your fault; it is I who have fallen short in my work."

Among Larsson's best-known works are *Music for Orchestra, Intimate Miniatures for String Quartet, Symphonic Sketch,* the suite *The Disguised God,* the Violin Concerto, and a Missa Brevis.

LARUETTE, Jean Louis. French tenor and composer (1731–1792). He and his wife, Mlle. Villette, were leading performers at the Paris Opéra-Comique. Laruette specialized in *buffo*

JAIME LAREDO

tenor parts and also composed many comic operas, which were among the earliest of the French school.

LASSALLE, Jean. French baritone (1847–1909). One of the famous singers of his time, he was a star of the Paris Opéra for twenty-three years and appeared in the important opera houses of the world, including the Metropolitan Opera, where he made his debut in 1892.

LASSO, Orlando di (Orlandus Lassus; also Roland de Lassus). Flemish composer (*c*. 1530–1594). As a boy Di Lasso sang in the choir of the Church of St. Nicholas, in Mons. His beautiful voice and expert musicianship were of such a quality that, according to several accounts, no fewer than three attempts to kidnap him were made by other churches in the vicinity who wanted him for their choirs.

In 1544 Fernando Gonzaga, the Viceroy of Sicily, heard the boy sing at St. Nicholas and requested him to be allowed to enter his service. Di Lasso accompanied Gonzaga first to France, then to Italy and Sicily. In 1550 he entered the service of the Marchese della Terra, a Neapolitan, but left his patron the following year and went to Rome where he attached himself to the household of Bishop Antonio Altovolti. Di Lasso remained with the Bishop until 1553, when he became choirmaster at the Cathedral of San Giovanni Laterano, a post he held until 1554.

ORLANDO DI LASSO

The following year he settled in Antwerp, immersing himself in the musical life of the city. His first works were published in Antwerp: a Book of Madrigals in 1555, and a Book of Motets in 1556. Both of these collections show that Di Lasso had begun to display a strongly individual talent in his compositions. The music displays a blend of the Italian and Netherlands schools, combining the gaiety and vitality of the Renaissance with the spiritual objectives of the Counter-Reformation.

In 1556 Di Lasso received an appointment to the court of Duke Albert V of Bavaria as chorister and musician to the ducal chapel, and two years later he married Regina Weckinger, the daughter of a lady of the court. During this period he wrote fewer secular works and began directing his energies toward the composing of sacred music. This was probably due to the influences that prevailed at the Bavarian court, which at that time was more in sympathy with the Roman Church than with the struggles of the Reformation.

In 1563 he was appointed chorus master to the court. His elevation was probably precipitated by the unpopular Lutheran sentiments expressed by his predecessor, Ludwig Daser. According to contemporary accounts this was the only logical reason for Daser's dismissal, since he otherwise seemed fully capable of carrying out his official duties. During this time Di Lasso wrote his famous *Seven Penitential Psalms, Sacrae Cantiones,* and *Sacrae Lectiones*.

In 1570 Maximilian, emperor of the Holy Roman Empire, conferred upon him a patent of nobility (which included the right to a coat-of-arms). The honor was a return favor for a motet Di Lasso had written for the Emperor on the occasion of his coronation, some years previously, as king of Bohemia and king of the Romans.

From 1570 until his death, Di Lasso's life was spent at various courts in France and Bavaria where he continued to compose prolifically (his total output consists of over 800 compositions). His works continued to develop in technical skill, and in profound emotional expression. Further honors were accorded him, and his exalted position has perhaps never been equaled by any other composer.

Di Lasso's music was also held in esteem by his contemporaries, and miraculous powers were even attributed to one of his works. In 1584 during the Feast of Corpus Christi a severe rainstorm threatened the cancellation of the procession of the Sacrament through the streets of Munich. As the Host was brought to the church porch the procession hesitated, but at that moment the choir—under Di Lasso's direction—began to sing his motet, *Gustate e Vidite (Taste and See)*. At the first notes the rain ceased and the sun came out, permitting the procession to proceed. This was regarded as a sign of Divine favor toward Di Lasso's music, and from then on, whenever an outdoor church procession was contemplated in Munich, this motet was sung to insure good weather.

Whereas his great contemporary, Palestrina, sought to express the general sentiments of the text in fluently melodious passages, Orlando di Lasso brought out the meaning of the individual words by rhythmic emphasis and surprising modulations and harmonic inversions. In this, he pointed the way toward Monteverdi's expressive style. Orlando di Lasso's somber pathos and passionate outcries form a sharp contrast to Palestrina's serenity and celestial purity of style. His counterpoint is also much freer than that of his predecessors. Many of his songs have appeal for modern ears. As Dyneley Hussey has written: "Last and greatest of the Flemish school, he transcends the bounds of school and nationality. . . . There is no form of vocal composition, sacred or profane, no depth of emotion, grave or gay, that he did not touch."

Best-known works:

SACRED CHORAL WORKS
Requiem
St. Matthew Passion
Seven Penitential Psalms
Mass, *Puisque j'ai perdu*

SECULAR SONGS
Audite Nova! (Die Martinsgans) (with chorus)
Matona, mia cara (Landsknechtsständchen)
 (4 voices) (1581)
Mon coeur se recommande à vous (5 voices) (1560)
Ola! O che bon eccho! (8 voices) (1581)
Quand mon mari vient du dehors (1564)
Neue Teutsche Lieder

LAST ROSE OF SUMMER, THE. Irish song with words by Thomas Moore, written in 1813. The tune was originally known as *The Grove of Blarney* and was attributed to Alfred Milliken; he, however, was only one year old when the song was first printed. It was used many years later by Flotow in the opera *Martha*. Beethoven

Orlando di Lasso (at the keyboard) with the musicians of the Duke of Bavaria's private chapel

Titlepage of Patrocinum Musices *by Orlando di Lasso, published between 1673–76*

JACOB LATEINER

made an arrangement of the melody and Mendelssohn wrote a piano fantasia based on it.

LATEINER, Jacob. American pianist (1928–). Born in Havana, he graduated from the Curtis Institute of Music, where he was a pupil of Isabelle Vengerova. He appeared with the Philadelphia Orchestra as winner of its Youth Competition and then was accompanist to Efrem Zimbalist. He has toured extensively in America and abroad and won high praise when he appeared with the New York Philharmonic Symphony in 1954.

LATTUADA, Felice. Italian composer (1882–). Lattuada has composed in all forms, but his chief interest is opera. He has written six works for the stage, including *La Tempesta* (1922), *Don Giovanni* (1929), and *Cain* (1957). Working within traditional forms, his operas reveal a broad lyric gift and a firm grasp in the handling of rich orchestral and vocal textures.

LAUBENTHAL, Rudolf. German tenor (1886–). A star of the Berlin Staatsoper, he became the leading Wagnerian tenor at the Metro-politan Opera in 1923 after his debut as Walther in *Die Meistersinger*. During ten seasons, he sang, in addition to many Wagnerian roles, the tenor leads in *Die ägyptische Helena, Jenufa,* and *Schwanda* at their American premières. He also sang at Covent Garden and the San Francisco Opera.

LAUDER, Sir Harry. Scottish comedian (1870–1950). Harry Lauder made his first professional appearance at Belfast, and in 1900 appeared successfully in London. He established his reputation at the Oxford Music Hall and the London Pavilion, and before long was the highest paid music-hall artist of his day.

Lauder made many tours of the United States and is best remembered through his recordings.

LAURI-VOLPI, Giacomo. Italian tenor (1893–). Lauri-Volpi studied singing at the Saint Cecilia Conservatory, made his debut in 1920 in *Manon* at the Teatro Costanzi in Rome,

Giacomo Lauri-Volpi in Massenet's Roi de Lahore

and afterward went to La Scala, Milan, and then to the Metropolitan in New York. Here he had enormous success in many parts, including those of Rodolfo in *La Bohème* and Calaf in *Turandot*. He remained with the Metropolitan for the next ten years, during which time he also toured North and South America.

A New York newspaper wrote about his first appearance in *Il Trovatore:* "Better performances have not been given since the fabulous days of Caruso. . . . His singing . . . was so spirited and white hot from the anvil of what seemed realistic passion that even the musicians in the orchestra lifted their jaded heads, and at the end of the scene rose in a body to join the general uproar of applause and cheers."

Since 1934 he has appeared mainly at La Scala, but has also given many concerts.

LAVALLE, Paul. American conductor and composer (1908–). Lavalle attended the Juilliard School of Music and made his symphonic debut with the New York Philharmonic Orchestra at Lewisohn Stadium in 1946. He is well known as a conductor on radio and has been guest conductor of several major symphony orchestras.

LA VIOLETTE, Wesley. American composer (1894–). He has been professor of theory and dean of the music department of Northwestern University. His works include an opera, *Shylock,* and choral music.

LAVRY, Marc. Latvian-Israeli composer and conductor (1903–). Born in Latvia, Lavry studied in Leipzig and worked on the staffs of several German opera houses. In 1932 he left Germany and reached Palestine via Riga and Stockholm. In 1951 he was appointed head of the Jerusalem broadcasting service. He has written an opera, symphonic works, ballets, and an oratorio.

LAWES, Henry. English singer and composer (1596–1662). He composed the music for Milton's *Comus* and sang the Attendant Spirit at the first performance in 1634. He composed many songs and was a much admired singer. His brother William (1602–1645) composed masques, songs, and instrumental pieces.

LAWRENCE, Marjorie. Australian dramatic

Marjorie Lawrence as Salome

soprano (1908–). After studying under Mme. Gilly in Paris, Marjorie Lawrence made her debut at Monte Carlo in 1932 as Elisabeth in *Tannhäuser.* She then appeared in leading roles in great opera houses all over the world, scoring triumph after triumph. She made her Metropolitan Opera debut in 1935 as Brünnhilde in *Die Walküre.*

In 1941 she was stricken by infantile paralysis, and it was thought that she would never sing again. However, through great courage and strength of will she returned to the concert stage in 1942, singing her recital from a wheel chair. In January, 1943, she returned to the Metropolitan Opera in the role of Venus in *Tannhäuser,* which requires little action. In March, 1944, she performed the exacting part of Isolde, where she remained seated for the first two acts and was carried on in the last act by Julius Huehn as Kurvenal. These appearances demonstrated that her voice had lost none of its former luster.

In 1944 she gave concerts for troops in Australia and Europe, and after the war she made regular appearances in recitals and opera. She has written an autobiography, *Interrupted Melody,* published in 1950.

At present she lives in Arkansas; she teaches, and has also formed an opera workshop there.

LAWRENCE, Robert. American conductor and critic (1912–). Lawrence's career has been divided between conducting and writing on musical subjects. After graduation from the College of the City of New York, he was a fellow at the Juilliard School. In 1940, he became a staff member of the New York *Herald Tribune's* music department. In 1948 he first conducted the New York Philharmonic Orchestra, and has appeared on its podium several times since. Among the other orchestras he has conducted are the Ballets Russes, Royal Opera, Rome, St. Cecilia Academy, Rome, and the Royal Philharmonic, London. He is co-author of *The Metropolitan Opera Guide* and wrote *The Victor Book of Ballets and Ballet Music* and *The World of Opera.* He is an expert on the works of Berlioz and is the founder and musical director of the Friends of French Opera.

LAZARO, Hipólito. Spanish tenor (1889–). He sang in European opera houses, including La Scala, and in South America. His career at the Metropolitan Opera began in 1918 as the Duke in *Rigoletto.*

LAZZARI, Sylvio. Italian composer (1857–1944). A pupil of Franck, he composed music for plays, including *Faust,* and orchestral works.

LAZZARI, Virgilio. Italian bass (1887–1953). After singing at La Scala, he was a member of the Chicago Opera for fifteen years and of the Metropolitan Opera for seventeen years. His most famous role was that of Leporello in *Don Giovanni.*

LEAGUE OF COMPOSERS. An American organization that commissioned and performed important contemporary works for concert and stage.

LEBRUN, Franziska Danzi. German soprano (1756–1791). She was one of the most famous singers in opera in the years before the advent of Gluck and Mozart. Her husband, Ludwig August Lebrun (1746–1790), was a famous oboist and composer of music for that instrument.

LECHNER, Frederick. German-American baritone (1904–). He came from a musical family and was trained in Berlin at the State Academy of Music. After distinguished engagements in Germany, Austria, Switzerland, and Belgium, he emigrated to America in 1936. He sang with the New York Philharmonic, the Boston Symphony, and many other major orchestras, then became Cantor of the Central Synagogue in New York. He also sang with the Metropolitan Opera for four seasons, scoring a particular success as Alberich in the *Ring* operas.

ERNESTO LECUÒNA

FREDERICK LECHNER

LECLAIR, Jean Marie. French composer and violinist (1697–1764). At first a ballet dancer, then a ballet master and composer, he studied violin with Somis in Italy and in 1728 became a successful violinist in Paris. He is among the foremost French writers of violin music; he wrote many sonatas for that instrument, as well as chamber music, and concertos.

LECOCQ, Alexandre Charles. French composer (1832–1918). He was a pupil of Halévy at the Paris Conservatory and became, like his master, an indefatigable composer of stage works. Success came slowly, and it was not until the production of *Fleur de thé* in 1868 that his reign in the Paris theaters began. Altogether, he composed forty-two operettas, of which only *La Fille de Mme. Angot* survives to this day. It ran 500 performances in its first production and has been revived many times since.

LECUÒNA, Ernesto. Cuban composer and pianist (1896–). Lecuòna toured widely as a pianist in the United States, Spain, and France following his graduation from the National Conservatory in Havana. He has composed several orchestral pieces including *Rhapsody Negra* (1943), and many songs in the rumba style among which the best known are *Malaguena* and *Siboney*.

LEDBETTER, Huddie ("Leadbelly"). American jazz singer and guitar player (*c.* 1885–1949). He spent a large part of his life in prison as a convicted murderer. Winning release in 1934 as a result of a performance given for the governor of Louisiana, he sang in night clubs, toured abroad, and recorded folk music for the archives of the Library of Congress. See *Folk Music.*

LEE, Dai-keong. American composer (1915–). Born in Hawaii, Lee studied with Roger Sessions, Frederick Jacobi, and Aaron Copland. He has written a one-act opera, orchestral works, chamber music, and choral compositions.

LEE, Peggy (Norma Jean Egstrom). American jazz singer and composer (1920–). Peggy Lee sang with the Benny Goodman band in the 1940s and turned to composition of several hit jazz songs. She appeared in the film *The Jazz Singer* and in other motion pictures and is a featured night-club and television performer.

BENJAMIN LEES

LEES, Benjamin. American composer (1924–). He was born in China of Russian parents but has spent most of his life in the United States. A pupil of George Antheil, he has received Fulbright, Guggenheim, and Copley Foundation awards. He composes chiefly in traditional forms in a style influenced by chromatic romanticism. His major works include two operas, *The Oracle* and *The Gilded Cage,* a large choral work, *Visions of Poets,* performed by the Seattle Symphony at the 1962 World's Fair, several concertos (a new violin concerto was premièred by the Boston Symphony in 1963), songs, chamber music, and piano works. His Second Symphony, commissioned by the Louisville Orchestra, was premièred by them and later performed by the Cleveland Orchestra under Szell, and over the Stockholm Radio. Also frequently performed are his Concerto for Orchestra, and Interlude for Strings.

LEGATO. Italian, "bound." A term indicating

Franz Lehár with Richard Tauber

that a passage is to be played or sung in a smooth, sustained manner without any perceptible interruption between the notes. The opposite of staccato, it is designated by a slur over the notes to be rendered thus.

LEGINSKA, Ethel. English-American composer, conductor, and pianist (1890–). Ethel Leginska has composed orchestral and vocal works among which are the one-act opera *Gale,* presented by the Chicago Opera in 1938. She studied at the Frankfurt Conservatory under Theodor Leschetizky and has toured Europe and the United States as a concert pianist.

LEHÁR, Franz. Hungarian composer of operettas (1870–1948). Lehár said about his early youth: "I was born the son of a soldier and was also to wear uniform for a time. During my early years my father was an army bandmaster at Komorn, a small Hungarian town, situated where the river Váh joins the Danube. Music had flowed from my father's veins into mine. But the first song I composed, I dedicated to my mother. I was six years old then. My father was anxious that I should be given a proper educa-

tion, and I was sent off to Budapest to attend college. If I had not played the organ so well during music lessons, I should surely have been expelled, for I was a lazy scamp who shunned schoolbooks."

At the Prague Conservatory Dvořák instructed Lehár in musical theory. "One day," Lehár tells us, "I plucked up my courage and showed Dvořák two sonatas which I had written. He glanced through them and said: 'Drop the violin and become a composer!' "

Lehár's father, however, wanted his son to take up a more practical career. Thus Franz was for a time engaged as a violinist by the theater at Barmen-Elberfeld. Later he joined the military band of the Hungarian garrison town of Losonc, where he augmented his very meager income by other musical activities, such as arranging Hungarian folk songs for military bands. He also composed marches, polkas, and waltzes. As military bandmaster he was transferred in turn to Pola, Trieste, and Budapest; his opera *Kukuscha* was performed in the last-named city successfully. Lehár next became orchestral conductor at Vienna's Theater an der Wien, where his first two operettas *Der Rastelbinder* and *Wiener Frauen* were performed in 1902.

The Merry Widow, which was to become the most successful operetta of all time, came next, making Lehár's name famous all over the world. He composed thirty operettas in all.

Lehár claimed that operettas need not necessarily be gay, and proved this with serious examples like *Frederica* and *The Land of Smiles.* He wanted to people his operettas with real-life men and women, not to imitate earlier composers who merely created dummies delivering melodious and catchy songs to make the audience laugh. For this reason he preferred the action to be laid in his own time. His intense interest in human beings led to his close understanding of different nations, and this left its mark on many of his operettas. Thus *Gypsy Love* was a gift to Hungary, *The Merry Widow* was his homage to Montenegro, *Frasquita* was his Spanish operetta, *Paganini* his Italian, *Frederica* his German, *Zarewitch* his Russian, and *The Land of Smiles* his Chinese operetta.

Lehár was a personal friend of Puccini. The two composers admired each other, and it was said jestingly about Lehár that he had "puccinitis."

Lehár's gaiety contains neither Offenbach's

lash of satirical malice nor the sly humor of J. Strauss. Lehár's humor is like sparkling champagne. Nevertheless, he possessed an exuberant bourgeois geniality and an honest and sound faculty for characterization. He gave new life to the operetta and created his own individual form of expression. He had been imitated by many, but very few have possessed his sincerity and sound taste.

Best-known works:

OPERETTAS

Der Rastelbinder (1920)
The Merry Widow (*Die lustige Witwe*) (1905)
The Count of Luxemburg (*Der Graf von Luxemburg*) (1909)
Gypsy Love (*Zigeunerliebe*) (1905)
Eva (1911)
Frasquita (1922)
Paganini (1925)
Der Zarewitch (1927)
Frederica (1928)
The Land of Smiles (*Das Land des Lächelns*) (1929)
Giuditta (1934)

ORCHESTRAL

Gold and Silver Waltz (1899)
Eva Waltz (*Wär' es auch nichts . . .*)
Merry Widow Waltz (*I Love You So . . .*)

LEHMANN, Fritz. German conductor (1904–1956). Well known in America through his recordings, he conducted many of the leading German orchestras and was for several years conductor of the opera at Göttingen and a professor at the Hochschule für Musik in Munich. He died in Munich while conducting a performance of Bach's *Easter Oratorio*.

LEHMANN, Lilli. German soprano (1848–1929). Her only teacher was her mother, a well-known singer at the Cassel Opera. Her sister, Marie, was also a talented singer. Lilli Lehmann's prodigious career began in Prague, after which she appeared in light soprano parts for fifteen years at the Berlin Hofoper. In 1876, she sang secondary roles under Wagner's direction at the first Bayreuth Festival, to which she was to return as a great star in 1896. Her London career began as Violetta in *La Traviata* at Her Majesty's Theatre in 1880. Five years later, she made her American debut at the Metropolitan Opera as Carmen. There she became established as a Wagnerian soprano when she sang Brünnhilde in the first Metropolitan perform-

ance of *Die Walküre* and the first American performances of *Siegfried* and *Die Götterdämmerung*. Her famous Isolde was also the first to be heard in America. She returned to the Metropolitan for a number of seasons until 1899, performing, in addition to Wagnerian roles, such amazingly diverse roles as Fidelio, Norma, Euryanthe, Aïda, Donna Anna in *Don Giovanni,* Rachel in *La Juive,* and Valentine in *Les Huguenots*. She proved her worth as a great lieder singer after the Kaiser barred her from German opera houses for some years, as punishment for singing abroad without his permission. In later life, she coached such famous singers as Fremstad and Farrar and wrote two books, *How To Sing* and *My Path Through Life*.

LEHMANN, Liza. English soprano and composer of German descent (1862–1918). She appeared regularly in London as soloist in the Monday Popular Concerts and performed with Clara Schumann. Upon her marriage in 1894, she gave up singing and devoted herself to composing. Though she composed an opera, *The*

LILLI LEHMANN

LOTTE LEHMANN

Vicar of Wakefield, a musical comedy, incidental music for several plays, and piano pieces, she achieved her greatest success with songs, particularly the cycles *In A Persian Garden, In Memoriam,* and *The Daisy-Chain.*

LEHMANN, Lotte. German-American soprano (1888–). Lotte Lehmann was trained at the Berlin Academy of Music. When she made her debut as Freia in *Das Rheingold* she was so nervous that the critics had no opportunity to gauge her possibilities. But the operatic director, Otto Klemperer, had faith in her and gave her the part of Elsa in *Lohengrin.* Of this she said: "On the evening of the performance I did not see the audience. I did not even see the face of the conductor. I forgot everything—where I was and what the evening meant for me. I was Elsa, that Elsa whom I now understood for the first time. Tears came into my eyes as the choir sang *Heil dir, Elsa von Brabant,* and I shall always sing *Heil dir* with all my heart to that great day which was the true beginning of my life."

She was soon given leading roles in French and Italian operas, and her interpretation of Sieglinde in *Die Walküre,* the Marschallin in *Der Rosenkavalier,* and *Leonora* in *Fidelio* secured her a special place among the opera singers of her time.

On the centenary of Beethoven's death (1927), the Paris Opéra was to present *Fidelio,* and Lotte Lehmann was the first German artist to be invited to sing the part in France since the war. Paris was still strongly anti-German, but before long the audience was carried away by enthusiasm, and at the end of the first act she received a great ovation. She regards this as her greatest personal triumph.

When in 1934 she sang for the first time at the Metropolitan, New York, in *Die Walküre,* one of the critics wrote: "Never before in the history of the Metropolitan has there been such a success."

But her versatility and artistry were shown perhaps even more clearly at her lieder concerts, particularly in her wonderful interpretations of Schubert, Schumann, and Hugo Wolf songs. In the more intimate atmosphere of the concert hall the audience could appreciate more fully her warm personality, the rich variety of her expression, and her charm.

Lotte Lehmann has considerable literary and artistic talents, and has published several books: *Eternal Flight, Midway in My Song, More Than Singing,* and *My Many Lives.* She also painted twenty-four illustrations to Schubert's song cycle *Die Winterreise.*

LEIBOWITZ, René. Polish-born French composer and conductor (1913–). Leibowitz is the leading exponent of the French twelve-tone school of composition. He studied with Arnold Schoenberg and Anton von Webern. He has written symphonic works, chamber music, and stage music, and is the author of *Schoenberg and His School,* and other books and articles on twelve-tone music.

LEICHTENTRITT, Hugo. German musicologist and composer (1874–1951). After studying at Harvard University with John Knowles Paine, Leichtentritt earned his doctorate in music at the Berlin Hochschule für Musik and taught at the Klindworth-Scharwenka Conservatory. He returned to the United States in 1933, lecturing at Harvard and New York universities. His considerable scholarship was shown in a number of biographical and musicological works, including *Music, History and Ideas* (1938), *Musical Form* (1951), and *Music of the Western Nations* (published posthumously, 1956). He composed in a number of forms.

LEIDER, Frida. German soprano (1888–). She is one of the great Isoldes of this century. Though her career was mainly as a star at the Bayreuth Festival and of the Berlin and Vienna State operas, she sang with the Chicago Opera for four seasons and at the Metropolitan for two. She also made frequent appearances in London at Covent Garden.

LEIGH, Adèle. English soprano (1928–). She studied at the Royal Academy of Dramatic Art, and with Maggie Teyte. In 1948, she made her debut at Covent Garden in London, where she was particularly successful in Mozart roles. In 1955 she created the role of Bella in Tippett's *The Midsummer Marriage*. She has given recitals all over the world with her husband, the bass-baritone James Pease, and they appeared together with the New York City Opera Company in 1961.

LEINSDORF, Erich. Austrian-American conductor (1912–). Educated in his native Vienna, Leinsdorf became an assistant in Salzburg for the 1934 Festival and remained in this post for three successive summers, working with such conductors as Bruno Walter and Arturo Toscanini. In 1938, he was engaged by the Metropolitan Opera as assistant to Artur Bodansky; two years later he became Bodansky's successor as conductor of the German repertoire. He also conducted symphony orchestras in Europe and the United States. In 1943, he was appointed principal conductor of the Cleveland Orchestra, and in 1947 he became musical director of the Rochester Philharmonic Orchestra.

Leinsdorf returned to opera in 1956 when he became director of the New York City Opera. In 1957 he rejoined the staff of the Metropolitan Opera, where he conducted notable performances until 1962, when he became musical director of the Boston Symphony.

LEITMOTIV. German, "leading motif." A short theme associated with a particular character, object, or idea, introduced at appropriate moments in an opera, or other work. The leitmotiv is used very flexibly, suffering changes in rhythm and even in harmonic construction to meet the requirements of its situation. The term was coined by E. von Wolzogen to describe Wagner's method of composition. Though Wagner was the first to use leitmotivs con-

sistently, he did not invent the idea, for they occur in works by Grétry, Mozart, Weber, and Berlioz. This musical device had a considerable influence on later opera, and on the symphonic poem.

LEJEUNE, Claude. French composer (1528–1600 or 1601). He was one of the masters of polyphonic church music. Although he composed in the conventional style, he was responsible for innovations in matters of harmony. His most celebrated work is a setting of the Genevan Psalter, edited by his sister after his death. He was attached to the French court and was a Huguenot sympathizer. His chansons, motets, madrigals, etc. can be ranked with those of Di Lasso.

LEKEU, Guillaume. Belgian composer (1870–1894). A pupil of Franck, he began to compose at fifteen and at twenty-one won the Prix de Rome with a cantata, *Andromède*. Though his early death left his great promise unfulfilled, he did manage in his short life to compose a surprising number of choral, chamber, piano, and symphonic works, two of which were completed by d'Indy after his death. The sonata he composed for Ysaÿe is still a favorite with many violinists.

Frida Leider as Brünnhilde in Die Walküre

Leonardo Leo, from Fedi's Il parnasso

LEONCAVALLO, Ruggiero. Italian composer (1858–1919). After studying at the Naples Conservatory, where he was considered a most promising composer, he spent some years wandering through Europe, giving piano and singing lessons, playing in cafés, and writing chansonettes for music-hall performers. A meeting with the famous baritone, Victor Maurel, led to an introduction to Ricordi, the powerful publishers, who encouraged him to compose a grandiose trilogy set in the Renaissance. However, they rejected the first of these, *I Medici.* Leoncavallo, who had already composed another unproduced opera, *Chatterton,* decided to emulate the *verismo* style of Mascagni and composed his masterpiece, *I Pagliacci,* which was produced with enormous success in Milan in 1892. Maurel sang the role of Tonio. So great was the popularity of *I Pagliacci,* for which Leoncavallo wrote his own libretto (as he did for all his operas), that his earlier works were now produced. Both were disastrous failures. Leoncavallo then had

LENTO. Italian, "slow"; a tempo indication. See *Music, Elements of.*

LENYA, Lotte. Austrian-American singer and actress. The daughter of a Viennese coachman, Lotte Lenya began her singing career at the age of four in a neighborhood carnival. Later she acted, performed as a tightrope walker, and danced, in Zurich and Berlin. She married Kurt Weill and, in 1928, created the leading role in Weill's *Dreigroschenoper (Threepenny Opera).* They fled the Nazis in 1933 and after two years in Paris settled in the United States. She has since appeared in motion pictures and in Broadway productions and has been the most effective exponent of her late husband's music, singing in concerts of his work, starring in the enormously successful revival of *The Threepenny Opera,* in his *Seven Deadly Sins* with the New York City Ballet, and lending her unique style and indispensable knowledge to the recording of his greatest work, *Mahagonny.*

LEO, Leonardo. Italian composer (1694–1744). An important figure in the early development of opera, he was a pupil of Alessandro Scarlatti at the Naples Conservatory and later was the teacher of Pergolesi. He composed fifty operas, both *seria* and *buffa,* which, though forgotten now, were greatly popular in his day. His first success was *Sofonisba* and others were *Farnace, L'Olimpiade,* and *La Contesta dell' Amore colla Virtù.*

LEONCAVALLO, Ruggiero. Italian composer (1858–1919). After studying at the Naples Conservatory, where he was considered a most promising composer, he spent some years wandering through Europe, giving piano and singing lessons, playing in cafés, and writing chansonettes for music-hall performers. A meeting with the famous baritone, Victor Maurel, led to an introduction to Ricordi, the powerful publishers, who encouraged him to compose a grandiose trilogy set in the Renaissance. However, they rejected the first of these, *I Medici.* Leoncavallo, who had already composed another unproduced opera, *Chatterton,* decided to emulate the *verissmo* style of Mascagni and composed his masterpiece, *I Pagliacci,* which was produced with enormous success in Milan in 1892. Maurel sang the role of Tonio. So great was the popularity of *I Pagliacci,* for which Leoncavallo wrote his own libretto (as he did for all his operas), that his earlier works were now produced. Both were disastrous failures. Leoncavallo then had

the bad luck to produce his *La Bohème,* a work
of considerable quality, a few months after
Puccini's version had created a sensation. For
the rest of his life, Leoncavallo struggled to
duplicate his one great success, composing
sixteen operas in all, of which only *Zaza*
achieved even mild popularity. Today, the only
one of his compositions besides *I Pagliacci* that
is known to the musical public is his famous
song, *La Mattinata.*

Disappointment and frustration finally ruined
Leoncavallo's health and led to his death.

LÉONIN, or Leoninus. French composer of
the twelfth century. He was choir master of
Notre Dame in Paris and composed the *Magnus
Liber Organi,* which survives only in versions
made by editors of a later time. This work contained about eighty settings of plainsong melodies for use in all the festival church services
of the year.

LEONORA OVERTURES. Altogether Beethoven wrote five overtures for his only opera

RUGGIERO LEONCAVALLO

Act I of Leoncavallo's Zaza *at a 1911 performance
conducted by the composer's brother*

Fidelio, originally called *Leonora, or Conjugal
Love.* Only four have been preserved. The first
three are known as *Leonora Overtures* Nos. 1,
2, and 3, and are all in C major, whereas the
fourth is called *Fidelio* Overture and is in E
major. The *Fidelio* Overture was composed in
1814 for the first performance of the opera, and
is generally played as the overture.

Leonora Overture No. 3, also Op. 72a, is regarded as
the most important of the overtures, and is the one most
frequently played. It was written for the performance of
the rewritten opera on March 29, 1806. Schindler says it
was a revised version of No. 2, written because Beethoven wanted to avoid some difficult brass parts.

The overture opens in a slow tempo with a melody
dropping in broad unison, as if to lead us into the dark
and sinister atmosphere of Florestan's prison cell. Then
we hear on clarinet and bassoon the famous tune from
the aria in which Florestan relates how suddenly the
happiness of his youth was torn to shreds.

Then very faintly comes the blithe Leonora theme
which opens the allegro part. Contrasting with the
ponderous theme of the slow introduction, this has a
lighter and happier air: it seems to soar, borne by
strength, hope, and trust.

The Leonora theme develops toward the Florestan
theme in the wind instruments: hope battles against
despair. It swells toward a climax when Leonora steps
before Florestan to make a shield against Pizarro's
rapier. Then suddenly there is a fanfare of trumpets
which announces that deliverance has come. It fades
away in a long, lingering note, relieved by a broad,
calm hymn of thanks. A brief allusion to the Florestan
theme casts a fleeting shadow, but it is swept away in
the surge of the coda which ends in all-embracing,
exultant joy.

JEAN FRANÇOIS LESUEUR

LEOPOLD I. Emperor of Austria (1640–1705). During his long reign (1658–1705), he frequently composed (two operas, church music, dance pieces), and was a great patron of music.

LERNER, Alan Jay. American lyricist (1918–). Lerner was graduated from Harvard University in 1940 and soon became one of the best-known lyricists and librettists of the American musical stage. His highly successful collaboration with Frederick Loewe resulted in the Broadway shows *The Day Before Spring, Brigadoon, Paint Your Wagon, My Fair Lady,* and *Camelot,* and the motion picture *Gigi,* an Academy Award winner for 1958. See *Loewe, Frederick.*

LE ROUX, Gaspard. French composer and harpsichordist (*c.* 1660–*c.* 1707). Though little is known of him, he was, apparently, a performer at court; he composed motets, as well as the *Pièces de clavessin* for which he gained his place in music history.

LEROUX, Xavier. French composer (1863–1919). A pupil of Massenet, he won the Prix de Rome with a cantata and later edited a journal, *Musica.* He composed thirteen operas, incidental music to plays, church music, and songs.

LE ROY, René. French flutist (1898–). One of the outstanding instrumentalists of our time, he has performed in many tours as soloist and head of his own chamber group, and also has participated in many recordings.

LESCHETIZKY, Theodor. Polish pianist, teacher, and conductor (1830–1915). Teacher of Paderewski, Leschetizky himself studied at the age of eleven with Carl Czerny. He became a famous concert pianist, performing in Austria, Germany, England, Poland, and Russia; he also conducted on tour. At various times he taught in St. Petersburg, Frankfurt, and Vienna, developing his own unique and famous method of instruction. Numerous later world-renowned pianists were among his pupils. He also composed operas, piano pieces, and other works.

LESSARD, John. American composer (1920–). A student at the age of fourteen of Elsie Belenky in San Francisco, Lessard also studied with Henry Cowell, and with Nadia Boulanger at the École Normale de Musique in Paris. He received a Guggenheim Fellowship in 1946 and a National Institute of Arts grant in 1952. He has composed works for orchestra, chamber music, songs, and choral and keyboard music.

LESUEUR, Jean François. French composer (1760–1837). Largely self-trained, he was musical director of the Cathedrals of Dijon, Le Mans, and Tours before assuming that post at Notre Dame in Paris, where he introduced the use of an orchestra at the services. This roused violent controversy that led to his eventual resignation. He now devoted himself to composing operas. After many reverses, he achieved a tremendous success at the Opéra with his *Ossian* (1804). Five years later, his *La Mort d'Adam* was almost equally successful. In later years, he was professor of composition at the Paris Conservatory, where one of his pupils was Berlioz.

LESUR, Daniel. French composer, pianist, and organist (1908–). Lesur studied at the Paris Conservatory and was assistant organist at the church of Sainte Clothilde from 1927 to 1937.

RAY LEV

From 1935 to 1939 he also was professor of counterpoint at the Schola Cantorum. In 1936, together with Yves Baudrier and Oliver Messiaen, he founded La Jeune France, an organization of contemporary French composers.

LETTVIN, Theodore. American pianist (1926–). Since 1952, Lettvin has appeared in more than four hundred recitals in the United States and abroad. He is head of the piano department of the Cleveland Music School Settlement. A scholarship student at the Curtis Institute, he studied with Rudolf Serkin and, upon graduation in 1949, served as apprentice conductor with the Buffalo Philharmonic Orchestra. He made his New York debut at Town Hall in 1948 and has appeared with the principal orchestras of the United States. He received the Naumburg Award (1948) and was a prize winner at the Belgian International Music Competition (1952).

LEV, Ray. American pianist (1912–). Ray Lev comes from a musical family. Her father, who was a cantor, gave her her first musical training. Her early piano studies were with Walter Ruell Cowles in New Haven, and she continued her instruction in New York with Rebecca Davidson, Gaston Dethier, and Alexander Lipsky, and in London with Tobias Matthay. Her winning of the New York Philharmonic Society Scholarship and of the American Matthay Prize (1930) facilitated the continuation of her studies in England.

She made her orchestral debut in 1931 at the Eastbourne Festival in England, and her solo debut at Wigmore Hall in London in 1932. Before returning to the United States, she gave recitals over the B.B.C. and was soloist at Wigmore Hall and at the Matthay Festival Queen's Hall concerts.

Her American debut was made at Carnegie Hall in 1933, when she appeared as soloist with Leon Barzin and the National Orchestral Association; her New York debut as a recitalist was at Town Hall in 1934. Since then she has made extensive tours in the United States, Canada, Europe, and Israel.

LEVANT, Oscar. American composer and pianist (1906–). After studying under Schoenberg and Sigismond Stojowski, Levant appeared as a pianist with several jazz orchestras, playing solo in many of the famous Gershwin concerts in New York and at the Hollywood Bowl.

He worked in Hollywood for several years,

OSCAR LEVANT

composing film music and appearing as pianist in films and radio. He has composed a nocturne and suite for orchestra (1936), two piano concertos (1936, 1943), chamber music, and songs (*Lady, Play Your Mandolin,* etc.). Oscar Levant is famous all over the world as an interpreter of the works of George Gershwin, with whom he was intimately acquainted. He owes his popularity to his excellent piano playing as well as to his colorful podium manner. He has also appeared as an actor in many motion pictures and conducted a television show.

LEVASSEUR, Nicholas Prosper. French bass (1791–1871). A famous performer for many years at the Paris Opéra, he created the bass roles in Rossini's *William Tell,* Halévy's *La Juive,* and three of Meyerbeer's operas: *Robert le Diable, Les Huguenots,* and *Le Prophète.*

LEVASSEUR, Rosalie. French soprano (1749–1826). She rose from small parts to stardom at the Paris Opéra, where she was greatly admired by Gluck, who composed for her the title roles in *Armide* and *Iphigenia in Tauris.*

LEVEY, Stanley (Stan). American jazz drummer (1925–). Levey, who came to prominence during the early days of bop, has played with many outstanding groups including those of Oscar Pettiford, Dizzy Gillespie, George Shearing, Charlie Ventura, Woody Herman, and Stan Kenton. He has recorded with his own group, and is equally at home backing East Coast or West Coast musicians.

LEVI, Hermann. German conductor (1839–1900). He was for a quarter-century conductor of the Hofoper in Munich. At Bayreuth on July 28, 1882, he conducted the world première of Wagner's *Parsifal.*

LEVITSKY, Micha. Russian pianist (1898–1941). One of the leading virtuosos of his time, he studied with Stojowski and Dohnányi. His recital tours took him throughout Europe, America, Australia, and the Orient. He composed many piano pieces; these he performed, and they are still played occasionally by other pianists.

LEVY, Marvin David. American composer (1932–). Levy studied piano with Carl Friedberg, musicology with Gustave Reese and Paul Henry Lang, and composition with Philip James and Otto Luening. He is a graduate of Columbia University. After serving as critic for several music magazines, he wrote music criticism for the New York *Herald Tribune* (1956–58). He is the recipient of a Guggenheim Fellowship (1960) and a Huntington Hartford Fellowship (1961).

Levy lists his major works as three operas, *The Tower, Sotoba Komachi,* and *Escorial;* an oratorio, *For the Time Being;* Symphony No. 1; *Kyros* (poem for orchestra); and *One Person* (alto and orchestra). A fourth opera, *Mourning Becomes Electra,* has been commissioned by the Metropolitan Opera Association.

LEWIS, Brenda. American soprano. After singing many roles with the Philadelphia and San Francisco operas, she joined the New York City Opera. She created the role of Birdie in Blitzstein's *Regina* on Broadway and later sang the title role with great success. At the Metropolitan Opera, where she made her debut in 1952, she has sung, among other roles, Carmen, Salome, Vanessa, Rosalinde in *Die Fledermaus,* and Marie in *Wozzeck.*

Brenda Lewis as the Marschallin

MARVIN DAVID LEVY

LEWIS, George. American jazz clarinetist and leader (1900–). A senior citizen of the jazz world, Lewis never took formal musical instruction and was playing professionally at sixteen years of age. Through the years he has played with Chris Kelly, Kid Rena, and Bunk Johnson, and toured at the head of his own New Orleans-style group.

LEWIS, John. American jazz arranger and pianist (1920–). Lewis is a well-known jazz arranger whose *Toccata for Trumpet and Orchestra* was performed at Carnegie Hall in 1947. He was pianist and arranger for the Dizzy Gillespie band and accompanist for Ella Fitzgerald. Since 1952 he has worked with the Modern Jazz Quartet.

LEWIS, Mary. American soprano (1900–1941). She went from the *Ziegfeld Follies* to the Metropolitan Opera, where from 1926 to 1930 she sang such roles as Mimi in *La Bohème* and Nedda in *Pagliacci*. Her much-publicized marriage to the famous baritone Michael Bohnen lasted but a short time.

LEWIS, Meade Lux. American jazz pianist (1905–). Originally a violinist, Lewis switched to piano and in 1929 recorded *Honky Tonk Blues,* the tune which made him famous. He was instrumental in reviving the boogie-woogie style during the late 1930s, and has appeared in night clubs and concerts with Albert Ammons, Pete Johnson, and others.

LEWIS, Richard. Welsh tenor (1914–). His career began as a boy soprano at Welsh festivals. Since 1948, when he came into prominence as Peter Grimes at Covent Garden, he has sung many roles there, including Troilus in Walton's *Troilus and Cressida* and Mark in Tippett's *The Midsummer Marriage* at their world premières. He has been featured in thirteen successive Glyndebourne festivals and in several seasons of the San Francisco Opera. As a major concert and oratorio singer, he has performed with many important orchestras in Europe and America, as well as in recitals. He re-created the role of Troilus in San Francisco at the American première.

LEWIS, Ted. American popular band leader (1892–). Lewis is a perennial of the American vaudeville stage. His band, well known throughout the United States, was the training place of

RICHARD LEWIS

Lewisohn Stadium in New York

many famous jazz musicians, among whom are Benny Goodman, Fats Waller, and Muggsy Spanier.

LEWIS, William. American tenor (1932–). He has performed in opera throughout the United States, appearing as Tamino in the NBC-TV Opera production of *The Magic Flute;* at the Stratford, Connecticut, Mozart Festival; with the New York City and New England opera companies; at the Festival of Two Worlds in Spoleto, Italy, at the invitation of Gian-Carlo Menotti; and with the American Opera Society in *The Trojans at Carthage* at Carnegie Hall.

He portrayed Andres in *Wozzeck,* Narraboth in *Salome,* and Rodolfo in *La Bohème* with the Metropolitan Opera company. At the composer's invitation Lewis sang in the American première of Stravinsky's *Threni* and in 1962 he sang in the première of Earl Wild's Easter cantata for television, *Revelation,* for which he also arranged the text.

LEWISOHN, Adolph. German-American philanthropist (1849–1938). Lewisohn was a prominent industrialist who was fervently interested in music. Among his great contributions to his beloved art was the donation of the Lewisohn Stadium on the campus of the College of the City of New York, which, since 1918, has been the scene of widely attended summer concerts.

LEWISOHN STADIUM CONCERTS. A series of open-air symphony, operatic, popular music, and dance concerts and recitals presented each summer at the Lewisohn Stadium on the campus of the College of the City of New York. The concerts were inaugurated in 1918 and, since then, more than seventeen million New Yorkers and summer visitors from all parts of the world have attended them.

Mrs. Minnie Guggenheimer has been the dynamic chairman of the Stadium Concerts ever since their inception. In her late seventies, she continues her tireless efforts, assuring performances by outstanding artists and raising the necessary funds needed to underwrite deficits.

The Stadium Concerts Orchestra is composed almost entirely of musicians from the New York

Philharmonic Orchestra. Conductors through the years have included Victor Herbert, Henry Hadley, William Van Hoogstraten, Frederick Stock, Dimitri Mitropoulos, Sir Thomas Beecham, Fritz Reiner, George Szell, Artur Rodzinski, José Iturbi, and Eugene Ormandy. One of the annual features is the all-Gershwin Concert, first presented in 1931 when George Gershwin himself was the soloist.

LHEVINNE, Josef. Russian-American pianist and teacher (1874–1944). Josef Lhevinne was a student of Safonov at the Moscow Conservatory, from which he was graduated in 1891. He taught at the Tiflis Conservatory and later joined the faculty of the Moscow Conservatory. He made his debut in New York with the Russian Symphony Orchestra conducted by Safonov in 1906, and, after living abroad for many years, returned to the United States in 1919 for extensive tours, orchestral appearances, and duo piano recitals with his wife, Rosina Lhevinne. He was a member of the Juilliard School faculty and, with his wife, conducted a studio in New York.

LHEVINNE, Rosina. Russian-American pianist and teacher (1880–). Rosina Lhevinne was graduated from the Kiev Conservatory in 1898 and performed as a soloist throughout Europe. She came to the United States with her husband, Josef Lhevinne, in 1919, joining him in duo piano recitals and establishing a studio in New York. She is an outstanding member of the Juilliard School faculty. Though now in her eighties, she still plays in public occasionally and recently enchanted critics and public alike with model performances of concertos by Mozart and Chopin.

LIADOV, Anatol. Russian composer (1855–1914). After studying at the St. Petersburg Conservatory, where Rimsky-Korsakov was his composition teacher, Liadov taught there. He wrote numerous graceful piano pieces influenced by Chopin but also of Russian flavor—the best known of these is *A Musical Snuff-Box*—and orchestral and choral works and songs. Among these *Eight Russian Folksongs* and his symphonic poems *Baba Yaga, The Enchanted Lake,* and *Kikimora* are occasionally performed.

Although Liadov's works are mostly short (he admitted that he was the laziest composer of all time, preferring rather to "think about composing than writing it"), his superb orchestration remains a model of its kind.

Rosina and Josef Lhevinne

Anatol Liadov, a portrait by Ilya Repin

LIBERACE, Wladziu Valentino. American pianist (1920–). He is the son of an Italian musician and a Polish-American mother whose own mother had been a pupil of Paderewski in Poland. His enormous popularity has been due very largely to television, which has brought his flamboyant personality and clever performances of popular classics, sentimental songs, and syncopated numbers to millions.

LIBRETTO. Italian, "booklet." The term for the text of an opera or other dramatic vocal work. Though mostly the librettist remains obscure, the ultimate success of an opera depends on him as much as on the composer. No opera with a weak libretto has survived in the repertory for long.

Masterpieces in this form were written by Da Ponte, Mozart's librettist; Boito, who worked with Verdi; and Von Hofmannsthal, who was Strauss' collaborator. Composers who wrote their own librettos include Wagner, Leoncavallo, and Gian-Carlo Menotti.

LIEBERMANN, Rolf. Swiss composer (1910–). Liebermann is an exponent of the twelve-tone system in a free and individual style. He was a student of Vladimir Vogel. He is presently general manager of the Hamburg State Opera. His orchestral piece *Furioso* won international recognition in 1947; his *Jazz Concerto* was first performed by the Chicago Symphony Orchestra in 1954; and his opera *School for Wives,* based on Molière's play, was commissioned and performed by the Louisville Orchestra in 1955, and was produced at the Salzburg Festival in 1957. He has also written works for orchestra and piano, and compositions (other than operas) for the musical theater.

LIEBERSON, Goddard. Anglo-American composer, critic, and recording-company executive (1911–). He is the president of Columbia Records and also a radio commentator, composer, and writer for musical journals and encyclopedias. His wife is the dancer Vera Zorina.

LIEBESFREUD *(Love's Joy).* Composition for violin and piano by Kreisler, published in 1910 together with two other violin compositions, *Caprice Viennois* and *Schöne Rosmarin (Fair Rosemary)*—"three pieces that will remain forever in the repertoire of violinists and in the

ROLF LIEBERMANN

Karl Liebl as Loge in Das Rheingold

George Balanchine's choreographic version of the Liebeslieder Waltzes, *danced by the New York City Ballet*

affections of their listeners" (Sigmund Spaeth).

LIEBESLEID *(Love's Sorrow).* Composition for violin and piano by Kreisler, written shortly after *Liebesfreud* (1910). It has been arranged as a song to the words *Die Liebe kommt, die Liebe geht (Love Comes, Love Goes)*. There is also an English translation which is a popular song.

LIEBESLEIDER WALTZES *(Love Song Waltzes).* Popular waltz songs (Op. 52), published in 1869 by Brahms. He composed them "as a sort of break" shortly after finishing his *Requiem*. The complete title is: *Liebeslieder für das Pianoforte zu vier Händen mit Gesang ad libitum (Love songs for the piano for four hands with song as desired).* Later Brahms arranged the waltzes for four hands without voice.

The words are taken from *Polydora,* a collection of foreign folk songs translated into German

by G. F. Daumer. In 1874 Brahms published a new collection of similar waltzes, also to words by Daumer. Here the words of the last song, *Zum Schluss,* are, however, taken from the epilogue to Goethe's comedy *Alexis und Dora.*

LIEBESTOD. See *Tristan und Isolde.*

LIEBL, Karl. German tenor. He is currently one of the leading Wagnerian tenors in European opera houses and at the Metropolitan Opera, where his roles include Tristan, which he often sings opposite Birgit Nilsson, Walther in *Die Meistersinger,* and Bacchus in Richard Strauss' *Ariadne auf Naxos.*

LIED. German, "song." A lied is simply a song with German words, but in other languages the word is used for the special type of German song associated particularly with the names of Schubert, Schumann, Brahms, and Hugo Wolf. Schubert is generally regarded as the incomparable master of lieder.

A section of a scroll by Hsu Tao-ning (fl. *eleventh century*), Fishing in a Mountain Stream. *William Rockhill Nelson Gallery of Art. Atkins Museum of Fine Arts, Kansas City, Missouri*

LIED VON DER ERDE, DAS *(The Song of the Earth)*. Symphony for tenor and contralto (or baritone) and orchestra, by Mahler. The work was completed in 1908 and first performed on November 10, 1911, at Munich. It is not a symphony in the usual sense, but a cycle of six solo songs with words from Hans Bethge's anthology of German translations of ancient Chinese poetry entitled *The Chinese Flute*. The poems are by Chang Chi, Li Po, Meng Hao-jan, and Wang-wei. Mahler himself regarded the work as a symphony, but, having written eight previous symphonies, he did not number it, since other great composers — Beethoven, Schubert, and Bruckner—had died shortly after completing their ninth symphonies. Mahler himself did not live to see the first performance of his own "ninth symphony," as he died in May, 1911.

A very personal work, *Das Lied* reflects at times a feeling of profound pessimism and bitter renunciation of the world. The mood of some of the poems is somber and the music dark and brooding though occasionally lit by vivid Oriental colors.

I. *Das Trinklied vom Jammer der Erde* (*The Drinking Songs of Earth's Sorrow*) is in praise of joy: the world is full of woe, but Heaven is eternal, life and death are unknown. Therefore pluck the lute and drain the golden cup!

II. *Der Einsame im Herbst* (*Autumn Loneliness*). Nature is shrouded in autumn fog . . . life's lamp is burning dimly, the poet's heart is full of melancholy and fear that the loving sun may nevermore dry his tears.

III. *Von der Jugend* (*Of Youth*). In the center of a lake lies an island with a pavilion of green and white porcelain. An arched bridge of jade spans the channel. In the pavilion young people are sitting talking, drinking, and writing verses. Everything is charmingly reflected upside down in the water.

IV. *Von der Schönheit* (*Of Beauty*) describes maidens picking lotus blossoms on the shore of the lake which reflects their slender limbs. Boys are riding across the flowers and grass, and one maiden gazes longingly after a boy as he gallops past with his horse's mane flying about him.

V. *Der Trunkene im Frühling* (*The Drunkard in Spring*) is about wine and spring. Why should I bother myself? Let me drink as long as I can, and then sleep. If spring comes how does it concern me? Let me drink and sleep and drink again!

VI. *Der Abschied* (*The Farewell*) concerns friendship. The poet is waiting for his friend. The sun has set, and weary people are returning home. "I am longing to enjoy the beauty of this evening with you, as I wander with my lute upon the grassy path." Then he arrives. "Fortune was not kind to me in this world. Where am I going? Into the mountains; I am seeking peace for my lonely heart. The earth flowers and spring is coming everywhere, and the shining blue distance is eternal."

LIEUTENANT KIJE.

Orchestral suite, Op. 60 (1934), by Prokofiev. The composer arranged the symphonic suite from his score to the film *Lieutenant Kije*. The plot of the film has its origin in an anecdote concerning Tsar Nicholas I. The Tsar misread a military dispatch to refer to a Lieutenant Kije. His courtiers, not wishing to risk the Tsar's displeasure by pointing out to him his error, invented a life for that nonexistent officer. The movements of the suite are:

1. The Birth of Kije (*allegro*), featuring cornet, fife, and drum.
2. Romance (*andante*). A solo in this movement is performed by tenor saxophone.
3. Kije's Wedding (*allegro fastoso*).
4. Troika (*moderato*), suggesting a Russian sleigh.
5. Burial of Kije (*andante assai*). Recalls the previous episodes.

LILLIBURLERO.

A popular song of the seventeenth century. Its strong Protestant tone gave it a great vogue during the Revolutionary period of 1688 onward, especially in Ireland. The doggerel words, dealing with the appointment of a new Lord Lieutenant of Ireland, were written in 1687 by the First Marquess of Wharton. He later boasted that *Lilliburlero* had "sung James II out of three kingdoms." The first verse runs:

Ho! broth-er Teague dost hear de de-cree?

Many other texts were later written to fit the tune, including *Protestant Boys,* an Orangemen's song.

The origin of the tune is not certain. It has been ascribed to Henry Purcell, for it appears as a piece for harpsichord in his *Music's Handmaid* (1689), but he may have merely used an already popular air.

A scene from Russian Soldier, *a ballet based on Prokofiev's* Lieutenant Kije

LINCKE, Paul.

German composer of operettas (1866–1946). Lincke became the leader of a small orchestra in Berlin when only eighteen years old. His first success as a composer was the sumptuously produced operetta *Venus auf Erden (Venus on Earth)*. This is so genuine a product of Berlin that it earned him the title of "the most Berlinlike of Berlin's composers."

For two years (1918–1920) he was leader of the orchestra at the Folies Bergère, Paris, but later returned to Berlin, where he had his own music-publishing business.

Best-known works:

OPERETTAS

Im Reiche des Indra (1899)
  Heimlich still und leise, kommt die Liebe
Frau Luna (1899)
  Ach Frühling, wie bist du so schön?
  Das ist die Berliner Luft, Luft, Luft
Nakiris Hochzeit (1902)
  Siamesischen Wachtparade
Lysistrata (1902)
  Glühwürmchen-Idyll: Wenn die Nacht sich
Berlinerluft (1906)
  Schenck mir doch ein kleines bischen Liebe

**LINCOLN CENTER FOR THE PERFORM-
ING ARTS.** Lincoln Center is being constructed
in New York City, northwest of Columbus Circle
in Manhattan, with funds derived from the city,
state, and federal governments and from private
sources. It will consist of the Metropolitan
Opera House, with a 3,800-seat theater, the new
home of the Metropolitan Opera; Philharmonic
Hall, seating 2,600, the new home of the New
York Philharmonic Orchestra; New York State
Theater, financed as the New York State contribution to the 1964–65 World's Fair, to seat
2,500; the Juilliard School of Music's new
quarters, including a Chamber Music and
Recital Hall; a 1,100-seat Repertory Theater
with a flexible stage, to house a new acting
company under leadership of Robert Whitehead
and Elia Kazan; and a Library-Museum building, to house the New York Public Library's
outstanding theater and dance collection and
many phonograph records and musical scores.

The Children's Theater will be in the Library-
Museum building. Ground was broken for
Lincoln Center on May 14, 1959, by President
Dwight D. Eisenhower.

Lincoln Center came into active existence on
September 23, 1962, when the first of its buildings, Philharmonic Hall, was opened to the
public. A gala concert by the New York Philharmonic Symphony was conducted by Leonard
Bernstein. Members of the audience included
the First Lady, Mrs. John F. Kennedy, the
Governor of New York, Nelson Rockefeller, and
his brother, John D. Rockefeller III, who is
chairman of the board of directors of the Center.
Also present were many famous musicians, including the president of Lincoln Center, William
Schumann. During the opening week, concerts
were given by the Boston Symphony, the Philadelphia Orchestra, the Cleveland Orchestra, and
the Metropolitan Opera. The opening-night
concert was televised coast to coast by CBS.

*Model of Lincoln Center for the Performing Arts, facing west from Columbus Avenue, New
York. Buildings* (clockwise from left) *are: New York State Theater, Metropolitan Opera House
and Opera Tower, Repertory Theater and Library-Museum, Juilliard School and Chamber Music
and Recital Hall, and Philharmonic Hall*

Above, right: *The proposed façade of the Metropolitan Opera House.* Above, left: *the interior of Philharmonic Hall on opening night.* Left: *The lobby of the New York State Theater.* Below: *the exterior of Philharmonic Hall, immediately after its completion*

LIND, Jenny (Johanna Maria). Swedish soprano (1820–1887). Jenny Lind, the "Swedish Nightingale," was born out of wedlock in Stockholm and christened in the name of her father, Jonas Niclas Lind. She grew up in very poor surroundings, but her neighbors soon noticed her remarkable talent and helped her to enter the Stockholm Dramatic School when she was nine years old.

She had her first success as a dramatic singer in 1838 at the age of eighteen, in *Der Freischütz.* She said herself that on this day she first realized that her calling as an artist was a gift and a duty sent from above. For the rest of her life she celebrated the anniversary of the day (March 7) with a quiet service.

Soon all Stockholm was at her feet. When only twenty, she became an honorary member of the Academy of Music, and King Oscar I made her

A portrait of Jenny Lind by L. Asher, in the National Museum, Stockholm

his "chief singer." She appeared at musical soirées at the palace, and a warm and lasting friendship bound her to the Swedish royal family.

She continued her training in Paris with García, the world-famous singing teacher, from 1841 to 1842. Her voice developed unique beauty and strength, with a wonderfully even quality over its whole range—a brilliant soprano with a register from low B to high G.

In 1844 she appeared in Berlin as Norma, and later as Vielka, the main role in Meyerbeer's *Das Feldlager in Schlesien (The Camp in Silesia),* which was especially written for her. These performances made her famous throughout Europe. Both the Emperor of Austria and the King of Prussia appointed her court singer; and the Danish fairy-tale writer, Hans Christian Andersen, commemorated her in his story "The Nightingale," in which she was the nightingale whose song brings health and life, balm and comfort. Andersen wrote of her effect upon him: "Only through Jenny Lind have I understood the secret of art. She is in truth the very manifestation of the world of art. No other person has had a greater and purer effect on me than Jenny Lind. One laughs, one weeps, one gains as much from listening to her as from going to church."

Andersen fell so much in love with her that he dared to propose. She replied that she valued his friendship highly, but could not love him.

Meanwhile, Jenny Lind had become friendly with Mendelssohn, and the development of their friendship was followed with lively interest by the whole world of art. She sang *On Wings of Song* for the first time at a Gewandhaus concert, and later she accompanied Mendelssohn to Aachen for a music festival, where she sang in Haydn's *Creation.* Brahms, who first heard her on that occasion, later wrote: "Every time I look at the score of *The Creation* Jenny Lind's singing shines with a golden light."

Chopin thought that her *mezza voce* and pianissimo trills were indescribably beautiful.

Mendelssohn's death in 1847 caused Jenny Lind deep and genuine sorrow. She gave up opera two years later, and began a new career as a concert singer. Her tour of the United States under the management of P. T. Barnum was a triumphal progress. But she tired of the noisy ovations that greeted her wherever she went, and abandoned the popular concert hall for religious music. She was particularly fond of

Messiah, The Creation, and *Elijah,* and gave an especially inspired interpretation of *I Know That My Redeemer Liveth* in *Messiah.*

In 1852 she married Otto Goldschmidt, a pupil of Mendelssohn and Chopin and director of the Bach Choir. It was mainly due to Jenny Lind that Bach's *St. Matthew Passion*—which she regarded as the greatest of all religious musical works—was performed for the first time in London, conducted by her husband. She was elected chief professor at the Royal College of Music in 1883.

On All Saints' Day, 1887, Jenny Lind died at her summer house at Malvern. She was buried in Malvern churchyard, and commemorated by a plaque in Westminster Abbey, between those of Shakespeare and Byron and just below Handel's. A memorial plaque also adorns her birthplace in Stockholm.

LINDA DI CHAMOUNIX. Opera in three acts by Donizetti, libretto by Gaetano Rossi, first performed in Vienna on May 19, 1842. Though this opera was one of Donizetti's greatest successes after *Lucia di Lammermoor,* it has been

Jenny Lind's first New York concert at the Castle Garden

revived since his time only infrequently. The title role has served as a vehicle for Patti, Albani, Clara Louise Kellogg, Galli-Curci, Toti Dal Monte, Lily Pons, and Antonietta Stella. The plot concerns a peasant girl who loves a nobleman who is disguised as a painter. She temporarily loses her wits when she thinks he has deserted her; but he returns to claim her and all ends happily.

LINLEY, Thomas. English composer (1733–1795). One of the best and most successful of English composers for the stage, he produced twenty-seven works: comic operas, ballad and pastoral operas, pantomimes, and incidental music for plays. His best-known work was *The Duenna,* an opera based on the play by Sheridan, who married Linley's daughter **Elizabeth** (1754–1792), a noted concert and oratorio singer.

LINZ SYMPHONY. Mozart's Symphony No. 36 in C major, K. 425, composed at the house of his friend, Count Thun, in the summer of 1783. Mozart's visit to his father to introduce his wife Constanze had not been a success, as his father did not approve of the marriage. On their return journey to Vienna, the young couple stopped at Linz and spent two enjoyable weeks with Count Thun.

The Count had arranged a concert for No-

Elizabeth Linley and her brother, by Gainsborough. J. Pierpont Morgan Collection, N. Y.

vember 4, 1783, and asked Mozart to contribute a symphony. Mozart wrote to his father: "On Thursday I am giving a concert in the theater, and as I have not got a single symphony with me I am writing a new one in a hurry, and it must be finished by then."

The *Linz* Symphony is written for a large orchestra, but the woodwinds consist of only oboes and bassoons.

I. *Adagio; Allegro spirituoso.* The *Linz* was the first of Mozart's symphonies to begin (like Haydn's) with a slow introduction. It starts with disjointed rhythm, strong dynamic contrasts, and chromatic figures. The change to the light main theme on the violins (*allegro spirituoso*) comes as a relief:

In the repetition for full orchestra this is dominated by Hallelujah fanfares on the harmonies C-F-C.

II. *Andante.* This is characterized by frequent changes between sharp dynamic accents and distinctive wind parts. The movement's idyllic intimate feeling and melancholy are not spoiled by the intrusion of trumpets and kettledrums.

III. *Menuetto.* The triad motif, together with marked rhythm and triumphant trills, creates the impression of festivity and pageantry. Against this background the

DINU LIPATTI

trio flows along easily in a repetition with a gay echo of the themes in the bassoons.

IV. *Finale, Presto.* This is reminiscent of an overture to an opera buffa. Written in sonata form, it is irresistible in its strength and vitality. The many quick dynamic changes may indicate that the gaiety is somewhat forced.

LIPATTI, Dinu. Romanian pianist and composer (1917–1950). Lipatti studied piano at the Bucharest Conservatory and, after winning an award at the Vienna international competition for pianists in 1933, with Alfred Cortot, Paul Dukas, and Nadia Boulanger in Paris. Shortly thereafter he became recognized in Europe as an exceptionally gifted concert pianist—powerful in technique and sensitive—performing in France, England, Switzerland, and the Low Countries. In 1943 he became professor of piano at the Geneva Conservatory. He composed works for piano, and for piano and orchestra.

LIPKIN, Arthur Bennett. American conductor and violinist. At the age of eighteen, he became the youngest member of the Philadelphia Orchestra and for twenty years was leader of the Philadelphia String Quartet. He became conductor of the Birmingham (Alabama) Symphony Orchestra in 1949, and has been guest conductor with the Dallas Symphony and the NBC Symphony.

LIPKIN, Seymour. American pianist and conductor (1927–). He studied piano at the Curtis Institute with David Saperton, Serkin, and Horszowski. At the Berkshire Music Center, he was a conducting student of Koussevitzky. He was accompanist to Heifetz on a USO tour abroad during World War II. In 1948, he won the Rachmaninoff Piano Contest. Since then, he has appeared as soloist with all the principal orchestras in the United States and has conducted the New York Philharmonic at Carnegie Hall and on tour, as assistant conductor to Leonard Bernstein. When the New York Philharmonic toured Russia in 1959, Lipkin was soloist in the Stravinsky Piano Concerto. He received a Ford Foundation Award in 1959-60 and has recently devoted more and more of his time to conducting, leading performances of the New York City Opera and other organizations.

LIPKOVSKA, Lydia. Russian soprano (1884–1955). After gaining prominence at the Maryinsky Theatre in St. Petersburg, she left Russia in 1910 to sing at Covent Garden in London, making her debut in the title role at the English première of *Il Segreto di Susanna*. She also sang at the Metropolitan Opera and with the Boston and Chicago opera companies. Her best role was that of Violetta in *La Traviata*.

LIPP, Wilma. Austrian soprano (1925–). A star of the Vienna State Opera and the Salzburg Festival, she sings roles in Mozart and Richard Strauss operas, Italian roles such as Gilda in *Rigoletto,* and others in modern works such as Hindemith's *Mathis der Maler*. She also is widely known as a concert and recording artist.

LIPTON, Martha. American mezzo-soprano (1919–). Martha Lipton received her first vocal instruction from her mother and studied at the Juilliard School of Music with Paul Reimers. Since 1944 she has been a member of the Metropolitan Opera company, with which she has appeared in many leading parts. She has performed as soloist with leading orchestras in the United States, has sung at the Vienna Opera (1954) and the Paris Opéra (1959), and has appeared at the

Martha Lipton as Mother Goose in the American première of Stravinsky's Rake's Progress

Emmanuel List as Hagen

Edinburgh Festival, the Holland Festival, and at the Teatro Municipal in Santiago, Chile. She is an associate professor at Indiana University.

LIST, Emmanuel. Austrian bass (1891–). A star at the Vienna State Opera, Covent Garden in London, and the Metropolitan Opera, where he sang for fourteen seasons, he was celebrated as Baron Ochs in *Der Rosenkavalier*. His deep bass also was used to great advantage in Wagnerian roles such as Hunding in *Die Walküre* and Hagen in *Die Götterdämmerung.*

LIST, Eugene. American pianist (1918–). List was born in Los Angeles, and made his debut with the Los Angeles Philharmonic Orchestra in 1930. Later he studied with Olga Samaroff and at the Juilliard School of Music. He made his New York debut playing the Shostakovitch Piano Concerto with the New York Philharmonic Orchestra in 1935. While a sergeant in the United States Army he performed at the Potsdam Conference in 1945, in the presence of Truman, Churchill, and Stalin. He frequently appears in the United States as soloist with leading orchestras and as recitalist. His wife is the violinist Carroll Glenn.

Franz Liszt

(OCTOBER 22, 1811–JULY 31, 1886)

LISZT'S father, Adam Liszt, was a lover of music and a skillful amateur. Through his employment in the management of the estates of Count Esterházy, who had his own orchestra, he came into contact with many musicians. Franz inherited his musical talent from his father, and from his mother he derived a religious outlook which led to close contact with the Church throughout his life. Franz was born at Raiding, Hungary.

His father gave Franz his first piano tuition, and he made such rapid progress that he played at a concert when only nine. Count Esterházy's attention was attracted, and he permitted the boy to give a concert at his palace in Pressburg, as a result of which five noblemen decided to sponsor Franz, each contributing six hundred Austrian gulden annually toward his further studies.

The Liszt family moved to Vienna, and Salieri became Franz's teacher of theory, while Karl Czerny took charge of his piano studies. The first time they visited the famous piano teacher, he had no time for new pupils, but when he heard the boy play he exclaimed, "I have not heard a talent like his since Schubert!" When Franz's father took the money to Czerny for the boy's first lesson it was refused: "I'll take no fee. The boy's tremendous ability is sufficient reward." After two years' intensive study, Franz was allowed to perform for the Viennese public, on December 1, 1823. Beethoven was present, and according to Schindler he clambered onto the platform, kissed Franz on the forehead, and exclaimed: "We shall hear more from him." In the same year the child prodigy made his debut as a composer with his variations on a waltz by Diabelli published in a collection entitled *Vaterländische Künstler-Verein.*

In 1823 Liszt went to Paris, furnished with an introduction from Prince Metternich, and applied for admission to the Conservatory. He described his interview thus: "We hastened to see Cherubini on the very day after our arrival. A letter of recommendation from Count Metternich was to pave our way. The clock struck ten as we arrived. Cherubini was already there. As we passed through the door—or, rather, the awe-inspiring portal—a wave of reverence swept over me. I thought to myself, 'This is the fatal place. Within these sacred walls reigns the tribunal which can either condemn or pardon.' I felt like falling on my knees before everyone I passed.

"At last, after a quarter of an hour filled with qualms, the suspense was brought to an end by a signal that we could now go in to the director. More dead than alive but, even so, possessed of superhuman powers, I lunged toward Cherubini with a desire to kiss his hand. I was suddenly struck by the thought that perhaps this was not the custom in France, and my eyes filled with tears. Fortunately, my quandary was soon cut short.

"I had previously been informed that I should meet with difficulties before I could be admitted to the Conservatory, but we were quite unaware of the existence of a law forbidding the admission of aliens. When Cherubini apprised us of this, it was like a thunderbolt, and I trembled from head to foot. We endeavored to stammer out a word or two, but the rules were inexorable. I was inconsolable; all seemed lost, even my honor, and I lost faith in everything. There was no end to my sobbing and lamentations. The

Right: *A portrait of Franz Liszt in the Goethe-Schiller-Archiv in Weimar*

The young Liszt (above) *after a lithograph by C. Molle, about 1825, and* (below) *a later drawing*

wounds were deep, and remained open for a long time."

Liszt then became the pupil of Reicha and Paër, and on the strength of his excellent references soon gained entry into the best circles. After one private concert, he gave a concert in the Paris opera house in 1824. On this occasion his father wrote to a friend: "This concert was a public triumph for my son. His appearance on the platform was the signal for a storm of applause, which continued unabated. At the end of each passage, murmurs of enthusiasm and admiration could be heard among the audience, and after each item he had to take two or three bows. Even before the concert the newspapers had issued reports of Franz's great talent, and afterward fourteen journalists vied with one another in singing his praises, and it is not over yet! He has been called a new Mozart! And do you know what I say to all this? I weep! Yes, just think, every evening we are invited to a party. He improvises wherever he goes and all are agreed that every time he plays they hear something new."

Newspaper reports of the concert on March 7, 1824, sounded like a fairy story. One newspaper stated: ". . . the members of the orchestra were so enthralled by Liszt's music that they forgot to attend to their own parts." "Le petit Liszt" was the sensation of Paris. The same thing happened in London, where he played at Drury Lane, and in Manchester. The following year Liszt's opera *Don Sancho* was an enormous success. (The manuscript was lost in a fire at the opera house in 1875.)

Liszt next toured the south of France and Switzerland. But his pleasure in performing in public had now diminished considerably. He felt lonely and turned to religion for comfort; he told his father of his desire to become a priest.

"You belong to Art and not to the Church!" his father replied. Nevertheless, Liszt immersed himself in the Bible and other religious books, reading day and night until his health was affected. The doctors in London, where he was then staying, prescribed rest and sea bathing, and in July, 1827, father and son journeyed to Boulogne. Liszt's health improved, but his father was suddenly taken ill, and died after three days. He took leave of his son with a warning. "On his deathbed in Boulogne, my father told me that I had plenty of common sense and a good heart, but he feared that women would come to play a dangerous part in my life. I was not a little taken aback at his suppositions. I was then only sixteen years old, and had no ideas about women. In my innocence I asked my father-confessor to enlighten me as to the meaning of the seventh and ninth Commandments, for fear that I had inadvertently broken them."

Liszt soon discovered the truth of his father's words, for before he was seventeen he had fallen deeply and earnestly in love. It happened in Paris, and the lady was no less a personage than the daughter of the French Minister of Commerce, the Countess Caroline St. Criq, who was the same age as Liszt and was one of his piano pupils. Her father would not hear of any friendship between them, and forbade them to see each other. This was such a heavy blow to Liszt that he became seriously ill and had to retire from public life for nearly two years. At this time, as so often later in life, he sought comfort and relief in religion, and once again seriously considered adopting the Church as his career.

He described this period of his life in a letter to George Sand written in 1837: "Young and arrogant as I was at that time, my heart was filled with a mystical desire for love and religion. Because I showed my true self, an enthusiastic child, a warm emotional artist, a conscientious believer—in short full of all those sentiments that an eighteen-year-old experiences when he loves God and mankind with all his heart—because I had no notion of play-acting, I gained a reputation for being an actor."

But the July Revolution turned his thoughts to other things. He plunged himself heart and soul into socialism, and his friends had difficulty in holding him back from the barricades.

Paganini gave his first performance in Paris in 1831. Liszt was present, and the event was of great significance in his development.

"For a whole fortnight my mind and fingers have been working like two lost spirits—Homer, the Bible, Plato, Locke, Byron, Hugo, Lamartine, Chateaubriand, Beethoven, Bach, Hum-

Liszt playing for a group of friends

Caricature of 1842, depicting the triumph of Liszt's style over "General Bass"

mel, Mozart, Weber are all around me. I study them, meditate on them, devour them with fury. 'I, too, am a painter!' Michelangelo exclaimed when he saw a masterpiece for the first time. Even though your friend is little and poor, he has constantly repeated these words ever since Paganini's concert. I practice four or five hours every day—exercises in thirds, sixths, eighths, tremolos, repetitions, cadenzas, etc. Ah, if I don't go mad, you will find an artist in me! Yes, an artist such as you desire, such as is needed nowadays."

As a result of this tremendous effort, Liszt developed an outstanding piano technique, and really approached the goal he had set himself— to became a Paganini of the piano, a master to whom all difficulties were mere child's play.

About this time Liszt became acquainted with the Countess Marie d'Agoult. He was twenty-two years old and she was twenty-eight. She

Women admirers thronged Liszt's concerts

later described her first impressions of him: "Tall, very slim, pale and with an illuminating fire shining forth from his sea-green eyes. His face has a suffering but strong expression. His gait is uncertain—he is seemingly lifted from the ground. He gives the impression of being distrait, uneasy, like a spirit waiting for the chime of a clock to herald its return to darkness and night. This is how I see the young genius— whose silence about his private life arouses curiosity, as his triumph provokes envy."

The friendship between Liszt and Marie d'Agoult blossomed into love, and she deserted her husband—who was twenty years her senior— and her children, and went with Liszt to Geneva where they made their home for four years. The Countess had pronounced literary and artistic interests, and with her Liszt pursued a course of intense study in philosophy, art, and architecture in Italy—a widening of his general education which came to have great importance for his art.

Liszt and the Countess d'Agoult had three children; their daughter Cosima became Wagner's second wife. Later in life, Marie d'Agoult made her name as an author under the pseudonym Daniel Stern. In her *Memoires* she wrote of Liszt and herself: "Strong affinities of race and temperament brought us together, but the extreme difference in our education and station in life necessarily raised innumerable difficulties between us, which finally made it impossible for us to live together."

During Liszt's absence from Paris a new piano virtuoso, the Austrian Sigismund Thalberg, became the idol of the public. Liszt's vanity was hurt, and he did his utmost to prove that he was the outstanding pianist of the time. The public was divided into two camps, and the climax was reached in a "musical duel" at a joint concert where Liszt and Thalberg played their own compositions. Liszt won, and henceforth maintained an unchallenged position as "king of the piano," or the "Pianist of the Future," as Berlioz termed him.

Between 1840 and 1848 Liszt was constantly engaged in concert tours, all of which resembled triumphal processions. People were overwhelmed by his extraordinary playing, his phenomenal technique, and his charming personality, and women adored him.

After a concert in Kiev in 1847, Liszt became acquainted with Princess Caroline von Sayn-

This picture by Schrams and Lafite shows Liszt playing before the Royal Family in Budapest in 1872

Wittgenstein. She was unhappily married to the Tsar's aide-de-camp, and tried to get a divorce in order to marry Liszt. But the Church rejected her appeal, although she and Liszt even petitioned the Pope.

By 1848 Liszt had grown weary of concert giving and lost interest in a virtuoso's life. He accepted a position as leader of the Grand Duke of Weimar's orchestra, and he and the Princess settled down at Weimar, which became his home for many years. There he concentrated all his efforts on his work as leader of the orchestra and on his activities as a composer. He was always anxious to help others, and as a conductor set himself to assist young unknown composers. Among the new works he performed were Berlioz' *Benvenuto Cellini* and Wagner's *Lohengrin*.

Liszt had been composing piano works all his life, and as a touring pianist had made effective though somewhat shallow piano arrangements of popular operatic melodies and similar works. His sense of the possibilities of the piano was such that he could transform even the mightiest orchestral works into excellent piano pieces. But gradually he transferred his interests to independent composition, and wrote a series of poetical piano pieces brilliant in style and technique. They form an art in themselves; with his glittering chromatic figures, complicated accompaniments in thirds and sixths, and powerful chord passages Liszt introduced a completely new piano style.

Simultaneously he turned his attention to the orchestra, and on the basis of Berlioz' program symphonies he created his own form, the one-movement symphonic poem.

His time at Weimar was one of abundant production. The compositions of this period include his piano concertos, his best piano pieces, including *Années de Pèlerinage (Years of Pilgrimage)*, the B minor Piano Sonata, the great piano studies, twelve symphonic poems, the *Faust* Symphony and the *Dante* Symphony. He also was planning an opera. He wrote in 1851 to a friend: "As far as concerns my opera, allow me

(Above) *Impressions of Liszt's various moods during a concert, and* (below) *a contemporary caricature of Liszt*

to thank you for the interest you are ready to take in it. For my own part I have made up my mind to work actively on the score." Unfortunately the opera was never written, or even sketched out to any degree.

In 1849 Wagner came to Weimar. A warm friendship sprang up between the two composers, and Liszt became one of Wagner's most ardent supporters during the difficult years before his music won acceptance. How well Liszt understood his friend's music is shown by these words of Wagner's: "I watched Liszt conducting a rehearsal of my *Tannhäuser,* and was astonished to recognize my 'second self' in him. What I had felt in composing the music, he felt in performing it; what I wanted to express in writing it down, he proclaimed in making it sound. Strange to say, through the love of my rarest friend I gained at the moment of becoming homeless a real home which I had longed and sought for always in the wrong places."

Liszt relinquished his position as orchestra leader at Weimar in 1859, and two years later left the town. The reason was partly that his compositions had not gained the recognition he had hoped for, and partly because the Princess's failure to procure her divorce prevented him from marrying her. In a letter to the Grand Duke, he declared: "Though I find it hard to leave you, I realize that I must find somewhere to live where things are not as difficult for me. I once dreamed of a new era in art in Weimar like that of the time of Charles Augustus. I thought that Wagner and I would become leaders similar to Goethe and Schiller, but unfavorable circumstances have caused my hopes to collapse."

Liszt moved to Rome, and took up close study of ecclesiastical questions. He was awarded the honorary title of Abbé in 1865, but was not consecrated until 1879. The Princess, too, devoted herself to religious work. Liszt was engaged for eight years in the improvement of Catholic church music and on such serious compositions as the oratorios *Christus* and *Saint Elizabeth.*

In 1869 he returned to Weimar and resumed his extensive activity as teacher; pianists traveled from all over the world to become his pupils. Naturally his creative activity suffered, and he wrote: "I must somehow get time to write at least a few pages of music. It will perhaps be difficult because half a dozen pianists have already come from Berlin, Hamburg, etc., and soon there will be a full dozen. Even more will join them later, and they will all be vying with one another for fame and success."

Liszt did not give "lessons" in the usual sense of the word. Felix Weingartner described his experience: "The first impression took one's breath away. While still on the stairway I could hear a dreadful scolding going on. When I opened the door, I caught sight of Liszt, standing in the midst of his students round the piano. There sat a pale young man who must certainly have been playing very badly, for Liszt berated him in no mean manner. 'What do you think I am here for—to wash your dirty underclothes?' he shouted, and flung the music on the piano lid. The young man crept away like a beaten dog.

"Liszt swung round and his glance fell at first casually and then inquisitively on me. I told him my name and referred to a letter I had previously written. 'That's good, that's good,' he growled, and gave me his hand. . . . Then followed a few quite ordinary samples of playing, constantly interrupted by Liszt's comments. Occasionally he played a bar or two himself, and it was astonishing to see how easily he overcame technical difficulties which tied other people's fingers in knots.

"The choice of who should perform, and what should be played, appeared to be quite haphazard. His remarks were brief, but pertinent. If there was a considerable display of talent, his appreciation was profuse. Criticism was frequently delivered in the form of sarcasm, and not all his hearers were intelligent enough to discover whether it was praise or blame.

"A beautiful young lady played a Chopin ballade in a completely trifling manner. Liszt strode cheerfully backward and forward, muttering: 'Holy bim-bam! Holy bim-bam!' Everybody was agog to see what would happen. When she had finished, Liszt went over to her, stroked her hair gently, kissed her brow and said with exquisite amiability: 'Get married very soon, my dear child. Adieu!' "

Liszt loved to be surrounded by young people. He liked to share their daily life and to be the central figure in all their excursions, and he would often be one of the last to bed after a merry evening.

In 1870 Liszt accepted the Emperor's offer of the directorship of a prospective State Academy of Music in Budapest. A number of famous

Liszt in advancing age

pianists became his pupils, and many of them have passed on his methods down to the present time. Liszt devoted the last years of his life entirely to teaching, although he still made some public appearances. After a brief tour of France, England, and Belgium, he arrived in Bayreuth in 1886. Despite a heavy cold, he insisted on attending a performance of *Tristan* at the Festival Hall on the evening of his arrival. Shortly afterward he developed pneumonia, and on February 28, at Bayreuth, he died. His last word was "Tristan."

Liszt was a strange mixture of worldliness and religion: "half gypsy and half Franciscan," as he himself said. Amy Fay, his American student, whose memoires offer a fascinating description of his master classes, described him thus: "Tall and slight, with deep-set eyes, shaggy eyebrows, and long iron-grey hair, which he parts in the middle. His mouth turns up at the corners, which gives him a most crafty and Mephistophelian expression when he smiles, and his whole appearance and manner have a sort of Jesuitical elegance and ease. His hands are very narrow, with long and slender fingers that look as if they had twice as many joints as other people's. They are so flexible and supple that it makes you nervous to look at them. I never saw anything like the polish of his manner. When he got up to leave, for instance, after making his adieux to the ladies he would lay his hand on his heart and make his final bow not with affectation, or in mere gallantry, but with a quiet courtliness that made you feel that no other way of bowing to a lady was right or proper. . . . But the most extraordinary thing about Liszt is his wonderful variety of facial expression. At one moment his face will look dreamy, shadowy, tragic. The next he will be insinuating, amiable, ironic, sardonic—but always with the same captivating grace of manner."

When asked why he had never written his memoirs, Liszt is said to have replied: "I could not write about my own life. I was always far too busy living it."

Liszt's significance in the history of music is immense. He was one of the most technically

Abbé Liszt playing for his admirers at Weimar

skillful pianists of all time, and one of the finest piano teachers the world has ever known. A pioneer of the exploitation of all the potentialities of the piano, and the creator of a completely new piano style, he advanced both technique and development of the piano more than any other musician.

He was an outstanding conductor, with a supreme gift of identifying himself with the music.

As a composer he created a new type of music in his *Hungarian Rhapsodies*. He was a bold reformer of harmonies, and his modulations and his use of chromatics brought about a great advance, for which Wagner was unjustly given the credit. Liszt was one of the few composers who really created new forms. His treatment of the sonata form was all his own, and he developed the one-movement symphonic poem. He used his unique position in European musical life in the most unselfish way by helping young and comparatively unknown composers, and his perception helped to further almost every new development in the European music of his time.

Many factors have prevented Liszt's receiving proper recognition as a composer. Many of his piano pieces are virtuoso works whose value can be rated only as fireworks. Their style is so brilliant that it disguises their more serious qualities. Also, many of his works are program music, and are condemned on that account. But this ought not to overshadow the poetry of his music, its fertility of expression, and its clear and pure form. Without Liszt the musical development of the nineteenth century would have pursued quite a different course, and many composers would have been restricted, if not checked, in their work.

Sacheverell Sitwell summarizes Liszt thus: "His transformation into a priest was the result of sincere religious feeling. The generosity of his character proved itself in his support of so many younger musicians: Dvořák, Grieg, Borodin, Tchaikovsky. All things considered, Liszt must remain among the phenomena of music. As a pianist he has never been equalled; he is a great, if neglected, composer; and he ranks with Byron among the most striking figures of the whole romantic epoch."

The Anglo-Greek music critic M. D. Calvocoressi said: "With regard to form, idiom and technique, his influence was universal. This is particularly discernible in Wagner and Richard

Liszt with his son-in-law, Wagner

LISZT'S BEST-KNOWN WORKS
ORCHESTRAL
Symphonies:

A Faust Symphony (with tenor and chorus)
  (1853–57)
Dante Symphony (with chorus) (1867)

Symphonic Poems:

Prometheus (1850)
Orpheus (1854)
Hungaria (1856)
Les Préludes (1854)
Mazeppa (1954)
Tasso (1856)
Two Episodes from Lenau's *Faust* (also arranged
  for piano) (1860–61)
  Mephisto Waltzes Nos. 1 and 2 (1860; 1880)

Piano Concertos:

No. 1, E flat major (1855)
No. 2, A major (1861)
Hungarian Fantasy (piano and orchestra) (1852)
Malediction (piano and strings) (1830–40)
Totentanz (piano and orchestra) (1859)

PIANO

12 *Études d'exécution transcendante*
Sonata, B minor
6 *Études d'exécution transcendante d'après Paganini*
Feux follets
Ricordanza
Concert Études
Waldesrauschen
Gnomenreigen
Années de Pèlerinage
Au bord d'une source
3 *Sonetti del Petrarca*
Venezia e Napoli, Suite
6 *Consolations*
Legend: St. Francis Walking on the Water
Polonaise, E major
Valses oubliées
Spanish Rhapsody
20 *Hungarian Rhapsodies* (also orchestral versions)
Valse Impromptu
Mazurka Brillante
12 *Grandes Études*
Berceuse
Les Jeux d'eau à la Villa d'Este
2 *Mephisto Waltzes* (originally for orchestra)
2 *Légendes*
Album d'un Voyageur
Fantasie and Fugue on the theme B.A.C.H.
Liebesträume, Op. 62

CHORAL

Christus (solists, chorus, orchestra, and organ)
  (1855–67)
The Legend of St. Elizabeth (soloists, chorus, orchestra,
  and organ) (1857–62)
Missa Choralis, in A minor (chorus and organ)
  (1865–69)
Missa Solemnis (*Gran Festival Mass*) (soloists, chorus,
  orchestra, and organ) (1855)
Hungarian Coronation Mass (soloists, chorus, organ,
  and orchestra) (1867–69)

Strauss, in all the leading French composers from Franck to Ravel, in all the Russians (from Balakirev to Borodin), and in our contemporary Hungarian composers."

Saint-Saëns said: "Liszt courageously followed the path that Beethoven and Berlioz had indicated, but had not themselves trodden, and produced the symphonic poem."

The French author G. Jean-Aubry emphasized Liszt's importance to the national schools of Europe, and showed that he supported and encouraged Borodin, Rimsky-Korsakov, César Franck, Saint-Saëns, Sgambati, Grieg, Smetana, Albéniz—in short, all those who founded the new national schools of Russia, France, Italy, Norway, Bohemia, and Spain. "The Germans ought to nourish a violent hatred of Liszt. For it was largely due to him that Germany's musical supremacy was overthrown."

Of Liszt's relationship to Wagner, the French author André Suarès writes: "Liszt forsook his own art in order to live in someone else's. Even further, he permitted himself to be plundered by Wagner, who read his symphonic poems in manuscript, appropriated them, used all Liszt's new discoveries, studied all that he had experimented on, and possessed himself of it with the speed of a genius. And when Wagner's triumph aroused the envy of all, Liszt was the only composer who did not begrudge him that triumph. Such self-sacrifice is unique."

PIANO TRANSCRIPTIONS

J. S. Bach:
  Fantasia and Fugue, G minor (piano)
  Prelude and Fugue, A minor (piano)
Beethoven:
  Fantasia on *Ruins of Athens* (piano and orchestra)
Chopin:
  Polish Songs:
    The Maiden's Wish, Op. 74, No. 1
    My Joys, Op. 74, No .12
Gounod:
  Faust, Waltz
Paganini:
  Andantino capriccioso, E flat major
  La Campanella (Rondo de la Clochette)
  La Chasse, E major
Schubert:
  The Wanderer Fantasy, C major, Op. 15 (piano and orchestra)
  Hungarian March No. 4 (originally piano, four hands, orchestra)
  Soirées de Vienne (piano)
  Songs:
    Hark, Hark the Lark (piano)
    Der Lindenbaum (piano)
Schumann:
  Widmung (piano)
Verdi:
  Rigoletto, Paraphrase de concert (quartet piano)
Wagner:
  Spinning Chorus
  Tannhäuser Overture

Göta Ljungberg as Elisabeth in Tannhäuser

LITOLFF, Henry. French composer and pianist (1818–1891). A pupil of Moscheles, he made his debut at twelve, then toured for some years before he became a music publisher and editor of an inexpensive edition of piano classics. He composed many works, including several operas, symphonies, concertos, chamber music, and piano pieces.

LITURGICAL MUSIC DRAMA. A form of religious service, containing musical and dramatic elements, that was developed in European churches in the period between 900 and 1200 A.D. Spoken and sung in Latin, they were important in the evolution of both music and the drama. Performed by clerics, they depicted religious mysteries and gradually worked into set forms after years of improvisation. Eventually, there were performed (with the use of simple scenic devices) plays of this kind for Christmas, Easter, Ascension, Pentecost, etc. In recent years, *The Play of Daniel* has been performed in churches and concert halls.

LITVINNE, Félia. (Françoise-Jeanne Schütz). Russian soprano (1861–1936). She studied with Victor Maurel and was the sister-in-law of Edouard De Reszké. With Jean De Reszké, she often sang in *Tristan und Isolde*. Her success was mostly in Wagnerian roles at La Scala, the Paris Opéra, Covent Garden, and, for one season, at the Metropolitan Opera.

LJUNGBERG, Göta. Swedish soprano (1893–1955). She was prominent, mostly in Wagnerian roles, at the Berlin Staatsoper, Covent Garden, and the Metropolitan Opera, where she sang the first Salome since Fremstad. Roles that she created were Goossens' Judith, and Lady Marigold in Hanson's *Merry Mount*.

LLOYD, David. American tenor. Since 1946, when he won the Philadelphia *Inquirer*'s "Voice of Tomorrow" contest, he has performed with many opera companies, including the New York City Opera, the Washington Opera Society, and the NBC-TV Opera, as well as at the Edinburgh and Glyndebourne festivals and in many European houses. He also has appeared with most of the major American symphony orchestras and on many recital tours. He became head of the vocal department at the University of Iowa in 1959.

LOCATELLI, Pietro. Italian composer and violinist (1695–1764). Locatelli studied with Corelli in Rome, and developed into an outstanding violin virtuoso. He is known for his sonatas, concerti grossi, and other music for violin and strings.

LOCH LOMOND. Scottish song. The words are attributed to Lady John Douglas Scott, who may also have written the tune. See *Annie Laurie*.

In 1937 an arrangement of the song was made by Claude Thornhill, which was sung with great success by Maxine Sullivan.

LOCKWOOD, Normand. American composer (1906–). Lockwood studied at the Michigan School of Music and later with Respighi, in Rome, and with Nadia Boulanger, in Paris. In 1930 he received a fellowship for study at the American Academy in Rome. He served on the faculties of Oberlin Conservatory, Columbia University, and the University of Wyoming. In 1938, he won the G. Schirmer prize for his choral work *Out of the Cradle, Endlessly Rocking* (after Walt Whitman) for mixed voices, and was a Guggenheim Fellow. His compositions include choral works, chamber music, the Concerto for Organ and Brasses, and compositions for piano and organ.

LOEFFLER, Charles Martin. American composer (1861–1935). Born in Alsace, he studied violin with Joachim and played in the Pasdeloup Orchestra in Paris before coming to the United States in 1881. He played under Theodore Thomas and Leopold Damrosch in New York and, in 1885, became first-desk violinist, with Franz Kneisel, of the newly organized Boston Symphony Orchestra, with which he served for twenty years. From 1903 until his death he spent his time composing and teaching.

Identified to a large extent with the impressionist movement, his style also contains modal and Slavic influences. He wrote choral, orchestral, chamber, instrumental, and vocal works. The best known of these are: *A Pagan Poem* (after Virgil), Op. 14; *Memories of My Childhood;* and Poem for Orchestra, *"La Bonne Chanson."*

LOEILLET, Jean Baptiste. Belgian composer (1680–1730). A member of a Flemish musical family, Loeillet became an excellent flute, oboe, and harpsichord player. He played in orchestras and taught music in England, where he must have been much in fashion, as he is known to have earned a good deal of money. He is credited with substituting the use of the transverse flute for that of the recorder, and it was probably due to him that the flute became the most popular instrument for amateur musicians of the gentry. His music includes many flute sonatas and suites for harpsichord. His brother **Jacques** (1685–1746), a musician of similar talents, was a court musician at Munich and Versailles and composed music that, until recently, was attributed to the "English" Loeillet.

LOESSER, Arthur. American pianist (1894–). Loesser studied at the Institute of Musical Art (now Juilliard School of Music) and made his professional debut as pianist in Berlin in 1913. He toured Australia and the Far East in 1920, and was assisting artist to Mischa Elman in Japan in 1921. In 1926 he joined the faculty of the Cleveland Institute of Music, of which he is now director of the piano department. He has appeared as soloist with leading American orchestras. He was a Japanese-language officer in the United States Army, and after World War II, was the first American musician in uniform to

PIETRO LOCATELLI

play for Japanese audiences. In 1954, his book, *Men, Women and Pianos,* met with considerable interest. His younger brother is Frank Loesser.

LOESSER, Frank. American composer, lyricist, producer, and publisher (1910–). The son of a German immigrant and an alumnus of New York City public schools, Frank Loesser worked as a reporter and vaudeville performer until he found his first success as a song writer, At first he wrote only lyrics; his first published song, *In Love with a Memory of You,* was written in 1931 with William H. Schuman, now director of Lincoln Center for the Performing Arts. His first Broadway show was *The Illustrators Revue* (1936).

In Hollywood, he wrote lyrics for such popular composers as Hoagy Carmichael, Burton Lane Arthur Schwartz, James McHugh, J. Fred Coots, and Jule Styne; among these were: *The Moon of Manakoora; See What the Boys in the Back Room Will Have; Jingle, Jangle, Jingle; Two Sleepy People; They're Either Too Young or Too Old.* By 1947 he was also writing the music for his songs, and his score to the film *The Perils of Pauline* contained several popular numbers.

In 1948 he returned to Broadway with the tremendously successful show *Where's Char-*

FRANK LOESSER

ley?, adapted from the farce *Charley's Aunt* and starring Ray Bolger. Since then, his activities have been divided between Hollywood and Broadway. For films he wrote the songs *Where Are You, Now That I Need You; Baby, It's Cold Outside; Tunnel of Love;* and the score to Danny Kaye's *Hans Christian Andersen.*

For Broadway he wrote *Guys and Dolls* (1950), *The Most Happy Fella* (1956) *Greenwillow* (1960), and *How To Succeed in Business Without Really Trying* (1961). Each is characterized by a freshly inventive attitude and a subtle relationship between music and text. *Guys and Dolls,* one of the finest of all American musicals, is written entirely in the Broadway honky-tonk vernacular of Damon Runyon, upon whose stories the show is based. *The Most Happy Fella* is an ambitious setting of Sidney Howard's *They Knew What They Wanted,* a tender love story of simple people in California's wine country. In it one musical number flows into the next with only occasional dialogue. The score contains a wide variety of musical styles: standard show tunes, chorales, the merry tunefulness of *opera buffa,* and the Italian aria. *Greenwillow* is an experiment with folk fantasy. *How To Succeed,* a riotous satire on big-business mores, won a Pulitzer Prize.

LOEWE, Carl. German composer, organist, conductor, and singer (1796–1869). Loewe was a protégé of Jerome Bonaparte and, as a consequence, was able to devote his talents to composing. He toured Europe extensively and wrote five operas, oratorios, and other works for voice. His most famous ballads are *Edward, Erlkönig,* and *Die Uhr.*

LOEWE, Frederick. Austrian-American composer (1904–). An outstanding composer of the current American musical theater, Loewe was born in Vienna, the son of a well-known operetta tenor. He studied music under Busoni, d'Albert, and Reznǐček, appeared as piano soloist with the Berlin Symphony Orchestra at thirteen, and at fifteen wrote a popular song which was a hit all over Europe. However, when he came to New York in 1924 he was unable to establish himself as a composer and for many years supported himself at odd jobs and by playing the piano in cafés. His one Broadway assignment, *Great Lady* (1937), ran for only twenty performances. The turning point came in 1942, when he formed the partnership with librettist Alan Jay Lerner that has resulted in the Broadway shows *The Day Before Spring* (1945), *Brigadoon* (1947), *Paint Your Wagon* (1951), *My Fair Lady* (1956), and *Camelot* (1960), and the film musical *Gigi* (1958).

Stemming in part from the Viennese operetta tradition, the Lerner and Loewe musicals have embellished it by remarkably skillful use of modern techniques—believable people and plots, united to scores that evoke the flavor of background and periods and songs that spring spontaneously from the action. *Brigadoon,* a fantasy about a village in Scotland which appears for one day once every hundred years, had an enchanting score; it was the first musical to win a Drama Critics' Circle award. *Paint Your Wagon* was set in California in gold-rush times, with songs that had the quality of authentic folk music. In *My Fair Lady,* the musical adaptation of Shaw's *Pygmalion,* Loewe's score, like Lerner's lyrics, is brilliantly attuned to Shaw's witty malice.

LOEWENGUTH, QUARTET. French string quartet of international repute consisting of Alfred Loewenguth and Maurice Fueri, violins; Roger Foche, viola; and Pierre Basseux, cello. The quartet was founded by Alfred Loewenguth in 1929 but it was not until 1936 that the four musicians felt ready for public appearance. In May of that year they gave their first concert and won immediate success. They have since toured Europe and the Americas, making their United States debut in 1937.

LOHENGRIN. Romantic opera in three acts by Wagner. After *Tannhäuser* Wagner had difficulty in finding fresh material suitable for a music drama. But while reading some medieval German poetry, he came across the legend of the son of Parsifal, the swan-knight Lohengrin, defender of the wrongfully persecuted.

What interested him particularly in this subject was the possibility of giving it a universal mythological character. But personal circum-

Act I of Lohengrin *from the Bayreuth production staged by Wieland Wagner, 1958*

Act II of Lohengrin *from the Bayreuth production staged by Wolfgang Wagner, 1953*

stances were also a decisive factor. As an artist, Wagner felt himself isolated from his age, and the figure of Lohengrin was an image of his own lonely position. Like Lohengrin, he longed for fellowship and communion with men, but they understood neither Lohengrin nor him.

Wagner wrote the music between 1846 and 1848, and *Lohengrin* was at once accepted by the Dresden Opera. But as Wagner took part in the political upheavals of 1848, he had to flee from Germany and the first performance was postponed; thanks to Liszt, however, the opera was performed two years later (August 28, 1850) at Weimar with Liszt himself conducting.

In *Lohengrin* Wagner freed himself from the conventional operatic form of the time, with its set arias and recitatives, but he had not yet found his final music-drama style. Like *Tannhäuser, Lohengrin* marks a new step forward in his development. The leitmotiv technique is used consistently, but in contrast to *Tristan,*

Lohengrin contains many sections which are complete in themselves—as, for example, *Elsa's Dream* (Act I), Lohengrin's *Story of the Grail* (last scene), and a number of choral and orchestral movements. But these occur as independent links in the whole; the action is not halted for them. In contrast to *Tristan,* the chorus plays an important part in *Lohengrin,* though the orchestra takes over a substantial part of the chorus' traditional task of commenting on the events that occur on the stage.

Wagner shows his individuality in his handling of the orchestra, in the important tasks he gives to the woodwinds, through the continual dividing of the strings into several sections, and through the use of special groups of instruments to describe individual characters or circumstances. Lohengrin, for example, is accompanied by high, ethereal violin tones. Elsa is characterized for the most part by the woodwinds, while the demoniacal Ortrud is accompanied by string tremolos and bass clarinet.

The prelude sets the mood of the whole work. A single theme is developed by various instruments, one after the other, each of the groups bringing in free counter-melodies as soon as the next takes over the theme. First we have the violins, *piano* in the highest register; then come flute, oboe, and clarinet; then viola, cello, horn, bassoon, trombone, and tuba *fortissimo;* lastly, the *decrescendo,* which ends *pianissimo* on violins and flute. Stephen Williams writes: "The prevailing color in *Lohengrin* is white—a vast, blinding radiance that seems to descend from another world. This is concentrated in the prelude which, if Wagner had written nothing else, would have proclaimed him a man of genius."

Time: *First half of the tenth century*

Place: *Antwerp*

ACT I

Scene: *A clearing by the banks of the Scheldt outside Antwerp*

King Henry the Fowler (bass) has called together the noblemen of Brabant. The Hungarians are threatening war and there is unrest in the country.

Count Frederick of Telramund (baritone) relates that the late Duke of Brabant had appointed him guardian of his two children, Elsa and Gottfried. One day, when Elsa went for a walk in the forest with her brother, she returned alone. Telramund accuses her of murdering her brother and demands the dukedom for himself. He has relinquished his claim to Elsa's hand and has taken to wife a woman of an old and princely race, Ortrud (contralto).

The King calls upon Elsa (soprano) to defend herself, and she tells of a dream she has had. In her loneliness and need, she says, she prayed to God for help. Then there appeared before her a knight in shining armor, who swore to fight for her and her cause:

Einsam in trü-ben Ta-gen hab' ich zu Gott ge-fleht,

Lonely in days of sadness, bowed by my load of care,
My heart's o'erwhelming anguish I poured to God in prayer:
Then rose from out my wailing, so full of pain, a cry,
Clear through the air resounding, piercing the clouds on high:
I heard it faintly echo, and dying far away;
Then gently closed my eyelids, in slumber sweet I lay.

Act III, Scene 1, of Lohengrin *from the Bayreuth production staged by Wieland Wagner in 1958*

The finale of Lohengrin, *Act III. Wolfgang Wagner's production at Bayreuth, 1953*

Telramund refuses to withdraw his accusation and asks the King to let the issue be decided before God by single combat between Telramund himself and anyone who is willing to defend Elsa's honor.

The Herald (baritone) calls repeatedly for one of the knights present to fight for Elsa, "who will do battle here in Heaven's name for Elsa of Brabant, let him appear!" But Telramund is feared and none offers himself. In despair Elsa prays to God to send the knight of her dreams.

A murmuring is heard among the crowd. A small boat, drawn by a snow-white swan, glides up the river with a knight in shining silver armor at the prow. The boat reaches the bank and the knight, Lohengrin (tenor), steps ashore and bids the swan depart.

Nun sei be-dankt, mein lie - ber Schwan!

Now thanks be thine, my faithful swan!
Wend back thy way across the main,
And seek the land where lies thy home;
Come once to bring us joy again!

The knight steps forward toward the astonished gathering and declares that Elsa is innocent and Tel-ramund's accusation false. He asks Elsa if she will accept his protection, and if she will be his wife if he wins the fight. For answer Elsa throws herself into his arms and thanks him for coming to her rescue. The knight immediately demands that she must make a vow never to ask who he is and whence he has come. If she breaks her vow he will have to leave her forever.

The Herald makes the arrangements for the combat and the King offers a prayer:

Mein Herr und Gott, nun ruf' ich dich, dass du

O Lord our God, on thee I call,
Now on this combat look Thou down!

In the combat the knight beats Telramund to the ground but spares his life. While Elsa and the knight are carried off in triumph, Telramund falls at his wife's feet, defeated and dishonored.

ACT II

Scene: *The courtyard of the King's castle in Antwerp*

It is night. In the shadows, on the steps of the King's

chapel, sit Telramund and Ortrud. The trumpets of the guard sound from the castle, where a feast is being held.

Telramund wants to go away, but his wife refuses. Furious, he blames her for the loss of his honor. It was she who made him accuse Elsa of the murder of her brother, and now the judgment of God has unveiled her as a liar. But Ortrud derides him and thinks that he lost the duel through cowardice. She has a plan: she will lure Elsa into breaking her vow to the strange knight. If he reveals who he is, his power will be broken.

Elsa comes out onto the terrace. She thanks Heaven for sending her a rescuer and sings of her happiness. Ortrud sends Telramund away and feigns grief by loudly bemoaning her fate. Full of compassion, Elsa hurries to console her. Ortrud pretends that she is anxious for Elsa and is convinced that the strange knight is a sorcerer. Elsa feels only pity for the wretched woman and takes her into the castle.

In the morning the Herald proclaims that Telramund has been declared an outlaw, and that the strange knight is to have Brabant in fief and Elsa to wife. The knight is to be called "not duke" but "protector" of Brabant.

After a procession of gaily clad court ladies has entered the chapel, Elsa comes from the castle. As she prepares to mount the chapel steps, Ortrud moves forward and places herself in her path. She shrieks that she and her husband have been unjustly dishonored and accuses the strange knight, who will not give his name, of sorcery.

The King and the knight enter, and the knight calms Ortrud. But as he is about to enter the chapel with his bride, Count Telramund appears and accuses him of practicing the black arts and demands that he tell his name. The knight rejects him, and says that Elsa is the only person to whom he will be accountable. Elsa declares that love conquers all doubt and, to the notes of the organ, she enters the chapel with Lohengrin.

ACT III

Scene 1: *The bridal chamber in the castle*

To the strains of the Bridal Chorus the King and the courtiers accompany the bridal pair to their chamber. But Elsa's happiness is not complete; the suspicion that Ortrud has set in her mind worries her, and finally she beseeches the knight to say who he is. Even if it means death, she must know.

At that moment Telramund bursts into the room with four men. Elsa hands her husband his sword and with one blow he fells Telramund. The Count's companions fall on their knees, and the knight commands them to lay the body before the King's throne. To Elsa he says that she has broken her vow and that he will answer her question before the King's throne.

Scene 2: *The clearing by the banks of the Scheldt*

The King has summoned his court. Before the throne there lies a covered bier with Telramund's body.

Pale and wretched, Elsa enters. When the strange knight appears he is acclaimed, but all are downcast when he declares that he can no longer be their protector. After telling of Telramund's assault, he says

that Elsa has broken her vow and that he will tell who he is and from whence he has come.

In a distant country, he says, lies the castle of Monsalvat, to which angels brought the blood of Christ in a cup. This cup is called the "Grail" and is guarded by a band of knights whose mission is to help those who are in need. But nobody must know who they are, for if their identity is divulged, they lose their divine power. Each year a dove appears, which renews the power of the cup. Parsifal, his father, is overlord of the castle, and he himself is called Lohengrin.

In fer-nem Land un-nah-bar eu-ren Schritten

A distant land, where none may come unbidden,
Holdeth a castle, Monsalvat 'tis named . . .

Out on the river the boat drawn by the swan appears. Lohengrin takes a sorrowful farewell of Elsa, who stands as if paralyzed. He confides to her that if his secret had been kept for one year, her brother would have returned. If he should come back nevertheless, Elsa is to give him Lohengrin's sword, horn, and ring.

As Lohengrin goes down to the river bank, Ortrud throws herself forward and shrieks triumphantly that the swan is Elsa's brother, whom she has bewitched. Lohengrin falls to his knees in silent prayer, and a white dove glides down over the boat. Lohengrin rises and releases the chain by which the swan draws the boat. The swan disappears under the water, and the next instant a young boy jumps up onto the bank. It is Elsa's lost brother. When Ortrud sees him, she swoons and falls to the ground.

Lohengrin steps into the boat, which gently glides out from the bank, drawn by the white dove. Elsa cries out after Lohengrin and sinks lifeless in her brother's arms.

LOLLI, Antonio. Italian composer and violinist (1730–1802). A great virtuoso and a tireless

Portrait of Antonio Lolli from Fedi's Il parnasso

traveler, he was attached to the court of the Duke of Württemberg and was a favorite of Catherine the Great at her court. He performed in Paris, Vienna, London, Copenhagen, and throughout Italy. He was reported to be a dazzling technician but a poor musician, and he was a notorious gambler. His concertos and violin sonatas are of indifferent quality; and it is believed that he actually composed only the violin parts in all of them.

LOMAX, Alan. American folk singer (1915–). From 1933 to 1942 Lomax, with his father, developed the Archive of American Folk Song, Library of Congress, becoming chief of that department in 1937. A pioneer collector of authentic folk songs, he was the first to introduce contemporary recording techniques (disc, 1933; tape, 1947; stereo, 1959) to field collecting of folk songs and the first to produce record albums of authentic folk songs. He and his father discovered Leadbelly in Louisiana. About half of the folk songs sung in the United States today were discovered, published, and taught to other balladeers by Lomax and his father. He has produced over one hundred record albums, and many books in this field, including

George London as Don Giovanni

Folk Songs of North America, Mister Jelly Roll (a biography of Jelly Roll Morton written on a Guggenheim Fellowship), *The Penguin Book of American Folk Songs,* and *USA, the Saga of American Folk Song.* He has concertized and lectured extensively in the United States and England.

LOMBARDO, Guy. Canadian-American band leader (1902–). Lombardo formed his band, The Royal Canadians, in 1919 with his three brothers, Carmen, Lebert, and Victor. The band has continued a popular favorite through the decades since, and its soft style has remained unchanged. The band has made an annual appearance at the Roosevelt Hotel in New York since 1929, has been a feature of radio and television shows, and has toured throughout the United States. During the past few years, Lombardo has produced musical shows at Jones Beach, New York, in co-operation with New York State.

LONDON, George. American bass-baritone (1920–). Born in Montreal and taken to Los Angeles as a child, George London studied under Enrico Rosali (who has coached Gigli) and won an engagement as a member of the Bel Canto Trio with Mario Lanza and Frances Yeend.

He went to Europe in 1949, and made his debut as Amonasro in *Aïda* with the Vienna State Opera. Other important roles—Escamillo, Boris Godunov, and Mephistopheles—followed and he scored success after success. He has since appeared at Edinburgh, Munich, Milan, and Bayreuth, and in 1953 returned to America to appear as Boris Godunov at the Metropolitan Opera.

In 1960, London became the first American singer to appear in the role of Boris Godunov at the Bolshoi Theater in Moscow, where he scored an outstanding success.

LONDONDERRY AIR. Irish traditional tune from county Derry, *Farewell to Cuchulain.* This Irish folk song was first published in the Petrie Collection, 1855, where it is stated that the composer is unknown.

The air has been arranged for practically every instrument—for violin and piano by Fritz Kreisler; for strings, horn, and also for chorus by Percy Grainger. Stanford used the melody in his first Irish Rhapsody, and at least five sets of

*London in the eighteenth century. The **prima donna** in the floating double bass carries a scroll reading:* I always sing out of tune (*courtesy The Bettmann Archive*)

words have been written to it, including the songs *Far Away* (by Dora Sigerson) and *Danny Boy* (by F. E. Weatherley).

LONDON SYMPHONIES. Name given to twelve symphonies, Nos. 93–104, by Haydn. He wrote these twelve symphonies (his last) to the order of the English-German violinist and impresario Johann Peter Salomon, and during his two stays in England, 1791–92 and 1794–95, he conducted them at a series of concerts in London. They contributed greatly to his fame and popularity in England.

The best known of these symphonies have been given names from some special feature, usually occurring in the second movement. It is not known for certain who originated the titles. The last of the series, No. 104, is itself often called the *London* Symphony.

The *London* Symphonies form the conclusion and the culmination of Haydn's symphonic output. Such a series of masterpieces, created in so short a time, is a phenomenon in the history of music. All the new techniques that Haydn had introduced in his earlier symphonies (see *Haydn, Symphonies*) now attained clarified ex-

pression, with inspired and perfected technical mastery.

This is particularly noticeable in the imaginative development sections of the first movements, and in the codas, where all the thematic threads are woven together to form an effective climax. In eight of the symphonies, the finales are worked out as a combination of rondo and sonata form, and Haydn solved this difficult task in such a richly varied manner that the compositions have become a source of inspiration for all later symphonists, above all Beethoven.

Some people think that the influence of Mozart can be traced in the more songlike character of the themes, though the themes are equally fully stamped with Haydn's own characteristic buoyancy and warm humor. Others see an inclination toward Romanticism, the new artistic trend stimulated by Rousseau which was rapidly becoming fashionable in Europe. The orchestra is no longer so markedly divided into groups, but individual instruments are given independent tasks, and the themes are divided among them. In many places Haydn boldly experimented with new combinations of sound, as when he gave the slow movement in the *Military* Symphony its special character by introducing percussion effects, and when he used muted brass in No. 102.

Johann Peter Salomon who commissioned Haydn's
London *Symphonies*

No. 93, in D major (1791).

Listed as No. 2 of the Salomon symphonies in the catalogue of the London Philharmonic Society, this work is notable for its intricate last movement, a sonata-rondo on two themes.

No. 94, in G major (1791).

Known as the *Surprise* Symphony, this symphony received its name because of the *fortissimo* outburst of the full orchestra in the second movement, just after the playing of the simple, quiet, and extremely popular main theme. Haydn himself, while composing it, is supposed to have remarked, "That's sure to make the ladies jump!" Haydn later used the theme again in *The Seasons.*

No. 95, in C minor (1791).

This symphony has an almost romantic character; only in the minuet does the Haydn humor break through. The first movement lacks the normal slow introduction. The second movement is in variation form. A remarkable feature of this symphony is the occurrence of solo passages for both the cello (in the trio of the minuet) and the violin.

No. 96, in D major (1791).

This symphony is relatively seldom played, and Haydn himself was not satisfied with the last movement. It is sometimes called the *Miracle,* because during the first performance a chandelier fell down but no one was injured. The waltzlike trio in the minuet is a beautiful episode. The finale-rondo is like a perpetuum mobile.

No. 97 in C major (1791–92).

The slow introduction to the first movement is in

this symphony thematically connected with the main section. In the third movement the recapitulation of the minuet section is written out fully, as it is varied. The last movement is rather singular in that, toward the end, in the midst of gaiety, it subsides into a gloomy interlude.

No. 98, in B major (1792).

This symphony contains the very mournful second movement, which has been characterized as Haydn's Requiem for the death of Mozart. But the minuet and especially the finale are again full of Haydn's brilliant gaiety.

No. 99, in E flat major (1793).

Also in this symphony (which was the first in which Haydn used clarinets) there is a very grave second movement—Karl Geiringer calls it "one of Haydn's most profound and most disturbing compositions"—by the side of the two unrestrainedly gay succeeding movements.

No. 100, in G major (1794).

This symphony is called the *Military* Symphony; both the first and second movements explain why. The allegro in the first movement begins with a theme introduced on a flute and two oboes, which gives it a droll, military guise. The second theme of the movement has a certain likeness both to the main theme of Mozart's G minor Symphony and to the *Radetzky March* of the elder Johann Strauss. The military character is further reinforced by the use of bass drum, cymbals, and triangle in the second and fourth movements. The main material of the second movement is a quiet march theme.

No. 101, in D major (1794). See *Clock Symphony.*

No. 102, in B flat major (1794–95).

Ralph Hill calls the melodious and calm largo which introduces this symphony "a pearl in miniature." The succeeding allegro vivace contains one of Haydn's richest and most imaginative development passages. The second movement, adagio, is a transcription of an older trio, but is one of Haydn's most beautiful symphonic movements. It has since been frequently used for church music. An unusual feature is the use of muted trumpets. The minuet is vigorous and robust, with an almost romantic trio, and the finale is full of genuine Haydn wit and caprice.

No. 103, in E flat major (1795).

This is called the *Drum Roll* Symphony because the first movement begins with a drum roll of one bar, after which the bassoon, cello, and bass enter with a portentous theme in unison, which returns later in the code of the allegro section. The second movement consists of variations on two alternating themes, one in C major and the other in C minor. The minuet has this theme:

Ralph Hill writes of the last movement that it "is unique in Haydn's output for being based throughout exclusively on one subject, and for a complete absence of repeats. The music drives along from start to finish in an unflagging torrent of inspiration." The basis of the whole movement is a characteristic main motif which comes right at the beginning.

No. 104, in D major (1795).

Often called the *London* Symphony, this is the last of the series and the last symphony Haydn wrote. It has a solemn adagio introduced in D minor, which Ralph Hill calls "the greatest of them all." After this, the main theme of the allegro section glides quietly in on the strings:

It dominates the whole movement, and the other themes play a small role. The second movement, andante, is also based on the variation of a single theme. The minuet is unusual, with the accents on the last beats of the measures, and the trio glides very originally and unconventionally over into B flat major from the main key of D major in the minuet. The main theme of the finale "is reminiscent of a peasant dance played on bagpipes" (Karl Geiringer). The movement is unusual because Haydn for once makes extensive use of tied notes as an accompaniment of the theme. The counterpoint in the development section of the movement has been a lesson to the composers of later ages.

LONG, Kathleen. British pianist (1896–). Kathleen Long first played in public at the age of eight, and later won a scholarship to the Royal College of Music, where she eventually became a member of the teaching staff. She made her London debut at the Aeolian Hall when she was nineteen, and has since played in America and many European countries.

Her repertoire is extensive, but she is best known for her interpretations of the Mozart concertos and of French music, particularly that of Gabriel Fauré, and has a reputation as a player of chamber music. She has been associated with many famous artists, including Casals, the French flutist René le Roy, Brosa, and Suggia, and has played frequently with the Pro-Arte Quartet.

LONG, Marguerite. French pianist and teacher (1874–). Marguerite Long studied with Mar-

montel and joined the faculty of the Paris Conservatory in 1906, becoming a professor in 1920. Ravel dedicated his Piano Concerto in G major to her in recognition of her outstanding service to modern French composers. Works by Debussy and Fauré were also written for and first played in public by her. She has lectured on contemporary French music and is the author of a book on the Beethoven quartets.

LONGO, Alessandro. Italian editor, composer, and pianist (1864–1945). A professor of piano at the Naples Conservatory and a composer of piano and other works, Longo is best known for his editions of the complete harpsichord works of Domenico Scarlatti and other old Italian keyboard compositions. Scarlatti's harpsichord sonatas are generally best identified by their Longo (L.) number. Longo's son **Achille** (1900–) is also a musician, and a composer of numerous works.

LOPATNIKOFF, Nicolai. Russian-American composer (1903–). After study at the Petrograd Conservatory, Lopatnikoff went to Finland and Germany, continuing his training at the Helsinki Conservatory and in Berlin where he worked with Ernest Toch and Grabner. He came to the United States in 1939 and in 1945 joined the music faculty of Carnegie Institute of Technology in Pittsburgh. He has written symphonic music, the opera *Danton,* and chamber music. He has received two Guggenheim Fellowships and a Koussevitzky Foundation commission.

LORELEI, DIE. Song by Friedrich Silcher, composed in 1837 to the poem by Heinrich Heine. According to legend, the Lorelei rock on the Rhine is haunted by a siren who with her song lures boatmen to their doom in the dangerous waters at this narrow part of the river. The poem describes the siren as she sits combing her beautiful long hair with a golden comb and chanting her magic song. The captain, unable to remove his eyes from her, wrecks his boat on the rock, and his men are drowned in the swift waters of the Rhine.

Ich weiss nicht was soll es be-deu-ten dass ich

I know not why, but my gladness
Hath utterly pass'd away. . . .

ALBERT LORTZING

LORENZ, Max. German tenor (1902–). In 1963, he sang his farewell at the Vienna State Opera after many years as one of its stars. His first success was in Dresden, as Menelaus in Strauss' *Die aegyptische Helena,* which he sang at the world première in 1928. After singing at the Berlin State Opera and the Metropolitan Opera, where he made his debut as Walther in *Die Meistersinger* in 1931, he began his long career in Vienna. He also sang Tristan and Siegfried at the Bayreuth Festival and appeared at La Scala and in South America. One of his best roles was Lohengrin.

LORTZING, Gustav Albert. German composer (1801–1851). He began acting as a child with his parents and later, after his marriage, the whole family performed together in various German cities. Lortzing also sang roles in light operas and was much influenced by the adaptations of French comic operas in which he performed, though his peculiar accomplishment was to transform the French style into something particularly German. Though his comic operas became popular and were produced ex-

tensively in Germany, he struggled all his life to support eleven children, working wherever he could as an actor, singer, or conductor. His most ambitious opera was a romantic one, *Undine,* which recently was revived in Europe. His *Zar und Zimmermann* and *Der Wildschütz* are still performed in Germany. Though none of his works is a masterpiece, they were important in the transitional stage of German opera development.

LOST CHORD, THE. Song by Sir Arthur Sullivan, written in 1877.

LOTTI, Antonio. Italian composer, organist, and singer (*c.* 1667–1740). Lotti studied in Venice with Giovanni Legrenzi, and eventually was elevated to first organist of St. Mark's. He wrote a great deal of church music, including masses and oratorios, in the eighteenth-century polyphonic tradition; numerous operas; arias, including *Pur dicesi;* and madrigals.

LOUIS FERDINAND, Prince of Prussia. (1772–1806). He was a nephew of Frederick the Great and one of the most talented of royal amateur musicians. His ability as a pianist was highly praised by Beethoven, who dedicated his Third Piano Concerto to him. The Prince composed much chamber music, some of it quite fine, and his Rondo in B major is used today as the theme music for a popular radio program.

LOUISE. Opera in four acts by Gustave Charpentier, first performed at the Paris Opéra-Comique in 1900. The composer wrote the libretto.

Charpentier tried to give a realistic picture of the life of contemporary artists and workers of Paris in this opera, the scenes being laid in a workingman's apartment, a street and a garden in Montmartre, and a dressmaker's workroom. The minor characters include an old-clothesman, ragpickers, peddlers, and night revelers.

The mere fact that *Louise* could drive home a topical issue was in itself an operatic achievement; the opera's theme reflects the realism at the start of the century. The musical idiom of the work is late nineteenth-century French Romantic lyricism.

The second act contains the much-admired episode in which Paris wakens to life and the street cries are heard. Three days after the first performance Debussy wrote of this scene: "Now, look what this man Charpentier has done! He has taken the Paris street cries which are so delightfully human and picturesque in character, and, like a wretched Prix de Rome scholar, has converted them into morbid cantilenas, and introduced harmonies which we—in order to be polite—will term parasites. The sly fox! It is ten times more conventional than *Les Huguenots*. Even though it may not appear to be the case, the technique there is the same. And they call this Life!"

Mary Garden made her operatic debut as Louise in Paris, and introduced the role to New York in 1907. *Louise* became part of the Metropolitan Opera repertory; famous in the title role have been Geraldine Farrar and Lucrezia Bori.

The story concerns a young seamstress, Louise, who falls in love with a poet, Julien, and leaves her parents to live with him. In the famous aria *Depuis le jour* she sings of the happiness she has experienced since she came to live with him. She returns home when her father is taken ill, but on his recovery he attempts to keep his daughter from rejoining her lover. Louise reminds him of his promise to allow her to return to Julien, but he wants Louise to remain the little girl she once was. Her mother furiously reproaches her, and finally her father beats her, but she runs off to Julien and the city.

A sequel to *Louise,* the opera *Julien,* was performed in 1913, but this was a much feebler work and met with no success.

LOUISVILLE SYMPHONY. See *Whitney, Robert.*

LOURIÉ, Arthur. Russian composer (1892–). Largely self-taught, he was at first a follower of Debussy and later of Schoenberg and Stravinsky. After the Russian revolution, he was for a time director of music for the Ministry of Public Instruction in the new régime. However, he left Russia in 1921 and settled in Paris, where he became prominent in the emigré society headed by Diaghiliev, Chaliapin, Stravinsky, etc. He has composed choral and chamber music and an opera.

LÖVBERG, Aase Nordmo. Norwegian soprano (1923–). She has performed at all the principal European opera houses, and with the Philadelphia Orchestra. She received her musical training in Oslo, Stockholm, Copenhagen, and New York and made her recital debut in

Act II of Louise, *showing the city of Paris from the heights of Montmartre. Munich State Opera production*

Oslo, in 1948, and her operatic debut in Stockholm in 1952 with the Royal Swedish Opera, as Elisabeth in *Tannhäuser*. Her Metropolitan Opera debut was in 1959 as Elsa in *Lohengrin*.

LOVE FOR THREE ORANGES, THE. Opera by Serge Prokofiev, libretto by the composer, after Gozzi. The work was commissioned and first produced by the Chicago Opera Company in 1921. Prokofiev conducted the world première and also led performances at the Manhattan Opera House in New York. The opera was sung in French. The libretto is a satirical fable with some of the singers impersonating an audience. The main action thus becomes a "play within a play." The prince, who loves three oranges, finds his princess in the third. When first introduced the opera was not a success. But in 1949, when the New York City Opera revived the work at City Center, it met with great acclaim.

LOVE OF THREE KINGS, THE (*L'amore dei tre re*). Opera by Italo Montemezzi, libretto by Sem Benelli. First performed at La Scala, Milan, April 10, 1913. The American première was at the Metropolitan, January 2, 1914. The

A scene from the NBC-TV Opera production of
The Love of Three Kings

opera has a medieval setting and concerns an aged king, Archibaldo, who is blind. Discovering that his son's wife Fiora, is unfaithful, he strangles her and sets a trap for her lover by poisoning her lips. The lover and Archibaldo's son both destroy themselves by kissing the dead Fiora, and the old king is left in his darkness of sight and mind.

LOW, Leo. Russian-American composer and conductor (1878–1960). A specialist in Jewish music, Leo Low took his early training at the Warsaw Conservatory and held posts in synagogues in Russia, Poland, and Romania. He first concertized in the United States in 1913, moving permanently to New York in 1920. Among his works are the cantata *A New World,* an operetta, *The Musical Village,* and a children's opera, *The Liberation of Spring.*

LOWE, Jack. American pianist (1918–). A member of the duo piano team of Whittemore and Lowe, he received his early training at Colorado College and was a student at the Eastman School of Music. There he met Arthur Whittemore and together they made their debut at Town Hall in 1940. They have since appeared with virtually all principal orchestras in the United States and abroad. Among contemporary composers whose works have been dedicated to them are Vaughan Williams, Poulenc, Gould, Křenek, Norton, and Rosenthal.

LOWE, Mundell. American jazz guitarist (1922–). An exponent of the "modern" jazz style, he has played with Jan Savitt, Ray McKinley, Dave Martin, Red Norvo, and Billy Taylor, and has headed his own group.

LUALDI, Adriano. Italian composer (1887–). A noted critic, essayist, and director of the Florence Conservatory, he has revived much old Italian music, and conducts his own chamber orchestra. His compositions include choral and chamber music, orchestral works, songs, and seven operas, for which he also wrote the librettos.

LUBIN, Germaine. French soprano (1890–). She was for more than a quarter century one of the stars of the Paris Opéra, where she sang all the Wagner heroines and other roles in operas by Gluck, Berlioz, Dukas, and Richard Strauss.

The wedding of Lucia and Lord Arthur. A scene from Franco Zeffirelli's production of Lucia di Lammermoor
at Covent Garden

LUBOFF, Norman. American choral conductor (1917–). Starting as a choirboy in Chicago, Luboff has become director of the ensemble which bears his name. He studied at the University of Chicago and after graduation taught at Central College. After army service, he became a successful arranger and conductor for radio, television, and motion pictures.

LUBOSHUTZ, Pierre. Russian-American pianist (1894–). A member of the famed duo piano team of Nemenoff and Luboshutz, he was educated at the Moscow Conservatory and later studied in Paris. He concertized as a solist with principal orchestras in Europe and the United States and was accompanist to virtuosos including Kreisler, Zimbalist, and Piatigorsky. He met Genia Nemenoff when she became one of his pupils in Paris and they soon married. They formed a duo piano team and, since 1936, have appeared before audiences the world over. See *Nemenoff, Genia.*

LUCA, Giuseppe De. See *De Luca, Giuseppe.*

LUCCA, Pauline. Austrian soprano of Italian descent (1841–1908). She first became famous in Prague and Berlin and was for eleven seasons the idol of London at Covent Garden. However, the greatest part of her career was in Vienna, though she also toured in America, Spain, and Russia. Her most famous roles, of the fifty that she sang, were Carmen, Cherubino in *The Marriage of Figaro,* and Sélika in *L'Africaine.* She was one of those rare singers in opera who had, in addition to a great voice, superb acting gifts and a bewitching personality.

LUCIA, Fernando de. Italian tenor (1860–1925). He was famous as Canio in *Pagliacci,* which he was the first to sing at Covent Garden and the Metropolitan Opera. Among his other roles was Fritz in the world première of Mascagni's *L'Amico Fritz* at Rome in 1891.

LUCIA DI LAMMERMOOR. Opera in three acts by Donizetti. The libretto by Salvatore Cammarano is based on Sir Walter Scott's novel *The Bride of Lammermoor.* It was first produced at the San Carlo opera house, Naples, in 1835, and was the second production of the Metropolitan Opera's first season, in 1883.

The scene is set in early eighteenth-century Scotland. Lord Henry Ashton of Lammermoor (baritone) for political reasons wishes to marry his sister Lucia (soprano) to Lord Arthur Bucklaw (tenor). But Lucia is secretly betrothed to Edgar of Ravenswood (tenor), although their two families have maintained a feud for years. While Edgar is away in France, Henry Ashton intercepts his letters to Lucia, and tricks her into thinking her lover has been unfaithful. She reluctantly agrees to marry Lord Arthur, and just as she has signed the contract Edgar returns. He charges her with infidelity, and he and Henry arrange to fight a duel. Lucia's wedding to Lord Arthur takes place, but the same night she goes mad and kills her husband. When Edgar hears of the tragedy and realizes the duplicity that brought it about he stabs himself.

The opera is often regarded merely as a vehicle for showing off some popular prima donna, but its melodies though simple possess genuine beauty. Lucia's *Mad Scene* in Act III reduced contemporary audiences to tears. To this coloratura aria, with flute obbligato, which is a *tour de force* for the singer, Donizetti gives pathos by introducing themes from Lucia's earlier arias, and the love duet between her and Edgar. Famous Lucias have included Marcella Sembrich, Jenny Lind, Nellie Melba, Adelina Patti, Lily Pons, Maria Callas, and Joan Sutherland.

LUDGIN, Chester. American baritone. Ludgin made his debut as Salvatore in the original production of Menotti's *The Saint of Bleecker Street* on Broadway. He has since sung with the New Orleans, Pittsburgh, and Baltimore Civic operas; at Central City, Colorado; Lewisohn Stadium, New York; the Hollywood Bowl; Chicago's Grant Park; the NBC-TV Opera; and other groups. He is a member of the New York City Opera, with which he has appeared in leading roles in several modern operas.

LUDUS TONALIS. A composition for piano by Paul Hindemith, composed in 1943. It consists chiefly of twelve fugues, each using one of the twelve tones of the chromatic scale as a tonal center.

LUENING, Otto. American composer and teacher (1900–). Luening has written many symphonic, choral, and instrumental works and the opera *Evangeline* (1932). He is presently experimenting, together with his colleague Vladimir Ussachevsky, in the field of electronic and tape-recorded music. He was head of the opera department at the Eastman School of Music, taught at the University of Arizona and Bennington College, and presently serves on the faculty of Columbia University. He was cofounder of the American Grand Opera Company in Chicago.

LUIGINI, Alexandre. French composer (1850–1906). Having studied the violin at the Paris Conservatory, he became conductor at a Lyons theater and later at the Opéra-Comique, Paris. His compositions included symphonies, chamber music, a cantata, and an opera, but he is remembered solely for his many ballets, which include the ever popular *Ballet égyptien,* also *Ballet russe, Carnaval truc,* and other pseudo-Oriental pieces.

LULLABY. See *Cradle Song.*

LULLY, Jean-Baptiste. French composer (1632–1687). The son of a miller of Florence, Lully received no regular education, but learned to read, and to play the guitar, from a monk. He taught himself to play the violin. When he was fourteen, his cheerfulness and the wholehearted way he entered into the festivities at a carnival attracted the notice of a French nobleman, the Chevalier de Guise, who took the boy to Paris. Here he was at first put to work in the kitchens of the King's cousin, Mlle. de Montpensier. Discovering his musical talent, Mlle. de Montpensier made him violinist in her small private orchestra, where he remained for six years. One day he repaid her kindness by making fun of her in a scurrilous song. His dismissal, however, was to his advantage, for he was immediately engaged by King Louis XIV, then a boy of fifteen.

Lully began his career at court as composer, ballet dancer, and violinist in the royal string orchestra, "The King's Twenty-four Violins." In this triple capacity he had great influence with the King, who was particularly interested in ballet and himself often performed as a dancer. Soon Lully had his own orchestra ("The King's Small Violins") which soon surpassed the older orchestra both in musicianship and technique. Lully wrote new ballets and plays for the royal entertainments at Versailles, composing, playing, and dancing his music for *le roi soleil.* Hermann Unger writes: "Lully, the creator of French opera, was always lively, energetic and

JEAN-BAPTISTE LULLY

Between 1660 and 1662 the operas of the Venetian composer Francesco Cavalli were performed at the French court, and Lully had an opportunity to study and assimilate the best qualities of the Italian style, particularly in its melody and instrumentation, and to adapt them to the French language.

Lully was in complete control of French opera, and in his twenty stage works created the French national opera, the basis of all French dramatic music. "In his operas Lully developed the importance of the accompanied recitative, replacing the *recitativo secco* favored by the Italians. He evolved a style of declamation eminently suited to the French language. He developed the operatic overture to a new degree of importance. He raised the standard of orchestral performance to a much higher level . . . and he demanded from his singers fidelity to the music as written by the composer. He was the first to introduce female dancers into the ballet" (Gilbert Chase).

Lully's importance in French opera is due to the great emphasis he placed on natural, lifelike, dramatic declamation. He studied the intonation of the great actors of the day at the Théâtre Français, and told his singers: "If you wish to

cheerful. He was a most accomplished mimic. When Molière had had difficulties at home, he would beg his friend Lully, 'Make me laugh!' And Lully succeeded every time. Louis XIV recognized this talent and often made use of it, and Lully thus gained increasing influence with the King."

In recognition of his work, Lully was appointed royal composer, royal chamber music composer, and musical director to the royal family. When he married, the royal family did him the rare honor of attending the ceremony.

In 1664 Lully began his collaboration with Molière in plays with ballets. Thanks to Lully, the musical element in these works became increasingly important, and the plays gradually became almost operas. At the same time the Frenchmen Perrin and Cambert sought to create a French opera based on Italian opera. Their enterprise failed, however, after a few years, and Lully secured a royal patent giving him the sole right to produce operas, other enterprises being forbidden to use more than two singers and six violins.

The titlepage of Lully's Armide

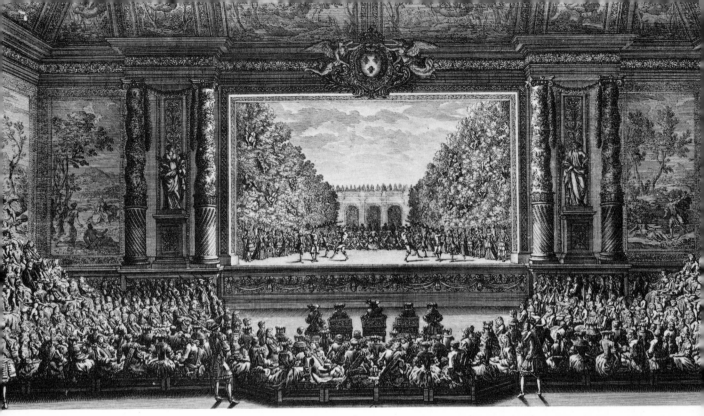

An opera-ballet by Lully performed at Versailles before Louis XIV and his court

sing my music well, go and listen to [the actress] La Champmesle."

He died in Paris following an accident that occurred while he was conducting a Te Deum after the King's recovery from a serious illness. He happened to strike his long heavy baton against his big toe. (In those days beat was indicated by thumping on the ground.) The wound resulted in blood poisoning, which proved fatal.

Lully died a rich and powerful man. Gifted equally as a politician and musician, his successful maneuverings and intrigues had made him one of the wealthiest and influential men in the French court. He was also one of the most-admired and least-liked men of his time: he was both feared and respected for his influence as a favorite of the king, and for his theatrical monopoly as director of the Opéra.

Lully's operatic overtures — the so-called "French" overture form—were, like the Italian, in three sections, but, while the Italian consisted of one quick, one slow, and then a quick movement, the sequence in the French was the opposite—a slow, a quick, and a slow movement.

Hermann Scherchen sums up Lully's importance in French opera thus: "He transformed music from a court pastime into a national art. . . . An unscrupulous and ambitious intriguer, he was not a good man, but no one can deny his greatness as a musician."

Although Lully's operas dominated the French opera stage for over a century, they are rarely performed today.

Best-known works:

OPERAS

Alceste, Prologue and 5 Acts (1674)
   Act IV: *Air de Caron: Il faut passer*
Amadis de Gaule, Prologue and 5 Acts (1684)
   Act II: *Air d'Amadis: Bois épais*
Armide et Renaud, 5 Acts (1686)
Acis et Galatée, 3 Acts (1686)

LUNCEFORD, Jimmie. American band leader (1902–1947). Lunceford first studied music under James Wilberforce Whiteman, father of Paul Whiteman, but later took a degree at Fisk University and began teaching English at Manassa High School, Memphis. There he organized a school orchestra, and when most of its members went on to Fisk University, he worked as head waiter in a restaurant to remain with them. In 1934 his band was engaged as a

The titlepage of Lully's Persée

thousand times in England and America, as well as many other places. At the Metropolitan, where she sang in 1894–95, she was Nanetta in *Falstaff* at its American première.

LUTCHER, Nellie. American jazz singer and pianist (1915–). Nellie Lutcher joined the Clarence Hart band when she was fifteen years old and later performed in night clubs and on tour with her own group. Many of her popular records are of songs she has composed.

LUTE. See *Stringed Instruments*.

LUTHER, Martin. German religious reformer and composer (1483–1546). Luther played the lute and the flute, and sang within the circle of his friends and family. In the process of his reformation of church services, he introduced congregation singing and altered the order of the German Mass. It is certain that he composed several hymns; a dozen others, including *Ein' feste Burg ist unser Gott (A Mighty Fortress Is Our God),* are attributed to him; and he arranged or adapted a number of other chorales.

Martin Luther, a portrait by Lucas Cranach. The Ufizzi Gallery, Florence

"fill-in" at the Cotton Club, New York, and scored a sensational success.

Lunceford's band was celebrated for the smoothness of its style and the originality of its arrangements. He made one very successful film, *Blues in the Night.* After his death his band was taken over by Joe Thomas.

LUR. Scandinavian wind instrument of the Bronze Age (1500–500 B.C.). About two yards long, shaped like an elongated S with a flat, ornamental disc at the end of the tube, it strikingly resembles a mammoth tusk, and is often found in symmetrically shaped pairs. See *Wind Instruments.*

LUSSAN, Zélie de. American mezzo-soprano of French descent (1863–1949). She was one of five famous Carmens (the others were Galli-Marié, Hauk, Calvé, and Lucca) who, with distinctly different impersonations, did much to bring about the great popularity of Bizet's opera. She was a protegée of Christine Nilsson and first sang Carmen in London at Covent Garden in 1888. She sang the role more than a

ALEXIS LVOV

LUTKIN, Peter. American composer and teacher (1858–1931). He was the founder and dean of the music department of Northwestern University and the organizer of the North Shore Music Festival in Chicago. He also served on a committee that revised the Episcopal Hymnal. His compositions include organ and choral works and chamber music.

LUVISI, Lee. American pianist (1937–). Luvisi studied with Dwight Anderson at the University of Louisville School of Music, and with Rudolf Serkin and Mieczyslaw Horszowski at the Curtis Institute. Upon graduation in 1957, he was appointed to the faculty as its youngest member. His debut was with the Philadelphia Orchestra under Eugene Ormandy in 1955, and he made his New York recital debut at Carnegie Hall in 1957. In 1958 he appeared as soloist with the New York Philharmonic Orchestra, Leonard Bernstein conducting, in Beethoven's *Emperor Concerto*. He received the Philadelphia Youth Award in 1955.

LVOV, Alexis. Russian violinist and composer (1798–1870). The son of a musicologist, he served in the army and then succeeded his father as director of the Imperial Chapel to Nicholas I. The string quartet that he organized in St. Petersburg became greatly celebrated. He composed three operas, church music, and violin pieces, as well as the melody for the national anthem of Imperial Russia.

LYFORD, Ralph. American composer and conductor (1882–1927). A student of Nikisch and George Chadwick, he conducted the Boston, San Carlo, and Cincinnati opera companies and was associate conductor of the Cincinnati Symphony. His compositions include an opera, a piano concerto, songs, and chamber music.

LYMPANY, Moura. English pianist (1916–). Moura Lympany started to learn the piano when she was at school in Belgium, and made her debut at Harrogate when she was twelve, playing Mendelssohn's G minor Piano Concerto under Basil Cameron's baton. She toured England and Belgium as a child prodigy, and a year later won the Ada Lewis Scholarship to the Royal Academy of Music, where she studied for three years. Later she studied under Paul Weingartner in Vienna.

In an international piano competition in Brussels in 1939, Moura Lympany won second prize from among nearly ninety competitors from twenty-four countries.

Moura Lympany has made many recordings, and has played with most of the leading orchestras in the United States, England, South America, and the Continent.

LYNE, Felice. American soprano (1887–1935). Her opera debut was in Hammerstein's season at his new London Opera House in 1911, when she sang Gilda to the Rigoletto of Renaud. Later, she sang with the Boston Opera.

LYRIC PIECES. Piano pieces by Grieg, totaling sixty-seven in number and published in ten books between 1867 and 1901. Short, simple, and tuneful, these pieces became so popular that Grieg called them his "hot cakes." Most of the pieces have general titles (Waltz, Berceuse, Folk Song, Elegy, etc.), but some depict aspects of nature (e.g. *Butterfly, Little Bird, To the Spring, The Little Brook*), and a few describe events of the Norwegian countryside (e.g. *Wedding Day at Troldhaugen*).

LYSENKO, Nicolai. Russian composer (1842–1912). A pupil of Rimsky-Korsakov, he was an authority on Russian folk music and a Ukrainian patriot. He composed four operas and five operettas, several of which were based on works of Gogol; all were set to Ukrainian texts.